2005
Magazine
Markets
for
Children's
Writers

Published by
Institute of Children's Literature

Acknowledgments

The editors of this directory appreciate the generous contributions of our instructors and students and the cooperation of the magazine editors who made clear their policies and practices.

MARNI MCNIFF, Editor

SUSAN TIERNEY, Articles Editor

HEATHER BURNS-DEMELO, Assistant Editor

JANINE MANGIAMELE, Assistant Editor

SHERRI KEEFE, Research Assistant

Contributing Writers: EILEEN BYRNE, BARBARA COLE, VICKI HAMBLETON, LOUANNE LANG, PAMELA PURRONE

Cover Art: HOWARD MUNCE

Contents

Contents (cont.)

Listings   39

This year's directory offers over 665 up-to-date listings, including 78 completely new listings.

How to Use the Listings   40
A section-by-section description of the listings.

Listings of Magazines   42

Additional Listings   283

Includes 144 short listings of additional markets.

Selected Contests and Awards   321

Provides basic guidelines for 48 magazine writing contests and awards.

Indexes   335

2005 Market News   336
Identifies new listings and deletions and name changes.

Fifty+ Freelance   338
Lists magazines that rely on freelance writers for at least 50% of the material they publish.

Category Index   339
Lists magazines under selected categories according to the type of material they are interested in acquiring.

Magazine and Contest Index   364
Cross references all magazines and contests listed; provides readership codes and page references.

Submissions Guide

Preparing to Sell

An idea has captivated you. You're sure it will be a fun and informative children's nonfiction article or an engaging story. Perhaps you've even written your piece and are ready for young readers to read it. Great! Your next step is to find those magazines whose editors and audiences will be most receptive to your writing.

You'll want to offer an editor the perfect match of quality, topic, and reader interest, making your work irresistible. Your goal is to identify the subjects those readers enjoy and then create material that engages them.

You might begin with a magazine you like and generate ideas for submissions specific to it, or begin with a good idea and no specific market in mind. Later you can research the topics of interest to various publications to find the best opportunities for placing your work. Here are some tips to launch your research.

What Captivates Young Readers?

You'll increase your publication odds if you know what topics interest children. Trust your own instincts, and hone these instincts throughout the market research process.

Researching potential subjects can begin by surveying the categories of magazines in *Magazine Markets for Children's Writers*. Start with the Category Index on pages 339-363, an excellent guide to finding magazines that publish the types of articles or stories you write on the subjects that interest you.

You'll find general interest publications, like *Highlights for Children* or *Spider*, and also special interest periodicals on topics such as health, sports, science, fiction, college, religion, history, and so on. Continue your research online or at libraries. Do Internet searches, and check the library or bookstores. What magazines are out there, for what ages, and what subjects do they cover? Along with magazines targeted specifically to children, be sure to check parenting, educational, and regional magazines.

You'll find that each magazine covers numerous subjects from month to month or year to year, even special interest publications that cover a niche more deeply than widely. Read several issues of each magazine to research which subjects a potential target magazine has covered recently and how it has approached particular subjects in the past. Begin to make a list of the magazines that cover subjects of interest to you. Use the Magazine Match List on page 7.

Roll Call: Who Are Your Readers?

Researching readers is intricately tied to subjects, but a magazine's target age and how the publication speaks to that age—voice, and purpose—are important factors in the market research you perform. Select subjects and slants based on age-appropriateness. If you'd like to take on the subject of animals' sleep habits, for example, you'd write an article or story for early readers with less specific information than you would for a middle-grader, and with a different tone.

Once again, go to the Internet and other media, as well as to schools and children's activities, to get a feel for the interests and developmental levels of the readership that is drawing you. For example, go to www.google.com and select the directory. Click Kids and Teens. Look at the websites under preschool, school time, teen life, and other categories. The arts section has many interesting sites that can give you additional insights into every age group.

Look Deeper: Magazine Specifications

Create a magazine market file that seems to be a match with your interests. Use index cards, a notebook, or your computer—to develop a file for each magazine for your initial list of publications. Request sample issues for the magazines and read them. Listings in *Magazine Markets for Children's Writers* will tell you if writers' guidelines, an editorial calendar, or a theme list are available, as well as the cost of a sample copy and the size of the envelope to send with your request. (See page 41 for a sample magazine listing.)

You may find the magazines you're targeting at your local library or newsstand, which will save you time and postage. Go to their websites—addresses are included in the listings.

Review each of the magazines in more detail for subjects related, or comparable, to yours. You should also check the *Reader's Guide to Periodical Literature* in your library to see if a target magazine has printed a piece similar to yours within the past two years. You may want to find another magazine or, depending on the publication, develop a new slant if you find that your topic is already well covered.

Study the Magazine and Its Guidelines

Sample issues. Use the Magazine Description Form (see example on page 8), to continue your detailed analysis of the publications, especially those you're beginning to hone in on as good matches. Record what you learn about each magazine. Evaluate how you could shape or present your manuscript to improve your chances of getting it published. If a particular idea or target magazine doesn't work out now, it may in the future—or it may lead to other ideas, angles, or possible markets. Review your market files periodically to generate ideas.

Writers' Guidelines. If the listing notes that a magazine offers writers' guidelines, you should send a letter requesting them with an SASE (see sample of page 9). Some magazines also list their writers' guidelines on their websites. This is specified in the listing. Read writers' guidelines, editorial calendars, and theme lists carefully. They may give you specific topics to write about,

but even if you're creating your own, take the guidelines seriously. They are key to the needs of publications and often new writers give them too little weight.

Some guidelines are more detailed and helpful than others, but virtually all will tell you something about the readership, philosophy, voice, and about such basics as word length requirements, submissions format, and payment. More than that, some guidelines can give writers specific insights into the immediate needs of a magazine. For example, *Odyssey* guidelines say, "The inclusion of primary research (interviews with scientists focusing on current research) are of primary interest to the magazine," while *Connecticut's County Kids* guidelines are directive in another way: "Use bullets and subheads to separate thoughts, especially in feature articles."

The guidelines will also indicate the rights a publication purchases, payment policies, and many more specifics, factors you'll consider as you get closer to submission. Many experienced writers do not sell all rights, unless the fee is high enough to be worth it; reselling articles or stories for reprint rights can be an additional source of income. (See the discussion of rights on page 21.)

Read with a Writer's Eye

Your review of sample magazines and guidelines should include:

Magazine Match List: Subjects

Idea Topic: _____

	Magazine	Audience Age	Similar/Related Subject	Slant	Date Published
1.	_____	_____
		_____
		_____
		_____
2.	_____	_____
		_____
		_____
		_____

- **Editorial objective.** Turn to the issue masthead, where the names of the editors are listed. Sometimes the magazine's editorial objective is also stated here. Does your story or article fit its purpose?

- **Audience.** What is the age range of the readers and the characters or children portrayed? For fiction, is your main character at the upper end of that range? Kids want to read about characters their own age or older.

- **Table of contents.** Study the table of contents. Usually, the stories and articles with bylines were written by freelancers like you. Compare the author names there with the editors and staff listed in the masthead to make sure that the publication is not primarily staff-written.

- **Article and story types.** Examine the types of articles and stories in the issue. Does one theme tie the articles and stories together? For example, does every article in a science magazine focus on plants, or do the articles cover a broader range of subjects? If the magazine issues a theme list, review it to see the range of topics. Think about the presentation as well: Is the magazine highly visual or does it rely primarily on text? Will photographs or illustrations be a consideration for you? Are there sidebars, and are you willing to provide those?

- **Style.** How is the writing impacted by the age of the audience? Read each story and article to get an idea of the style and tone the magazine prefers. Are there numerous three-syllable words, or mostly simpler words? Are most sentences simple or complex, or a mixture of both? Is the tone upbeat and casual, or informative and educational? Do the writers speak directly to readers in a conversational way, or is the voice appropriately authoritative?

- **Editor's comments.** Note in the writers' guidelines particularly what *feel* for the magazine the editors provide. *Ladybug*'s guidelines include this important request: "[We] look for beauty of lan-

---

Magazine Description Form

Name of Magazine: U*S*Kids   **Editor:** Daniel Lee
Address: Children's Better Health Institute, 1100 Waterway Boulevard, P.O. Box 567, Indianapolis, IN 42606-0567

Freelance Percentage: 50%   **Percentage of Authors Who Are New to the Magazine:** 70%

Description
What subjects does this magazine cover? U*S*Kids features articles, stories, and activities related to health and fitness, science and nature, and multicultural and ethnic issues.

Readership
Who are the magazine's typical readers? Children ages 6 to 8

Articles and Stories
What particular slants or distinctive characteristics do its articles or stories emphasize? Articles and stories that spark a child's imagination and creativity while they learn something new.

Potential Market
Is this magazine a potential market? Yes. I have an article and activity to submit.

Ideas for Articles or Stories
What article, story, or department idea could be submitted? Submit an article on different types of physical fitness activities for young children.

guage and a sense of joy or wonder." *Magazine Markets for Children's Writers* includes a section called Editor's Comments in each listing. Study this section carefully as well. The editors give you tips on what they most want to see, or don't need.

Refine Your Magazine List

After you analyze your selected magazines, rank them by how well they match your idea, article or story's subject, style, and target age. Then return to the listings to examine other factors, such as the magazine's freelance potential, its receptivity to new or unpublished writers, rights purchased, and payment.

These facts reveal significant details about the magazine that you can use to your advantage as a freelance writer. For example, many published writers prefer magazines that:

- Publish a high percentage of authors who are new to the magazine;
- Respond in one month as opposed to three;
- Pay on acceptance rather than on publication.

If you're not yet published, however, writing for a nonpaying market may be worth the effort to earn the clips to build published credits. Once you've acquired credentials in these markets, you can list these published pieces in your queries to paying markets.

What to do if a magazine requests clips, but you've never been published before?

Many editors are open to new writers, so don't be discouraged if you haven't yet seen your name in a byline and think it's a vicious circle editors spin: To get published you need clips, but you can't have clips until you're published.

First, consider whether in fact you have been "published." Have you written anything substantial for a school or church newsletter (not a 100-word piece on the school lunch choices for the week), or a volunteer organization? If it's good, it might reveal your style well. If not, gather together unpublished samples. Try to select those that will be closest to the piece you're proposing, or include a portion of the piece itself. Be sure your samples are well written and have no errors.

Be honest with the editor in your query and call them *writing samples*, not *clips*; clips are published items.

Sample Guidelines Request

Name
Address
City, State, ZIP

Date

Dear (Name of Current Editor):

I would like to request a copy of your writers' guidelines and editorial calendar. I have provided a self-addressed, stamped envelope for your convenience.

Sincerely,

Your name

Submitting Your Work to an Editor

Your market study will prepare you to draft a query or cover letter that convinces the right editor of why your idea is suitable for the magazine and why *you* are the person to write it. When do you send a query, and when a cover letter and manuscript? Should a query be accompanied by an outline or synopsis or other materials? Is a query ever appropriate for fiction?

In your research, you should already have begun to see the variety of submissions possibilities. Let's sort them out.

Know What Editors Want

Some editors want the query alone; it's efficient and provides them with enough information to make a decision about the article's appeal to their readers. Others want queries accompanied by a synopsis, outline, or other information for an article. Yet other editors prefer to have a complete article or story before them to get a full sense of the work you do and whether the subject is a match for them. Expect that the editor who accepts a complete, unsolicited manuscript may require even more revisions or rewrites than if you had queried first.

In reality, queries for magazine fiction are rare, although they've become somewhat more common for book-length fiction. Magazine stories are short enough without being too much for an editor to review.

If the editor asks for a:	*Send:*
Query (nonfiction)	• One-page letter indicating article topic, slant, target readership, word count • Bibliography of research sources • One-page résumé (if requested) • SASE
Query (fiction)	• One-page letter containing a brief synopsis of the plot, indicating target readership and word count • SASE
Complete manuscript (nonfiction)	• Brief cover letter • Manuscript • Bibliography of research sources • List of people interviewed • SASE
Complete manuscript (fiction)	• Brief cover letter • Manuscript • SASE

Keys to Writing a Query Letter

A query tells the editor why your idea is appropriate for the magazine and why *you* are the person to write it. There are several advantages to using a query letter:

- Editors generally respond faster to queries than manuscripts.
- Your chances for a sale are increased because the piece is still in the "planning stage" and the editor can give you suggestions that help you tailor the article to the magazine.
- You save research and writing time by knowing exactly what the editor wants.

Do Your Homework

Before you write your query letter, refine your idea based on the sample issues you've read and the requirements described in the guidelines. Know the word limit the magazine prefers and whether or not it requires a bibliography of your sources. Most editors like articles with quotes from experts in the field you're writing about. Be prepared to tell the editor who you'll interview for the piece. For example, if you plan to write a science article and the magazine wants resourced and quoted articles, gather pertinent facts and include names of authorities you plan to interview. Know whether you can obtain photos—this can often swing a sale.

What Makes a Good Query Letter

A good query letter is short and to the point. If you can't get your idea across in one page or less, you're not yet ready to write the article.

Below are the basic steps in writing a query (see the examples on pages 12, 13, and 14):

- Direct your query to a specific editor.
- Begin with a lead paragraph that captures the editor's interest, conveys your slant, and reflects your knowledge of the editorial focus and writing style of the magazine.
- Include a one- or two-line description of your article that conveys your central idea. This should be very narrow in focus.

- Show how your idea meets the editorial goals of the targeted magazine.
- Indicate word length.
- Provide details as to what will be in the article —anecdotes, case histories, statistics, etc.
- Cite sources, research resources, and interviews to be done.
- Indicate number and type of photographs or illustrations available. If you can't provide any, don't mention them at all.
- List your publishing credentials briefly and, if enclosed, refer to your résumé, clips or writing samples. No need to tell the editor if you are unpublished.
- Close by asking if the magazine is interested; mention whether your query represents a simultaneous submission.
- Include other information if requested, such as an outline or bibliography.

Tips for Making a Good First Impression

Your query is the first impression the editor will have of you and your work, so take a few extra minutes to make sure it's ready to send.

- Use good quality bond paper (not erasable paper).
- Your font should be close to Courier or Times Roman 12. Type that's too small is hard on the eyes; large type is distracting. Only amateurs use script or other fancy type styles.
- Use a letter-quality printout, not dot matrix, and be sure your type is crisp and dark.
- Margins frame your words, so leave 1 to 1¼-inch margins on all four sides. Single spacing is preferred for query letters.
- Proofread for grammar, spelling, punctuation, and typos. If you're careless with this simple step, the editor will wonder if you're careless with your research, too.
- Make sure your name, address, phone number, and email address are on the query in case the editor wants to contact you. Always include a self-addressed, stamped envelope or postcard for the editor's reply.

Query Letter—Checklist

Your query letter will make the difference between a sale and a rejection in today's magazine market. The following checklist and sample query letter offer tips on how to avoid simple mistakes that can cost you a sale.

❶ Verify that you are writing to the current editor and correct address; double-check the spelling of the name and address. This is extremely important.

❷ Phrase the letter as if the article is in the planning stage. Editors prefer pieces written specifically for their publication, not generic articles.

❸ Give enough examples of what you will cover to allow the editor to get a feel for the article. Include any unique material, interviews, or primary sources that you will use.

❹ Note any background or experience you have that gives you credibility in writing this piece for this particular audience. **Include publishing credits if available.**

❺ No need to tell the editor if you are unpublished; let your work speak for you. If you have been published, give the editor your publishing history—but keep it brief.

Street Address
City, State ZIP
Phone Number
Email Address
Date

❶

(Name of Current Editor)
Cobblestone Publishing
Suite C, 30 Grove Street
Peterborough, NH 03458

Dear (Name of Current Editor):

❷

Blue eye feathers? A red, green, and orange beak? How do some of Venezuela's birds become so colorful? Why are others mostly black or gray?

For your January issue of *Faces* devoted to Venezuela and Guyana, I propose retelling, in 750 words or less, the Arawak/Taio folktale, "How the Birds Changed Their Colors."

❸

The story begins when the world is new and all the birds are gray. The the cormorant catches a brightly colored water snake and lays it on the river bank. Many species of birds peck pieces of color from the snake's skin and joyfully decorate themselves. Those arriving first, the toucans and hummingbirds, take the brightest colors. The guinea fowl and the jabiru stork, arriving later, have fewer shades to choose from. The cormorant and the heron are left with only gray, black, and white.

❹
❺

Formerly an elementary school media specialist, I am now a full-time writer, and a member of the Society of Children's Book Writers and Illustrators. My most recent publishing credits include articles in *Boys' Quest*, *Highlights*, and *Spider*.

❻

I have enclosed a bibliography for my story proposal, in addition to a postage-paid return envelope. I have also enclosed a writing clip for your review.

Sincerely,

Gale S. Jacob

❻ Keep the closing brief and professional; remember to include an SASE.

Sample Query & Article Outline

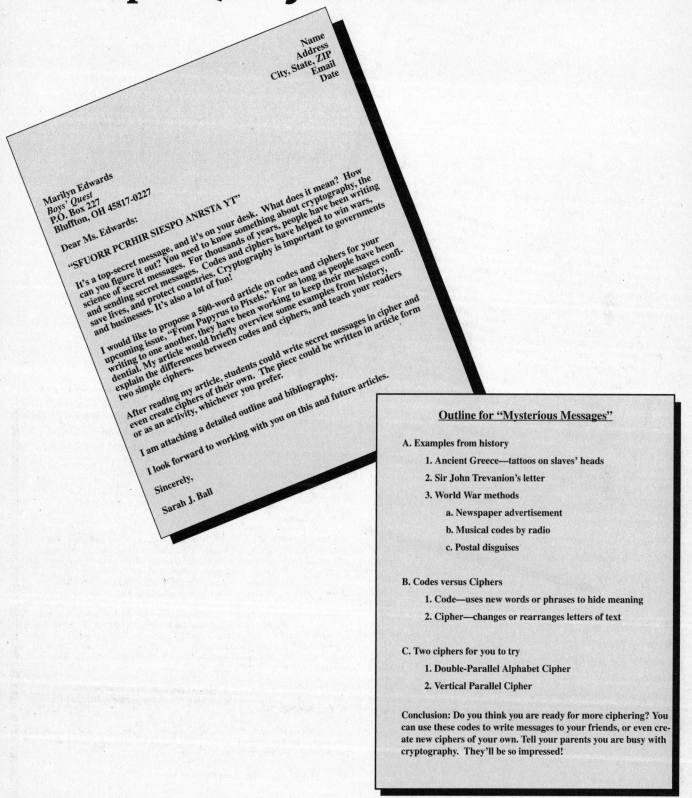

Name
Address
City, State, ZIP
Email
Date

Marilyn Edwards
Boys' Quest
P.O. Box 227
Bluffton, OH 45817-0227

Dear Ms. Edwards:

"SFUORR PCRHIR SIESPO ANRSTA YT"

It's a top-secret message, and it's on your desk. What does it mean? How can you figure it out? You need to know something about cryptography, the science of secret messages. For thousands of years, people have been writing and sending secret messages. Codes and ciphers have helped to win wars, save lives, and protect countries. Cryptography is important to governments and businesses. It's also a lot of fun!

I would like to propose a 500-word article on codes and ciphers for your upcoming issue, "From Papyrus to Pixels." For as long as people have been writing to one another, they have been working to keep their messages confidential. My article would briefly overview some examples from history, explain the differences between codes and ciphers, and teach your readers two simple ciphers.

After reading my article, students could write secret messages in cipher and even create ciphers of their own. The piece could be written in article form or as an activity, whichever you prefer.

I am attaching a detailed outline and bibliography.

I look forward to working with you on this and future articles.

Sincerely,

Sarah J. Ball

Outline for "Mysterious Messages"

A. Examples from history

   1. Ancient Greece—tattoos on slaves' heads

   2. Sir John Trevanion's letter

   3. World War methods

      a. Newspaper advertisement

      b. Musical codes by radio

      c. Postal disguises

B. Codes versus Ciphers

   1. Code—uses new words or phrases to hide meaning

   2. Cipher—changes or rearranges letters of text

C. Two ciphers for you to try

   1. Double-Parallel Alphabet Cipher

   2. Vertical Parallel Cipher

Conclusion: Do you think you are ready for more ciphering? You can use these codes to write messages to your friends, or even create new ciphers of your own. Tell your parents you are busy with cryptography. They'll be so impressed!

Sample Query Letters

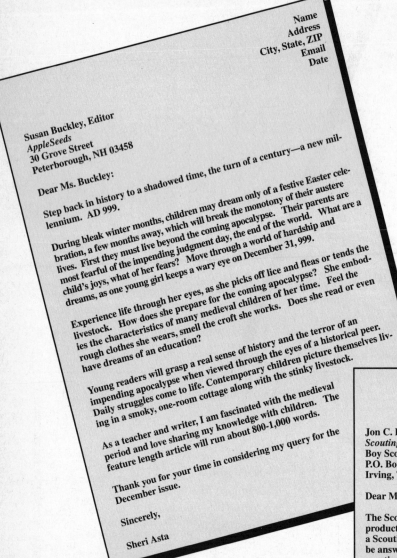

Name
Address
City, State, ZIP
Email
Date

Susan Buckley, Editor
AppleSeeds
30 Grove Street
Peterborough, NH 03458

Dear Ms. Buckley:

Step back in history to a shadowed time, the turn of a century—a new millennium. AD 999.

During bleak winter months, children may dream only of a festive Easter celebration, a few months away, which will break the monotony of their austere lives. First they must live beyond the coming apocalypse. Their parents are most fearful of the impending judgment day, the end of the world. What are a child's joys, what of her fears? Move through a world of hardship and dreams, as one young girl keeps a wary eye on December 31, 999.

Experience life through her eyes, as she picks off lice and fleas or tends the livestock. How does she prepare for the coming apocalypse? She embodies the characteristics of many medieval children of her time. Feel the rough clothes she wears, smell the croft she works. Does she read or even have dreams of an education?

Young readers will grasp a real sense of history and the terror of an impending apocalypse when viewed through the eyes of a historical peer. Daily struggles come to life. Contemporary children picture themselves living in a smoky, one-room cottage along with the stinky livestock.

As a teacher and writer, I am fascinated with the medieval period and love sharing my knowledge with children. The feature length article will run about 800-1,000 words.

Thank you for your time in considering my query for the December issue.

Sincerely,

Sheri Asta

Street Address
City, State ZIP
Phone Number
Email
Date

Jon C. Halter, Editor
Scouting
Boy Scouts of America
P.O. Box 152079
Irving, TX 75015-2079

Dear Mr. Halter:

The Scouting years of a boy's life build memories that last a lifetime. The by-products of those memories: badges, pins, uniforms, etc., add up throughout a Scouting career. At some point in a Scout's life the inevitable question must be answered: "What am I going to do with all of this?" I married into a scouting family and know firsthand the thrill of moving these memories out of boxes and onto the walls where they can be enjoyed.

I would like to submit an article on preserving and displaying Scouting memorabilia. This article will give parents and Scout leaders creative and practical ways to store and enjoy these Scouting memories. This article will include quotes and ideas from scouting families and will be approximately 700 words in length. It will also encourage the readers to use items sold by the Boy Scouts of America for storing Scouting items.

This article will focus on items that are too large to fit in photo albums. It will not include scrapbooking, which was covered in an excellent article in the October 2001 issue.

I am a freelance writer and have been published in *Parents & Kids, Carolina Parenting,* and *Pittsburgh Parents.* I have enclosed recent clips of my work and an SASE for your response.

I look forward to hearing from you.

Sincerely,

Erin E. Ulerich

Sample Bibliography

Bibliography for "How the Birds Changed Their Colors"

Arnott, Kathleen. <u>Animal Folk Tales Around the World.</u> Henry Z. Walck, 1970. pp. 100–103.

Hilty, Steven L. <u>Birds of Venezuela.</u> Princeton University Press, 2002.

Ingersoll, Ernest. <u>Birds in Legend, Fable and Folklore.</u> Longmans Green & Co., 1923. p. 229.

Minnesota University. "Arawak."
http://emuseum.mnsu.edu/cultural/southamerica/arawak.html

Troughton, Joanna, ret. <u>How the Birds Changed Their Feathers: A South American Indian Folk Tale.</u> Peter Bedrick, 1976.

Bibliography

A solid indication of the sources you have identified is more and more a requirement of submissions to children's magazines. Much less common for fiction, with the possible exception of historical fiction, than for nonfiction, bibliographies show an editor that you have already thought through the viability of the project, that the finished piece is likely to be supported by strong evidence and research, and give the editor the tools to fact-check your work and feel confident it is of high quality.

Primary sources, interviews with experts or other relevant individuals (a profile subject and those who know him or her, for example), and a strong synthesis of research that is presented with a clarity and language your target age will appreciate—those are the strict demands of writing well for magazines for children. Articles on science or history or any other nonfiction subject, and stories with factual bases as well, can't rest on secondhand or encyclopedia-level information.

A well-constructed and balanced bibliography is an important tool in selling your writing to an editor. Several references are available and generally accepted for bibliographic format. Investing in one of these is highly recommended for writers: *The Chicago Manual of Style; Modern Language Association (MLA) Handbook;* or handbooks by such news organizations as the *New York Times* or Associated Press.

Preparing a Manuscript Package

The following guide shows how to prepare and mail a professional-looking manuscript package. However, you should always adhere to individual magazine's submission requirements as detailed in its writers' guidelines and its listing in this directory.

Cover Letter Tips

Always keep your cover letter concise and to the point. Provide essential information only.

If the letter accompanies an unsolicited manuscript submission (see below), indicate that your manuscript is enclosed and mention its title and word length. If you're sending the manuscript after the editor responded favorably to your query letter, indicate that the editor requested to see the enclosed manuscript.

Provide a *brief* description of the piece and a short explanation of how it fits the editor's needs. List any publishing credits or other pertinent qualifications. If requested in the guidelines or listing, note any material or sources you can provide. Indicate if the manuscript is being sent to other magazines as well (a simultaneous submission). Mention that you have enclosed a self-addressed, stamped envelope for return of the manuscript.

Sample Cover Letter

Street Address
City, State Zip
Phone Number
Email Address
Date

Manuscript Submissions
Highlights for Children
803 Church Street
Honesdale, PA 18431

Dear (Name of Current Editor):

If most chocolate chip cookie receipes include pretty much the same ingredients, why are some cookies crispy and thin with little hard nuggets of chocolate while others are chewy and moist, bursting with gooey melted chocolate?

The answer is a matter of science.

I have enclosed a 570-word nonfiction article entitled "Cookie Science." Almost everyone loves chocolate chip cookies, and I believe your older readers would enjoy learning about the chemical reactions involved in baking a great cookie.

I am a member of SCBWI and an enthusiastic, experienced baker. I have taught writing at the high school and community college levels.

I have enclosed an SASE for the return of the manuscript if it does not meet your needs at this time.

Thank you for your consideration.

Sincerely,

Ann Marie Pace

Subject/ Specifications: A brief description of the topic and its potential interest to the magazine's readers. Word lengths, age range, availability of photos, and other submission details.

Publishing Credits or relevant experience

Closing: Be formal and direct.

Put Your Best Foot Forward

Magazine editors prefer to receive a typewritten manuscript or a clear, letter-quality computer printout. Be sure your type is clear and not faded.

Use high-quality 8½ x 11 white bond paper. If acceptable, you may send clear photocopies or submissions on a computer disk. For disk submissions, make sure your disk size and software system are compatible with the publication's—and always include a hard (paper) copy of the manuscript.

Some editors accept electronic (email) submissions. When this is the case, the publication's email address is given in its listing.

If requested in the guidelines or listing, include artwork according to specifications, a list of sources, a bibliography, or a biography.

Standard Manuscript Format

The format for preparing manuscripts is fairly standard—an example is shown below. Double- space manuscript text, leaving 1- to 1½-inch margins on the top, bottom, and sides. Indent 5 spaces for paragraphs.

In the upper left corner of the first page (also known as the title page), single space your name, address, phone number, and email address. In the upper right corner of that page, place your word count.

Center the title with your byline below it halfway down the page, approximately 5 inches. Then begin the manuscript text 4 lines below your byline.

In the upper left corner of the following pages, type your last name, the page number, and a word or two of your title. Then, space down 4 lines and continue the text of the manuscript.

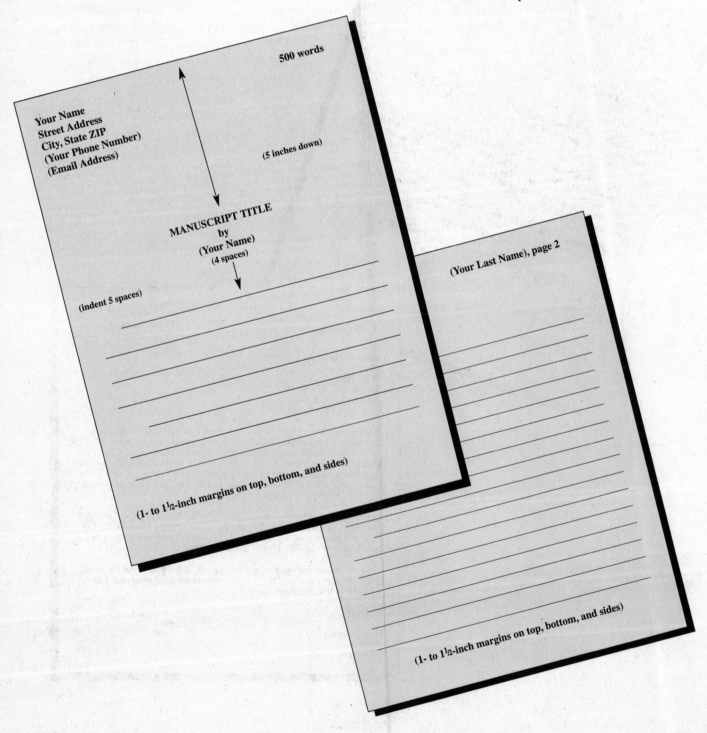

500 words

Your Name
Street Address
  City, State ZIP
  (Your Phone Number)
  (Email Address)

(5 inches down)

MANUSCRIPT TITLE
by
(Your Name)
(4 spaces)

(indent 5 spaces)

(1- to 1½-inch margins on top, bottom, and sides)

(Your Last Name), page 2

(1- to 1½-inch margins on top, bottom, and sides)

Sample Cover Letters

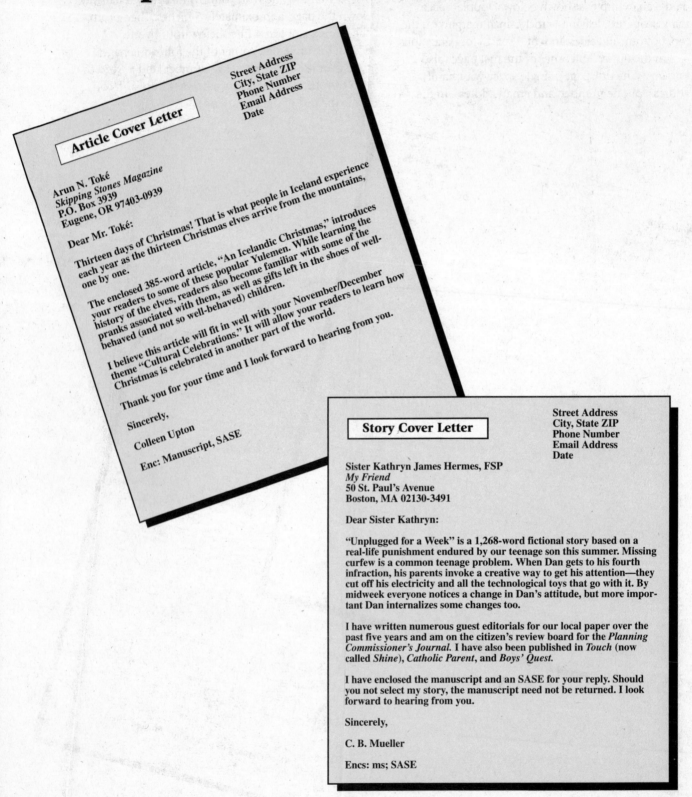

Article Cover Letter

Street Address
City, State ZIP
Phone Number
Email Address
Date

Arun N. Toké
Skipping Stones Magazine
P.O. Box 3939
Eugene, OR 97403-0939

Dear Mr. Toké:

Thirteen days of Christmas! That is what people in Iceland experience each year as the thirteen Christmas elves arrive from the mountains, one by one.

The enclosed 385-word article, "An Icelandic Christmas," introduces your readers to some of these popular Yulemen. While learning the history of the elves, readers also become familiar with some of the pranks associated with them, as well as gifts left in the shoes of well-behaved (and not so well-behaved) children.

I believe this article will fit in well with your November/December theme "Cultural Celebrations." It will allow your readers to learn how Christmas is celebrated in another part of the world.

Thank you for your time and I look forward to hearing from you.

Sincerely,

Colleen Upton

Enc: Manuscript, SASE

Story Cover Letter

Street Address
City, State ZIP
Phone Number
Email Address
Date

Sister Kathryn James Hermes, FSP
My Friend
50 St. Paul's Avenue
Boston, MA 02130-3491

Dear Sister Kathryn:

"Unplugged for a Week" is a 1,268-word fictional story based on a real-life punishment endured by our teenage son this summer. Missing curfew is a common teenage problem. When Dan gets to his fourth infraction, his parents invoke a creative way to get his attention—they cut off his electricity and all the technological toys that go with it. By midweek everyone notices a change in Dan's attitude, but more important Dan internalizes some changes too.

I have written numerous guest editorials for our local paper over the past five years and am on the citizen's review board for the *Planning Commissioner's Journal*. I have also been published in *Touch* (now called *Shine*), *Catholic Parent*, and *Boys' Quest*.

I have enclosed the manuscript and an SASE for your reply. Should you not select my story, the manuscript need not be returned. I look forward to hearing from you.

Sincerely,

C. B. Mueller

Encs: ms; SASE

Sample Cover Letters

Marilyn Edwards
Boys' Quest
P.O. Box 227
Bluffton, OH 45817-0227

Street Address
City, State ZIP
Phone Number
Email Address
Date

Dear Ms. Edwards:

The American buffalo has played an important role in "manifest destiny" in the United States. During this history-making time, buffalo were nearly annihilated to only about 1,000 animals by the late 1880's.

Though most middle-grade students are aware of the near extinction of the buffalo, the enclosed article explains how people are restoring buffalo to native grassland throughout the United States. Native Americans, individual ranchers, and U.S. National Parks play an important role in this endeavor.

I did not find the noble buffalo (bison) on your theme list. I hope you will consider my article for a future publication. I am enclosing a photo downloaded from the Theodore Roosevelt National Park website, as well as a stamped, self-addressed envelope for your reply. I look forward to hearing from you.

Sincerely,

Marilyn J. Faulhaber

Enc: Manuscript
      SASE

Street Address
City, State ZIP
Phone Number
Email Address

Date

Mary Lou Carney, Editor
Guideposts for Kids
P.O. Box 538A
Chesterton, IN 46304

Dear Ms. Carney:

Lurlene McDaniel returned my fiction manuscript THE AMBULANCE RIDE recently and asked me to rework it per her suggestions and resubmit it to you. So please find enclosed the revised manuscript, now titled TOM JORDAN.

Tom Jordan nearly dies of embarrassment when his antique-dealer mother drags him around with her in a big pink van named Ellabelle to sort through people's trash for treasures. In fact, his mother, by her mere existence, embarrasses Tom horribly. Nothing worse could happen to a sixth-grade boy, right? Wrong.

He could end up pinned in crumpled Ellabelle, with the flood waters of Brushy Creek rising fast. He could end up responsible for saving his mother's life or letting her drown. He could end up with no way to get help except for a string of Christmas lights that probably didn't work.

Thank you for giving me the opportunity to rewrite the story and resubmit it to you. If you would like further changes, I'd be glad to work with you. I've enclosed an SASE for your response.

I look forward to hearing from you.

Very truly yours,

Sharelle Byars Moranville

Preparing a Résumé

Several publications in this directory request that prospective writers send a list of publishing credits or enclose a résumé with their submission. As you read through the listings, you will notice that some editors want to see a résumé only, while others may request a résumé with a query letter, writing samples, or a complete manuscript.

By reviewing a résumé, an editor can determine if a prospective writer has the necessary experience to research and write material for that publication.

A résumé that you submit to a magazine is different from one you would submit when applying for a job, because it emphasizes writing experience, memberships in writing associations, and education. This type of résumé does not list all of your work experience or every association to which you belong, but should include only those credentials that demonstrate experience related to the magazine's editorial requirements. In the case of educational or special interest publications, be sure to include pertinent work experience.

No one style is preferred, but make sure your name and email address (if you have one) appear at the top of the page. Keep your résumé short and concise—it should not be more than one page long.

Sample Résumés

```
                Joanna Coates
                   Address
               City, State ZIP
                    Phone
                Email Address

EDUCATION:
                University of Missouri, Columbia, MO
    1980        M.Ed. Reading
    1975        B.A. English Education

Missouri Certified Teacher of English and Reading
Specialist

TEACHING EXPERIENCE:
  1997-present  Instructor
                Adult Continuing Education ESL Classes
                Springfield College, Springfield, MO

  1981-1995     Classroom Teacher
                Middle School English and Reading
                John Jay Middle School, Thornfield, MO

EDUCATIONAL MATERIAL PUBLISHED:
                Educational Insights
    1995        FUN WITH READING II
                   Story/activity kit
    1993        FUN WITH READING I
                   Story/activity kit
MEMBERSHIP:
Society of Children's Book Writers and Illustrators
```

```
                Maria Lital
                  Address
              City, State ZIP
                   Phone
               Email Address

EDUCATION:
    1989        Bachelor of Arts
                History/Journalism
                University of North Carolina,
                Chapel Hill, North Carolina

WORK EXPERIENCE:
  1998-present  Media Sales Representative,
                Clarkson Ledger, Ripley, Tennessee

  1996-1998     Researcher/Librarian, Station
                WBXI, Danville, Kentucky

  1993-1996     Researcher, Family News, Raleigh,
                North Carolina

  1990-1993     Assistant Librarian, Public
                Library; Edenton, North Carolina

RELATED ACTIVITIES:
  1998-present  Newsletter Editor, St. James
                Church, Ripley, Tennessee

  1998-present  Historical Tour Guide, Ripley,
                Tennessee, Historical Association

  1996-present  Active in Civil War Reenactments

MEMBERSHIP:
  1996-present  American Library Association
```

Copyright and Permissions

In the literary field, a copyright is legal ownership of an original written work. The owner or writer has the legal right to decide how a work is reproduced, and, for certain works, how it is performed or displayed. According to the Copyright Act of 1976 (effective January 1, 1978), this protection exists from the moment the work is recorded in a tangible medium, such as computer file or on paper, without any need for legal action or counsel.

As a result of the Copyright Term Extension Act of 1998, you now own all rights to work you created during or after 1978 for your lifetime plus 70 years, until you choose to sell all or part of the copyright for this work. But remember that it is only your unique combination of words—how you wrote something—that the law protects and considers copyrighted. Ideas or facts that are expressed in your work cannot be copyrighted.

Do You Need to Register Your Work?

Once your manuscript is completed, your work is protected by the current copyright laws. You don't need to register your work with the United States Copyright Office. Editors want to buy your work; they have no need to steal it. A copy of the manuscript and a dated record of your submission will provide proof of creation.

Most editors view an author's copyright notice on manuscripts as a sign of amateurism, or a signal that the author doesn't trust the publication. However, if you decide to register your work, obtain an application form and directions on the correct way to file your copyright application. Write to the Library of Congress, Copyright Office, 101 Independence Ave. S. E., Washington, DC 20559-6000. These forms and directions are also available online in Adobe Acrobat format at: www.copyright.gov/forms. Copyright registration fees are currently $30.

If you have registered your unpublished manuscript with the Library of Congress, notify your editor of that fact once it is accepted for publication.

Rights Purchased by Magazines

Magazines request and purchase certain rights to publish manuscripts. A publisher is restricted by an agreement with you on when, how, and where he or she may publish your manuscript. Below is a list of common rights that are purchased by magazines:

All World Rights: The publisher purchases all rights to publish your work anywhere in the world any number of times. This includes all forms of media (both current and those which may be developed later). The publisher also has the right to all future use of the work, including reprints, syndication, creation of derivative works, and use in databases. You no longer have the right to sell or reproduce the work, unless you can negotiate for the return of certain rights (for example, book rights).

All World Serial Rights: The publisher purchases all rights to publish your work in newspapers, magazines, and other serial publications throughout the world any number of times. You retain all other rights, such as the right to use it as a chapter in a book.

First Rights: A publisher acquires the right to publish your work for the first time in any specified media. Electronic and nontraditional markets often seek these rights. All other rights, including reprint rights, belong to you.

Electronic Rights: Publishers use this as a catch-all for inclusion in any type of electronic publication, such as CD-ROM, websites, ezines or in an electronic databases.

First North American Serial Rights: The publisher can publish your work for the first time in a U.S. or Canadian periodical. You retain the book and North American reprint rights, as well as first rights to a foreign market.

Second or Reprint Rights: This allows a publication non-exclusive rights to print the material for the second time. You may not authorize second publication to occur until alter the work has appeared in print by the publisher who bought First Rights.

One-time Rights: Often bought by regional publications, this means the publication has bought the right to use the material once. You may continue to sell the material elsewhere; however, you should inform the publisher if this work is being simultaneously considered for publication in a competing magazine.

You should be aware that an agreement may limit a publisher to the right to publish your work in certain media (e.g., magazines and other periodicals only) or the agreement may include wider-ranging rights (e.g., the right to publish the manuscript in a book or an audio-cassette). The right may be limited to publishing within a specific geographic region or in a specific language. Any rights you retain allow you to resell the manuscript within the parameters of your agreement.

It is becoming increasingly common for magazines to purchase all rights, especially those who host Internet sites and make archives of previously published articles available to readers. Unless you have extensive publishing credentials, you may not want to jeopardize the opportunity to be published by insisting on selling limited rights.

Contracts and Agreements

Typically, when a publisher indicates an interest in your manuscript, he or she specifies what rights the publication will acquire. Then usually, but not always, a publisher will send you a letter of agreement or a standard written contract spelling out the terms of the agreement.

If a publisher does not send you a written contract or agreement and appears to be relying on oral consent, you need to consider your options. While an oral agreement may be legally binding, it is not as easy to enforce as a written one. To protect your interests, draft a letter outlining the terms as you understand them (e.g., a 500-word article without photos, first North American serial rights, paying on acceptance at $.05 a word). Send two copies of the letter to the editor (with a self-addressed, stamped envelope), asking him or her to sign one and return it to you if the terms are correct.

Work Made for Hire

Another term that is appearing more frequently in contracts is work made for hire. As a freelance writer, most editors treat you as an independent contractor (not an employee) who writes articles for their publication. Magazine editors can assign or commission articles to freelancers as works-made-for-hire, making the finished article property of the publisher.

Under current copyright laws, only certain types of commissioned works are considered works-made-for-hire, and only when both the publisher and the commissioned writer agree in writing. These works typically include items such contributions to "collec-tive works" such as magazines. A contract or agreement clearly stating that the material is a work-made-for-hire must be signed by both parties and be in place before the material is written. Once a writer agrees to these terms, he or she no longer has any rights to the work.

Note that a pre-existing piece, such as an unsolicited manuscript that is accepted for publication is not considered a commissioned work.

Guidelines for Permission to Quote

When you want to quote another writer's words in a manuscript you're preparing, you must get that writer's permission. If you don't, you could be sued for copyright infringement. Here are some guidelines:

- Any writing published in the U.S. prior to 1923 is in the public domain, as are works created by the U.S. government. Such material may be quoted without permission, but the source should be cited.

- No specific limits are set as to the length of permitted quotations in your articles: different publishers have various requirements. Generally, if you quote more than a handful of words, you should seek permission. Always remember to credit your sources.

- The doctrine of "fair use" allows quoting portions of a copyrighted work for certain purposes, as in a review, news reporting, nonprofit educational uses, or research. Contrary to popular belief, there is no absolute word limit on fair use. But as a general rule, never quote more than a few successive paragraphs from a book or article and credit the source.

- If you're submitting a manuscript that contains quoted material, you'll need to obtain permission from the source to quote the material before it is published. If you're uncertain about what to do, your editor should be able to advise you.

Resources

Interested in finding out more about writers and their rights under the law? Check these sources for further information:

The Publishing Law Center
www.publaw.com/legal.html
The Copyright Handbook: How to Protect and Use Written Works, 6th Edition by Attorney Stephen Fishman. Nolo, 2002.
The Writer's Legal Guide, 2nd Edition by Tad Crawford. Allworth Press, 1998

Last Steps and Follow Up

Before mailing your manuscript, check the pages for neatness, readability, and proper page order. Proofread for typographical errors. Redo pages if necessary. Keep a copy of the manuscript for your records.

Mailing Requirements

Assemble the pages (unstapled) and place your cover letter on top of the first page.

Send manuscripts over 5 pages in length in a 9x12 or 10x13 manila envelope. Include a same-size SASE marked "First Class." If submitting to a foreign magazine, enclose the proper amount of International Reply Coupons (IRC) for return postage. Mail manuscripts under 5 pages in a large business-size envelope with a same-size SASE folded inside.

Package your material carefully and address the outer envelope to the magazine editor. Send your submission via first-class or priority mail. Don't use certified or registered mail. (See Postage Information, page 26.)

Follow up with the Editor

Some writers contend that waiting for an editor to respond is the hardest part of writing. But wait you must. Editors usually respond within the time period specified in the listings.

If you don't receive a response by the stated response time, allow at least three weeks to pass before you contact the editor. At that time, send a letter with a self-addressed, stamped envelope requesting to know the status of your submission.

The exception to this general rule is when you send a return postcard with a manuscript. In that case, look for your postcard about three weeks after mailing the manuscript. If you don't receive it by then, write to the editor requesting confirmation that it was received.

If more than two months pass after the stated response time and you don't receive any response, send a letter withdrawing your work from consideration. At that point, you can send your query or manuscript to the next publication on your list.

What You Can Expect

The most common responses to a submission are an impersonal rejection letter, a personalized rejection letter, an offer to look at your material "on speculation," or an assignment.

If you receive an impersonal rejection note, revise your manuscript if necessary, and send your work to the next editor on your list. If you receive a personal note, send a thank-you note. If you receive either of the last two responses, you know what to do!

Set up a Tracking System

To help you keep track of the status of your submissions, you may want to establish a system in a notebook, in a computer file, or on file cards (see below).

This will keep you organized and up-to-date on the status of your queries and manuscripts and on the need to follow up with certain editors.

SENT QUERIES TO THE FOLLOWING PUBLICATIONS

Editor	Publication	Topic	Date Sent	Postage	Accepted/ Rejected	Rights Offered

SENT MANUSCRIPTS TO THE FOLLOWING PUBLICATIONS

Editor	Publication	Title	Date Sent	Postage	Accepted/ Rejected	Rights Offered

Frequently Asked Questions

How do I request a sample copy and writers' guidelines?

Write a brief note to the magazine: *"Please send me a recent sample copy and writers' guidelines. If there is any charge, please enclose an invoice and I will pay upon receipt."* The magazine's website, if it has one, offers a faster and less expensive alternative. Many companies put a part of the magazine, writers' guidelines, and sometimes a theme list or editorial calendar on the Internet.

How do I calculate the amount of postage for a sample copy?

Check the listing in this directory. In some cases the amount of postage will be listed. If the number of pages is given, use that to estimate the amount of postage by using the postage chart at the end of this section. For more information on postage and how to obtain stamps, see page 26.

I need to include a bibliography with my article proposal. How do I set one up?

The reference section of your local library can provide several sources that will help you set up a bibliography. A style manual such as *The Chicago Manual of Style* will show you the proper format for citing all your sources, including unpublished material, interviews, and Internet material. For information on bibliographies, see page 15.

What do I put in a cover letter if I have no publishing credits or relevant personal experience?

In this case, you may want to forego a formal cover letter and send your manuscript with a brief letter stating: *"Enclosed is my manuscript, [Insert Title], for your review."* For more information on cover letters, see pages 18 and 19.

How long should I wait before contacting an editor after I have submitted my manuscript?

The response time given in the listings can vary, and it's a good idea to wait three to four weeks after the stated response time before sending a brief note to the editor asking about the status of your manuscript. You might use this opportunity to add a new sales pitch or include additional material to show that the topic is continuing to generate interest. If you do not get a satisfactory response or you want to send your manuscript elsewhere, send a certified letter to the editor withdrawing the work from consideration and requesting its return. You are then free to submit the work to another magazine.

I don't need my manuscript returned. How do I indicate that to an editor?

With the capability to store manuscripts electronically and print out additional copies easily, some writers keep postage costs down by enclosing a self-addressed, stamped postcard (SASP) saying, *"No need to return my manuscript. Please use this postcard to advise me of the status of my manuscript. Thank you."*

Common Publishing Terms

All rights: Contractual agreement by which a publisher acquires the copyright and all use of author's material (see page 21).

Anthology: A collection of selected literary pieces.

Anthropomorphization: Attributing human form or personality to things not human (i.e., animals).

Assignment: Manuscript commissioned by an editor for a stated fee.

Bimonthly: A publication that appears every two months.

Biweekly: A publication issued every two weeks.

Byline: Author's name credited at the heading of an article.

Caption: Description or text accompanying an illustration or photograph.

CD-ROM (compact disc read-only-memory)**:** Non-erasable compact disc containing data that can be read by a computer.

Clip: Sample of a published work.

Contributor's copies: Copies of the publication issue in which the writer's work appears.

Copyedit: To edit with close attention to style and mechanics.

Copyright: Legal rights that protect an author's work (see page 21).

Cover letter: Brief letter sent with a manuscript introducing the writer and presenting the materials enclosed (see pages 18 and 19).

Disk submission: Manuscript that is submitted on a computer disk.

Early readers: Children 4 to 7 years.

Editorial calendar: List of topics, themes, or special sections that are planned for upcoming issues for a specific time period.

Electronic submission: Manuscript transmitted to an editor from one computer to another through a modem.

Email (electronic mail)**:** Messages sent from one computer to another via computer network or modem.

English-language rights: The right to publish a manuscript in any English-speaking country.

Filler: Short item that fills out a page (e.g., joke, light verse, or fun fact).

First serial rights: The right to publish a work for the first time in a periodical; often limited to a specific geographical region (e.g., North America or Canada) [see page 21].

Genre: Category of fiction characterized by a particular style, form, or content, such as mystery or fantasy.

Glossy: Photo printed on shiny rather than matte-finish paper.

Guidelines: See **Writers' guidelines.**

In-house: See **Staff written.**

International Reply Coupon (IRC): Coupon exchangeable in any foreign country for postage on a single-rate, surface-mailed letter.

Kill fee: Percentage of the agreed-upon fee paid to a writer if an editor decides not to use a purchased manuscript.

Layout: Plan for the arrangement of text and artwork on a printed page.

Lead: Beginning of an article.

Lead time: Length of time between assembling and printing an issue.

Libel: Any false published statement intended to expose another to public ridicule or personal loss.

Manuscript: A typewritten or computer-printed version of a document (as opposed to a published version).

Masthead: The printed matter in a newspaper or periodical that gives the title and pertinent details of ownership, advertising rates, and subscription rates.

Middle-grade readers: Children 8 to 12 years.

Modem: An internal device or a small electrical box that plugs into a computer; used to transmit data between computers, often via telephone lines.

Ms/mss: Manuscript/manuscripts.

One-time rights: The right to publish a piece once, often not the first time (see page 21).

On spec: Refers to writing "on speculation," without an editor's commitment to purchase the manuscript.

Outline: Summary of a manuscript's contents, usually nonfiction, organized under subheadings with descriptive sentences under each.

Payment on acceptance: Author is paid following an editor's decision to accept a manuscript.

Payment on publication: Author is paid following the publication of the manuscript.

Pen name/pseudonym: Fictitious name used by an author.

Pre-K: Children under 5 years of age; also known as *preschool.*

Proofread: To read and mark errors, usually in printed text.

Query: Letter to an editor to promote interest in a manuscript or an idea.

Rebus story: A "see and say" story form, using pictures followed by the written words; often written for pre-readers.

Refereed journal: Publication that requires all manuscripts be reviewed by an editorial or advisory board.

Reprint: Another printing of an article or story; can be in a different magazine format, such as an anthology.

Reprint rights: See **Second serial rights.**

Response time: Average length of time for an editor to accept or reject a submission and contact the writer with his or her decision.

Résumé: Account of one's qualifications, including educational and professional background, as well as publishing credits.

SAE: Self-addressed envelope (no postage).

SASE: Self-addressed, stamped envelope.

SASP: Self-addressed stamped postcard.

Second serial rights: The right to publish a manuscript that has appeared in another publication; also known as *Reprint rights* (see page 21).

Semiannual: Occurring every six months or twice a year.

Semimonthly: Occurring twice a month.

Semiweekly: Occurring twice a week.

Serial: A publication issued as one of a consecutively numbered and indefinitely continued series.

Serial rights: See **First serial rights.**

Sidebar: A short article that accompanies a feature article and highlights one aspect of the feature's subject.

Simultaneous submission: Manuscript submitted to more than one publisher at the same time; also known as multiple submission.

Slant: Specific approach to a subject to appeal to a certain readership.

Slush pile: Term used within the publishing industry to describe unsolicited manuscripts.

Solicited manuscript: Manuscript that an editor has requested or agreed to consider.

Staff written: Prepared by members of the magazine's staff; also known as *in-house*.

Syndication rights: The right to distribute serial rights to a given work through a syndicate of periodicals.

Synopsis: Condensed description or summary of a manuscript.

Tabloid: Publication printed on an ordinary newspaper page, turned sideways and folded in half.

Tearsheet: A page from a newspaper or magazine (periodical) containing a printed story or article.

Theme list: See **Editorial calendar.**

Transparencies: Color slides, not color prints.

Unsolicited manuscript: Any manuscript not specifically requested by an editor.

Work-made-for-hire: Work specifically ordered, commissioned, and owned by a publisher for its exclusive use (see page 22).

World rights: Contractual agreement whereby the publisher acquires the right to reproduce the work throughout the world (see page 21); also known as *all rights*.

Writers' guidelines: Publisher's editorial objectives or specifications, which usually include word lengths, readership level, and subject matter.

Writing sample: Example of your writing style, tone, and skills; may be a published or unpublished piece.

Young adult: Readers 12 to 18 years

Postage Information

How Much Postage?

When you're sending a manuscript to a magazine, enclose a self-addressed, stamped envelope with sufficient postage; this way, if the editor does not want to use your manuscript, it can be returned to you. To help you calculate the proper amount of postage for your SASE, here are the US postal rates for first-class mailings in the US and from the US to Canada based on the latest increase (2002). Rates are expected to increase again, so please check with your local Post Office, or check the US Postal Service website at usps.com.

Ounces	9x12 Envelope (Approx. no. of pages)	US First-Class Postage Rate	Rate from US to Canada
1	1–5	$ 0.37	$ 0.60
2	6–10	0.60	0.85
3	11–15	0.83	1.10
4	16–20	1.06	1.35
5	21–25	1.29	1.60
6	26–30	1.52	1.85
7	31–35	1.75	2.10
8	36–40	1.98	2.35

The amount of postage and size of envelope necessary to receive a sample copy and writers' guidelines are usually stated in the magazine listing. If this information is not provided, use the chart above to help gauge the proper amount of postage.

How to Obtain Stamps

People living in the US, Canada, or overseas can acquire US stamps through the mail from the Philately Fulfillment Service Center. Call 800-STAMP-24 (800-782-6724) to request a catalogue or place an order. For overseas, the telephone number is 816-545-1100. You pay the cost of the stamps plus a postage and handling fee based on the value of the stamps ordered, and the stamps are shipped to you. Credit card information (MasterCard, Visa, and Discover cards only) is required for fax orders. The fax number is 816-545-1212. If you order through the catalogue, you can pay with a US check or an American Money Order. Allow 3–4 weeks for delivery.

Gateway to
the Markets

Golden Years, Golden Opportunities for Middle-Grade Fiction

By Pamela Holtz Beres

Your friend tells you she has finally found success writing fiction. Her readers, she says, are in the golden years. You wrinkle your forehead. "The golden years?" you ask. "Grandmas and grandpas in conflict at the bingo hall?"

Your friend laughs. "No. My readers are kids between the ages of 8 and 12. Those are the golden years for reading."

The light goes on. You remember all of those dog-eared copies of *American Girl, Children's Digest, Boys' Quest,* and *Cricket* on the library shelves. You think about your niece, who likes to tell you about her favorite story in the current issue of *New Moon.* Then you remember all of the Sunday-school magazines your own kids have brought home over the years—*Pockets, My Friend, Shine Brightly.* Your pulse picks up speed. If your friend can crack this market, maybe you can, too!

Who Are the Golden Girls—and Boys?

By the age of eight, most children are able to read on their own. They're confident in their skills and eager to practice independently of teachers or parents. During the next four years, many of them will spend more time reading "just for fun" than at any other period of their lives. The child's mind is open. Opinions, morals, and values begin to take shape. While parents still have the greatest influence on their ideas, stories can enhance what they learn, and expand their world.

For the middle-grade reader, the world is larger than it was just a couple of years ago. School is no longer a new experience and classmates are no longer incidental companions. Rather, classmates are people through whom they will learn the ins and outs of friendship and getting along with others. While they long for the support and approval of the adults in their lives, their focus shifts from family to friends. They like independence, are ready to accept responsibility, and strive to work through their problems without running to their parents or teachers. While some see the middle-grade years as the calm before the storm of adolescence, the issues children this age face are complex. And this age won't settle for easy answers. Writers for this audience share an awesome responsibility. Their words will forever shape the minds of their readers.

Pamela Holtz Beres's middle-grade fiction has appeared in a wide variety of magazines, including *Children's Digest, Jack And Jill, My Friend, On the Line,* and *Pockets.* She is the author of *Timber Lake Road,* a monthly fiction series published in *Pockets.*

The Heart of Fiction

While the middle-grade reader craves action, the stories they read must have a main character with whom they can identify and to follow through the story. A single point of view is vital. Since children like to read about kids the same age or slightly older than they are, the main character is usually 12 or 13 years old.

Children should see themselves in the character you create but that character should be unique enough to stand out in your reader's mind. Consider giving your character a "tag"—something to identify him or her as different from other characters. Perhaps Mandy always flicks her head to get her overgrown bangs off her face. Maybe super-sleuth Quinn snaps his fingers and points at his companion each time he comes up with one of his brilliant ideas. Or what if Rosa has a habit of humming, to the great annoyance of her friends? Choose your character tags carefully. They should serve to individualize your character or perhaps even play a role in the story's plot. Rosa's friends may be annoyed by her humming, but when all three of them are alone in an elevator stuck between floors, her tunes have a calming effect as they wait for help to arrive.

The best compliment a writer can get is to have a reader say that they feel as though the character in your story is their new best friend. To achieve that level of reality, you must know your main character well before you begin writing. Some writers find it helpful to create a profile of their main character. Note your character's name, age, hair color and style, eye color, and body size and build. Know their personality. Is Dakota popular, easy-going, kind, helpful, loud, boisterous, leap-before-looking or quiet, withdrawn, thoughtful, insightful, loyal and true? By knowing your character inside and out, he or she will lead the way through your story and bring your reader along for the ride. Since stories for the middle-grade market usually top out around 1,200 words or less, you will undoubtedly know more about your main character than you will show in your story. But never underestimate the sophistication of your readers. Characters created with little thought will be rejected, if not by editors, surely by your audience!

Action!

Ask a fourth-grade teacher what her worst nightmare is and she might tell you, "cancelled recess." Running, jumping, climbing, biking, hiking, swimming, collecting, building, exploring: Life moves quickly for middle-grade readers. To keep their attention long enough to read your story, it, too, must be action-filled and move at a rapid pace. Strong verbs and abundant sensory detail will bring your story to life and let your reader experience it just as your main character does.

Description must never be static. If your story begins with, "Mandy has brown eyes, long, straight blond hair and an annoying habit of always turning her head to get the hair out of her eyes," your reader will yawn and either skip to the next paragraph where she hopes something will happen, or worse yet, she'll set the magazine down and pick up the video game controller. Description must be blended with action. Start your story instead with something like this: "Mandy's brown eyes filled with tears as she stood face to face with Kelly. She flicked her head to get her overgrown bangs off her face, but they fell right back down." Your reader still learns that Mandy has brown eyes and likes to turn her head to get her bangs off her face, but your reader hardly knows they've read description. They've watched the action, absorbed the details, and will read on to find out why Mandy is crying.

Remember that your reader has five senses and when all are engaged, he or she is totally immersed in your world. It's not enough to sprinkle in a few sight details, such as a red and white striped shirt or a blue calico quilt on a bed. In real life, your reader also hears, tastes, smells, and feels through touch. Let him experience those things in your fictional world as well.

Problems and Solutions

No matter how likable your main character or great your sensory detail, something must happen in your story. A writer can submit a 1,200-word, action-filled manuscript and have it rejected because there is nothing for your reader to care about. Your main character may swim across the river, hike through a forest, and then go home and clean his room. Whew! That would be a busy, action-filled day! But would your reader care? No. He would be wondering why your character did all of those things. What was his goal? What did he want? What was he trying to accomplish?

What if you let your reader know that your main character's goal was to prove he could do all of those things, or maybe win a bet with his friend? Will the reader be satisfied now? Not yet. You got his attention, but your demanding young audience expects even more. They expect your main character to struggle.

Something must stand in the way of success. Set your stakes high and then increase the tension as the story progresses. Then, you'll have a satisfied reader. He or she will bond with the character and will root and cheer, hoping for success. Keep in mind, too, that children read to feel empowered. No matter how big the problem, your main character must play a central role in resolving it.

Does that mean that all of your stories must show a 12-year-old beating unbearable odds in order to satisfy the reader? Of course not. Slip into the shoes of your audience. Everyday life poses challenges that are new and exciting and sometimes puzzling, intimidating, or scary. To an adult, a thunderstorm is an ordinary occurrence. Even a temporary power outage raises little concern. But to a 12-year-old left home in charge of his siblings, it's a frightening experience. Kids this age are eager to prove their sense of responsibility. The reader will want to know how this character faces the challenge and overcomes the struggle. If your main character could do it, your reader will reason that he or she could, too.

Maintaining friendships, getting along with brothers and sisters, and learning about cooperation and teamwork through school, sports, and other activities, including plain old-fashioned messing around, are all fodder for exciting middle-grade stories. Even if your story takes place in another time or another country, at the heart of your story will be experiences common to all middle-grade children. If your main character's best friend chooses a new best friend for no reason at all, your reader will sympathize and identify with that character, whether he or she lives in twenty-first century Cleveland, ancient Egypt, or some unknown galaxy in the distant future.

What the Editors Say about Middle-Grade Fiction

♦ Marilyn Edwards, Editor, *Boys' Quest, Fun For Kidz, Hopscotch,* page 66.

♦ Penny Rasdall, Editor, *Children's Digest,* page 85.

♦ Sister Maria Grace Dateno, Editor, *My Friend,* page 179.

♦ Lacey Louwagie, Editor, *New Moon,* page 183.

Taboos and Other Do's and Don'ts

While the issues kids face are complex, and technological advances have exposed them to the harsher realities of life, editors of middle-grade children's magazines strive to keep their publications wholesome and fun. Cursing and swearing are out. So are violence, derogatory humor, and sexual content. Some magazines allow simple crushes while others prefer to keep boy/girl relationships platonic. Editors of religious or health-themed magazines might choose to show the consequences of making poor choices regarding drugs, cigarettes, and alcohol, but usually it's an older character who imbibes, with the main character learning through observation. Unwise choices always have consequences in middle-grade fiction.

The goal for middle-grade magazine editors is simply to publish stories that help today's kids face and solve everyday problems. In any story, the main character must learn and grow. But despite the need for the reader to "learn" through the story, editors are adamant that the stories they publish should not be "preachy." The message or take-away value must be woven into the plot with the main character making discoveries or coming to conclusions through their own thought process. For the religious market, Biblical references obviously are accepted, yet each editor has distinct ideas on how many and the manner in which they are incorporated. One editor might find that your main character's reciting a specific Bible passage is the perfect way to impart a certain truth while another editor might see it as unnatural.

Of course, the best way to know what's acceptable and what's taboo is to read the publication you want to write for and know the editorial guidelines. While generalizations exist, each market has its own mission and method of carrying it out. Get to know the market, and then cash in on a golden opportunity by writing for kids in the golden years of reading.

Short Subjects: The Market for Activities, Games, & Filler

By Mark Haverstock

When it comes to magazine submissions, most writers think of feature articles or fictional stories. But in reality, a sizeable portion of popular children's and teen magazines are made up of shorter pieces—quizzes, puzzles, crafts, or departments. A recent issue of *Highlights for Children*, for example, contained 19 shorter pieces.

With numbers like these, editors are always hungry for a reliable pool of writers to handle short subjects, many fewer than 200 words. "We don't get enough, especially of the quality we are looking for," says Kim T. Griswell, Coordinating Editor for *Highlights*. "We're always trying to encourage writers to send in these smaller pieces."

For writers new to the game, it's a good way to begin a career, especially if you don't have any writing credits. "Submitting a puzzle, craft, or activity can help you get your foot in the door," says Griswell. "It gets you noticed by editors, and if you do a number of quality submissions of those kind, we start looking at you to do longer pieces for us."

Filling the Gap

Griswell's wish list includes more seasonal materials, as well as visual and other types of puzzles for the inside back cover of the magazine. "We do one short section on page five of the magazine, usually a how-to or activity-based article, and we're always looking for these," she explains. "They're a little bit longer than an individual activity and have to be more meaty." In particular, Griswell looks for submissions that are related to holidays, cultures, in addition to anything that's activity-based and has broad appeal for our readers from the younger readers up to the older readers.

If you plan to write puzzles or quizzes of any kind, note that *Highlights* doesn't publish anything in the magazine that requires you to mark on the page. Activities can't be fill-in-the-blank or any other form in which readers would have to write on the page. They have to be something that you can do visually, in your mind, or on a separate sheet of paper. "Keep your audience in mind—the age levels broadly being from 2 to 12, with the core audience being 6 to 8," says Griswell. "Write things that appeal to that range of readers."

"I still don't get enough activity pieces on the lesser holidays," says Susan Reith Swan, Editor of *Story Friends*. "What surprises me for a Christian magazine is that I don't get enough on Easter. Everyone thinks Christmas. I don't get a whole lot on Valentine's Day, Mother's Day, or Father's Day either." Since *Story Friends* is a Mennonite publication and the denomination is pacifist, pieces relating to patriotic holidays, such as the Fourth of July, aren't accepted. The magazine has a large readership

Mark Haverstock is the author of more than 450 articles, including how-to's, quizzes, and activities. He has written for *Boys' Life*, *Guideposts for Teens*, *Guideposts for Kids*, *Cobblestone*, *Highlights for Children*, *National Geographic Kids*, *Parenting Teens*, and is a regular contributor to *Children's Writer* and *Children's Writer Guide*.

Picture Perfect

Many of the larger, well-established magazines have art directors or hire photographers and illustrators to handle the graphics that go with filler pieces. But smaller magazines with limited budgets often welcome clear photos and illustrations from those who have an artistic flair.

"Most of our puzzle and activity submissions don't come in illustrated, and the chances of acceptance are better if accompanied with quality photos or drawings," says *Hopscotch* Editor Marilyn Edwards. "For example, one author sent clear pictures for each step in making a lei, along with her text. We were so impressed that we came up with a new issue theme to accommodate the project."

As for *Wee Ones*, they won't accept crafts or projects unless they come with a photo or a graphic. "In the beginning we would get craft ideas, do the craft, and take a picture of it," says Editor Jennifer Reed. "Later we came to the conclusion if the author is doing the craft, chances are that they have a picture of it or actually have the craft made. That's when we decided to let them handle that part." Since *Wee Ones* is an online magazine, digital photos are encouraged because they're easier to format and post on the Web.

Illustrators might want to consider writing short activities and filler as a supplement to their income. "I believe a lot of them think all they can do is illustrate, and here's an easy opportunity for them to break into writing," says Edwards. "It's also a way to make things simpler for us."

in Canada, so Swan also avoids holidays specific to the United States.

According to Lou Waryncia, Managing Editor of *Cobblestone*, the American history magazine isn't lacking in quantity of activities and filler, but he'd like to see more variety. "We could use a little more complexity, especially in the word puzzles, or more mind-challenging activities," he says. "Sometimes all we'll get are word searches or crossword puzzles—not that there's anything wrong with those, but there are so many other things that can be done."

No matter what the activity, Waryncia looks for connections to *Cobblestone*'s monthly themes, which appear on its website, along with writers' guidelines.

"For example, if we were doing an issue on Native Americans and if there was a game that a particular tribe created, then we might want to recreate that game as an activity—or perhaps show a modern version of that game to make a connection from past to present," he says.

Do It Yourself

One of the most popular activities for older children and teens are projects they can make themselves. "We try to put a do-it-yourself (DIY) feature in each issue of *Teen*," says Damon Romaine, Deputy Editor. They specifically look for fashion do-it-yourselfs, room makeover projects, back-to-school crafts, and anything else that would be appropriate for tween girls. Note that *Teen* now targets the 12- to 16-year-old crowd and is now published quarterly.

Romaine looks for crafty people who can also give clear explanations. "It's great to find that artist who can create a great project and be able to write it in a way that a 12-year-old can understand." Romaine suggests writers query, with pictures of the project and a writing sample.

Justine, a new entry into the teen market, will be looking for craft and room decorating pieces in the near future. "One of the best responses from any of the sections we publish is for Just Made," says Jana Pettey, Publisher. "We would certainly welcome some new ideas for crafts that are relatively simple to make and don't require a major investment in tools." Their preview issue included four nifty projects, including a key ring and a stiletto earring.

"We're hoping to include more DIY projects," says Betsy Kohn, Editor of *Guideposts Sweet 16* (formerly *Guideposts for Teens*). "Girls love them and they're very popular. I'm always looking for them." On their wish list are things that would appeal to the *Trading Spaces* crowd: cool pillows, lamps, and other room decor items. In addition, they're seeking fun fashion and beauty DIYs. "In one issue, we did a whole spread on ribbons—ribbon purses, ribbon place mats, ribbon necklaces, a watch band made out of ribbons—a whole spread of projects ranging from very simple to more complicated," says Kohn.

Kohn asks for text copy and/or directions, with a snapshot. "If we're interested in the project we'll work together, polish it, and have you send us the finished product so we can photograph it."

Highlights buys craft pieces for their Crafts You Can Make, a two-page spread of craft activities combining contributions from several authors. "We want them to use materials you can commonly find around the house," says Griswell. "Think about things kids can do alone. We don't recommend cooking anything or using hot glue guns." She prefers simple, sequential projects that don't have more than five steps. Instead of a query, send a photo or a finished sample that they can evaluate.

Because *Fun For Kidz* is written for both boys and girls, Editor Marilyn Edwards tries to include at least a craft and a building project that could appeal to both. "In our American Indian issue, we had a project on how to make a scale model birchbark canoe." With most of these projects, a parent is likely to get involved since their core readers ages eight to nine might require some help.

Recipes for Success

Edwards also seeks creative recipes for *Hopscotch* and *Fun For Kidz*. "They have to fit the issue theme and be original, or at least a new twist on a conventional recipe," she says. "Instead of making the traditional s'more, we published a recipe for making s'mores in a cupcake holder. When we did the doll issue for *Hopscotch*, someone sent in an idea for a salad that looked like a Raggedy Ann doll." Edwards looks for recipes that kids can do easily with commonly found ingredients.

Cricket also looks for recipes, crafts, and experiments with a unique spin. "Be aware of what's been done before—and done to death," says Senior Editor Tracy Schoenle. "If it's a recipe, are the ingredients easy to find in most grocery stores? Does the recipe offer something out of the ordinary? Does it have any specific cultural meaning?" Schoenle says her readers are asking for more vegetarian recipes from any culture. Ingredients (or substitutions) should be readily available in most grocery stores.

Q & A

A staple of many teen and tween magazines are quizzes that expose facts about your personal preferences and your "real" self.

"We love quizzes and games at *Teen*, so it would be nice to see more of those," says Romaine. "Our quizzes are based on things our tween readers like: friendship, boys, and beauty." These quizzes should be personality-based and the answers should be revealing to the reader. Quizzes can take multiple formats but the most common formats are multiple choice and the flow chart (i.e., if yes, go this direction, if no, go this way).

Want a Sidebar with That?

Though they're normally purchased with an article instead of à la carte, sidebars can help sell an article, or even provide a little more in your check. Sidebars often overlap with the category of filler, adding fast facts or a related activity to a piece. For almost every feature you write, you can usually find additional information that will enhance its value, as well as its readability.

"For instance, I just assigned a first-person story about a musician who was being bullied—the whole *Mean Girls* thing," says Betsy Kohn, Editor of *Guideposts Sweet 16*. "Kids were spray painting graffiti in the halls about her; they were really mean to her because she was successful." Kohn asked the writer not only to write the article together with the young musician, but to pitch the editor some ideas about sidebars, such as a mean girl quiz or what to do when you're bullied.

So what makes a sidebar that catches the attention of editors? According to Kohn, they should be short, engaging, and provide a unique angle that's not in the main text. "It needs to be able to stand alone," she says. It also needs to be written specifically as a sidebar: Don't write extra material into the text and expect the editor to glean sidebar material from it.

Sidebars also address the short attention spans of young readers who aren't inclined to read the continuous blocks of text that adults take for granted. "We don't want our readers to think it's work to read our stories. This is a magazine, it's not a textbook!" says Kohn. "We want it to be visually fun—eye candy. A sidebar may be the only thing that reluctant readers will look at."

Examples of recent quiz topics in *Teen* include "Are You What You Eat?" (health); "Are You Too Sensitive?" (personality); "What Kind of Friend Are You?" (friendship); "Is He the One?" (boys); "Are You Sabotaging Your Skin?" (beauty).

"We're committed to doing two quizzes per issue because we know teen girls love quizzes," says Kohn. "One is more graphically based, like a flow chart, the other a more narrative-type quiz." They're always looking for good quiz material, especially on topics they haven't done or revisited a dozen times. She's also seeking new ideas for graphically based quiz formats.

According to Kohn, *Guideposts Sweet 16* receives many quizzes with a voice that's just wrong for them. "They're too preachy or the answers are too obvious, or it's too obvious how you're supposed to answer," she says. "The most fun quizzes are not right or wrong, but more like 'Are You the Shy Type or Outgoing Type' or 'What Kind of Shoe Are You?' Humor is an important element."

The Bottom Line

All the editors suggested that prospective contributors always examine back issues of their magazines to get a feel for their style, content, and the types of filler they routinely use. Always kid-test your activities before submitting them. "It's important! The last thing we want to happen is someone emailing us saying the project didn't work," says Jennifer Reed, Editor of *Wee Ones*.

Clarity and detailed directions are also a must with queries and submissions. "With activities, it's important that you explain. We need to be able to test it," says Waryncia. "There's nothing more frustrating to an editor than trying to figure out an activity. If I'm totally confused, how is a 10-year-old going to figure it out?"

You won't get rich writing activities and filler, but you can usually produce several of them in the time it would take you to do a typical feature or fiction story. Payment varies among the magazines surveyed—from $10 for short activities in the smaller markets up to $400 for a two-pager in a major publication. Other factors may include the type of piece, whether it includes photos or illustrations, or how long a writer has worked with the particular publication. Several of the editors surveyed note that their regular contributors often earn more.

So while your latest story manuscript is making the rounds, or you're between projects, why not try a change of pace? Write an activity that kids—and editors—are sure to like.

Help Us Help Them: "Support" Publications Aid Children & Families

By Pegi Deitz Shea

This year's *Magazine Markets for Children's Writers* is full of publications aimed at child readers. But writers who focus on children have even more opportunities to write and sell to magazines aimed at adults who help, encourage, and care for children. These magazines, newsletters, and journals have a constant need for nonfiction and range across a wider spectrum than most writers ever consider. Teaching and home schooling journals and newsletters cover educational matters for grades K-12. Regional parenting monthlies cover local news and events. Look more closely, however, at the number of magazines that help parents and care providers deal with specific situations or lifestyles. In those niches are often overlooked opportunities to publish.

Tools of Organizations

Many support publications are the voices of large organizations. The print vehicle represents what an organization stands for and advocates. It updates members on news, events, people, perhaps advances in a field, and provides guidance and advice.

U Magazine, published by the United States Automobile Association (USAA), has a whopping 440,000 circulation. Its mission is to improve rela-tionships between parents and children, and promote good citizenship. It also uses the magazines to help families build solid financial futures.

A quarterly, *U* has four annual themes that correspond with the seasons: safety, family, community, future, and puts each issue to bed six months in advance. Despite that long lead time, Editor Shari Biediger says, "Current events and people are always our best subjects, so timeliness is preferred over evergreen copy. Stories that profile or feature our members (young or adult) are very desirable, but not absolutely necessary." Biediger adds that the magazine also needs games, activities, quizzes, lists, and factoids.

The organization has two other publications. While *U* is aimed at members with children ages 9 to 12, *U.25* targets members between ages 18 to 25, and *U-Turn* targets kids 13 to 17. *U-Turn*, with an international circulation of 545,000, addresses topics such as cars, driving, education, community service, leadership, financial planning, and business, says Biediger. Many of the readers of *U* are military families.

"These readers are very interested in what's happening in the world around them. So we try to give them a forum for world issues, from elections and

Pegi Deitz Shea is an award-winning children's book author specializing in multicultural stories for all ages. She has also published more than 250 poems, essays, and articles for adult readers. Pegi is a mother of two, wife of one, soccer and softball coach, gardener, and world-traveler.

war to pop culture and the future," she explains. "Upcoming topics we'd like to address: athletics/fitness (social/emotional issues), reality vs. myth concerning careers, long-distance relationships, transitioning from military to civilian life and schools, entering a military academy."

Editors of these USAA magazines often assign topics to regular writers. Authors are encouraged to send queries, published clips, and résumés if they wish to write for these publications.

The Canada Safety Council comes out with *Living Safety*, a 32-page quarterly, targeted at families. Editor in Chief Jack Smith says, "We do not have any direct competitors in Canada. The only publication that even comes close charges more than four times the single issue price and is an animated-type presentation."

While daily newspapers might have occasional articles on, say, barbecuing, *Living Safety*'s mission is to prevent accidents all year round. It covers the whole country's concerns, so the magazine runs articles on farm safety, boating precautions, city security, sports injury prevention, and school-related hazards. It also tracks legislation, and its effects on citizens. The organization's member newsletter, *Safety Canada*, takes on traffic and occupational safety.

Americans are no slouches when it comes to public safety. *Family Safety & Health*, a quarterly published by the National Council of Safety, covers the same issues. This can be a tough market, but the publication will consider queries. Check out the theme list on its website, review past volumes, and propose a fresh new idea it can't refuse.

The American Automobile Association and Exxon/Mobile also publish family magazines, heavy on travel, of course. Other publications from organizations include: *Children's Voice* (Child Welfare League of America); *Children's Advocate Newsmagazine* (Action Alliance for Children); *Circles of Peace, Circles of Justice* (Institute for Peace and Justice); *National Pal Copsnkids Chronicles* (National Association of Police Athletic Leagues).

Check out some of the organizations you belong to. Chances are, they may have publications you can submit to.

Religious Guidance

Religious organizations publish hundreds of magazines and pamphlets for children attending Sunday school, reading on their own at a parochial or secular school, or tackling tough issues in teen youth groups. But the inspiring doesn't stop at age 18. Parents and educators who want to guide their children's spiritual and moral growth can subscribe to publications aimed directly at their concerns.

LifeWay Church Resources is there to help. LifeWay sells books, films, music, career and workplace tools, and more. And it publishes five magazines to help Christians find "biblical solutions" to life's challenges.

The first is *HomeLife*, 50 years old, which begot new magazines as the market splintered into age groups along the way: *ParentLife, Living with Teenagers, Christian Single,* and *Mature Living*. "*ParentLife* readers tend to be women ages 20 to 39 who have at least one preschooler at home," says William Summey, Editor in Chief.

Living with Teenagers can help parents cope as their children gain independence and face difficult choices. "From every corner, teenagers are being told to succeed, to excel, to grow up fast," Editor Sherrie Thomas has written on the website. *Living with Teenagers* provides articles that will help parents "guide today's teens to become well-grounded Christian adults."

According to Summey, most readers receive copies of *ParentLife* through their churches. "*ParentLife* is sold to churches of over 20 different denominations, but Southern Baptist churches are the largest group."

Other religious publications also provide support information for parents and others involved with youth. Among the nondenominational publications are *Christian Parenting Today, Leaders in Action, Today's Christian Parent;* and *Youth & Christian Education Leadership*.

But many adults wish to emphasize their own denomination's beliefs with their children. Resources exist for those parents and educators as well. Here's a sampling: *Catholic Parent* and *Momentum* (Roman Catholic); *Children's Mission* and the *Journal of Adventist Education* (Seventh-day Adventist Church); *Dovetail* (Dovetail Institute for Jewish/Christian Families); *The EMMC Recorder* (Evangelical Mennonite Faith); *Resource* (Wesleyan-Holiness); *Your Child* (Judaism).

Special Situations & Lifestyles

If you're dealing with a special situation, such as raising or teaching a learning disabled daughter, or being a homosexual parent, *you* have something to contribute to the number of magazines that cover these challenges.

For instance, *Adoptive Families* needs articles and

first-person stories about transracial adoption, adoptive parent support groups, and other topics. The magazine has many departments open to submission, including At Home, Single Parent, About Birthparents, and Parent Exchange. Its core coverage includes health issues, school and education, parenting tips and guidelines, and preparing for adoption. Current hot topics include foster adoption, adoptive parents of color, and middle-schoolers and teenagers going through their own adoption issues,

Accepting about 100 freelance submissions annually, *Adoptive Families* is a great choice if you've just come back from China with a baby girl. Readers would love to know, for instance, if you should keep an open return flight date in case of delays. Better yet, how do you prepare for your trip to avoid bureaucratic delays? As all editors say, though, make sure you are familiar with the magazine so your submission can *fit*.

If you're familiar with *ADDitude*, sister publication under New Hope Media, you'll know they don't accept unsolicited manuscripts. Editors at both publications prefer queries, with *Adoptive Families* more receptive to submissions by lay people. *ADDitude* covers research, treatment, and life issues regarding Attention Deficit Disorder and Attention Deficit Hyperactive Disorder. It prefers using journalists to cover topics. Both magazines have writers' guidelines on their websites.

For some publications, your age situation matters most. Young People's Press (YPP), a North American online news service, only accepts nonfiction submissions from writers between the ages of 14 to 24, according to Editor Ken Sitter. Editors work with young authors on their first-person accounts, opinion pieces, music and movie reviews, or profiles of outstanding young people. YPP offers writing and media-literacy workshops and conducts contests as well. As a free news service, YPP makes your work available to other media outlets.

No Crime, YPP's semi-annual ezine, is celebrating its tenth edition. Its articles include "Young Offenders Learn Hard Lessons," "One-Man Play Explores Drug World," and "Breaking up Families."

In the USAA's *U-Turn*, half of the content is youth-written. "*U-Turn* magazine reinforces the importance of its readers' voices and ideas," Biediger says. "In addition, a large and active teen panel comprised of readers is vital to *U-Turn*'s editorial mission."

Other special situation publications include *Adoption, Exceptional Parent, Multiple Moments, Single Mother* (National Organization of Single Mothers); *Vegetarian Baby & Child, Working Mother, Fostering Families Today; In the Family* (homosexual lifestyle); *Volta Voices* (Alexander Graham Bell Association for the Deaf).

Education/Day Care

The print world has recognized that teaching children goes on in a multitude of locations other than schools. Not just home schools, but in day-care facilities, home-based day care situations, latch-key programs, alternative schools, and in libraries.

VOYA (Voice of Youth Advocates) is published by Scarecrow Press, part of the Rowman and Little-field Publishing Group. Unlike religious and organizational magazines that control and shape the information to serve themselves and their slice of subscribers, *VOYA* can be scene as an *anti-niche* publication. "We are an intellectual freedom journal," says Editor Cathi Dunn MacRae. "We are anti-filtering and anti-censorship."

VOYA's subscribers are youth-serving professionals, including coordinators of teen programming, teen counselors, media specialists, and both public and school librarians. These people want the teens they work with to have total access to information. A favorite annual issue is the September/October *VOYA* listing banned books.

"Our readers guide and mentor teens, but do not direct them," McRae says. Readers share *VOYA*'s philosophy, stated on their website: "Young adults have rights to free and equal access to information in print, nonprint, and electronic media."

In addition to accepting articles from practitioners in the field of teen service, *VOYA* also accepts

---

What the Editors Say about "Support" Markets

◆ Bonnie Neugebauer, Editor, *Child Care Information Exchange*, page 82.

◆ Jack Smith, General Manager, *Living Safety*, page 168.

◆ William Summey, Editor in Chief, *ParentLife*, page 195.

◆ Cathi Dunn MacRae, Editor, *VOYA*, page 264.

youth-written submissions for its column, Notes from the Teenage Underground. Here, teens can share "secrets" regarding books, entertainment, and identity. *VOYA* also conducts teen-written poetry and photography contests.

Researching publications online has distinct advantages for print writers. Look at the website of *Child Care Exchange,* which shows that for this group and publication, "more is more." Access to information seems boundless. "*Exchange* is the only publication focusing on the needs and interests of early childhood administrators," says Marketing Director Bruce Schon. A recent issue illustrates the bimonthly's variety. Articles include "Energizing Your Staff," "Early Signs of Burnout," and "All Germs Are Not Bad Germs."

Ninety percent of *Exchange* readers own or direct early childhood centers, with nearly half of these centers caring for more than 100 children. Sponsorship of these centers run the gamut from nonprofit to profit, from religious to secular, and employer to government. Examples include churches, YMCAs, public or government sites housing a Head Start program. Readership is international.

According to Schon, authors should be practitioners, professionals, providers, consultants or recognized experts in the field of early child care and education. Most editors of the magazines interviewed here prefer that you have personal or professional experience in the care of children. However, if you can get great interviews with any of the above and can fashion an informing and entertaining article, you can still break into these magazines.

Other day-care or specialized education publications include: *Early Childhood Education; Gifted Education Press Quarterly; MOMSense* (from the organization, Mothers of Preschoolers); *Montessori Life* (American Montessori Society), *Music Educators Journal* (National Association for Music Education); *Our Children* (National PTA); *Relational Child and Youth Care Practice; School Library Media Activities Monthly; Sharing Space* (Creative Response to Conflict); *Teaching Tolerance* (Southern Poverty Law Review); *Teachers of Vision* (Christian Educators Association International); and Child Care Business.

Whether you run your own in-home day care of the neighbor's children, or you're an adoptive parent or have a doctorate in early childhood education, you have a lot to offer. So check out these publications, study the submission guidelines and theme lists, and get writing!

Listings

How to Use the Listings

The pages that follow feature profiles of 618 magazines that publish articles and stories for, about, or of interest to children and young adults. Throughout the year, we stay on top of the latest happenings in children's magazines to bring you new and different publishing outlets. This year, our research yielded over 78 additional markets for your writing. They are easy to find; look for the listings with a star in the upper right corner.

A Variety of Freelance Opportunities

This year's new listings reflect the interests of today's magazine audience. You'll find magazines targeted to readers interested in nature, the environment, computers, mysteries, child care, careers, different cultures, family activities, and many other topics.

Along with many entertaining and educational magazines aimed at young readers, we list related publications such as national and regional magazines for parents and teachers. Hobby and special interest magazines generally thought of as adult fare but read by many teenagers are listed too.

In the market listings, the Freelance Potential section helps you judge each magazine's receptivity to freelance writers. This section offers information about the number of freelance submissions published each year.

Further opportunities for selling your writing appear in the Additional Listings section on page 283. This section profiles a range of magazines that publish a limited amount of material targeted to children, young adults, parents, or teachers. Other outlets for your writing can be found in the Selected Contests and Awards section, beginning on page 321.

Using Other Sections of the Directory

If you are planning to write for a specific publication, turn to the Magazine and Contest Index beginning on page 364 to locate the listing page. The Category Index, beginning on page 339, will guide you to magazines that publish in your areas of interest. This year, the Category Index also gives the age range of each publication's readership. To find the magazines most open to freelance submissions, turn to the Fifty+ Freelance index on page 338, which lists magazines that rely on freelance writers for over 50% of the material they publish.

Check the Market News, beginning on page 336, to find out what's newly listed, what's not listed and why, and to identify changes in the market that have occurred during the past year.

About the Listings

We revisited last year's listings and, through a series of mailed surveys and phone interviews, verified editors' names, mailing addresses, submissions and payment policies, and current editorial needs. All entries are accurate and up-to-date when we send this market directory to press. Magazine publishing is a fast-moving industry, though, and it is not unusual for facts to change before or shortly after this guide reaches your hands. Magazines close, are sold to new owners, or move; they hire new editors or change their editorial focus. Keep up-to-date by requesting sample copies and writers' guidelines.

Note that we do *not* list:

- Magazines that did not respond to our questionnaires or phone queries. Know that we make every effort to contact each editor before press date.

- Magazines that *never* accept freelance submissions or work with freelance writers.

To get a real sense of a magazine and its editorial slant, we recommend that you read several recent sample issues cover to cover. This is the best way to be certain a magazine is right for you.

Cadet Quest

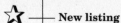 — New listing

Calvinist Cadet Corps
P.O. Box 7259
Grand Rapids, MI 49510

Who to contact —— Editor: G. Richard Broene

Description and Readership

Profiles the publication, its interests, and readers —

Formerly known as *Crusader*, this magazine targets members of the Calvinist Cadet Corps, a Christian organization that includes pre-teen and teenage boys from a number of Protestant denominations. It teaches Christian principles through stories and articles about sports, nature, and animals.

• **Audience:** 9–14 years
• **Frequency:** 7 times each year
• **Distribution:** 100% subscription
• **Circulation:** 10,000
• **Website:** www.calvinistcadets.org

Freelance Potential

70% written by nonstaff writers. Publishes 20 freelance submissions yearly; 5% by unpublished writers, 10% by authors who are new to the magazine. Receives 50 unsolicited mss monthly.

Designates the amount and type of freelance submissions published each year; highlights the publication's receptivity to unpublished writers

Provides guidelines for submitting material; lists word lengths and types of material accepted from freelance writers —

Submissions

Send complete ms. Accepts photocopies, computer printouts, and simultaneous submissions if identified. SASE. Responds in 1 month.

Articles: 400–1,000 words. Informational and factual articles; profiles; and interviews. Topics include religion, spirituality, sports, camping, crafts, and animals.

Fiction: 900–1,600 words. Features adventure and sports stories and humor—all written from a Christian perspective.

Depts/columns: Word length varies. Cadet Corps news and Bible stories.

Other: Puzzles, and cartoons.

Sample Issue

24 pages (5% advertising): 4 articles; 3 stories; 2 depts/columns; 2 activities. Sample copy, free with 9x12 SASE ($1.01 postage). Guidelines and theme list available.

• "Truth or Consequences." Story about a boy who stretches the truth after he forgets to close the door to his uncle's chicken coop.
• "What Good Are Insects Anyway?" Articles offers facts about the importance of honeybees and the role fruit flies have played in medical research.

Analyzes a recent sample copy of the publication; briefly describes selected articles, stories, departments, etc.

Rights and Payment

Lists types of rights acquired, payment rate, and number of copies provided to freelance writers —

First and second rights. Written material, $.04–$.05 per word. Other material, payment rate varies. Pays on acceptance. Provides 1 contributor's copy.

Editor's Comments

We look for material that will appeal to all adolescent boys, not just those in the Calvinist Cadet Corps. Our readers are active, inquisitive, and imaginative.

Offers advice from the editor about the publication's writing style, freelance needs, audience, etc.

Icon Key

☆ New Listing   🖰 Epublisher   ⊗ Not currently accepting submissions

Abilities

Suite 650
340 College Street
Toronto, Ontario, M5T 3A9
Canada

Managing Editor: Lisa Bendall

Description and Readership

Distributed nationally and internationally, this lifestyle magazine offers informative articles and resources for people with disabilities and their families.
- **Audience:** People and families of people with disabilities
- **Frequency:** Quarterly
- **Distribution:** 80% controlled; 10% newsstand; 10% other
- **Circulation:** 45,000
- **Website:** www.abilities.ca

Freelance Potential

50% written by nonstaff writers. Publishes 30–40 freelance submissions yearly; 5–10% by unpublished writers, 75% by authors who are new to the magazine. Receives 10 queries, 42 unsolicited mss monthly.

Submissions

Query with writing samples; or send complete ms with photos. Accepts photocopies, computer printouts, and email to lisa@abilities.ca. SAE/IRC. Responds in 2–3 months.
Articles: 1,500–2,000 words. Informational, self-help, and how-to articles; personal experience and opinion pieces; profiles; interviews; and humor. Topics include health, travel, recreation, sports, employment, housing, social policy, family life, women's issues, youth, and sexuality.
Depts/columns: 500–1,200 words. Crafts and cooking.

Sample Issue

68 pages (50% advertising): 5 articles; 22 depts/columns. Writers' guidelines available.
- "Trading Spaces." Article discusses the author's joyful experiences and challenges during a vacation home exchange for people with disabilities.
- "Access Guide Canada." Article takes a look at several points of interest in Canada that are accessible venues.
- Sample dept/column: "The Lighter Side" essay takes a humorous look at the changes in airport security.

Rights and Payment

First and electronic rights. Written material, $25–$350 Canadian. Pays 30 days after publication. Kill fee, 50%. Provides 2 contributor's copies.

Editor's Comments

The style of our magazine is "conversational," in that it is important for each article to be appreciated by as many readers as possible. Articles on travel resources, vacation ideas, information on employment, and issues related to education, health, social policy, and housing are always needed. We look for material that provides readers with resources to become more independent.

Able Ezine

Suite 200
110 Eglinton Avenue West
Toronto, Ontario M4R 1A3
Canada

Managing Editor

Description and Readership

Young adults seeking to share their experiences and concerns about living with a disability find a forum for their work in *Able Ezine*. Published by Young People's Press, it targets readers between the ages of 14 and 24 and welcomes material from writers in that age group.
- **Audience:** YA–Adult
- **Frequency:** 5 times each year
- **Distribution:** 100% Internet
- **Hits per month:** Unavailable
- **Website:** www.able-ezine.org

Freelance Potential

95% written by nonstaff writers. Publishes 150–200 freelance submissions yearly; 70% by unpublished writers, 75% by authors who are new to the magazine.

Submissions

Send complete ms. Accepts email submissions to writeus@ypp.net. Responds immediately.
Articles: 500–1,500 words. Informational articles and personal experience pieces. Topics include physical disability, personal growth, and health.
Artwork: JPEG and GIF images.
Other: Poetry, no line limit; to 3 poems per submission. Comics.

Sample Issue

12 pages. Guidelines available at website.
- "Living with Cancer." Essay written by a young woman describes how her experience with cancer changed her life and made her a better person.
- "The Cards You Are Dealt." Article reports on a man who returned to his job as a city planner after a car accident left him a quadriplegic and the inspiring effect he's had on other disabled people who want to re-enter the workplace.
- "In My Prayers." Essay reveals the thoughts of a young woman as she reaches the brink of suicide.

Rights and Payment

Rights, payment policy, and payment rates vary.

Editor's Comments

We at Young People's Press are interested in publishing the writing as well as the artwork of the youth of Canada. We sponsor a variety of e-zines in addition to *Able Ezine*, and all of them are open to submissions from 14- to 24-year-old artists and writers. If you need help with your article or essay, or if you're looking for more specific guidelines for our publications, visit writeus@ypp.net.

ADDitude Magazine

Suite 901
42 West 38th Street
New York, NY 10018

Editor & Publisher: Susan Caughman

Description and Readership

This publication describes itself as "the happy, healthy lifestyle magazine for people with ADD." Its purpose is to improve the academic, vocational, and social outcomes for adults and children with Attention Deficit Disorder.
- **Audience:** Adults
- **Frequency:** 6 times each year
- **Distribution:** Subscription; other
- **Circulation:** Unavailable
- **Website:** www.additudemag.com

Freelance Potential

80% written by nonstaff writers. Publishes 25 freelance submissions yearly; 30% by unpublished writers, 30% by authors who are new to the magazine. Receives 4 queries each month.

Submissions

Query. No unsolicited mss. Accepts email submissions to susan@additudemag.com. SASE. Response time varies.
Articles: To 2,000 words. Informational articles and personal experience pieces. Topics include Attention Deficit Disorder, education, recreation, and child development.
Depts/columns: Word length varies. Profiles of schools and teachers; first-person experiences from parents; and AD/HD news and notes.

Sample Issue

62 pages (33% advertising): 5 articles; 17 depts/columns. Sample copy, $4.95. Guidelines available.
- "Behavior Therapy: It Works!" Article cites research that shows that medication used in conjunction with behavior therapy results in the greatest improvement in children's AD/HD symptoms.
- "How to Survive Summer Vacation." Article suggests ways parents of kids with AD/HD can balance free time with planned time to give kids the structure they need.
- Sample dept/column: "Job Fair" outlines strategies parents can use to help their AD/HD teen survive and thrive at a summer job.

Rights and Payment

First rights. Pays on publication. All material, payment rate varies. Kill fee, $75.

Editor's Comments

We strive to be a national voice for people with AD/HD, many of whom are children who have difficulty speaking for themselves and asserting their rights. We also want to be a credible resource for parents and professionals interested in AD/HD.

Adoptalk

North American Council on Adoptable Children
Suite 106
970 Raymond Street
St. Paul, MN 55114-1149

Communications Specialist: Diane Riggs

Description and Readership

This publication gets right to the heart of issues surrounding adoption, foster care, and special needs children. It is factual and straightforward in its style and format, and each issue contains several profiles of children waiting to be adopted. Parents and professionals read it for information and news.
- **Audience:** Adults
- **Frequency:** Quarterly
- **Distribution:** 100% controlled
- **Circulation:** 3,700
- **Website:** www.nacac.org

Freelance Potential

40% written by nonstaff writers. Publishes 6–8 freelance submissions yearly; 10% by unpublished writers, 50% by authors who are new to the magazine. Receives 1 query or unsolicited ms monthly.

Submissions

Query or send complete ms with bibliography. Accepts photocopies, computer printouts, and email submissions to dianeriggs@nacac.org. SASE. Responds in 2–3 weeks.
Articles: To 2,000 words. Informational articles; profiles; and personal experience pieces. Topics include parenting, recruitment of adoptive and foster parents, adoption news, conference updates, and NACAC membership news.
Depts/columns: Word length varies. Book reviews.

Sample Issue

20 pages (no advertising): 4 articles; 3 depts/columns; 1 book review. Sample copy, free with 9x12 SASE ($.83 postage). Guidelines available.
- "Award Winners Inspire All." Article profiles several persons who have received awards for untiring work serving children and families in their communities.
- Sample dept/column: "Recruitment Update" assesses the success of a website for Alberta's Children's Services that features photos and descriptions of children.

Rights and Payment

Rights policy varies. No payment. Provides 5 author's copies.

Editor's Comments

Everything in our publication is related to adoption and foster care. We are interested in articles that provide parenting insights from persons caring for adopted children who have special behavioral, emotional, or psychological needs. Tell us what you do in everyday situations to help your child or children develop, mature, and handle challenging experiences.

Adoptive Families

Suite 901
42 West 38th Street
New York, NY 10018

Editor: Rochelle Green

Description and Readership

This award-winning publication is a leading informational resource for families prior to, during, and after the adoption process. Each issue is built around stories of adoption, presented in a reader-friendly format.
- **Audience:** Adoptive families
- **Frequency:** 6 times each year
- **Distribution:** 80% subscription; 20% other
- **Circulation:** 35,000
- **Website:** www.adoptivefamilies.com

Freelance Potential

75% written by nonstaff writers. Publishes 100 freelance submissions yearly; 20% by unpublished writers, 50% by authors who are new to the magazine. Receives 42–50 unsolicited mss each month.

Submissions

Query or send complete ms. Accepts photocopies, computer printouts, Macintosh disk submissions (Microsoft Word), and email submissions to beth@adoptivefamilies.com. SASE. Responds in 4–6 weeks.
Articles: 500–1,800 words. Self-help, personal experience, and how-to articles; humor; and interviews. Topics include family issues, child development, health, teen topics, education, learning disabilities, careers, and multicultural issues.
Depts/columns: To 1,200 words. Opinion and personal experience pieces focusing on adoption, single parenting, and birth-parent issues; book and media reviews.
Other: Material on ethnic holidays, National Adoption Month, and Martin Luther King, Jr. Day.

Sample Issue

78 pages (40% advertising): 5 articles; 16 depts/columns; 1 calendar. Sample copy, $4. Guidelines available.
- "The Color of Life." Article tells the stories, joys, and challenges of three families who have created transracial families through adoption.
- Sample dept/column: "Single Parent" recounts a single woman's transformation from an adoring daughter to an adoring, adoptive mother.

Rights and Payment

All rights. All material, payment rate varies. Provides 2 contributor's copies.

Editor's Comments

We currently need articles on middle-school and teen years, relatives and community, adoptive parent support groups, school, foster adoption, and domestic adoption.

Alateen Talk

Al-Anon Family Group
1600 Corporate Landing Parkway
Virginia Beach, VA 23454-5617

Associate Director, Member Services/Alateen:
Barbara Older

Description and Readership

This newsletter is written by and for members of Alateen, a fellowship of young Al-Anon members whose lives have been affected by the problem drinking of a relative or friend. All of the material printed in *Alateen Talk* is written by members only, most of whom are teenagers.
- **Audience:** 6–18 years
- **Frequency:** Quarterly
- **Distribution:** 100% subscription
- **Circulation:** 4,000
- **Website:** www.al-anon.alateen.org

Freelance Potential

90% written by nonstaff writers. Publishes 80–100 freelance submissions yearly; 100% by unpublished writers, 80% by authors who are new to the magazine. Receives 10 unsolicited mss monthly.

Submissions

Accepts material from Alateen members only. Send complete ms. SASE. Responds in 2 weeks.
Articles: Word length varies. Self-help articles and personal experience pieces. Topics include alcoholism and its effects on friends and family members.
Depts/columns: Staff written.
Artwork: B/W line art.
Other: Poetry.

Sample Issue

8 pages (no advertising): 30 articles. Sample copy, free with 9x12 SASE ($.87 postage). Guidelines available to Alateen members.
- "A Perfect Place to Be." Essay describes how a teen felt acceptance, encouragement, and comfort at Alateen meetings.
- "Focus on the Solution." Personal experience piece reveals that one teen finds hope by focusing on the positive outcomes and success stories that other members share.
- "One Day at a Time." Essay tells how a young person learned, through attendance at Alateen meetings, to take life one day at a time and how this philosophy has improved the teen's outlook on life.

Rights and Payment

All rights. No payment.

Editor's Comments

We provide a safe forum for our young members to express their feelings about the alcoholism of a relative or friend and to share their opinions of the Alateen program. Submissions written by non-members are not used.

American Adrenaline ☆

The National Youth Wrestling Magazine

P.O. Box 683
Centerville, IA 52544

Submissions Editor

Description and Readership

This magazine covers youth wrestling at the kindergarten through eighth-grade level, which is a large and growing segment of the wrestling community. It is the only magazine of its kind to target this group exclusively. The mission of *American Adrenaline* is to report, promote, and inspire wrestling excellence through grassroots efforts and family unity.
- **Audience:** 5–14 years; parents; coaches
- **Frequency:** 9 times each year
- **Distribution:** Subscription; newsstand
- **Circulation:** Unavailable
- **Website:** www.americanadrenaline.com

Freelance Potential

50–66% written by nonstaff writers.

Submissions

Send complete ms. Accepts computer printouts and email submissions to john@americanadrenaline.com. SASE. Response time varies.
Articles: Word length varies. Informational articles; profiles; and interviews. Topics include health, fitness, and coaching.
Fiction: Word length varies. Wrestling-related stories.
Depts/columns: Word length varies. National and state tournament reviews, reports on wrestling camps and clubs, and coaching tips.
Other: Puzzles, activities, games, and wrestling tips.

Sample Issue

18 pages (28% advertising): 5 articles; 5 depts/columns; 1 activity page. Sample copy, $4 with 9x12 SASE.
- "Five-Time Triple Crown Winner." Article profiles a boy in junior high school who has won the World of Wrestling Triple Crown five times.
- "Antibiotic-Resistant Skin Infections in Athletes on the Rise, Officials Say." Article reports on a contagious infection, once common only in hospitals and prisons, that is now gaining ground among players of contact sports such as wrestling and football.
- Sample dept/column: "Kids Corner" features word-search puzzles, a maze, a comic, and a wrestling tip.

Rights and Payment

Rights vary. Provides 1-year subscription in lieu of payment.

Editor's Comments

The only guidelines we have are that submissions should be geared to our youth readers, their coaches, or their parents, and that all material must be related to wrestling, fitness, or health. We would love to have a fiction story submitted.

American Baby

16th Floor
125 Park Avenue
New York, NY 10012

Editorial Assistant: Sarah Jones

Description and Readership

This magazine strives to provide helpful, supportive information on preconception, pregnancy, and the care of infants. It is read by parents with children under the age of two.
- **Audience:** Parents
- **Frequency:** Monthly
- **Distribution:** 50% subscription; 50% controlled
- **Circulation:** 2.1 million
- **Website:** www.americanbaby.com

Freelance Potential

55% written by nonstaff writers. Publishes 24 freelance submissions yearly; 20% by unpublished writers. Receives 83 unsolicited mss monthly.

Submissions

Query with clips or writing samples; or send complete ms. Accepts photocopies, computer printouts, and simultaneous submissions if identified. SASE. Responds in 2 months.
Articles: 1,000–2,000 words. Informational and how-to articles; profiles; interviews; humor; and personal experience pieces. Topics include pregnancy, preconception, infants, child care, child development, and adoption.
Depts/columns: 1,000 words. Relationships, new product information, fashion, and medical updates.
Other: Submit seasonal material 3 months in advance.

Sample Issue

110 pages (50% advertising): 5 articles; 11 depts/columns. Sample copy, free with 9x12 SASE ($2 postage). Writers' guidelines available.
- "Beyond the Baby Blues." Article discusses the warning signs of postpartum depression, which affects 10 to 20 percent of new mothers, and tells how to get help.
- "Is It Wise to Circumcise?" Article reports on the continuing debate over whether the circumcision of infant boys is healthy or uneccesary.
- Sample dept/column: "Nutrition Now" reports on the health benefits of green tea.

Rights and Payment

First serial rights. Articles, to $2,000. Depts/columns, to $1,000. Pays on acceptance. Provides 5 contributor's copies.

Editor's Comments

We try to provide our readers with a source they can trust as they begin the hectic, joyful, and satisfying journey of parenting. We look for focused, concise articles that deal with topics such as balancing work and family, breastfeeding, postpartum issues, infant care, and adoption.

American Careers

6701 West 64th Street
Overland Park, KS 66202

Editor: Mary Pitchford

Description and Readership
Information in this magazine is intended to help middle and high school students understand what is needed for various careers and what to expect in the job market. It includes links to websites for information on careers, self-assessments, and other practical information designed to promote career development.
- **Audience:** 12–18 years
- **Frequency:** 1 time each year for high school students; 1 time each year for middle school students
- **Distribution:** 99% schools; 1% other
- **Circulation:** 400,000
- **Website:** www.carcom.com

Freelance Potential
90% written by nonstaff writers. Publishes 15 freelance submissions yearly; 20% by unpublished writers, 40% by authors who are new to the magazine. Receives 20+ queries each month.

Submissions
Query with résumé and clips. Accepts photocopies and computer printouts. SASE. Responds in 2 months.
Articles: 300–750 words. Informational and how-to articles and profiles. Topics include careers, education, and job-related skills.
Depts/columns: Word length varies. "Reality Check" offers facts and figures related to career choices, life-planning assessments, and information on current job opportunities.
Artwork: Color prints, transparencies, or digital photos.
Other: Quizzes.

Sample Issue
48 pages (no advertising): 17 articles; 7 depts/columns. Sample copy, $4 with 9x12 SASE (5 first-class stamps). Writers' guidelines available.
- "There's Something for Everyone in Software Engineering." Article describes what is involved in a software engineering career and includes websites for information.
- Sample dept/column: "Future Prep" provides solid information about building critical thinking skills, a necessary tool for anyone looking for a job.

Rights and Payment
All rights. All material, payment rate varies. Pays on publication. Provides 2 contributor's copies.

Editor's Comments
We seek articles with a national focus that are balanced, written at a seventh-grade reading level, and pertain to careers in logistics, government, and finance. Please do not submit articles on "how to interview" or on employability skills.

American Cheerleader

23rd Floor
110 William Street
New York, NY 10038

Managing Editor: Sheila Noone

Description and Readership
The only national magazine written for more than 3 million young people involved in cheerleading, *American Cheerleader* fills its pages with practical information on health, fitness, routines, helpful advice, and fashion and beauty tips.
- **Audience:** 13–18 years
- **Frequency:** 6 times each year
- **Distribution:** Subscription; newsstand
- **Circulation:** 200,000
- **Website:** www.americancheerleader.com

Freelance Potential
50% written by nonstaff writers. Publishes 10 freelance submissions yearly; 20% by unpublished writers, 20% by authors who are new to the magazine. Receives 1–2 queries and unsolicited mss monthly.

Submissions
Query with clips or send complete ms. Accepts computer printouts, Macintosh disk submissions, and email submissions to snoone@lifestyleventures.com. SASE. Responds in 3 months.
Articles: To 1,000 words. Informational and how-to articles; profiles; personal experience pieces; and photo essays. Topics include cheerleading, workouts, competitions, scholarships, fitness, college, careers, and popular culture.
Depts/columns: Word length varies. Product news, safety issues, health, nutrition, fundraising, beauty, and fashion.
Artwork: High-resolution digital images; 35mm color slides.

Sample Issue
144 pages (40% advertising): 9 articles; 15 depts/columns; 1 camp guide; 1 special section. Sample copy, $3.99 with 9x12 SASE ($1.70 postage). Editorial calendar available.
- "Learning to Shine." Article tells how one dedicated cheerleader was able to overcome discrimination in order to get back to the sport she loves.
- "Sharing the Spirit." Article demonstrates how a cheerleading squad finds time for community service and gives tips on how others can accomplish the same goal.

Rights and Payment
All rights. All material, payment rate varies. Pays 2 months after acceptance. Provides 1 contributor's copy.

Editor's Comments
We would like to receive more submissions on cheerleading skills, all-star college cheer programs, general health, and beauty. All material must relate directly to cheerleading.

American Cheerleader Junior

23rd Floor
110 William Street
New York, NY 10038

Submissions Editor: Sheila Noone

Description and Readership
This colorful publication is a lively presentation of cheers, routines, ideas, featured cheerleaders, and tips for young girls interested in this sport. Competitions, competition results, new products, and activities are also included.
- **Audience:** 7–12 years
- **Frequency:** Quarterly
- **Distribution:** Subscription; newsstand
- **Circulation:** 65,000
- **Website:** www.americancheerleaderjunior.com

Freelance Potential
35% written by nonstaff writers. Publishes 10 freelance submissions yearly; 20% by unpublished writers, 30% by new authors. Receives 6 queries and 2 unsolicited mss monthly.

Submissions
Query with clips; or send complete ms. Accepts computer printouts, Macintosh disk submissions, and email submissions to snoone@lifestyleventures.com. SASE. Responds in 3 months.
Articles: To 1,000 words. Informational and how-to articles; profiles; photo essays; and personal experience pieces. Topics include cheerleading, fitness, health, and popular culture.
Depts/columns: Word length varies. Cooking, information for parents, and fund-raising.
Artwork: High-resolution digital images; 35mm color slides.
Other: Activities, games, and crafts. Poetry.

Sample Issue
72 pages (40% advertising): 7 articles; 5 depts/columns; 1 contest; 2 activities. Sample copy, $4.99 with 9x12 SASE ($.77 postage). Guidelines available.
- "Why Raven Rocks." Article describes the cheerleader who received the AC Junior's Honorary Cheerleader Award and the reasons behind her win.
- "Back to Basics." Article includes tips from experienced cheerleaders for those trying out for the first time.
- Sample dept/column: "Dance Class" demonstrates through pictures a routine that can be added to an existing cheer.

Rights and Payment
All rights. All material, payment rate varies. Pays 2 months after acceptance. Provides 1 contributor's copy.

Editor's Comments
We would like to receive more articles on how to ace tryouts and behind the scene looks at the cheerleading experience. Potential writers should currently be part of the cheerleading world.

American Girl

Pleasant Company Publications
8400 Fairway Place
Middleton, WI 53562

Department Assistant

Description and Readership
Readers of *American Girl* are girls in their formative years who dream big dreams. The publication's goal is to encourage girls to set goals, and to reinforce self-confidence, curiosity, and self-esteem in order to develop into successful young women.
- **Audience:** 8–12 years
- **Frequency:** 7 times each year
- **Distribution:** Subscription; newsstand; schools
- **Circulation:** 700,000
- **Website:** www.americangirl.com

Freelance Potential
10% written by nonstaff writers. Publishes 5–10 freelance submissions yearly; 5% by unpublished writers, 5% by authors who are new to the magazine. Receives 150 queries and unsolicited mss monthly.

Submissions
Query for nonfiction. Send complete ms for fiction. Accepts photocopies, computer printouts, and simultaneous submissions if identified. SASE. Responds in 4 months.
Articles: 500–1,000 words. Informational articles; profiles; and interviews. Topics include crafts, hobbies, nature, and sports.
Fiction: To 2,300 words. Genres include mysteries and historical, contemporary, and multicultural fiction.
Depts/columns: "Girls Express" uses profiles of girls, how-to articles, and easy craft ideas, to 175 words.
Other: Word games, mazes.

Sample Issue
48 pages (no advertising): 4 articles; 1 story; 6 depts/columns; 1 activity; 1 quiz. Sample copy, $3.95 with 9x12 SASE ($1.93 postage). Guidelines available.
- "Rebecca's Story." Article celebrates 12-year-old Rebecca who does not let the fact that she is legally blind stop her from aiming high and living life to its fullest.
- "The Parsley Problem or the Story of How My Mother Lost Her Head." Story reminisces about the habits of a very embarrassing mother.
- Sample dept/column: "Cooking" shows how to make puffy marshmallow treats that look like miniature slippers.

Rights and Payment
First North American serial rights. Written material, payment rate varies. Pays on acceptance. Provides 1 contributor's copy.

Editor's Comments
Please submit material that serves the developing interests and intellectual and emotional needs of our audience while reinforcing positive social and moral values.

American Journal of Health Education

1900 Association Drive
Reston, VA 20191

Editor: Jackie Lance

Description and Readership
Targeting health educators in schools and colleges, community and public health agencies, and health care settings in the workplace, this journal provides readers with up-to-date information on what is going on in the health field.
- **Audience:** Health educators
- **Frequency:** 6 times each year
- **Distribution:** 100% subscription
- **Circulation:** 8,000
- **Website:** www.aahperd.org/aahe

Freelance Potential
100% written by nonstaff writers. Publishes 50 freelance submissions yearly; 10% by unpublished writers. Receives 12 unsolicited mss monthly.

Submissions
Send complete ms. Accepts email submissions only through an on-line journal submission and review process at www.journalsubmit.com. Responds in 2 months.
Articles: 2–15 pages. Informational articles on initiation, development, and conduct of programs in health, leisure, and movement-related activities.
Depts/columns: 4–5 pages. Health news, and strategies and ideas for teachers.

Sample Issue
192 pages (3–5% advertising): 7 articles; 3 depts/columns. Guidelines available.
- "Reducing Subclinical Symptoms of Anxiety and Depression." Article examines the results from two courses on reducing stress and anxiety symptoms in college students.
- "'The Thrill is Gone' from Teaching Human Sexuality Education." Article discusses the change in teaching human sexuality due those who are uncomfortable with the subject.
- Sample dept/column: "Teaching Ideas" offers a teaching strategy that allow students to discover their health history.

Rights and Payment
All rights. No payment. Provides 2 contributor's copies.

Editor's Comments
We accept practical, theoretical, technical, historical, or controversial articles. Material should have a broad general application and implications for health education. We encourage writers to submit health education and promotional manuscripts related to community development, policy, and awareness strategies; professional and instructional programs; and individual health enhancement and maintenance methods.

American Kids Parenting Magazine

P.O. Box 66
West Alexandria, OH 45381

Editor: Jennifer Beam

Description and Readership
This regional parenting magazine covers topics related to raising children up to the age of 16. It is interested in topics that pertain to family life and parenting on local and global levels.
- **Audience:** Parents
- **Frequency:** Monthly
- **Distribution:** 50% controlled; 50% other
- **Circulation:** 75,000
- **Website:** www.americankids.net

Freelance Potential
50% written by nonstaff writers. Publishes 5 freelance submissions yearly; 30% by unpublished writers, 70% by authors who are new to the magazine. Receives 12–15 queries each month.

Submissions
Query with published clips. Accepts simultaneous submissions and email queries (Microsoft Word in body of email) to editor@americankids.net. Responds in 1 month if interested.
Articles: To 1,000 words. Informational and how-to articles and personal experience pieces. Topics include gifted education, humor arts, music, travel, sports, health and fitness, social issues, and regional news.
Depts/columns: 500 words. News and reviews.

Sample Issue
16 pages (50% advertising): 2 articles; 11 depts/columns. Guidelines available at website.
- "Ready or Not, Here I Come." Article addresses the issues that arise when a child heads off to school for the first time.
- "Early Language Learning." Article looks at the benefits of beginning the study of a foreign language at a young age.
- Sample dept/column: "Project Read" suggests ways kids can entertain themselves with books and reading projects during the cold winter months.

Rights and Payment
One-time and reprint rights. Articles, to $35. Depts/columns, $10. Pays on publication. Provides 1 contributor's copy.

Editor's Comments
Our readers are involved with children as parents, educators, and mentors. We provide information and resources to improve the quality and outcome of that involvement. Readers do not need to be convinced that they should be better parents. Don't send us anything that is "preachy"—only straightforward information. We look for material that has real value, not just simple how-tos.

American Libraries

American Library Association
50 East Huron Street
Chicago, IL 60611

Acquisitions Editor: Beverly Goldberg

Description and Readership
Members of the American Library Association, which include library and information workers at all levels, are kept informed of issues affecting public, private, and school libraries through the articles and reports in this publication.
- **Audience:** Librarians and library media specialists
- **Frequency:** 11 times each year
- **Distribution:** 100% membership
- **Circulation:** 56,000
- **Website:** www.ala.org/alonline

Freelance Potential
50% written by nonstaff writers. Publishes 30 freelance submissions yearly; 20% by unpublished writers, 60% by authors who are new to the magazine. Receives 30 unsolicited mss each month.

Submissions
Send complete ms. Accepts computer printouts and IBM disk submissions (Microsoft Word). No simultaneous submissions. SASE. Responds in 8–10 weeks.
Articles: 600–2,500 words. Informational articles; profiles; and interviews. Topics include modern libraries, new technologies, and intellectual freedom.
Depts/columns: Word length varies. The Internet, books about library management, new technology, and opinion pieces.

Sample Issue
72 pages (27% advertising): 9 articles; 16 depts/columns. Sample copy, $6. Guidelines available.
- "Saving Ourselves: Plural Funding for Public Libraries." Article questions whether libraries can break their dependence on tax dollars by adopting the funding strategies of National Public Radio and other nonprofit cultural institutions.
- "A Brief History of Library Service to African Americans." Article examines the development of library services for African Americans since the 1800s.
- Sample dept/column: "Grassroots Report" looks at a successful fundraising program instituted by the New York Public Library that asks patrons for small contributions.

Rights and Payment
First North American serial rights. Written material, $50–$400. Pays on acceptance. Provides 1+ contributor's copies.

Editor's Comments
Write in an informal style. Factual articles should be inviting and readable, but all statements must be backed up by responsible research and interviews. Avoid excessive footnotes.

American School & University

9800 Metcalf Avenue
Overland Park, KS 66212

Managing Editor: Susan Lustig

Description and Readership
The content of *American School & University* is geared exclusively to education administrators and other professionals such as architects who are responsible for business decisions and facility design and maintenance. Articles provide new insight into appropriate markets and guidelines to help readers through a design, planning, or renovation process.
- **Audience:** School administrators
- **Frequency:** Monthly
- **Distribution:** 100% controlled
- **Circulation:** 63,000
- **Website:** www.asumag.com

Freelance Potential
35% written by nonstaff writers. Publishes 40 freelance submissions yearly; 30% by authors who are new to the magazine. Receives 15 queries monthly.

Submissions
Query with outline. Prefers email submissions to slustig@primediabusiness.com. Will accept photocopies, computer printouts, disk submissions (Microsoft Word or ASCII). Responds in 2 weeks.
Articles: 1,200 words. Informational and how-to articles. Topics include facilities management, maintenance, technology, energy, furnishings, and security.
Depts/columns: 250–350 words. New technologies, case histories, and new product information.

Sample Issue
70 pages (55% advertising): 5 articles; 1 special section; 6 depts/columns. Sample copy, $10. Guidelines and editorial calendar available.
- "Paying for Protection." Article examines possible solutions of increased security demands for school campuses.
- "Building Knowledge." Article shows how new computerized management systems help schools and universities gather data needed to manage buildings.
- Sample dept/column: "Product Solutions" keeps readers updated on the newest innovations.

Rights and Payment
All rights. Payment rates and policy vary. Provides 2 contributor's copies.

Editor's Comments
A visit to our website will help answer questions and clarify our specific needs and readership. We do not include information of specific companies—articles are non-proprietary and written in general terms.

American Secondary Education

Ashland University, Weltmer Center
401 College Avenue
Ashland, OH 44805

Editor: James A. Rycik

Description and Readership
This scholarly journal examines current issues in secondary education and is read by professionals in that educational strata. The practical and erudite mix of articles serves those in both public and private secondary education. Topics include educational theory, practice, and policy.
- **Audience:** Secondary school educators
- **Frequency:** 3 times each year
- **Distribution:** 70% colleges and universities; 30% subscription
- **Circulation:** 450
- **Website:** www.ashland.edu/ase.html

Freelance Potential
100% written by nonstaff writers. Publishes 15 freelance submissions yearly. Receives 1 unsolicited ms monthly.

Submissions
Send 3 copies of complete ms with disk and 100-word abstract. No simultaneous submissions. SASE. Response time varies.
Articles: 10–30 double-spaced manuscript pages. Informational articles. Topics include secondary education research and practice.
Depts/columns: Book reviews, word length varies.

Sample Issue
100 pages (no advertising): 5 articles; 2 book reviews. Sample copy, free. Guidelines available.
- "Middle and High School Students with Learning Disabilities: Practical Academic Interventions for General Education Teachers—A Review of the Literature." Article considers the trend of mainstreaming more and more students with learning disabilities into general educational settings.
- "The Influence of Peer Status and Peer Relationships on School-Related Behaviors, Attitudes, and Intentions among Alternative High School Students." Article explores the links between peer relationship and school-related variables.
- "Book Review." Review details a book concerned with the challenging focus on education today and the increasing expectations placed on teachers.

Rights and Payment
All rights. No payment. Provides 1 contributor's copy.

Editor's Comments
Our journal features articles by practitioners and researchers who address current theories, research, and practice in secondary education. When submitting material, please include your educational affiliation and title, along with other pertinent qualifications or experience.

American String Teacher

4153 Chain Bridge Road
Fairfax, VA 22030

Editor: Tami O'Brien

Description and Readership
This highly professional magazine is published by the American String Teachers Association and covers a wide range of information beneficial to teachers and performers of violin, cello, viola, bass, guitar, and harp. Readers find practical tips on how to enhance techniques and musicality, as well as association and educational news.
- **Audience:** String teachers and performers
- **Frequency:** Quarterly
- **Distribution:** 100% subscription
- **Circulation:** 11,500
- **Website:** www.astaweb.com

Freelance Potential
75% written by nonstaff writers. Publishes 30 freelance submissions yearly; 5% by unpublished writers, 50% by authors who are new to the magazine. Receives 2–3 queries and unsolicited mss monthly.

Submissions
Prefers query; accepts 5 copies of complete ms. Accepts photocopies and computer printouts. No simultaneous submissions. SASE. Responds in 3 months.
Articles: 1,000–3,000 words. Informational and factual articles; profiles; and association news. Topics include teaching methodology, techniques, competitions, and auditions.
Depts/columns: Word length varies. Teaching tips, opinion pieces, and industry news.

Sample Issue
140 pages (45% advertising): 9 depts/columns. Sample copy, free with 9x12 SASE ($3.25 postage). Guidelines available.
- "Where Exactly Is the Music?" Article reminds readers of the importance of learning the basics on the road to mastering an instrument.
- "Yes, Virginia, There Really Are Jazz Violists." Article highlights the history of these neglected and little-known artists, and profiles two contrasting personalities.
- Sample dept/column: "Teaching Tips" describes why David Popper's Opus 73 is often referred to as the Bible of cello playing.

Rights and Payment
All rights. No payment. Provides 5 contributor's copies.

Editor's Comments
We prefer in-depth treatment of a subject that presents both sides of an issue rather than a broad overview. Articles should be based on research that emphasizes a practical application to string teaching.

America's Moms

101 Walton Green Way
Kennesaw, GA 30144

Submissions: Alicia Hagan

Description and Readership
This monthly online publication provides good, practical information for experienced and expectant parents to help them navigate the childrearing years with as little upset as possible. It includes articles on general parenting, education, adoption, family issues, finances, health, and pregnancy.
- **Audience:** Parents
- **Frequency:** Monthly
- **Distribution:** 100% Internet
- **Hits per month:** Unavailable
- **Website:** www.parentinguniverse.com

Freelance Potential
90% written by nonstaff writers. Publishes 1,000+ freelance submissions yearly. Receives 417 queries, 12–13 unsolicited mss monthly.

Submissions
Query or send complete ms. Accepts photocopies, computer printouts, and email submissions to marketing@ bestparentresources.com. Prefers online submissions through website. SASE. Response time varies.
Articles: Word length varies. Informational and how-to articles; profiles; interviews; reviews; and personal experience pieces. Topics include gifted education, health, fitness, recreation, self-help, and special education.
Depts/columns: Word length varies. Parenting tips, guides.

Sample Issue
Sample issue available at website.
- "Handling Unwanted Advice." Article lists several suggestions for parents to use to counteract unwanted advice from in-laws, parents, friends, and others.
- "Should I Let My Baby Cry it Out?" Article offers practical questions that parents can ask themselves about a baby who has trouble falling asleep in order to determine what steps might be taken to alleviate the situation.
- "Control Your Children's Clutter!" Article gives easy-to-use suggestions for eliminating the constant mess caused by items brought home every day by school-aged children.

Rights and Payment
Electronic rights. Written material, payment rate varies. Pays on publication. Provides 2 contributor's copies.

Editor's Comments
We are looking for more submissions on general parenting, children's health, adoption, toddler activities, crafts, and family finances. We look for a fresh approach on issues that families face, written in a warm, conversational voice.

Analog Science Fiction and Fact

Dell Magazine Fiction Group
475 Park Avenue South
New York, NY 10016

Editor: Stanley Schmidt

Description and Readership
Basically, this digest is all about science fiction. All stories have an element of future science or technology that is integrated into the plot. It brings readers the best of the genre's new and established writers.
- **Audience:** YA–Adult
- **Frequency:** 10 times each year
- **Distribution:** 80% subscription; 20% newsstand
- **Circulation:** 60,000
- **Website:** www.analogsf.com

Freelance Potential
100% written by nonstaff writers. Publishes 80–100 freelance submissions yearly; 10% by unpublished writers, 10% by authors who are new to the magazine. Receives 500 unsolicited mss monthly.

Submissions
Query for serials. Send complete ms for shorter works. Accepts computer printouts. SASE. Responds in 6 weeks.
Articles: To 6,000 words. Informational articles about science and technology.
Fiction: Serials, 40,000–80,000 words; novellas and novelettes, 10,000–20,000 words; short stories, 2,000–7,000 words. Future science and technology must be integral to the plot of the story.
Depts/columns: Staff written.

Sample Issue
144 pages (7% advertising): 1 article; 1 novella; 3 novelettes; 3 short stories; 5 depts/columns. Sample copy, $5 with 6x9 SASE. Guidelines available.
- "The Transience of Memory: We Really *Can* Remember It for You Wholesale." Article looks at the reasons that people's memories are not always correct.
- "The Bistro of Alternate Realities." Story considers the possibility of numerous universes and one's relationship to them.
- "On the Tip of My Tongue." Novellete delves into the relationship between two friends.

Rights and Payment
First North American serial and nonexclusive rights. Written material, $.05–$.08 per word; $.04 per word for serials. Pays on acceptance. Provides 2 contributor's copies.

Editor's Comments
We would like to see more stories accurately applying realistic science but in unusual settings. We currently have enough stories about 9/11 and asteroid mining. Send us something that seeks to predict what the near future may bring.

And Baby

481 Van Brunt Street
Brooklyn, NY 11231

Submissions Editor: Deanne Musolf-Crouch

Description and Readership
Focusing on non-traditional and traditional families, this colorful glossy features articles for parents of children of all ages. It provides resourceful information to families on topics related to finances, modern parenting, news, and marriage.
- **Audience:** Parents
- **Frequency:** 6 times each year
- **Distribution:** Newsstand; subscription
- **Circulation:** 100,000
- **Website:** www.andbabymag.com

Freelance Potential
100% written by nonstaff writers. Publishes several freelance submissions yearly.

Submissions
Query with résumé and clips. Email clips (or sample stories), copied into the email (not as attachment) and a list of publications you have written for to info@andbabymag.com. Also accepts photocopies and computer printouts. SASE. Response time varies.
Articles: Word length varies. Informational, factual, how-to, and self-help articles; and personal experience pieces. Topics include gay and lesbian family life, child care, family finances, education, social issues, current events, assisted fertility, and multicultural and ethnic issues.
Depts/columns: Word length varies. Book reviews and travel pieces.

Sample Issue
96 pages (15% advertising): 6 articles; 14 depts/columns. Sample copy, $4.99 at newsstands.
- "Dual-Faith Families." Article discusses ways for parents of different faiths to successfully celebrate and explain religions in the home.
- "So You Want to Get Pregnant?" Article offers fertility suggestions for lesbians over the age of 35 who want to get pregnant.
- Sample dept/column: "Nesting" discusses creating a family fun room.

Rights and Payment
Rights negotiable. Payment policy and rates vary.

Editor's Comments
We strive to present information that helps families create a positive family environment to promote growth, self-respect, and acceptance of others. We provide parenting information and resources that appeal to a broad audience. While some of our readers are gay and lesbians, some are not. All of our stories are written by assignment, work-for-hire projects.

AppleSeeds

Cobblestone Publishing Company
30 Grove Street
Peterborough, NH 03458

Editor: Susan Buckley

Description and Readership
All articles revolve around a central theme in this social studies publication for third and fourth grade students. Articles, written in a lively manner, encourage discussion and curiosity.
- **Audience:** 7–10 years
- **Frequency:** 9 times each year
- **Distribution:** 100% subscription
- **Circulation:** 5,000
- **Website:** www.cobblestonepub.com

Freelance Potential
90% written by nonstaff writers. Publishes 90–100 freelance submissions yearly; 20% by unpublished writers, 35% by authors who are new to the magazine. Receives 42 queries each month.

Submissions
Query. Prefers email submissions to swbuc@aol.com. Responds in 2–3 months.
Articles: 300–700 words. Factual articles; profiles; interviews; and personal experience pieces. Topics include nature, animals, pets, the environment, the arts, biography, crafts, hobbies, health, fitness, history, mathematics, multicultural and ethnic subjects, popular culture, science, social issues, sports, and travel.
Fiction: Word length varies. Genres include folklore. Also publishes poetry.
Depts/columns: 150–300 words. Theme-related activities and profiles.

Sample Issue
32 pages (no advertising): 11 articles; 4 depts/columns. Guidelines and theme list available at website.
- "Harriet Tubman: The Moses of Her People." Article relates the fascinating story of a woman who courageously worked to help many slaves gain freedom.
- "The Underground Railroad: A Path to Freedom." Article explains how the underground railroad worked to help slaves escape before the Emancipation Proclamation.
- Sample dept/column: "From the Source" quotes from a letter written by abolitionist Thomas Garrett.

Rights and Payment
All rights. Written material, $50 per page. Pays on publication. Provides 2 contributor's copies.

Editor's Comments
It is important that all submissions be historically and scientifically accurate, and we urge writers to use primary sources. Please visit our website for upcoming themes.

Aquila

P.O. Box 2518
Eastbourne
East Sussex BN21 2BR
United Kingdom

Editor: Jackie Berry

Description and Readership

This British magazine caters to the interests of bright, caring children with enquiring minds. Its articles encourage readers to explore facts and discover the world for themselves.
- **Audience:** 8–13 years
- **Frequency:** Monthly
- **Distribution:** 100% subscription
- **Circulation:** 8,000
- **Website:** www.aquila.co.uk

Freelance Potential

40% written by nonstaff writers. Publishes 4 freelance submissions yearly; 25% by unpublished writers, 25% by authors who are new to the magazine. Receives 16–20 queries monthly.

Submissions

Query with résumé. Accepts computer printouts and email queries to info@aquila.co.uk (Microsoft Word). SAE/IRC. Responds in 2–4 months.
Articles: 750–800 words. Informational and how-to articles; profiles; and interviews. Topics include pets, animals, the arts, crafts, hobbies, history, mathematics, nature, the environment, science, and technology.
Fiction: To 1,000 words. Genres include historical and contemporary fiction, science fiction, folklore, folktales, mystery, adventure, and horror. Also publishes animal stories.
Artwork: Color prints and transparencies.
Other: Arts and crafts activities. Submit seasonal material 3 months in advance.

Sample Issue

24 pages (no advertising): 5 articles; 1 story; 8 activities. Sample copy, £2.60 with 9x12 SAE/IRC. Guidelines and editorial calendar available.
- "Golf." Informative article explains the sport of golf, how to get involved in the sport, and highlights some of the top players in the field.
- "Queen Elizabeth I . . . . Who Died 400 Years Ago." Article examines the the life and accomplishments of the daughter of Henry VIII.

Rights and Payment

First rights. Articles and fiction, £60–£80. Artwork, payment rate varies. Pays on publication. Provides up to 6 copies.

Editor's Comments

We need educational and entertaining material that engages young readers with a mix of facts, puzzles, and fun. No contemporary pop culture topics, please.

Arizona Parenting

Suite 100
4041 North Central Avenue
Phoenix, AZ 85012

Editor: Linda Exley

Description and Readership

With a strong regional focus, this publication is read by parents and families as well as educators who live and work in Arizona. Its editors are interested in writers who are familiar with the state and its parent-friendly resources.
- **Audience:** Parents
- **Frequency:** Monthly
- **Distribution:** 100% other
- **Circulation:** 80,000
- **Website:** www.azparenting.com

Freelance Potential

50% written by nonstaff writers. Publishes 20 freelance submissions yearly; 5% by unpublished writers, 25% by authors who are new to the magazine. Receives 35 queries, 25 unsolicited mss monthly.

Submissions

Query or send complete ms. Accepts photocopies and disk submissions. SASE. Responds to queries in 2–3 months.
Articles: 850–2,400 words. Informational articles; profiles; interviews; and humor. Topics include parenting, education, finances, health, travel, sports, recreation, and fitness.
Depts/columns: 400–850 words. Child development, short news items, and family forums.
Artwork: B/W prints and transparencies. Line art.

Sample Issue

58 pages (50% advertising): 4 articles; 2 depts/columns; 1 calendar. Sample copy, free with 9x12 SASE ($2 postage). Editorial calendar available.
- "Theme Parkin' It." Article offers practical tips to maximize a theme park vacation.
- "Diet Wars." Article compares and contrasts a high protein diet with a high carbohydrate diet.
- Sample dept/column: "Family F.Y.I." features information on asthma relief, safety around fireworks, and recent recalls.

Rights and Payment

First North American serial and electronic rights. Written material, $100+. Artwork, payment rate varies. Pays on publication. Provides 2–3 contributor's copies.

Editor's Comments

We consider ourselves to be a complete family resource. We publish articles on a wide variety of topics—all related to raising children in general and in Arizona in particular. Our articles follow a seasonal schedule. For example, issues printed in the summer months, include topics such as summer school, family get-aways, and water safety.

Art Education

Virginia Commonwealth University
1916 Association Drive
Reston, VA 20191-1590

Editor: B. Carpenter II

Description and Readership
The audience for this publication includes art educators who teach art in grades K–12, educators in museums and art centers, university art education professors and instructors, art administrators, and art education students.
- **Audience:** Art teachers, grades K–12
- **Frequency:** 6 times each year
- **Distribution:** 70% subscription; 30% newsstand
- **Circulation:** 20,000

Freelance Potential
100% written by nonstaff writers. Publishes 36 freelance submissions yearly; 25% by unpublished writers, 5% by authors who are new to the magazine. Receives 10 mss monthly.

Submissions
Send 3 copies of complete ms. Accepts photocopies, computer printouts, disk submissions, and simultaneous submissions if identified. SASE. Responds in 8–10 weeks.
Articles: To 3,000 words. Interviews; profiles; and personal experience pieces. Topics include art history, art criticism, curriculum and studio planning, and other issues of interest to art educators.
Depts/columns: To 2,750 words. "Instructional Resources" features suggestions for lesson plans.
Artwork: 8x10 or 5x7 B/W prints, slides, or digital images.

Sample Issue
54 pages: 6 articles; 1 dept/column. Sample copy, $1.25 with 9x12 SASE ($.87 postage). Guidelines available.
- "The Adventures of Artemis and the Llama." Article by an educator explores the use of fictional narrative in working with art objects.
- "Music, Libraries, and Public Television." Article stresses the need for museums, libraries, and public television stations to act as significant sources of public information in this age of technology.
- Sample dept/column: "Instructional Resources" discusses teaching with public art.

Rights and Payment
All rights. No payment. Provides 2 contributor's copies.

Editor's Comments
Most of our writers are involved in art education and we are always interested in hearing from teachers about successful classroom techniques in a variety of art forms. Keep in mind that we prefer material that is instructional in nature; though profiles and interviews with well-known art educators are also welcome.

Art & Activities

12345 World Trade Drive
San Diego, CA 92128

Editor-in-Chief: Maryellen Bridge

Description and Readership
This well-known publication is read by art teachers working with students in all grades, kindergarten through high school. It features practical articles on successful art programs as well as personal experience pieces.
- **Audience:** Art educators, grades K–12
- **Frequency:** 10 times each year
- **Distribution:** 100% subscription
- **Circulation:** 20,000
- **Website:** www.artsandactivities.com

Freelance Potential
95% written by nonstaff writers. Publishes 100–125 freelance submissions yearly; 70% by unpublished writers, 50% by authors who are new to the magazine. Receives 25 unsolicited mss monthly.

Submissions
Send complete ms. Accepts photocopies, computer printouts, and disk submissions with hard copy. No simultaneous submissions. SASE. Responds in 2–6 months.
Articles: Word length varies. Practical application and how-to articles and personal experience pieces. Topics include art education, program development, art history, and visual perception.
Depts/columns: Word length varies. New product information, short news items, and book reviews.
Other: Lesson plans for classroom projects.

Sample Issue
70 pages (29% advertising): 10 articles; 7 depts/columns. Sample copy, $3 with 9x12 SASE ($2 postage). Guidelines and editorial calendar available.
- "George Caitlin and His Indian Gallery." Article profiles a unique exhibit of American Indian life featuring paintings collected by Caitlin in the 1800s.
- Sample dept/column: "Media Reviews" offers reviews on new books and videos related to art.

Rights and Payment
First North American serial rights. Pays on publication. All material, payment rate varies. Provides 3 contributor's copies.

Editor's Comments
We are currently seeking reviews of notable collections or exhibitions and profiles of artists and collectors. Most of our editorial is comprised of personal experience pieces from educators interested in sharing their ideas with other professionals. If you have a successful classroom project, we'd like to hear about it.

Asimov's Science Fiction ☆

Floor 11
475 Park Avenue South
New York, NY 10016

Editor: Sheila Williams

Description and Readership
In the science fiction stories published by this digest-sized magazine, the characters rather than the science, provide the main focus for the reader's interest. While fiction accounts for 90% of the contents of each issue, some poetry, reviews, and commentary also appear regularly.
- **Audience:** YA–Adult
- **Frequency:** 10 times each year
- **Distribution:** 87% subscription; 13% newsstand
- **Circulation:** 60,000
- **Website:** www.asimovs.com

Freelance Potential
97% written by nonstaff writers. Publishes 85 freelance submissions yearly; 10% by unpublished writers, 30% by authors who are new to the magazine. Receives 800 unsolicited mss each month.

Submissions
Send complete ms. No queries. Accepts photocopies and computer printouts. No simultaneous submissions. SASE. Responds in 6–8 weeks.
Fiction: To 20,000 words. Genres include science fiction and fantasy. Also publishes novellas and novelettes.
Depts/columns: Word length varies. Reviews of books and e-zines.
Other: Poetry, to 40 lines.

Sample Issue
144 pages (10% advertising): 8 stories; 3 poems; 1 novelette, 4 depts/columns. Sample copy, $5. Guidelines available.
- "Yard Sale." Short story revolves around two sisters who are cleaning out the home of their deceased parents.
- "Chicken Soup for Mars and Venus." Story focuses on an encounter in space between a long-haul trucker bound for Mars and a hostile patrolling space vehicle.
- Sample dept/column: "Reflections" discusses trilobites, marine creatures that dominated Earth for three hundred million years—longer than any other lifeform.

Rights and Payment
First North American serial rights. Fiction, $.06–$.08 per word. Poetry, $1 per line. Depts/columns, payment rate varies. Pays on acceptance. Provides 2 contributor's copies.

Editor's Comments
Serious, thoughtful, yet accessible fiction constitutes the majority of our purchases, but there's always room for the humorous as well. Borderline fantasy is fine, but please don't submit Sword & Sorcery stories. Explicit sex or violence are not welcome.

Atlanta Baby

Suite 101
2346 Perimeter Park
Atlanta, GA 30341

Managing Editor: Amy Dusek

Description and Readership
Practical topics aimed at helping new and expecting parents are found in this publication. Its advice focuses on parents with children up to two years of age and on various issues encountered in pregnancy. All problems presented are accompanied by a solution.
- **Audience:** Parents
- **Frequency:** Twice each year
- **Distribution:** 100% controlled
- **Circulation:** 30,000
- **Website:** www.atlantaparent.com

Freelance Potential
25% written by nonstaff writers. Publishes 50 freelance submissions yearly; 5% by unpublished writers, 30% by new authors. Receives 260 unsolicited mss each month.

Submissions
Send complete ms. Accepts photocopies, disk submissions (Word Perfect or ASCII), and email submissions to adusek@ atlantaparent.com. SASE. Responds in 6 months.
Articles: 600–1,200 words. Informational and how-to articles; and humor. Topics include pregnancy, childbirth, child development, early education, health and fitness, and parenting.
Depts/columns: Word length varies. Short essays and resource guides.
Other: Submit holiday material 6 months in advance.

Sample Issue
34 pages (50% advertising): 5 articles; 3 depts/columns. Sample copy, $2 with 9x12 SASE. Guidelines available.
- "The Name Game." Article clarifies the five stumbling blocks that can change the name a parent "always wanted" to use for a child.
- "Chiropractic Care During Pregnancy." Article considers chiropractic care during pregnancy as a means to ease headaches, back pain, and heartburn.
- Sample dept/column: "Nursery Giggles" provides a humorous side to the foibles of pregnancy.

Rights and Payment
One-time rights. Written material, $35–$50. Pays on publication. Provides 1 tearsheet.

Editor's Comments
Our editorial style is reader-friendly with the intention of helping parents through the first two years of childrearing. When including professional resources, use quotes from either local experts, or experts from other parts of the country. Keep instructions short, to the point, and accurate.

Atlanta Parent

Suite 101
2346 Perimeter Park Drive
Atlanta, GA 30341

Managing Editor: Amy Dusek

Description and Readership

Available free of charge throughout the Atlanta metropolitan area, *Atlanta Parent* is a resource for families with children up to the age of 16. Its articles provide parents with the latest information on education, child care, and health-related topics. A monthly calendar that highlights local events and attractions is a major feature of each issue.
- **Audience:** Parents
- **Frequency:** Monthly
- **Distribution:** 100% controlled
- **Circulation:** 100,000
- **Website:** www.atlantaparent.com

Freelance Potential

25% written by nonstaff writers. Publishes 50 freelance submissions yearly; 5% by unpublished writers, 30% by authors who are new to the magazine. Receives 22 mss monthly.

Submissions

Send complete ms. Accepts photocopies, disk submissions (WordPerfect or ASCII), and email submissions to adusek@atlantaparent.com. SASE. Responds in 6 months.
Articles: 600–1,200 words. Informational and how-to articles and humorous pieces. Topics include education, child care, child development, health, fitness, and parenting issues.
Depts/columns: Word length varies. Short essays and resource guides.
Other: Submit secular holiday material 6 months in advance.

Sample Issue

90 pages (50% advertising): 4 articles; 8 depts/columns; 1 special section. Sample copy, $2 with 9x12 SASE. Writers' guidelines available.
- "Discover Downtown." Article surveys the many family-vacation destinations in downtown Atlanta.
- "The Quest for Quality Childcare." Article follows three area moms as they search for a family child-care home, a child-care center, and a nanny.
- Sample dept/column: "It's a Woman's World" features a book review and short items on designer merchandise, customized beauty products, and business networking.

Rights and Payment

One-time rights. Pays on publication. Written material, $35–$50. Provides 1 tearsheet.

Editor's Comments

In addition to informational articles, our readers like to see articles that are activity-based. If you try your hand at one of these, keep the instructions short and to the point.

Austin Family

P.O. Box 7559
Round Rock, TX 78684-7559

Editor: Betty Richardson

Description and Readership

Parenting tips and information about local events, services, and activities help make this regional tabloid useful for families living in the Austin area. Articles on health, camps, creative family projects, and education add to the resource mix.
- **Audience:** Adults
- **Frequency:** Monthly
- **Distribution:** 80% controlled; 10% schools; 5% subscription; 5% other
- **Circulation:** 35,000
- **Website:** www.austinfamily.com

Freelance Potential

70% written by nonstaff writers. Publishes 15 freelance submissions yearly; 10% by unpublished writers, 50% by authors who are new to the magazine. Receives 67 queries and unsolicited mss monthly.

Submissions

Query or send complete ms. Accepts photocopies, computer printouts, simultaneous submissions, and email submissions to editor@austinfamily.com. Artwork improves chance of acceptance. SASE. Responds in 3 months.
Articles: 800 words. Informational, practical application, and how-to articles. Topics include parenting, family, the environment, recreation, multicultural issues, hobbies, crafts, careers, college, pets, current events, health, and fitness.
Depts/columns: 800 words. Local news and events, humor, and parenting tips.
Artwork: B/W prints.
Other: Submit seasonal material 6 months in advance.

Sample Issue

40 pages (50% advertising): 4 articles; 10 depts/columns. Sample copy, free.
- "Scouting for Austin." Article spotlights an Austin teen who proves kids can get involved with a community to support a common goal.
- "Preparing to Be Parents: Are You Ready?" Interview offers tips from pediatrician T. Berry Brazelton.
- Sample dept/column: "Healthy Homes" presents creative ideas for bringing spring indoors.

Rights and Payment

First and second serial rights. Payment rates and payment policy vary.

Editor's Comments

We would like to see a wide variety of parenting topics, not just pieces on birthing and maternity.

BabagaNewz

90 Oak Street
Newton, MA 02464

Managing Editor: Ina Lerman

Description and Readership
This lively, colorful classroom magazine is targeted specifically to 4th- through 7th-grade students in Jewish schools. With the subtitle "Jewish Kids Exploring the World," it accurately and thoughtfully presents and analyzes major news stories, religious holidays, cultural events, and youth trends that play an important part in the lives of Jewish youngsters. It is published by the AVI CHAI Foundation.
- **Audience:** 9–13 years
- **Frequency:** 9 times each year
- **Distribution:** Schools; subscription
- **Circulation:** Unavailable
- **Website:** www.babaganewz.com

Freelance Potential
All articles are written on assignment.

Submissions
Query or send complete ms. Accepts photocopies and computer printouts. SASE. Response time varies.
Articles: Word length varies. Informational and how-to articles; profiles; and interviews. Topics include education, health, fitness, sports, social issues, and current events—all with Jewish themes.
Depts/columns: Word length varies. Science updates, news, and short profiles.

Sample Issue
20 pages (no advertising): 2 articles; 8 depts/columns; 1 activity page. Guidelines available by email to ina@babaganewz.com.
- "Face-Off at Emek Ha'Elah." Article takes the reader to the famous battlefield where David struck down the "mighty giant," Goliath.
- "Eyewitness to History." Article relives the capture of Jerusalem from the Arabs in 1967 from the viewpoint of a soldier who was part of the Israeli army.
- Sample dept/column: "Spotlight" chronicles the life of an archaeologist who is literally digging up Jewish history in biblical regions of Israel.

Rights and Payment
All rights. Written material, payment rate varies. Pays on acceptance. Provides contributor's copies.

Editor's Comments
Each issue revolves around a specific Jewish value and all of our articles are written on assignment—most of them by freelance writers. In addition to writers who understand Jewish culture, we are looking for illustrators who are familiar with the symbols used in Jewish holidays.

Babybug

Cricket Magazine Group
P.O. Box 300
315 Fifth Street
Peru, IL 61354

Submissions Editor

Description and Readership
Babybug, published by the renowned Cricket family of children's magazines, is a listening and looking magazine for infants and toddlers. It features very short stories and poems composed of simple words and concepts that help youngsters learn about the world around them.
- **Audience:** 6 months–2 years
- **Frequency:** 10 times each year
- **Distribution:** 90% subscription; 10% newsstand
- **Circulation:** 46,000
- **Website:** www.cricketmag.com

Freelance Potential
90% written by nonstaff writers. Publishes 45–50 freelance submissions yearly; 50% by authors who are new to the magazine. Receives 200 unsolicited mss monthly.

Submissions
Send complete ms. Accepts photocopies, computer printouts, and simultaneous submissions if identified. SASE. Responds in 3–4 months.
Articles: 10 words. Basic conceptual ideas to be illustrated.
Fiction: 3–6 short sentences. Simple, concrete stories. Humor should be age-appropriate.
Other: Rhyming and rhythmic poetry, to 8 lines. Activities calling for parent/child interaction.

Sample Issue
22 pages (no advertising): 3 stories; 3 poems. Sample copy, $5. Guidelines available.
- "Ways of Going." Story connects children's natural interest in motion to an exploration of sounds and sound making.
- "Kim and Carrots." Story parlays a pair of new shoes into an exercise session and the shoe box into a bed for a pet.
- "I Have Wheels." Poem demonstrates that making something move using muscles is better than relying on batteries.

Rights and Payment
Rights vary. Written material, $25 minimum. Pays on publication. Provides 6 contributor's copies.

Editor's Comments
The stories in *Babybug* are meant to be read aloud and shared between child and adult. It's imperative that writers submitting pieces to *Babybug* become familiar with the publication and the nuances, instincts, and characteristics of infants and toddlers. Understand the way they learn, how they're motivated, and entertained. As simple as the pieces are, they are meant to enable parents to utilize fun sounds and voices as one way to teach their children.

Baby Dallas

Lauren Publications
Suite 146
4275 Kellway Circle
Addison, TX 75001

Editor: Shelley Pate

Description and Readership

A handy reference for information relating to pregnancy and early child care, *Baby Dallas* is distributed free of charge to the greater Dallas community. Articles are written in a practical and straightforward tone.
- **Audience:** Parents
- **Frequency:** Twice each year
- **Distribution:** 90% controlled; 10% subscription
- **Circulation:** 120,000
- **Website:** www.dallaschild.com

Freelance Potential

25% written by nonstaff writers. Publishes 12–15 freelance submissions yearly; 20% by authors who are new to the magazine. Receives 20 queries monthly.

Submissions

Query with résumé. Accepts photocopies, computer printouts, simultaneous submissions if identified, and email queries to editorial@dallaschild.com. SASE. Responds in 2–3 months.
Articles: 1,000–2,500 words. Informational, self-help, and how-to articles; profiles; interviews; humor; and personal experience pieces. Topics include parenting, education, current events, social issues, multicultural and ethnic issues, health, fitness, crafts, and computers.
Depts/columns: 800 words. Health updates, safety issues, baby care, and parent resources.

Sample Issue

30 pages (14% advertising): 1 article; 7 depts/columns. Sample copy, free with 9x12 SASE. Guidelines available.
- "The Many Emotions of Motherhood." Article delves into the extensive range of emotions associated with new motherhood from ecstatic joy immediately following birth to depression often brought on by too little sleep and an overwhelming feeling of losing control.
- Sample dept/column: "Safety" provides tips for parents on safely using baby products such as strollers and car seats.
- Sample dept/column: "Health" offers suggestions on how yoga can help pregnant women stay in shape and reduce the stress of being pregnant.

Rights and Payment

First rights. Written material, payment rate varies. Pays on publication. Provides contributor's copies on request.

Editor's Comments

Most of our information is targeted at new mothers. We want to help make first-time parenting a positive experience.

Baby Talk

The Parenting Group
3rd Floor
530 5th Avenue
New York, NY 10036

Senior Editor: Patty Onderko

Description and Readership

Baby Talk is filled with practical information for pregnant women and for parents of children under 18 months old. Its crisp style plainly tells readers what they need to know about pregnancy, baby care, and personal issues revolving around infants and their development.
- **Audience:** Parents
- **Frequency:** 10 times each year
- **Distribution:** 100% controlled
- **Circulation:** 2 million
- **Website:** www.babytalk.com

Freelance Potential

70% written by nonstaff writers. Publishes 40 freelance submissions yearly; 20% by authors who are new to the magazine. Receives 42 queries monthly.

Submissions

Query with clips or writing samples. No simultaneous submissions. SASE. Responds in 2 months.
Articles: 1,500–2,000 words. Informational and how-to articles; and personal experience pieces. Topics include pregnancy, baby care, infant health, juvenile equipment and toys, day care, marriage, and relationships.
Depts/columns: 500–1,200 words. News, advice, women's and infant health, and personal experiences from new parents.

Sample Issue

92 pages (50% advertising): 6 articles; 10 depts/columns. Sample copy, free with 9x12 SASE ($1.60 postage). Guidelines and theme list available.
- "What Your Baby's Telling You." Article explains how to interpret an infant's repertoire of sounds and behaviors and match them with an appropriate response.
- "New Mom Care." Article demonstrates how important it is for a new mom to have help and how to get it.
- Sample dept/column: "Table for 2" covers nutrition news for babies and mothers.

Rights and Payment

First rights. Articles, $1,000–$2,000. Depts/columns, $300–$1,200. Pays on acceptance. Provides 2–4 contributor's copies.

Editor's Comments

Every topic we cover is approached from a how-to service perspective for new parents to give them easy-to-follow guidelines from experts and people who have been there. Our goal is to help instill confidence in parents who are either new to parenthood, or who want to discover the latest information, products, ideas, and advice on rearing babies and toddlers.

Baltimore's Child

11 Dutton Court
Baltimore, MD 21228

Editor: Dianne R. McCann

Description and Readership
Parents of children from newborns to teens turn to this magazine for positive, constructive, practical advice that helps them make informed choices. Stories with local angles point readers toward places, events, resources, and activities for families in the Baltimore metropolitan area.
- **Audience:** Parents
- **Frequency:** Monthly
- **Distribution:** Unavailable
- **Circulation:** Unavailable
- **Website:** www.baltimoreschild.com

Freelance Potential
95% written by nonstaff writers. Publishes 250 freelance submissions yearly.

Submissions
Prefers query; accepts complete ms. Accepts photocopies, computer printouts, and email submissions to baltochild@aol.com. SASE. Response time varies.
Articles: 1,000–1,500 words. Informational articles. Topics include parenting issues, education, health, fitness, child care, social issues, and regional news.
Depts/columns: Word length varies. Family issues, travel, opinion, baby care, book and music reviews, new product reviews, parenting teens, and parenting children with special needs.

Sample Issue
74 pages: 5 articles; 14 depts/columns; 1 directory; 4 calendars. Guidelines available.
- "The Growing Problem of Childhood Obesity." Article shows how to confront this national trend by balancing a child's free time with physical activity.
- "Is Your Child's Backpack Too Big a Burden?" Article lists warning sign that indicate a child's backpack is heavier than the recommended maximum 15 percent of body weight.
- Sample dept/column: "Focus on Fathers" reviews a book written to help dads understand their daughters.

Rights and Payment
One-time rights. Written material, payment policy and rates vary.

Editor's Comments
We're seeking stories with a local angle that offer specific resources and information. For example, an article about teaching children how to swim must include a list of places in the Baltimore area that provide swimming lessons.

Bay Area Baby

Suite 120
2280 Vehicle Drive
Rancho Cordova, CA 95670

Regional Editor: Corrie Pelc

Description and Readership
Distributed free throughout the San Francisco Bay area, this publication for new and expectant parents focuses exclusively on issues associated with pregnancy, childbirth, and infant care. It mixes informational articles with material about local events, resources, and services.
- **Audience:** Parents
- **Frequency:** 3 times each year
- **Distribution:** 100% controlled
- **Circulation:** 80,000
- **Website:** www.bayareaparent.com

Freelance Potential
50% written by nonstaff writers. Publishes 21 freelance submissions yearly; 50% by authors who are new to the magazine. Receives 8 queries and unsolicited mss monthly.

Submissions
Query or send complete ms. Accepts photocopies, computer printouts, and simultaneous submissions if identified. SASE. Responds in 1–2 months.
Articles: 1,200–1,400 words. Informational, self-help, and how-to articles; profiles; interviews; humor; and personal experience pieces. Topics include pregnancy, prenatal care, childbirth, and infant care.
Depts/columns: 800 words. Parenting updates.
Artwork: 8x10 B/W or color prints. No slides.
Other: Submit seasonal material 6 months in advance.

Sample Issue
36 pages: 5 articles; 2 depts/columns. Sample copy, free with 9x12 SASE (5 first-class stamps). Guidelines available.
- "Bilingual in the Bay Area: How Families Benefit, Plus Tips for Raising Bilingual Kids." Article profiles 3 families whose children are growing up with a second language.
- "Beyond Stranger Danger: Teaching Kids How to Avoid Abduction." Article reports on ways to give kids the tools they need to stay safe.
- "Baby Signs: Want to Know What Baby's Thinking?" Article describes the sign language used by infants.

Rights and Payment
Regional rights. Written material, payment rate varies. Pays on publication. Provides 1 contributor's copy.

Editor's Comments
We try to present our readers with information they can't get from national parenting publications. We want to see features that include the personal experiences of Bay area parents or interviews with local experts.

Bay Area Parent

Suite 4
987 University Avenue
Los Gatos, CA 95036

Regional Editor: Richard Cornett

Description and Readership

Families living in the Silicon Valley area of California turn to this parenting tabloid for its newsworthy articles, information on local goods and services, and articles on issues that impact family lives.
- **Audience:** Parents
- **Frequency:** Monthly
- **Distribution:** 99% controlled; 1% subscription
- **Circulation:** 55,000
- **Website:** www.parenthood.com

Freelance Potential

50% written by nonstaff writers. Publishes 20 freelance submissions yearly; 20% by authors who are new to the magazine. Receives 30+ queries and unsolicited mss monthly.

Submissions

Query or send complete ms. Accepts photocopies, computer printouts, and simultaneous submissions if identified. SASE. Responds in 2 months.
Articles: 1,200–1,400 words. Informational, self-help, and how-to articles; profiles; interviews; humor; and personal experience pieces. Topics include family issues, health, fitness, social and multicultural issues, and gifted and special education.
Depts/columns: Word length varies. Opinion, news, travel, and profiles.
Artwork: B/W and color prints.
Other: Submit seasonal material 6 months in advance.

Sample Issue

106 pages: 5 articles; 9 depts/columns; 1 calendar. Sample copy, free with 9x12 SASE (5 first-class stamps). Guidelines and theme list available.
- "Family Resort Vacation." Article discusses aspects of resort vacations that can help you determine if its the right type of vacation for you and your family.
- "The 12 Toughest Questions You'll Ever Ask." Local professionals answer the questions that frequently stump parents.
- Sample dept/column: "Teen Focus" looks at the growing trend towards gastric bypass surgery as a weight loss solution for obese teenagers.

Rights and Payment

One-time rights. Written material, $.06 per word. Artwork, $10–$15. Pays on publication. Provides 1 contributor's copy.

Editor's Comments

We are always interested in hearing from writers who can deliver a feature on a tried and true parenting topic (i.e. teething) that offers a new approach or a fresh twist.

Bay State Parent

P.O. Box 617
Holden, MA 01520

Editor: Susan Scully Petroni

Description and Readership

Formerly known as *Today's Parent*, this free regional tabloid is read by families living in Massachusetts who have an interest in issues and events related to raising children. Its readership concentrates on families with children up to the age of 13.
- **Audience:** Parents
- **Frequency:** Monthly
- **Distribution:** Newsstand; subscription; libraries
- **Circulation:** 44,000

Freelance Potential

80% written by nonstaff writers. Publishes 15 freelance submissions yearly; 10% by unpublished writers, 25% by authors who are new to the magazine. Receives 8–10 queries and unsolicited mss monthly.

Submissions

Query with writing samples; or send complete ms. Accepts email submissions to spetrani@rcn.com. Responds in 3 months.
Articles: 800–1,200 words. Informational and how-to articles and humorous pieces. Topics include regional and local events, health, education, travel, books, the arts, crafts, family finance, and computers.
Depts/columns: Word length varies.
Artwork: B/W or color prints

Sample Issue

76 pages: 8 articles; 13 depts/columns; 1 activity. Writers' guidelines available.
- "So You Think Being a Mom Is Tough?" Article profiles a mother who is in charge of running a house for a family of ten, and does so with ease.
- "Swift Tips for Juggling Career and Family" Article features interview with former Massachusetts governor, Jane Swift, who is also a mother of three.
- Sample dept/column: "The Parent Review" discusses how to evaluate newborn behavior and development.

Rights and Payment

First North American serial rights. Articles, $50–$125. Pays 30 days after publication.

Editor's Comments

Right now we are seeing too many first-person stories. We need more news articles that take a serious look at issues in the headlines, relating to family life and children. Keep in mind that as a regional publication, we always look for the local connection that will hook our readers into a piece, no matter what the topic.

Beckett Publications

15850 Dallas Parkway
Dallas, TX 75248

Editorial Department

Description and Readership

Baseball Card Monthly, Beckett Basketball Monthly, Beckett Focus on Future Stars, Beckett Racing Monthly, Beckett Football Monthly, and *Beckett Hockey Monthly* are other titles published by Beckett Publications. Each is a source of information on players, products, and news.
- **Audience:** YA–Adult
- **Frequency:** Monthly
- **Distribution:** 80% newsstand; 20% subscription
- **Circulation:** 2 million (combined)
- **Website:** www.beckett.com

Freelance Potential

50% written by nonstaff writers. Publishes 100 freelance submissions yearly; 1% by unpublished writers, 10% by authors who are new to the magazine. Receives 30 queries, 30 unsolicited mss monthly.

Submissions

Prefers query with outline and clips. Accepts complete ms. Accepts photocopies and computer printouts. No simultaneous submissions. SASE. Responds in 1–2 months.
Articles: 500–2,000 words. Informational articles and profiles. Topics include sporting events, sports stars, card and memorabilia collecting. All-Star games and Hall of Fame inductions.
Fiction: Word length varies. Stories about sports.
Depts/columns: 500–750 words. News related to sports memorabilia collecting.

Sample Issue

Beckett Baseball: 120 pages (20% advertising): 4 articles; 9 depts/columns; 1 show calendar; 6 price guides. Sample copy, $4.95. Guidelines available.
- "Small Ball." Article describes MLB SportsClix, a popular 3-D, collectible, tradable, and playable baseball game, as one of the hottest items today with gamers and collectors.
- Sample dept/column: "Signing Session" follows the progress of hitter Albert Pujols from willing signer to elusive baseball star.

Rights and Payment

First North American serial rights. Articles and fiction, $250–$500. Depts/columns, $100–$200. Pays on acceptance. Provides 2 contributor's copies.

Editor's Comments

Articles on sports, sports players, and out-of-the-ordinary collections are always of interest to us. Please note that we prefer queries over complete manuscripts.

Better Homes and Gardens

Meredith Corporation
1716 Locust Street
Des Moines, IA 50309-3023

Department Editor

Description and Readership

Read primarily by active women, this well-known home and family magazine features practical articles on decorating, crafts, entertaining, cooking, and gardening.
- **Audience:** Adults
- **Frequency:** Monthly
- **Distribution:** Subscription; newsstand
- **Circulation:** 7.6 million
- **Website:** www.bhg.com

Freelance Potential

10% written by nonstaff writers. Publishes 25–30 freelance submissions yearly; 25% by authors who are new to the magazine. Receives 20 queries monthly.

Submissions

Query with résumé and clips or writing samples. No unsolicited mss. Accepts photocopies and computer printouts. SASE. Responds in 1 month.
Articles: Word length varies. Informational and how-to articles; personal experience pieces; and profiles. Topics include food and nutrition, home design, gardening and outdoor living, travel, the environment, health, fitness, holidays, education, parenting, and child development.

Sample Issue

284 pages: 34 articles. Sample copy, $2.99 at newsstands. Guidelines available.
- "Relax," Article suggests growing herbs for a relaxing aromatherapy treatment.
- "Color Comes of Age." Article describes an enterprising couple's plans for updating an older home with a sophisticated color scheme.
- Sample dept/column: "Then and Now" offers an opinion that childhood off-the-cuff home performances are a sneak preview of the future.

Rights and Payment

All rights. Written material, payment rate varies. Pays on acceptance. Provides 1 contributor's copy.

Editor's Comments

Please be sure to address your query to the appropriate editor—see our masthead for current names and departments. A freelancer's best chances are in the areas of travel, health, parenting, and education. Send us material that takes a tired subject and injects it with a contemporary twist. Our "BH&G Kids" department needs interviews and profiles of children from across the nation.

Big Apple Parent

4th Floor
9 East 38th Street
New York, NY 10016

Editor: Kirsten Matthew

Description and Readership

This well-known tabloid targets parents and family members with children to the age of 16. Each issue of Big Apple Parent brings readers the latest news and research about topics related to raising children as well as detailed listings of local events and attractions. The mother company also produces parenting papers for Queens, Brooklyn, and Westchester, New York.
- **Audience:** Parents
- **Frequency:** Monthly
- **Distribution:** 100% controlled
- **Circulation:** 70,000
- **Website:** www.parentsknow.com

Freelance Potential

95% written by nonstaff writers. Publishes 450 freelance submissions yearly; 25% by authors who are new to the magazine. Receives 75 queries, 75 unsolicited mss monthly.

Submissions

Query or send complete ms. Accepts photocopies, computer printouts, and email to hellonwheels@parentsknow.com. SASE. Responds to queries in 1 week.
Articles: 800–1,000 words. Informational and how-to articles; profiles; interviews; humor; and personal experience pieces. Topics include family issues, health, nutrition, fitness, crafts, current events, gifted and special education, nature, and regional news.
Depts/columns: 750 words. News and reviews.
Other: Submit seasonal material 4 months in advance.

Sample Issue

120 pages: 8 articles; 10 depts/columns. Sample copy, free with 10x13 SASE. Guidelines available.
- "When Girls Bully Girls." Article offers suggestions for parents and teachers to help them curb the trend of "mean girls" in junior and senior high school.
- Sample dept/column: "Education" discusses the benefits of smaller schools, such as those now in New York that are funded by the Gates Foundation.

Rights and Payment

First New York area rights. Articles, $50. Pays 2 months after publication. Provides 1 contributor's copy.

Editor's Comments

We are currently in the market for submissions tackling news issues important to parents as well as investigative articles looking at controversial topics. We are not currently accepting submissions related to travel, humor, personal experience essays, or general articles on child raising.

Biography Today

615 Griswold Street
Detroit, MI 48226

Managing Editor: Cherie D. Abbey

Description and Readership

Profiles of authors, musicians, political leaders, sports figures, movie actors, scientists, astronauts, television personalities, and other popular figures can be found in this unique publication. With input by teachers and librarians who work with children, it provides young readers with the life history on personalities they want to know about.
- **Audience:** 9–14 years
- **Frequency:** 6 times each year
- **Distribution:** 100% subscription
- **Circulation:** 9,000
- **Website:** www.omnigraphics.com

Freelance Potential

50% written by nonstaff writers. Publishes several freelance submissions yearly. Receives 1 query monthly.

Submissions

Query with résumé. SASE. Responds in 2 months.
Articles: 2,000–5,000 words. Biographical sketches of people in the news. Covers individuals young readers want to know more about, according to teachers and librarians. They include entertainers, authors, political leaders, athletes, scientists, sports figures, musicians, and astronauts.

Sample Issue

188 pages (no advertising): 10 articles. Sample copy, $19 with 8x10 SASE. Guidelines available.
- "Ashton Kutcher." Article profiles the career of this popular American actor and producer who has starred in both television shows and movies.
- "Tony Blair." Article chronicles the childhood, education, career highlights, and political career of the Prime Minister of the United Kindgom as well as the challenges he faces in the position.
- "Will Wright." Profile looks at the early life and career of an American game designer who created the best-selling computer games "Sim City," "The Sims," and "The Sims Online."

Rights and Payment

All rights. Payment policy and rates vary depending on author's experience. Provides 2 contributor's copies.

Editor's Comments

We offer readers a complete look at a person's life. Detail is provided, but not overly so. Kids enjoy our tell-all style, while teachers, librarians, and parents like our clever format, and intelligent and informative text. We provide information about a celebrity's early life and experiences, including stories about family, education, hobbies, activities, and career highlights.

Birmingham Christian Family

P.O. Box 382724
Birmingham, AL 35238

President: Laurie Stroud

Description and Readership
This regional publication is used as a resource for information on family issues from parenting and finances to health and local personalities. In addition to having a local flavor, the material also reinforces Christian values.
- **Audience:** Families
- **Frequency:** Monthly
- **Distribution:** 95% newsstand; 5% subscription
- **Circulation:** 35,000
- **Website:** www.birminghamchristian.com

Freelance Potential
50% written by nonstaff writers. Publishes 60 freelance submissions yearly; 5% by unpublished writers, 2–3% by authors who are new to the magazine. Receives 8–9 queries monthly.

Submissions
Query with photos if applicable. Accepts email submissions to laurie@birminghamchristian.com. Availability of artwork improves chance of acceptance. SASE. Responds in 1 month.
Articles: To 500 words. Informational, self-help, and how-to articles; profiles, personal experience pieces; and interviews. Topics include animals, pets, the arts, crafts, hobbies, current events, fitness, music, recreation, religion, travel, and sports.
Fiction: To 500 words. Features inspirational fiction and humorous stories.
Depts/columns: To 500 words. Book and music reviews, regional news, humor, money matters, and recipes.
Artwork: Color prints and transparencies. Line art.
Other: Activities. Submit seasonal material on Christmas, Easter, and summer 2 months in advance.

Sample Issue
30 pages (25% advertising): 3 articles;16 depts/columns; 1 guide. Sample copy, free with 9x12 SASE ($3.00 postage). Editorial calendar available.
- "Alabama's Cowboy, Lee Roy Jordan." Article highlights the professional and personal life of the Dallas Cowboy star and relates his success to Christian values.
- Sample dept/column: "Healthy Living" focuses on building a healthy marriage.

Rights and Payment
Rights vary. No payment.

Editor's Comments
We provide information on local events, news, personalities, and family issues. We are interested in submissions that show what families and individuals in the area are doing to improve their spiritual lives.

The Black Collegian

34th Floor
909 Poydras Street
New Orleans, LA 70112

Editorial Assistant: Caroline Wilson

Description and Readership
This magazine targets African American students who are graduating from college and considering further education or career opportunities. It regularly covers topics related to career, education, job opportunities, and self-development. The publication appears twice each year.
- **Audience:** African Americans, 18–22 years
- **Frequency:** 2 times each year
- **Distribution:** Internet; college campuses
- **Circulation:** 122,000
- **Website:** www.black-collegian.com

Freelance Potential
90% written by nonstaff writers. Publishes 20 freelance submissions yearly; 33% by authors who are new to the magazine. Receives 2 queries monthly.

Submissions
Query. Accepts photocopies, computer printouts, and IBM disk submissions (Microsoft Word 97). SASE. Responds in 3 months.
Articles: 1,500–2,000 words. Informational, how-to, and self-help articles; profiles; and personal experience pieces. Topics include careers, personal development, job hunting, colleges, financial aid, history, technology, and multicultural and ethnic issues.
Depts/columns: Word length varies. Health issues and African American book and art reviews.
Artwork: 5x7 and 11x14 B/W and color transparencies. B/W and color line art.

Sample Issue
102 pages: 22 articles; 3 depts/columns. Guidelines available.
- "The Pharmaceutical Industry." Article reports on the latest career opportunities in this field and what kinds of experience is necessary for finding employment.
- "How to Evaluate a Job Offer." A director of a university career center gives tips to help students decide if a job is right for them.
- Sample dept/column: "Art of the African World" showcases award-winning artwork from the Historically Black Colleges and Universities Student Art Competition.

Rights and Payment
One-time rights. Written material, payment rate varies. Pays after publication. Provides 1 contributor's copy.

Editor's Comments
We are interested in practical, informational pieces that will bring our readers the facts they need to make decisions about their career, education, or self-development.

Blackgirl Magazine

P.O. Box 90729
Atlanta, GA 30364

Editorial Director: Kenya James

Description and Readership

An interesting mix of information pertinent to today's African American girls and young women, *Blackgirl Magazine* also provides broad historical and ethnic viewpoints for its readers.
- **Audience:** 9–21 years
- **Frequency:** 6 times each year
- **Distribution:** 50% subscription; 20% newsstand; 30% other
- **Circulation:** 7,000
- **Website:** www.blackgirlmagazine.com

Freelance Potential

40% written by nonstaff writers. Publishes several submissions yearly; 70% by unpublished writers, 50% by authors who are new to the magazine.

Submissions

Query. Accepts computer printouts and email submissions to editor@blackgirlmagazine.com. SASE. Responds in 6 weeks.
Articles: 1,000–1,500 words. Informational, factual, and self-help articles; profiles; interviews; and reviews. Topics include the arts, crafts, hobbies, current events, history, multicultural and ethnic issues, music, popular culture, and social issues.
Fiction: Word length varies. Multicultural and ethnic fiction, folklore, and folktales.
Depts/columns: Word length varies. Sports and advice.
Artwork: B/W and color prints and transparencies. Line art.
Other: Activities, games, jokes, puzzles, and poetry.

Sample Issue

20 pages (15% advertising): 2 articles; 1 story; 4 depts/columns; 3 interviews; 1 book review. Sample copy, $4. Guidelines and editorial calendar available.
- "Remembering Emmett Till." Article describes the incident of 14-year-old Emmett Till's kidnapping and murder in Mississippi during the '50s and its coverage by PBS.
- "Cheating Never Pays." Short story revolves around a cheating incident in school and the effect it had on the involved students—some innocent, some not.
- Sample dept/column: "First Fruits: Our Elders Speak" provides a world perspective from the older generation.

Rights and Payment

All rights. No payment. Provides 3 contributor's copies.

Editor's Comments

Our publication focuses on contributions to and from our target audience of African American pre-teens, teens, and young adults. We include current social issues and events that impact their lives, but avoid articles on sex and make-up.

Book Links

American Library Association
50 East Huron Street
Chicago, IL 60611

Editor: Laura Tillotson

Description and Readership

This magazine is designed for teachers, librarians, library media specialists, parents, and other adults interested in connecting children with books. By linking books on similar themes and providing bibliographies, it is considered a good resource for child-care centers and public libraries.
- **Audience:** Librarians, teachers, and parents
- **Frequency:** 6 times each year
- **Distribution:** 98% subscription; 2% controlled
- **Circulation:** 20,577
- **Website:** www.ala.org/BookLinks

Freelance Potential

90% written by nonstaff writers. Publishes 60 freelance submissions yearly; 20% by unpublished writers, 30% by authors who are new to the magazine. Receives 8 queries monthly.

Submissions

Query. No unsolicited ms. SASE. Response time varies.
Articles: Word length varies. Interviews; profiles; and personal experience pieces. Topics include children's books, current and historical events, nature, the environment, and ethnic and multicultural subjects.
Depts/columns: Ideas for using children's books in the classroom, 800–1,200 words. Book lists for specific countries or locales, and themes/ideas with title lists, 250–300 words. Interviews with authors and illustrators, word length varies.

Sample Issue

56 pages (28% advertising): 9 articles; 4 depts/columns. Sample copy, $6. Guidelines and theme list available.
- "B Is for Book Buddies: Alphabet Books in the Classroom." Article looks at the many levels of alphabet books that enrich children and classroom projects.
- "Beyond Superman: Superheroes in Picture Books." Article analyzes the role played by literary superheroes in helping young readers believe that they can be brave, dream big dreams, and meet great challenges.
- Sample dept/column: "Spotlight on the Stars" helps readers keep up with the best and brightest new children's titles.

Rights and Payment

All rights. Articles, $100. Interviews, $150. Pays on publication. Provides 2 contributor's copies.

Editor's Comments

Please review our publication before submitting a manuscript. We look for authors who have a strong background in children's literature in order to accommodate our goals.

Bop

Suite 700
6430 Sunset Boulevard
Hollywood, CA 90028

Editor: Leesa Coble

Description and Readership
Tween readers enjoy this high-energy magazine for the latest news, features, and gossip on today's hottest teen market celebrities. It also includes poetry, artwork, posters, and crafts.
- **Audience:** 10–16 years
- **Frequency:** Monthly
- **Distribution:** 75% newsstand; 25% subscription
- **Circulation:** 200,000
- **Website:** www.bopmag.com

Freelance Potential
10% written by nonstaff writers. Publishes 10 freelance submissions yearly; 5% by unpublished writers, 10% by authors who are new to the magazine. Receives 2 queries monthly.

Submissions
Query with résumé and clips. Accepts photocopies, computer printouts, and simultaneous submissions if identified. SASE. Responds 2 months.
Articles: To 700 words. Celebrity interviews; profiles of film and television personalities and recording stars; and behind-the-scenes reports on the entertainment industry.
Depts/columns: Word length varies. Media reviews, celebrity news, gossip, trivia, song lyrics, beauty tips, fashion, and celebrity advice.
Other: Poetry, quizzes, and puzzles. Submit seasonal material 3–5 months in advance.

Sample Issue
82 pages (15% advertising): 16 articles; 21 depts/columns; 16 pin-up posters. Sample copy, $3.99 at newsstands.
- "Can Hillary Handle the Stress?" Article discusses the busy lifestyle of superstar Hillary Duff and offers tips on ways to deal with stress.
- "Ashton Gets Serious." Article profiles the many sides of actor Ashton Kutcher including his most recent dramatic movie, his new comedy, and his role as a producer.
- Sample dept/column: "The Bop Closet" takes a look at the popular look in "geek chic."

Rights and Payment
All rights. Written material, payment rate varies. Pays on publication. Provides 2 contributor's copies.

Editor's Comments
We are interested in exclusive interviews with top-tier celebrities in the teen market. Our readers turn to us to keep them abreast of what's going on with their favorite young film, television, and music personalities. If you have an inside connection that will get you a hot interview, send us a query.

The Boston Parents' Paper

370 Centre Street
Jamaica Plain, MA 02130

Senior Editor: Dierdre Wilson

Description and Readership
Focusing on families in the Boston area, this parenting magazine covers programs, services, and activities for all ages as well as informative articles on parenting, child development, and education.
- **Audience:** Parents
- **Frequency:** Monthly
- **Distribution:** 98% controlled; 2% subscription
- **Circulation:** 70,000
- **Website:** www.bostonparentspaper.com

Freelance Potential
75% written by nonstaff writers. Publishes 3 freelance submissions yearly; 10% by unpublished writers, 20% by authors who are new to the magazine. Receives 21 queries monthly.

Submissions
Query with clips or writing samples. Accepts photocopies and computer printouts. Availability of artwork improves chance of acceptance. SASE. Response time varies.
Articles: Word length varies. Information articles; profiles; and interviews. Topics include child development, education, parenting, family issues, fitness, and health.
Depts/columns: To 1,800 words. Short news items, parenting, and profiles.
Artwork: B/W prints. Line art.
Other: Submit seasonal material 6 months in advance.

Sample Issue
68 pages (45% advertising): 3 articles; 9 depts/columns; 1 calendar of events. Guidelines and theme list available.
- "Birth Order." Article discusses the significance of birth order and how it can affect family dynamics.
- "The Family Bed." Article examines and risks and rewards of co-sleeping with young children.
- Sample dept/column: "Dining without Whining" suggests children-friendly places to have a traditional "high tea" party.

Rights and Payment
First North American serial and electronic rights. All material, payment rate varies. Pays within 30 days of publication. Provides 5 contributor's copies.

Editor's Comments
Quick-reading, high-interest, and informative articles are what we prefer. Our audience is comprised of busy parents, so we need to give them the information they need in an accessible format. Writers with parenting experience are encouraged to send us material on what to do and see in the Boston area, as well as community and educational issues.

Boys' Life

Boy Scouts of America
P.O. Box 152079
1325 West Walnut Hill Lane
Irving, TX 75015-2079

Senior Editor: Michael Goldman

Description and Readership
In print for over 90 years, this colorful magazine includes fiction and nonfiction articles on general-interest topics for boys in kindergarten through grade twelve. It also offers reviews, cartoons, and puzzles.
- **Audience:** 6–18 years
- **Frequency:** Monthly
- **Distribution:** 95% subscription; 5% other
- **Circulation:** 1.3 million
- **Website:** www.boyslife.org

Freelance Potential
80% written by nonstaff writers. Publishes 50 freelance submissions yearly; 1% by unpublished writers, 25% by authors who are new to the magazine. Receives 8+ queries monthly.

Submissions
Query for articles and depts/columns. Query or send complete ms for fiction. Accepts computer printouts. SASE. Responds to queries in 4–6 weeks, to unsolicited mss in 6–8 weeks.
Articles: 500–1,500 words. Informational and how-to articles; profiles; and humor. Topics include sports, science, American history, geography, animals, nature, and the environment.
Fiction: 1,000–1,500 words. Genres include mystery, adventure, humor, and science fiction.
Depts/columns: 300–750 words. Book reviews, cars, music, collecting, science, and history.
Other: Puzzles and cartoons.

Sample Issue
54 pages (18% advertising): 5 articles; 1 story; 6 depts/columns; 5 comics. Sample copy, $3.60 with 9x12 SASE. Writers' guidelines available.
- "Smart Trekking." Article reports on the decisions and planning of one troop's five-day, 50-mile backpacking trip in the rugged Sierra Nevada backcountry.
- "D-Day." Story features two young boys who risk their lives to cut German phone lines in their village during D-Day.
- Sample dept/column: "Collecting" tells of a new stamp set that features images of American Indian artifacts.

Rights and Payment
First rights. Articles, $400–$1,500. Fiction, $750+. Depts/columns, $150–$400. Pays on acceptance. Provides 2 copies.

Editor's Comments
We are interested in articles and stories on American history that are educational and entertaining. Also, how-to articles that would benefit scouts on outdoor activities such as hiking, camping, and canoeing.

Hands-on Adventure for Boys
Marilyn Edwards, Editor
Boys' Quest

Knowing that middle-grade boys are less likely to sit down with a magazine than middle-grade girls, the editors at *Boys' Quest* go out of their way to grab the attention of this action-minded audience. By using graphics that are simple and direct, readers are pulled into articles and stories that are fun, exciting, and written with their interests in mind. Each issue is theme-oriented and features such topics as dogs, horses, hand sports, trains, cars, space, frogs, snakes, and even "nifty" rodents. Activities strategically placed between the articles and stories keep the reader involved and curious enough to read more. "*Boys' Quest*," says Editor Marilyn Edwards, "is designed to inspire boys to develop an interest in reading at an early age."

For fiction, Edwards finds that mystery, adventure, and humor are equally popular. "Stories must be short," she says, and usually run around 500 words. While not all of the stories in *Boys' Quest* are directly tied to an activity, if it does it's a plus. For example, Edwards remembers one story where a boy comes home and finds some interesting-looking cookies on the counter. The "cookies" turn out to be dog biscuits and a recipe for making the biscuits followed the story.

Competition at *Boys' Quest* is keen as Edwards receives far more fiction than nonfiction. Writers can increase their chances by writing to a theme way ahead of the issue's publication date and also by studying the magazine. An attention-grabbing beginning is essential, and of course, the story must feature a boy as the main character. Then, lead him on an adventure that will have him coming back for more!

Boys' Quest

P.O. Box 227
Bluffton, OH 45817-0227

Associate Editor: Virginia Edwards

Description and Readership
This magazine wants to encourage literacy and reading comprehension through exciting, lively articles and projects that promote the development of the individual spirit.
- **Audience:** 6–13 years
- **Frequency:** 6 times each year
- **Distribution:** 60% school libraries; 40% newsstand
- **Circulation:** 10,000
- **Website:** www.boysquest.com

Freelance Potential
100% written by nonstaff writers. Publishes 100 freelance submissions yearly; 20% by unpublished writers, 50% by new authors. Receives 208 queries and unsolicited mss monthly.

Submissions
Prefers complete ms. Accepts photocopies, computer printouts, and simultaneous submissions if identified. SASE. Responds to queries in 1–2 weeks, to mss in 2–3 months.
Articles: 500 words. Informational and how-to articles; profiles; humor; and personal experience pieces. Topics include nature, animals, hobbies, science, and sports.
Fiction: 500 words. Genres include adventure, mystery, suspense, and multicultural fiction; rebus stories; and stories about animals, sports, and nature.
Depts/columns: 300–500 words. Science projects.
Artwork: Prefers B/W prints to accompany nonfiction; accepts color prints. No photocopies of photographs.
Other: Puzzles, activities, riddles, and cartoons. Submit seasonal material 6–12 months in advance.

Sample Issue
48 pages (no advertising): 4 articles; 5 poems; 8 depts/columns; 1 science project; 9 puzzles and activities; 1 comic. Sample copy, $4 with 9x12 SASE. Guidelines and open theme list available with #10 SASE.
- "Space Camp Adventurers." Article explains the U.S. Space Camp program for children.
- Sample dept/column: "Cooking" offers shooting star sandwiches to tie in with the space theme.

Rights and Payment
First and second rights. Articles and fiction, $.05 per word. Depts/columns, $35. Photos, $5–$10. Color slides, $5. Poems and activities, $10+. Pays on publication. Provides 1 contributor's copy.

Editor's Comments
We are looking for lively writing, most of it from a young boy's point of view, that directly involves the reader.

Bread for God's Children

P.O. Box 1017
Arcadia, FL 34265-1017

Editorial Secretary: Donna Wade

Description and Readership
The purpose of *Bread for God's Children* magazine is to help Christian families learn to apply the word of God in their everyday living. Each issue contains articles and stories written for families, but from a child's point of view.
- **Audience:** Families
- **Frequency:** 6–8 times each year
- **Distribution:** 100% subscription
- **Circulation:** 10,000
- **Website:** www.breadministries.com

Freelance Potential
30% written by nonstaff writers. Publishes 15–20 freelance submissions yearly; 10–20% by unpublished writers, 10–20% by authors who are new to the magazine. Receives 25 unsolicited mss monthly.

Submissions
Send complete ms. Accepts photocopies, computer printouts, and simultaneous submissions if identified. No email submissions. SASE. Responds in 2–3 months.
Articles: 600–800 words. Informational and personal experiences that inspire readers to grow in their spiritual lives.
Fiction: Christian theme-based stories for younger children, 500–800 words. Stories for middle-grade and young adult readers, 800–1,000 words.
Depts/columns: To 800 words. Parenting issues, family activities, and issues of interest to teens.
Other: Filler and crafts.

Sample Issue
28 pages (no advertising): 3 stories; 7 depts/columns; 1 Bible story. Sample copy, free with 9x12 SASE (5 first-class stamps). Guidelines available at website.
- "Snakes Alive." True story about a young boy who sees the good God brings to life.
- Sample dept/column: "Bible Study" looks at the word faith and its meaning in the Scripture.

Rights and Payment
First rights. Pays on publication. Articles, $25. Fiction, $40–$50. Short filler, $10. Provides 3 contributor's copies.

Editor's Comments
We are looking for writers who have a solid knowledge of biblical principles and are concerned about the youth of today keeping those principles. The stories must be written from a child's viewpoint with the story itself getting the message across. The plot and characters need to be realistic.

Breakaway

Focus on the Family
8605 Explorer Drive
Colorado Springs, CO 80920

Editor: Mike Ross

Description and Readership
Teenage boys are the target audience for *Breakaway*'s concentration on making the Bible and scriptural advice relevant in today's world. It is a source of spiritual nourishment for readers, written in a fast-paced and concise style.
- **Audience:** 12–18 years
- **Frequency:** Monthly
- **Distribution:** 97% subscription; 3% other
- **Circulation:** 95,000
- **Website:** www.breakawaymag.com

Freelance Potential
20% written by nonstaff writers. Publishes 5 freelance submissions yearly; 1% by unpublished writers, 1% by new authors. Receives 50 unsolicited mss monthly.

Submissions
Send complete ms. Accepts photocopies and computer printouts. SASE. Responds in 8–10 weeks.
Articles: 600–1,200 words. How-to and self-help articles; personal experience pieces; profiles; interviews; and humor. Topics include religion, sports, and multicultural issues.
Fiction: 1,500–2,200 words. Contemporary and inspirational fiction; suspense; adventure; and stories about sports.
Depts/columns: Word length varies. Advice, scripture readings, and Bible facts.
Other: Filler. Submit seasonal material about religious holidays 6–8 months in advance.

Sample Issue
32 pages (9% advertising): 4 articles; 1 story; 6 depts/columns. Sample copy, $1.75 with 9x12 SASE (2 first-class stamps). Guidelines available.
- "*Breakaway* Tours the World." Article explores the gradual change in a teenage boy who at first did not want to accompany his parents and siblings on a short-term mission.
- "Fish Wars." Story teases the reader with a humorous not-quite-true account of how a young man became a Christian.
- Sample dept/column: "Truth Encounter" looks at the reasons for having rules and guidelines for sex, while acknowledging its importance in life.

Rights and Payment
First or one-time rights. Written material, $.15 per word. Pays on acceptance. Provides 5 contributor's copies.

Editor's Comments
Instead of fiction, we need more articles based on real-life situations that have Christian applications, provide role models, and help build self-esteem.

Brilliant Star

1233 Central Street
Evanston, IL 60201

Senior Editor: Hoda Movagh

Description and Readership
This magazine is directed to children of the Bahá'í faith, and its goal is to develop age-appropriate, as well as culturally and racially diverse, content that addresses today's current issues.
- **Audience:** 8–12 years
- **Frequency:** 6 times each year
- **Distribution:** 75% subscription; 25% other
- **Circulation:** 3,000

Freelance Potential
5% written by nonstaff writers. Publishes 5–6 freelance submissions yearly; 30% by unpublished writers, 90% by authors who are new to the magazine. Receives 10 queries and unsolicited mss monthly.

Submissions
Query with clips for nonfiction. Send complete ms for fiction. Accepts photocopies, computer printouts, and simultaneous submissions if identified. SASE. Responds in 6–8 weeks.
Articles: To 700 words. Informational and how-to articles; personal experience pieces; profiles, and biographies. Topics include the Bahá'í faith, historical Bahá'í figures, religion, history, social issues, travel, music, and nature.
Fiction: To 700 words. Early reader fiction. Genres include multicultural, historical, contemporary, and problem-solving fiction.
Depts/columns: To 600 words. Religion and ethics.
Other: Puzzles, activities, games, and recipes. Poetry.

Sample Issue
30 pages (no advertising): 3 articles; 1 story; 3 depts/columns; 1 comic; 1 song; 2 calendars. Sample copy, $3 with 9x12 SASE (5 first-class stamps). Guidelines, theme list, and editorial calendar available.
- "'Alí-Akbar Furútan." Article profiles the life of an Iranian who converted to the Bahá'í faith as a youngster and who worked for its success his entire life.
- "Jerome Vincent: Super Kid." Story features a young boy who has to decide whether or not to tell his parents about disturbing things going on in his friend's home.
- Sample dept/column: "Radiant Stars" introduces kids from around the world.

Rights and Payment
All or one-time rights. No payment. Provides 2 contributor's copies.

Editor's Comments
We try to offer spiritual Bahá'í perspectives or universal values to children and youth in fun, engaging, and dynamic ways.

Brio

Focus on the Family
8605 Explorer Drive
Colorado Springs, CO 80920

Associate Editor: Marty Kasza

Description and Readership

The magazine's dual goal is to assist young teens to develop spirituality and a healthy self-concept. Its compelling style is a blend of creativity and entertainment that challenges readers to attain those attributes without being preachy.
- **Audience:** 12–15 years
- **Frequency:** Monthly
- **Distribution:** Subscription; newsstand
- **Circulation:** 200,000
- **Website:** www.briomag.com

Freelance Potential

10% written by nonstaff writers. Publishes 20–30 freelance submissions yearly; 1% by unpublished writers, 5% by authors who are new to the magazine. Receives 25 queries, 25 unsolicited mss monthly.

Submissions

Query or send complete ms. Accepts photocopies and computer printouts. SASE. Responds in 4–6 weeks.
Articles: To 2,000 words. Informational and how-to articles; profiles; interviews; and personal experience pieces. Topics include Christian living, family life, and contemporary issues.
Fiction: To 2,000 words. Genres include contemporary fiction, romance, and humor with Christian themes.
Depts/columns: Staff written.
Other: Cartoons, anecdotes, and quizzes.

Sample Issue

48 pages (6% advertising): 6 articles; 1 story; 7 depts/columns; 2 reviews; 1 comic; 1 quiz. Sample copy, $1.50 with 9x12 SASE ($.52 postage). Guidelines available.
- "Not Just Dirty Diapers." Article offers helpful hints to teens that will help turn babysitting jobs into positive experiences for everyone involved.
- "The Amazing Adventures of Scripture Man." Story solves the mysterious appearance of scriptural quotes appearing on school walls.

Rights and Payment

First rights. Written material, $.08–$.15 per word. Pays on acceptance. Provides 3 contributor's copies.

Editor's Comments

We are looking for more quizzes and less fiction. How-to articles for teen girls are always welcome. Pertinent topics include how to talk with members of the opposite sex; how to relate to parents or other people in authority; or how to handle spending money. We can also use biographical articles on or interviews with persons admired by teens.

Brio and Beyond

Focus on the Family
8605 Explorer Drive
Colorado Springs, CO 80920

Associate Editor: Marty Kasza

Description and Readership

The issues, joys, and responsibilities of living a Christian lifestyle are tackled in this magazine as it offers solutions and guidance to older teens. It recognizes the problems encountered in today's world and offers encouragement to stay on target by keeping faith in everyday living.
- **Audience:** 16–20 years
- **Frequency:** Monthly
- **Distribution:** 100% subscription
- **Circulation:** Unavailable
- **Website:** www.briomag.com

Freelance Potential

10% written by nonstaff writers. Publishes 20–30 freelance submissions yearly; 70% by unpublished writers, 50% by authors who are new to the magazine.

Submissions

Send complete ms. Accepts computer printouts, disk submissions, and email submissions to brio@macmail.fotf.org. Availability of artwork improves chance of acceptance. SASE. Responds in 1 month.
Articles: Word length varies. Informational and how-to articles; profiles; interviews; reviews; and personal experience pieces. Topics include college, careers, hobbies, health, fitness, music, popular culture, religion, multicultural and social issues, sports, and travel. Also publishes humorous pieces.
Fiction: Word length varies.
Depts/columns: Staff written.
Artwork: Color prints or transparencies. Line art.
Other: Submit seasonal material 6 months in advance.

Sample Issue

48 pages (no advertising): 7 articles; 1 story; 3 depts/columns; 1 quiz; 1 comic. Sample copy, free. Guidelines available.
- "Living God's Dream." Article tells the story of a teen gymnast and her difficult decision to forego Olympic dreams.
- "Regrets" Article follows a young woman's struggle with her sexual decisions as a high school student.
- "The Amazing Adventures of Scripture Man." Story weaves scriptural references into a mystery set in a high school.

Rights and Payment

First or reprint rights. All material, payment rate varies. Pays on acceptance. Provides 3–5 contributor's copies.

Editor's Comments

Our readers are familiar with the real world and articles and stories should be written with this in mind. Use a teen-friendly tone that recognizes issues faced by this age group.

Brooklyn Parent

25 Eighth Avenue
Brooklyn, NY 11217

Editor

Description and Readership

This regional parenting tabloid is the latest offering from the company that publishes Big Apple Parent, Queens Parent, and Westchester Parent. It often features some of the same articles as the other publications. Topics covered regularly include birth, pregnancy, and raising children, as well as stories about local goods and services.
- **Audience:** Parents
- **Frequency:** Monthly
- **Distribution:** 100% controlled
- **Circulation:** 68,000
- **Website:** www.parentsknow.com

Freelance Potential

95% written by nonstaff writers. Publishes 450 freelance submissions yearly; 25% by authors who are new to the magazine. Receives 75 queries, 75 unsolicited mss monthly.

Submissions

Query or send complete ms. Accepts photocopies, computer printouts, and email submissions to hellonwheels@parentsknow.com. SASE. Responds in 1 week.
Articles: 800–1,000 words. Informational articles; profiles; interviews; and personal experience pieces. Topics include family issues, health, nutrition, fitness, crafts, current events, gifted education, humor, nature, and regional news.
Depts/columns: 750 words. News and reviews.
Other: Submit seasonal material 4 months in advance.

Sample Issue

76 pages: 6 articles; 2 depts/columns. Sample copy, free with 10x13 SASE. Guidelines available.
- "Getting Suspended or Expelled from School." A new study recommends that schools work with local health experts to provide evaluation, support, and assistance for students with disciplinary problems.
- Sample dept/column: "Reviews" covers new books, music, board games, toys, and video games.

Rights and Payment

First New York area rights. Articles, $50. Dept/columns, payment rate varies. Pays 2 months after publication. Provides 1 contributor's copy.

Editor's Comments

We like to see submissions that report on controversial issues in the field of parenting. Articles on the latest news in health care, educational opportunities, and childhood development. We rely on regional experts and businesses to back up a story and give it regional significance.

Busy Family Network

Publisher: Gina Ritter

Description and Readership

This website sponsors several online publications, including Natural Family Online, Busy Parents Online, and Busy Homeschool magazine. Each e-zine targets a specific parenting and family niche—from natural to mainstream, from home-schoolers to gradeschoolers.
- **Audience:** Parents
- **Frequency:** Monthly
- **Distribution:** 100% Internet
- **Hits per month:** 10,000
- **Website:** www.busyfamilynetwork.com

Freelance Potential

95% written by nonstaff writers. Publishes 140 freelance submissions yearly; 5% by unpublished writers, 50% by authors who are new to the magazine. Receives 20 unsolicited mss each month.

Submissions

Send complete ms with brief author bio via email only to publisher@busyfamilynetwork.com. No attachments. Responds in 1–3 months.
Articles: 700–1,000 words. Informational, how-to, and self-help articles; profiles; photoessays; and personal experience pieces. Topics include nature, animals, crafts, hobbies, gifted and special education, health, fitness, popular culture, multicultural and ethnic issues, social issues, sports, and travel.
Fiction: 500–3,000 words. Genres include adventure; contemporary, historical, and multicultural fiction; folktales; and stories about sports. Also features read-aloud stories.
Depts/columns: 500–1,000 words.
Other: Filler, activities, and games. Interviews and profiles, 500–1,000 words.

Sample Issue

Sample copies of each publication, along with individual guidelines and editorial calendars, available at website.
- "An Introduction to Freezer Meals." Article provides tips on making a month's worth of meals to store in the freezer.
- "Need an End of the Day Pick-Me-Up?" Article describes a yoga position that will leave you refreshed and relaxed.

Rights and Payment

First North American serial or reprint rights and 1-year archival rights. Payment policy and rates vary.

Editor's Comments

Please don't submit extremely negative or close-minded material. We don't want articles that advocate spanking, or articles that speak against homeschooling or public schools.

ByLine

P.O. Box 5240
Edmond, OK 73083-5240

Articles Editor: Marcia Preston
Fiction Editor: Carolyn Wall; Poetry Editor: Sandra Soli

Description and Readership
For more than 20 years, this informational publication has been bringing writers ideas to help them in their craft. It has also served as a showcase for the first works of many established writers. Each issue incudes instructional articles as well as essays, fiction, and poetry.
- **Audience:** Writers
- **Frequency:** 11 times each year
- **Distribution:** 100% subscription
- **Circulation:** 3,500
- **Website:** www.bylinemag.com

Freelance Potential
80% written by nonstaff writers. Publishes 198 freelance submissions yearly. Receives 300 queries and mss monthly.

Submissions
Query or send complete ms. Accepts photocopies, computer printouts, and simultaneous submissions if identified. SASE. Responds in 1–2 months.
Articles: 1,500–1,800 words. Informational and how-to articles. Topics include writing and marketing fiction, nonfiction, and poetry.
Fiction: 2,000–4,000 words. Genres include mainstream, literary, and contemporary fiction.
Depts/columns: 200–400 words. Humor, marketing tips, and contest information.
Other: Poetry, to 30 lines.

Sample Issue
36 pages (8% advertising): 3 articles; 2 stories; 1 essay; 8 depts/columns. Sample copy, $4 with 9x12 SASE. Writers' guidelines available.
- "Writing for *Guideposts for Teens*." Article features an interview with magazine editor-in-chief Mary Lou Carney about what works for this magazine.
- "Writing Without a Net." Examines the question of whether or not a writer should take work on speculation.
- Sample dept/column: "Markets" features news about new magazines and tips on pubications' current editorial needs.

Rights and Payment
First rights. Articles, $75. Fiction, $100. Depts/columns, $15–$35. Pays on acceptance. Provides 1–3 contributor's copies.

Editor's Comments
Our message to writers has always been: "Believe in yourself and keep trying." We buy the work of beginners and veterans alike. Each issue offers a wealth of information on varied topics and we welcome submissions on any and all of them.

BYU Magazine

218 UPB
Provo, UT 84602

Editor: Jeff McClellan

Description and Readership
Articles that inform, stimulate thought, and promote spiritual growth for alumni and students of Bringham Young University fill the pages of this magazine. It strives to provide an insightful look into college life at BYU and create a supportive community of present and past students.
- **Audience:** YA–Adult
- **Frequency:** Quarterly
- **Distribution:** 98% controlled; 2% schools
- **Circulation:** 180,000
- **Website:** www.magazine.byu.edu

Freelance Potential
45% written by nonstaff writers. Publishes 5 freelance submissions yearly; 5% by authors who are new to the magazine. Receives 4 queries monthly.

Submissions
Query with writing samples. Accepts photocopies and computer printouts. SASE. Responds in 6–12 months.
Articles: 2,000–4,000 words. Informational, factual, and how-to articles; self-help and personal experience pieces; and humor. Topics include college life, careers, computers, current events, health, religion, science, sports, and family issues.
Depts/columns: To 1,500 words. Campus news, book reviews, commentary, and alumni updates.
Artwork: 35mm color prints or transparencies.
Other: Word length varies. BYU trivia.

Sample Issue
72 pages (15% advertising): 3 articles; 12 depts/columns. Sample copy, free.
- "Born for Glory." Article discusses how God has chosen us to lead the final days of glory, and has given us the ability to learn spiritually and increase access to the power of God.
- "Point of Arrival." Article takes a look at composer Stephen Jones, and the world premiere of his work at the Chicago Symphony Orchestra's Symphony Center.
- Sample dept/column: "First Person" shares memories of alumni studying abroad.

Rights and Payment
First North American serial rights. Articles, $.35 per word. Pays on publication. Provides 10 contributor's copies.

Editor's Comments
We seek articles that capture the BYU experience, and inspire readers to get involved. New writers have the best chance at publication with a personal essay for our departments "After All," or "First Person," or news about campus life.

Cadet Quest

Calvinist Cadet Corps
P.O. Box 7259
Grand Rapids, MI 49510

Editor: G. Richard Broene

Description and Readership

Formerly known as *Crusader*, this magazine targets members of the Calvinist Cadet Corps, a Christian organization that includes pre-teen and teenage boys from a number of Protestant denominations. It teaches Christian principles through stories and articles about sports, nature, and animals.
- **Audience:** 9–14 years
- **Frequency:** 7 times each year
- **Distribution:** 100% subscription
- **Circulation:** 10,000
- **Website:** www.calvinistcadets.org

Freelance Potential

70% written by nonstaff writers. Publishes 20 freelance submissions yearly; 5% by unpublished writers, 10% by authors who are new to the magazine. Receives 50 unsolicited mss monthly.

Submissions

Send complete ms. Accepts photocopies, computer printouts, and simultaneous submissions if identified. SASE. Responds in 1 month.
Articles: 400–1,000 words. Informational and factual articles; profiles; and interviews. Topics include religion, spirituality, sports, camping, crafts, and animals.
Fiction: 900–1,600 words. Features adventure and sports stories and humor—all written from a Christian perspective.
Depts/columns: Word length varies. Cadet Corps news and Bible stories.
Other: Puzzles, and cartoons.

Sample Issue

24 pages (5% advertising): 4 articles; 3 stories; 2 depts/columns; 2 activities. Sample copy, free with 9x12 SASE ($1.01 postage). Guidelines and theme list available.
- "Truth or Consequences." Story about a boy who lies after he forgets to close the door to his uncle's chicken coop.
- "What Good Are Insects Anyway?" Articles offers facts about the importance of honeybees and the role fruit flies have played in medical research.

Rights and Payment

First and second rights. Written material, $.04–$.05 per word. Other material, payment rate varies. Pays on acceptance. Provides 1 contributor's copy.

Editor's Comments

We look for material that will appeal to all adolescent boys, not just those in the Calvinist Cadet Corps. Our readers are active, inquisitive, and imaginative.

Calliope

Exploring World History

Cobblestone Publishing
Suite C, 30 Grove Street
Peterborough, NH 03458

Co-Editor: Rosalie F. Baker

Description and Readership

This award-winning publication features articles, colorful artwork, and stories. Written in thematic form, it offers students in the middle grades a look at the history of the world in an exciting and enriching way.
- **Audience:** 8–14 years
- **Frequency:** 9 times each year
- **Distribution:** 100% subscription
- **Circulation:** 11,000
- **Website:** www.cobblestonepub.com

Freelance Potential

95% written by nonstaff writers. Publishes 75 freelance submissions yearly; 25% by unpublished writers, 75% by authors who are new to the magazine. Receives 8 queries monthly.

Submissions

Query with outline, bibliography, and clips or writing samples. All material submitted must relate to upcoming themes. SASE. Responds in 2 months.
Articles: Features, 700–800 words; sidebars, 300–600 words. Informational articles and profiles. Topics include Western and Eastern history.
Fiction: To 800 words. Historical and biographical fiction, adventure, retold legends, and plays.
Depts/columns: 300–600 words. Current events, archaeology, languages, and book reviews.
Artwork: B/W or color prints and slides. B/W or color line art.
Other: Poetry, to 100 lines. Activities, games, crafts, puzzles, and recipes, to 700 words.

Sample Issue

50 pages (no advertising): 14 articles; 6 depts/columns; 5 activities. Sample copy, $4.95 with 9x12 SASE ($2 postage). Writers' guidelines and theme list available.
- "The Roman Inquisition." Article explains the formation of the Inquisition and its role in the Catholic church.
- Sample dept/column: "Time Line" looks at the life of Galileo Galilei.

Rights and Payment

All rights. Articles and fiction, $.20–$.25 per word. Other material, payment rate varies. Pays on publication. Provides 2 contributor's copies.

Editor's Comments

Please remember that all of our issues are theme related and that no two issues are alike. We look for educational material about world history that is entertaining and engaging.

Camping Magazine

American Camping Association
5000 State Road 67 North
Martinsville, IN 46151-7902

Editor-in-Chief: Harriet Gamble

Description and Readership
Professionals who work in recreational camps for children and youth find the latest information on trends in the business in *Camping Magazine*. Articles cover current research in the area of youth development, present innovative programming ideas, and offer management strategies.
- **Audience:** Camp managers and educators
- **Frequency:** 6 times each year
- **Distribution:** 100% subscription
- **Circulation:** 6,500
- **Website:** www.ACAcamps.org

Freelance Potential
98% written by nonstaff writers. Publishes 30 freelance submissions yearly; 50% by unpublished writers, 50% by authors who are new to the magazine. Receives 8 queries each month.

Submissions
Query with outline. Accepts photocopies, computer printouts, IBM disk submissions, simultaneous submissions if identified, and email submissions to magazine@acacamps.org. SASE. Response time varies.
Articles: 1,500–4,000 words. Informational and how-to articles. Topics include camp management, special education, social issues, careers, health, recreation, crafts, and hobbies.
Depts/columns: 800–1,000 words. Health issues related to camping, marketing ideas, building and construction information, and opinion pieces.
Artwork: B/W and color prints and slides.

Sample Issue
56 pages (20% advertising): 6 articles; 13 depts/columns. Sample copy, $4.50 with 9x12 SASE. Guidelines and editorial calendar available.
- "Breaking the Chains." Article describes the programs at special camps for children of prisoners.
- "Outreaching to Diverse Communities." Article reports on new camp opportunities for Hispanic youth made possible by The Boys and Girls Clubs of America.
- Sample dept/column: "In the Trenches" discusses seven skills of highly effective counselors.

Rights and Payment
All rights. No payment. Provides 2 contributor's copies.

Editor's Comments
Please do not mistake us for an RV campground magazine. Our focus is on organized children's camps, and many of our articles are written by professionals in this field.

Campus Life

Christianity Today
465 Gunderson Drive
Carol Stream, IL 60188

Editor: Chris Lutes

Description and Readership
Christian values are emphasized throughout this magazine to help teens keep their faith while navigating through their adolescent years. Male and female readers are inspired by accounts of personal growth and overcoming negative lifestyles, and by absorbing the pointers given to help readers make correct choices in challenging situations.
- **Audience:** 13–19 years
- **Frequency:** 9 times each year
- **Distribution:** 100% subscription
- **Circulation:** 100,000
- **Website:** www.campuslife.com

Freelance Potential
50% written by nonstaff writers. Publishes 50 freelance submissions yearly; 80% by unpublished writers, 20% by authors who are new to the magazine. Receives 25 queries monthly.

Submissions
Query with one-page synopsis. No unsolicited mss. Accepts photocopies, computer printouts, and simultaneous submissions if identified. SASE. Responds in 3–6 weeks.
Articles: 750–1,500 words. Personal experience pieces and humor. Topics include Christian values, beliefs, and education.
Fiction: 1,000–1,500 words. Genres include contemporary fiction with religious themes.
Depts/columns: Staff written.

Sample Issue
64 pages (30% advertising): 7 articles; 22 depts/columns. Sample copy, $3 with 9x12 SASE (3 first-class stamps). Writers' guidelines available.
- "Smart Dating." Article provides thoughtful questions teens should ask themselves before becoming involved in a potentially serious relationship.
- "What If I Die?" Article chronicles a teen's journey from drug addiction to a positive lifestyle.
- "All Alone?" Story tells of a daughter's desire for her father's approval of her performance.

Rights and Payment
First rights. Written material, $.15–$.25 per word. Pays on acceptance. Provides 2 contributor's copies.

Editor's Comments
Understanding our unique style and editorial philosophy is a must for writers submitting pieces. While we emphasize Christian values, we don't offer simplistic religious answers or preachy articles. We find first-person stories are most widely accepted by our readers.

Canadian Children's Literature

4th Floor, MacKinnon Building, University of Guelph
Guelph, Ontario N1G 2W1
Canada

Administrator: Benjamin Lefebvre

Description and Readership

Scholarly articles on children's literature and articles that examine the boundaries of "national" literature in general and of children's literature in particular are found in each issue of this academic journal. A major feature is its extensive review section which covers recent Canadian books, drama, and other media for children and young adults.
- **Audience:** Educators; scholars; and librarians
- **Frequency:** Quarterly
- **Distribution:** 70% subscription; 3% newsstand
  27% other
- **Circulation:** 900
- **Website:** www.uoguelph.ca/ccl

Freelance Potential

99% written by nonstaff writers. Publishes 100 freelance submissions yearly; 10% by unpublished writers, 40% by authors who are new to the magazine. Receives 10 unsolicited mss monthly.

Submissions

Query with summary; or send 3 copies of complete ms. Accepts photocopies, computer printouts, and email submissions to ccl@uoguelph.ca. SAE/IRC. Responds to queries in 6 weeks, to mss in 6 months.
Articles: 2,000–6,000 words. Informational articles; reviews; profiles; and interviews. Topics include children's literature; film, videos, and drama for children; and children's authors.

Sample Issue

96 pages (2% advertising): 5 articles; 16 reviews; 6 mini reviews. Sample copy, $10. Guidelines and theme list/editorial calendar available.
- "Reading Mainstream Possibilities." Abstract focuses on the subject of Canadian young adult fiction with lesbian and gay characters.
- "Weaving the Self." Article examines the struggle for identity in Martine Bates's *Marmawell* trilogy.
- "The Mirror's New Message?" Article discusses gender in the adolescent, postmodern fairy tale.

Rights and Payment

First serial rights. No payment. Provides 1 contributor's copy.

Editor's Comments

Ours is an academic journal, and all submissions are sent for peer review. We publish both theme issues and general issues; please see our website for more information on what issues are currently in preparation.

Canadian Guider

50 Merton Street
Toronto, Ontario M4S 1A3
Canada

Publications Manager: Catherine Bryant

Description and Readership

Canadian Guider is the official publication of the Girl Guides of Canada, and provides its readers with thought-provoking articles, resources for leaders and others involved with the organization, and practical hands-on material. Regular subjects include camping, life skills, innovative ideas, leadership tips and experiences, outdoor skills, and health and fitness.
- **Audience:** Girl Guide leaders
- **Frequency:** Quarterly
- **Distribution:** 100% controlled
- **Circulation:** 40,000
- **Website:** www.girlguides.ca/guider

Freelance Potential

20% written by nonstaff writers. Publishes 3–5 freelance submissions yearly. Receives 2 queries monthly.

Submissions

Query with résumé. SAE/IRC. Responds in 1 month.
Articles: To 200 words. Informational and how-to articles. Topics include fitness, health, camping, nature, the environment, the arts, social issues, and leadership and life skills.
Depts/columns: Word length varies. Activity ideas and leadership tips.
Artwork: B/W and color photos; digital images. Submission information at our website.

Sample Issue

48 pages (12% advertising): 13 articles; 9 depts/columns; 1 guide. Sample copy, $3 with 9x12 SAE/IRC. Editorial calendar and theme list available.
- "Live from Camp Carter." Article describes the annual May camp in Cape Breton coastal area and what makes it the most memorable event each year.
- "In Their Words . . . . Guiders on Guiding." Article compiles stories from several volunteers highlighting their experiences and histories as guiders.
- Sample dept/column: "Global Guiding" states some of the issues addressed by international guiding groups.

Rights and Payment

All rights. No payment. Provides 2 contributor's copies.

Editor's Comments

We look forward to receiving submissions from Girl Guide leaders and others who work with the organization. Please familiarize yourself with the straightforward, conversational style of the articles. Our goal is to give our readers innovative ideas that have been successfully used, and information they can incorporate into their own group.

Careers & Colleges

P.O. Box 22
Keyport, NJ 07735

Editor-in-Chief: Don Rauf

Description and Readership
Careers & Colleges provides much-needed information to high school students who are considering further education. Most of its information is geared to college and campus life, but other types of education are also considered. Four color and glossy, its content is thoughtfully presented in thematic issues.
- **Audience:** 14–18 years
- **Frequency:** 4 times each school year
- **Distribution:** 99% schools; 1% subscription
- **Circulation:** 752,000
- **Website:** www.careersandcolleges.com

Freelance Potential
80% written by nonstaff writers. Publishes 4 freelance submissions yearly; 10% by authors who are new to the magazine. Receives 8 queries monthly.

Submissions
Query with clips or writing samples. No unsolicited mss. Accepts photocopies and computer printouts. SASE. Responds in 2 months.
Articles: 800–2,400 words. Informational and how-to articles; profiles; interviews; and personal experience pieces. Topics include careers, post-secondary education, independent living, and personal growth.
Depts/columns: Staff written.

Sample Issue
48 pages (29% advertising): 8 articles; 2 depts/columns. Sample copy, $6.95 with 10x13 SASE ($1.75 postage). Writers' guidelines available.
- "Are Liberal Arts Dead?" Article reveals the strengths of a liberal arts education and the growing interest in the emphasis on independent study and research.
- "4 Alternatives to a 4-Year Degree." Article explores rewarding alternative educational paths such as apprenticeships and community colleges.
- "SAT/ACT Survival Guide." Article suggests ways to prepare for these important tests and what to expect from them.

Rights and Payment
First North American serial and electronic rights. Articles, $300–$800. Pays 2 months after acceptance. Provides 2 contributor's copies.

Editor's Comments
We would like to see articles on college life, students' accounts of their success at college, and more submissions addressing some of the prevalent issues on campus such as drinking and drug use.

Career World

Weekly Reader Corporation
200 First Stamford Place
P.O. Box 120023
Stamford, CT 06912

Senior Editor: Anne Flaunders

Description and Readership
Like Weekly Reader Corporation's other publications, *Career World* is distributed through schools. It targets middle school and high school students who are beginning to think about life after graduation. College selection and future employment opportunities are the focus of its articles.
- **Audience:** 12–18 years
- **Frequency:** 6 times each year
- **Distribution:** 100% subscription
- **Circulation:** 200,000
- **Website:** www.weeklyreader.com

Freelance Potential
50% written by nonstaff writers. Publishes 20–30 freelance submissions yearly; 30% by authors who are new to the magazine. Receives 3–4 queries monthly.

Submissions
Query with résumé and clips or writing samples. No unsolicited mss. SASE. Response time varies.
Articles: To 2,500 words. Informational, how-to, and self-help articles and job profiles. Topics include college preparation and selection, technical and vocational job opportunities, careers, résumé and interview preparation, and guidance.
Depts/columns: Word length varies. Scholarship search tips, reports on hot jobs, news, and trends.

Sample Issue
30 pages (1% advertising): 8 articles; 4 depts/columns. Sample copy available. Guidelines provided on assignment.
- "Out of the Lab and into the World." Article provides an overview of how common scientific principles are used in a broad spectrum of careers.
- "You've Gotta Have a Plan." Article chronicles one girl's experience researching and creating an inventory of her career interests.
- Sample depts/column: "Tips, News, & Trends" talks about the popularity of on-campus housing at community colleges.

Rights and Payment
All rights. Articles, $1 per word. Pays on publication. Provides 2 contributor's copies.

Editor's Comments
We want fresh, up-to-date ideas that explore educational and career opportunities for middle school and high school students. Send us a query that includes credentials and clips that demonstrate your ability to write in an engaging style for students in this age range.

Catholic Digest

185 Willow Street
P.O. Box 6001
Mystic, CT 06355

Articles Editor: Julie Rattey

Description and Readership
Catholic Digest presents material that encourages readers to live each day with faith, hope, and meaning. Its features draw on Catholic values, teachings, and traditions to help readers meet life's everyday challenges.
• **Audience:** Adults
• **Frequency:** Monthly
• **Distribution:** 92% subscription; 8% other
• **Circulation:** 350,000
• **Website:** www.catholicdigest.com

Freelance Potential
50% written by nonstaff writers. Publishes 100–200 freelance submissions yearly; 10% by unpublished writers. Receives 400 unsolicited mss monthly.

Submissions
Send complete ms. Accepts computer printouts, disk, and email submissions to cdsubmissions@bayardpubs.com. No simultaneous submissions. SASE. Responds in 6–8 weeks.
Articles: 1,000–3,500 words. Informational articles; profiles; and personal experience pieces. Topics include religion, prayer, spirituality, relationships, family issues, history, science, and nostalgia.
Depts/columns: 50–500 words. True stories about faith, spotlights of community organizations, and profiles of volunteers.
Other: Filler, to 500 words.

Sample Issue
126 pages (13% advertising): 7 articles; 17 depts/columns. Sample copy, free with 6x9 SASE ($1 postage). Writers' guidelines available.
• "Spice of Life for Afghanistan." Article discusses how saffron and other crops are bringing hope to this war-ravaged nation.
• "Song for a Loved One." Article describes the author's quest for solace in helping her dying friend.
• "He's Not Bad, He Just Has a Temper." Article demonstrates ways of coping with loved ones who have anger problems.

Rights and Payment
One-time rights. Articles, $100–$400. Depts/columns, $2 per published page. Pays on publication. Provides 2 copies.

Editor's Comments
Your article should be tightly focused on one specific topic that is illustrated for the reader through a well-developed series of true-life, interconnected vignettes. An anecdotal approach works best for us; you will see what we mean when you study back issues to get a sense of our tone and style.

Catholic Forester

P.O. Box 3012
335 Shuman Boulevard
Naperville, IL 60566-7012

Associate Editor: Patricia Baron

Description and Readership
This magazine offers articles on health and wellness, parenting, inspiration, career, and senior issues, as well as some light fiction. Targeting members of the Catholic Order of Foresters, it also provides organizational news and updates.
• **Audience:** Catholic Forester members
• **Frequency:** Quarterly
• **Distribution:** 100% controlled
• **Circulation:** 100,000
• **Website:** www.catholicforester.com

Freelance Potential
20% written by nonstaff writers. Publishes 4–8 freelance submissions yearly; 5% by unpublished writers, 20% by authors who are new to the magazine. Receives 20 unsolicited mss each month.

Submissions
Send complete ms. Accepts computer printouts. SASE. Responds in 3–4 months.
Articles: 1,000 words. Informational and inspirational articles. Topics include money management, fitness, health, family life, senior issues, careers, parenting, and nostalgia.
Fiction: 1,000 words. Genres include inspirational, humorous, and light fiction.
Depts/columns: Word length varies. Cooking, kids, activities, and membership news.
Artwork: B/W prints. Line art.
Other: Cartoons.

Sample Issue
40 pages (no advertising): 10 articles; 1 story; 7 depts/columns. Sample copy, free with 9x12 SASE (3 first-class stamps). Guidelines available.
• "First Aid for Grief." Article discusses ways for easing grief's turmoils including support groups and maintaining hope.
• "Brother Trouble." Story features a boy who tries to outwit his older brother, and learns something surprising.
• Sample dept/column: "The Prayer Basket" offers an essay about a prayer basket that connects parishioners.

Rights and Payment
First North American serial rights. Written material, $.30 per word. Cartoons, one-time rights, $30. Pays on acceptance. Provides 3 contributor's copies.

Editor's Comments
Although most of our material is nonfiction, a good children's story that is entertaining and educational would interest us.

Catholic Library World ☆

Suite 224
100 North Street
Pittsfield, MA 01201-5109

Editor: Mary S. Gallagher, SSJ

Description and Readership

Catholic Library World was established in 1929 and is read by library-science students, professional librarians, volunteers, and others who are interested in librarianship. Its goal is to provide information on books that are appropriate for inclusion in Catholic libraries.
- **Audience:** Adults
- **Frequency:** Quarterly
- **Distribution:** 99% subscription; 1% other
- **Circulation:** 1,100
- **Website:** www.cathla.org

Freelance Potential

25% written by nonstaff writers. Publishes 12 freelance submissions yearly.

Submissions

Query or send complete ms. Accepts photocopies, computer printouts, and email submissions (Microsoft word attachments) to cla@cathla.org. SASE.
Articles: Word length varies. Informational articles; reviews. Topics include books, reading, library science, and Catholic Library Association news.
Reviews: 150–300 words. Topics include theology, spirituality, pastoral issues, church history, education, history, literature, library science, philosophy, and reference; children's and young adult topics include biography, fiction, multicultural issues, picture books, reference, science, social studies, and values.
Artwork: B/W and color prints and transparencies. Line art.

Sample Issue

78 pages (2% advertising): 5 articles; 144 book reviews; 8 media reviews. Sample copy, $15. Reviewers' guidelines available.
- "Does Anyone Use a Playpen Anymore? Discipline or the Lack of It—How Does It Affect the Love of Books?" Article relates the discipline symbolized by a playpen to the determination needed to find the wisdom contained in well-written books.
- "Those Old Books. . . ?" Article reminds librarians that old books may be valuable rare books.
- "Reviews" offer summaries and book reviews of recently released titles in line with the teachings of the Catholic church.

Rights and Payment

No payment. Provides 1 contributor's copy.

Editor's Comments

Topics of interest include libraries, archives, and library education. Reviews of juvenile works should contain a critical evaluation of content, physical format, organization, and illustrations. We do not accept or review adult fiction.

Catholic Parent

Our Sunday Visitor
200 Noll Plaza
Huntington, IN 46750-4304

Associate Editor: York Young

Description and Readership

Practical, anecdotal articles speak to the concerns of parents trying to raise children with solid, timeless values in this publication from Our Sunday Visitor.
- **Audience:** Parents
- **Frequency:** 6 times each year
- **Distribution:** 95% subscription; 5% religious instruction
- **Circulation:** 30,000
- **Website:** www.osv.com

Freelance Potential

95% written by nonstaff writers. Of the freelance submissions published yearly, 10% are by authors who are new to the magazine. Receives 200 queries and unsolicited mss each month.

Submissions

Query or send complete ms. Accepts photocopies and computer printouts. SASE. Responds to queries in 3 months, to mss in 3–6 months.
Articles: To 1,200 words. Informational and how-to articles. Topics include religion, relationships, marriage, family life, teen issues, and child development.
Depts/columns: Word length varies. Short news items, media reviews, and parenting tips.
Other: Submit seasonal material 8 months in advance.

Sample Issue

50 pages (27% advertising): 13 articles; 7 depts/columns. Sample copy, $5. Guidelines available.
- "The Sandwich Generation." Article lists tips for managing the demands of our aging parents, growing children, spouse, employer, and friends while still finding time for personal renewal.
- "Is Your Room Clean Yet?" Article suggests ways to make this task easier for grade-school children.
- Sample dept/column: "Keep the Faith" offers ideas for faith-based summertime activities.

Rights and Payment

First rights. Written material, payment rate varies. Pays on acceptance.

Editor's Comments

We're primarily an assignment-only publication, but queries are welcome. Published clips of representative work should be included with your query. We will consider first-person accounts if they are well-written and directly tied to the concerns and needs of other parents. Scholarly material and argumentative or theological essays are not accepted.

Celebrate

6401 The Paseo
Kansas City, MO 64131

Editor: Melissa Hammer

Description and Readership

The child-friendly, colorful format of *Celebrate* ties in perfectly with its young audience. Published weekly, it is used in correlation with the WordAction Sunday School curriculum to help children understand the connection between what they learn in Sunday school and their daily living experiences.
- **Audience:** 3–6 years
- **Frequency:** Weekly
- **Distribution:** 100% subscription
- **Circulation:** 40,000
- **Website:** www.wordaction.com

Freelance Potential

40% written by nonstaff writers. Publishes 50 freelance submissions yearly; 30% by unpublished writers, 35% by authors who are new to the magazine. Receives 10 queries monthly.

Submissions

Query. Accepts photocopies, computer printouts, and email queries to mhammer@nazarene.org (Microsoft Word attachments). SASE. Responds in 2–4 weeks.
Other: Poetry, 4–8 lines. Songs, finger plays, action rhymes, crafts, activities, and recipes.

Sample Issue

4 pages (no advertising): 2 Bible stories; 1 poem; 1 recipe; 2 activities. Sample copy, free with #10 SASE (1 first-class stamp). Guidelines and theme list available.
- "Simeon and Anna Thank God." Story relates the Bible incident when Joseph and Mary took Jesus to the temple in Jerusalem and met Simeon and Anna there.
- "Christmas Trees." Activity includes a recipe for making and decorating Christmas tree cookies.
- "At Home." Activity helps preschooler to learn the names of persons prominent in a Bible story by drawing lines from the name to the person's picture.
- "Happy, Happy Day." Poem connects the joy of receiving a Christmas gift with celebrating baby Jesus' birthday.

Rights and Payment

Multiple-use rights. Written material, payment rate varies. Pays on acceptance. Provides 2 contributor's copies.

Editor's Comments

Please refer to our guidelines before submitting a query. We accept poems, preferably with rhythmic patterns and word pictures; piggyback songs utilizing a Bible verse set to a familiar children's tune; finger plays or action rhymes that demonstrate character building or scriptural application; simple crafts doable with parental help; and basic recipes.

Central Penn Parent

101 North Second Street, 2nd Floor
Harrisburg, PA 17101

Editor: Karren Johnson

Description and Readership

Feature articles on education, family activities, and children's health appear along with a comprehensive events calendar in *Central Penn Parent*. It is the only parenting tabloid that serves Pennsylvania's Dauphin, Lancaster, Cumberland, and York counties.
- **Audience:** Parents
- **Frequency:** Monthly
- **Distribution:** 100% controlled
- **Circulation:** 35,000
- **Website:** www.centralpennparent.com

Freelance Potential

50% written by nonstaff writers. Publishes 10 freelance submissions yearly; 20% by unpublished writers, 10% by authors who are new to the magazine. Receives 8 queries monthly.

Submissions

Request guidelines first. Query. Accepts email submissions to karrenm@journalpub.com. Availability of artwork improves chance of acceptance. SASE. Responds in 2 weeks.
Articles: 1,200–1,500 words. Informational articles and reviews. Topics include local family events and activities, health, nutrition, travel, education, home life, technology, literature, parenting issues, and discipline.
Depts/columns: 700 words. Parenting and health news, infants, family finances, and perspectives from fathers.
Artwork: Color prints and transparencies. Line art.
Other: Submit seasonal material at least 2 months in advance.

Sample Issue

24 pages (50% advertising): 3 articles; 7 depts/columns. Sample copy, free. Guidelines available.
- "Kids and Drugs, Part II: Under Our Noses." Article examines the ways kids are abusing drugs, from household products to prescription and over-the-counter drugs.
- "Birthday Party Overload: How Much Is Too Much." Offers tips for keeping parties simple, yet fun.
- Sample dept/column: "How-To" tells how to make a patriotic candle jar.

Rights and Payment

All rights. Articles, $35–$125. Depts/columns, $30. Pays on publication. Provides contributor's copies on request.

Editor's Comments

We're looking for ideas, activities, and reports on products and services that will help busy parents with kids from newborns to age 15 improve the quality of their family lives. Send us something on raising happy, healthy children.

Characters

Kids Short Story and Poetry Outlet

P.O. Box 708
Newport, NH 03773

Editor: Cindy Davis

Description and Readership

Formerly listed as *PEEKS & valleys*, this publication includes fiction and poetry in a variety of genres and prefers to showcase the works of children and young adults.
- **Audience:** 7–18 years
- **Frequency:** Quarterly
- **Distribution:** 100% subscription
- **Circulation:** Unavailable

Freelance Potential

100% written by nonstaff writers. Publishes 40–50 freelance submissions yearly; 50% by unpublished writers, 75% by authors who are new to the magazine. Receives 50 unsolicited mss monthly.

Submissions

Send complete ms with short biography. Accepts email submissions to hotdog@nhvt.net (no attachments), and simultaneous submissions. SASE. Responds 2–4 weeks.
Fiction: 1,500 words. Genres include mystery, adventure, Westerns, romance, fantasy, and historical and science fiction. It also publishes humorous stories and stories that have nature themes.
Other: Poetry, to 20 lines; to 3 poems per submission.

Sample Issue

36 pages (no advertising): 7 stories; 6 poems. Sample copy, $5.75. Writers' guidelines available.
- "Handprint Mystery." Story tells of a boy who finds the meaning behind a strange, glowing handprint on the wall of his new room.
- "The Consequences of Being Popular." Story features two friends who learn a valuable lesson about lying, and the dangers of trying to impress others.
- "Jake." Story shares author's remembrance of a childhood friendship, and the sadness he felt when the friend dies unexpectedly from an illness.

Rights and Payment

One-time and electronic rights. Written material, $5. Payment policy varies. Provides contributor's copies.

Editor's Comments

We are hoping to see more submissions from kids themselves. Please check to be sure the vocabulary in your story matches that of your target market. If your main character is a child, he should not only speak like one, but also narrate like one. Please do not send queries—send the whole story or poem. Currently, we are seeking more humorous stories and mysteries.

Charlotte Parent

Suite 201
1100 South Mint Street
Charlotte, NC 28230

Editor: Elaine Heitman

Description and Readership

This tabloid is a compilation of parenting tips, and local news and events for parents in Charlotte's seven-county metro region. Each month's issue features a different theme.
- **Audience:** Parents
- **Frequency:** Monthly
- **Distribution:** 54% controlled; 35% schools; 10% libraries; 1% subscription
- **Circulation:** 55,000
- **Website:** www.charlotteparent.com

Freelance Potential

40% written by nonstaff writers. Publishes 60 freelance submissions yearly; 15% by unpublished writers, 25% by authors who are new to the magazine. Receives 25 queries, 50 unsolicited mss monthly.

Submissions

Query with résumé, outline/synopsis, and clips or writing samples; or send complete ms with resume and bibliography. Prefers email to family@charlotteparent.com. Accepts photocopies. Macintosh disk submissions, and simultaneous submissions. SASE. Responds if interested.
Articles: 500–1,000 words. Informational and how-to articles. Topics include parenting, family life, finances, education, health, fitness, vacations, entertainment, regional activities, and the environment.
Depts/columns: Word length varies. Restaurant and media reviews; children's health, ages, and stages.
Artwork: High-density, Macintosh format.
Other: Activities. Submit seasonal material 2–3 months in advance.

Sample Issue

84 pages (35% advertising): 7 articles; 2 reviews, 15 depts/columns. Sample copy, free with 9x12 SASE (5 first-class stamps). Guidelines and editorial calendar available at website.
- "Out-of-Home Care." Article examines child-care options to help parents find the solution that fits their circumstances.
- Sample dept/column: "Family Matters" includes several quick parenting tips and short informational items.

Rights and Payment

First rights. Written material, payment rate varies. Pays on publication. Provides 1 contributor's copy.

Editor's Comments

We prefer articles and essays with a local relevancy for our primary audience. Submit more articles on health-related topics and fewer humorous Mom and Dad situations.

ChemMatters

American Chemical Society
1155 16th Street NW
Washington, DC 20036

Editor: Kevin McCue

Description and Readership

Chemistry can be fun and exciting and this publication for teens proves it. Articles feature real-world applications of high school textbook concepts. *ChemMatters* is more interested in exploring how a theory is used in everyday living than in the underlying theoretical concept itself.

- **Audience:** 14–18 years
- **Frequency:** 5 times each year
- **Distribution:** 80% schools; 20% subscription
- **Circulation:** 40,000
- **Website:** www.chemistry.org/education/chemmatters.html

Freelance Potential

80% written by nonstaff writers. Publishes 20 freelance submissions yearly; 5% by unpublished writers, 30% by authors who are new to the magazine. Receives 2–3 queries monthly.

Submissions

Query with abstract, outline, related material that conveys the scientific content, and a writing sample. Accepts photocopies and email queries to chemmatters@acs.org. SASE. Responds in 5 days.
Articles: 1,400–2,100 words. Informational articles. Topics include the human body, food, history, current events, and chemical matters.
Depts/columns: 1,400–2,100 words. News and reviews.
Artwork: JPEG or GIF line art.
Other: Chemistry-oriented puzzles and activities.

Sample Issue

20 pages (no advertising): 5 articles; 2 depts/columns. Sample copy, $2.50. Guidelines and theme list available.
- "Building a Better Bleach." Article compares the effectiveness and environmental impact of chlorine and nonchlorine bleaches and their different chemical formulas.
- "Can Chemistry Stop What's Bugging You?" Article scrutinizes the different compositions of bug killers.
- Sample dept/column: "Question from the Classroom" features an interesting slant to lightening and electricity.

Rights and Payment

All rights. Articles, $500–$1,000. Pays on acceptance. Provides 5 contributor's copies.

Editor's Comments

We need more science topics that relate directly to a high school chemistry curriculum such as solutions, acids, bases, metals and reactions, written to stimulate a student to learn about chemistry. We currently have enough material on organic chemistry and biochemistry.

Chesapeake Family

Suite 100
102 West Street
Annapolis, MD 21401

Editor

Description and Readership

Families with young children living in the Chesapeake Bay area read this parenting tabloid for its how-to and informational articles and personal experience pieces on topics important to parents. All its material includes a strong regional angle and offers local resources and services.

- **Audience:** Parents
- **Frequency:** Monthly
- **Distribution:** 55% schools; 15% newsstand; 5% subscription; 25% other
- **Circulation:** 40,000
- **Website:** www.chesapeakefamily.com

Freelance Potential

85% written by nonstaff writers. Publishes 4–6 freelance submissions yearly; 5% by unpublished writers, 10% by authors who are new to the magazine. Receives 20 mss monthly.

Submissions

Send complete ms. Accepts photocopies and computer printouts. SASE. Response time varies.
Articles: 1,000–1,500 words. Informational and how-to articles and profiles. Topics include parenting, the environment, music, regional news, current events, education, entertainment, health, and family travel destinations.
Fiction: "Just for Kids" features stories and poems by local 4- to 17-year-old children.
Depts/columns: 700–900 words. Education, child development, and health.
Other: Submit seasonal material 3–6 months in advance.

Sample Issue

54 pages (45% advertising): 4 articles; 6 depts/columns; 3 calendars. Guidelines and editorial calendar available.
- "Dater-Aid." Article stresses the need for real communication and understanding when it comes to dating for inexperienced teens.
- "Summer Adventures along Rt. 2." Article features a detailed itinerary of places for families to enjoy together on a summer road trip in the state.

Rights and Payment

Geographic print rights; electronic rights negotiable. Payment policy varies. Features, $75–$110. Depts/columns, $50. Reprints, $35.

Editor's Comments

Any topic of interest to parents that includes a regional angle will be reviewed by our editors.

Chess Life

U.S. Chess Federation
Suite 100
3068 US Route 9W
New Windsor, NY 12553

Editor: Kalev Pehne

Description and Readership

Chess Life covers the world of chess for everyone interested in the game, from professional grandmasters to amateurs and hobbyists. Instructional articles, profiles of chess personalities, and the use of chess in other fields—such as computer science and psychology—are among its features. It also reports on major chess events.
- **Audience:** YA–Adult
- **Frequency:** Monthly
- **Distribution:** 90% subscription; 10% newsstand
- **Circulation:** 60,000–80,000
- **Website:** www.uschess.org

Freelance Potential

45% written by nonstaff writers. Publishes 30 freelance submissions yearly; 30% by unpublished writers. Receives 30–50 queries monthly.

Submissions

Query with clips or writing samples. Accepts photocopies, computer printouts, and IBM disk submissions (ASCII). SASE. Responds in 1–3 months.
Articles: 800–3,000 words. Informational, how-to, and historical articles; profiles; humor; and personal experience and opinion pieces. Topics include chess playing, tournaments, and events.
Depts/columns: To 1,000 words. Book and product reviews, short how-to's, and player profiles.
Other: Chess-oriented cartoons, contests, and games.

Sample Issue

66 pages (16% advertising): 4 articles; 16 depts/columns. Sample copy, free with 9x12 SASE. Guidelines available.
- "Fischer's War Ends in Self-Mate in One." Article reviews a new book about the famous chess player, Bobby Fischer.
- "The Little Sweden Chess Festival." Article reports on a 10-day, four-tournament festival held in Lindsborg, Kansas.
- Sample dept/column: "Opening Secrets" discusses the Chigorin defense.

Rights and Payment

All rights. Pays on publication. Written material, $100 per page. Kill fee, 50%. Provides 2 contributor's copies.

Editor's Comments

The game of chess or personalities involved with the game are central every piece we publish. Freelancers may try breaking in with a profile of a chess player or a tournament report. Filler, poems, puzzles, and cartoons related to chess may be submitted without a query.

Chicago Parent

141 South Oak Park Avenue
Chicago, IL 60302

Editor: Susy Schultz

Description and Readership

Parents living in Chicago's metropolitan area with children 14 years old and younger are the prime target for this publication. It covers topics on education, profiles of remarkable local people, local news and reviews, and the joys and challenges of typical Chicago parents.
- **Audience:** Parents
- **Frequency:** Monthly
- **Distribution:** 90% controlled; 10% subscription
- **Circulation:** 138,000
- **Website:** www.chicagoparent.com

Freelance Potential

85% written by nonstaff writers. Publishes 100–200 freelance submissions yearly; 10% by unpublished writers, 40% by authors who are new to the magazine. Receives 40–50 queries monthly.

Submissions

Query with résumé and clips. Accepts photocopies, computer printouts, and emails to spedersen@chicagoparent.com. SASE. Responds in 6 weeks.
Articles: 1,500–2,500 words. Informational articles and profiles. Topics include local resources, regional events, parenting, grandparenting, maternity, foster care, child development, adoption, day care, careers, education, and family issues.
Depts/columns: 850 words. Opinion pieces, children's health, media reviews, travel, and fathering.
Other: Submit seasonal material 2 months in advance.

Sample Issue

110 pages (60% advertising): 13 articles; 12 depts/columns. Sample copy, $3.95. Guidelines and editorial calendar available.
- "The Right Time for the Next Baby." Article presents the pros and cons of waiting and not waiting to have the next child.
- "Living on One Income in a Two-Income World." Article reveals strategies from parents who survive on one income.
- Sample dept/column: "Getaways" explores various locations for vacations with or without children.

Rights and Payment

One-time and Illinois exclusive rights. Articles, $125–$350. Depts/columns, $75-$100. Kill fee, 10%. Pays on publication. Provides contributor's copies on request.

Editor's Comments

Timely articles should be submitted 2–3 months in advance; we are always happy to respond to queries. Keep in mind we are a regional publication and prefer information featuring people and events from the greater Chicago area.

Child

Gruner + Jahr USA Publishing
9th Floor
375 Lexington Avenue
New York, NY 10017-4024

Submissions Editor

Description and Readership

A lifestyle magazine for sophisticated parents, *Child* presents the latest news on child development, pediatric medicine, nutrition, and education. Articles that offer inspiring ideas for home, entertaining, and family travel round out each issue.
- **Audience:** Parents
- **Frequency:** 10 times each year
- **Distribution:** 92% subscription; 8% newsstand
- **Circulation:** 1,020,000
- **Website:** www.child.com

Freelance Potential

65% written by nonstaff writers. Publishes 50 freelance submissions yearly; 10% by unpublished writers, 30% by authors who are new to the magazine. Receives 150 queries each month.

Submissions

Query with published clips. Accepts computer printouts. SASE. Responds in 2 months.
Articles: Word length varies. Informational and how-to articles, profiles, interviews, and personal experience pieces. Topics include pets, computers, crafts, hobbies, current events, gifted and special education, health, fitness, popular culture, science, sports, travel, fashion, and lifestyles.
Depts/columns: Word length varies. Media reviews, safety, beauty, food, nutrition, and dining out.
Other: Submit seasonal material 6–8 months in advance.

Sample Issue

164 pages (47% advertising): 10 articles; 29 depts/columns. Sample copy, $3.50 at newsstands. Guidelines and editorial calendar available.
- "The New Pediatric Scare." Article reports that chronic diseases that previously developed in adults only are now striking children in epidemic numbers.
- "Fabulous First Birthday." Article offers ideas for party food and fun.
- Sample dept/column: "Elegant Expectations" spotlights maternity clothes that combine comfort and high style.

Rights and Payment

First-time rights. Written material, payment rate varies. Pays on acceptance. Provides contributor's copies.

Editor's Comments

Established writers who have been published in national magazines or newspapers are invited to query on the following topics: children's health, behavior, and development; education; relationship issues; family travel; and pregnancy.

Connecting & Informing
Bonnie Neugebauer, Editor
Child Care Information Exchange

In the 1970s, women flooded the workplace, making two-income households the norm. As a result, what used to be called *babysitting* blossomed into the day-care business. In 1978, *Child Care Information Exchange* stepped up to connect and inform caregivers on a variety of topics, from first aid and feeding to education and behavior.

Editor Bonnie Neugebauer says that she needs "articles that draw information from a range of sources and include practical information as well as insights from other fields that inspire more creative thinking." At the same time, she says, "We are trying to strengthen our work with family child care providers. We need their support for our work, so we're trying harder to include their issues and voices."

While the circulation of its newsletter is 28,000, the Washington State company now connects day-care providers and early childhood educators around the world even more with its website. Want to know how to train new employees? You can access articles with a mere click. Need to stimulate creativity in the children? You've come to the right place.

Bruce Schon, Marketing Director, says that their authors "can be practitioners, professionals, providers, consultants, or recognized experts in the field of early care and education." Neugebauer adds, however, "The voice of experience is much stronger for our audience than that of people who imagine and plan, but haven't tried their ideas out in real life. We support the voices of our authors and encourage them to write with personality and real stories."

The *Exchange*'s editorial calendar for the coming year is posted on the website in September. The 2005 calendar is currently up, and Schon recommends writers submit for a particular issue at least six months in advance.

Child Care Information Exchange

P.O. Box 3249
Redmond, WA 98073-3249

Editor: Bonnie Neugebauer

Description and Readership

Early childhood professionals are the audience for this publication. *Child Care Information Exchange* focuses on child-care center management. It mixes practical, how-to information for operating child-care centers with discussions of current events and social issues as they relate to the field.
- **Audience:** Child-care professionals
- **Frequency:** 6 times each year
- **Distribution:** 100% subscription
- **Circulation:** 26,000
- **Website:** www.childcareexchange.com

Freelance Potential

65–75% written by nonstaff writers. Publishes 75 freelance submissions yearly; 50% by unpublished writers, 60% by authors who are new to the magazine. Receives 12 queries each month.

Submissions

Query with outline and writing samples. Accepts photocopies, computer printouts, and Macintosh disk submissions. SASE. Responds in 1 week.
Articles: 1,500 words. How-to, self-help, and practical-application articles. Topics include education, current events, multicultural and ethnic subjects, and social issues.
Depts/columns: Word length varies. Infant and toddler care, staff training and development, and perspectives from parents.

Sample Issue

88 pages: 9 articles; 7 depts/columns. Sample copy, $8. Guidelines and theme list available.
- "Conferencing with Parents of Infants." Article explains why conferences form the foundation of the communication system between parents and providers of infant care.
- "What to Expect When Staff Is Expecting." Article details how to develop a pregnancy plan for employees.
- Sample dept/column: "Ideas for Training Staff" offers an opinion on broadening the scope of professional development for child-care workers.

Rights and Payment

All rights. Articles, $300. Other material, payment rate varies. Pays on publication. Provides 2 contributor's copies.

Editor's Comments

We are committed to supporting early childhood professionals in their efforts to craft early childhood environments where adults and children thrive. We try to publish material that helps our readers create child-care centers that foster friendship, curiosity, self-esteem, joy, and respect.

Childhood Education

Association for Childhood Education International
Suite 215
17904 Georgia Avenue
Olney, MD 20832

Editor: Anne W. Bauer

Description and Readership

This professional journal is published in thematic issues and targets classroom teachers, teachers-in-training, teacher educators, parents, child-care workers, librarians, supervisors, and educational administrators.
- **Audience:** Educators and child-care professionals
- **Frequency:** 5 times each year
- **Distribution:** 100% controlled
- **Circulation:** 12,000
- **Website:** www.acei.org

Freelance Potential

98% written by nonstaff writers. Publishes 40 freelance submissions yearly; 75% by authors who are new to the magazine. Receives 10 unsolicited mss monthly.

Submissions

Send 4 copies of complete ms. Accepts photocopies, computer printouts, and Macintosh or IBM disk submissions. SASE. Responds in 3 months.
Articles: 1,400–3,500 words. Informational articles. Topics include innovative learning strategies, the teaching profession, research findings, parenting and family issues, communities, drug education, prenatal drug exposure, and safe environments for children.
Depts/columns: 1,000 words. Classroom technology, reviews of professional books and books for children, and current educational issues.
Artwork: 8x10 B/W glossy prints and color transparencies.
Other: Hands-on classroom activities.

Sample Issue

63 pages (15% advertising): 6 articles; 10 depts/columns. Sample copy, free with 9x12 SASE (3 first-class stamps). Guidelines and editorial calendar available.
- "Create Rewarding Circle Times by Working with Toddlers, Not against Them." Article describes two classroom's circle times and explains why one is more rewarding and less frustrating for toddlers than the other.
- "Teaching Elements of Story through Drama to First-Graders." Describes a successful integration of drama with other content areas in a Title 1 school.

Rights and Payment

All rights. No payment. Provides 5 contributor's copies.

Editor's Comments

Articles on innovative classroom topics, discussions of timely issues, and interviews with leaders in education or allied fields will be considered.

Children and Families

1651 Prince Street
Alexandra, VA 22310

Associate Editor: Julie Konieczny

Description and Readership
Published by the National Head Start Association (NHSA), this magazine offers early childhood care professionals and education practioners working for Head Start and Early Start with information on program development, teaching and parenting skills, advocacy strategies, and solutions to problems in the field.
- **Audience:** Early child care professionals and educators
- **Frequency:** Quarterly
- **Distribution:** 90% subscription; 10% other
- **Circulation:** 16,000
- **Website:** www.nhsa.org

Freelance Potential
75% written by nonstaff writers. Publishes 25 freelance submissions yearly; 70% by unpublished writers, 70% by new authors. Receives 2 unsolicited mss monthly.

Submissions
Send complete ms. Accepts email submissions to julie@nhsa.org. SASE. Responds in 1–12 weeks.
Articles: 1,600–4,000 words. Informational and how-to articles. Topics include computers, gifted education, health, fitness, mathematics, multicultural issues, music, science and technology, and special education.
Depts/columns: 500–1,400 words. Crafts and cooking.
Artwork: Color prints or transparencies.
Other: Submit seasonal material 4 months in advance.

Sample Issue
76 pages (25% advertising): 6 articles; 9 depts/columns. Writers' guidelines and theme list available.
- "Literacy in Early Childhood Education." Article discusses finding a balance between literacy and other domains of development in early childhood education.
- "On the Path to Literacy." Article takes a look at the language-literacy connection and offers strategies to develop early literacy skills.
- Sample dept/column: "How Children Learn" offers strategies for involving boys in activities in which they can succeed.

Rights and Payment
First rights. No payment. Provides 2+ contributor's copies.

Editor's Comments
We are looking for articles that cover special education needs. New writers have the best chance with a feature or our "Child Health Talk" section. Please note that although we are a serious publication, we are not an academic journal. Articles should be written in a first or second person, with a conversational style.

Children's Advocate Newsmagazine

Action Alliance for Children, The Hunt House
1201 Martin Luther King, Jr. Way
Oakland, CA 94612-1217

Editor: Jean Tepperman

Description and Readership
This newsmagazine deals exclusively with current trends and public policy issues that affect young children in California. Professionals dealing with children's rights and caring for children read this publication for ideas and reports on statewide programs. It is published in English and Spanish.
- **Audience:** Children's advocates
- **Frequency:** 6 times each year
- **Distribution:** 50% newsstand; 30% subscription; 20% controlled
- **Circulation:** 15,000
- **Website:** www.4children.org

Freelance Potential
40% written by nonstaff writers. Publishes 18 freelance submissions yearly; none by authors who are new to the magazine or previously unpublished. Receives few queries monthly.

Submissions
All articles assigned. Send résumé with clips or writing samples. Accepts photocopies and computer printouts. SASE. Responds in 1 month.
Articles: 500–1,500 words. Informational articles; program descriptions; policy analysis pieces; and how-to articles. Topics include families, foster care, child care, education, child welfare, violence prevention, nutrition, poverty, and mental health.
Depts/columns: Short news items. 300–500 words. Public policy analysis, 500–1,100 words. Book reviews, word length varies.

Sample Issue
16 pages (4% advertising): 8 articles; 4 depts/columns. Sample copy, $3. Guidelines available.
- "Preschool for All: Key Questions" Article looks at the possibility of providing high-quality preschool programs for all California children.
- "My Future Is a Little Brighter." Article provides information on tax assistance programs that can boost family income.
- Sample dept/column: "Grassroots Snapshot" details the efforts and components that turned a community coalition spending plan into a successful venture.

Rights and Payment
First North American serial rights. Written material, to $.25 per word. Pays on acceptance. Provides 3 contributor's copies.

Editor's Comments
We would like to see more submissions dealing with multicultural education and social or health programs with accompanying outcome data.

Kids in Pursuit of Excellence
Penny Rasdall, Editor
Children's Digest

At Children's Better Health Institute, publisher of *Children's Digest* and *Jack And Jill* magazines, health, fitness, and nutrition are more than just buzzwords. They're a way of life, and editors hope readers will pursue that lifestyle.

While this theme is carried throughout the magazines, Editor Penny Rasdall says, "It's hard to find fiction with that particular kind of message." The message should be woven into the story, yet the story should be fun. As examples of stories that have worked for her, Rasdall cites one in which a young boy encourages his father to join him in his jogging activity. Another featured a gardening theme. Even this kind of activity—bending, squatting, beautifying the environment— encourages exercise.

While a wide range of stories are accepted, Rasdall says that adventure stories work particularly well for her. One story featured a child who had been teased by his friends when he chose to spend his time training for a marathon rather than playing video games. But when one of them becomes stuck in a ravine during a hiking trip, it is the child who trained for the marathon who is able to find help quickly and rescue the trapped friend. The message was strong, yet the story was fun and exciting for the reader. Rasdall also appreciates it when a fiction story features a health issue, such as juvenile diabetes and is accompanied by a factual sidebar.

Rasdall sees her audience as "bright with a lot of common sense." She likes her readers to feel challenged rather than catered to and for that reason, the content of *Children's Digest* is aimed at the 12-year-old at the upper end of her readership age, while the content of *Jack And Jill* is aimed at the 10-year-old.

Children's Digest

Children's Better Health Institute
1100 Waterway Boulevard
Indianapolis, IN 46202

Editor: Penny Rasdall

Description and Readership
Children's Digest uses factual features to educate youth about good health habits. Its pages include articles, stories, and activities that promote a healthy and active lifestyle.
- **Audience:** Pre-teens
- **Frequency:** 6 times each year
- **Distribution:** 100% subscription
- **Circulation:** 85,000
- **Website:** www.childrensdigest.com

Freelance Potential
50% written by nonstaff writers. Publishes 30 freelance submissions yearly; 70% by unpublished writers. Receives 100 unsolicited mss monthly.

Submissions
Query only. No unsolicited mss. Accepts photocopies and computer printouts. SASE. Responds in 3 months.
Articles: To 1,200 words. Informational and how-to articles; profiles; interviews; and personal experience pieces. Topics include health, exercise, safety, and nutrition.
Fiction: To 1,500 words. Genres include multicultural and ethnic fiction, science fiction, fantasy, adventure, mystery, humor, and stories about animals and sports.
Depts/columns: To 1,200 words. Book reviews, recipes, and information on personal health.
Other: Puzzles, activities, and games. Poetry, to 25 lines. Submit seasonal material 8 months in advance.

Sample Issue
34 pages (6% advertising): 3 stories; 1 article; 3 poems; 3 depts/columns; 1 page of jokes; 1 page of puzzles; 1 contest. Sample copy, $1.25 with 9x12 SASE. Guidelines available.
- "Mr. Greenlaw's Red Felt Hat." Story about a boy who comes to terms with an elderly friend's death.
- "Planting Potatoes." Article explains how to plant and grow potatoes.
- Sample dept/column: "Ask Dr. Corey" answers readers' questions on health issues..

Rights and Payment
All rights; returns book rights upon request. Written material, $.12 per word. Pays prior to publication. Provides 10 contributor's copies.

Editor's Comments
Information on health can be presented in a variety of formats—fiction, nonfiction, poems, and puzzles. We are especially interested in material concerning sports and fitness; including profiles of professional and amateur athletes.

Children's Magic Window

P.O. Box 390
Perham, MN 56573

Editor-in-Chief: Joan Foster

Description and Readership

Every page is chock full in this colorful and fast-paced publication filled with fiction, nonfiction, recipes, jokes, and activities. Social issues, violence, drugs, alcohol, and sex are avoided.
- **Audience:** 5–12 years
- **Frequency:** 6 times each year
- **Distribution:** 95% subscription; 5% schools
- **Circulation:** 20,000
- **Website:** www.childrensmagicwindow.com

Freelance Potential

90% written by nonstaff writers. Publishes 150 freelance submissions yearly; 15% by unpublished writers, 50% by new authors. Receives 40 unsolicited mss monthly.

Submissions

Query with outline; or send complete manuscript with illustrations if needed. Accepts photocopies and computer printouts. Availability of artwork improves chance of acceptance. SASE. Responds to queries in 5–8 weeks; to mss in 6–10 weeks.
Articles: To 1,000 words. Informational and how-to articles; humor; and profiles. Topics include animals, pets, computers, crafts, hobbies, health, fitness, history, math, nature, the environment, multicultural and ethnic issues, popular culture, recreation, science, technology, sports, and travel.
Fiction: To 1,000 words. Humor, adventure, fantasy, folk tales, folklore, mystery, suspense, stories about nature and the environment, and historical fiction.
Depts/columns: "Fun Facts" to 100 words.
Artwork: Line art.
Other: Games, jokes, puzzles, crafts, and rebus stories.

Sample Issue

112 pages (no advertising): 5 articles; 6 stories; 11 depts/columns; 12 activities. Sample copy, $5. Guidelines available.
- "Wilbur Goes Fishing." Story tells a whopper of a tale about a boy and his dad during an unusual fishing experience.
- Sample dept/column: "State by State" gives pertinent facts about the featured state.

Rights and Payment

All or one-time rights. Articles and fiction, to $400. Depts/columns, to $50. Pays on publication. Provides 1 copy.

Editor's Comments

We believe that our content must compete with videos, electronic games, and other stimulating forms of entertainment. Information should be challenging yet fun in order to motivate children to explore other types of written material.

Children's Ministry

1515 Cascade Avenue
P.O. Box 481
Loveland, CO 80539-0481

Associate Editor: Jennifer Hooks

Description and Readership

This publication is packed with useful and practical information to help anyone who is involved with teaching or working with children. It includes inspirational pieces and ideas for guiding children's spiritual development.
- **Audience:** Adults who work with children in a church setting
- **Frequency:** 6 times each year
- **Distribution:** Subscription; other
- **Circulation:** 90,000
- **Website:** www.cmmag.com

Freelance Potential

70% written by nonstaff writers. Publishes 60–80 freelance submissions yearly; 45% by unpublished writers, 55% by authors who are new to the magazine.

Submissions

Query or send complete ms. Accepts computer printouts. SASE. Responds in 2–3 months.
Articles: 500–1,700 words. Informational and how-to articles. Topics include Christian education, family issues, and child development.
Depts/columns: 50–150 words. Educational issues, activities, devotionals, family ministry, and reviews.
Other: Activities, crafts, games, and tips. Submit seasonal material 6–8 months in advance.

Sample Issue

146 pages (50% advertising): 10 articles; 1 story; 16 depts/columns. Sample copy, $2 with 9x12 SASE. Writers' guidelines available.
- "They Are in Our Midst." Article discusses sexually abused children in our society, and how to identify, report, and help them.
- "Those Terrific Toddlers." Article explores the world of children under three years of age and describes what's within the realm of normal behavior and personality traits.
- Sample dept/column: "Special Needs" examines learning disabilities and practical ways to minister to children who have been identified as having them.

Rights and Payment

All rights. Articles, to $350. Depts/columns, $40. Pays on acceptance. Provides 1 contributor's copy.

Editor's Comments

We would like to see more submissions on outreach, family ministry, volunteer management, seasonal and holiday material, and tips for teachers and parents. We don't accept fiction or poetry, or material unrelated to our magazine.

Children's Mission

12501 Old Columbia Pike
Silver Spring, MD 20904-6600

Editor: Charlotte Ishkanian

Description and Readership
Seventh-day Adventist Sunday school leaders who work with elementary school students are the target audience of this publication. Each issue of *Children's Mission* is devoted to a specific area or country that is served by Seventh-day Adventist missionaries, and includes articles, stories, and activities related to that country.
- **Audience:** 5–10 years; teachers; parents
- **Frequency:** Quarterly
- **Distribution:** 100% controlled
- **Circulation:** 35,000
- **Website:** http://sspm.gc.adventist.org

Freelance Potential
10% written by nonstaff writers. Publishes 3–8 freelance submissions yearly; 10% by authors who are new to the magazine. Receives less than 1 query monthly.

Submissions
All material is written in-house or on assignment.
Articles: 600–800 words. Informational articles; profiles; interviews; and personal experience pieces. Topics include the Seventh-day Adventist church, mission work, faith, spirituality, and children served by missions.
Depts/columns: Word length varies. Media reviews.
Artwork: B/W and color prints or transparencies.
Other: Activities, crafts, games, and recipes.

Sample Issue
30 pages (no advertising): 7 articles; 14 activities; 3 recipes.
- "Children's Mission News." Article explains the meaning behind the preparations for celebrating the Jewish Sabbath.
- "Night Rescue." True story about the trust one young man placed in God when he suffered a sailing mishap.
- "Make a Snowflake." How-to article explains how to fold and cut a decorative paper snowflake.

Rights and Payment
First rights. Articles, $30. Other material, payment rate varies. Pays on acceptance. Provides 3+ contributor's copies.

Editor's Comments
Because each issue of our magazine relates to a specific country or region, all material is written on assignment. The majority of our authors are members of the Seventh-day Adventist church. This year, we need more articles and information on the spiritual conversions of children in their featured country, their beliefs, and their experiences; as well as recipes and activities from that country.

Children's Playmate

Children's Better Health Institute
1100 Waterway Boulevard
P.O. Box 567
Indianapolis, IN 46206-0567

Editor: Terry Harshman

Description and Readership
Young readers enjoy this magazine for its interesting articles, entertaining stories, poetry, and fun crafts, puzzles, and activities. All material has a link to fitness, health, or science.
- **Audience:** 6–8 years
- **Frequency:** 6 times each year
- **Distribution:** 100% subscription
- **Circulation:** 115,000
- **Website:** www.childrensplaymatemag.org

Freelance Potential
40% written by nonstaff writers. Publishes 40–50 freelance submissions yearly; 10% by unpublished writers, 50% by authors who are new to the magazine. Receives 75 unsolicited mss monthly.

Submissions
Send complete ms. Accepts photocopies and computer printouts. SASE. Responds in 2–3 months.
Articles: To 500 words. Humorous and how-to articles. Topics include health, fitness, nature, the environment, science, hobbies, crafts, multicultural and ethnic subjects, and sports.
Fiction: To 100 words. Rebus stories.
Depts/columns: Staff written.
Other: Puzzles, activities, games, and recipes. Poetry, to 20 lines. Submit seasonal material about unusual holidays 8 months in advance.

Sample Issue
36 pages (no advertising): 1 article; 2 stories; 11 activities; 1 depts/column; 12 poems; 1 rebus. Sample copy, $1.75 with 9x12 SASE. Guidelines available.
- "Mitch's Itch." Story tells of a boy who gets itchy red bumps on his arms, and discovers he caught poison ivy from playing in the woods.
- "Skin-Sational Skin Facts." Article takes a look at interesting facts about our skin.
- "A Salute to Animal Fathers." Article examines different types of animal fathers and their roles as caregivers.

Rights and Payment
All rights; will return book rights on request. Written material, $.17 per word. Pays on publication. Provides up to 10 contributor's copies.

Editor's Comments
We seek articles and activities that educate children about health, fitness, and science in an entertaining and fun way. Easy recipes and crafts that are age-appropriate interest us as well. The only fiction we are looking for are rebus stories.

Children's Voice

3rd Floor
440 First Street NE
Washington, DC 20001-2085

Editor-in-Chief: Steven Boehm

Description and Readership
This peer-reviewed journal targets child welfare professionals with its articles on child advocacy, juvenile justice, education, health, and mental health. It is published by the Child Welfare League of America, the nation's largest membership-based child welfare organization.
- **Audience:** Child-welfare professionals
- **Frequency:** 6 times each year
- **Distribution:** Subscription; membership
- **Circulation:** 15,000
- **Website:** www.cwla.org

Freelance Potential
5% written by nonstaff writers. Publishes 2–3 freelance submissions yearly; 25% by authors who are new to the magazine. Receives 6+ queries monthly.

Submissions
Query. Accepts photocopies, computer printouts, Macintosh disk submissions with hard copy, and email queries (text only) to voice@cwla.org. Availability of artwork improves chance of acceptance. SASE. Responds in 1 week.
Articles: 1,000–2,000 words. Informational and how-to articles; profiles; interviews; and personal experience pieces. Topics include social issues, current events, and regional news as they relate to children and child-welfare issues.
Depts/columns: 100–200 words. Legislative updates; agency and organizational news.

Sample Issue
38 pages (20% advertising): 4 articles; 5 depts/columns; 2 parenting pages. Sample copy, $10. Guidelines available.
- "Is There a Therapeutic Value to Physical Restraint?" Article cites current reasearch on whether it is best for residential treatment programs for children to be restraint and seclusion-free.
- "No More Eye for an Eye." Article tells how families of murder victims have been speaking out in opposition to the death penalty for minors.
- "Better Governance for Nonprofits." Article explains the Sarbanes-Oxley Act and its relevance for nonprofits.

Rights and Payment
All rights. No payment. Provides contributor's copies.

Editor's Comments
We primarily use articles by professionals, for professionals on topics such as juvenile justice, child welfare, and behavioral health. Most of the accepted submissions are backed up by current research. Reports on successful programs and proven interventions are always of interest.

Children's Writer

Institute of Children's Literature
95 Long Ridge Road
West Redding, CT 06896-1124

Editor: Susan Tierney

Description and Readership
Beginning writers as well as published professionals consult this newsletter for information on the juvenile publishing industry. It offers articles on the writing process and updates on publishing trends along with solidly researched market reports on children's magazine and book publishers.
- **Audience:** Children's writers
- **Frequency:** Monthly
- **Distribution:** 100% subscription
- **Circulation:** 14,000
- **Website:** www.childrenswriter.com

Freelance Potential
100% written by nonstaff writers. Publishes 75 freelance submissions yearly; 10% by unpublished writers, 15% by authors who are new to the magazine. Receives 5+ queries monthly.

Submissions
Query with outline/synopsis and résumé. Prefers email submissions through website. Accepts disk submissions with hard copy. SASE. Responds in 2 months.
Articles: 1,500–2,000 words. Reports on children's book and magazine publishing markets that include interviews with editors and writers. Topics include industry trends, new markets, and publishers. Also publishes features on writing technique, research, motivation, and business issues.
Depts/columns: To 750 words, plus 125-word sidebar. Practical pieces about writing technique and careers; inside tips; and information about children's publishing.

Sample Issue
12 pages (no advertising): 3 articles; 4 depts/columns. Sample copy, free with #10 SASE (1 first-class stamp). Guidelines available with SASE or at website.
- "Friendship (Writing) Is Evergreen." Article maintains that the theme of friendship in stories and articles is perennially popular with kids, and therefore with editors as well.
- Sample dept/column: "Craft" looks at the issue of voice—a compilation of heart, mind, and soul unique to every writer—and includes exercises to help it emerge.

Rights and Payment
First North American serial rights. Articles, $135–$350. Pays on publication.

Editor's Comments
We consider queries on all aspects of the writing process, from inspiration, to final polish, and finding an appropriate market. Quotes from experts, including editors, writers, booksellers, and educators, are a required component of our articles.

Child Welfare Report

E3430 Mountainview Lane
P.O. Box 322
Waupaca, IL 54981

Editor: Mike Jacquard

Description and Readership

Professionals who work with at-risk youth read this newsletter for its practical and informational articles on subjects related to gifted and special education, family life, social issues, teens, parenting, and psychology. Each issue includes two inserts: one for parents and one on teen issues.
- **Audience:** Child Welfare Professionals
- **Frequency:** Monthly
- **Distribution:** 100% subscription
- **Circulation:** 500
- **Website:** www.impact-publications.com

Freelance Potential

60% written by nonstaff writers. Publishes 8 freelance submissions yearly; 50% by unpublished writers, 95% by authors who are new to the magazine. Receives 1 query monthly.

Submissions

Query with outline. Accepts photocopies, computer print-outs, and IBM disk submissions (Microsoft Word). SASE. Responds in 1 month.
Articles: Word length varies. Informational and how-to articles; personal experience and opinion pieces; interviews; and new product information. Topics include gifted and special education, disabilities, government programs, foster care, career choices, family life, parenting, psychology, mentoring, and multicultural and ethnic subjects.

Sample Issue

8 pages (15% advertising): 7 articles; 2 inserts; 1 resource page; 1 conference guide. Sample copy, guidelines, and editorial calendar, $6.95 with #10 SASE (1 first-class stamp).
- "Views Are Changing about Herbal Medications." Article looks at the increase in parents' use of herbs for medicinal purposes.
- "Ecstasy, Other Drug Use Declines."Article reviews new figures on the positive correlation between telling teens about the ill effects of drugs and their choice to abstain.
- Sample dept/column: "Parent Talk" looks at a trainer who uses Playstation to get kids in better physical shape.

Rights and Payment

First North American serial rights. Written material, payment rate varies. Pays on publication. Provides 5 author's copies.

Editor's Comments

If your background is in child welfare or if you have experience writing about issues important to welfare professionals, we are interested in hearing from you. We are also always looking for submissions specifically for our insert on teen issues or our parents insert.

Christian Camp & Conference Journal

P.O. Box 62189
Colorado Springs, CO 80962-2189

Editor: Alison Hayhoe

Description and Readership

This journal is published by Christian Camping International/USA and seeks to inform, inspire, and motivate all personnel serving in Christian camps and conferences. Readers discover practical information and how God works through Christian camp and conference ministries.
- **Audience:** Adults
- **Frequency:** 6 times each year
- **Distribution:** 95% subscription; 5% other
- **Circulation:** 9,000
- **Website:** www.christiancamping.org

Freelance Potential

90% written by nonstaff writers. Publishes 2 freelance submissions yearly. Receives 1–2 unsolicited queries monthly.

Submissions

Query with résumé and writing samples. Accepts email submissions to editor@cciusa.org. Availability of artwork may improve chance of acceptance. Responds in 1 month.
Articles: 800–1,500 words. Informational and how-to articles; profiles; and interviews. Topics include biography, crafts, hobbies, health and fitness, multicultural and ethnic issues, nature, environment, popular culture, recreation, religion, social issues, and sports.
Depts/columns: Staff written.
Artwork: B/W and color prints and transparencies.
Other: Submit seasonal material 6 months in advance.

Sample Issue

38 pages (25% advertising): 7 articles; 8 depts/columns. Sample copy, $4.95 with 9x12 SASE ($1.40 postage). Guidelines and theme list available.
- "Show Me the Money." Article examines different methods camp counselors can use to help young campers develop a sense of fiscal responsibility.
- "In Sixty Minutes." Article emphasizes the importance of counselors using the first day of camp to set the tone for a successful camping experience.

Rights and Payment

First rights. Written material, $.16 per word. Artwork, $25–$250. Pays on publication. Provides 1 contributor's copy.

Editor's Comments

We need more articles on programming, marketing, camp facility management, finances, human resources, and guest services. We would also like to see issues related to spiritual development, ministry, fund raising, and health care.

Christian Home & School

3350 East Paris Avenue SE
Grand Rapids, MI 49512-3054

Senior Editor: Roger Schmurr

Description and Readership
This magazine is published for parents who send their children to Christian schools. It addresses a wide range of topics that are faced by parents everywhere, such as helping children make good choices and teaching a child self-control.
- **Audience:** Christian parents
- **Frequency:** 6 times each year
- **Distribution:** 95% schools; 5% subscription
- **Circulation:** 68,000
- **Website:** www.csionline.org/chs

Freelance Potential
75% written by nonstaff writers. Publishes 40–45 freelance submissions yearly; 10% by unpublished writers, 30% by authors who are new to the magazine. Receives 5 queries, 25 unsolicited mss monthly.

Submissions
Query or send complete ms. Accepts photocopies, computer printouts, and simultaneous submissions if identified, and email to RogerS@csionline.org. SASE. Responds to queries in 1 week, to mss in 10 days.
Articles: 1,000–2,000 words. Informational, how-to and self-help articles; and personal experience pieces. Topics include education, parenting, family issues, college, careers, current events, and entertainment.
Fiction: Word length varies. Christian stories and first-person narratives depicting Christian life.
Depts/columns: Word length varies. Media reviews. "Parentstuff" uses parenting tips, 100–250 words.

Sample Issue
34 pages (15% advertising): 4 articles; 10 depts/columns. Sample copy, free with 9x12 SASE ($1.06 postage). Writers' guidelines available.
- "You Want to Date Whom?" Article presents practical advice for parents whose children are beginning to date.
- "Window Moments." Article reminds parents to take advantage of the times when children open up their hearts.
- Sample dept/column: "Parentstuff" covers good hugs, sibling conflict, simple family excursions, and computer control.

Rights and Payment
First rights. Written material, $175–$250. "Parentstuff," $25–$40. Pays on publication. Provides 5 contributor's copies.

Editor's Comments
Our magazine aims to promote Christian education. We are interested in current parenting issues, presented in a lively style that incorporates a biblical point of view.

Christian Parenting Today

Christianity Today Inc.
465 Gundersen Drive
Carol Stream, IL 60188

Editor: Carla Barnhill

Description and Readership
Guidance for building families based on Christian values is found throughout this magazine. Emphasis is on good parenting skills and solid relationships between parents and their infant through teenage children. Included are activities to help build family bonds.
- **Audience:** Parents
- **Frequency:** Quarterly
- **Distribution:** 85% subscription; 15% newsstand
- **Circulation:** 90,000
- **Website:** www.christianparenting.net

Freelance Potential
90% written by nonstaff writers. Publishes 24–30 freelance submissions yearly; 20% by unpublished writers, 20% by authors who are new to the magazine. Receives 100–125 queries monthly.

Submissions
Query with résumé, outline, and clips or writing samples. Accepts photocopies and computer printouts. SASE. Responds in 6–8 weeks.
Articles: 1,000–2,000 words. Informational articles and humor. Topics include parenting, family life, spiritual development, personal values, and discipline.
Depts/columns: Word length varies. Single parenting, child development, and faith.
Other: Submit seasonal material 6 months in advance.

Sample Issue
64 pages (40% advertising): 6 articles; 12 depts/columns. Sample copy, $3.95 at newsstands. Guidelines available at website.
- "Why Kids Misbehave." Article contends that there are a few main reasons a child misbehaves and that those reasons are linked to the child's personality type.
- "Moms in Ministry." Article describes five women in ministry and how they juggle obligations with motherhood.
- Sample dept/column: "Home Pages" tackles the tough question of when to tell children they are adopted.

Rights and Payment
First North American serial rights. Articles, $.12–$.25 per word. Other material, $25–$250. Pays on acceptance for articles; on publication for depts/columns. Provides 1 copy.

Editor's Comments
Fresh, new approaches to family life are always welcome. Our audience is comprised of parents working to instill Christian ideals in their children using everyday situations.

Church Educator

165 Plaza Drive
Prescott, AZ 86303

Editor: Linda Davidson

Description and Readership
Church Educator is a monthly publication serving an ecumenical readership of Christian educators. It is comprehensive in scope, presenting relevant and practical education resources for large and small churches alike.
- **Audience:** Christian educators
- **Frequency:** Monthly
- **Distribution:** 100% subscription
- **Circulation:** 3,000
- **Website:** www.educationalministries.com

Freelance Potential
90% written by nonstaff writers. Publishes 100 freelance submissions yearly; 10% by unpublished writers, 5% by authors who are new to the magazine. Receives 25 mss monthly.

Submissions
Send complete ms. Accepts computer printouts. SASE. Responds in 1 month.
Articles: 500–1,500 words. How-to articles. Topics include faith education, spirituality, and religion.

Sample Issue
32 pages: 12 articles. Sample copy, free with 9x12 SASE ($.83 postage). Guidelines and theme list available.
- "Composing a Life." Article is based on personal experience and offers constructive suggestions for how to find the right teachers for a church school.
- "Who, Me?" Article offers suggestions on how to bring youth to minister to each other.
- "Teaching the Psalms." Article offers practical suggestions on how to bring the ideas behind a Psalm to life for young children.

Rights and Payment
One-time rights. Written material, $.03 per word. Pays on publication. Provides 2 contributor's copies.

Editor's Comments
The freelance articles we publish in each issue of *Church Educator* may be grouped into four broad categories—two of which, apply to children and youth. In our "Children's Ministry" category we are interested in general educational features; ideas and lesson plans on seasonal and special themes; stories, prayers and liturgies to help children celebrate God's love; as well as easy crafts, activities, and other projects designed to enhance the lesson being taught. For our "Youth Ministry" category we want youth programs and program outlines that provide tips for beginning, continuing, and concluding sessions— including discussion starters and activities.

Church Worship

165 Plaza Drive
Prescott, AZ 86303

Editor: Linda Davidson

Description and Readership
This monthly magazine is used as a resource for innovative services. It follows a liberal viewpoint intended for mainline Protestant pastors, and requires material and sermons that will encourage thinking and questioning in congregations and children's groups.
- **Audience:** Adults
- **Frequency:** Monthly
- **Distribution:** 100% subscription
- **Circulation:** 1,000
- **Website:** www.educationalministries.com

Freelance Potential
100% written by nonstaff writers. Publishes 50 freelance submissions yearly. Receives 4 queries and 15 unsolicited mss each month.

Submissions
Send complete ms. Accepts computer printouts. SASE. Responds to queries in 1 week, to mss in 1–2 months.
Articles: 300–1,500 words. Dialogue sermons; readers' theater scripts; children's sermons; and youth worship services. Topics include congregational participation in worship, the power of prayer in congregational worship, and mime/clowning in worship.
Other: Submit seasonal material 4 months in advance.

Sample Issue
24 pages (no advertising): 1 article; 1 service; 2 lessons; 1 hymn; 4 sermons. Sample copy, free with 9x12 SASE ($.60 postage). Editorial calendar available.
- "Pentecost." Service contains information for children's time, a sermon, and other elements for a Pentecostal liturgy.
- "Reader's Theatre." Article explains the role of theater in worship and includes a short dramatization.
- "The Ring of Power." Sermon revolves around *The Lord of the Rings* trilogy to make its point about the use and abuse of power in recent history.

Rights and Payment
First rights. Written material, $.03 per word. Pays on publication. Provides 2 contributor's copies.

Editor's Comments
New writers will find the best chance for acceptance by submitting complete worship services. We are looking for material that goes out of the box to make people think. We have a need for informal services for weekday occasions, youth programs, retreats, women's fellowship groups, and prayer groups as well as formal Sunday morning services.

Cicada

Cricket Magazine Group
P.O. Box 300
315 Fifth Street
Peru, IL 61354

Submissions Editor

Description and Readership
Part of the Cricket Magazine Group, *Cicada* is a literary magazine for teens and young adults featuring top-notch fiction by young authors and established writers. Contents include short stories, poems, novellas, essays, and personal experiences.
- **Audience:** 14–21 years
- **Frequency:** 6 times each year
- **Distribution:** 95% subscription; 5% newsstand
- **Circulation:** 18,500
- **Website:** www.cricketmag.com

Freelance Potential
98% written by nonstaff writers.

Submissions
Send complete ms. Accepts photocopies, computer printouts, and simultaneous submissions if identified. SASE. Responds in 2–3 months.
Articles: To 5,000 words. Essays and personal experience pieces.
Fiction: To 5,000 words. Genres include adventure; fantasy; humor; and historical, contemporary, and science fiction. Plays and stories presented in a sophisticated cartoon format. Novellas, to 15,000 words.
Depts/columns: 350–1,000 words. Social and cultural issues, school life, and book reviews.
Other: Cartoons. Poetry, to 25 lines.

Sample Issue
128 pages (no advertising): 8 stories; 4 poems; 1 book review; 1 dept/column. Sample copy, $8.50. Writers' guidelines available.
- "Egg." A tale about unique creatures and dragon slayers facing dilemmas and challenges similar to thoses confronting modern teens.
- "You Cannot Have All the Answers." Story reveals a coming-of-age experience set in India.
- Sample dept/column: "World View" relates a teen's interesting experiences revolving around her parents' tradition of collecting plates from different countries.

Rights and Payment
All rights. Payment rate varies. Pays on publication.

Editor's Comments
We would like to see more pieces with humor, romance, or adventure themes. Main characters should reflect the readers' age range and have a genuine teen/young adult sensibility. Fantasy, science fiction, and contemporary topics are also accepted.

Circle K

Circle K International
3636 Woodview Trace
Indianapolis, IN 46268-3196

Executive Editor: Shanna Mooney

Description and Readership
Bright college students interested in community service and leadership development are the target of this publication. Articles address broad areas of interest to all college students, but most specifically to those who are service minded.
- **Audience:** YA–Adult
- **Frequency:** 5 times each year
- **Distribution:** Subscription; schools; controlled
- **Circulation:** 15,000
- **Website:** www.circlek.org

Freelance Potential
40% written by nonstaff writers. Publishes 8 freelance submissions yearly; 10% by unpublished writers, 35% by authors who are new to the magazine. Receives 8 queries and unsolicited mss monthly.

Submissions
Prefers query with clips or writing samples. Accepts complete ms. Accepts photocopies and computer printouts. SASE. Responds in 6 weeks.
Articles: 1,000–1,800 words. Informational and self-help articles. Topics include current social and collegiate trends, community involvement, leadership, and career development.
Depts/columns: Word length varies. News and information about Circle K activities.
Artwork: 5x7 or 8x10 glossy prints or emailed TIFF or JPEG files of 300 dpi or better.

Sample Issue
16 pages (no advertising): 3 articles; 4 depts/columns. Sample copy, $.75 with 9x12 SASE ($.75 postage). Writers' guidelines available.
- "Break Down Barriers." Article discusses rules that will help a volunteer feel more comfortable when the opportunity arises to work with someone who has a disability.
- Sample dept/column: "Spotlight" features several Circle K clubs with details of their successful programs and projects.

Rights and Payment
First North American serial rights. Written material, $150–$400. Artwork, payment rate varies. Pays on acceptance. Provides 3 contributor's copies.

Editor's Comments
We are looking for articles covering topics of leadership, fellowship, and issues that are applicable to the lives and concerns of today's college students. Submissions must be based on multiple interviews and research; not personal insights or experiences.

Circles of Peace, Circles of Justice

Institute of Peace and Justice
4144 Lindell Boulevard #408
St. Louis, MO 63108

Editor: Kathy McGinnis

Description and Readership
The Institute of Peace and Justice publishes this newsletter. It is written for parents, educators, and others in the community who work with children and are interested in promoting justice. It also discusses educational opportunities and resources.
- **Audience:** Parents
- **Frequency:** Quarterly
- **Distribution:** 100% subscription
- **Circulation:** 2,000
- **Website:** www.ipj.ppj.org

Freelance Potential
50% written by nonstaff writers. Publishes 10 freelance submissions yearly; 25% by unpublished writers, 75% by authors who are new to the magazine. Receives 1 query monthly.

Submissions
Query. SASE. Responds in 2 months.
Articles: To 750 words. Informational, educational, and how-to articles; profiles; and reviews. Topics include social and family issues, parenting, popular culture, religion, nonviolence, and multicultural and ethnic issues.
Fiction: To 1,000 words. Genres include mystery, adventure, and historical and multicultural fiction.
Depts/columns: Word length varies. Organization news, resources, and advocacy.

Sample Issue
8 pages (no advertising): 4 articles; 3 depts/columns. Sample copy, free.
- "Still Trying . . . . After All These Years." First-person article looks at how one family deals with the pull of the consumer culture.
- "Families Challenging Materialism." Article offers practical tips on how families can enjoy a quality life without being greedy consumers.
- Sample dept/column: "What's Happening at the Institute for Peace & Justice" offers information on publications, programs, and other resources of interest to families.

Rights and Payment
First or one-time rights. No payment. Provides 1 copy.

Editor's Comments
While we welcome freelance submissions, our focus is a narrow one and we often receive queries on topics that simply do not fit in with our editorial mission. We want to see queries that deal with issues strictly related to justice, human rights, and peace. Reports on organizations that have this goal, as well as first-person stories, are welcome here.

City Parent

467 Speers Road
Oakville, Ontario L6K 3S4
Canada

Editor-in-Chief: Jane Muller

Description and Readership
Canada's largest regional parenting publication offers timely advice on issues of concern to parents, such as children's health, education, and family safety. It also publicizes upcoming family-oriented events and activities in the area. Published in tabloid format, it may be picked up free of charge in grocery stores, bookstores, schools, and shopping malls.
- **Audience:** Parents
- **Frequency:** Monthly
- **Distribution:** Newsstand; subscription; libraries; schools; other
- **Circulation:** 285,000
- **Website:** www.cityparent.com

Freelance Potential
100% written by nonstaff writers. Publishes 12 freelance submissions yearly; 20% by authors who are new to the magazine. Receives 17 queries monthly.

Submissions
Query with outline and clips or writing samples. SAE/IRC. Responds in 2 months.
Articles: 1,000–1,250 words. Informational and how-to articles and self-help pieces. Topics include parenting, education, family life, health, fitness, recreation, entertainment, current events, computers, audio, video, music, nature, science, crafts, travel, technology, and animals.
Depts/columns: 500–700 words. Computers, cooking, news, opinion pieces, parenting, and book reviews.

Sample Issue
48 pages (50% advertising): 16 articles; 6 depts/columns; 1 calendar of events. Guidelines available.
- "Bonding Basics—Life Before Birth." Article explains how expectant parents can bond with their babies in the womb through music, massage, and conversation.
- "Vacations Are Good Medicine." Article looks at a study that revealed regular vacations contribute to better health.
- "Practical Pool Pointers." Article points out the dangers of backyard pools and outlines an action plan for pool safety.

Rights and Payment
First rights. Written material, $.10 per word. Pays on publication. Provides 5 contributor's copies.

Editor's Comments
We expect our writers to be prepared to back up their research with notes or tapes if called upon to do so. Writers are asked to work with our editors to approve or oppose any substantive changes we feel their work may require.

The Claremont Review

4980 Wesley Road
Victoria, British Columbia V8Y 1Y9
Canada

Business Manager: Sue Field

Description and Readership
This literary journal publishes the work of young adult writers, most of whom are Canadian. Poems, short plays, short stories, graphic art, photography, and interviews are featured in each issue.
- **Audience:** 13–19 years
- **Frequency:** Twice each year
- **Distribution:** 20% newsstand; 20% schools; 15% subscription; 45% other
- **Circulation:** 600
- **Website:** www.theClaremontReview.com

Freelance Potential
100% written by nonstaff writers. Publishes 120 freelance submissions yearly; 50% by unpublished writers, 90% by authors who are new to the magazine. Receives 67 unsolicited mss monthly.

Submissions
Send complete ms with biography. Accepts photocopies and computer printouts. SAE/IRC. Responds in 1 month.
Articles: Word length varies. Interviews with contemporary authors and editors.
Fiction: To 5,000 words. Genres include traditional, literary, experimental, and contemporary fiction. Also publishes adventure and sports stories.
Artwork: B/W and color prints and transparencies.
Other: Poetry, no line limit.

Sample Issue
112 pages (2% advertising): 15 stories; 45 poems. Sample copy, $6 with 9x12 SAE/IRC. Guidelines available at website.
- "Climbing the Water Tower." Story reveals the thoughts a young woman has about herself and her relationship with a life-long friend.
- "Close Enough for Sunset." Story focuses on one working day in the life of a young waitress at South Coast Coffee.
- "Falling in Love with James." Story revolves around a homeless young man and the narrator's fantasies about him.

Rights and Payment
Rights vary. All material, payment rate varies. Provides 1 contributor's copy.

Editor's Comments
Although most of the work we publish is written by Canadians, we welcome submissions from 13- to 19-year-old writers throughout the English speaking world. All submissions accompanied by an SAE/IRC receive a written comment on their work.

The Clearing House

Heldref Publications
1319 18th Street
Washington, DC 20036

Managing Editor: Sarah Cyaussi

Description and Readership
Self-described as "a journal of educational strategies, issues, and ideas," this bimonthly is read by educators working in middle school and high school. Its editorial content focuses on new innovations in education, teaching strategies, and standardized testing.
- **Audience:** Educators
- **Frequency:** 6 times each year
- **Distribution:** Subscription; other
- **Circulation:** 1,500
- **Website:** www.heldref.org/tch.php

Freelance Potential
100% written by nonstaff writers. Publishes 65 freelance submissions yearly; 5% by unpublished writers, 50% by authors who are new to the magazine. Receives 10 mss monthly.

Submissions
Send 2 copies of complete ms. Accepts photocopies and computer printouts. Does not return mss. Responds in 3–4 months.
Articles: To 2,500 words. Informational and how-to articles. Topics include teaching methods, special education, learning styles, and testing and measurement.
Depts/columns: Word length varies. Opinion pieces and education news.

Sample Issue
50 pages (no advertising): 9 articles; 1 dept/column. Sample copy, $14.50. Guidelines available in each issue.
- "Playing Indian at Halftime." Article addresses the recent controversy over the use of mascots and other school symbols related to Native Americans.
- "Bibliotheraphy for Gay and Lesbian Youth." Article reports on the use of reading to foster understanding of self, as related to teens who consider themselves to be gay or lesbian.
- "Encouraged or Discouraged?" Article discusses the fact that in relation to the large number of women who choose to be teachers, very few choose to train for administrative positions.

Rights and Payment
All rights. No payment. Provides 2 contributor's copies.

Editor's Comments
Our mission is to keep our readers as current as possible on news and information related to teaching in middle and high school. We are interested in submissions on practical experience subjects, as well as material that addresses the issues facing educators in today's world.

Cleveland/Akron Family

Suite 224
35475 Vine Street
Eastlake, OH 44095-3147

Editor: Frances Richards

Description and Readership

Distributed to greater metropolitan Cleveland and Akron, this magazine offers a wealth of information on parenting, family issues, health, and entertainment. It also provides up-to-date material on resources and events in the region.
- **Audience:** Parents
- **Frequency:** Monthly
- **Distribution:** 100% controlled
- **Circulation:** 65,000
- **Website:** www.clevelandakronfamily.com

Freelance Potential

75% written by nonstaff writers. Publishes 30 freelance submissions yearly; 33% by authors who are new to the magazine. Receives 25 queries monthly.

Submissions

Query. Accepts email to editor@tntpublications.com. Responds only if interested.
Articles: 500+ words. Informational, self-help, and how-to articles; profiles; and reviews. Topics include animals, the arts, computers, crafts, health, fitness, gifted education, popular culture, sports, the environment, religion, and regional issues.
Depts/columns: Word length varies. Media reviews, health, and education.
Artwork: High resolution JPEG and TIFF files.

Sample Issue

46 pages (50% advertising): 6 articles; 9 depts/columns. Editorial calendar available.
- "Read Across America." Article discusses the benefits of reading and offers tips for parents to help their children develop a love of reading.
- "Early Intervention Helps Kids." Article offers a review of early intervention programs and activities for children that have a developmental delay.
- Sample dept/column: "Family Doctor" tells of a study on Type 2 diabetes, and ways to help prevent medical errors.

Rights and Payment

Exclusive rights. Written material, payment rate varies. Pays on publication. Provides 1 contributor's copy.

Editor's Comments

Our focus is on issues that affect families with children from birth to 18. Since our readers look to us to provide them with parenting information, we are always on the lookout for well-written articles on topics that are related to child development, parenting issues, health, local news, resources that are available in the region, and travel pieces that highlight family-friendly destinations.

Click

Cricket Magazine Group
Suite 1100
332 South Michigan Avenue
Chicago, IL 60604

Submissions Editor

Description and Readership

Click introduces young children to many of the same phenomena and questions about the world that intrigue adults. It also endeavors to introduce the processes of investigation and observation to encourage youngsters to become active participants in the world around them.
- **Audience:** 3–7 years
- **Frequency:** 9 times each year
- **Distribution:** Subscription; newsstand
- **Circulation:** 50,000
- **Website:** www.cricketmag.com

Freelance Potential

75% written by nonstaff writers. Publishes 1–2 freelance submissions yearly; 15% by authors who are new to the magazine. Receives 35 unsolicited mss monthly.

Submissions

Send complete ms with bibliography. Accepts photocopies and computer printouts. SASE. Responds in 3 months.
Articles: 200–400 words. Informational articles. Topics include science, nature, technology, math, history, the arts, and social sciences.
Fiction: 600-1,000 words. Stories about the arts, technology, the environment, and animals.

Sample Issue

38 pages (no advertising): 3 articles; 3 stories; 1 interview; 1 comic; 2 activities. Sample copy, $5. Writers' guidelines and theme list available.
- "Is It an Insect?" Article explains exactly what type of body constitutes an insect and profiles some of the different insects common to our own backyards.
- "It's a Ball of Poop." Article spotlights dung beetles and various aspects of their lifestyles.
- "The Great Peacock Moth." Story shares childhood memories of Paul Fabre, son of the famous French explorer Jean Henri Fabre.

Rights and Payment

All rights. Written material, $.25 per word. Pays on publication.

Editor's Comments

Prospective authors should study the magazine closely, then submit a manuscript for a particular theme five months in advance of publication date. Each issue revolves around a central nonfiction theme, explored through a variety of formats including stories, articles, poems, activities, interviews, and photo essays. Stories should help readers discover information about the universe and encourage questioning of what is seen.

Club Connection

Assemblies of God
1445 North Boonville Avenue
Springfield, MO 65802-1894

Associate Editor: Kelly Kirksy

Description and Readership
An underlying message of salvation forms the basis of this four-color magazine for Missionettes. Information covers interests that are common to all girls in the target age group from school, friends, and music to religion and family relationships. While inspirational, its format presents an upbeat and fun style for readers. Also included is an idea resource section for Missionettes' leaders.
- **Audience:** 6–12 years
- **Frequency:** Quarterly
- **Distribution:** 100% subscription
- **Circulation:** 12,000
- **Website:** www.clubconnection.ag.org

Freelance Potential
60% written by nonstaff writers. Publishes 30 freelance submissions yearly; 45% by unpublished writers, 80% by authors who are new to the magazine. Receives 15–17 unsolicited mss monthly.

Submissions
Send complete ms. Accepts photocopies, computer printouts, and simultaneous submissions if identified. SASE. Responds in 1–2 months.
Articles: 300–700 words. Profiles; interviews; and biographical pieces. Topics include religion, missions, hobbies, health, fitness, music, nature, the environment, multicultural and ethnic subjects, camping, pets, sports, recreation, science, and technology.
Depts/columns: Word length varies. Advice, science, fun, club news, and book and music reviews.
Other: Puzzles, games, trivia, and recipes.

Sample Issue
32 pages (5% advertising): 6 articles; 10 depts/columns; 3 devotionals; 3 games; 2 crafts. Sample copy, $2 with 9x12 SASE ($.77 postage). Guidelines and editorial calendar available.
- "Gabriela: World Traveler." Article relates a teen's experience with a different culture during a visit to Uzbekistan.
- Sample dept/column: "Craft Creation" gives recipes for making spring flowers, confetti-filled eggs, homemade bubbles and bubble wands, and Easter baskets.

Rights and Payment
First or one-time rights. Articles, $25–$50. Pays on publication. Provides 2 contributor's copies.

Editor's Comments
We would like to see more inspirational articles and fewer that are based on nature and related topics.

Cobblestone
Discover American History

Cobblestone Publishing
Suite C, 30 Grove Street
Peterborough, NH 03458

Editor: Meg Chorlian

Description and Readership
Thoroughly researched, this publication gives middle school children an in-depth look into periods and events in America's historical past. All issues revolve around a central theme.
- **Audience:** 8–14 years
- **Frequency:** 9 times each year
- **Distribution:** 100% subscription
- **Circulation:** 29,000
- **Website:** www.cobblestonepub.com

Freelance Potential
85% written by nonstaff writers. Publishes 90 freelance submissions yearly; 20% by unpublished writers, 20% by authors who are new to the magazine. Receives 50 queries monthly.

Submissions
Query with outline, bibliography, and clips or writing samples. All queries must relate to a specific theme. Accepts photocopies and computer printouts. SASE. Responds in 5 months.
Articles: Features, 700–800 words. Sidebars, 300–400 words. Informational articles; interviews; and profiles of historical figures—all as they relate to American history.
Fiction: To 800 words. Historical, multicultural, and biographical fiction; retold legends; and adventure.
Artwork: Color prints and slides. Line art.
Other: Puzzles, activities, and games. Poetry relating to the issue's theme.

Sample Issue
48 pages (no advertising): 10 articles; 7 depts/columns; 2 activities; 1 cartoon. Sample copy, $4.95 with 9x12 SASE ($1.24 postage). Guidelines available.
- "The Path to War: A Time Line of Major Events." Article gives a progressive account of the events that led up to the Revolutionary War.
- "The Battle of Lexington." Article recounts the battle that hosted the "shot that was heard around the world" and initiated the Revolutionary War.
- Sample dept/column, "Digging Deeper" suggests books to read that will provide further information on the issue's theme.

Rights and Payment
All rights. Written material, $.20–$.25 per word. Artwork, rate varies. Pays on publication. Provides 2 contributor's copies.

Editor's Comments
Articles must be historically accurate and thoroughly researched. Whenever possible, events should be seen through the eyes of participants. New writers, please read past issues.

College Bound Teen Magazine

Suite 202
1200 South Avenue
Staten Island, NY 10314

Editor-in-Chief: Gina LaGuardia

Description and Readership
High school students read this magazine to discover the ins and outs of life on a college campus. It relates real-life experiences and information needed to find and apply to a college that matches the reader's needs. All aspects of college life are addressed.
- **Audience:** 14–18 years
- **Frequency:** Monthly for regional editions; 2 times each year for national edition
- **Distribution:** 85% schools; 15% subscription
- **Circulation:** 755,000 national; 100,000 regional
- **Website:** www.collegeboundmag.com

Freelance Potential
60% written by nonstaff writers. Publishes 175 freelance submissions yearly; 60% by unpublished writers, 60% by authors who are new to the magazine. Receives 50 queries monthly.

Submissions
Query with clips or writing samples. Accepts photocopies and email queries to editorial@collegebound.net. SASE. Responds in 6–8 weeks.
Articles: 600–1,000 words. Informational and how-to articles; profiles; interviews; and personal experience pieces. Topics include choosing a college, college survival, dorm life, joining a fraternity or sorority, and scholarships.
Depts/columns: Word length varies. Reviews of college guides and resources, financial aid, lifestyle issues, and athletics.
Other: Submit seasonal material 4 months in advance.

Sample Issue
80 pages (48% advertising): 12 articles; 12 depts/columns. Sample copy, free with 9x12 SASE. Guidelines available.
- "High School vs. College." Article readies a high school student for the transition to college life.
- "Break Out of the Wallflower Syndrome." Article combines a student's real-life experience as a shy person with information on how to break the cycle.
- Sample dept/column: "Cash Crunch" suggests different approaches to take when looking for available scholarships and monetary awards.

Rights and Payment
First and second rights. Articles, $50–$100. Depts/columns, $15–$70. Pays on publication. Provides 3–5 copies.

Editor's Comments
Specific topics needed include trend stories with real teen sources, and unusual college classes, activities, and campus happenings. Combine teen lingo and down-to-earth authority.

College Outlook

20 East Gregory Boulevard
Kansas City, MO 64114-1145

Editor: December Lambeth

Description and Readership
This magazine helps its readers select a college, obtain financial aid, and choose a career. It also covers topics such as money management and extracurricular activities.
- **Audience:** College-bound students
- **Frequency:** Twice each year
- **Distribution:** 100% controlled
- **Circulation:** Spring, 440,000; fall, 710,000
- **Website:** www.townsend-outlook.com

Freelance Potential
60% written by nonstaff writers. Publishes 5–10 freelance submissions yearly; 95% by unpublished writers, 95% by authors who are new to the magazine. Receives 8 queries and unsolicited mss monthly.

Submissions
Query with clips or writing samples; or send complete ms. Accepts photocopies and computer printouts. SASE. Responds in 1 month.
Articles: To 1,500 words. How-to articles; personal experience pieces; and humor. Topics include school selection, financial aid, scholarships, student life, extracurricular activities, money management, and college admissions procedures.
Artwork: 5x7 B/W and color transparencies.
Other: Gazette items on campus subjects, including fads, politics, classroom news, current events, leisure activities, and careers.

Sample Issue
48 pages (15% advertising): 4 articles; 1 academic chart. Sample copy, free. Guidelines available.
- "Career Planning." Article provides a step-by-step guide for finding a career based on your values, interests, skills, and aptitudes.
- "Developing the Skills for a Successful Musical Career." Article explores a number of career possibilities for students interested in studying music.
- "Grades: What Really Counts When Applying to Art School." Article discusses what admissions counselors look for when evaluating a portfolio.

Rights and Payment
All rights. No payment. Provides 2 contributor's copies.

Editor's Comments
We're looking for informative, entertaining, and easy-to-read pieces. The key is: if you have fun writing it, it'll be fun to read. Articles should not be biased toward any one school.

Columbus Parent Connect

Suite F
670 Lakeview Plaza Boulevard
Worthington, OH 43085

Editor: Donna Willis

Description and Readership

Parents in the Columbus region find helpful information in *Columbus Parent* for raising healthy, happy children. While content covers children through late teen years, most of the articles focus on infants through pre-teen years.
- **Audience:** Parents
- **Frequency:** Monthly
- **Distribution:** 90% newsstand; 10% subscription
- **Circulation:** 125,000
- **Website:** www.columbusparent.com

Freelance Potential

50% written by nonstaff writers. Publishes 50 freelance submissions yearly; 100% by authors who are new to the magazine. Receives 83 queries and 40 unsolicited mss monthly.

Submissions

Query. Accepts email submissions to dwillis@thisweeknews.com.
Articles: 700 words. Informational and how-to articles; profiles; interviews; and reviews. Topics include the arts, current events, health and fitness, humor, music, recreation, self-help, and travel.
Fiction: 300 words. Humor.
Depts/columns: 300 words. Local events, food, health, book reviews, travel, and local personalities.
Artwork: Color prints and transparencies.
Other: Submit seasonal material 2 months in advance.

Sample Issue

60 pages (50% advertising): 4 articles; 10 depts/columns; 1 guide. Sample copy, free at newsstands. Guidelines and theme list available.
- "Young Yogis." Article details the benefits of yoga for children and its popularity among children of all ages in the Columbus region.
- "Less than Perfect Athlete Role Models: What Parents Can Do." Article explains how to handle situations that arise when a child's favorite athlete exhibits bad behavior.
- Sample dept/column: "Growing up Healthy" tackles the problems of menstrual cramps in teenage girls from school absences to painful symptoms.

Rights and Payment

No rights. Written material, $.10 per word. Pays on publication.

Editor's Comments

We are a regional publication, so every item has a local twist. New writers will find the best chance for acceptance in our feature section.

P.O. Box 60
Brattleboro, CT 05302-0060

Associate Editor: Heather Taylor

Description and Readership

This publication is filled with ideas and innovations for math, science, and technology teachers. It is used as a resource for hands-on learning, developing strong problem-solving skills in students, and bringing excitement for these subjects back to the classroom. Each issue focuses on a single theme, explored from different angles.
- **Audience:** Teachers, grades K–8
- **Frequency:** 5 times each year
- **Distribution:** 100% subscription
- **Circulation:** 2,000
- **Website:** www.synergylearning.com

Freelance Potential

90% written by nonstaff writers. Publishes 25 freelance submissions yearly; 60% by unpublished writers, 75% by authors who are new to the magazine. Receives 3–4 queries and unsolicited mss monthly.

Submissions

Query or send complete ms with résumé. Accepts photocopies, computer printouts, Macintosh disk submissions, and email submissions to connect@synergylearning.org. SASE. Responds in 1 month.
Articles: To 1,400 words. Personal experience pieces; how-to articles; and interviews. Topics include math, science, nature, the environment, and technology.
Depts/columns: Book reviews and news, word lengths vary. Resource reviews, 50–300 words.
Other: Activities, 250–300 words.

Sample Issue

25 pages (no advertising): 7 articles; 4 depts/columns. Sample copy, free with 9x12 SASE. Guidelines available.
- "Science Side Trips." Article demonstrates the use of math and science to empower both subjects for students.
- "Technology for Learning." Article lists a number of Internet sites that provide real data to students integrating math and science projects.
- Sample dept/column: "Literature Links" reviews books that make math and science problem solving fun for children.

Rights and Payment

First rights. Honorarium for published full-length articles. Provides 5 contributor's copies and a 1-year subscription.

Editor's Comments

We are looking for material that is engaging and stimulating for teachers and students, is easy to understand, and stresses interdisciplinary instruction.

Connect for Kids

125 K Street NW
Washington, DC 20006

Editor: Susan Phillips

Description and Readership

This resourceful online publication offers articles on topics related to building healthy, strong communities for families and children. It provides inspiring information on how to get involved and become a more active citizen.
• **Audience:** Children and families
• **Frequency:** Weekly
• **Distribution:** Online
• **Hits per month:** Unavailable
• **Website:** www.connectforkids.org

Freelance Potential

15% written by nonstaff writers. Publishes 12 freelance submissions yearly; 50% by authors who are new to the magazine. Receives 10 unsolicited mss monthly.

Submissions

Query. Accepts photocopies, computer printouts, and email to susan@connectforkids.org. SASE. Response time varies.
Articles: 900–1,500 words. Informational articles; profiles; reviews; and photoessays. Topics include adoption, foster care, the arts, child abuse and neglect, health, child care and early development, kids and politics, community building, learning disabilities, crime and violence prevention, parent involvement in education, development, out of school time, diversity and awareness, parenting, education, family income and poverty, and volunteering and mentoring.

Sample Issue

Guidelines available at website.
• "Assessing Foster Care from the Inside." Article takes a look at how the experience of foster care affects individuals in their adult life.
• "On the Alert for Toxins in Preschools." Article examines possible environmental hazards in preschools, and offers tips for creating a safe environment for children.
• "A Passport to Better Health, Better Grades." Article reports on new technology that helps manage health and education records for youths in foster care.

Rights and Payment

All rights. Payment rates and policies vary.

Editor's Comments

We are currently seeking more articles on early childhood learning and development, quality infant child care, diversity in schools, preschools, and communities, and mental health issues of children. We do not need any material covering mentoring/tutoring program profiles as we already have enough of these. Please note that we are exclusively an online publication.

Connecticut Parent

Suite 18
420 East Main Street
Branford, CT 06405

Editor & Publisher: Joel MacClaren

Description and Readership

Similar to other regional publications, *Connecticut Parent* maintains a local spin to its contents. It's a resource guide with timely information on local events, programs, camps, and schools. Also included are timeless topics covering good parenting, travel tips, personal improvement, and recipes.
• **Audience:** Parents
• **Frequency:** Monthly
• **Distribution:** 95% controlled; 5% subscription
• **Circulation:** 50,000
• **Website:** www.ctparent.com

Freelance Potential

20% written by nonstaff writers. Publishes 36 freelance submissions yearly; 25% by unpublished writers. Receives 50 unsolicited mss monthly.

Submissions

Send complete ms. Accepts photocopies and computer printouts. SASE. Response time varies.
Articles: 500–1,000 words. Self-help articles; profiles; interviews; and reviews. Topics include parenting, regional news, family relationships, social issues, education, special education, health, fitness, entertainment, and travel.
Depts/columns: 600 words. Family news, new product information, and media reviews.

Sample Issue

92 pages (60% advertising): 5 articles; 7 depts/columns. Sample copy, $5 with 9x12 SASE. Guidelines available.
• "What Kind of Homework Helper Are You?" Article discusses positive ways parents can help their children with homework without actually doing it.
• "Room to Grow: Creating a Children's Play Space." Article contains several tips for organizing a special area for play.
• Sample dept/column: "Party Planner" lists several places in Connecticut specializing in birthday parties geared toward energetic children.

Rights and Payment

One-time rights. All material, payment rate varies. Pays on publication. Provides 1 contributor's tearsheet.

Editor's Comments

Ours is a statewide publication targeted to families with children, prenatal to age 12. We look for articles that have a new slant on topics of interest to Connecticut parents. In addition to the monthly focus, we look for general information such as children's crafts, keeping a marriage alive, birthing, single parenting, health, holidays, and humor.

Connecticut's County Kids

877 Post Road East
Westport, CT 06880

Editor: Linda Greco

Description and Readership

This award-winning publication provides information to parents on child rearing, available resources, and events in Fairfield and New Haven counties in Connecticut.
- **Audience:** Parents
- **Frequency:** Monthly
- **Distribution:** 99% controlled; 1% subscription
- **Circulation:** 32,000
- **Website:** www.countykids.com

Freelance Potential

100% written by nonstaff writers. Publishes 50–60 freelance submissions yearly; 5% by unpublished writers, 10% by authors who are new to the magazine. Receives 42 queries and unsolicited mss monthly.

Submissions

Query or send complete ms. Prefers email submissions to countykids@ctcentral.com. Accepts photocopies. Responds only if interested.
Articles: 600–1,200 words. Informational, self-help, and how-to articles; profiles; and interviews. Topics include family issues, parenting, education, current events, regional news, recreation, sports, travel, hobbies, the media, music, fitness, and multicultural issues.
Depts/columns: 500–800 words. "Partyline" offers party ideas. Also uses essays on parenting and updates on pediatric health issues.

Sample Issue

42 pages (50% advertising): 8 articles; 14 depts/columns. Sample copy, free with 10x13 SASE. Writers' guidelines and editorial calendar available.
- "Fitness: It's a Family Affair." Article discusses ways to be active with your kids to help keep them physically fit.
- "Computers Are for Kids." Article reports on what to expect from computer camps.
- Sample dept/column: "Pediatric Health" offers ways for parents to advocate for their children during a hospital stay.

Rights and Payment

First North American serial rights. Pays 30 days after publication. Written material, payment rate varies. Reprints, $25–$40. Provides 1 contributor's copy.

Editor's Comments

We are seeking more articles on family and parenting issues, education, health, regional sports, and recreation. Writing style should be casual, and in an easy-to-read format. Please don't send material on ADHD, fitness, obesity, or travel.

The Conqueror

United Pentecostal Church International
8855 Dunn Road
Hazelwood, MO 63042-2299

Editor: Travis Miller

Description and Readership

The Conqueror gives teens a basis for building their lives on Christian principals and ideals. Its contents focus on social reality, everyday situations, and reports on missionary work.
- **Audience:** 12–18 years
- **Frequency:** 6 times each year
- **Distribution:** 80% churches; 20% subscription
- **Circulation:** 5,200
- **Website:** http://pentecostalyouth.org

Freelance Potential

95% written by nonstaff writers. Publishes 55 freelance submissions yearly; 5% by unpublished writers, 5% by authors who are new to the magazine. Receives 10 unsolicited mss each month.

Submissions

Send complete ms. Accepts photocopies, computer printouts, and simultaneous submissions if identified. SASE. Responds in 3 months.
Articles: Features, 1,200–1,800 words. Shorter articles, 600–800 words. Personal experience pieces and profiles. Topics include religion, missionary-related subjects, spiritual growth, social issues, and current events.
Fiction: 600–900 words. Real-life fiction with Christian themes. Genres include humor and romance.
Depts/columns: Word length varies. Book and music reviews, opinion pieces and first-person pieces by teens, and reports on church events.

Sample Issue

16 pages (11% advertising): 4 articles; 1 story; 4 depts/columns. Sample copy, free with 9x12 SASE (2 first-class stamps). Guidelines available.
- "What Then?" Article relates a true incident of a teen saving a pregnant woman after a roof collapsed and realizing that every fetus is a real person from conception.
- "Sweet Temptations." Story pursues the thought that overcoming temptation builds overall character strength.
- Sample dept/column: "Time Out for Truth" reminds us that a hasty word spoken in anger can never be recalled.

Rights and Payment

All rights. All material, $15–$50. Pays on publication. Provides 1 contributor's copy.

Editor's Comments

We are looking for material on spiritual growth and development, Christian fiction, character studies, personal testimonies and experiences, and current events.

CosmoGirl!

3rd Floor
224 West 57th Street
New York, NY 10019

Associate Editor: Lauren A. Greene

Description and Readership
Teenage girls find feature articles with news angles that pertain to their lives, quizzes, relationship stories, and dynamic first-person stories in *CosmoGirl!* All the material it presents promotes a positive self-image and encourages girls to reach for their goals and dreams.
- **Audience:** 12–17 years
- **Frequency:** 10 times each year
- **Distribution:** Subscription; newsstand
- **Circulation:** 1.35 million
- **Website:** www.cosmogirl.com

Freelance Potential
25% written by nonstaff writers. Publishes 10 freelance submissions yearly; 5% by unpublished writers, 40% by authors who are new to the magazine.

Submissions
Query with résumé and clips. Accepts photocopies. SASE. Responds in 2 months.
Articles: 1,200 words. Informational and how-to articles; profiles; and personal experience pieces. Topics include relationships, entertainment, fashion, fitness, beauty, and social issues.
Depts/columns: Word length varies. Beauty advice, health, fitness, and celebrity news.
Other: Submit seasonal material on Halloween, proms, graduation, and summer events and activities 4 months in advance.

Sample Issue
206 pages (25% advertising): 5 articles; 30 depts/columns; 3 quizzes; 1 calendar; 1 special section. Sample copy, $2.99 at newsstands. Guidelines available.
- "Be Your Own Hero." Article suggests that girls can better themselves by tapping into the wisdom and values of their role models and mentors.
- "Why Is She in Prison for His Crime?" Article details how one unfortunate mistake sent a young woman to jail for her boyfriend's crime.
- Sample dept/column: "Project 2024" presents pointers from Madeleine Albright on commanding respect.

Rights and Payment
All rights. Written material, $1 per word. Pays on publication. Provides 1 contributor's copy.

Editor's Comments
We expect writers to draw information for their articles from industry experts. Consult experts on the cutting edge of their field; the more specific their area of expertise, the better.

Creative Kids

Prufrock Press
P.O. Box 8813
Waco, TX 76714

Editor: Libby Goolsby

Description and Readership
Showcasing work by children and young adults, this magazine includes articles, stories, poetry, songs, plays, activities and artwork. It first appeared in 1980.
- **Audience:** 6–14 years
- **Frequency:** Quarterly
- **Distribution:** Subscription; schools
- **Circulation:** 3,600
- **Website:** www.prufrock.com

Freelance Potential
97% written by nonstaff writers. Publishes 150 freelance submissions yearly; 95% by unpublished writers, 80% by authors who are new to the magazine. Receives 500 unsolicited mss monthly.

Submissions
Send complete ms. Accepts photocopies, computer printouts, disk submissions, email submissions to lindsey@prufrock.com, and simultaneous submissions if identified. Availability of artwork improves the chances of acceptance. SASE. Responds in 4–6 weeks.
Articles: 800–900 words. Informational, self-help, and how-to articles; humor; photoessays; and personal experience pieces. Topics include animals, pets, social issues, sports, travel, and gifted education.
Fiction: 800–900 words. Genres include real-life and problem-solving stories; inspirational, historical, and multicultural fiction; mystery; suspense; folktales; humor; and stories about sports and animals.
Artwork: B/W and color prints and transparencies. Line art on 8½x11 white paper.
Other: Poetry, songs, word puzzles, games, and cartoons. Submit seasonal material 1 year in advance.

Sample Issue
34 pages (no advertising): 4 articles; 1 story; 4 depts/columns; 26 poems; 6 games. Writers' guidelines available.
- "The Unexpected." Essay tells of a girl walking home from school who finds an abandoned kitten and brings it home.
- "A Journey for Food in Occupied Holland." Essay recalls how a girl and her sister bravely search for food for their family in Holland during World War II.

Rights and Payment
Rights vary. No payment. Provides 3–4 contributor's copies.

Editor's Comments
We are looking for fresh, top-notch stories, poems, games, activities, and artwork by kids ages 8–14.

Cricket

Cricket Magazine Group
P.O. Box 300
315 Fifth Street
Peru, IL 61354

Submissions Editor

Description and Readership

High-quality writing is a hallmark of this popular magazine for pre- and early teens. Its award-winning format is a mix of fiction and nonfiction, thought-provoking poetry and activities. Fables, folktales, and cultural information are often found within its pages.
- **Audience:** 9–14 years
- **Frequency:** Monthly
- **Distribution:** 92% subscription; 8% newsstand
- **Circulation:** 70,000
- **Website:** www.cricketmag.com

Freelance Potential

100% written by nonstaff writers. Publishes 150 freelance submissions yearly; 30% by unpublished writers, 50% by authors who are new to the magazine. Receives 1,000 unsolicited mss monthly.

Submissions

Send complete ms; include bibliography for nonfiction. Accepts photocopies, computer printouts, and simultaneous submissions. SASE. Responds in 2–3 months.
Articles: 200–1,500 words. Informational and how-to articles; biographies; and profiles. Topics include science, technology, history, social science, archeology, architecture, geography, foreign culture, travel, adventure, and sports.
Fiction: 200–2,000 words. Genres include humor, mystery, fantasy, science fiction, folktales, fairy tales, mythology, and historical and contemporary fiction.
Depts/columns: Staff written.
Other: Poetry, to 25 lines. Puzzles, games, crafts, recipes, and science experiments, word length varies.

Sample Issue

64 pages (no advertising): 3 articles; 9 stories; 3 poems; 1 puzzle. Sample copy, $5 with 9x12 SAE. Guidelines available.
- "Jeremy Goes Shopping." Story illustrates a change of heart in a boy resentful of spending his summer in a small town.
- "Farm Fable." Story weaves a tale of an extraordinary farm event based on a true story.
- "The Ballad of a Prairie Blacksmith." Article describes the life of John Deere and the company he founded.

Rights and Payment

Rights vary. Articles and fiction, to $.25 per word. Poetry, to $3 per line. Pays on publication. Provides 6 copies.

Editor's Comments

We are looking for well-written science fiction, fantasy, and humor appropriate for our readers.

Crinkles

17 East Henrietta Street
Baltimore, MD 21230-3910

Publisher: Paula Montgomery

Description and Readership

Crinkles is written for children between the ages of seven and eleven. All of its material is designed to develop critical thinking skills in children and to teach them to develop good study habits and a comfort with independent research.
- **Audience:** 7–11 years
- **Frequency:** 6 times each year
- **Distribution:** Subscription
- **Circulation:** 6,000
- **Website:** www.crinkles.com

Freelance Potential

70% written by nonstaff writers. Publishes 2–3 freelance submissions yearly; 30% by authors who are new to the magazine. Receives 3 queries monthly.

Submissions

Query with résumé. Accepts computer printouts. SASE. Responds in 1 month.
Articles: Word length varies. Informational articles. Topics include history, culture, multicultural and ethnic subjects, social issues, science, animals, nature, the arts, and sports.
Other: Puzzles, games, and crafts.

Sample Issue

50 pages (no advertising): 13 articles; 13 activities.
- "Troll Tales." Article looks at the myths behind these fantastic creatures, and how they developed.
- "Yarn and More." Article looks at the tradition of knitting and its origins.
- "The Kingdom of Norway." Article looks at why Norway was chosen by the United Nations as the best country in which to live.

Rights and Payment

All rights. Payment policy varies. Written material, $150. Provides contributor's copies.

Editor's Comments

Our mission is to bring children articles that will ignite their curiosity and give them a desire to learn more about the world around them, and the events that have shaped it. We welcome submissions from writers at ease with writing for a young audience in such a way that will both inform and entertain. All of our material is meticulously researched and connects with appropriate school curricula. Keep in mind that the more "add-ons" you can include with your article, the better. We look for accompanying activities, puzzles, games, and quizzes. Whatever your imagination can come up with that will hook readers into your articles will help your chances of publication here.

Current Health 1

Weekly Reader Corporation
P.O. Box 120023
200 First Stamford Place
Stamford, CT 06912-0023

Editorial Director: Sabrina McCaughin

Description and Readership
Schools use this publication from the Weekly Reader Corporation as part of their health curriculum. *Current Health 1* includes articles on health, fitness, safety, and nutrition written for students in fourth through seventh grade.
- **Audience:** Grades 4–7
- **Frequency:** 8 times each year
- **Distribution:** 100% schools
- **Circulation:** 163,793
- **Website:** www.weeklyreader.com

Freelance Potential
90% written by nonstaff writers. Publishes 64 freelance submissions yearly; 30% by authors who are new to the magazine.

Submissions
All articles are assigned. Query with letter of introduction, list of areas of expertise, publishing credits, and clips. No unsolicited mss. Responds 1–4 months.
Articles: 850–2,000 words. Informational articles about subjects related to the middle-grade health curriculum. Topics include health, fitness, safety, first aid, nutrition, disease, drug education, psychology, and relationships.
Depts/columns: Activities, Q&A, and health updates.

Sample Issue
32 pages (no advertising): 8 articles; 3 depts/columns. Sample copy available. Writer's guidelines provided upon agreement.
- "Putting Your Best Feet Forward." Article includes interesting facts about feet, covers some common foot problems, and offers tips for promoting foot health.
- "Get Ready, Get Fit, Go!" Article features advice for kids about how to get started with an exercise, fitness, and weight-loss regimen.
- Sample dept/column: "Health Notes" describes some of the hidden dangers of microwave cooking and tells what to look for in healthy smoothies.

Rights and Payment
All rights. Articles, $150+. Provides 2 contributor's copies.

Editor's Comments
We are looking for experienced writers who have expertise in childhood health and who can present information to kids in fun and educational ways. All of the articles that appear in our magazine are written by assignment. We suggest you contact us with a letter of introduction that describes your skills and areas of knowledge. You may also include a brief bio and/or writing samples. To get a feel for our tone and the types of material we are interested in, read a copy of our publication.

Current Health 2

Weekly Reader Corporation
P.O. Box 120023
200 First Stamford Place
Stamford, CT 06912-0023

Senior Managing Editor: Hugh Vestrup

Description and Readership
Topics such as substance abuse, fitness, nutrition, and psychology are covered in this magazine for preteens and teens. Provided as a curriculum supplement to middle school and high school health classes, it also offers optional material on human sexuality.
- **Audience:** Grades 7–12
- **Frequency:** 8 times each year
- **Distribution:** 100% schools
- **Circulation:** 232,000
- **Website:** www.weeklyreader.com

Freelance Potential
90% written by nonstaff writers. Publishes 64 freelance submissions yearly; 30% by authors who are new to the magazine. Receives 5 queries monthly.

Submissions
Query with letter of introduction listing areas of expertise, publishing credits, and clips. No unsolicited mss. SASE. Responds to queries in 1–4 months.
Articles: 900–2,500 words. Informational articles on subjects related to the middle school and high school curricula. Topics include fitness, exercise, nutrition, disease, psychology, first aid, safety, and human sexuality.
Depts/columns: Word length varies. Health updates and Q&A on health-related issues.

Sample Issue
32 pages (1% advertising): 8 articles; 2 depts/columns. Sample copy available. Guidelines provided upon assignment.
- "In Search of Happiness: Finding Your Strengths." Article discusses how finding and exploring your talents builds confidence and leads to greater happiness.
- "What You Need to Know about Fad Diets." Article examines the promises and pitfalls of some of today's more popular fad diets.
- Sample dept/column: "Health Beat" features short pieces on SARS and organic foods.

Rights and Payment
All rights. Articles, $150+. Pays on publication. Provides 2 contributor's copies.

Editor's Comments
The goal of our publication is to use current news to make topics relevant to students and to help them make healthier choices. Many of the articles we publish explain the health effects of drugs, alcohol, and tobacco use and offer suggestions on how to help students resist peer pressure.

Current Science

Weekly Reader Corporation
P.O. Box 120023
200 First Stamford Place
Stamford, CT 06912-0023

Managing Editor: Hugh Westrup

Description and Readership

Striving to make science fun, this magazine offers exciting and engaging learning activities that cover life, earth, and physical science as well as information on health and technology. It is distributed in middle school classrooms.
- **Audience:** 11–17 years
- **Frequency:** 16 times each year
- **Distribution:** 100% schools
- **Circulation:** 1 million
- **Website:** www.weeklyreader.com/features/cs.html

Freelance Potential

40% written by nonstaff writers. Publishes 30 freelance submissions yearly; 10% by authors who are new to the magazine. Receives 2 queries monthly.

Submissions

Query with résumé. No unsolicited mss. Availability of artwork improves the chances of acceptance. SASE. Response time varies.
Articles: Word length varies. Informational articles. Topics include nature, science, the environment, technology, animals, physics, and earth science.
Depts/columns: Word length varies. Science-related news briefs and answers to science questions.
Artwork: Color prints.
Other: Science-related photos, trivia, and puzzles.

Sample Issue

16 pages (no advertising): 4 articles; 2 depts/columns; 2 games. Sample copy, free with 9x12 SASE.
- "Flights of Fancy?" Article discusses several conspiracy theorists who insist that the moon missions were a hoax.
- "Steer Clear?" Article takes a look at the origin of mad cow disease, how it works, and what precautions are being taken to prevent future outbreaks in the U.S.
- "Rocket Boy." Article reports on a teen who is competing to be the first teen in space on a rocket built by a private aerospace company.

Rights and Payment

All rights. Written material, payment rate varies. Pays on acceptance. Provides contributor's copies.

Editor's Comments

We link today's news to students in a way that excites them and gets them involved. The topics include themes teachers will find useful in the classroom. We provide skill-building techniques that include thought-provoking exercises to help students learn about the great world of science.

Curriculum Review

Paperclip Communications
125 Patterson Avenue
Little Falls, NJ 07424

Publisher: Andy McLaughlin

Description and Readership

The editorial objective of *Curriculum Review* is to help teachers hone their craft through mutual support and the sharing of ideas. Its pages are devoted to news of successful programs and teaching strategies in use in schools today.
- **Audience:** Teachers and school administrators
- **Frequency:** 9 times each year
- **Distribution:** 100% subscription
- **Circulation:** 5,000
- **Website:** www.curriculumreview.com or
  www.paper-clip.com

Freelance Potential

2% written by nonstaff writers. Publishes 10 freelance submissions yearly. Receives 2 unsolicited mss monthly.

Submissions

Send complete ms. Responds in 1 month.
Articles: To 4,000 words. Informational articles; resource reviews; and conference reports. Teaching techniques and classroom ideas, to 500 words.
Depts/columns: Word length varies. Short news items about educational programs and practices; interviews with educators and administrators.

Sample Issue

16 pages (no advertising): 28 articles; 6 depts/columns.
Sample copy, free with 9x12 SASE (2 first-class stamps).
- "Zero-Tolerance Policy Causes a Major Headache." Article reports on a Shreveport, Louisiana, sophomore who could face a one-year suspension from school for being caught with Advil in her purse.
- "Promote Literacy—and Many Other Skills—Through Board Games." Article reports on the use of board games at a Virginia elementary school and their positive effect in developing communication, sportsmanship, math, social studies, and critical thinking skills.
- Sample dept/column: "Q&A" presents an interview with a college professor who discusses strategies for improving the safety of school science labs.

Rights and Payment

One-time rights. Written material, payment rate varies. Provides contributor's copies.

Editor's Comments

Submissions that appeal to us are those that encourage teachers as they face the challenges and reap the rewards of working with students in kindergarten through high school. If you have a strategy or program to share, we'd like to see it.

Dallas Child

Lauren Publications
Suite 146
4275 Kellway Circle
Addison, TX 75001

Editor: Shelley Hawes Pate

Description and Readership
This award-winning parenting magazine offers informative and inspirational articles on issues affecting families. Distributed free to parents throughout the Dallas metropolitan area, it focuses on children from prenatal through adolescence.
- **Audience:** Parents
- **Frequency:** Monthly
- **Distribution:** 90% controlled; 10% subscription
- **Circulation:** 120,000
- **Website:** www.dallaschild.com

Freelance Potential
50% written by nonstaff writers. Publishes 10–20 freelance submissions yearly; 20% by authors who are new to the magazine. Receives 33 queries monthly.

Submissions
Query with résumé. Accepts photocopies, computer print-outs, and simultaneous submissions if identified. SASE. Responds in 2–3 months.
Articles: 1,000–2,500 words. Informational, self-help, and how-to articles; profiles; interviews; humor; and personal experience pieces. Topics include parenting, education, family travel, regional news, recreation, entertainment, current events, social issues, multicultural and ethnic subjects, health, fitness, and crafts.
Depts/columns: 800 words. Local events, travel destinations, and health updates.

Sample Issue
86 pages (14% advertising): 2 articles; 9 depts/columns. Sample copy, free with 9x12 SASE. Guidelines available.
- "Look Who's (Not) Squawking Now." Article discusses calming techniques for infant crying.
- "North Texas' Best Family-Friendly Companies 2004." Article presents companies in North Texas that have the best commitment to work/life practices.
- Sample dept/column: "Mom-Mobile Reviews" offers practical car reviews for moms.

Rights and Payment
First rights. Written material, payment rate varies. Pays on publication. Provides author's copies upon request.

Editor's Comments
We like to present guidelines, advice, and comfort with a dose of humor, as well as accurate, up-to-date information on health and safety issues. We look for fresh voices, ideas, and perspectives on parenting. Stories should have a local focus and be from writers in the Dallas area.

Dance Magazine

11th Floor
333 7th Avenue
New York, NY 10001

Editor-in-Chief: Wendy Perron

Description and Readership
Revolving around the world of dance, this publication offers a professional look at dance personalities, techniques, classes, choreography, trends, international news, advice, and corps reviews. It appeals to dancers of every age.
- **Audience:** YA–Adult
- **Frequency:** Monthly
- **Distribution:** Subscription; newsstand
- **Circulation:** 45,000
- **Website:** www.dancemagazine.com

Freelance Potential
75% written by nonstaff writers. Publishes 5 freelance submissions yearly; 20% by unpublished writers, 50% by authors who are new to the magazine. Receives 83 queries and unsolicited mss monthly.

Submissions
Query or send complete ms. Response time varies.
Articles: Word length varies. Informational articles; profiles; and interviews. Topics include dance, dance instruction, choreography, the arts, and family and health issues as they relate to dance.
Depts/columns: Word length varies. New product information, reviews, news from the dance world, and information on dance education.

Sample Issue
98 pages (33% advertising): 8 articles; 9 depts/columns; 1 interview; 1 directory. Sample copy, $4.95 with 9x12 SASE. Guidelines available.
- "Baby Boom." Article focuses on the growing tendency of pregnancy among dancers.
- "Mind Your Body." Article looks at The Feldenkrais Method for dancers that provides techniques for dancers to use to ease bodily pains associated with dance workouts.
- Sample dept/column: "Education Matters" details the experiences of a Russian dance teacher and her evolving philosophies that she passes on to her students.

Rights and Payment
Rights negotiable. Written material, approximately $.30 per word. Payment policy varies.

Editor's Comments
Our magazine covers all types of dance from classic to modern, and is a source of information and trends for our readers. We are interested in all topics relating to dance, including health issues and interviews with dance professionals. We are also looking for material for "The Young Dancer," written for teens and children.

Dance Teacher

Lifestyle Ventures
Suite 420
250 West 57th Street
New York, NY 10107

Associate Editor: Katia Bachko

Description and Readership
Covering all aspects of the dance world, *Dance Teacher* provides information on dance techniques, instructions, new steps, nutrition, and business management. Articles are professionally beneficial to teachers and serious students.
- **Audience:** Dance teachers and students
- **Frequency:** Monthly
- **Distribution:** 100% subscription
- **Circulation:** 20,000
- **Website:** www.dance-teacher.com

Freelance Potential
50% written by nonstaff writers. Publishes 75 freelance submissions yearly; 10% by unpublished writers, 15% by authors who are new to the magazine. Receives 12 queries monthly.

Submissions
Query. Accepts computer printouts, email submissions to kbachko@lifestylemedia.com, and disk submissions. Availability of artwork improves chance of acceptance. SASE. Responds in 2 months.
Articles: 1,000–2,000 words. Topics include dance education, nutrition, health, publicity, and management as it relates to dance businesses.
Depts/columns: 700–1,200 words. Media reviews and news from the dance world.
Artwork: Slides, transparencies, and prints; prefers color, accepts B/W.

Sample Issue
126 pages (50% advertising): 7 articles; 15 depts/columns; 1 calendar of events. Sample copy, free with 9x12 SASE ($1.37 postage). Writers' guidelines and theme list available.
- "Bare-bone Facts about Bone Health." Article talks about the risk of osteoporosis and how teachers can safeguard themselves and their students against it.
- "Eat to Compete." Article shares nutritional tips from experienced teachers that keep their competitive dancers fit.
- Sample dept/column: "Supporting All Learners" discusses differentiated instruction strategies for varied aptitudes.

Rights and Payment
All rights. Articles, $200–$300. Depts/columns, $100–$150. Pays on acceptance. Provides 1 contributor's copy.

Editor's Comments
We would welcome more articles about practical issues, and tips-oriented pieces on dance, pedagogy, and health issues. We would also like to see how-to submissions on the business aspects of dance, and on anatomical topics.

Dane County Kids

P.O. Box 45050
Madison, WI 53744-5050

Editor-in-Chief: Justine Kessler

Description and Readership
Parents, grandparents, and other providers of child care living in and around Madison, Wisconsin, read this tabloid for information on local events, resources, education, and everyday child-rearing situations.
- **Audience:** Parents
- **Frequency:** Monthly
- **Distribution:** 100% controlled
- **Circulation:** 28,000
- **Website:** www.ericksonpublishing.com

Freelance Potential
80% written by nonstaff writers. Publishes 40 freelance submissions yearly; 70% by authors who are new to the magazine. Receives 20 queries and unsolicited mss monthly.

Submissions
Query or send complete ms. Accepts photocopies, computer printouts, and disk submissions (RTF format). SASE. Response time varies.
Articles: To 1,000 words. Informational articles; personal experience pieces; profiles; and interviews. Topics include parenting, family issues, gifted and special education, multicultural issues, hobbies and crafts, animals, computers, and careers.
Depts/columns: To 750 words. Personal experiences, local school news, health and safety issues, and book reviews.

Sample Issue
32 pages (50% advertising): 8 articles; 13 depts/columns; 1 book review. Sample copy, $2. Guidelines and theme list/editorial calendar available.
- "Let's Scrapbook!" Article outlines the reasons to make scrapbooks and provides information on the best ways to preserve photos and momentos.
- "Lost in Cyberspace?" Article emphasizes online research as the best first step in planning a great vacation.
- Sample dept/column: "Slices of Motherhood" takes one aspect of raising children, looks at the problems, then offers practical solutions that worked for the author.

Rights and Payment
Rights negotiable. All material, payment rate varies. Pays on publication.

Editor's Comments
We particularly like practical information with a touch of humor. We also look for pieces on local resources, and new slants on solving problems in short, to-the-point articles that are lively and easy to read. Check our editorial calendar for our selected monthly topics.

Daughters

3754 Pleasant Avenue South
Minneapolis, MN 55409

Editor: Lynette Lamb

Description and Readership
Daughters provides parents with material that will help them raise strong, self-confident daughters. It tackles issues that are important to today's pre-teen and teen girls and doesn't shy away from controversial subjects pertinent to that age group.
- **Audience:** Parents of 8- to 16-year-old girls
- **Frequency:** 6 times each year
- **Distribution:** 100% subscription
- **Circulation:** 25,000
- **Website:** www.daughters.com

Freelance Potential
65% written by nonstaff writers. Publishes 10 freelance submissions yearly; 90% by unpublished writers, 10% by authors who are new to the magazine. Receives 2–3 queries and unsolicited mss monthly.

Submissions
Send complete ms for "Mothering Journey" and "Fathering Journey." Query for all other articles. Accepts email submissions to editor@daughters.com (Microsoft Word attachments). SASE. Responds in 1–2 months.
Articles: 600 words. Informational and self-help articles; profiles; interviews; and personal experience pieces. Topics include health, fitness, social issues, and parenting, all as related to adolescent girls.
Depts/columns: 375 words. First-person pieces about mothering and fathering adolescent girls.

Sample Issue
16 pages (no advertising): 8 articles; 1 interview; 4 depts/columns. Guidelines available.
- "Babysitting: Is Your Daughter Ready?" Article helps parents assess whether or not a child is ready to start babysitting.
- "Carol Eagle on the Brother Factor." Interview compares the differences between girls who grow up with brothers and those who don't.
- Sample dept/column: "Mothering Journey" depicts an incident between a mother and her daughter.

Rights and Payment
All rights. Written material, $.30–$.50 per word. Depts/columns, $.35 per word. Pays on publication. Provides 3 copies.

Editor's Comments
Two columns always open to submissions are "Mothering Journey" and "Fathering Journey," both written in the first-person and relate parent-daughter stories that provide tips and information other parents can use. We are also eager to learn of new research and resources for parents.

Devo'Zine

P.O. Box 340004
1908 Grand Avenue
Nashville, TN 37203-0004

Editor: Sandy Miller

Description and Readership
Young adults seeking to develop a relationship with God find guidance and inspiration in this magazine of daily devotional meditations.
- **Audience:** YA
- **Frequency:** 6 times each year
- **Distribution:** 100% subscription
- **Circulation:** 105,000
- **Website:** www.devozine.org

Freelance Potential
100% written by nonstaff writers. Publishes 378 freelance submissions yearly; 50% by authors who are new to the magazine.

Submissions
Query. Accepts photocopies, computer printouts, disk submissions, and email submissions to devozine@ upperroom.org. SASE. Responds in 4 months.
Articles: 150–500 words. Daily meditations, 150–250 words. Informational articles; personal experience pieces; and profiles. Topics include Christian faith, mentoring, independence, courage, teen parenting, creativity, social issues, and relationships.
Fiction: 150–250 words. Inspirational short stories.
Other: Prayers and poetry, 10–20 lines. Submit seasonal material 6–8 months in advance.

Sample Issue
64 pages (no advertising): 60 devotionals. Sample copy, $3.90. Guidelines and theme list available.
- "Living and Dying by Faith." Article relates the story of Dietrich Bonhoeffer, a German critic of the Nazis who believed Christians and Jews should stand together to bring down Hitler's regime.
- "For These Things I Pray." A prayer written in poetry form draws on the biblical injunction to pray about everything; includes a journal activity.
- "Love." Poem reflects on the Bible verse that we show love for our friends by truly helping them, not just by talking about it.

Rights and Payment
First and second rights. Pays on acceptance. Features, $100. Meditations, $25.

Editor's Comments
We depend on contributions from our readers to fill our pages. If you have an experience you want to share, write a mediation about it and query us.

Dig

Suite C
Cobblestone Publishing
30 Grove Street
Peterborough, NH 03458

Editor: Rosalie F. Baker

Description and Readership

Fascinating facts and figures relating to archaeology fill this lively publication with information geared to middle-grade readers. The in-depth contents of each issue all revolve around a specific theme.
- **Audience:** 9–14 years
- **Frequency:** 9 times each year
- **Distribution:** Subscription; newsstand
- **Circulation:** 21,000
- **Website:** www.cobblestonepub.com

Freelance Potential

80% written by nonstaff writers. Publishes 40 freelance submissions yearly; 40% by unpublished writers, 60% by authors who are new to the magazine. Receives 8 queries monthly.

Submissions

All submissions must relate to an upcoming theme. Query with outline, bibliography, and clips or writing samples. SASE. Responds in 2 months.
Articles: Word length varies. Informational articles and photo essays. Topics include nature, animals, science, and technology.
Fiction: Word length varies. Stories relate to the theme of each issue.
Depts/columns: Word length varies. Art, archaeology facts, quizzes, and projects.

Sample Issue

34 pages (no advertising): 7 articles; 7 depts/columns. Sample copy, $4.95 at newsstands. Guidelines available.
- "Preserving the Excavated Past." Article demonstrates the inherent problems in finding ancient wall paintings and the techniques used to preserve them.
- "Food for Thought." Article analyzes the process of figuring out an ancient people's diet from the food remnants and plants found at archaeological sites, and the way that molars are worn down.
- Sample dept/column: "Project" gives step-by-step instructions for making an obsidian mirror similar to those found at ancient burial sites.

Rights and Payment

First rights. Written material, $.20–$.25 per word. Pays on publication. Provides 2 contributor's copies.

Editor's Comments

We only accept queries that are related to the theme of an upcoming issue. Please send for a theme list and become acquainted with our publication's format and style before sending a submission.

Dimensions

1908 Association Drive
Reston, VA 20191

Assistant Editor: Courtney Reyers

Description and Readership

DECA, an association of students and teachers of marketing, management, and entrepreneurship, publishes this journal of business-related articles for knowledgeable students who are planning to become successful leaders in the business world.
- **Audience:** 14–18 years
- **Frequency:** Quarterly
- **Distribution:** Unavailable
- **Circulation:** 165,000
- **Website:** www.deca.org

Freelance Potential

60% written by nonstaff writers. Publishes 9 freelance submissions yearly; 50% by unpublished writers, 50% by authors who are new to the magazine.

Submissions

Query or send complete ms with short author bio. Accepts photocopies, computer printouts, Macintosh disk submissions (RTF files), simultaneous submissions if identified, and email submissions to courtney_reyers@deca.org. SASE. Response time varies.
Articles: 800–1,200 words. Informational and how-to articles, profiles, interviews, and personal experience pieces. Topics include general business, management, marketing trends (domestic and international), sales, ethics, leadership development, entrepreneurship, franchising, personal finance, advertising, e-commerce, technology, careers, college admissions, and school-to-work incentives.
Depts/columns: 400–600 words. DECA chapter news and short business news items.

Sample Issue

32 pages (45% advertising): 12 articles; 6 depts/columns. Sample copy, free with 9x12 SASE. Guidelines available.
- "Sense and Sensibility." Article offers guidelines for students who, like most Americans, are confused about appropriate business attire in today's world.
- "Start a Business Now." Article profiles several young people who have started their own successful businesses and outlines key steps for others considering a business venture.

Rights and Payment

First North American serial rights. Pays on publication. Written material, payment rate varies.

Editor's Comments

Don't talk down to our knowledgeable readers. They expect valuable, timely information that they can learn from and refer back to as they move into the business world.

Dimensions of Early Childhood

Southern Early Childhood Association
P.O. Box 55930
Little Rock, AR 72215-5930

Executive Director: Glenda Bean

Description and Readership
The articles published in this journal address the interests of early childhood professionals and present the latest information relevant to the field. Theme issues about timely, critical topics are published occasionally. In addition to early childhood educators, its audience also includes researchers, child-care providers, social workers, and education policy makers.
- **Audience:** Early childhood professionals
- **Frequency:** Quarterly
- **Distribution:** 100% subscription
- **Circulation:** 19,000
- **Website:** www.SouthernEarlyChildhood.org

Freelance Potential
99% written by nonstaff writers. Publishes 40 freelance submissions yearly; 90% by unpublished writers, 80% by authors who are new to the magazine. Receives 7 unsolicited mss monthly.

Submissions
Send 4 copies of complete ms with bibliography. Accepts photocopies and disk submissions. SASE. Responds in 3–4 months.
Articles: Word length varies. Informational articles. Topics include early childhood care, day care, parent education, developmental curricula, personnel management, health, safety, and the moral, ethical, and spiritual development of children.
Depts/columns: Word length varies. Southern Early Childhood Association updates.

Sample Issue
40 pages (20% advertising): 5 articles; 4 depts/columns. Sample copy, $5. Guidelines available.
- "Paper Dolls: Back to Basics, with a Contemporary Twist." Article maintains that the use of personalized paper dolls can promote problem solving and creativity.
- "Camera in Action!" Article reports on a classroom observation that showed toddlers as competent and curious.
- Sample dept/column: "Book Reviews" looks at recent titles for early childhood educators.

Rights and Payment
All rights. No payment. Provides 1 contributor's copy.

Editor's Comments
Prospective authors must be familiar with our members' interests. Practical information that will advance the knowledge base of our profession is what we're looking for.

Dogs for Kids

P.O. Box 6050
Mission Viejo, CA 92690-6050

Managing Editor: Roger Sipe

Description and Readership
Kids and dogs have a natural affinity for each other and this magazine is a resource for making that association a positive one. Readers find information on different breeds, traveling with dogs, tips on the care of dogs, and different methods of training dogs.
- **Audience:** 10–15 years
- **Frequency:** Quarterly
- **Distribution:** Subscription; newsstand
- **Circulation:** Unavailable
- **Website:** www.dogsforkids.com

Freelance Potential
50% written by nonstaff writers. Publishes 15–25 freelance submissions yearly; 70% by authors who are new to the magazine. Receives 100 queries monthly.

Submissions
Query with writing samples. Accepts photocopies and computer printouts. SASE. Responds in 8–10 weeks.
Articles: 1,200–1,800 words. Informational and how-to articles; profiles; photoessays; and personal experience pieces. Topics include animals and pets.
Depts/columns: To 650 words. Tips on dog behavior, health, breeds, nutrition, and new products.
Other: Puzzles, activities, and games.

Sample Issue
48 pages (10% advertising): 5 articles; 7 depts/columns; 3 activities; 1 humorous page. Sample copy, $2.99 with 9x12 SASE. Guidelines available.
- "Camp Canine." Article touts the merits of a summer camp that is geared to kids and canines and teaching children about responsible dog ownership.
- "What's Up, Doc?" Article explains the profession of veterinary technician and the benefits and responsibilities that are part of the job.
- Sample dept/column: "Breed Files" profiles several different types of dogs from different groups, and gives their characteristics, personality traits, and needs.

Rights and Payment
First North American serial rights. All material, payment rate varies. Pays on publication. Provides 2 author's copies.

Editor's Comments
Please gear writing to pre- and early teens who own dogs. We cover different breeds, training, and a variety of opportunities available for expanding associations of kids and dogs.

Dolphin Log

The Cousteau Society
710 Settlers Landing Road
Hampton, VA 23669-4035

Editor: Lisa Rao

Description and Readership

The Cousteau Society, founded in 1974 by the famed underwater explorer Jacques Cousteau, publishes this magazine to educate children about the world's oceans and their diverse life forms.
• **Audience:** 7–13 years
• **Frequency:** 6 times each year
• **Distribution:** 100% membership
• **Circulation:** 80,000
• **Website:** www.dolphinlog.org

Freelance Potential

40% written by nonstaff writers. Publishes 4 freelance submissions yearly; 50% by authors who are new to the magazine. Receives 4 queries monthly.

Submissions

Query. Accepts photocopies, computer printouts, and simultaneous submissions if identified. SASE. Responds in 4–6 weeks.
Articles: 400–600 words. Shorter pieces, to 250 words. Informational articles. Topics include unique aquatic organisms, underwater habitats, ocean phenomena and environments, and the physical properties of water.
Depts/columns: Staff written.
Artwork: Color slides (duplicates only).
Other: Games based on scientific fact, original science experiments, or art projects related to an ocean theme.

Sample Issue

24 pages (no advertising): 5 articles; 1 comic strip; 1 quiz; 2 depts/columns. Sample copy, $2 with 9x12 SASE (3 first-class stamps). Guidelines available.
• "Return of the Killer Blob." Article reports on a patch of black water off the coast of Florida that proved deadly to fish and other forms of sea life.
• "Gulls Gulls Gulls." Article looks at some of the many species in this family of birds.

Rights and Payment

One-time and reprint rights; worldwide translation rights for use in other Cousteau Society publications. Pays on publication. Articles, $100–$300. Shorter pieces, $15–$100. Artwork, payment rate varies. Provides 3 contributor's copies.

Editor's Comments

By making children aware of the treasures of our oceans, we hope to instill an environmental awareness that they will carry into adulthood. We hope they will become advocates for protection of the oceans and their fragile ecosystems.

Dovetail

A Journal By and For Jewish/Christian Families

775 Simon Greenwell Lane
Boston, KY 40107

Editor: Debi Tenner

Description and Readership

The Dovetail Institute for Interfaith Family Resources, a nonprofit organization, publishes this newsletter to help Jewish and Christian partners explore the spiritual and religious dimensions of an interfaith household. It achieves this goal through articles free of proselytizing, pressure, or judgment.
• **Audience:** Interfaith families
• **Frequency:** 6 times each year
• **Distribution:** Subscription; other
• **Circulation:** 800
• **Website:** www.dovetailinstitute.org

Freelance Potential

80% written by nonstaff writers. Publishes 18 freelance submissions yearly; 90% by unpublished writers, 80% by authors who are new to the magazine. Receives 4 queries and unsolicited mss monthly.

Submissions

Query or send complete ms. Accepts photocopies, computer printouts, Macintosh and text file submissions, email submissions to DebiT4RLS@aol.com and simultaneous submissions if identified. SASE. Responds in 1–2 months.
Articles: 800–1,000 words. Informational articles, profiles, interviews, personal experience pieces, and reviews. Topics include interfaith marriage, parenting, family issues, social issues, and education.
Other: Poetry.

Sample Issue

16 pages (no advertising): 5 articles; 1 poem. Sample copy, $5.50 with 9x12 SASE ($.78 postage). Guidelines and theme list available.
• "Turning Differences into Opportunities." Personal experience piece recounts how a Catholic/Jewish couple draw from both of their religious traditions to keep God and an ethical way of life as their focus.
• "Planning an Interfaith Marriage Ceremony." Article advises couples on ways to include the best of two traditions in one harmonious ceremony.

Rights and Payment

One-time rights. Pays on publication. Articles, $25. Reviews, $15. Provides 2 contributor's copies.

Editor's Comments

We strive to be open to all ideas and opinions regarding the questions interfaith couples face. We respect the perspectives of both Jewish and Christian partners, as well as those of the parents and children of interfaith couples.

Dragon Magazine

Suite 110
3245 146th Place SE
Bellevue, WA 98007

Editor-in-Chief: Matthew Sernett

Description and Readership
This magazine is the source of official Dungeons & Dragons material for players and Dungeon Masters. With its emphasis on useful game content, *Dragon*'s articles introduce new game elements and provide tips on world or character building, game design, and roleplaying.
- **Audience:** YA–Adult
- **Frequency:** Monthly
- **Distribution:** Subscription; newsstand
- **Circulation:** 55,000
- **Website:** www.paizo.com/dragon

Freelance Potential
80% written by nonstaff writers. Publishes 350 freelance submissions yearly.

Submissions
Query with clips. Accepts photocopies and computer printouts. Prefers email submissions to dragon@paizo.com. No simultaneous submissions. SASE. Responds in 3 months.
Articles: Word length varies. Informational articles that provide new feats, weapons, spells, magic items, equipment, or prestige classes.
Depts/columns: Word length varies. Game strategies, advice.
Other: Comics.

Sample Issue
106 pages: 11 articles; 5 depts/columns; 3 comics. Sample copy, $5.99 at newsstands. Guidelines available at website.
- "The Way of the Gun." Article describes in detail several gunpowder weapons for D&D.
- "Planer Dragons." Article introduces five new planer dragons from the Outer Planes, which differ from dragons that dwell on the Material Planes.
- Sample dept/column: "DM's Toolbox" looks at the issue of dramatic irony—how to use or avoid it in your game.

Rights and Payment
All rights. Written material, $.05 per word. Pays on publication.

Editor's Comments
It's easier and almost always better to write about subjects that interest you. Writing for us can be an easy, fantastic experience, but you must do your homework before writing and familiarize yourself with our guidelines and the ways to write for the D&D system. Note that we will not publish an article written in the first person. If you must refer to some example from personal experience, do not use the first person to do so. The more work you do to adhere to our rules and formats, the greater your chance for acceptance.

Dramatics

Educational Theatre Association
2343 Auburn Avenue
Cincinnati, OH 45219

Editor: Donald Corathers

Description and Readership
Readers find information on drama, production, acting tips, industry news and events, and other topics that help improve the quality of secondary school theatre. Published by the International Thespian Society and read primarily by high school students, *Dramatics* helps students make an informed decision whether or not to pursue a career in theatre.
- **Audience:** High school students and teachers
- **Frequency:** 9 times each year
- **Distribution:** 100% subscription
- **Circulation:** 37,000
- **Website:** www.edta.org

Freelance Potential
90% written by nonstaff writers. Publishes 41 freelance submissions yearly; 5% by unpublished writers; 50% by authors who are new to the magazine. Receives 15 unsolicited mss each month.

Submissions
Send complete ms. Accepts photocopies and email submissions to dcorathers@edta.org. SASE. Responds 2–4 months.
Articles: 750–4,000 words. Informational articles; profiles; and interviews; and book reviews. Topics include playwriting, musical theater, acting, auditions, stage makeup, set design, and production.
Fiction: 500–3,500 words. Full-length and one-act plays suitable for high school audiences.
Artwork: 5x7 or larger B/W prints or 35mm or larger color transparencies. B/W line art. High-resolution JPGs or TIFFs.

Sample Issue
60 pages (40% advertising): 4 articles; 1 dept/column; 1 play. Sample copy, $2.50 with 9x12 SASE. Guidelines available.
- "Telling the Story" Article explores how actors can use conflict to assist them in effectively playing their character.
- "Korczak's Children." Play profiles a Polish pediatrician, who sheltered Jewish orphans during World War II.
- Sample dept/column: "Strut and Fret" compiles newsy items from the theatre industry.

Rights and Payment
First rights. Written material, $50–$400. Pays on acceptance. Provides 5 contributor's copies.

Editor's Comments
We are looking for more articles about the technical aspects of theatre production, and legitimate topics in film written by authors with experience in that field. Plays should be written with live theatre production in mind.

Drink Smart

Suite 200
110 Eglinton Avenue W
Toronto, Ontario M4R 1A3
Canada

Managing Editor: Julie Crljen

Description and Readership
Published exclusively on the Internet by the Young People's Press, *Drink Smart* addresses issues related to alcohol abuse and addiction. It advocates responsible drinking for young people of all ages and backgrounds.
- **Audience:** YA–Adult
- **Frequency:** Unavailable
- **Distribution:** 100% Internet
- **Hits per month:** Unavailable
- **Website:** www.drinksmart.org

Freelance Potential
95% written by nonstaff writers. Publishes 150–200 freelance submissions yearly; 70% by unpublished writers, 75% by authors who are new to the magazine.

Submissions
Send complete ms. Accepts email submissions to writeus@ypp.net. Responds immediately.
Articles: Word length varies. Informational articles; opinion and personal experience pieces. Topics include alcohol culture, responsible drinking, the effects of alcohol consumption, drinking and driving, domestic abuse, and the effects of alcohol abuse on careers, health, and relationships.

Sample Issue
Guidelines available at website.
- "Don't Do It." First-person essay tells the experiences of a youth who is pulled over for suspected drunk driving and the nightmare he faces if he is convicted.
- "Lessons Learned." Personal experience essay explains why a young man started drinking seriously when he was only 15 years old.
- "You Don't Drink!?" Essay explains one woman's challenges as she tries to fit in as a non-drinking Freshman in college.

Rights and Payment
Rights, payment rates, and payment policies vary.

Editor's Comments
Drinking has been a double-edged sword, and especially difficult for young people to understand. Our goal is to help young people learn the effects of drinking alcohol and to call for responsible drinking. Most of our writers are young people who use the e-zine as a forum in which to share their personal experiences and stories. We would like to see submissions that offer a positive message, if not a cautionary one. Tips for our readers about how to resist peer pressure or live a life of abstinence from alcohol are also welcome. Other topics covered are personal experiences with alcoholism, drunk driving, society's acceptance of drinking, and the culture of alcohol consumption.

Earlychildhood News

Suite 125
2 Lower Ragsdale
Monterey, CA 93940

Director of Publishing: Megan Shaw

Description and Readership
In addition to regular articles and departments, each issue of *Earlychildhood News* contains two approved CEU articles. Readers are parents, teachers, and other professionals who are involved with children to age eight. Education and curriculum information as well as development and behavioral issues are routinely covered in its content.
- **Audience:** Early childhood professionals and parents
- **Frequency:** 6 times each year
- **Distribution:** Subscription; controlled
- **Circulation:** 50,000
- **Website:** www.earlychildhoodnews.com

Freelance Potential
80% written by nonstaff writers. Publishes 35 freelance submissions yearly; 4% by unpublished writers, 10% by authors who are new to the magazine. Receives 3–4 queries and unsolicited mss monthly.

Submissions
Query with clips or writing samples; or send complete ms. Accepts photocopies, computer printouts, Macintosh disk submissions, or email to mshaw@excelligencemail.com. SASE. Responds in 2 months.
Articles: 600–1,200 words. Informational and self-help articles; success stories; and interviews. Topics include early childhood education; health and safety; advocacy; testing; multicultural subjects; family, social, and emotional issues; parenting; and professional development.
Depts/columns: 500 words. Crafts, cooking, and science activities.

Sample Issue
60 pages (50% advertising): 4 articles; 4 depts/columns; 2 CEU program articles. Sample copy, $3. Writers' guidelines and editorial calendar available.
- "Arts & Crafts." Article includes activities for infants, toddlers, preschoolers, and school-age children.
- Sample dept/column: "The Problem-Solving Parent" addresses the importance of play as an educational tool.

Rights and Payment
First rights. Articles, $75–$200. Depts/columns, payment rate varies. Pays on acceptance. Provides 1 copy.

Editor's Comments
We would like to receive submissions concerned with infant and toddler issues, math, childhood obesity, health-related articles, and music. We do not need articles on literacy at this time. Please refer to our guidelines for potential CEU articles.

Early Childhood Today

Scholastic Inc.
5th Floor
557 Broadway
New York, NY 10012-3999

Editor-in-Chief: Diane Ohanesian

Description and Readership

A valuable resource for early childhood educators, this magazine offers articles on issues related to child development, family, health, and safety. It also includes information on curriculum development and ideas for activity plans.
- **Audience:** Early childhood professionals
- **Frequency:** 8 times each year
- **Distribution:** Subscription; schools
- **Circulation:** 55,000
- **Website:** www.scholastic.com

Freelance Potential

85% written by nonstaff writers. Publishes 100 freelance submissions yearly; 5% by unpublished writers, 20% by authors who are new to the magazine. Receives 25 queries monthly.

Submissions

Query. Accepts computer printouts. SASE. Responds in 1 month.
Articles: Word length varies. Informational, educational, and how-to articles. Topics include child advocacy, child development, special needs education, family issues, health, music, computers, technology, and multicultural issues.
Depts/columns: Word length varies. News about early childhood issues, teaching tips, and teaching with technology.

Sample Issue

86 pages (8% advertising): 8 articles; 6 depts/columns. Sample copy, $3 with SASE. Guidelines available.
- "Exploring Science with Young Children." Interview with early childhood teacher, Kristal Rice, who shares her science curriculum and ideas to get children interested in science.
- "Teaching Science through the Visual Arts and Music." Article discusses how exploring materials helps children discover the wonders of the world.
- Sample dept/column: "Tough Talks" discusses children's challenging behaviors.

Rights and Payment

All rights. Written material, payment rate varies. Pays on acceptance. Provides 3 contributor's copies.

Editor's Comments

We provide teachers with the resources they need to meet the daily challenges they face in the classroom, and enhance their professional development. We seek articles and tips that are practical and informational and can be easily adapted in the classroom or at home. Make sure writing is friendly and conversational in tone, and that you have examples to support the information being presented. Most of our material comes from professionals in the field of early childhood education.

East of the Web

361 Manhattan Building
Fairfield Road
London E32UL
England

Editor: Alex Patterson

Description and Readership

East of the Web provides an opportunity for short story writers to have their work read by more readers than any other short story publication. The site is also frequented by agents, film makers, schools, universities, and the press, giving writers overall access to talent scouts. It also offers a link for writers to have their pieces critiqued before publication.
- **Audience:** All ages
- **Frequency:** Unavailable
- **Distribution:** 100% Internet
- **Hits per month:** 40,000+
- **Website:** www.eastoftheweb.com

Freelance Potential

96% written by nonstaff writers. Publishes 150 freelance submissions yearly; 50% by unpublished writers, 85% by authors who are new to the magazine. Receives 500+ unsolicited mss monthly.

Submissions

Send complete ms. Accepts email submissions to submissions@eastoftheweb.com (TEXT, RTF files, or Microsoft Word attachments). Responds in 3–4 months.
Fiction: Word length varies. Genres include contemporary fiction, mystery, folktales, fairy tales, humor, science fiction, and stories about animals.

Sample Issue

Guidelines available at website.
- "The Devoted Friend." Story weaves a message of the importance of friendship and how it can be taken advantage of by unscrupulous people who have a false sense of themselves.
- "High and Lifted Up." Story tells a tale of a young boy who becomes a leaf in autumn to play with his new friends and learns a life lesson in the process.
- "Marmalade." Story promotes the message that gardens, trees, and friends need attention and care to thrive and be able to offer their gifts, and if they don't receive this affection, their gifts will slowly disappear—just like them.

Rights and Payment

Non-exclusive rights. No payment.

Editor's Comments

Our site provides a high quality, respected setting for writers, and includes feedback from readers and other publishers. We do not publish every submission we receive, but we do read them all. Please include a brief biography.

Eclectic Homeschool Online

P.O. Box 50188
Sparks, NV 89435-0188

Acquisitions Editor

Description and Readership
Presented from a Christian perspective, this e-zine publishes encouraging, practical, insightful articles that reflect a creative and individual approach to homeschooling. Typical articles deal with real-life responses to homeschooling issues, choosing and using curricula or resources, and homeschooling as a Christian lifestyle.
• **Audience:** Adults
• **Frequency:** Monthly
• **Distribution:** 100% Internet
• **Hits per month:** Unavailable
• **Website:** www.eho.org

Freelance Potential
30% written by nonstaff writers. Publishes 30 freelance submissions yearly.

Submissions
Send complete ms; include 20- to 30-word author bio. Accepts email submissions to articles@eho.org. Responds in 2–3 months.
Articles: 1,000–3,000 words. Informational and how-to articles; profiles; interviews; personal experience pieces; and reviews. Topics include gifted and special education, music, sports, homeschooling issues, educational resource information, and Christian living.
Depts/columns: 400–700 words. Math, critical thinking, science, social studies, language arts, the arts, crafts, home and family, the Bible, computers, technology, college, and careers.
Other: Resources such as homeschool forms, charts, teacher's aids, and documents.

Sample Issue
Sample copy and guidelines available at website.
• "Motivation Tips." Article shares a homeschooling mother's advice for getting morning sessions started on time.
• "A Love of Writing." Article suggests that one of the best ways to teach writing to children is to have them copy down portions of good writing; this emulates the self-teaching method used by Jack London and Benjamin Franklin.

Rights and Payment
First and non-exclusive electronic rights. Articles, $100. Depts/columns, $35. Resources, payment rate negotiable. Payment policy varies.

Editor's Comments
We are a Christian publication, and although we do not limit ourselves to Christian material, we will not accept articles that include proselytizing other religions or worldviews.

The Edge

The Salvation Army
2 Overlea Boulevard
Toronto, Ontario M4H 1P4
Canada

Editor: John McAlister

Description and Readership
The Edge addresses real-life issues that are common among today's teens, and presents a Christian perspective on those issues. Interviews and profiles of Christian athletes, musicians, and entertainers are included in its editorial mix, giving readers positive role models who are successful in society.
• **Audience:** 14–18 years
• **Frequency:** 10 times each year
• **Distribution:** 90% controlled; 10% subscription
• **Circulation:** 5,000

Freelance Potential
80% written by nonstaff writers. Publishes 20 freelance submissions yearly; 50% by unpublished writers, 50% by authors who are new to the magazine. Receives 4 queries and unsolicited mss monthly.

Submissions
Query or send complete ms. Accepts disk submissions (Microsoft Word attachments) and email submissions to edge@can.salvationarmy.org. Availability of artwork may improve chance of acceptance. SAE/IRC. Responds in 2 weeks.
Articles: 400–500 words. How-to articles; profiles; and personal experience pieces. Topics include biography, humor, health, music, the environment, religion, social issues, sports, popular culture, computers, and college.
Fiction: 300 words. Problem-solving stories, humor, inspirational fiction, and stories about sports.
Depts/columns: 200 words. Advice and reviews.
Artwork: Color prints or transparencies.

Sample Issue
24 pages (no advertising): 10 articles;1 dept/column. Guidelines available.
• "Friendship Fix." Article examines how to build a bridge to reinstate a relationship after a falling out has occurred.
• "Chill Out." Article suggests ways to decrease the stresses common to teen years, including taking concerns to God.
• Sample dept/column: "Listen Up" critiques new music CDs.

Rights and Payment
First rights. All material, payment rate varies. Pays on publication. Provides 3 contributor's copies.

Editor's Comments
Our publication celebrates youth and encourages them in their spiritual growth. Articles should contain Christian truths or application without preaching or giving the impression of writing down to our readers. Conclusions or solutions presented should be consistent with biblical principles.

Edge for Kids

The Salvation Army
2 Overlea Boulevard
Toronto, Ontario M4H 1P4
Canada

Coordinator: Miriam Mills

Description and Readership
Articles, stories, puzzles, and activities for children fill the pages of this Canadian publication. Readers include children involved with the Salvation Army and its programs. Printed in digest-sized format, its focus is to create an awareness and spread the word of God.
- **Audience:** 7–12 years
- **Frequency:** Weekly
- **Distribution:** 100% controlled
- **Circulation:** 17,500
- **Website:** www.salvationarmy.ca

Freelance Potential
10% written by nonstaff writers. Publishes 12–15 freelance submissions yearly; 75% by authors who are new to the magazine. Receives 5–10 queries and unsolicited mss monthly.

Submissions
Query or send complete ms. Accepts photocopies, computer printouts, and simultaneous submissions if identified. SAE/IRC. Response time varies.
Articles: 200–300 words. Informational articles related to service and faith.
Fiction: 400–500 words. Inspirational and religious fiction.
Other: Puzzles, activities, and poetry.

Sample Issue
10 pages: 1 article; 2 stories; 4 puzzles; 6 activities. Sample copy, free. Guidelines available.
- "My Feelings Count." Story tells how a young boy who is feeling sad at school is reminded through examples in the Bible to pray to God for help.
- "When Sin Started." Article takes a look at how sin started in the Garden of Eden, and reminds readers that God forgives us for our sins.
- Sample dept/column: "Treasure Hunt" asks readers to find hidden objects in a picture.

Rights and Payment
Rights and payment policy vary. Provides copies.

Editor's Comments
We offer children a fun way to learn about the messages of God. Activities that teach a biblical lesson, and enforce Christian meaning are of interest to us. Most of our pages include puzzles, coloring pictures, math quizzes, mazes, and rhyming and matching games. We also use crafts and recipes. Although we are a Christian publication, we welcome submissions from all faiths.

Educational Horizons

Pi Lambda Theta
P.O. Box 6626
4101 East Third Street
Bloomington, IN 47407-6626

Managing Editor

Description and Readership
The International Honor Society, Pi Lambda Theta, publishes this magazine and through it strives to bring its readers articles that provide new insight into some aspect of education.
- **Audience:** Pi Lambda Theta members
- **Frequency:** Quarterly
- **Distribution:** 90% controlled; 10% subscription
- **Circulation:** 17,000
- **Website:** www.pilambda.org

Freelance Potential
95% written by nonstaff writers. Publishes 3 freelance submissions yearly; 80% by authors who are new to the magazine. Receives 5 queries, 10 unsolicited mss monthly.

Submissions
Query with outline/synopsis; or send complete ms with biography. Accepts photocopies, computer printouts, and simultaneous submissions if identified. Availability of artwork improves chance of acceptance. SASE. Responds to queries in 1 month, to mss in 3–4 months.
Articles: 3,500–5,000 words. Informational articles; research reports; and scholarly essays on national and international trends.
Depts/columns: 500–750 words. Multicultural education, educational topics in the news, international perspectives on education, legal issues, and book reviews.
Artwork: B/W prints and camera-ready illustrations.

Sample Issue
80 pages (4% advertising): 6 articles; 6 depts/columns. Sample copy, $5 with 9x12 SASE ($.87 postage). Guidelines and theme list available at website.
- "No Child Left Behind: The Mathematics of Guaranteed Failure." Article explores the new bill signed into law, and questions its ability to improve education.
- "Will Students with Disabilities Be Scapegoats for School Failures?" Article addresses the pros and cons of new federal legislation to improve education, and its possible negative impact on disabled students.
- Sample dept/column: "On Balance" features an essay on the new and developing relationship between liberal arts departments and schools of education.

Rights and Payment
First rights. No payment. Provides 5 contributor's copies.

Editor's Comments
We welcome educational papers that touch on some aspect of the international or national field of education.

Educational Leadership

1703 North Beauregard Street
Alexandria, VA 22311-1714

Editor: Margaret Scherer

Description and Readership
Focusing on all areas of education, this thematic publication offers articles on professional development, educational leadership, and capacity building. It is produced by the Association for Supervision and Curriculum Development and targets teachers, principals, superintendents, and other professionals and leaders interested in education.
- **Audience:** Educators
- **Frequency:** 8 times each year
- **Distribution:** 90% subscription; 10% schools
- **Circulation:** 170,000
- **Website:** www.ascd.org

Freelance Potential
90% written by nonstaff writers. Publishes 200 freelance submissions yearly; 50% by unpublished writers. Receives 125 unsolicited mss monthly.

Submissions
Send complete ms. Accepts computer printouts. SASE. Does not return mss. Responds in 1–2 months.
Articles: 1,500–2,500 words. How-to articles and personal experience pieces. Topics include health, fitness, computers, special and gifted education, social issues, religion, nature, science, technology, and multicultural and ethnic subjects.
Depts/columns: Word length varies. Association and education news, and opinion pieces. Also includes policy, book, and website reviews.

Sample Issue
96 pages (25% advertising): 16 articles; 5 depts/columns. Sample copy, $6. Guidelines and theme list available at website.
- "Partnering with Families and Communities." Article discusses the benefits of forming a school-learning community to improve schools and learning opportunities.
- "The Magic of Mentoring." Article takes a look at a what makes a mentoring program successful.
- Sample dept/column: "Research Link" takes a look at how a community influences a young person's school success.

Rights and Payment
First rights. No payment. Provides 5 contributor's copies.

Editor's Comments
Our readers cover the entire spectrum of educators; which our material reflects by offering multiple perspectives on key educational policies. Material should include practical examples, which highlight the key points. Each issue is organized around a theme and contains articles, reports, interpretations of research, and books reviews.

Education Forum

60 Mobile Drive
Toronto, Ontario M4A 2P3
Canada

Managing Editor: Marianne Clayton

Description and Readership
This educational publication is sponsored by Ontario's Secondary School Teacher's Federation. Its mission is to bring educators information on the latest teaching strategies, trends, education issues, and education in foreign countries, as well as profiles of successful teachers.
- **Audience:** Teachers
- **Frequency:** 3 times each year
- **Distribution:** 90% membership; 10% subscription
- **Circulation:** 48,000
- **Website:** www.osstf.on.ca

Freelance Potential
90% written by nonstaff writers. Publishes 35 freelance submissions yearly; 20% by unpublished writers, 80% by authors who are new to the magazine. Receives 4 queries and unsolicited mss monthly.

Submissions
Query with clips or writing samples; or send complete ms. Accepts photocopies. No simultaneous submissions. SAE/IRC. Responds in 1–2 months.
Articles: To 2,500 words. How-to and practical application articles on education trends; discussions of controversial issues; and teaching techniques for use in secondary school classrooms.
Depts/columns: "Openers" features news and opinion pieces, to 300 words. "Forum Picks" uses media and software reviews.
Artwork: B/W prints and line art for nonfiction pieces. Color prints and transparencies.
Other: Classroom activities, puzzles, and games. Submit seasonal material 8 months in advance.

Sample Issue
38 pages (18% advertising): 3 articles; 7 depts/columns. Sample copy, free with 9x12 SAE/IRC (Canadian postage). Guidelines available.
- "Gerard Kennedy." Article profiles the new Canadian educational minister.
- Sample dept/column: "International Perspective" features a look at the state of education in Cameroon.

Rights and Payment
First North American serial rights. No payment. Provides 5 contributor's copies.

Editor's Comments
We are interested in hands-on pieces on teaching strategies, articles on controversial issues facing teachers today, and first-person accounts of education in foreign countries.

Education Week

Suite 100
6935 Arlington Road
Bethesda, MD 20814-5233

Managing Editor: Greg Chronister

Description and Readership

First appearing in 1981, this tabloid offers articles on issues and developments in the field of education. It is read by educational professionals in elementary and secondary schools.
- **Audience:** Educators
- **Frequency:** Weekly
- **Distribution:** Subscription; schools; newsstand
- **Circulation:** 50,000
- **Website:** www.edweek.org

Freelance Potential

8% written by nonstaff writers. Publishes 125 freelance submissions yearly; 80% by unpublished writers, 75% by authors who are new to the magazine. Receives 50 unsolicited mss each month.

Submissions

Send complete ms. Accepts IBM disk submissions (WordPerfect or Microsoft Word) and Macintosh disk submissions (plain text). SASE. Responds in 6–8 weeks.
Articles: 1,200–1,500 words. Essays on child development and education related to grades K–12, for use in "Commentary" section.
Depts/columns: Staff written.

Sample Issue

52 pages (25% advertising): 24 articles; 15 depts/columns. Sample copy, $3 with 9x12 SASE ($1 postage). Writers' guidelines available.
- "Spotlight Shining on Overlooked Paraeducators." Article discusses the possible effects of the new requirements for paraeducators set by the federal government.
- "Study Finds Benefits in Teach for America." Article reports on the success of a program which recruits liberal-arts graduates to teach in disadvantaged rural and inner-city schools.
- "Faith Groups Express Belief in Federal Aid." Article takes a look at possible controversy over government supported faith group programs.

Rights and Payment

First rights. "Commentary," $200. Pays on publication. Provides 2 contributor's copies.

Editor's Comments

The only freelance materials we will consider are opinion essays for inclusion in our "Commentary" section. Most of our readers are already aware of basic issues in education; for this reason we usually accept only essays that treat specific topics in a detailed and analytical way. Check our guidelines for specific style rules before submitting.

Elementary School Writer

Writer Publications
P.O. Box 718
Grand Rapids, MN 55744-0718

Editor: Emily Benes

Description and Readership

Memories, past events, social issues, school and life experiences, imaginative stories, and poetry of all lengths make up this publication that showcases works by elementary school students for their peers throughout the country.
- **Audience:** Elementary school students
- **Frequency:** 6 times each year
- **Distribution:** 100% schools
- **Circulation:** Unavailable

Freelance Potential

100% written by nonstaff writers. Publishes 300 freelance submissions yearly; 95% by unpublished writers, 75% by authors who are new to the magazine. Receives 3,000 unsolicited mss each month.

Submissions

Accepts submissions from students of subscribing teachers in elementary school only. Send complete ms. Accepts photocopies, computer printouts, email submissions to writer@mx3.com (ASCII text only), and simultaneous submissions if identified. SASE. Response time varies.
Articles: To 1,000 words. Informational and how-to articles; profiles; and personal experience pieces. Topics include current events, humor, multicultural and ethnic issues, nature, the environment, popular culture, recreation, sports, and travel.
Fiction: To 1,000 words. Genres include humor and science fiction; and stories about nature, the environment, and sports.
Other: Poetry, no line limit. Seasonal material.

Sample Issue

8 pages (no advertising): 11 articles; 12 stories; 19 poems. Sample copy, free. Guidelines available in each issue.
- "Hating Hussein." Article examines the life and character of Saddam Hussein.
- "Pete Rose." Article puts forth the statistics of Pete Rose's baseball career and argues that his terrific record makes him a deserving candidate for the Baseball Hall of Fame.
- "Saving Bill." Story tells a tale of a magic carpet ride that brings the rider to a young boy who had been lost for a year, and brings them both back to safety.

Rights and Payment

One-time rights. No payment.

Editor's Comments

We are interested in bringing the efforts of young students to light. We only accept submissions by students whose teachers are subscribers to the publication. All material must be original, or with proper credit when appropriate.

Ellery Queen's Mystery Magazine

475 Park Avenue South
New York, NY 10016

Editor: Janet Hutchings

Description and Readership
Established in 1941, this magazine publishes all types of mystery short stories, including psychological suspense tales, deductive puzzles, and both realistic and imaginative crime fiction.
- **Audience:** YA–Adult
- **Frequency:** 11 times each year
- **Distribution:** 90% subscription; 10% newsstand
- **Circulation:** 180,780
- **Website:** www.themysteryplace.com

Freelance Potential
100% written by nonstaff writers. Publishes 125 freelance submissions yearly; 7% by unpublished writers, 20% by authors who are new to the magazine. Receives 200 unsolicited mss each month.

Submissions
Send complete ms. Accepts computer printouts and simultaneous submissions if identified. SASE. Responds in 2–3 months.
Fiction: 2,000–12,000 words. "Minute Mysteries," 250 words. Novellas by established authors, to 20,000 words. Genres include crime and psychological fiction; mystery; suspense; and detective and private-eye stories.
Other: Poetry, line length varies.

Sample Issue
144 pages (6% advertising): 8 stories; 3 interviews; 1 article. Sample copy, $5. Guidelines available.
- "The Wedding Gig." Tale of revenge about an overweight bride, the mob, and justice.
- "Cold Call." Agatha Christie-style story that takes place during a country manorhouse dinner party.
- "Director's Cut." Interview with film director David Koepp.

Rights and Payment
First and anthology rights. All material, $.05–$.08 per word. Pays on acceptance. Provides 3 contributor's copies.

Editor's Comments
We always need hard-boiled stories, from realistic police procedure-type stories to the more imaginative "locked room" and "impossible crime" stories. Note that we are not interested in true crime stories. With the exception of book reviews, we do not publish nonfiction. Our editors are especially happy to consider stories by authors who have never published fiction, as well as submissions by experienced writers. We have a distinct style that requires strong writing and an original plot.

The EMMC Recorder

P.O. Box 52059
Winnipeg, Manitoba R2M 5P9
Canada

Editor: Lil Goertzen

Description and Readership
Published by the Evangelical Mennonite Mission Conference, this newsletter provides church members with articles on theology, interviews with church leaders, and reports on local church events.
- **Audience:** YA–Adult
- **Frequency:** Monthly
- **Distribution:** 100% controlled
- **Circulation:** 3,100
- **Website:** www.emmc.ca

Freelance Potential
75% written by nonstaff writers. Publishes 100 freelance submissions yearly; 100% by unpublished writers, 70% by authors who are new to the magazine. Receives 13 unsolicited mss monthly.

Submissions
Send complete ms with photos. Accepts email submissions to info@emmc.ca. SAE/IRC. Responds in 1 week.
Articles: To 1,000 words. Informational articles; profiles; interviews; and personal experience pieces. Topics include religion, social issues, celebrating faith and tradition, family life, and regional news.
Artwork: B/W TIF or JPEG files.
Other: Puzzles, activities, and games. Submit seasonal material 6 months in advance.

Sample Issue
12 pages (16% advertising): 9 articles; 4 poems. Sample copy, free with #10 SAE/IRC ($.48 postage). Guidelines available.
- "Window on Our Churches." Article reports on local happenings among Evangelical Mennonite churches.
- "Rave for Youth." Article looks at current reality TV programs and suggests that true reality is reflected in the word of God.
- Sample dept/column: "Stewardship Today" emphasizes a donation plan for church members.

Rights and Payment
First rights. Pays on publication. Written material, $.05 per word. Artwork, payment rate varies.

Editor's Comments
Our newsletter focuses on what is currently happening in local EMMC churches and how those events relate to the EMMC as a whole. We would like to see more information on Christian literature for children ages five to twelve, as well as seasonal material on Easter, Mother's Day, Father's Day, Thanksgiving, and Christmas.

Encounter

Standard Publishing
8121 Hamilton Avenue
Cincinnati, OH 45231

Editor: Kelly Carr

Description and Readership
All the material in this weekly publication is written to help teens understand their Christian faith and to strengthen their ability to live a positive lifestyle.
- **Audience:** 13–19 years
- **Frequency:** Quarterly, in weekly editions
- **Distribution:** Churches, Christian bookstores
- **Circulation:** 30,000

Freelance Potential
90% written by nonstaff writers. Publishes 160 freelance submissions yearly; 15% by unpublished writers, 20% by authors who are new to the magazine. Receives 83 unsolicited mss each month.

Submissions
Query or send complete ms. Prefers email submissions to kcarr@standardpub.com. Accepts simultaneous submissions if identified. Responds in 1–2 months.
Articles: To 1,000 words. Self-help, how-to, and personal experience pieces; profiles; interviews; and humor. Topics include dating, friends, school, part-time jobs, current events, music, recreation, social issues, health, sports, and fitness.
Fiction: To 1,100 words. Problem-solving stories; contemporary, religious, inspirational, and ethnic fiction; humor; and stories about sports.
Other: Poetry written by teens only. Submit seasonal material 9–12 months in advance.

Sample Issue
8 pages (no advertising): 2 articles; 1 interview; 1 Bible lesson. Sample copy, free with 9x12 SASE (2 first-class stamps.). Guidelines and theme list available.
- "Why I Read the Bible." Article follows the progress of a young woman who first resisted, then found solace and interest in Scriptures.
- "Embodyment: Ministering Through Hard Rock." Interview shows how bass player Jason Lindquist found Jesus.
- Sample Dept/Column: "Walk in the Light" provides a week's worth of Scriptural readings and interpretations for each day.

Rights and Payment
First or one-time rights. Articles and fiction, $.06–$.08 per word. Pays on acceptance. Provides 5 contributor's copies.

Editor's Comments
We need nonfiction and fiction written to interest teens and exemplify a Christian point of view.

English Journal

English Department, 359 Eddy Hall
Colorado State University
1773 Campus Delivery
Fort Collins, CO 80523-1773

Editor: Dr. Louann Reid

Description and Readership
Articles on all aspects of teaching English language arts in junior high and high school are the focus of this professional journal. It also includes reviews of professional books and materials for teachers.
- **Audience:** English teachers
- **Frequency:** 6 times each year
- **Distribution:** 100% subscription
- **Circulation:** 40,000
- **Website:** www.ncte.org/ej

Freelance Potential
80% written by nonstaff writers. Publishes 75 freelance submissions yearly; 60% by unpublished writers, 75% by authors who are new to the magazine. Receives 50 unsolicited mss each month.

Submissions
Send 3 copies of complete ms; include a statement guaranteeing ms has not been published elsewhere. Accepts photocopies, computer printouts, and IBM disk submissions (WordPerfect 5.1 or higher) No simultaneous submissions. SASE. Responds in 2–3 months.
Articles: To 4,000 words. Informational articles; personal experience pieces; and position papers. Topics include teaching language arts, communication, grammar, classroom practice, young adult literature, and teaching materials.
Depts/columns: 1,500–2,000 words. Opinion pieces, book reviews, and classroom ideas.
Artwork: 8x10 B/W glossy prints. Line art.
Other: Poetry, to 40 lines. Original puzzles, cartoons, and games.

Sample Issue
128 pages (8% advertising): 11 articles; 14 depts/columns; 14 poems. Sample copy, $10. Guidelines and theme list available in each issue.
- "Transforming Seniors Who Don't Read into Graduates Who Do." Article explains how one teacher designed a senior English class to help students develop comprehension, fluency, and speed.
- Sample dept/column: "Speaking My Mind" offers a view of what teaching was like in the years prior to 1984.

Rights and Payment
First rights. No payment. Provides 2 contributor's copies.

Editor's Comments
We are looking for opinions, discussions, and arguments on teaching English language arts, as well as ideas for innovative classroom practices.

ePregnancy

P.O. Box 2102
Orinda, CA 94563

Editors: Nancy Price & Betsey Gartrell-Judd

Description and Readership
ePregnancy is both an online and a printed publication that addresses any issue relating to preconception, pregnancy, and the post-natal period. Health, fashion, relationships, careers, profiles, mental health, and beauty are all tackled.
- **Audience:** Expectant parents
- **Frequency:** Monthly
- **Distribution:** Internet, newsstand; subscription
- **Circulation:** 466,000
- **Website:** www.epregnancy.com

Freelance Potential
95% written by nonstaff writers. Publishes 300 freelance submissions yearly. Receives 80 queries and unsolicited mss each month.

Submissions
Prefers query. Accepts ms. Accepts photocopies, computer printouts, and submissions through the website. SASE. Response time varies.
Articles: 500–2,500 words. Informational, self-help, and how-to articles; profiles; interviews; humor; and reviews. Topics include preconception, pregnancy, and postpartum issues; health; fitness; social issues; education; and travel.
Depts/columns: Word length varies. Expert advice, fitness, and personal essays.

Sample Issue
128 pages: 20 articles; 14 depts/columns. Sample copy, $4.99 at newsstands. Guidelines available at website.
- "Amnios Need to Know." Article describes the process of having an anmiocentisis test done during the second trimester of pregnancy and the benefits and drawbacks of the procedure.
- "Pregnant? Or Not?" Article examines common symptoms of pregnancy and discusses what else they might mean.
- "Treat Your Feet!" Article recounts all the ways that pampered feet—from massages to warming socks—can help relieve the stress of pregnancy.

Rights and Payment
First print rights. Written material, $25–$50; $10 for reprints and first-person essays. Pays on publication.

Editor's Comments
We welcome freelance submissions, but discourage personal essays and opinion pieces. Check our website to discover our current needs and subject ideas. Plan to research the subject well, interview parents or experts, and complete the article in a writing style that is friendly and approachable.

eSchoolNews

Suite 900
7920 Norfolk Avenue
Bethesda, MD 20814

Editor: Greg Downey

Description and Readership
This publication is dedicated to providing the latest news and information to assist educational professionals in choosing the technology and tools needed to help their schools achieve their educational goals. Appearing in both print and electronically, it offers articles on technology, strategies, the Internet, services, and political issues that effect technology in schools.
- **Audience:** K–12 educators
- **Frequency:** Monthly
- **Distribution:** 100% subscription
- **Hits per month:** Unavailable
- **Website:** www.eschoolnews.com

Freelance Potential
20% written by nonstaff writers. Publishes 6–8 freelance submissions yearly. Receives 1 submission monthly.

Submissions
Prefers query. Accepts ms. Accepts photocopies, computer printouts, and email to GDowney@eschoolnews.com. SASE. Response time varies.
Articles: Word length varies. Informational and how-to articles; profiles; and reviews. Topics include gifted children, science, technology, social issues, and special education.
Depts/columns: Word length varies. News, reviews, grants and funding, community relations, and technology.

Sample Issue
62 pages (45% advertising): 2 articles; 25 depts/columns.
- "FBI Hits Schools, Colleges." Article discusses recent school raids, which are believed to be part of a larger crackdown on internet piracy.
- "Texas School Swaps Textbooks for Laptops." Article reports on a program that provides schools with laptops for learning to increase student interest in learning.
- Sample dept/column: "Netwatch" offers the latest in instructional resources on the Internet.

Rights and Payment
Rights vary. Payment rates vary. Pays on acceptance.

Editor's Comments
We provide school administrators and technological professionals with the information they need to make the best choices possible with regards to technology and the Internet. Our reporting covers all aspects of school technology news, events, issues, key players, products, services, and strategies as well as the business and political issues impacting school technology. Articles on topics related technology and gifted education, social issues, and special education are of interest to us.

Evangelizing Today's Child

Child Evangelism Fellowship
P.O. Box 348
Warrenton, MO 63383-0348

Editor: Elsie Lippy

Description and Readership

This resource for Sunday school teachers, Christian education leaders, and children's workers in every phase of Christian ministry for children 4 to 11 years of age, provides inspiration and ideas for them to use in teaching situations.
- **Audience:** Christian educators
- **Frequency:** 6 times each year
- **Distribution:** 75% subscription; 25% other
- **Circulation:** 14,000
- **Website:** www.etczine.com

Freelance Potential

50% written by nonstaff writers. Publishes 50 freelance submissions yearly; 5% by unpublished writers, 20% by authors who are new to the magazine. Receives 8–9 queries and unsolicited mss monthly.

Submissions

Query with outline; or send complete ms. Accepts photocopies, computer printouts, and email submissions to etceditor@cefonline.com. SASE. Responds to queries in 1 month, to mss in 2 months.
Articles: 1,000–2,000 words. How-to, factual, and personal experience pieces. Topics include Christian education, religion, teaching techniques, and crafts.
Fiction: 800–900 words for stories written at the third-and fourth-grade level. Features contemporary stories with scriptural solutions to problems faced by children.
Depts/columns: "Impact" uses human interest stories about people who, as children, find Jesus. "Resource Center" uses activities, ideas, object lessons, and seasonal material for Sunday schools and Bible clubs, 250–300 words.

Sample Issue

64 pages (25% advertising): 4 articles; 12 depts/columns; 1 skit; 7 teaching ideas; 5 reproducibles. Guidelines available.
- "We Give Because We Love." Article demonstrates how to instill a passion for lifelong giving in children.
- Sample dept/column: "Preteen Connection" shows how to awaken students' creativity and enjoyment of the arts.

Rights and Payment

All, first, one-time, or electronic rights. Written material, payment rate varies. Pays within 60 days of acceptance. Provides 1 contributor's copy.

Editor's Comments

We are interested in stories for children facing challenges in their homes, schools, and neighborhoods. Scriptural solutions should be worked into the text in a natural and believable style.

Exceptional Parent

65 East Route 4
Riveredge, NJ 07661

Editor-in-Chief: Dr. Rick Rader

Description and Readership

Exceptional Parent publishes articles on a broad variety of social, psychological, and educational concerns faced by individuals with disabilities and those who care for them.
- **Audience:** Parents, teachers, and professionals
- **Frequency:** Monthly
- **Distribution:** Subscription; controlled
- **Circulation:** 70,000
- **Website:** www.eparent.com

Freelance Potential

70% written by nonstaff writers. Publishes 40–50 freelance submissions yearly; 50% by unpublished writers, 50% by authors who are new to the magazine. Receives 8+ queries each month.

Submissions

Prefers query. Accepts photocopies, computer printouts, and Macintosh disk submissions. SASE. Accepts email to epedit@aol.com. Responds to queries in 3 weeks.
Articles: To 2,000 words. Informational articles; profiles; interviews; and personal experience pieces. Topics include the social, psychological, legal, political, technological, financial, and educational concerns of families with disabled members.
Depts/columns: Word length varies. Opinion and personal experience pieces, news items, and media reviews.

Sample Issue

98 pages (50% advertising): 10 articles; 12 depts/columns. Sample copy, $4.99 with 9x12 SASE ($2 postage). Guidelines and editorial calendar available.
- "Promoting Successful Transition from Pediatric to Adult-Oriented Health Care." Article offers tips on helping teenagers with special health care needs.
- "Parent Power 2004." Article stresses the importance of parental involvement in the ongoing care for children with special needs.
- Sample dept/column: "Idea Notebook" discusses how to ensure that recreation continues to be a regular part of the lives of special-needs children.

Rights and Payment

First North American serial rights. Written material, to $60. Provides 2 contributor's copies. Pays on acceptance.

Editor's Comments

Most of our material comes from individuals with disabilities, caregivers, physicians, or industry leaders with issues related to disabilities. Our tone is "how to work together." We seek useful material that is well researched and practical.

Faces

Cobblestone Publishing Company
Suite C
30 Grove Street
Peterborough, NH 03458

Editor: Elizabeth Carpentiere

Description and Readership

In each issue, *Faces* chooses one country or culture to present in a comprehensive manner. It's award-winning format introduces readers to foods, customs, languages, religions, cities, and histories from around the world.
- **Audience:** 9–14 years
- **Frequency:** 9 times each year
- **Distribution:** 100% subscription
- **Circulation:** 15,000
- **Website:** www.cobblestonepub.com

Freelance Potential

80% written by nonstaff writers. Publishes 80 freelance submissions yearly; 10% by unpublished writers, 35% by authors who are new to the magazine. Receives 30 queries monthly.

Submissions

Query with outline, bibliography and clips or writing samples. Accepts email queries to facesmag@yahoo.com. Availability of artwork improves chance of acceptance. SASE. Responds in 5 months.
Articles: 800 words. Informational articles and personal experience pieces related to the theme of each issue. Supplemental articles, 300–600 words.
Fiction: To 800 words. Stories, legends, and folktales from countries around the world, related to each issue.
Depts/columns: Staff written.
Artwork: Color prints and transparencies.
Other: Games, crafts, puzzles, and activities, to 700 words. Poetry, to 100 lines.

Sample Issue

48 pages (no advertising): 10 articles; 9 depts/columns; 1 activity. Sample copy, $4.95 with 9x12 SASE ($2 postage). Writers' guidelines and theme list available at website.
- "Bread With Everything: The Foods of Jordan." Article describes the foods that are typically found and served in Jordan, usually accompanied by a type of pita bread.
- "Traditional Culture: Etiquette and Body Language." Article stresses the importance of understanding accepted gestures and behavior when visiting a foreign country.

Rights and Payment

All rights. Articles and fiction, $.20–$.25 per word. Pays on publication. Provides 2 contributor's copies.

Editor's Comments

We would like more crafts and activities that are related to the theme of each issue.

Face Up

75 Orwell Road
Rathgar, Dublin 6
Ireland

Editor: Gerard Moloney

Description and Readership

The Irish Redemptorists, a religious order of men with a mission to spread the word of God through the print media, publish this magazine for "teens who want something deeper." It is one of several magazines produced by Redemptorist Publications.
- **Audience:** 14–18 years
- **Frequency:** 10 times each year
- **Distribution:** 80% schools; 15% subscription; 5% newsstand
- **Circulation:** 12,000
- **Website:** www.faceup.ie

Freelance Potential

100% written by nonstaff writers. Publishes 60 freelance submissions yearly; 30% by unpublished writers, 70% by authors who are new to the magazine. Receives 42 unsolicited mss each month.

Submissions

Send complete ms. Accepts email submissions to info@faceup.ie. Availability of artwork improves chance of acceptance. SAE/IRC. Responds in 1 month.
Articles: 900 words. Informational and how-to articles; profiles; interviews; and personal experience pieces. Topics include college, careers, current events, health, fitness, music, popular culture, and sports.
Depts/columns: 500 words. The Internet, health issues, opinion pieces, advice, and reviews.
Artwork: Color prints or transparencies.
Other: Submit seasonal material on Christmas, Easter, and final exams 3 months in advance.

Sample Issue

40 pages (5% advertising): 13 articles; 7 depts/columns. Sample copy, guidelines, and theme list available.
- "Roughing It." Article reports on the annual Christmas sleep out, a program that students from Dublin's Belvedere College take part in to raise money for the homeless.
- "Body Beautiful." Article promotes the goal of nutritionists who are trying to change the idea that stick-thin is normal and healthy.

Rights and Payment

Rights vary. All material, payment rate varies. Pays on publication. Provides 2 contributor's copies.

Editor's Comments

Our magazine delves into a variety of topics of importance in a teen's world with its thoughtful, insightful articles.

Family Circle

Gruner + Jahr Publishing
375 Lexington Avenue
New York, NY 10017

Senior Editor: Angela Ebron

Description and Readership

Every aspect of women's lives is covered in *Family Circle*, from parenting and cooking to fashion and decor. Articles focus on making life better, easier, healthier, more beautiful, more fulfilling, and more enjoyable. How-to information fills its pages along with helpful tips and recipes.
- **Audience:** Families
- **Frequency:** 15 times each year
- **Distribution:** 50% subscription; 50% newsstand
- **Circulation:** 5 million
- **Website:** www.familycircle.com

Freelance Potential

80% written by nonstaff writers. Publishes 50 freelance submissions yearly; 50% by unpublished writers, 20% by authors who are new to the magazine. Receives 25 queries monthly.

Submissions

Query with outline and 2 clips or writing samples. No simultaneous submissions. SASE. Responds in 6–8 weeks.
Articles: 2,000–2,500 words. Profiles of women who make a difference; reports on contemporary family issues; and real-life inspirational issues.
Depts/columns: 750–1,500 words. Beauty, fashion, health, legal issues, parenting, relationships, home decorating, food, and fitness.

Sample Issue

202 pages (48% advertising): 16 articles; 6 depts/columns; 1 mini-magazine. Sample copy, $2.50 at newsstands. Guidelines available.
- "From the Heart: Deep in the Heart of Texas." Article tells the story of families in a small town in Texas that have adopted 70 children.
- "What Makes Tweens Tick?" Article delves into the changes that occur in 9-to-12 year-old tweens.
- Sample dept/column: "FC Good Life" offers short items on food, fashion, entertainment, and other lifestyle trends.

Rights and Payment

Rights negotiable. Written material, $1 per word. Kill fee, 10%. Pays on acceptance. Provides 1 contributor's copy.

Editor's Comments

We are always looking for new contributors. We are a magazine with a focus on family issues. Accounts of women who have made a difference in their community are of special interest to us. We are also looking for dramatic personal experiences, and news and information on health, child care, and relationships.

The Family Digest

P.O. Box 40137
Fort Wayne, IN 46804

Manuscript Editor: Corine B. Erlandson

Description and Readership

This bimonthly publication is written for Catholic families interested in articles on church traditions, prayer, and spirituality. It also offers stories that demonstrate the many ways faith in God is part of the events of our everyday lives. It does not publish fiction.
- **Audience:** Families
- **Frequency:** 6 times each year
- **Distribution:** 100% controlled
- **Circulation:** 150,000

Freelance Potential

95% written by nonstaff writers. Publishes 60 freelance submissions yearly; 40% by authors who are new to the magazine. Receives 100 unsolicited mss monthly.

Submissions

Send complete ms. Accepts photocopies and computer printouts. No simultaneous submissions; previously published material will be considered. SASE. Responds in 1–2 months.
Articles: 750–1,300 words. Informational, how-to, inspirational, and self-help articles; and personal experience pieces. Topics include family life, parish life, prayer, spirituality, Catholic church traditions, and friendship.
Other: Humorous anecdotes, 25–100 words. Cartoons. Submit seasonal material 7 months in advance.

Sample Issue

48 pages (no advertising): 10 articles; 5 depts/columns. Sample copy, free with 6x9 SASE (2 first-class stamps). Writers' guidelines available.
- "Are You a Good Neighbor?" Article offers ideas for how to connect with your community by reaching out to neighbors.
- "Practical Prayer." The many roles prayer can play in daily life are covered here.
- "Our Cat Got Us Through Hard Times." Essay on how a cat's entertainment helped a family through illness and death by keeping them laughing in spite of the odds.

Rights and Payment

First North American serial rights. Articles, $40–$60. Anecdotes, $25. Pays 1–2 months after acceptance. Provides 2 contributor's copies.

Editor's Comments

Our publication is dedicated to the joy and fullfillment of Catholic family life. We like to see an upbeat message in all of our articles. Topics of interest incude prayer and family life, spirituality, saints' biographies, seasonal celebrations, and church traditions.

Family Digest Baby

Suite 349
696 San Ramon Valley
Danville, CA 94256

Editor

Description and Readership
This magazine focuses exclusively on pregnancy, infancy, and toddlerhood. It targets an audience of African American parents.
- **Audience:** Parents
- **Frequency:** Quarterly
- **Distribution:** 80% subscription; 20% newsstand
- **Circulation:** Unavailable
- **Website:** www.familydigestbaby.com

Freelance Potential
90% written by nonstaff writers. Publishes 100 freelance submissions yearly; 20% by unpublished writers, 20% by authors who are new to the magazine. Receives 60 queries monthly.

Submissions
Query with clips or writing samples. Accepts email submissions to editor@familydigestbaby.com. SASE. Response time varies.
Articles: 1,000–2,000 words. Informational and how-to articles. Topics include baby and toddler care, child development, pregnancy, relationships, and multicultural issues.
Depts/columns: 800–1,400 words. Health issues of babies and mothers, Q&As.
Artwork: Color prints or transparencies.
Other: Filler, activities, and games.

Sample Issue
100 pages (35% advertising): 3 articles; 8 depts/columns. Sample copy, $3. Guidelines available.
- "The Importance of Letting Your Child Know You Love Them." Article explains that children need unconditional love from their parents in order to develop into happy, well-adjusted adults.
- "What to Do When Your Baby Is Vomiting." Article discusses causes, treatments, and the various ailments connected with this symptom.
- "Marriage Makeover." Article looks at the ways children and work can cause a relationship to wither.

Rights and Payment
All rights. All material, payment rate varies. Pays on publication. Provides 2 contributor's copies.

Editor's Comments
We encourage a mix of approaches to article writing, such as narratives, profiles, how-to's, and Q&As. Please indicate in your query which approach you would like to use. We suggest potential writers send for a sample copy prior to submitting material to us. Most of our rejections are for inappropriate submissions.

Family Doctor

P.O. Box 38790
Colorado Springs, CO 80937-8790

Managing Editor: Leigh Ann Hubbard

Description and Readership
Subtitled "The Magazine that Makes Housecalls," this publication is a source for upbeat, reliable medical information and advice. It focuses on mainstream medicine and looks at alternative treatments from a scientific, studied point of view.
- **Audience:** Women
- **Frequency:** 6 times each year
- **Distribution:** Unavailable
- **Circulation:** 10,000
- **Website:** www.familydoctormag.com

Freelance Potential
100% written by nonstaff writers. Publishes 100 freelance submissions yearly; 1% by unpublished writers, 15% by authors who are new to the magazine. Receives 12 queries and unsolicited mss monthly.

Submissions
Query with writing samples. Prefers email submissions to managingeditor@familydoctormag.com. Accepts photocopies and computer printouts. SASE. Responds in 1 month.
Articles: 1,500 words. Informational articles and personal experience pieces. Topics include health, fitness, nutrition, preventive medicine, lifestyles, and safety.
Depts/columns: 200–500 words. Medical studies and medical breakthroughs.
Other: Filler, 250 words.

Sample Issue
66 pages (2% advertising): 8 articles; 14 depts/columns; 1 calendar. Sample copy available at newsstand. Writers' guidelines available.
- "29 Ways to Build a Better Relationship with Your Physician." Article compiles suggestions from several physicians.
- "Stop the Pain." Article details the advances in available chronic-pain treatments.
- Sample dept/column: "Living With" relates a young woman's experience with her eating disorder.

Rights and Payment
First North American serial, exclusive syndication for one year, and non-exclusive rights. Written material, $.30 per word. Pays on publication.

Editor's Comments
Most of our material is written by physicians or other healthcare professionals. Non-healthcare contributors should focus on personal stories for our "Living With" column, or on recent medical studies, techniques, or developments that can be covered in 500 words or less.

FamilyFun

Disney Publishing Company
244 Main Street
Northampton, MA 01060

Jean Graham

Description and Readership

This colorful, fast-paced publication concentrates on activities families can enjoy together. It also includes views on family relationships, travel ideas, book and video reviews, and delicious recipes for the entire family.

- **Audience:** Parents
- **Frequency:** 10 times each year
- **Distribution:** Subscription; newsstand
- **Circulation:** 1.85 million
- **Website:** www.familyfun.com

Freelance Potential

50% written by nonstaff writers. Publishes 100+ freelance submissions yearly; 1% by unpublished writers, 5% by authors who are new to the magazine. Receives 450 unsolicited mss each month.

Submissions

Query with clips or writing samples. No unsolicited mss. Accepts photocopies and letter-quality computer printouts. SASE. Responds in 2–3 months.

Articles: 850–3,000 words. Informational and how-to articles. Topics include cooking, games, activities, crafts, educational projects, sports, holiday parties, travel, and creative solutions to household problems.

Depts/columns: 1,500 words. News items about family travel, media reviews, and inspirational or humorous pieces focusing on family life.

Other: Submit seasonal material 6 months in advance.

Sample Issue

112 pages (47% advertising): 6 articles; 9 depts/columns. Sample copy, $3.50 at newsstands. Guidelines available.

- "Secrets of Organized Moms." Article dishes up uncommonly sensible ideas for organizing a home.
- "A Fabulous Flower Party." Article gives step-by-step instructions for a girl's birthday party that includes ideas for food, decorations, refreshments, and games.
- Sample dept/column: "Family Ties" presents thoughtful insights from a mother who finally recognizes the abilities of her middle child.

Rights and Payment

All rights. Articles, $.50–$1 per word. Other material, payment rate varies. Pays on acceptance.

Editor's Comments

We take fun seriously and look for fun-loving, creative ideas that are inexpensive and easy to do. Travel information is kept within the United States.

FamilyWorks Magazine

4 Joseph Court
San Rafael, CA 94903

Editor: Lew Tremaine

Description and Readership

This magazine serves as an outreach program for its parent company, the nonprofit agency FamilyWorks. Its editorial content furthers the agency's mission to strengthen families and promote healthy communities in California's Marin and Sonoma Counties.

- **Audience:** Parents, caregivers, and professionals
- **Frequency:** Monthly
- **Distribution:** 50% newsstand; 40% schools; 10% subscription
- **Circulation:** 30,000
- **Website:** www.familyworks.org

Freelance Potential

90% written by nonstaff writers. Publishes 18 freelance submissions yearly; 25% by unpublished writers, 25% by authors who are new to the magazine. Receives 8 unsolicited mss monthly.

Submissions

Send complete ms. Accepts computer printouts, Macintosh disk submissions, and email submissions to familynews@ familyworks.org. Availability of artwork improves chance of acceptance. SASE. Responds in 1 month.

Articles: 1,000 words. Informational articles; profiles; and interviews. Topics include parenting, family issues, recreation, education, finance, crafts, hobbies, sports, health, fitness, nature, and the environment.

Depts/columns: Word length varies. Reviews and organizational news.

Artwork: B/W and color prints.

Sample Issue

40 pages (46% advertising): 5 articles; 8 depts/columns. Sample copy, free. Guidelines available.

- "Reducing Junk Food Reaps Unexpected Benefits." Article reports that restricting student access to junk food in schools has not only curbed childhood obesity, but has also resulted in better behavior and concentration.
- "Angry Spinach and Other Green Things." Humorous essay describes how one woman discreetly introduced healthy foods into her family's diet.

Rights and Payment

One-time rights. No payment. Provides 3 contributor's copies.

Editor's Comments

Our contributors submit material that entertains, informs, or encourages our readers. Insightful first-person stories about family members or group interactions are welcome.

Faze Teen

Suite 2400
4936 Yonge Street
Toronto, Ontario M2N 6S3
Canada

Editor: Lorraine Zander

Description and Readership
Targeting Canadian teenagers, this exciting magazine offers readers an inspiring and insightful look at real-life issues, current events, entertainment, science, technology, business, and health and fitness. It is read by both boys and girls, and is available online and in print.
- **Audience:** 13–18 years
- **Frequency:** Quarterly
- **Distribution:** Subscription; newsstand; school libraries; Internet
- **Circulation:** 250,000
- **Website:** www.fazeteen.com

Freelance Potential
80% written by nonstaff writers. Publishes 50 freelance submissions yearly; 90% by authors who are new to the magazine. Receives 8 queries, 2 unsolicited mss monthly.

Submissions
Query or send complete ms. SAE/IRC. Response time varies.
Articles: Word length varies. Informational and factual articles; personal experience pieces; profiles; and interviews. Topics include current affairs, real-life issues, famous people, entertainment, science, travel, business, technology, and health.
Depts/columns: Word length varies. Media reviews.

Sample Issue
66 pages (3% advertising): 13 articles; 7 depts/columns. Sample copy, $3.50 Canadian. Guidelines available at website.
- "Psst . . ." Article discusses the long term effects gossiping has on victims, the history of gossip, and ways to respond to hearing it.
- "Hillary Duff." Article takes a look at the challenging life of this teen actress/singer.
- Sample dept/column: "Tech Talk" takes a look at the growing trend of using abbreviated sentences for communicating electronically.

Rights and Payment
All rights. No payment.

Editor's Comments
We offer readers an alternative to teen magazines that are filled with the usual pop culture by offering well-written real-life stories, empowering informational pieces, investigative reports, and profiles of interesting people. A good part of our material is written by teens and other young adults. Our publication is responsive and evolves according to the wishes of our teen readers. Send us something that is fresh and entertaining but also inspirational and thought provoking.

FitPregnancy

21100 Erwin Street
Woodland Hills, CA 91367

Executive Editor: Sharon Cohen

Description and Readership
Expectant mothers find articles on health, nutrition, exercise, psychology, food, fashion, and beauty related to pregnancy in this magazine. New mothers with babies up to the age of two also read *FitPregnancy* for information on fitness, lifestyle issues, and baby and toddler care.
- **Audience:** Adults
- **Frequency:** 6 times each year
- **Distribution:** 60% subscription; 40% newsstand
- **Circulation:** 500,000
- **Website:** www.fitpregnancy.com

Freelance Potential
75% written by nonstaff writers. Publishes 50 freelance submissions yearly; 3% by unpublished writers, 5% by authors who are new to the magazine. Receives 30 queries monthly.

Submissions
Query with clips. Accepts photocopies and computer printouts. SASE. Responds in 1 month if interested.
Articles: 1,200–2,400 words. Informational articles and personal experience pieces. Topics include health, fitness, family issues, psychology, postpartum issues, and breastfeeding.
Fiction: Word length varies. Publishes humorous fiction.
Depts/columns: 600 words. Nutrition, baby care, food, fashion, beauty, news items, and new product information.

Sample Issue
132 pages (42% advertising): 9 articles; 17 depts/columns. Sample copy, $4.95 at newsstands. Guidelines available.
- "A Perfect Plan." Article compiles a shopping list, five-day meal plan, and recipes for complete and easy pregnancy nutrition.
- "Surf & Turf." Article recommends a plan for walking workouts on land and in the water.
- Sample dept/column: "Health" outlines what you need to know if you're over 40 and thinking of getting pregnant.

Rights and Payment
Rights vary. Written material, payment rate varies. Pays on publication. Provides 2 contributor's copies.

Editor's Comments
Our articles are meant to encourage women to stay healthy and fit during pregnancy. When it comes to caring for their newborns, we want to let new moms know they can trust themselves and their instincts. Our articles are informative, but never written in a condescending tone. Queries should be specific. Read our magazine and tell us whether you are presenting an idea for a feature or for a specific column.

Florida Leader

Oxendine Publishing
P.O. Box 14081
Gainesville, FL 32604-2081

Associate Editor: Stephanie Reck

Description and Readership
This special-interest journal is read by students interested in attending colleges and universities in Florida. Each issue includes stories related to leadership, college life, student government, and other subjects related to volunteers and leaders in college.
- **Audience:** 15–22 years
- **Frequency:** 3 times each year
- **Distribution:** 95% schools; 5% subscription
- **Circulation:** 45,000
- **Website:** www.floridaleader.com

Freelance Potential
10% written by nonstaff writers. Publishes 5 freelance submissions yearly; 50% by unpublished writers, 80% by authors who are new to the magazine. Receives 12 queries monthly.

Submissions
Query. No unsolicited mss. Accepts photocopies, computer printouts, and simultaneous submissions if identified. SASE. Responds in 3 weeks.
Articles: 1,000 words. Informational, self-help, and how-to articles. Topics include colleges, universities, undergraduate life, financial aid, admissions requirements, majors, and student leadership.
Depts/columns: Word length varies. Information on careers and education.
Artwork: B/W and color prints and slides.

Sample Issue
30 pages (50% advertising): 11 articles. Sample copy, guidelines, and editorial calendar available.
- "It's a Green Thing." Article profiles collegiate environmental groups that are making a difference.
- "Make It Happen!" Article features tips on how to plan and achieve goals.
- "Eight Is Enough." Article profiles eight very different students who came together to help their college community.

Rights and Payment
All rights. Pays on publication. All material, payment rate varies. Provides 2 contributor's copies.

Editor's Comments
We will consider articles for graduating high school students and those students already in college or university. We look for writers who can bring solid research to our readers in a way that is hands-on and entertaining. Personal essays on topics like "my first year at college" are not what we are looking for. Send us an idea that will motivate others to move on your original idea.

Focus on the Family Clubhouse

8605 Explorer Drive
Colorado Springs, CO 80902

Associate Editor: Suzanne Hadley

Description and Readership
A strong Christian theme runs through this magazine for middle-grade readers. Stories utilize situations relevant to the target audience to make a moral point. Content blends parents' desire for wholesome, scriptural inspiration with an element of adventure, action, or humor.
- **Audience:** 8–12 years
- **Frequency:** Monthly
- **Distribution:** 100% subscription
- **Circulation:** 115,000
- **Website:** www.clubhousemagazine.com

Freelance Potential
20% written by nonstaff writers. Publishes 12–15 freelance submissions yearly; 5% by unpublished writers, 5% by authors who are new to the magazine. Receives 95 unsolicited mss each month.

Submissions
Send complete ms. Accepts photocopies and computer printouts. SASE. Responds in 4–6 weeks.
Articles: 800–1,000 words. Informational how-to, and factual articles; interviews; personal experience pieces; and humor. Topics include sports, nature, history, fantasy, religion, current events, and multicultural issues.
Fiction: 800–1,400 words. Genres include historical, contemporary, and religious fiction; parables; and mystery.
Other: Activities and Bible-related comics. Submit Christian holiday material 7 months in advance.

Sample Issue
24 pages (5% advertising): 4 articles; 3 stories; 1 dept/column; 1 poem; 3 activities; 1 comic. Sample copy, $1.50 with 9x12 SASE (2 first-class stamps). Guidelines available.
- "Hiding Out." Article showcases a variety of interesting insects in their habitats.
- "The Right Answer." Story demonstrates the importance of standing up for strong personal beliefs.
- Sample dept/column: "God's Secret Garden" explores life on the ocean floor.

Rights and Payment
First rights. Written material, to $200. Pays on acceptance. Provides 5 contributor's copies.

Editor's Comments
We would like to see more seasonal pieces and a variety of cultural stories that provide insight into the types of diversity prevalent in today's world. We are not looking for fiction about middle-class lifestyles, poetry, or stories about boy-girl relationships.

Focus on the Family Clubhouse Jr.

8605 Explorer Drive
Colorado Springs, CO 80920

Associate Editor: Suzanne Hadley

Description and Readership
Christian beliefs and family values form the basis of this magazine's content. Stories and articles are designed to teach and entertain young readers while inspiring them to emulate the positive examples.
- **Audience:** 4–8 years
- **Frequency:** Monthly
- **Distribution:** 98% subscription; 2% newsstand
- **Circulation:** 105,000
- **Website:** www.clubhousemagazine.org

Freelance Potential
20% written by nonstaff writers. Publishes 6–12 freelance submissions yearly; 1% by unpublished writers, 5% by authors who are new to the magazine. Receives 60 unsolicited mss each month.

Submissions
Send complete ms. Accepts photocopies and computer printouts. No simultaneous submissions. SASE. Responds in 4–6 weeks.
Articles: 200–500 words. Informational articles. Topics include the environment, nature, hobbies, health, and fitness.
Fiction: 25–1,000 words. Genres include Bible stories; humor; folktales; and religious, contemporary, and historical fiction.
Other: Puzzles, activities, games, cartoons, and poetry with biblical themes. Submit seasonal material 6 months in advance.

Sample Issue
16 pages (no advertising): 3 articles; 1 story; 1 activity; 1 book review; 1 comic; 1 poem. Sample copy, $1.50 with 9x12 SASE (2 first-class stamps). Guidelines available.
- "Amazing Ride." Article describes what Alaska's famous Iditarod race is all about.
- "Puppy Love." Article expands the Iditarod theme by featuring two girls in Alaska who help their dad with racing dogs.
- "Peep, Cheep, and Quack!" Story utilizes a familiar barnyard scene to demonstrate a Christian principle.

Rights and Payment
First North American one-time rights. Written material, to $200. Pays on acceptance. Provides 5 contributor's copies.

Editor's Comments
Activities are important to our young audience, and we are looking for seasonal items, poetry, rebus stories, puzzles, and recipes. Poems should be biblically based and reflect real-life experiences of young children. Humorous, descriptive poetry is a plus.

Footsteps
African American History

Cobblestone Publishing
Suite C, 3 Grove Street
Peterborough, NH 03458

Associate Editor: Rosalie F. Baker

Description and Readership
This educational publication was developed by Cobblestone Publishing and focuses on African American history and covers a wide range of related topics. All issues are themed-based and an editorial calendar is available at the company's website.
- **Audience:** 9–14 years
- **Frequency:** 5 times each year
- **Distribution:** 100% subscription
- **Circulation:** 6,000
- **Website:** www.footstepsmagazine.com

Freelance Potential
80% written by nonstaff writers. Publishes 100 freelance submissions yearly; 40% by unpublished writers, 60% by authors who are new to the magazine. Receives 8 queries monthly.

Submissions
Query with résumé. Accepts photocopies, computer printouts, and Macintosh disk submissions. SASE. Responds in 1–3 months.
Articles: 200–1,000 words. Informational articles; profiles; and interviews. Topics include history and multicultural issues. Also publishes biographies.
Depts/columns: 200–1,000 words. Reviews and reader's poems and artwork.
Artwork: B/W and color prints or transparencies. Line art.
Other: Theme-related activities.

Sample Issue
50 pages (no advertising): 13 articles; 6 depts/columns; 3 activities. Sample copy, $4.50 with 9x12 SASE ($1.24 postage). Guidelines and theme list available.
- "Learning the Best from Charles Hamilton Houston." Article profiles a lawyer who was a legal crusader against racial discrimination.
- "Face to Face with Prejudice." Article chronicles the early years of Supreme Court Justice Thurgood Marshall.
- Sample dept/column: "Descendants" features an interview with John W. Marshall, son of Thurgood Marshall.

Rights and Payment
All rights. Pays on publication. Written material, $.20 per word. Artwork, payment rate varies. Provides 2 copies.

Editor's Comments
All of our material follows our editorial calendar, and we are only interested in queries related to these topics. We work many months ahead of publication so if you are interested, please review topics well before the issue is published.

Fort Worth Child

Lauren Publications
Suite 146
4275 Kellway Circle
Addison, TX 75001

Editor: Shelley Pate

Description and Readership

Parents who are expecting, as well as families with children are the target audience of this regional publication. *Fort Worth Child* strives to meet the needs of parents on all fronts—from child care to education, health, and travel.
- **Audience:** Parents
- **Frequency:** Monthly
- **Distribution:** 90% controlled; 10% subscription
- **Circulation:** 120,000
- **Website:** www.fortworthchild.com

Freelance Potential

25% written by nonstaff writers. Publishes 12–15 freelance submissions yearly; 20% by authors who are new to the magazine. Receives 20 queries monthly.

Submissions

Query with resume. Accepts photocopies, computer printouts, and simultaneous submissions if identified. SASE. Responds in 2–3 months.
Articles: 1,000–2,500 words. Informational, self-help, how-to articles; humor; profiles; and personal experience pieces. Topics include family, parenting, education, health, nutrition, exercise, travel, crafts, hobbies, computers, regional news, and multicultural and ethnic issues.
Depts/columns: 800 words. Health news and reviews.

Sample Issue

46 pages (14% advertising): 2 articles; 8 depts/columns. Sample copy, free with 9x12 SASE. Guidelines available.
- "Trading Spaces." Article addresses the new exodus of families back into downtown Fort Worth.
- "Kids Bored?" Outdoor activities and adventures for the family are profiled in this article.
- Sample dept/column: "In the Know" discusses the connection between TV watching and ADHD; poison control; shoes for babies; and water safety for kids.

Rights and Payment

First rights. Written material, payment rate varies. Pays on publication. Provides contributor's copies upon request.

Editor's Comments

Our goal is to keep families current on the issues that concern the Fort Worth area and have an impact on their lives. All of our features have a strong local or regional angle, no matter what the subject. We like to hear from writers who can deliver stories that are timely and informative and if you can provide a new twist on familiar topic, so much the better. Any topic that relates to parenting is of interest to us but serious issues take priority.

Fostering Families Today

Unit N
541 East Garden Drive
Windsor, CO 80550

Editor

Description and Readership

Informational and educational material on topics related to adoption and foster care fill the pages of this resourceful magazine. It offers articles and essays for families and individuals interested in international, national, and domestic adoption and foster care.
- **Audience:** Parents
- **Frequency:** 4 times each year
- **Distribution:** Subscription
- **Circulation:** Unavailable
- **Website:** www.adoptinfo.net

Freelance Potential

50% written by nonstaff writers. Publishes several freelance submissions yearly.

Submissions

Send complete ms. Accepts photocopies, computer printouts, IBM disk submissions (Microsoft Word or ASCIII), and email to fft@netcarrier.com. SASE. Response time varies.
Articles: 1,200 words. Informational and how-to articles; profiles; and personal experience pieces. Topics include parenting, pertinent research, health and family, adoption, single parenting, adolescence, special-needs children, foster parenting, multicultural families, issues in education, and legal issues.
Depts/columns: Word length varies. Parenting topics, events, cultural information, identity formation, and reviews.

Sample Issue

62 pages (no advertising): 17 articles; 12 depts/columns. Guidelines available.
- "I Was That Child." Essay reflects on the author's thoughts of the foster care system, which she was in as a child for ten years, and her determination to help children.
- "A Day at the Clinic." Article tells of a foster mother's difficulty in attending to her child's needs and keeping a good relationship with the baby's parents during a clinic visit.
- Sample dept/column: "Crossing the Line" takes a look at the importance of getting the flu shot early.

Rights and Payment

Rights vary. Payment rates and policies vary. Provides 2 contributor's copies.

Editor's Comments

We seek articles and personal experience pieces that deal with issues such as multicultural families, parenting, children with special needs, and health issues. Families turn to us to keep them up-to-date with legal issues, and other issues on adoption and fostering.

Fox Valley Kids

P.O. Box 45050
Madison, WI 53744-5050

Editor: Barb Schmitz

Description and Readership

Parents living in the Wisconsin communities of Appleton, Oshkosh, Neenah, Menasha, Kimberly, Kaukauna, Little Chute, Fond du Lac, and Darboy turn to this tabloid for its articles and news about children, parenting, and family life.
- **Audience:** Parents
- **Frequency:** Monthly
- **Distribution:** Schools; libraries; other
- **Circulation:** 24,000
- **Website:** www.ericksonpublishing.com

Freelance Potential

70% written by nonstaff writers. Publishes 60 freelance submissions yearly; 10% by unpublished writers, 60% by authors who are new to the magazine. Receives 83 queries and unsolicited mss monthly.

Submissions

Query or send complete ms. Accepts photocopies, computer printouts, and disk submissions (RTF files). SASE. Response time varies.
Articles: To 750 words. Informational articles and humorous pieces. Topics include parenting, family issues, education, gifted and special education, regional and national news, crafts, hobbies, music, the arts, health, fitness, sports, animals, pets, travel, popular culture, and multicultural and ethnic issues.
Depts/columns: To 750 words. Women's and children's health, school news, and personal experience essays.
Artwork: B/W and color prints. Line art.
Other: Submit seasonal material 4 months in advance.

Sample Issue

16 pages (60% advertising): 2 articles; 5 depts/columns; 1 events calendar. Sample copy, free with 9x12 SASE. Writers' guidelines and editorial calendar available.
- "Expecting the Unexpected." Article describes the challenges a family experiences when they find out a child has Down's syndrome.
- "Get Scrapping." Article takes a look at the joys of scrapbooking and offers tips on getting started.
- Sample dept/column: "Money Matters" discusses college savings plans.

Rights and Payment

Rights negotiable. All material, payment rate varies. Pays on publication. Provides 2 contributor's copies.

Editor's Comments

We are always looking for fresh ideas for articles and news on issues relating to parenting as well as activity-oriented items.

The Friend

The Church of Jesus Christ of Latter-day Saints
24th Floor
50 East North Temple
Salt Lake City, UT 84150

Managing Editor: Vivian Paulsen

Description and Readership

The teachings of the Mormon church are fortified in this publication for young children, through stories based on true events, activities, comics, articles, and poems. Without using a preachy tone, focus is on building a strong character and special emphasis on conflict resolution.
- **Audience:** 3–11 years
- **Frequency:** Monthly
- **Distribution:** 100% subscription
- **Circulation:** 245,000

Freelance Potential

60% written by nonstaff writers.

Submissions

Send complete ms. Accepts photocopies and computer printouts. SASE. Responds in 2 months.
Articles: To 1,200 words. Informational and factual articles; profiles; personal experience pieces; and true stories. Topics include spirituality, the Mormon church, personal faith, and conflict resolution.
Depts/columns: Word length varies. Profiles of Mormon elders and children from different countries.
Other: Poetry, word length varies. Puzzles, activities, crafts, and cartoons. Submit seasonal material 8 months in advance.

Sample Issue

48 pages (no advertising): 2 articles; 6 stories; 1 poem; 7 depts/columns; 7 activities; 1 comic. Sample copy, $1.50 with 9x12 SASE (4 first-class stamps). Guidelines available.
- "Feleti Vimahi of Pangai, Tonga." Article introduces a 10-year-old boy who lives in the Kingdom of Tonga, comprised of several islands in the South Pacific.
- "Aren't You a Mormon?" Story describes a wrong choice made by a young school girl and her attempts to rectify it with God and her classmates.
- Sample dept/column: "Sharing Time" gives an example of how parents can instill positive values in young children.

Rights and Payment

All rights. Articles, 200–300 words, $100; 400+ words, $250. Poems, $50. Other material, $15+. Pays on acceptance. Provides 2 contributor's copies.

Editor's Comments

We are interested in material with universal settings. We are particularly interested in stories with substance for younger children, and poems with catchy cadences suitable for preschoolers. Appropriate humor is always needed. We do not need any more stories based on science or nature.

Fun For Kidz

P.O. Box 227
Bluffton, OH 45817

Associate Editor: Virginia Edwards

Description and Readership
Fun For Kidz is a companion to *Boys' Quest* and *Hopscotch*, appearing in the alternate months, and providing activities for its readers. Its target audience are 8-, 9-, and 10-year-old children, although it is designed for a broader age range.
- **Audience:** 6–13 years
- **Frequency:** 6 times each year
- **Distribution:** 80% subscription; 20% newsstand
- **Circulation:** 3,000
- **Website:** www.funforkidz.com

Freelance Potential
100% written by nonstaff writers. Publishes many freelance submissions yearly; 5% by unpublished writers, 15% by authors who are new to the magazine.

Submissions
Send complete ms. Accepts computer printouts and simultaneous submissions if identified. Availability of artwork improves chance of acceptance. SASE. Responds in 4–6 weeks.
Articles: 500 words. How-to articles. Topics include crafts and hobbies.
Fiction: 500 words. Features stories about animals, adventure; and humorous fiction.
Artwork: B/W and color prints or transparencies. Line art.
Other: Activities, filler, games, jokes, and puzzles. Submit seasonal material 6–12 months in advance.

Sample Issue
50 pages (no advertising): 2 articles; 2 stories; 5 depts/columns; 7 activities and puzzles; 2 comics; 2 poems; 1 recipe. Sample copy, $4. Guidelines and theme list available.
- "Get Rid of That Cold Germ." Article shows how to make a game out of old playing cards and a few drawings.
- "Cookies for Blackie." Story depicts a cookie-baking session that turns into an experiment for making healthy dog treats.
- Sample dept/column: "Sports Hunt" gives tips to children who collect old sporting equipment.

Rights and Payment
First or reprint rights. Written material, $.05 per word. Artwork, payment rate varies. Pays on publication. Provides 1 contributor's copy.

Editor's Comments
We are looking for lively writing that involves an activity that is wholesome and unusual. We are a theme-based publication and deal with topics that relate to and are enjoyed by children, such as pets, nature, science, games, simple cooking, sports, and games.

Games

7002 West Butler Pike
Ambler, PA 19002

Editor-in-Chief: Wayne R. Schmittberger

Description and Readership
Individuals who enjoy the pleasure and challenge of solving puzzles of all kinds are the target audience of this magazine. Its editorial offers a wealth of puzzles as well as informational articles about games and reviews of new products.
- **Audience:** YA–Adult
- **Frequency:** 10 times each year
- **Distribution:** 70% subscription; 30% newsstand
- **Circulation:** 80,000

Freelance Potential
86% written by nonstaff writers. Publishes 200+ freelance submissions yearly; 10% by unpublished writers, 50% by authors who are new to the magazine. Receives 80+ queries and unsolicited mss monthly.

Submissions
Query with outline for articles. Send complete ms for shorter pieces. Accepts photocopies and computer printouts. SASE. Responds in 6–8 weeks.
Articles: 2,000–2,500 words. Informational articles; humor; and profiles. Topics include game-related events and people, wordplay, and human ingenuity in all its guises. Game reviews are by assignment only.
Depts/columns: Staff written, except for "Gamebits."
Other: Visual and verbal puzzles, quizzes, contests, two-play games, and fake advertisements.

Sample Issue
80 pages (8% advertising): 5 articles; 10 depts/columns; 19 activities. Sample copy, $4.50 with 9x12 SASE ($1.24 postage). Guidelines available.
- "Just the Right Fit." Article profiles a young man who makes wooden jigsaw puzzles.
- Sample dept/column: "Game Views" explores the world of electronic crossword puzzles. "They're All Greek to Me" challenges readers to identify well-known personalities of Greek descent.

Rights and Payment
All rights. Articles, $1,500–$1,750. "Gamebits," $150–$250. Pays on publication. Provides 1 contributor's copy.

Editor's Comments
We are a very unique publication and our readers expect to be entertained as well as challenged. Most of our writers have considerable experience writing about all kinds of games as well as playing them. If this description fits you, we welcome your submission. Remember that we only consider manuscripts for short items.

Genesee Valley Parent Magazine

Suite 204
1 Grove Street
Pittsford, NY 14534

Managing Editor: Barbara Melnyk

Description and Readership

Established in 1994, this magazine is published for expectant parents and parents of young children in the Greater Rochester, New York area. Its articles are a source of information on topics relating to raising children today.
- **Audience:** Parents
- **Frequency:** Monthly
- **Distribution:** 65% controlled; 30% schools; 5% other
- **Circulation:** 37,000
- **Website:** www.gvparent.com

Freelance Potential

75% written by nonstaff writers. Publishes 50 freelance submissions yearly; 5% by authors who are new to the magazine. Receives 20 queries monthly.

Submissions

Query with clips or writing samples. Accepts photocopies and simultaneous submissions if identified. SASE. Responds in 1–3 months.
Articles: 700–1,200 words. Informational and how-to articles; personal experience pieces; interviews; reviews; and humor. Topics include regional events and concerns, special and gifted education, social issues, family problems, health, fitness, and parenting.
Depts/columns: 500–600 words. Short news items, health, and family finances.
Other: Submit seasonal material 4 months in advance.

Sample Issue

50 pages (50% advertising): 4 articles; 8 depts/columns; 1 calendar of events. Guidelines and editorial calendar available.
- "Raising Kids on One Salary." Article describes how to budget expenses to allow for a full-time stay-at-home parent.
- "A Day for Dad." Article offers ideas to make Father's Day a day to remember.
- Sample dept/column: "Active Child" extols the benefits of family swim time.

Rights and Payment

Second rights. Articles, $30–$45. Depts/columns, $25–$30. Pays on publication. Provides 1 tearsheet.

Editor's Comments

We generally work with established writers in the Greater Rochester area, we will consider others who can provide a researched feature about a topic related to parenting. Local resources should be cited in all articles. New writers have the best chance of acceptance with a piece on local and regional events, community resources, and book and product reviews.

GeoParent

719 Octavia Street
New Orleans, LA 70115

Editor: Jennifer Newton Reents

Description and Readership

Practical information for parents of toddlers to teens is found online at this website. Content includes parenting tips and ideas, as well as information on family health, relationships, lifestyles, and community activities.
- **Audience:** Parents
- **Frequency:** Weekly
- **Distribution:** 100% Internet
- **Hits per month:** 700,000
- **Websites:** www.geoparent.com; www.coincide.com

Freelance Potential

90% written by nonstaff writers. Publishes 50 freelance submissions yearly. Receives 50 queries and unsolicited mss each month.

Submissions

Prefers query. Accepts complete ms. Accepts photocopies, computer printouts, email submissions to feedback@ coincide.com, and submissions through their website. SASE. Response time varies.
Articles: 500–2,500 words. Informational articles and advice. Topics include family issues, parenting, child development, child care, gifted education, and special education.
Depts/columns: Word length varies. Parenting advice.

Sample Issue

Sample copy and guidelines available at website.
- "Smooth Teen Years by Being an Involved Parent." Article drives home the importance of communication between teens and their parents and provides several suggestions to help parents accomplish that goal.
- "Teaching Your Child What to Do in an Emergency." Article details the steps to take to prepare children to handle an emergency situation.
- "Musical Activities for Guaranteed Fun." Article describes activities that introduce children and their friends to the pleasures of music.

Rights and Payment

Rights vary. Written material, $25–$50; $10 for reprints. Pays on publication.

Editor's Comments

We are continually looking for information, community interaction, and entertainment that will help our readers improve their lives. Most of our material is written by freelancers and experts in a variety of fields. Currently we would like to receive more submissions on issues faced by parents of children up to 18 years of age, pregnancy, and fashion.

Georgia Family

523 Sioux Drive
Macon, GA 31210

Managing Editor: Veronique Saiya

Description and Readership
Committed to the children, families, and community of central Georgia, this magazine serves as a local resource for raising happy, healthy families. Parents find features on issues that concern them, such as child care, family life, private and public education, summer camps, and birthday parties.
- **Audience:** Parents
- **Frequency:** Monthly
- **Distribution:** 65% controlled; 30% schools; 5% subscription
- **Circulation:** 23,000
- **Website:** www.georgiafamily.com

Freelance Potential
50% written by nonstaff writers. Publishes 120 freelance submissions yearly; 60% by authors who are new to the magazine. Receives 12 unsolicited mss monthly.

Submissions
Send complete ms. Accepts disk submissions. Prefers email submissions to publisher@georgiafamily.com. Availability of artwork improves chance of acceptance. SASE. Responds in 1 month.
Articles: 500–1,200 words. Informational, how-to, and self-help articles; profiles; interviews; reviews; and personal experience pieces. Topics include parenting, popular culture, regional news, social issues, gifted and special education, college, careers, computers, health, travel, and ethnic and multicultural issues.
Depts/columns: 400 words. Restaurant and book reviews, education highlights, health, and safety.
Artwork: B/W prints or transparencies. Line art.

Sample Issue
46 pages (20% advertising): 8 articles; 6 depts/columns; 1 calendar. Sample copy, $2 with 9x12 SASE.
- "Choosing a Day Camp." Article offers guidelines parents can use to find a camp that fits their child's personality.
- "Understanding Autism." Article looks at alternate treatments, programs, and resources for autistic children.

Rights and Payment
One-time and reprint rights. All material, $10–$30. Pays on publication. Provides 1 contributor's copy.

Editor's Comments
Our features require careful research, independent reporting, and well-developed story lines. We prefer articles that pertain to parenting in our area, but do consider general articles that relate to the family.

Gifted Education Press Quarterly

P.O. Box 1586, 10201 Yuma Court
Manassas, VA 20109

Editor & Publisher: Maurice D. Fisher

Description and Readership
In print for over 18 years, this quarterly newsletter offers useful, informative articles on the education of gifted children and educational resources. It targets teachers, parents, and school administrators.
- **Audience:** Parents, educators, school administrators
- **Frequency:** Quarterly
- **Distribution:** 100% subscription
- **Circulation:** 1,500
- **Website:** www.giftededpress.com

Freelance Potential
75% written by nonstaff writers. Publishes 12 freelance submissions yearly; 75% by authors who are new to the magazine. Receives 5 queries monthly.

Submissions
Query. SASE. Responds in 2 weeks.
Articles: 3,000–5,000 words. Informational, how-to, and personal experience articles; profiles; and interviews. Topics include gifted education, homeschooling, multiple intelligence, parent advocates in the school system, social issues, science, history, the environment, and popular culture.

Sample Issue
12 pages (no advertising): 6 articles. Sample copy, $4 with 9x12 SASE.
- "Do the Gifted Need Gifted Education?" Article explores the risks involved with separating gifted children already thriving in a regular school program, as well as the selection procedures for gifted programs.
- "Hemingway's *A Moveable Feast* and the Sensibility of Giftedness." Essay discusses and provides insight into Ernest Hemingway's book, *A Moveable Feast*.
- "Another Look at Cleveland's Major Work Program." Article discusses the history, development, and demise of one of Ohio's premier programs for the gifted.

Rights and Payment
All rights. No payment. Provides 5 contributor's copies and a free subscription upon publication.

Editor's Comments
Articles that outline the issues in identifying and teaching the gifted are of interest to us. We look for well-written and well-documented material from writers who have extensive knowledge in the field that can be applied both in and out of the classroom. We continue to monitor the impact of legislation on gifted children and are interested in articles relating to these important issues.

Girls' Life

4517 Harford Road
Baltimore, MD 21214

Executive Editor: Lizzie Skurnick

Description and Readership

Jam-packed with tween survival information, *Girls' Life* provides its readers with upbeat tips and information on relationships, school, and family issues. Sprinkled inbetween those pages are quizzes and pieces on fashion, beauty, and health all written with a positive tone.
- **Audience:** 10–14 years
- **Frequency:** 6 times each year
- **Distribution:** Subscription; newsstand
- **Circulation:** 400,000
- **Website:** www.girlslife.com

Freelance Potential

40–50% written by nonstaff writers. Publishes 100+ freelance submissions yearly; 10% by unpublished writers, 10% by authors who are new to the magazine. Receives 83 unsolicited mss monthly.

Submissions

Query or send complete ms with résumé and 2 clips. SASE. Responds in 3 months.
Articles: 1,200–2,500 words. Informational, service-oriented articles. Topics include self-esteem, body image, friendships, crushes and dating, divorce, sibling rivalry, school success, facing challenges, and setting goals.
Depts/columns: 300–800 words. Celebrity spotlights; newsworthy stories on real girls; service pieces on friends, guys, and life; decorating tips; and easy-to-do crafts and activities.

Sample Issue

96 pages (30% advertising): 5 articles; 20 depts/columns; 3 quizzes. Sample copy, $5. Guidelines and editorial calendar available at website or with SASE.
- "Wipe out Guilt." Article provides several tips on how to get rid of constricting guilt and free up the path to happiness.
- "The Secret Life of an Overweight Teenager." Article features one teenager's struggle with obesity and the road she took to overcome the problem.
- Sample dept/column: "Guys" offers ideas on how to get over the fact that your crush doesn't like you in return.

Rights and Payment

All or first rights. All material, payment rate varies. Pays on publication. Provides 1 contributor's copy.

Editor's Comments

We would like to receive more nonfiction feature stories, fiction, and short submissions suitable for GL Fun. We concentrate on fun information that has constructive content suitable for helping girls navigate through these developmental years.

Go-Girl

Rumholtz Publishing
Suite 202
1200 South Avenue
Staten Island, NY 10314

Editor-in-Chief: Gina LaGuardia

Description and Readership

Addressing the social and academic needs of teen girls, this unique website provides up-to-date information on beauty, fashion, health, sports, social issues, careers, and college life. It features entertaining and informational articles and tips.
- **Audience:** 14–18 years
- **Frequency:** 6 times each year
- **Distribution:** Internet
- **Circulation:** 350,000
- **Website:** www.go-girl.com

Freelance Potential

50% written by nonstaff writers. Publishes 100 freelance submissions yearly; 50% by unpublished writers, 70% by authors who are new to the magazine. Receives 42 queries monthly.

Submissions

Query with clips. Accepts email queries to editorial@ collegebound.net, and photocopies. SASE. Responds in 5 weeks.
Articles: 200–600 words. Informational, factual, and how-to articles; profiles; interviews; and personal experience pieces. Topics include fashion, beauty, health, fitness, relationships, family, friends, celebrities, hobbies, college, careers, sports, music, popular culture, and education.
Depts/columns: 100–300 words. Fashion, beauty, health, fitness, entertainment, and academic advice.

Sample Issue

Guidelines available at website.
- "Girls Give Daring Sports a Go." Article discusses the trend in teen girls to try extreme sports such as skateboarding, snowboarding, windsurfing, and rock climbing.
- "Be Sun Savvy." Article takes a look at the pros and cons of sun bathing and tanning products.
- "10 Things You Need to Know." Article reports on things you should know before going away to college.

Rights and Payment

All or first rights. Written material, $50–$75. Depts/columns, $25–$40. Pays on publication.

Editor's Comments

We provide empowering articles for teen girls, and encourage them to be "all that they can be." Articles that portray real-life experiences that they can relate to; as well as entertainment pieces on personalities they admire are of interest to us. We want our readers to know they should feel good about themselves, and boost their intelligence. If you have an idea for a hip article, that teens can relate to, send us a query. Please keep writing light and fun, and feel free to use teen lingo.

Going Forth

P.O. Box 108
San Pedro, CA 90733

Editor: Jessica Ralph

Description and Readership

Going Forth is an online Christian publication established with the intent to reach youth throughout the United States and the world. Its website includes articles to enhance readers' relationships with God, increase self-esteem, and promote reaching out to others.
• **Audience:** 14–18 years
• **Frequency:** Updated quarterly
• **Distribution:** 100% Internet
• **Hits per month:** Unavailable
• **Website:** www.goingforth.net

Freelance Potential

50% written by nonstaff writers. Publishes 25–35 freelance submissions yearly; 50% by unpublished writers, 50% by authors who are new to the magazine. Receives 4–10 queries each month.

Submissions

Query or send complete ms. Accepts email submissions to submissions@goingforth.net (accepts attachments). Responds in 1 week.
Articles: To 1,000 words. Personal experience pieces; interviews; profiles; humor; and reviews. Topics include popular culture, multicultural and ethnic issues, music, religion, devotionals, and prayer.
Other: Jokes. Submit Christmas, Mother's Day, and Father's Day material 1–3 months in advance.

Sample Issue

Sample copy and writers' guidelines available at website.
• "Don't Forget Your Appointment with God." Article encourages readers to find and maintain a special time to communicate with God.
• "Lifting up the Countries in Prayer." Article discusses how Christians in Africa are being persecuted for their beliefs.
• "Wanna Get Saved?" Article explains how a simple act of repentance can result in permanent fulfillment.

Rights and Payment

No rights. No payment.

Editor's Comments

Our editors are looking for dedicated writers who are able to compose devotionals and profiles of Christian celebrities, interview young adults on popular topics, recommend Christian books, and suggest ideas for youth groups, as well as develop original general-interest articles. Material that discusses tests, trials, and tribulations of being Christian will be considered.

Great Lakes Family Magazine

P.O. Box 714
Kalamazoo, MI 49004

Editor & Publisher: Cynthia L. Schrauben

Description and Readership

Family-centered articles that feature information from local and national sources appear along with columns by medical experts and event calendars in this regional tabloid for parents living in Southwest Michigan.
• **Audience:** Parents living in the Michigan counties of Barry, Kent, Calhoun, Allegan, and Kalamazoo
• **Frequency:** 6 times each year
• **Distribution:** Subscription; newsstand
• **Circulation:** 47,000
• **Website:** www.glfamily.com

Freelance Potential

90% written by nonstaff writers. Publishes 18–20 freelance submissions yearly. Receives 100+ queries, 100+ unsolicited mss monthly.

Submissions

Query or send complete ms. Accepts photocopies, computer printouts, and email submissions to editor@glfamily.com. SASE. Response time varies.
Articles: Word length varies. Informational articles. Topics include infant and child care, health and fitness, family safety, and family travel destinations.
Fiction: Word length varies. Contemporary fiction.
Depts/columns: Word length varies. Updates on local events, book reviews, and family recipes.

Sample Issue

32 pages: 4 articles; 8 depts/columns. Sample copy available.
• "Parents, Kids Get Failing Grade in Child Helmet Use." Article reports on the results of a survey on helmet use and discusses their importance in preventing head injuries.
• "Seven Steps to a Safer Playground." Article explains ways parents can make public playgrounds safer.
• Sample dept/column: "Parenting with Success" explores the issues of jealously, competition, favoritism, and sharing as they relate to sibling rivalry.

Rights and Payment

Rights vary. Written material, payment rate varies. Pays on publication.

Editor's Comments

We're looking for editorial content that will appeal to expectant parents, parents of babies and toddlers, and older children. Our primary goal is to help parents address their concerns and problems by presenting information that is obtained from local and national experts. We want our readers to turn to us for the advice they need to raise healthy, well-adjusted children.

Green Teacher

95 Robert Street
Toronto, Ontario M5S 2K5
Canada

Co-Editors: Tim Grant & Gail Littlejohn

Description and Readership
Educators seeking to put forth environmental education programs find articles and cross-curricular activities suitable for use with kindergarten through high school students in *Green Teacher*. Each issue offers teaching strategies, examples of successful programs other teachers have used, and reviews of the latest teaching resources.
- **Audience:** Teachers, grades K–12
- **Frequency:** Quarterly
- **Distribution:** 50% newsstand; 40% subscription 10% other
- **Circulation:** 7,000
- **Website:** www.greenteacher.com

Freelance Potential
90% written by nonstaff writers. Publishes 40 freelance submissions yearly; 90% by unpublished writers, 90% by authors who are new to the magazine. Receives 5 mss monthly.

Submissions
Send complete ms. Accepts photocopies, computer printouts, disk submissions (ASCII) with hard copy, fax submissions to 416-925-3474, and email submissions to greentea@ web.net. Availability of artwork improves chance of acceptance. SAE/IRC. Responds in 2 months.
Articles: 1,500–2,500 words. Informational and how-to articles. Topics include the environment, science, education, and mathematics.
Depts/columns: Word length varies. Resources, reviews, and announcements.
Artwork: B/W and color prints and transparencies. Line art.
Other: Submit material for Earth Day 6 months in advance.

Sample Issue
52 pages (12% advertising): 8 articles; 4 depts/columns. Sample copy, $6. Guidelines available.
- "Teaching about Salt Marshes." Article outlines a teaching plan for a field trip that encourages respect for the often neglected and sometimes abused tidal wetlands.
- "Winter Treasures." Article reports on a program that involves a one-day environmental experience along with pre-trip and post-trip classroom activities.

Rights and Payment
Rights negotiable. No payment. Provides 5 author's copies.

Editor's Comments
We're less formal than academic journals. Write clearly, avoid jargon, and don't hesitate to use humor or personal reflections if your subject calls for it.

Grit

1503 SW 42nd Street
Topeka, KS 66609-1265

Editor-in-Chief: Ann Crahan

Description and Readership
A national publication, *Grit* includes a wide range of topics that are of interest to today's families. Subjects include American values, interesting people and places, travel, and nostalgia.
- **Audience:** Families
- **Frequency:** 12 times each year
- **Distribution:** 100% subscription
- **Circulation:** 90,000
- **Website:** www.gritmagazine.com

Freelance Potential
85% written by nonstaff writers. Publishes 500–600 freelance submissions yearly; 90% by unpublished writers. Receives 1,000 unsolicited mss monthly.

Submissions
Send complete ms with photos, résumé, and clips or writing samples. Accepts Macintosh disk submissions. SASE. Response time varies.
Articles: 800–1,500 words. Factual and how-to articles; profiles; and personal experience pieces. Topics include American history, family lifestyles, parenting, pets, arts and crafts, community involvement, and antiques.
Fiction: 1,000+ words. Serials, romance, mysteries, Westerns, and stories with strong moral principles.
Depts/columns: 500–1,500 words. Topics include pets, nostalgia, true stories, family issues, health, cooking, and gardening.
Artwork: Color slides. B/W prints for nostalgia pieces.
Other: Poetry. Submit seasonal material 6 months in advance.

Sample Issue
64 pages (40% advertising): 14 articles; 2 stories; 10 depts/columns; 1 poem. Sample copy, $4. Guidelines available.
- "Equestrians Ride for Fun and History." Article describes a group of women who love to ride horses and who have formed Wild Women of the Frontier equestrian group.
- "Tiger Eyes." Story features a Connecticut woman who is unexpectedly visited by a tiger that walks into her home.
- Sample dept/column: "Best Friends" recounts heartwarming experiences with pets and other animals.

Rights and Payment
First rights. Articles, to $.15 per word. Depts/columns, payment rate varies. Artwork, $15–$25 for color photos. Pays on publication. Provides 1 contributor's copy.

Editor's Comments
We need more submissions about the eastern region of the United States. We currently have enough material relating to the Old West.

Group

Group Publishing, Inc.
P.O. Box 481
Loveland, CO 80539-0481

Associate Editor: Kathy Dieterich

Description and Readership

Group is an interdenominational magazine for youth ministers. It serves its readership through articles that outline successful youth ministry strategies and covers topics such as recruiting adult leaders, serving parents, and understanding kids. It also provides articles that seek to enhance the personal and professional lives of youth ministers.

- **Audience:** Adults
- **Frequency:** 6 times each year
- **Distribution:** 100% subscription
- **Circulation:** 55,000
- **Website:** www.grouppublishing.com

Freelance Potential

60% written by nonstaff writers. Publishes 200 freelance submissions yearly; 50% by unpublished writers, 80% by authors who are new to the magazine. Receives 25 queries each month.

Submissions

Query with outline/synopsis and clips or writing samples. Accepts photocopies and computer printouts. State if artwork is available. SASE. Responds in 8–10 weeks.

Articles: 500–1,700 words. Informational and how-to articles. Topics include youth ministry strategies, recruiting and training adult leaders, understanding youth culture, professionalism, time management, leadership skills, and professional and spiritual growth of youth ministers.

Depts/columns: "Try This One," to 300 words. "Hands-On Help," to 175 words.

Artwork: B/W or color illustration samples. Send artwork to art department. No photographs.

Sample Issue

102 pages (30% advertising): 6 articles; 11 depts/columns. Sample copy, $2 with 9x12 SASE. Guidelines available.

- "The Dirty Little Secret about Mission Trips." Article questions the value of short-term mission trips and maintains that an everyday commitment to service is more important.
- "Moving Parents off the Bench." Personal experience piece explains how one minister came to understand the valuable role parents play in his ministry.

Rights and Payment

All rights. Articles, $125–$225. Dept/columns, $40. Pays on acceptance.

Editor's Comments

If you have an idea for an article that will help youth leaders become more effective in their ministry, send us your query.

Guide

Review and Herald Publishing Association
55 West Oak Ridge Drive
Hagerstown, MD 21740

Assistant Editor: Rachel Whitaker

Description and Readership

Pre-teens and early teens find inspiration in the true life experiences presented in this publication. Stories, which are told with a sense of adventure, demonstrate character-building principles in action. Readers are encouraged to incorporate these Christian values into their own lives.

- **Audience:** 10–14 years
- **Frequency:** Weekly
- **Distribution:** 100% subscription
- **Circulation:** 32,000
- **Website:** www.guidemagazine.org

Freelance Potential

95% written by nonstaff writers. Publishes 300 freelance submissions yearly; 10% by unpublished writers, 30% by authors who are new to the magazine. Receives 60–85 unsolicited mss each month.

Submissions

Send complete ms. Prefers email to guide@rhpa.org. Accepts photocopies, computer printouts, and simultaneous submissions if identified. SASE. Responds in 4–6 months.

Articles: To 1,200 words. True stories with inspirational and personal growth themes; true adventure pieces; and humor. Nature articles with a religious emphasis, 750 words.

Other: Puzzles, activities, and games. Submit seasonal material about Thanksgiving, Christmas, Mother's Day, and Father's Day 8 months in advance.

Sample Issue

32 pages (no advertising): 4 true stories; 1 serial; 2 Bible lessons; 2 activities. Sample copy, free with 9x12 SASE (2 first-class stamps). Guidelines available.

- "Kids in Jail." Story narrates a true story about a young teen boy and his friends who learned a hard lesson about fake guns and real violence.
- "Disguised for Death." Story describes an incident in A.D. 303 when Albanus, a new Christian convert in Britain, gave up his life so a priest could live.
- "When Jesus Got Thirsty." Lesson brings to life a Bible story by retelling it in today's language.

Rights and Payment

First and second rights. Written material, $.06–$.12 per word. Pays on acceptance. Provides 3 contributor's copies.

Editor's Comments

Protagonists should be 10- to 14-year-old children in stories that contain a good deal of mystery, action, and discovery while illustrating biblical principles.

Guideposts for Kids Online

Suite 6
1050 Broadway
Chesterton, IN 46304

Managing Editor: Rosanne Tolin

Description and Readership
Articles, stories, poetry, and activities for children can be found on this online magazine. It offers a place for kids to learn, play, and express themselves while providing them with reliable resources, information, and tips on kid-friendly topics.
- **Audience:** 6–12 years
- **Frequency:** Unavailable
- **Distribution:** Internet
- **Hits per month:** 3.5 million
- **Website:** www.gp4k.com

Freelance Potential
90% written by nonstaff writers. Publishes 150 freelance submissions yearly; 20% by authors who are new to the magazine. Receives 125 queries and unsolicited mss monthly.

Submissions
Query for nonfiction. Send complete ms for fiction. Accepts photocopies, computer printouts, and email submissions to rtolin@guideposts.org. SASE. Responds in 2–3 months.
Articles: To 700 words. Thought-provoking, issue-oriented articles. Topics include current events, science, animals, school, sports, and general subjects of interest to kids.
Fiction: To 900 words. Historical and contemporary fiction and mysteries. Stories must convey strong values.
Depts/columns: Profiles of 6- to 12-year-old kids who volunteer in their communities, 50–150. "Tips from the Top" features profiles of athletes and other celebrities, 500 words.
Other: Puzzles, jokes, trivia, quizzes, crafts, poetry, and recipes. Submit seasonal material 5 months in advance.

Sample Issue
Writers' guidelines available at website or with SASE sent to 39 Seminary Hill Road, Carmel, NY 10512.
- "Bohemian Valentine." Story tells how a boy's great aunt from Eastern Europe helps him make special homemade valentines for the girls in his class.
- "There's a Bear in My Room." Story features a young girl who remembers a song about God's protection when she and a cousin are faced with fear.

Rights and Payment
Electronic and non-exclusive print rights. All material, payment rate varies. Pays on acceptance.

Editor's Comments
We need more crafts and fashion/beauty articles that are of interest to tweens. Also, we are still looking for nonfiction pieces that cover school and sports. Send us something that is interactive, creative, and fun.

Guideposts Sweet 16

Suite 6
1050 Broadway
Chesterton, IN 46304

Associate Editor: Allison Payne

Description and Readership
This re-designed, re-named magazine for girls offers true, first-person stories about real teens; no fiction is included. Most of the content is geared to girls, although an occasional boy-narrated story is included. Uplifting rather than inspirational is the mood or tone desired by the publishers.
- **Audience:** 12–18 years
- **Frequency:** 6 times each year
- **Distribution:** 100% subscription
- **Circulation:** 250,000
- **Website:** www.gp4teens.com

Freelance Potential
90% written by nonstaff writers. Publishes 80 freelance submissions yearly; 40% by authors who are new to the magazine.

Submissions
Query. Accepts photocopies and email submissions to gp4twriters@guideposts.org. SASE. Responds in 1 month.
Articles: 750–1,500 words. First-person true stories by teens. Topics include action/adventure, relationships, and real-life teen issues such as dating, friendship, and peer pressure.
Depts/columns: 300–500 words. Fashion, beauty, miracle stories, teen profiles, and quizzes.

Sample Issue
46 pages (no advertising): 11 articles; 2 quizzes; 9 depts/columns. Sample copy, $4.50. Guidelines available.
- "Wild Child." Article follows the progress of a teen as she turns her life around from a downward spiral to fighting wildfires while serving time in a youth camp.
- "Something to Celebrate." Article recounts a teen's out-of-control reaction to life after a drive-by shooting narrowly misses her.
- Sample dept/column: "In the Know" assembles information and helpful tips for teens as they maneuver through life.

Rights and Payment
All rights. Articles, $150–$500. Depts/columns, $175–$400. Pays on acceptance. Provides 2–5 copies.

Editor's Comments
Submissions should be written in the first person and focus on one specific event or happening in a teen's life. We prefer a narrative style that is dramatic with content that contains conflict and resolution. We are always looking for strange-but-true stories and unexplained coincidences as well as light stories and catch-in-the-throat stories. Language and subject matter must be current—and please, no preaching.

Gumbo Magazine Happiness

1818 North Dr. Martin Luther King Drive
Milwaukee, WI 53212

Managing Editor: Amy Muehlbauer

Description and Readership
This magazine provides a forum for teens to educate their peers, explore social and political issues, and voice their opinions. It is a multicultural magazine targeted at both male and female teens.
• **Audience:** 14–18 years
• **Frequency:** 6 times each year
• **Distribution:** 50% schools; 40% libraries; 10% subscription
• **Circulation:** 25,000
• **Website:** www.mygumbo.com

Freelance Potential
15% written by nonstaff writers. Publishes 60 freelance submissions yearly; 95% by unpublished writers, 90% by authors who are new to the magazine. Receives 100 queries monthly.

Submissions
Query. Accepts email queries to amy@mygumbo.com. SASE. Responds in 2 weeks.
Articles: 700–1,000 words. Personal experience pieces; profiles, interviews, and reviews. Topics include college; career; computers, current events, health, fitness, music, popular culture; recreation; science; technology; sports; and self-help; and multicultural and social issues.
Articles: Word length varies. Current events, technology, fashion, book and music reviews.
Other: Poetry, less than 500 words. Submit seasonal material 6 months in advance.

Sample Issue
50 pages (30% advertising): 17 articles; 6 depts/columns; 1 poem. Sample copy, $3 with 8x10 ($1.23 postage). SASE. Guidelines and theme list available.
• "Crossing out Smoke." Article informs readers what is involved in the production of tobacco; including children working on tobacco farms.
• "Grandparents Shouldn't Raise Our Children." Article offers a teen's opinion on the responsibility of being a parent.
• Sample dept/column: "Fashion" offers creative accessories to maximize prom style.

Rights and Payment
One-time rights. Written material, $25. Pays on publication. Provides 10 contributor's copies.

Editor's Comments
We are interested in seeing more articles on money management, careers, and sports. Material should be written in a youthful tone, with proper grammar.

P.O. Box 388
Portland, TN 37148

Editor: Sue Fuller

Description and Readership
Happiness is a weekly television guide with uplifting material that builds character and a positive approach to living. Stories and articles emphasize self-improvement and a more fulfilling life in health, personal pursuits, and behavior.
• **Audience:** Families
• **Frequency:** Weekly
• **Distribution:** Subscription
• **Circulation:** Unavailable
• **Website:** www.happiness.com

Freelance Potential
50% written by nonstaff writers.

Submissions
Send complete ms. Accepts computer printouts. SASE. Availability of artwork improves chance of acceptance. Responds in 3 months.
Articles: 500 words. Informational, how-to, self-help, and inspirational articles and personal experience pieces. Topics include education, health, fitness, crafts, hobbies, animals, pets, nature, the environment, recreation, and travel. Also publishes humor and biographical articles.
Fiction: 500 words. Inspirational fiction, real-life stories, and stories about animals.
Depts/columns: 25–75 words. Crafts, cooking, and tips from readers.
Artwork: Color prints.
Other: Puzzles, activities, and poetry. Submit seasonal material 4 months in advance.

Sample Issue
48 pages (no advertising): 6 articles; 5 depts/columns; 8 activities. Guidelines available.
• "Seven Ways to Be Happier at Work." Article concentrates on developing a positive perception of and attitude toward the work we do.
• "Suggestions for Becoming a Good Neighbor." Article lists several ideas we can incorporate into our daily lives for improving our neighborly relationships.
• Sample dept/column: "The Front Porch" shares memories from readers that carry an inspirational punch.

Rights and Payment
First rights. All material, payment rates vary. Pays on publication.

Editor's Comments
Submissions should be positive and upbeat in nature, without a specific religious slant. We do not accept references to evolution, mythology, mystical powers, or negativism.

High Adventure

The General Council of the Assemblies of God
1445 North Boonville Avenue
Springfield, MO 65802-1894

Editor: Jerry Parks

Description and Readership
The spirit of the Royal Rangers ministry comes through all the material in this periodical for boys in kindergarten through high school. Stories, illustrations, crafts, comics, and informational articles are all used to challenge readers to higher ideals and greater spiritual dedication.
- **Audience:** Boys grades K–12
- **Frequency:** Quarterly
- **Distribution:** 95% charter; 5% subscription
- **Circulation:** 87,000
- **Website:** www.royalrangers.ag.org

Freelance Potential
50% written by nonstaff writers. Publishes 125 freelance submissions yearly; 5% by unpublished writers, 30% by authors who are new to the magazine. Receives 4–5 mss monthly.

Submissions
Send complete ms. Accepts photocopies, computer printouts, IBM disk submissions, email submissions to jparks@ag.org, and simultaneous submissions. SASE. Responds in 1–2 months.
Articles: To 1,000 words. Informational, how-to, and self-help articles; profiles; humor; and personal experience pieces. Topics include religion, geography, nature, travel, sports, college, and multicultural subjects.
Fiction: 1,000 words. Genres include inspirational, historical, religious, adventure, and multicultural fiction, problem-solving stories, and humor.
Depts/columns: Word length varies. News and views of interest to Royal Rangers.
Artwork: Color prints.
Other: Puzzles, activities, games, and jokes. Submit seasonal material 6 months in advance.

Sample Issue
16 pages (no advertising): 2 articles; 2 stories; 2 depts/columns; 1 comic. Sample copy, free with 9x12 SASE. Writers' guidelines available.
- "Flying High." Article relates how the Montgolfier brothers in France invented hot air balloons.
- "The Surprise Prize." Story articulates that the unexpected discoveries of real life often transcend electronic games.

Rights and Payment
First or all rights. All material, payment rate varies. Pays on publication. Provides 2 contributor's copies.

Editor's Comments
We would like to receive interesting nonfiction that deals with significant historical events.

Highlights for Children

803 Church Street
Honesdale, PA 18431

Manuscript Submissions

Description and Readership
This popular publication has been teaching children about their world since 1946. Its goal is to help children increase their knowledge, and develop creativity, skills, and ideals through a variety of formats and activities.
- **Audience:** 2–12 years
- **Frequency:** Monthly
- **Distribution:** 100% subscription
- **Circulation:** More than 2.5 million
- **Website:** www.highlights.com

Freelance Potential
98% written by nonstaff writers. Publishes 200 freelance submissions yearly; 30% by unpublished writers, 40% by authors who are new to the magazine. Receives 665 unsolicited mss monthly.

Submissions
Send complete ms. Accepts photocopies, computer printouts, and simultaneous submissions. SASE. Responds in 4–6 weeks.
Articles: To 800 words. Informational articles; interviews; profiles; and personal experience pieces. Topics include nature, animals, science, crafts, hobbies, world culture, and sports.
Fiction: To 400 words for ages 3–7; to 800 words for ages 8–12. Rebuses, to 120 words. Genres include mystery, adventure, and multicultural fiction. Also features stories about sports and retellings of traditional stories.
Depts/columns: Word length varies. Science, crafts, and pets.
Other: Puzzles, activities, riddles, games, and jokes.

Sample Issue
44 pages (no advertising): 5 articles; 5 stories; 9 depts/columns; 13 activities; 2 poems; 1 comic. Sample copy, free. Guidelines and theme list available.
- "Free at Last." Article contrasts the experiences a Kurdish family had in Turkey, its old homeland, with those it had in the United States, its new home.
- "Riding the Whale." Story depicts a young girl's move to a new house via the family car nicknamed the Blue Whale.
- Sample dept/column: "You Can Make It" shows several projects and crafts appropriate for children to make and use.

Rights and Payment
All rights. Written material, payment rate varies. Pays on acceptance. Provides 2 contributor's copies.

Editor's Comments
We need more nonfiction articles for our younger readers and contemporary stories using lively language and strong characterizations that are set in other cultures.

High School Writer

Junior High Edition

Writer Publications
P.O. Box 718
Grand Rapids, MN 55744-0718

Editor: Emily Benes

Description and Readership
This publication seeks to encourage junior high and middle school students to write creatively by publishing their efforts for peer review. Submissions to *High School Writer* come through teachers throughout the country who subscribe to the paper and send in their students' work.
- **Audience:** Junior high school students
- **Frequency:** 6 times each year
- **Distribution:** 100% schools
- **Circulation:** 44,000

Freelance Potential
100% written by nonstaff writers. Publishes 300 freelance submissions yearly; 95% by unpublished writers, 75% by authors who are new to the magazine. Receives 3,000 unsolicited mss each month.

Submissions
Accepts submissions from students of subscribing teachers in junior high school only. Send complete ms. Accepts photocopies, computer printouts, and simultaneous submissions if identified. SASE. Response time varies.
Articles: To 2,000 words. Informational and how-to articles; profiles; and personal experience pieces. Topics include family, religion, health, social issues, careers, college, multicultural issues, travel, nature, the environment, science, and computers.
Fiction: To 2,000 words. Genres include historical and contemporary fiction, science fiction, drama, adventure, suspense, mystery, humor, fantasy, and stories about sports and nature.
Artwork: B/W line art.
Other: Poetry, no line limit.

Sample Issue
8 pages (15% advertising): 10 articles; 5 stories; 24 poems; 1 review. Sample copy, free. Guidelines available in each issue.
- "Huntington Disease." Article explains what Huntington's disease is, how a person acquires it, its symptoms, and current research being conducted.
- "Raining Cats and Dogs." Story weaves between a dream world and reality as the young author unfolds a situation that has cats and dogs falling out of the sky.

Rights and Payment
One-time rights. No payment.

Editor's Comments
We accept articles, fiction, stories, life experiences, poetry, and artwork. Almost any topic is accepted—if it interests you there is a good chance it will interest your peers. We look for good writing and good taste.

High School Writer

Senior High Edition

Writer Publications
P.O. Box 718
Grand Rapids, MN 55744-0718

Editor: Emily Benes

Description and Readership
This publication is completely written by students and includes a mix of true stories, fiction, and poetry. It is used as a vehicle to spotlight the literary talents of senior high students throughout the country.
- **Audience:** Senior high school students
- **Frequency:** 6 times each year
- **Distribution:** 100% schools
- **Circulation:** 44,000

Freelance Potential
100% written by nonstaff writers. Publishes 300 freelance submissions yearly; 95% by unpublished writers, 75% by authors who are new to the magazine. Receives 3,000 unsolicited mss each month.

Submissions
Accepts submissions from students of subscribing teachers in senior high school only. Send complete ms. Accepts photocopies, computer printouts, email submissions to writer@ mx3.com (ASCII text), and simultaneous submissions if identified. SASE. Response time varies.
Articles: To 2,000 words. Informational and how-to articles; profiles; and personal experience pieces. Topics include current events, humor, mutlicultural and ethnic issues, nature, the environment, popular culture, recreation, sports, and travel.
Fiction: To 2,000 words. Genres include humor, science fiction, adventure, and stories about sports.
Other: Poetry, no line limit. Seasonal material.

Sample Issue
8 pages (no advertising): 9 articles; 9 stories; 21 poems. Sample copy, free. Guidelines available in each issue.
- "Unconditional Animal Love." Article relates an incident of a young boy who was babysitting when a black bear broke into the house and was chased away by the family's dog.
- "Tradition Remembered." Article shares a remembered Christmas that involved an unusual Norwegian custom, fondly recalled by family members.
- "Alternative Motives." Story reinvents the tale of Grendel making the protagonist a young, modern boy living in the classic underwater domain.

Rights and Payment
One-time rights. No payment.

Editor's Comments
Virtually every subject or issue is fair game for publication as long as it is presented in good taste. All submissions must include a statement of originality or proper credit if due.

Alfred Hitchcock's Mystery Magazine

475 Park Avenue South
New York, NY 10016

Editor: Linda Landrigan

Description and Readership

Every type of fictional mystery is included in this magazine from classic crime detection to the intriguing worlds of espionage and suspense. It does not accept stories based on real crimes or other events. Occasionally a story with a supernatural theme will be included, but only if it is connected to a crime or threat of one.

- **Audience:** YA–Adult
- **Frequency:** 10 times each year
- **Distribution:** Subscription; newsstand
- **Circulation:** Unavailable
- **Website:** www.themysteryplace.com

Freelance Potential

97% written by nonstaff writers. Publishes 96–110 freelance submissions yearly; 10% by unpublished writers, 10% by authors who are new to the magazine. Receives 300 unsolicited mss monthly.

Submissions

Send complete ms. Accepts photocopies. No simultaneous submissions. SASE. Responds in 3 months.

Fiction: To 12,000 words. Mysteries that revolve around a crime or the threat of a crime, including police procedurals, detective stories, private eye tales, suspense, courtroom dramas, and stories of espionage.

Depts/columns: Word length varies. Reviews; puzzles; mystery bookstore profiles.

Sample Issue

144 pages (2% advertising): 6 stories; 1 mystery classic; 7 depts/columns. Sample copy, $5. Guidelines available.

- "Peat." Story unravels a murder mystery in the British Isles after a body that has been missing for two years is found in a peat bog.
- "Aces and Eights." Story follows mysterious events in the Texas Panhandle that start out with a troublesome card game.
- Sample dept/column: "Conversation" features a short interview with Kathy Lynn Emerson.

Rights and Payment

First serial, anthology, and foreign rights. Written material, payment rate varies. Pays on acceptance. Provides 3 author's copies.

Editor's Comments

We welcome submissions from new writers and look forward to reading their works. We are looking for stories that have not been previously published elsewhere, and for ideas and presentations that are fresh, well-told, and absorbing. All stories should be entirely fictional.

Hit Parader

Suite 211
210 Route 4 East
Paramus, NJ 07652

Managing Editor: Renée Daigle

Description and Readership

The world of hard rock, heavy metal, and underground bands comes alive in *Hit Parader*. Readers find information on trends, the current status of musical groups, and critiques of albums, sound equipment, and emerging bands.

- **Audience:** YA
- **Frequency:** Monthly
- **Distribution:** Subscription; newsstand
- **Circulation:** 150,000
- **Website:** www.hitparader.com

Freelance Potential

10% written by nonstaff writers. Publishes 10 freelance submissions yearly; 50% by authors who are new to the magazine.

Submissions

Query. Accepts computer printouts. Availability of artwork improves chance of acceptance. SASE. Responds in 1–3 months.

Articles: 1,000 words. Lifestyle articles; profiles; and interviews. Topics include hard rock and heavy metal musicians and popular bands.

Depts/columns: Word length varies. Reports on instruments and sound equipment; profiles of new bands; and reviews of video games, music videos, and new music releases.

Artwork: 3x5 and 5x7 B/W prints and color transparencies.

Other: Submit seasonal material about anniversaries or notable events 4 months in advance.

Sample Issue

98 pages (50% advertising): 11 articles; 14 depts/columns. Sample copy, $4.99 at newsstands. Guidelines available.

- "Red Tape: Out from Under." Article talks about the Red Tape band and its newest album, *Radioactivist*.
- "All-Time Top 100 Metal Guitarists." Article lists the *Hit Parader*'s version of the best guitarists in heavy metal bands.
- Sample dept/column: "Pick Hit" profiles the rock group Element 80 and describes its style and impact on today's evolving music scene.

Rights and Payment

First rights. Articles, $75–$100. Other material, payment rate varies. Pays on publication. Provides 1 contributor's copy.

Editor's Comments

Please do not send reviews of any type—we will not use them. A good way to catch our attention is to interview an up-and-coming group or musician and present the information in a style that is compatible with our magazine.

Home Education Magazine

P.O. Box 1083
Tonasket, WA 98855

Managing Editor: Helen Hegener

Description and Readership
One of the purposes of this magazine is to empower families who homeschool their children. Its widely diverse readers also find that the publication takes an active political stance in its editorial focus.
- **Audience:** Parents
- **Frequency:** 6 times each year
- **Distribution:** 50% subscription; 20% controlled; 30% other
- **Circulation:** 60,000
- **Website:** www.home-ed-magazine.com

Freelance Potential
90% written by nonstaff writers. Publishes 50 freelance submissions yearly; 25% by unpublished writers, 50% by authors who are new to the magazine. Receives 42 unsolicited queries and mss monthly.

Submissions
Query or send complete ms with résumé. Accepts photocopies, computer printouts, and email submissions to editor@home-ed-magazine.com. SASE. Responds in 1–2 months.
Articles: 1,000–1,500 words. Informational, how-to, and personal experience articles. Topics include homeschooling, education, and parenting.
Depts/columns: Staff written.
Artwork: B/W prints and color slides.

Sample Issue
66 pages (13% advertising): 8 articles; 13 depts/columns. Sample copy, $4.50 with 9x12 SASE. Guidelines available.
- "People Different from Ourselves." Article compares opportunities to meet children of different backgrounds in homeschooling and public education.
- "Beyond Statistics: A Real Look at African American Homeschoolers." Article delves into the growing number of African American children being taught at home.
- Sample dept/column: "Taking Charge" examines the misinformation about homeschooling provided by the media.

Rights and Payment
First North American serial and electronic rights. Articles, $50–$100. Artwork, $10–$100. Pays on acceptance. Provides 1 contributor's copy.

Editor's Comments
We would like to see more informative articles about real-life experiences written by parents who are homeschooling. We are not interested in pieces by teachers or ex-teachers who are not homeschooling their children.

Homeschooling Today

P.O. Box 436
Barker, TX 77413

Editor-in-Chief: Stacy McDonald

Description and Readership
This educational magazine offers practical, hands-on ideas for parents who homeschool their children and covers all age groups up to college. While it is not a religious publication, per se, many of the features found in the magazine are written with a Christian perspective.
- **Audience:** Parents
- **Frequency:** 6 times each year
- **Distribution:** Subscription; newsstand
- **Circulation:** 30,000
- **Website:** www.homeschoolingtoday.com

Freelance Potential
90% written by nonstaff writers. Publishes 10–20 freelance submissions yearly; 10% by unpublished writers, 5% by authors who are new to the magazine. Receives 5–10 unsolicited mss monthly.

Submissions
Send complete ms. Accepts photocopies and email submissions to editor@homeschoolingtoday.com (Microsoft Word or RTF attachments). SASE. Responds to queries in 3–6 months.
Articles: 1,000–2,500 words. Informational and how-to articles; profiles; interviews; and personal experience pieces. Topics include education, music, special education, the arts, history, mathematics, and science. Also publishes self-help articles.
Depts/columns: Word length varies. Study units, media and book reviews, and new product information.

Sample Issue
88 pages: 8 articles; 14 depts/columns. Sample copy, $5.95. Guidelines available.
- "What Makes a Book Good?" Article offers suggestions of books that will instill both a love of reading and a love of good literature in children.
- "Run with Endurance." Article profiles Congressman and Mrs. Jim Ryan.
- Sample dept/column: "Understanding the Arts" looks at the artwork of American impressionist Mary Cassatt.

Rights and Payment
First rights. Written material, $.08 per word. Pays on publication. Provides 1 contributor's copy.

Editor's Comments
Most of our writers come from a Christian background and in general, we prefer material that features a Christian perspective. We try and bring our readers practical ideas for use in their education program at home. Ideas that have been used successfully are the best.

Home Times

Suite 16
3676 Collin Drive
West Palm Beach, FL 33406

Editor: Dennis Lombard

Description and Readership

This tabloid covers a wide range of topics including the home, the arts, family life, arts and entertainment, national and international news, and religion. While it is nondenominational, the paper does present issues with a biblical perspective in mind.
- **Audience:** Families
- **Frequency:** 2 times a month
- **Distribution:** 100% controlled
- **Circulation:** 9,000
- **Website:** www.hometimes.org

Freelance Potential

80% written by nonstaff writers. Publishes 25 freelance submissions yearly; 75% by authors who are new to the magazine. Receives 60 unsolicited mss monthly.

Submissions

Send complete ms. Accepts photocopies, computer printouts, and simultaneous submissions if identified. SASE. Responds in 1 month.
Articles: 500–750 words. Informational and how-to articles; profiles; and interviews. Topics include family life, current events, entertainment, religion, and personalities.
Fiction: 500–750 words. Genres include contemporary, humorous, and historical and inspirational fiction.
Depts/columns: Word length varies. News, local issues, community events, book reviews, and entertainment.

Sample Issue

24 pages: 15 articles; 6 depts/columns. Sample copy, $3. Guidelines available.
- "Bush Victorious in Midst of Campaign Battle." Article examines the president's campaign.
- "House of Friends. Article profiles a synagogue congregation in Florida that provides a nurturing atmosphere.
- Sample dept/column: "Newswatch" discusses previous Bin Laden escapes.

Rights and Payment

One-time and electronic rights. Pays on publication. All material, payment rate varies. Provides 1 contributor's copy.

Editor's Comments

We are currently interested in seeing more profiles of interesting people from all walks of life, as well as personal testimonies. Articles that can present an idea or subject with a humorous point of view are always a plus. Please do not send any poetry submissions—we rarely use them and get far too many in the mail. We are a unique publication in that we publish every day topics with a mildly religious slant.

Hopscotch

P.O. Box 164
103 North Main Street
Bluffton, OH 45817-0164

Associate Editor: Virginia Edwards

Description and Readership

This theme-related publication is geared toward wholesome and unique subjects that appeal to young girls, and involve them directly in activities. There is no dating or fashion.
- **Audience:** 6–13 years
- **Frequency:** 6 times each year
- **Distribution:** 70% subscription; 30% newsstand
- **Circulation:** 15,000
- **Website:** www.hopscotchmagazine.com

Freelance Potential

100% written by nonstaff writers. Publishes 100–200 freelance submissions yearly; 20% by unpublished writers, 50% by authors who are new to the magazine. Receives more than 400 queries and unsolicited mss monthly.

Submissions

Query or send complete ms. Include photographs with nonfiction. Accepts photocopies, computer printouts, and simultaneous submissions if identified. SASE. Responds to queries in 1–2 weeks, to mss in 2–3 months.
Articles: To 500 words. Informational articles; profiles; and personal experience pieces. Topics include nature, animals, crafts, hobbies, ethnic subjects, and sports.
Fiction: To 1,000 words. Genres include mystery, adventure, and historical and multicultural fiction.
Depts/columns: 500 words. Crafts, cooking, and science activities.
Artwork: Prefers B/W prints to accompany nonfiction. Accepts color prints. No photocopies of photographs.
Other: Puzzles, activities, and poetry.

Sample Issue

50 pages (no advertising): 5 articles; 4 stories; 7 depts/columns; 2 poems; 6 activities; 1 joke page. Sample copy, $4 with 9x12 SASE. Guidelines and open theme list available with #10 SASE.
- "Grow Flowers Year Around." Article gives instructions on how to start flowering bulbs in indoor pots.
- "The Prize." Story recounts the efforts of a Japanese girl who has an opportunity to grow a prize chrysanthemum.
- Sample dept/column: "Science" tells how to grow potatoes.

Rights and Payment

First and second rights. Written material, $.05 per word. Artwork, payment rate varies. Pays on publication. Provides 1 contributor's copy.

Editor's Comments

Our upcoming themes include dollars and sense, babies, sports, and pioneers. No Halloween or fantasy pieces are accepted.

The Horn Book Magazine

Suite 200
56 Roland Street
Boston, MA 02129

Editor-in-Chief: Roger Sutton

Description and Readership

This journal of children's literature includes articles of a critical nature related to children's books and reading. Each issue features reviews of current books for children and young adults. *The Horn Book Magazine* is published for parents, teachers, librarians, artists, writers, and other adults interested in children's literature.
- **Audience:** Parents, teachers, and librarians
- **Frequency:** 6 times each year
- **Distribution:** 70% subscription; 10% newsstand
  20% other
- **Circulation:** 16,000
- **Website:** www.hbook.com

Freelance Potential

70% written by nonstaff writers. Publishes 12–15 freelance submissions yearly; 10% by unpublished writers, 25% by authors who are new to the magazine. Receives 20 queries, 10 unsolicited mss monthly.

Submissions

Query or send complete ms. Accepts photocopies and computer printouts. SASE. Responds in 4 months.
Articles: To 2,800 words. Interviews with children's authors, illustrators, and editors; critical articles about children's and young adult literature; and book reviews.
Depts/columns: Word length varies. Perspectives from illustrators; children's publishing updates; and special columns.

Sample Issue

140 pages (20% advertising): 8 articles; 67 reviews; 1 poem. Sample copy, free with 9x12 SASE. Guidelines and editorial calendar available.
- "Cutting the Cheese." Article looks at the proliferation of adult titles that are being re-worked as children's books.
- "Holden at Sixteen." Article discusses the reasons why *The Catcher in the Rye* would likely be published as a young adult novel in today's publishing world and how Holden Caulfield works as a young adult protagonist while so many others fail.

Rights and Payment

All rights. Pays on publication. Written material, payment rate varies. Provides 1 contributor's copy.

Editor's Comments

All of our articles relate to children's literature, whether they be discussions of authors or illustrators, book selection/criticism, or trends in children's and young adult publishing.

Horsemen's Yankee Pedlar

83 Leicester Street
North Oxford, MA 01537

Editor: Molly Johns

Description and Readership

This publication is an essential resource for New England's horse owners, trainers, and riders with information on events, training and discipline tips, care and feeding of horses, new products, industry updates, and breeds.
- **Audience:** YA–Adult
- **Frequency:** Monthly
- **Distribution:** Newsstand; subscription; schools
- **Circulation:** 50,000
- **Website:** www.pedlar.com

Freelance Potential

50% written by nonstaff writers. Publishes 40 freelance submissions yearly; 5% by authors who are new to the magazine. Receives 30 queries, 20 unsolicited mss monthly.

Submissions

Query or send complete ms. Accepts photocopies, computer printouts, and simultaneous submissions if identified. SASE. Responds to queries in 1–2 weeks, to mss in 2–3 months.
Articles: 500–800 words. Informational and how-to articles; personal experience pieces; interviews; and reviews. Topics include horse breeds, disciplines, training, health care, and equestrian equipment.
Depts/columns: Word length varies. Regional news, book reviews, business issues, nutrition, and legal issues.
Artwork: B/W and color prints.

Sample Issue

236 pages (75% advertising): 46 articles; 10 depts/columns. Sample copy, $2.75 with 9x12 SASE (7 first-class stamps). Guidelines available.
- "Appy Trails: Spring at Last!" Article features Appaloosa horses in the news—some from past glories, some in current activities, and some with famous owners.
- Sample dept/column: "Dressage News: July, 2004" lists summer events including Olympic happenings in Greece.

Rights and Payment

First North American serial rights. Written material, $2 per published column inch. Show coverage, $75 per day. Pays 30 days after publication. Provides 1 tearsheet.

Editor's Comments

The northeast region is our beat, so writers submitting material must have an understanding of horsemanship in that part of the United States. All facets of the equine industry and all breeds and disciplines are covered in our publication. If you write well and are familiar with New England's horse scene, we'd like to receive your submissions.

Horsepower

P.O. Box 670
Aurora, Ontario L4G 4J9
Canada

Managing Editor: Susan Stafford

Description and Readership
Horsepower is read by kids with a passion for horses. Each issue offers fiction with horse themes, as well as games, how-to articles, and informational articles on topics such as equine health, training, feeding, and horse care.
• **Audience:** 8–16 years
• **Frequency:** 6 times each year
• **Distribution:** 80% subscription; 10% schools; 10% controlled
• **Circulation:** 10,000
• **Website:** www.horse-canada.com

Freelance Potential
80% written by nonstaff writers. Publishes 10–12 freelance submissions yearly; 10% by unpublished writers, 10% by new authors. Receives 2–3 unsolicited mss monthly.

Submissions
Query with outline or synopsis; or send complete ms with résumé. Accepts photocopies, computer printouts, IBM disk submissions (ASCII or WordPerfect), and email submissions to info@horse-canada.com. SAE/IRC. Responds to queries in 1–2 weeks, to mss in 2–3 months.
Articles: 500–1,000 words. Informational and how-to articles; profiles; and humor. Topics include breeds, training, stable skills, equine health, and tack.
Fiction: 500 words. Adventure, humorous stories, and sports stories related to horses.
Depts/columns: Staff written.
Artwork: B/W and color prints.
Other: Horse-themed activities, games, and puzzles.

Sample Issue
44 pages (20% advertising): 7 articles; 5 depts/columns. Sample copy, $3.95. Guidelines and theme list available.
• "Summer Riding Camps." Article offers information on various camps with riding programs.
• "Competition." Story about a boy who tries to get the attention of a girl who only has horses on her mind.
• "A 'Rosie' Future." Article tells how chiropractic treatment helped an injured filly.

Rights and Payment
First North American serial rights. Pays on publication. Written material, $50–$90. Artwork, $10–$75. Provides 1 copy.

Editor's Comments
Please don't send us any fiction—we have too much already. We need articles on horse care and equine health, horse apparel, safety, grooming, and gift ideas for horse lovers.

Hudson Valley & Capital District Parent

174 South Street
Newburgh, NY 12550

Editor: Leah Black

Description and Readership
Articles that focus on parenting issues, resources, and events fill the pages of this tabloid. It is a free publication that is available to residents in the Mid-Hudson Valley and Capital District of New York State.
• **Audience:** Parents
• **Frequency:** Monthly
• **Distribution:** 100% other
• **Circulation:** 70,000
• **Website:** www.excitingread.com

Freelance Potential
90% written by nonstaff writers. Publishes 120 freelance submissions yearly; 50% by unpublished writers, 50% by authors who are new to the magazine. Receives 8 queries and unsolicited mss monthly.

Submissions
Query with writing samples; or send complete ms. Prefers email submissions to editor@excitingread.com. SASE. Responds in 3–6 weeks.
Articles: 700–1,200 words. Practical application and how-to articles. Topics include parenting, grandparenting, recreation, computers, technology, health, sports, hobbies, and the home.
Depts/columns: 700 words. Health topics, education, and adolescent issues.
Artwork: JPEG digital photos.
Other: Submit seasonal material 6 months in advance. New Spanish section, "Vida y Familia Hispana."

Sample Issue
62 pages (50% advertising): 6 articles; 8 depts/columns. Sample copy, free with 9x12 SASE. Writers' guidelines and editorial calendar available.
• "Making the Grade." Article features organizations that offer extra-curricular tutoring.
• "Six Tips for Better Parent/Teacher Conferences." Article offers tips to ensure a successful parent/teacher meeting.
• Sample dept/column: "Kid-Friendly Kitchen" provides an easy, kid-friendly recipe for chocolate pie.

Rights and Payment
One-time rights. Written material, $25–$70. Pays on publication. Provides contributor's copies.

Editor's Comments
We are currently seeking more articles on couples/marriage issues. Articles with local information using local sources are preferred. Make sure your writing is clear and concise. When possible send photographs that are applicable to the article.

Humpty Dumpty's Magazine

Children's Better Health Institute
1100 Waterway Boulevard, P.O Box 567
Indianapolis, IN 46206-0567

Editor: Phyllis Lybarger

Description and Readership

This publication is designed to educate and entertain readers while promoting good health and fitness. Through its editorial mix it encourages children of all races and cultures to strive for excellence in academics, personal fitness, and science.
- **Audience:** 4–6 years
- **Frequency:** 6 times each year
- **Distribution:** 100% subscription
- **Circulation:** 236,000
- **Website:** www.humptydumptymag.com

Freelance Potential

70% written by nonstaff writers. Publishes 25 freelance submissions yearly; 10% by unpublished writers, 25% by authors who are new to the magazine.

Submissions

Send complete ms. Accepts photocopies and computer printouts. SASE. Responds in 10–12 weeks.
Articles: To 250 words. Factual, observational, and how-to articles. Topics include health, fitness, sports, science, nature, the environment, animals, crafts, hobbies, and multicultural and ethnic subjects.
Fiction: To 300 words. Genres include early reader contemporary and multicultural fiction; stories about sports; fantasy; folktales; mystery; drama; and humor.
Depts/columns: Word length varies. Recipes and health and fitness news.
Other: Puzzles, activities, and games. Submit seasonal material 8 months in advance.

Sample Issue

36 pages (2% advertising): 4 articles; 1 story; 1 dept/column; 12 activities. Sample copy, $1.25. Writers' guidelines available.
- "Our Friend the Earthworm." Article demonstrates why earthworms are called "the gardener's best friend" by showing how they aerate and nourish soil.
- "The Zebra Who Didn't Like His Stripes." Story shows how a young zebra who wanted to have spots like a leopard, spots like a peacock, and spots like a giraffe finally realizes it's best just to be himself.

Rights and Payment

All rights. Written material, to $.22 per word. Pays on publication. Provides 10 contributor's copies.

Editor's Comments

Although our emphasis is on health, we certainly use material with more general themes and would like to see more holiday stories, articles, and activities.

Imperial Valley Family

P.O. Box 1397
El Centro, CA 92243

Publisher: Cheryl Von Flue

Description and Readership

Distributed free in stores, schools, medical offices, and family-related businesses and agencies, this tabloid serves parents living in Imperial County, California, including the communities of Niland, Ocotillo, Winterhaven, and Calexico. Parenting articles, resource lists, and schedules for libraries, parks, and swimming pools appear in its pages. Much of its material is published in both English and Spanish.
- **Audience:** Parents
- **Frequency:** Monthly
- **Distribution:** 50% schools; 50% other
- **Circulation:** 40,000
- **Website:** www.imperialvalleyfamily.org

Freelance Potential

40% written by nonstaff writers. Publishes 10–20 freelance submissions yearly; 10% by unpublished writers, 10% by authors who are new to the magazine. Receives 5–10 unsolicited mss monthly.

Submissions

Send complete ms. Accepts photocopies, computer printouts, and email submissions to impvalleyfamily@aol.com. SASE. Responds in 2 weeks.
Articles: 500–600 words. Informational and how-to articles; profiles; personal experience pieces; humor; and photo essays. Topics include parenting, family issues, recreation, popular culture, music, nature, the environment, social issues, college, and careers.
Depts/columns: 500–600 words. Book reviews.
Artwork: B/W prints or transparencies.
Other: Filler, activities, games.

Sample Issue

12 pages: 3 articles; 3 depts/columns; 1 community calendar. Sample copy, free with 9x12 SASE.
- "It's Summer and What's a Kid to Do?" Article lists ways to have fun, learn, and be safe over the summer.
- "Ten Common Sense Rules for Fathers." Article offers tips for improving relationships between dads and kids.
- "Travel'n Tots, Teens, and Tweens." Explains how to prepare children for a vacation.

Rights and Payment

All rights. Payment rates and policies vary. Provides 1 copy.

Editor's Comments

Our mission is to provide families living in Imperial County a resourceful and supportive medium for issues related to education, community, and business.

Indy's Child

1901 Broad Ripple Avenue
Indianapolis, IN 46220

Editorial Assistant: Lynette Rowland

Description and Readership
Parents with children from birth to age ten read this regional tabloid for its informational articles and its news and resources on Indianapolis and its surrounding suburbs. The tabloid is also a resource for local educators and caregivers working with children.
- **Audience:** Parents
- **Frequency:** Monthly
- **Distribution:** 50% newsstand; 30% controlled; 10% religious instruction; 10% schools
- **Circulation:** 144,000
- **Website:** www.indyschild.com

Freelance Potential
98% written by nonstaff writers. Publishes 75 freelance submissions yearly; 20% by authors who are new to the magazine. Receives 83 unsolicited mss monthly.

Submissions
Send complete ms. Accepts Macintosh disk submissions and email submissions to editor@indyschild.com. SASE. Responds 3–4 months.
Articles: 1,000–2,000+ words. Informational and self-help articles; profiles; interviews; humor; and personal experience pieces. Topics include the arts, colleges, careers, crafts, hobbies, current events, gifted and special education, health, fitness, multicultural and ethnic subjects, music, popular culture, recreation, social issues, sports, and travel.
Depts/columns: To 1,000 words. Women's and family health, single parenting, and museum reviews.
Artwork: Color prints, transparencies, or digital images.
Other: Puzzles, activities, filler, games, and jokes.

Sample Issue
46 pages (50% advertising): 6 articles; 9 depts/columns; 1 column. Sample copy, free. Guidelines available.
- "Dino Might." Article profiles a new dinosphere at the Children's Museum of Indianapolis.
- Sample dept/column: "News You Can Use" features brief items on the low-carb craze, practical products for pet owners, and why parents should let their children get dirty.

Rights and Payment
First or second rights. Written material, $100. Pays on publication. Provides 1–50 contributor's copies.

Editor's Comments
We welcome submissions from writers who are new to us and are familiar with our needs. Keep in mind that all of our features have a strong regional angle.

Insight

55 West Oak Ridge Drive
Hagerstown, MD 21740-7390

Editor: Dwain Neilson Esmond

Description and Readership
The Seventh-day Adventist Church produces this publication for Christian teens. It covers a wide range of topics that impact teens' lives.
- **Audience:** 14–21 years
- **Frequency:** Weekly
- **Distribution:** 10% subscription; 90% other
- **Circulation:** 20,000
- **Website:** www.insightmagazine.org

Freelance Potential
99% written by nonstaff writers. Publishes 150 freelance submissions yearly; 50% by unpublished writers, 70% by authors who are new to the magazine. Receives 83 mss monthly.

Submissions
Send complete ms. Accepts photocopies, computer printouts, disk submissions (Microsoft Word), and email submissions to insight@rhpa.org. SASE. Responds in 1–3 months.
Articles: 500–1,500 words. Informational articles; profiles; biographies; reports on volunteer and mission trips; and humor. Topics include social issues, religion, music, and careers.
Depts/columns: Word length varies. True-to-life stories and personal experience pieces.
Other: Submit material about Christmas, Easter, Mother's Day, Father's Day, and Valentine's Day 6 months in advance.

Sample Issue
16 pages (2% advertising): 6 articles; 1 dept/column. Sample copy, $2 with 9x12 SASE (2 first-class stamps). Writers' guidelines available.
- "The Spice of Life." Story relates how a young, homeless girl has a positive impact on another girl's life.
- "Rapid Number." A young missionary takes a challenging ride down a river in a kayak and prays for God's help.
- Sample dept/column: "Love and Relationships." offers a discussion about when couples should marry, and how they will know if they have received God's blessing.

Rights and Payment
First rights. Written material, $50–$125. Pays on acceptance. Provides 3 contributor's copies.

Editor's Comments
Our readers are teens who are looking for answers to the tough questions that relate to faith and growing up. We want to see stories that are upbeat and show the many ways God can impact teens' daily lives. We are not interested in stories that are full of "shoulds." Send us a submission that shows how the main character grows though an experience.

Instructor

Scholastic Inc.
524 Broadway
New York, NY 10012

Manuscript Editor

Description and Readership
Instructor gives teachers in kindergarten through eighth grade tips on everything from lesson plans and organization to professional development, activities, and educational trends.
- **Audience:** Teachers
- **Frequency:** 8 times each year
- **Distribution:** 40% subscription; 30% newsstand; 30% schools
- **Circulation:** 250,000
- **Website:** www.scholastic.com/instructor

Freelance Potential
75% written by nonstaff writers. Publishes 50 freelance submissions yearly; 20% by unpublished writers, 25% by authors who are new to the magazine. Receives 40 unsolicited mss monthly.

Submissions
Send complete ms. Accepts photocopies. Availability of artwork improves chance of acceptance. SASE. Responds in 3–4 months.
Articles: 1,200 words. Informational, how-to, and factual articles; and personal experience pieces. Topics include animals, pets, the arts, biographies, college, career, computers, current events, mathematics, science, music, nature, the environment, and special education.
Depts/columns: Short news items, questions and answers, computers, and testing. Word length varies. Classroom activities, to 250 words. Humorous or poignant personal essays, to 400 words.
Artwork: Color prints or transparencies. Line art.
Other: Games, puzzles, and activities, 400–800 words. Submit seasonal material 6 weeks in advance.

Sample Issue
72 pages (40% advertising): 3 articles; 5 depts/columns; 8 activities. Sample copy, $3 with 9x12 SASE. Guidelines and theme list available.
- "10 Big Math Ideas." Article shares a teacher's ideas that encourage children to better enjoy and understand math.
- Sample activity. "How to Paint Like Georgia O'Keeffe" provides instructions for children to duplicate her technique.

Rights and Payment
All rights. Articles, $600. Depts/columns, $250–$300. Pays on publication. Provides 2 contributor's copies.

Editor's Comments
We like to receive activities and teaching ideas that have worked well in classroom settings; written in a natural voice rather than academic prose.

InTeen

P.O. Box 436987
Chicago, IL 60643

Editor: Katara A. Washington

Description and Readership
This Christian magazine is designed to help inner-city African American teens cope with the daily challenges they face. It is filled with Bible lessons and Bible study guides. Fictional stories that illustrate biblical principles are incorporated into the lessons.
- **Audience:** 15–17 years
- **Frequency:** Quarterly
- **Distribution:** 80% subscription; 20% newsstand
- **Circulation:** 75,000
- **Website:** www.urbanministries.com

Freelance Potential
95% written by nonstaff writers. Publishes 52 freelance submissions yearly; 60% by unpublished writers, 50% by authors who are new to the magazine. Receives 30 queries monthly.

Submissions
All material is written on assignment. Send résumé with writing samples. SASE. Responds in 3–6 months.
Articles: Word length varies. Bible study guides and Bible lessons; how-to articles; profiles; interviews; and reviews. Topics include religion, biography, colleges, careers, black history, multicultural and ethnic subjects, social issues, and music.
Fiction: Word length varies. Stories are sometimes included as part of study plans. Includes inspirational, multicultural, and ethnic fiction, as well as real-life and problem-solving stories.
Other: Puzzles, activities, and poetry. Submit seasonal material 1 year in advance.

Sample Issue
32 pages (no advertising): 2 articles; 14 Bible study guides; 1 activity; 1 poem. Guidelines available.
- "Putting God First." Bible study guide includes a Scripture reading from Haggai as well as a story about a teen girl who gets so involved in activities she forgets about God.
- "Restored and Renewed." Article talks about God's willingness to forgive and restore us, even after we have turned away from his teachings.

Rights and Payment
All rights for work-for-hire material. One-time rights for features and poetry. Written material, payment rate varies. Artwork, payment rate varies. Pays 2 months after acceptance. Provides 2 contributor's copies.

Editor's Comments
We want to see submissions from writers who can present interesting and theologically sound explanations of Scripture. All of our Bible study guides reflect the African American worldview.

InTeen Teacher

P.O. Box 436987
Chicago, IL 60643

Editor: Katara A. Washington

Description and Readership
This magazine is published by Urban Ministries, Inc., the largest African American owned and operated Christian media company. It publishes lesson plans to be used with the Bible lessons that appear in *InTeen*.
- **Audience:** Religious educators
- **Frequency:** Quarterly
- **Distribution:** 80% subscription; 20% newsstand
- **Circulation:** 75,000
- **Website:** www.urbanministries.com

Freelance Potential
95% written by nonstaff writers. Publishes 52 freelance submissions yearly; 60% by unpublished writers, 50% by authors who are new to the magazine. Receives 30 queries monthly.

Submissions
All material is written on assignment. Send résumé with writing samples. SASE. Responds in 3–6 months.
Articles: Word length varies. Offers Bible study plans and teaching guides for teaching Christian values to African American teens.
Fiction: Word length varies. Stories are sometimes included as part of study plans. Includes inspirational, multicultural, and ethnic fiction, as well as real-life and problem-solving stories.
Other: Puzzles, activities, and poetry. Submit seasonal material 1 year in advance.

Sample Issue
80 pages (no advertising): 14 teaching plans; 14 Bible study guides. Guidelines available.
- "Hope for a New Era." Bible study guide teaches students how to articulate Zechariah's vision to the new world and obtain the requirement to participate in it.
- "Rejoice!" Teaching plan includes a fictional scenario about a talent contest that teaches a lesson on the importance of gaining a spiritual perspective on life.

Rights and Payment
All rights for work-for-hire material. One-time rights for features and poetry. Written material, payment rate varies. Artwork, payment rate varies. Pays 2 months after acceptance. Provides 2 contributor's copies.

Editor's Comments
Our products are developed by Christian educators who have experienced the African and African American worldview. Material you submit to us must be age appropriate, culturally relevant, and offer theologically sound explanations of Bible passages.

International Gymnast

P.O. Box 721020
Norman, OK 73070

Editor: Dwight Normile

Description and Readership
Information on gymnastic personalities, training, fitness, techniques, and competitions is written to engage and appeal to young gymnasts as well as their coaches and parents. It also includes innovations in the sport, guest opinions, and psychology along with some fiction.
- **Audience:** 10–16 years
- **Frequency:** 10 times each year
- **Distribution:** 95% subscription; 5% newsstand
- **Circulation:** 17,000
- **Website:** www.intlgymnast.com

Freelance Potential
10% written by nonstaff writers. Publishes 5 freelance submissions yearly; 50% by unpublished writers, 50% by authors who are new to the magazine. Receives fewer than 1 unsolicited ms monthly.

Submissions
Send complete ms. Accepts photocopies, computer printouts, and simultaneous submissions if identified. SASE. Responds in 1 month.
Articles: 1,000–2,250 words. Informational articles; profiles; and interviews. Topics include gymnastics competitions and coaching and personalities involved in the sport.
Fiction: To 1,500 words. Stories about gymnastics.
Depts/columns: 700–1,000 words. News, training tips, and opinion pieces.
Artwork: B/W prints. 35mm color slides for cover.

Sample Issue
46 pages (14% advertising): 5 articles; 1 story; 7 depts/columns. Sample copy, $5 with 9x12 SASE. Guidelines available.
- "Memoirs of a Gymnast." Article relates the ups and downs and personal experiences of Olympian Michelle Campi.
- "Standout." Article features China's Zhang Nan who made history for her country in the competition before going on to the Athens' Olympic Games.
- Sample dept/column: "All Around the World" profiles several international gymnasts in short vignettes.

Rights and Payment
All rights. Written material, $15–$25. Artwork, $5–$50. Pays on publication. Provides 1 contributor's copy.

Editor's Comments
All material should be geared to informing, improving, or uplifting young gymnasts and others associated with the sport. Unusual, humorous, and fiction stories are also accepted.

In the Family

Suite 114
7850 North Silverbell Road
PMB 188
Tucson, AZ 85743

Editor: Laura Markowitz

Description and Readership

This award-winning publication explores the variety and complexity of gay, lesbian, bisexual, and transgender (LGBT) family relationships. Informational and personal experiences are included in its mix.
- **Audience:** Gays and lesbians
- **Frequency:** Quarterly
- **Distribution:** Unavailable
- **Circulation:** 1,000
- **Website:** www.inthefamily.com

Freelance Potential

90% written by nonstaff writers. Publishes 12 freelance submissions yearly; 20% by previously unpublished writers; 30% by authors who are new to the magazine. Receives 50 queries and unsolicited mss each month.

Submissions

Query or send complete ms. Accepts photocopies and computer printouts. SASE. Response time varies.
Articles: Word length varies. Informational articles; profiles; and personal experience pieces. Topics include relationships, case presentations, and personal essays.
Fiction: To 4,000 words. Fiction should fit into our overall LGBT theme.
Depts/columns: Word length varies. Book reviews and lifestyles.
Other: Poetry. Up to 5 poems.

Sample Issue

28 pages (5% advertising): 3 articles; 1 story; 6 depts/columns. Sample copy, $6.50. Guidelines available at website.
- "Coming to Terms." Article chronicles the life of a young boy as he grows up, and the woman with whom his mother developed a relationship with after leaving his father.
- "The Prodigal Father." Story explores the relationship of a minister who initially renounces his son upon being told he's gay.
- Sample dept/column: "Out There" highlights several items relating to the LGBT lifestyle.

Rights and Payment

First rights. Written material, $35. Poetry, $35. Pays on publication. Provides 5 contributor's copies.

Editor's Comments

We would like to see more submissions on the perspectives of straight people regarding parenting, who are related to or working with gay, lesbian, bisexual, and transgender people. We invite feature articles, personal essays, and case presentations.

Iowa Parent

P.O. Box 957
Des Moines, IA 50304

Editor: Roberta J. Peterson

Description and Readership

Created to serve families living in central Iowa, this tabloid offers preschool, day care, and camp directories, along with activity calendars and practical articles on raising children. Each issue of *Iowa Parent* addresses a specific parenting theme.
- **Audience:** Parents
- **Frequency:** Monthly
- **Distribution:** 100% controlled
- **Circulation:** 26,000
- **Website:** www.iowaparent.com

Freelance Potential

20% written by nonstaff writers. Publishes less than 10 freelance submissions yearly; 50% by unpublished writers, 10% by authors who are new to the magazine. Receives 50 unsolicited mss monthly.

Submissions

Send complete ms. Accepts disk submissions and email submissions to editor@iowaparent.com. SASE. Response time varies.
Articles: 700–800 words. Informational, self-help, and how-to articles, and profiles. Topics include family issues, recreation, gifted and special education, summer camps, careers, college, the arts, music, entertainment, travel, crafts, sports, social issues, and popular culture.
Depts/columns: 700–800 words. Essays on family life; advice from physicians; and party planning.

Sample Issue

16 pages (50% advertising): 5 articles; 4 depts/columns; 2 directories; 1 activities calendar. Sample copy, $2 with 10x12 SASE. Guidelines and theme list available.
- "Are We There Yet?" Article features ideas for keeping kids occupied on long car or plane trips.
- "Hop into Spring with Great Craft Ideas." Article includes ideas and instructions for easy, fun Easter crafts adults can make with kids.
- Sample dept/column: "The Party Page" tells how to plan a safe and fun party for teens.

Rights and Payment

One-time, non-exclusive rights. Articles, $25. Pays on publication. Provides 2 contributor's copies.

Editor's Comments

If you want to write for us, we suggest you obtain a copy of our editorial calendar and theme list. We primarily use seasonal and holiday material in line with the topics listed on our calendar.

Jack And Jill

Children's Better Health Institute
1100 Waterway Boulevard
P.O. Box 567
Indianapolis, IN 46206-0567

Editor: Daniel Lee

Description and Readership

Stories, articles, activities, games, and poems fill the pages of this magazine that targets second- and third- grade readers. It aims to provide material focused on health and nutrition and is published by the Children's Better Health Institute.
• **Audience:** 7–10 years
• **Frequency:** 6 times each year
• **Distribution:** 100% subscription
• **Circulation:** 200,000
• **Website:** www.jackandjillmag.org

Freelance Potential

50% written by nonstaff writers. Publishes 10 freelance submissions yearly; 70% by authors who are new to the magazine. Receives 100 unsolicited mss monthly.

Submissions

Send complete ms. Accepts photocopies and computer printouts. SASE. Responds in 3 months.
Articles: 500–600 words. Informational and how-to articles; humor; profiles; and biographies. Topics include sports, health, exercise, safety, nutrition, and hygiene.
Fiction: 500–900 words. Genres include mystery, fantasy, folktales, humor, science fiction, as well as stories about sports and animals.
Artwork: Submit sketches to Andrea O'Shea, art director; photos to Daniel Lee, editor.
Other: Poetry, games, puzzles, activities, and cartoons. Submit seasonal material 8 months in advance.

Sample Issue

36 pages (4% advertising): 5 articles; 2 stories; 8 activities; 1 cartoon; 3 poems. Sample copy, $6.50 ($2 postage). Guidelines available.
• "Green Beans." Story tells of a boy who tries to avoid eating the string beans his mother gives him for dinner.
• "Bearobics" Article describes a bear game that includes exercising while stretching like a bear.

Rights and Payment

All rights. Articles and fiction, to $.17 per word. Other material, payment rate varies. Pays on publication. Provides 10 contributor's copies.

Editor's Comments

We seek articles that help kids lead a healthy lifestyle, including activities that make exercise fun, and interesting facts about healthy foods. Humorous stories are especially welcome. New writers have the best chance of publication with fiction.

Jackson Christian Family

PMB 346
6069 Old Canton Road
Jackson, MS 39211

Editor: Marilyn Smith

Description and Readership

Residents in the Jackson, Mississippi, area read this tabloid for local information and news. It also provides a great deal of inspirational material for Christian living by highlighting people of faith and other community leaders.
• **Audience:** Parents
• **Frequency:** Monthly
• **Distribution:** 95% newsstand; 5% subscription
• **Circulation:** 10,000

Freelance Potential

30% written by nonstaff writers. Publishes 60 freelance submissions yearly; 5% by unpublished writers, 2–3% by authors who are new to the magazine. Receives 8 queries monthly.

Submissions

Query with photos if applicable. Accepts photocopies and computer printouts. SASE. Responds in 1 month.
Articles: 500 words. Informational, self-help, and how-to articles; profiles; humor; and personal experience pieces. Topics include current events, health, fitness, music, recreation, regional news, religion, and social issues.
Fiction: 500 words. Genres include inspirational and humorous fiction.
Depts/columns: 500 words. Mission work, church leaders, legal issues, and healthy living.
Artwork: Color prints or transparencies.
Other: Activities. Submit seasonal material 2 months in advance.

Sample Issue

30 pages (35% advertising): 2 articles; 20 depts/columns; 1 calendar. Sample copy, free with 9x12 SASE ($3 postage). Editorial calendar available.
• "Hero Dads." Article profiles several area fathers who have provided their children and community with examples of integrity and courage.
• "Chris and Carla Snopek: Faith and Family." Article features the head of Jackson's Performance Sports Academy and the Christian influences that helped shape his success.
• Sample dept/column: "Inspirational Thoughts" relates a father's heartbreaking and heartwarming experiences with his daughter to the parable about the prodigal son.

Rights and Payment

Rights vary. No payment. Provides 1 contributor's copy.

Editor's Comments

We look for submissions that are uplifting and that provide individuals and families with positive examples. We also look for current issues and events that relate to the Jackson area.

Journal of Adolescent & Adult Literacy

International Reading Association
800 Barksdale Road, P.O. Box 8139
Newark, DE 19714-8139

Editorial Assistant: Rebecca Zell

Description and Readership
This journal, the official publication of the International Reading Association, promotes high levels of literacy by improving the quality of reading instruction, disseminating research and information about reading, and encouraging the lifetime habit of reading.
- **Audience:** Reading education professionals
- **Frequency:** 8 times each year
- **Distribution:** 100% subscription
- **Circulation:** 16,000
- **Website:** www.reading.org

Freelance Potential
100% written by nonstaff writers. Publishes 50 freelance submissions yearly; 20% by unpublished writers, 10% by authors who are new to the magazine. Receives 21 unsolicited mss monthly.

Submissions
Send 2 copies of complete ms with disk and hard copy. SASE. Responds in 2–3 months.
Articles: 1,000–6,000 words. How-to, informational, and personal experience articles. Topics include reading theory, research, and practice; and trends in teaching literacy.
Depts/columns: Word length varies. Opinion pieces, reviews, and technology information.

Sample Issue
96 pages (7% advertising): 5 articles; 6 depts/columns; 12 book reviews. Sample copy, $10. Guidelines available.
- "Chasing the Albatross: Gendering Theory and Reading with Dual-Voiced Journals." Article provides insight on differing male and female responses to the same works of literature.
- "Helping 'Struggling' Students Achieve Success." Article suggests cognitive approaches to help students make connections with their out-of-school experiences.
- Sample dept/column: "Literacy & Identity" offers an opinion on what it means to be a "reader."

Rights and Payment
All rights. No payment. Provides 5 contributor's copies for articles; 2 copies for depts/columns.

Editor's Comments
Our audience consists of classroom teachers, reading specialists, consultants, administrators, researchers, librarians, and parents. We are interested in receiving material that enhances the professional development of our audience, improves reading instruction, encourages the interests of reading professionals, and supports research that promotes informed decision making by policy makers.

Journal of Adventist Education

12501 Old Columbia Pike
Silver Spring, MD 20904-6600

Editor: Beverly J. Rumble

Description and Readership
Published by the Seventh-day Adventist Church, this magazine targets educators working with students in kindergarten through college. It publishes articles on educational theory and practice, with an emphasis on practical teaching ideas. It is available in English, French, Spanish, and Portuguese versions.
- **Audience:** Educators, school board members
- **Frequency:** 5 times each year
- **Distribution:** Subscription; religious instruction; controlled
- **Circulation:** 15,000
- **Website:** http://education.gc.adventist.org/JAE

Freelance Potential
90% written by nonstaff writers. Publishes 30–40 freelance submissions yearly. Receives 2–4 queries monthly.

Submissions
Query. Accepts photocopies and computer printouts. Availability of artwork improves chance of acceptance. SASE. Responds in 3 weeks.
Articles: To 2,000 words. Informational and how-to articles. Topics include parochial, gifted, and special education; mathematics; religion; science; and technology.
Artwork: B/W and color prints and transparencies. Line art.

Sample Issue
46 pages (5% advertising): 7 articles; 1 dept/column. Sample copy, $3.50 with 9x12 SASE ($.68 postage). Writers' guidelines available.
- "Student Success: How to Help Your Child." Article offers a primer for parents on working productively with educators and teaching their children to love to learn.
- "Binge Drinking: A New College Epidemic." Articles reports that high-risk alcohol and drug use is now considered the most widespread health problem on college campuses.
- "Theology for Children." Article offers ideas for teaching abstract theological concepts to younger children.

Rights and Payment
First North American serial rights. Articles, to $100. Artwork, payment rate varies. Pays on publication. Provides 2 contributor's copies.

Editor's Comments
Please remember that we have an international readership. We like to see articles that offer a call for action on a particular problem such as drug use, violence, or hazards at school. We'll also consider articles on church projects related to education, educational administration, extracurricular activities, and students with special needs and learning disabilities.

Journal of School Health

P.O. Box 708
7263 State Route 43
Kent, OH 44240-0708

Managing Editor: Tom Reed

Description and Readership

Since its establishment in 1930, the *Journal of School Health* has been publishing research papers, position papers, articles on teaching techniques, and informational articles that address the interests of health teachers, school nurses, physical education teachers, counselors, and other health professionals who work in day-care centers and schools.
- **Audience:** School health professionals
- **Frequency:** 10 times each year
- **Distribution:** Subscription
- **Circulation:** 5,000
- **Website:** www.ashaweb.com

Freelance Potential

90% written by nonstaff writers. Publishes 60 freelance submissions yearly; 90% by authors who are new to the magazine. Receives 10 queries monthly.

Submissions

Query or send 4 copies of complete ms; include 150-word abstract for articles and research papers. SASE. Responds to queries in 2 weeks, to mss in 3–4 months.
Articles: 2,500 words. Informational articles, research papers, commentaries, teaching techniques, and health service application pieces. Topics include health services in day-care centers, preschools, and elementary and secondary schools; teaching techniques; school nursing; medicine; and dentistry.

Sample Issue

34 pages (no advertising): 3 articles; 2 research papers; 1 health service application. Sample copy, $8.50 with 9x12 SASE. Guidelines available.
- "Physical Activity, Dietary Practices, and Other Health Behaviors of At-Risk Youth Attending Alternative High Schools." Article cites a study that reveals that the environment of alternative schools does not support physical activity and healthful eating, but that most administrators are interested in implementing programs to correct this.
- "Mental Health Services at Selected Private Schools." Article reports on a project that surveyed the type and frequency of mental health problems experienced by students at 11 private schools in Connecticut.

Rights and Payment

All rights. No payment. Provides 2 contributor's copies.

Editor's Comments

Please send for our detailed guidelines before preparing a submission for us. Failure to follow our guidelines completely may delay or prevent us from considering your work.

Juco Review

P.O. Box 7305
Colorado Springs, CO 80933-7305

Submissions: Wayne Baker

Description and Readership

Members of the National Junior College Athletic Association read this magazine for its articles on nutrition and health information, association news, and college sporting events.
- **Audience:** YA–Adult
- **Frequency:** 9 times each year
- **Distribution:** 90% controlled; 10% subscription
- **Circulation:** 2,700
- **Website:** www.njcaa.org

Freelance Potential

10% written by nonstaff writers. Publishes 5–7 freelance submissions yearly; 90% by unpublished writers, 80% by authors who are new to the magazine. Receives less than 1 unsolicited ms monthly.

Submissions

Send complete ms. Accepts photocopies and computer print-outs. Availability of artwork improves chance of acceptance. SASE. Responds in 2 months.
Articles: 1,500–2,000 words. Informational articles. Topics include sports, college, careers, health, fitness, and NJCAA organizational news.
Artwork: B/W prints and transparencies.

Sample Issue

22 pages (25% advertising): 8 articles. Sample copy, $4 for current issue; $3 for back issue with 9x12 SASE. Editorial calendar available.
- "NJCAA Basketball Hall of Famers Honored." Article reports on four retired basketball players from Hannibal-LaGrange College who were honored and had their jerseys retired.
- "2004 NJCAA Baseball Hall of Fame." Article spotlights four baseball head coaches that were inducted into the Juco Baseball Hall of Fame in the year 2004.

Rights and Payment

All rights. No payment. Provides 5 contributor's copies.

Editor's Comments

The majority of the pages of our publication are filled with timely information covering male and female athletes, college sports and events, and association news. We also, at times, include an article on health, nutrition, or an issue related to sports. If you have a unique story about a specific school, coach, or student athlete who is a member of the NJCAA, send us your manuscript. The best way to get know the type of material we use is to review our magazine.

Juniorway

P.O. Box 436987
Chicago, IL 60643

Editor: Katherine Steward

Description and Readership
This magazine is distributed to Christian African American youth in urban areas. Its articles promote evangelism, discipline, and service to Christ. *Juniorway* can be used as an aid to Bible study.
- **Audience:** 9–11 years
- **Frequency:** Quarterly
- **Distribution:** 100% religious instruction
- **Circulation:** 75,000
- **Website:** www.urbanministries.com

Freelance Potential
95% written by nonstaff writers. Publishes 52 freelance submissions yearly. Receives 20 queries monthly.

Submissions
Send résumé and writing samples. All material is written on assignment. Response time varies.
Articles: Word length varies. Personal experience pieces; photo essays; and humor. Topics include religion, social issues, ethnic and multicultural subjects, hobbies, crafts, nature, the environment, pets, and African American studies.
Fiction: Word length varies. Inspirational stories with multicultural themes; adventure stories; humor; and folktales.
Artwork: B/W and color prints and tranparencies.
Other: Activities, games, puzzles, jokes, and filler. Accepts seasonal material for vacation Bible school.

Sample Issue
32 pages (no advertising): 13 Bible lessons; 1 article; 4 puzzles. Sample copy, $1.90. Guidelines and theme list available.
- "Pathfinders." Article lists several courageous people who found a way to do what they believe is right.
- "Obedience Is a Choice." Lesson about a girl's choice to accept Jesus as her savior.
- "A Promise That Can't Be Broken." Lesson examines the consequences of broken promises.

Rights and Payment
All rights. Pays on publication. All material, payment rate varies.

Editor's Comments
Prospective writers must have the following qualifications and characteristics: be practicing Christians with a knowledge of the Bible; have an understanding of the African American experience and its relationship with the Bible; possess ability to clearly express ideas and thoughts; be familiar with formal Sunday school curriculum; and have experience in teaching Sunday school. We are looking for material that helps urban youth cope and make good decisions about everyday issues.

Juniorway Teacher

P.O. Box 436987
Chicago, IL 60643

Editor: Katherine Steward

Description and Readership
Juniorway Teacher contains 13 Bible study lessons for teachers to use with urban black middle school children. It provides religious teachers with lesson plans, study guides, discussion ideas, and other helpful information for conducting classes.
- **Audience:** Religious educators
- **Frequency:** Quarterly
- **Distribution:** 100% religious instruction
- **Circulation:** Unavailable
- **Website:** www.urbanministries.com

Freelance Potential
95% written by nonstaff writers. Publishes 52 freelance submissions yearly. Receives 20 queries monthly.

Submissions
Query with résumé. All material is written on assignment. Response time varies.
Articles: Word length varies. Informational and how-to articles; personal experience pieces; and teaching guides. Topics include religion, science, technology, social issues, crafts, hobbies, animals, pets, and African American history.
Artwork: B/W and color prints and transparencies.

Sample Issue
96 pages (no advertising): 3 articles; 13 teaching plans; 13 Bible study guides. Sample copy, $1.90. Guidelines and theme list available.
- "Teaching Juniors to Live the Christian Life." Article describes a change in attitude that happened when a teacher stopped telling children what to do and instead, started setting an example.
- "Obedience Is a Choice." Teaching plan sets out the theme of being faithful and obedient, and backs it up with several steps for specific instruction.
- "Be Faithful: Obey!" Bible study guide relates the theme to the teaching plan with Bible verses and a discussion pertinent to today's society.

Rights and Payment
All rights. All material, payment rate varies. Pays on publication.

Editor's Comments
We build each issue around a quarterly focus based on Bible verses. We also include tips and ideas from religious educators that have successfully improved the demeanor of students or aided in classroom teaching. Our mission is to provide quality Christian educational products and other services that will enhance instruction in Christian principles for teachers and students in a classroom setting.

Kansas School Naturalist

Department of Biological Sciences
Emporia State University
1200 Commercial Street
Emporia, KS 66801-5087

Editor: John Richard Schrock

Description and Readership
Each issue of *Kansas School Naturalist* is devoted to one article that considers an aspect of natural science or natural history. It is published on an irregular basis, and distributed free of charge upon request to teachers, school administrators, public and other school librarians, youth leaders, conservationists, and other persons interested in natural history and nature education who reside in Kansas. All material has some type of relationship to Kansas.
- **Audience:** Teachers, librarians, and conservationists
- **Frequency:** Irregular
- **Distribution:** 70% schools; 30% other
- **Circulation:** 9,300
- **Website:** www.emporia.edu/ksn

Freelance Potential
75% written by nonstaff writers. Publishes 100–200 freelance submissions yearly; 50% by authors who are new to the magazine. Receives 2 unsolicited mss yearly.

Submissions
Query or send complete ms. Accepts computer printouts and IBM disk submissions. SASE. Response time varies.
Articles: Word length varies. Informational and how-to articles. Topics include natural history, nature, science, technology, animals, health, and education—all with a Kansas focus.
Artwork: B/W and color prints and transparencies.
Other: Seasonal material.

Sample Issue
16 pages (no advertising): 1 article. Sample copy, free.
- "Pseudoscience of Animals and Plants: A Teachers Guide to Nonscientific Beliefs." Article goes in depth discussing how to answer students' questions concerning the scientific validity of everyday claims made by persons who may or may not be stating the facts accurately.

Rights and Payment
All rights. No payment. Provides contributor's copies.

Editor's Comments
Although most of our material is written by scientists, we do accept queries or manuscripts from others who are qualified to write on pertinent subjects. Write in a conversational and informative style, but please understand that all material must be backed up by exacting, scientific research. Students comprise a large part of our audience, so an engaging tone is important in order to keep their attention. Also bear in mind that the material we publish relates in some way to the nature or natural history of Kansas.

Keynoter

Key Club International
3636 Woodview Trace
Indianapolis, IN 46268-3196

Executive Editor: Shanna Mooney

Description and Readership
Kiwanis International Key Clubs distributes *Keynoter* to all of its service members to keep them informed of the latest news and updates within the organization. It also offers ideas for service projects, tips on leadership, and general information.
- **Audience:** 14–18 years
- **Frequency:** Quarterly
- **Distribution:** 100% membership
- **Circulation:** 200,000
- **Website:** www.keyclub.org

Freelance Potential
65% written by nonstaff writers. Publishes 16 freelance submissions yearly; 10% by unpublished writers, 40% by authors who are new to the magazine. Receives 10 queries monthly.

Submissions
Query with outline/synopsis and clips or writing samples. Accepts photocopies, computer printouts, and simultaneous submissions if identified. SASE. Responds in 1 month.
Articles: 1,200–1,500 words. Informational, self-help, and service-related articles focusing on problems faced by teens. Topics include education, current events, careers, and nature.
Depts/columns: Staff written.
Artwork: Color prints and illustrations.
Other: Submit material about college, back-to-school, and summer activities 3–7 months in advance.

Sample Issue
20 pages (5% advertising): 3 articles; 3 depts/columns. Sample copy, free with 9x12 SASE ($.65 postage). Guidelines available.
- "Service Scores." Article uses examples of several Kiwanis Clubs that have very successful sports projects involving young children in their communities.
- "Part-Time Jobs, Full-Time Fun." Article provides several sources that teens can tap when looking for a summer or part-time job that goes beyond fast food restaurants.
- "Remember to Floss—Your Mind?" Article profiles former Key Club members who created a magazine that educates and entertains.

Rights and Payment
First North American serial rights. Articles, $150–$350 (artwork fee may be included). Pays on acceptance. Provides 3 contributor's copies.

Editor's Comments
Our publication is written for young people who are interested in improving their lives through serving others. Articles should be written with a service slant for that age group.

Keys for Kids

Children's Bible Hour
Box 1
Grand Rapids, MI 49510

Editor: Hazel Marett

Description and Readership
Spiritual stories that reveal God's Word and help children build a personal faith in Jesus Christ fill the pages of this digest-sized publication. Each issue also includes daily devotionals that are based on Scripture passages, as well as passages to memorize.
- **Audience:** 6–14 years
- **Frequency:** 6 times each year
- **Distribution:** Sent upon request
- **Circulation:** 100,000
- **Website:** www.cbhministries.org

Freelance Potential
90% written by nonstaff writers. Publishes 75 freelance submissions yearly; 10% by unpublished writers, 10% by authors who are new to the magazine. Receives 8 unsolicited mss each month.

Submissions
Send complete ms. Accepts photocopies, computer printouts, and simultaneous submissions if identified. SASE. Responds in 2 months.
Articles: 400–425 words. Features devotionals consisting of 4 sections: "To Read" is a short Scripture passage followed by an illustrative story; "How About You?" applies the story and Scripture passage to children's lives; "To Memorize" offers Bible quotes in full; and "A Key" summarizes the point of the devotional. Topics include contemporary problems and peer pressure.

Sample Issue
74 pages (no advertising): 61 devotionals. Sample copy, free with 6x9 SASE. Writers' guidelines available.
- "A Helping Hand." Story teaches children the importance of lending a helping hand to others in need.
- "A Protective Love." Story discusses how God cares and protects each of his children.
- "Ten Feet Tall." Story explains how God makes each of us unique and every person is special.

Rights and Payment
First and second rights. Devotionals, $20–$25. Pays on acceptance.

Editor's Comments
We would like to see more stories that focus on current issues. Writing should include an everyday happening or object that illustrates a spiritual or biblical truth. Make sure each story teaches only one lesson and includes some action. If possible, include some humor and try to keep your story simple.

Kids Domain

Suite 1400
505 University Avenue
Toronto, Ontario M5G 1X3
Canada

Editor

Description and Readership
Kids Domain is a critically acclaimed educational and entertainment online destination for kids, parents, grandparents, caregivers, and educators in search of child-safe Internet content. It offers safe surfing tips, articles on effective teaching, thousands of downloads, contests, and experiential learning resources to educate and entertain children.
- **Audience:** Parents, educators, child caregivers, children
- **Frequency:** Updated weekly
- **Distribution:** 100% Internet
- **Hits per month:** Unavailable
- **Website:** www.kidsdomain.com

Freelance Potential
10% written by nonstaff writers. Publishes 10 freelance submissions yearly; 90% by unpublished writers. Receives 1 query each month.

Submissions
Query after completing an application and interview. Accepts email submissions to cindy@kidsdomain.com. Response time varies.
Articles: Word length varies. Informational and how-to articles; and reviews. Topics include effective teaching, safety, entertainment, parenting information, family issues, and product reviews.
Fiction: Word length varies. Publishes animal and holiday stories.
Depts/columns: Word length varies.
Artwork: GIF and JPEG formats.
Other: Interactive games, holiday activities.

Sample Issue
Sample copy available at website.
- "Painless Pointers for Packing." Article provides helpful hints on organized packing for every member of the family for short or long trips.
- "Activity Books." Article shows how to make an activity binder that is simple, easy-to-use, and a great idea for kids traveling in a car.

Rights and Payment
All rights. Written material, payment rate varies. Product reviews, no payment. Payment policy varies.

Editor's Comments
We need writers for 200–400 word reviews on products for families and children, including books, games, toys, and software. There is no payment, but the reviewer can keep the product.

Kids Life Magazine

3014 11th Avenue East
Tuscaloosa, AL 33405

Publisher: Mary Jane Turner

Description and Readership

Kids Life Magazine is a free publication for families in West Alabama. It features information on child-related events and family activities in the Tuscaloosa area. The publisher has also just launched a *Kids Life* for Birmingham, Alabama.
- **Audience:** Parents
- **Frequency:** 6 times each year
- **Distribution:** Subscription; newsstand; schools
- **Circulation:** 30,000
- **Website:** www.kidslifemagazine.com

Freelance Potential

100% written by nonstaff writers. Publishes 30 freelance submissions yearly; 50% by unpublished writers, 50% by authors who are new to the magazine. Receives 200 queries and unsolicited mss monthly.

Submissions

Query or send complete ms. Accepts computer printouts and email submissions to kidslife@comcast.net. SASE. Responds to email in 2 weeks.
Articles: 1,000 words. Informational articles; reviews; and personal experience pieces. Topics include parenting, education, child care, religion, cooking, crafts, health, and current events.
Artwork: Color prints or transparencies. Line art.
Other: Puzzles, activities, games, and filler.

Sample Issue

38 pages (60% advertising): 7 articles. Sample copy, free.
- "Choose Camp . . . And Choose Carefully."Article reviews issues to consider in choosing a camp for a child.
- "Ship of Dreams." A new exhibit about the *Titanic* featured at a local museum is reviewed.
- Sample dept/column: "Happy Birthday to You" showcases pictures of local kids with birthdays in the issue month.

Rights and Payment

Rights policy varies. Written material, to $30. Pays on publication. Provides 1 contributor's copy.

Editor's Comments

We are first and foremost a magazine for parents and families in Alabama. All of the material we publish has a focus on some aspect of our state. Topics that we cover routinely include family issues, parenting, education, and religion. If you have a story or idea that will interest our family readers, then we are interested in hearing from you. We understand that many parenting topics are not new, but a good writer can give a tried and true subject like bedtime a new and fresh perspective.

Kids Tribute

71 Barber Greene Road
Don Mills, Ontario M3C 2A2
Canada

Editor: Robin Stevenson

Description and Readership

Kids Tribute is a popular culture and entertainment magazine for children and adolescents. Movies for families and kids, television shows, videos, video and computer games, books, and music are all covered. It includes celebrity profiles, reviews, and activities, as well as occasional articles on nature, animals, and the environment.
- **Audience:** 8–14 years
- **Frequency:** Quarterly
- **Distribution:** 90% newsstand; 10% subscription
- **Circulation:** 310,000
- **Website:** www.tribute.ca

Freelance Potential

10% written by nonstaff writers. Publishes 5–10 freelance submissions yearly; 1% by authors who are new to the magazine. Receives 2 queries monthly.

Submissions

Query with clips or writing samples. No unsolicited mss. Availability of artwork improves chance of acceptance. SAE/IRC. Responds in 1–2 months.
Articles: 400–500 words. Informational articles; profiles; photo essays; and personal experience pieces. Topics include entertainment, popular culture, music, the arts, video and computer games, nature, animals, and the environment.
Depts/columns: Word length varies. Media reviews.
Artwork: Color prints and transparencies.
Other: Puzzles, activities, and games.

Sample Issue

45 pages (50% advertising): 11 articles; 5 depts/columns; 6 activities; 1 pull-out poster. Sample copy, $2.95 Canadian with 9x12 SAE/IRC ($.86 Canadian postage).
- "A Cinderella Story . . . Without the Glass Slipper." Article profiles teen superstar Hilary Duff.
- "Are You Ready for the Return of Spidey?" Article provides behind-the-scenes information about the making of a superhero movie sequel.
- Sample dept/column: "Take a Byte" reviews four new video games.

Rights and Payment

First North American serial rights. Written material, $75–$100 Canadian. Artwork, payment rate varies. Pays on acceptance. Provides 1 contributor's copy.

Editor's Comments

We want writers who can provide kids with insider information on the movie, music, and entertainment scenes.

Kids VT

10½ Alfred Street
Burlington, VT 05401

Editor: Susan Holson

Description and Readership
This regional tabloid likes to keep its material local, and prefers to quote parents from the Vermont area. Subjects are covered thoroughly to provide as much information as possible to readers. Parenting issues and local resources make up the majority of this publication's content.
- **Audience:** Parents
- **Frequency:** 10 times each year
- **Distribution:** 100% other
- **Circulation:** 22,000
- **Website:** www.kidsvt.com

Freelance Potential
75% written by nonstaff writers. Publishes 50 freelance submissions yearly; 25–50% by authors who are new to the magazine. Receives 40–80 unsolicited mss monthly.

Submissions
Send complete ms. Accepts faxes to 802-865-0595, email to editorial@kidsvt.com, and simultaneous submissions if identified. Response time varies.
Articles: 500–1,500 words. Informational articles; profiles; interviews; and humor. Topics include the arts, education, recreation, nature, the environment, music, camps, maternity issues, and infancy.
Depts/columns: Word length varies. News and book reviews.
Other: Activities and games. Submit seasonal material 2 months in advance.

Sample Issue
32 pages (50% advertising): 8 articles; 7 depts/columns. Theme list available.
- "The Family That Skis Together Freeze Together." Article gives lots of advice and humorous episodes related to skiing with young children.
- "A Cook's Confession." Article outlines why the author likes to cook from scratch with fresh foods, even if it's not a "cool" pursuit today.
- Sample dept/column: "Parenting With Success" shares an expert's advice and experiences to help new parents raise their children.

Rights and Payment
Exclusive Vermont rights. Written material, $15–$40. Pays on publication. Provides 1–2 contributor's copies.

Editor's Comments
Our publication serves as a parenting guide for local families. Submissions should emphasize information that helps make parenting a positive and enjoyable experience.

Kid Zone

450 Benson Building
Sioux City, IA 51101

Editor-in-Chief: Jennifer Winquist

Description and Readership
The motive of this colorful, fast-paced magazine is to entice young minds via interesting projects and activities, many of which are tied into short, informational articles. It's not just for kids, but also for teachers, parents, and day-care providers who find this publication useful.
- **Audience:** 4–12 years
- **Frequency:** 6 times each year
- **Distribution:** Unavailable
- **Circulation:** 100,000
- **Website:** www.kidzonemag.com

Freelance Potential
30% written by nonstaff writers. Publishes 12–18 freelance submissions yearly; 25% by authors who are new to the magazine. Receives 12 unsolicited mss monthly.

Submissions
Send complete ms. Accepts photocopies, computer printouts, and email submissions to jwinquist@scottpublications.com (no attachments). SASE. Responds in 1 month.
Articles: 500–1,500 words. Informational articles. Topics include recycling, food, nature, various cultures, and animals.
Depts/columns: Word length varies. Crafts, cooking, nature, and activities.
Artwork: Color prints and transparencies. Line art.
Other: Submit seasonal material 4 months in advance.

Sample Issue
66 pages (12% advertising): 4 articles; 10 depts/columns; 14 games and puzzles. Sample copy, $4.99 with 9x12 SASE ($1.73 postage). Guidelines available.
- "New Zealand." Article introduces the reader to facts about New Zealand, including the animals, the land, the location, the culture, and some of the Maori words and phrases.
- "Morph Zone." Article begins with a short history of fabric, then demonstrates how to recycle old clothes to make fun, new accessories.
- Sample dept/column: "Info Zone" gives several short wind-related informational bites, followed by an activity showing how wind works.

Rights and Payment
World rights. All material, payment rate varies. Pays on publication. Provides 1 contributor's copy.

Editor's Comments
We are looking for well-rounded features that include information in a fun format, with applicable crafts and games. We have enough bug material, and we don't accept fiction.

Know Your World Extra

200 First Stamford Place
Stamford, CT 06912

Senior Managing Editor: Deb Nevins

Description and Readership

Striving to engage below-level readers with lively and informative content, this educational magazine offers articles, stories, and activities that target middle-grade students.
- **Audience:** 10–18 years
- **Frequency:** Monthly
- **Distribution:** 50% controlled; 50% schools
- **Circulation:** 80,000
- **Website:** www.weeklyreader.com

Freelance Potential

40% written by nonstaff writers. Of the freelance submissions published yearly; 20% are by unpublished writers, 50% are by authors who are new to the magazine. Receives 10 queries each month.

Submissions

Query with samples. SASE. Response time varies.
Articles: 350–500 words. How-to articles, plays, profiles, and interviews. Topics include animals, current events, health and fitness, history, humor, music, popular culture, science, technology, and sports.
Fiction: 1,200 words. Genres include adventure, contemporary, fantasy, horror, humor, inspirational, multicultural, real-life issues, science fiction, and sports.
Depts/columns: 150–200 words. Current events, health, animals, and sports.
Other: Crosswords, riddles, and puzzles.

Sample Issue

16 pages (no advertising): 2 articles; 9 depts/columns. Sample copy, free with 9x12 SASE. Guidelines available.
- "All Juiced Up." Article discusses the issue of steroids being used by athletes.
- "The Racket." Play features a garage band that struggles to find its signature sound.
- Sample dept/column: "Reality Check" talks about the benefits of volunteering during summer vacation and offers a list of volunteer ideas.

Rights and Payment

One-time rights. Written material, payment rate varies. Pays on approval. Provides 5 contributor's copies.

Editor's Comments

We look for issues that interest young teens such as celebrities and music. New writers have the best chance with a read-aloud play, cover stories, and our department "real teens." In order to meet the needs of our readers, writing should be in a conversational tone, compelling, but uncomplicated.

☆ Ladies' Home Journal

Meredith Corporation
125 Park Avenue
New York, NY 10017

Editor: Caroline Stanley

Description and Readership

This well-known lifestyle magazine is read primarily by women. Each issue of *Ladies' Home Journal* brings readers articles on fashion, fitness, family, parenting, child development, health, and careers.
- **Audience:** Women
- **Frequency:** Monthly
- **Distribution:** Newsstand; subscription
- **Circulation:** 4.1 million
- **Website:** www.lhj.com

Freelance Potential

50% written by nonstaff writers. Publishes 50 freelance submissions yearly; 5% by unpublished writers, 10–20% by authors who are new to the magazine. Receives 200 queries monthly.

Submissions

Query with résumé, outline, and clips or writing samples for nonfiction. Accepts fiction through literary agents only. SASE. Responds in 1–3 months.
Articles: 1,500–2,000 words. Informational, how-to, and personal experience articles; profiles; and interviews. Topics include family issues, parenting, social concerns, fashion, beauty, and women's health.
Fiction: Word length varies. Accepts agented submissions only.
Depts/columns: Word length varies. Short news items, fashion and beauty advice, and marriage and family issues.

Sample Issue

224 pages: 18 articles; 17 depts/columns. Sample copy, $2.49 at newsstands.
- "This Home Saved My Son's Life." Article highlights the benefits of Habitat for Humanity homes for families in need.
- "The Birth Controller." Article profiles a woman who advocates sterilization for drug addicts.
- Sample dept/column: "Inner Life" suggests that luck requires a winning attitude.

Rights and Payment

All rights. All material, payment rate varies. Pays on acceptance. Provides 2 contributor's copies.

Editor's Comments

We will consider true accounts of dramatic events and first-person pieces about moments that have changed lives. Freelancers are invited to submit material for our "First Person" department, as well as timely pieces with sidebars about contemporary issues. Family and parenting concerns take priority with our editors.

Ladybug

The Magazine for Young Children

Cricket Magazine Group
P.O. Box 300, 315 Fifth Street
Peru, IL 61354

Submissions Editor

Description and Readership

Young children love this magazine for its colorful stories, poems, songs, and activities. In print for over 14 years, it features different types of stories including read-aloud, early reader, and picture stories.
- **Audience:** 2–6 years
- **Frequency:** Monthly
- **Distribution:** 92% subscription; 8% other
- **Circulation:** 145,000
- **Website:** www.cricketmag.com

Freelance Potential

90% written by nonstaff writers. Publishes 120 freelance submissions yearly; 50% by authors who are new to the magazine. Receives 200 unsolicited mss monthly.

Submissions

Send complete ms with exact word count. Accepts photocopies, computer printouts, and simultaneous submissions if identified. SASE. Responds in 3–4 months.
Articles: To 300 words. Informational, humorous, and how-to pieces. Topics include nature, animals, family, the environment, and other age-appropriate topics.
Fiction: 100–800 words. Read-aloud, early reader, picture, and rebus stories. Genres include adventure, humor, mild suspense, folktales, and contemporary fiction.
Other: Puzzles, activities, games, crafts, finger plays, songs, and short poems.

Sample Issue

36 pages (no advertising): 6 stories; 1 poem; 2 cartoons; 1 song; 1 activity. Sample copy, $5. Guidelines available.
- "Dog Talk." Story features a dog who provides insight into what sounds and actions by dogs really mean.
- "Rahul's Cat." Story tells of a young boy's desire to keep a stray cat, and how with the help of his grandmother, he gains acceptance from his mother.
- "The Secret Project." Story tells of a girl who gathers things from her house to make a project for birds.

Rights and Payment

Rights vary. Articles and fiction, $.25 per word. Other material, payment rate varies. Pays on publication. Provides 6 copies.

Editor's Comments

We only print top-notch material. Make sure your writing style matches our target age group. Humorous pieces are always welcome. Remember, we want to provide children with entertaining stories that help foster a love of reading, and make reading time fun.

Language Arts

University of Arizona
515 College of Education
Tucson, AZ 85721

Editor: Kathy G. Short

Description and Readership

Language Arts is the journal of the elementary section of the National Council of Teachers of English. As such, it publishes original articles on all facets of language arts learning and teaching, focusing primarily on children preschool through middle school.
- **Audience:** Teachers
- **Frequency:** 6 times each year
- **Distribution:** 100% subscription
- **Circulation:** 22,000
- **Website:** www.ncte.org

Freelance Potential

85% written by nonstaff writers. Publishes 35–40 freelance submissions yearly; 15% by unpublished writers, 25% by authors who are new to the magazine. Receives 20 unsolicited mss monthly.

Submissions

Send 5 copies of complete ms along with an electronic Word or pdf file. Accepts photocopies, computer printouts, and IBM or Macintosh disk submissions. SASE. Responds in 3–9 months.
Articles: 2,500–6,500 words. Research articles; position papers; personal experiences; and opinion pieces. Topics include language arts, linguistics, literacy, and educational psychology.
Depts/columns: Word length varies. Profiles of children's authors and illustrators; reviews of instructional material, children's trade books, and professional resources; and theme-related research papers.

Sample Issue

95 pages (8% advertising): 6 articles; 4 depts/columns. Sample copy, $5 with 9x12 SASE. Writers' guidelines and theme list available.
- "Art and Literacy with Bilingual Children." Article reveals how a teacher uses art projects and book discussions to develop students' literary skills.
- Sample dept/column: "Profile" presents four retired English teachers who courageously decided to attend a literary forum just a few days following the September 11th tragedy.

Rights and Payment

All rights. No payment. Provides 2 contributor's copies.

Editor's Comments

We would like more cutting-edge pieces on classroom practice, technology, and literacy. When possible please include charts, children's artifacts, bulleted points, and graphs. We have too many pieces on rubrics and mandates.

Launch Pad

Teen Missions International
885 East Hall Road
Merritt Island, FL 32953

Senior Editor: Linda Maher

Description and Readership

Teen Missions International uses this tabloid to showcase the efforts of their missionaries around the world. It is full of pictures and real-life experiences of these young people, focusing not only on their successes, but on the people they serve. It also contains information on current and future mission sites.
• **Audience:** YA–Adult
• **Frequency:** Twice a year
• **Distribution:** Unavailable
• **Circulation:** Unavailable
• **Website:** www.teenmissions.org

Freelance Potential

10% written by nonstaff writers. Publishes 10 freelance submissions yearly; 15% by unpublished writers, 15% by authors who are new to the magazine. Receives 8–10 queries monthly.

Submissions

Query. Accepts photocopies and computer printouts. SASE. Response time varies.
Articles: Word length varies. Informational and factual articles; personal experience pieces; profiles; interviews; and photo essays. Topics include mission work and teen evangelism in different countries.
Fiction: Word length varies. Inspirational, multicultural, and ethnic fiction.
Depts/columns: Word length varies. Alumni news and teen mission opportunities.

Sample Issue

8 pages (5% advertising): 2 articles; 4 depts/columns.
Sample copy available.
• "Summer Success Stories." Article relates the positive experiences of several young missionaries.
• "Overseas Boot Camps." Article describes a variety of boot camp successes throughout the world.
• Sample dept/column: "Rescue Unit Update" brings readers up to date on the status of the Sub-Sahara Africa AIDS Orphans Rescue Units.

Rights and Payment

Rights policy varies. No payment.

Editor's Comments

We would like to see more articles concentrating on how to live a Christian life, written by teens and children for teens and children. Life-changing mission experiences are always welcome if they are upbeat—but please do not send stories of healing experiences or accounts of heart-wrenching testimonies.

Leadership for Student Activities

National Association of Secondary School Principals
1904 Association Drive
Reston, VA 20191-1537

Editor: Lyn Fiscus

Description and Readership

This publication provides practical and useful information, including challenges met and overcome, for student activities advisors and leaders at middle and high school levels.
• **Audience:** Student leaders and advisors
• **Frequency:** 9 times each year
• **Distribution:** 95% subscription; 5% other
• **Circulation:** 51,000
• **Website:** www.nhs.us/leadershipmag

Freelance Potential

67% written by nonstaff writers. Publishes 18–25 freelance submissions yearly; 75% by unpublished writers, 50% by authors who are new to the magazine. Receives 1–2 queries, 4 unsolicited mss monthly.

Submissions

Query with clips; or send complete ms. Accepts photocopies, computer printouts, Macintosh disk submissions, and email submissions to FiscusL@principal.org. SASE. Responds to queries in 2 weeks, to mss in 1 month.
Articles: 1,200–1,700 words. Informational and how-to articles; profiles; and interviews. Topics include student activities, leadership development, and careers.
Depts/columns: Reports on special events, 100–350 words; advice for and by activity advisors, 1,000–1,500 words; national and regional news, leadership plans, and opinion pieces, word length varies.
Artwork: B/W and color prints and transparencies.
Other: Submit homecoming, graduation, and other seasonal material 4 months in advance.

Sample Issue

52 pages (21% advertising): 6 articles; 11 depts/columns.
Sample copy, free with 9x12 SASE ($1.24 postage).
Guidelines and theme list available.
• "Travel Tension." Article chronicles the detailed planning needed for an overseas trip with students or other school-connected travelers.
• Sample dept/column: "Middle Level Activities" shows how starting as a middle school student council leader gave the author good skills that have lasted beyond college years.

Rights and Payment

All rights. Payment policy and rates vary. Provides 5 contributor's copies.

Editor's Comments

We are always looking for exciting articles and ideas to share with our readers. Don't forget to include the difficulties!

Leading Edge

3146 JKHB
Provo, UT 84602

Fiction Director: Jillena O'Brien

Description and Readership
New and upcoming talent is presented in this magazine dedicated to science fiction and fantasy. Readers find novellas, novelettes, short stories, and poetry in its pages—all written with an underlying purpose to uphold traditional family values.
- **Audience:** YA–Adult
- **Frequency:** Twice each year
- **Distribution:** 30% subscription; 70% other
- **Circulation:** 500
- **Website:** http://tle.byu.edu

Freelance Potential
85% written by nonstaff writers. Publishes 15 freelance submissions yearly; 75% by unpublished writers, 100% by authors who are new to the magazine. Receives 50 unsolicited mss monthly.

Submissions
Send complete ms. Accepts photocopies and computer printouts. No simultaneous submissions. SASE. Responds in 2–3 months.
Articles: 1,000–10,000 words. Informational articles; interviews; and book reviews. Topics include science fiction, fantasy, and mythology.
Fiction: To 17,000 words. Science fiction and fantasy.
Depts/columns: Staff written.
Other: Poetry, no line limit.

Sample Issue
170 pages (no advertising): 2 articles; 8 stories; 3 poems; 4 depts/columns. Sample copy, $4.95. Guidelines available.
- "Goodbye, Me!" Article delves into the author's psyche, as he tries to determine how his self-identity makes sense in his world.
- "The Bones Don't Lie." Story ties together ancient myths and coming-of-age responsibilities in a gripping science fiction mystery format.

Rights and Payment
First rights. Written material, $.05 per word. Artwork, payment rate varies. Pays on publication. Provides 2 contributor's copies.

Editor's Comments
We accept nonfiction articles on subjects such as mythology, speculative anthropology, science, fantasy, and science fiction. Interviews with current popular authors writing in the science fiction or fantasy genre are also welcome. We do not accept submissions that contain excessive violence, profanity or sex, or that belittle religion or values.

Leading Student Ministry

One Life Way Plaza
Nashville, TN 37234-0174

Editor-in-Chief: Paul Turner

Description and Readership
The mission of this magazine is "to equip vocational and volunteer leaders for faithful and effective ministry to students by providing practical tools for life and ministry." In each issue, ministers and leaders find practical information to assist them in their work with young people in seventh grade through college.
- **Audience:** Youth ministers and leaders
- **Frequency:** Quarterly
- **Distribution:** Unavailable
- **Circulation:** 10,000
- **Website:** www.lifeway.com

Freelance Potential
85% written by nonstaff writers.

Submissions
Query or send complete ms with résumé. Accepts email submissions to paul.turner@lifeway.com (Microsoft Word documents). SASE. Responds to queries in 2–3 days, to mss in 2–3 weeks.
Articles: 1,000–1,800 words. How-to articles, profiles, interviews, and personal experience pieces. Topics include college, careers, current events, health, fitness, music, popular culture, religion, adolescent ministry, and parenting teens. Also publishes humorous articles.
Depts/columns: 500–1,000 words. Youth culture, adolescent development and counseling, college ministry, parent ministry, teaching tips, and resource reviews.
Artwork: B/W and color prints and transparencies. Line art.
Other: Jokes. Submit seasonal material 3 months in advance.

Sample Issue
62 pages (no advertising): 7 articles; 8 depts/columns. Sample copy, $3.95. Guidelines available.
- "Getting off the Roller Coaster." Article maintains that carrying the momentum of summer youth activities into the fall programs will result in more effective ministries.
- Sample dept/column: "Parent Ministry" advises ministers and parents to be aware of and sensitive to the developmental changes that teens are going through.

Rights and Payment
All rights. Pays on acceptance. Written material, $.10 per word. Artwork, payment rate varies. Provides 3 copies.

Editor's Comments
We suggest using a warm, conversational tone in your writing. Our goal is to encourage student ministry leaders, and we do that by addressing personal as well as professional issues.

Learning and Leading With Technology

International Society for Technology in Education
480 Charnelton Street
Eugene, OR 97401-2626

Editor: Kate Conley

Description and Readership
Practical articles relating to technology in the classroom appear in this magazine from the International Society for Technology in Education (ISTE). It features material about educational policy, leadership, and curriculum development.
- **Audience:** Educators
- **Frequency:** 8 times each year
- **Distribution:** 90% subscription; 10% libraries
- **Circulation:** 12,000
- **Website:** www.iste.org/LL

Freelance Potential
90% written by nonstaff writers. Publishes 50 freelance submissions yearly; 50% by unpublished writers. Receives 8 unsolicited mss monthly.

Submissions
Check website for latest submissions information. Send 2 copies of complete ms with resources and author biography. Accepts photocopies, computer printouts, disk submissions, email submissions to submission@iste.org, and simultaneous submissions if identified. SASE. Response time varies.
Articles: 600–2,000 words. Informational and how-to articles; and personal experience pieces. Topics include computers, software, technology, teaching methods, and telecommunications.
Depts/columns: Word length varies. Research, software reviews, and curriculum ideas.
Artwork: B/W prints. Line art.

Sample Issue
64 pages (20% advertising): 3 articles; 13 depts/columns. Sample copy, free with 9x12 SASE (3 first-class stamps). Guidelines and editorial calendar available at website.
- "Leading Through Advocacy." Interview with ISTE CEO Don Knezek discusses his thoughts on educational technology leadership and leadership development.
- "Sine Qua Non." Article offers several indispensable resources for educational technology professionals.
- Sample dept/column: "Student Voices" highlights the work of a student-produced multimedia broadcasting station.

Rights and Payment
All rights; returns limited rights to author upon request. No payment. Provides 3 contributor's copies.

Editor's Comments
We like to see practical information on using technology where it can make a difference in teaching and motivating students. Send us material for varying levels of student ability and learning styles.

The Learning Edge

Clonlara School
1289 Jewett
Ann Arbor, MI 48104

Editor: Susan Andrews

Description and Readership
The Clonlara School publishes this newsletter to keep its participants informed of school news and events, as well as member activities and accomplishments. Committed to educational rights and freedoms, this school offers advice, support, and curriculum materials to parents who choose to home-school their children.
- **Audience:** Clonlara School members
- **Frequency:** 6 times each year
- **Distribution:** 100% subscription
- **Circulation:** 3,000
- **Website:** www.clonlara.org

Freelance Potential
25% written by nonstaff writers. Publishes 10 freelance submissions yearly; 25% by unpublished writers, 5% by authors who are new to the magazine. Receives 3 queries monthly.

Submissions
Query. Accepts photocopies and computer printouts. SASE. Responds in 2 months.
Articles: Word length varies. Informational and how-to articles; profiles; and personal experience pieces. Topics include homeschooling, education, computers, careers, and college.
Depts/columns: Word length varies. School programs, membership information, and curriculum resources.
Other: Puzzles and activities.

Sample Issue
12 pages (no advertising): 3 articles; 4 depts/columns; 4 poems. Sample copy available upon request.
- "Alternative Education: A Springboard for College." Article relates the alternative education experiences of a young man in the secondary program who was accepted at his three top-choice universities.
- "Walkabouts Help Student Realize a Dream." Article by a parent reports on her son's success, which she believes was aided by homeschooling and the support of Clonlara.
- Sample dept/column: "News from Our Families" offers poetry and artwork by members and announcements of member accomplishments.

Rights and Payment
All rights. No payment.

Editor's Comments
We encourage our families to consider writing articles about their experiences. Material of general interest to home educators is welcome, particularly on the subject of mathematics. Query us with your ideas.

Learning Guide

321 North Pine
Lansing, MI 48933

Office Manager: Jan Mason

Description and Readership

Learning Guide equips parents to evaluate their children's educational progress, understand their learning styles, choose the school that best meets their needs, and get involved in helping that school succeed.
- **Audience:** Parents
- **Frequency:** Quarterly
- **Distribution:** 50% subscription; 50% schools
- **Circulation:** 10,000+
- **Website:** www.partnershipforlearning.org

Freelance Potential

85% written by nonstaff writers. Publishes 25–30 freelance submissions yearly; 10% by unpublished writers, 60% by authors who are new to the magazine. Receives 4 unsolicited mss monthly.

Submissions

Send complete ms. Accepts computer printouts and email submissions to jan@partnershipforlearning.org. SASE. Responds in 4–6 weeks.
Articles: 500–1,000 words. Informational and how-to articles; profiles; interviews; and personal experience pieces. Topics include the arts, college, careers, computers, gifted education, health, fitness, history, humor, mathematics, music, science, technology, special education, and issues related to elementary and secondary education.
Depts/columns: Word length varies. Advice and opinion pieces.
Artwork: Color prints and transparencies. Line art.
Other: Reviews, 200 words. Submit seasonal material 3 months in advance.

Sample Issue

16 pages (no advertising): 3 articles; 2 depts/columns; 3 reviews. Sample copy, $3 with 9x12 SASE ($1 postage). Guidelines and theme list/editorial calendar available.
- "Low-Cost Outings." Article presents a list of low-cost or no-cost activities parents can do with their kids.
- "A Summer To-Do List for Parents." Article suggests ways parents can prepare themselves for the next school year.

Rights and Payment

First or reprint rights. All material, payment rate varies. Pays on acceptance. Provides 5 contributor's copies.

Editor's Comments

Any topic related to kindergarten through twelfth-grade education interests us. Avoid educational jargon and write concisely; we strive to reach everyone, including reluctant readers.

Lexington Family Magazine

3529 Cornwall Drive
Lexington, KY 40503

Publisher: Dana Tackett

Description and Readership

This magazine offers articles and stories on parenting issues, child development, education, and health, as well as information on events and resources in the region. It is distributed free of charge to families living in the Lexington, Kentucky, area.
- **Audience:** Parents and women
- **Frequency:** Monthly
- **Distribution:** 50% schools; 50% other
- **Circulation:** 30,000
- **Website:** www.lexingtonfamily.com

Freelance Potential

40% written by nonstaff writers. Publishes 24 freelance submissions yearly; 20% by unpublished writers, 30% by authors who are new to the magazine. Receives 8 queries and unsolicited mss monthly.

Submissions

Query or send complete ms. Accepts photocopies and computer printouts. SASE. Response time varies.
Articles: 500–1,500 words. Informational and how-to articles. Topics include the arts, computers, crafts, hobbies, current events, gifted and special education, health, fitness, history, mathematics, multicultural issues, popular culture, recreation, regional news, science, technology, and family travel.
Depts/columns: 800 words. Media reviews and news; pediatric updates.
Artwork: 8x10 B/W and color prints. Line art.
Other: Puzzles, activities, and poetry.

Sample Issue

36 pages (50% advertising): 6 articles; 6 depts/columns. Sample copy, free with 9x12 SASE ($1.50 postage). Guidelines and theme list available.
- "Enrichment Camps." Article discusses the learning experiences for children that are offered by today's summer camps.
- "Get Energized." Article offers a list of ways to increase your energy level.
- Sample dept/column: "Short Stuff" looks at a space exhibit at a children's museum, and ways to celebrate Arbor Day.

Rights and Payment

All rights. All material, payment rate varies. Pays on publication. Provides 25 contributor's copies.

Editor's Comments

We are seeking travel stories and articles covering women's issues: health, balancing work and family, leisure activities, and crafts. We also need more articles on the "sandwich generation"—families caring for kids and their elderly parents.

Library Media Connection

Suite L
40 East Wilson Bridge Road
Worthington, OH 43085

Editor: Shelley Glantz

Description and Readership
The management and operation of libraries in elementary and secondary schools is the focus of this publication. It covers topics such as integrating library programs into the curriculum, technology in media centers, and library advocacy.
- **Audience:** School librarians and technology specialists
- **Frequency:** 7 times each year
- **Distribution:** 100% subscription
- **Circulation:** 15,000
- **Website:** www.linworth.com

Freelance Potential
100% written by nonstaff writers. Publishes 215 freelance submissions yearly; 75% by unpublished writers, 25% by authors who are new to the magazine. Receives 12 queries, 12 unsolicited mss monthly.

Submissions
Query or send complete ms with résumé. Accepts computer printouts, disk submissions (ASCII, Microsoft Word), and email submissions to linworth@linworthpublishing.com. SASE. Responds in 2 weeks.
Articles: Word length varies. Informational and how-to articles; personal experience pieces; and opinions. Topics include library science, research, technology, education, computers, and media services.
Depts/columns: Word length varies. Teaching tips, handouts, reviews, and opinion pieces.
Other: Submit seasonal material 6 months in advance.

Sample Issue
110 pages (15% advertising): 11 articles; 13 depts/columns. Sample copy, $11 with 9x12 SASE. Guidelines and theme list available.
- "Destination Information: A Road Map for the Journey." Article presents research models for information literacy.
- "A Tale of Two Libraries: School and Public Librarians Working Together." Article explains how public librarians can help high school students with research.
- Sample dept/column: "Copyright Questions of the Month" discusses puppet show adaptations.

Rights and Payment
All rights. All material, payment rate varies. Pays on publication. Provides 4 contributor's copies.

Editor's Comments
We are primarily interested in practical and creative ideas that school librarians and media specialists can use to benefit their students and make learning fun.

Library Sparks

P.O. Box 800
W5527 State Road 106
Fort Atkinson, WI 53580

Editor: Michelle McCardell

Description and Readership
Subtitled "Activities to Encourage Lifelong Readers," this publication for librarians and teachers is designed to help educators teach library skills, integrate literature across curricula, and motivate students to read. It provides resources and activities for use in elementary through high school, and each issue addresses a theme, such as back-to-school, fall, or family.
- **Audience:** Librarians and teachers
- **Frequency:** 9 times each year
- **Distribution:** Subscription; other
- **Circulation:** Unavailable
- **Website:** www.librarysparks.com

Freelance Potential
90% written by nonstaff writers. Publishes 100 freelance submissions yearly.

Submissions
Query or send complete ms. Accepts photocopies, computer printouts, and email submissions to librarysparks@highsmithpress.com. SASE. Response time varies.
Articles: Word length varies. Informational articles and profiles. Topics include connecting literature to the curriculum, lesson plans for librarians, library skills, children's authors and illustrators, and ideas for motivating students to read.
Depts/columns: Word length varies. Reading skills and book review activities, ready-made lessons, fingerplays and storytelling activities, booktalks, and reader's theater scripts.
Other: Reproducible games and activities, craft projects.

Sample Issue
50 pages (no advertising): 1 article; 11 depts/columns. Sample copy, free at website. Writers' guidelines available.
- "From Crop to Crunch." Article provides a list of books and Web resources that explore how fruits and vegetables are grown and shipped to grocery stores.
- Sample dept/column: "Meet the Author" presents an interview with Saxton Freymann, an illustrator and author who develops children's books that feature edible art.

Rights and Payment
Rights vary. Written material, payment rate varies. Pays on publication. Provides 1 contributor's copy.

Editor's Comments
We're looking for practical, ready-to-use lessons and activities for all areas of our magazine. We want fun and engaging programming ideas. We're also interested in hearing from teachers and librarians who have helpful hints and five-minute fillers that they want to share.

Listen Magazine

55 West Oak Ridge Drive
Hagerstown, MD 21740

Editor: Céleste Perrino-Walker

Description and Readership
Listen features articles and stories that teach young adults about the consequences of drugs, offer help to those already involved, and promote the benefits of healthy living.
- **Audience:** 12–18 years
- **Frequency:** 9 times each year
- **Distribution:** 60% subscription; 40% newsstand
- **Circulation:** 40,000
- **Website:** www.listenmagazine.org

Freelance Potential
90% written by nonstaff writers. Publishes 45 freelance submissions yearly; 10% by unpublished writers, 20% by authors who are new to the magazine. Receives 50 queries, 50 unsolicited mss monthly.

Submissions
Query or send complete ms. Accepts photocopies, computer printouts, email submissions to editor@listenmag.org, and simultaneous submissions. SASE. Responds in 6 weeks.
Articles: 1,000–1,100 words. Informational articles; self-help pieces; and profiles. Topics include peer pressure, family conflict, self-discipline, self-esteem, suicide, and hobbies.
Fiction: 1,000–1,100 words. Contemporary fiction based on true events.
Depts/columns: Word length varies. Opinion pieces and short pieces on social issues.
Other: Poetry, word length varies.

Sample Issue
28 pages (no advertising): 8 articles; 8 depts/columns; 5 poems. Sample copy, $2 with 9x12 SASE (2 first-class stamps). Guidelines and editorial calendar available.
- "Gym Candy." Story about the pitfalls of taking steroids to increase athletic prowess.
- "Room for Improvement" Article suggests that the benefits of a clean room outweigh the work involved.
- Sample dept/column: "Ask Gary" answers readers' questions about substance abuse.

Rights and Payment
All rights. Pays on acceptance. Written material, $.05–$.10 per word. Provides 3 contributor's copies.

Editor's Comments
Although our readers are usually teenagers, we have some younger and older subscribers as well. We base our editorial philosophy of primary drug prevention on total abstinence from tobacco, alcohol, and other drugs. Articles and stories with overt religious emphasis are discouraged.

Live

The General Council of the Assemblies of God
1445 North Boonville Avenue
Springfield, MO 65802-1894

Senior Editor: Paul Smith

Description and Readership
A mix of nonfiction, true-to-life inspirational stories, and poetry are included in this Christian publication. It is distributed weekly in adult Sunday school classes.
- **Audience:** College level and up
- **Frequency:** Quarterly in weekly sections
- **Distribution:** 100% religious instruction
- **Circulation:** 155,000
- **Website:** www.radiantlife.org

Freelance Potential
100% written by nonstaff writers. Publishes 110 freelance submissions yearly; 20% by unpublished writers, 50% by authors who are new to the magazine. Receives 180 unsolicited mss each month.

Submissions
Query or send complete ms. Accepts photocopies, computer printouts, and simultaneous submissions if identified. SASE. Responds in 6 weeks.
Articles: 800–1,600 words. Informational articles; personal experience pieces; and humor. Topics include family issues, parenting, and religious history.
Fiction: 800–1,600 words. Historical, inspirational, problem-solving, and adventure fiction; stories about family life, including celebrations and traditions.
Other: Poetry, 12–25 lines. Filler, 200–700 words. Submit seasonal material 1 year in advance.

Sample Issue
8 pages (no advertising): 3 articles. Sample copy, free with #10 SASE ($.37 postage). Guidelines available.
- "The Promise." Article tells how a teacher of incarcerated teens helps a student reconnect with his father who abandoned him as a child.
- "The Mathematics of Love." Essay reflects on how God puts man and woman together in marriage to put aside differences and be joined as one.
- "My Barber." Essay reflects on the author's trips to the barber as a youth.

Rights and Payment
First and second rights. Written material, $.10 per word for first rights, $.07 for second rights. Pays on acceptance. Provides 2 contributor's copies.

Editor's Comments
We seek upbeat stories that show realistic characters finding resolutions to everyday problems through the Scriptures. Material should be encouraging, humorous, and challenging.

Living

1251 Virginia Avenue
Harrisburg, VA 22802

Editor: Melodie Davis

Description and Readership

This tabloid offers inspirational articles that provide hope and encouragement to families in dealing with the issues they face in the home, workplace, and community. All material is written with a Christian slant. It is distributed free to families that live in select communities in Virginia.

- **Audience:** Families
- **Frequency:** Quarterly
- **Distribution:** 100% controlled
- **Circulation:** 250,000
- **Website:** www.churchoutreach.com

Freelance Potential

85% written by nonstaff writers. Publishes 55 freelance submissions yearly; 5% by unpublished writers, 30% by authors who are new to the magazine. Receives 50 unsolicited mss monthly.

Submissions

Send complete ms. Accepts email submissions to melodiemd@msn.com. Include name of magazine and title of article in the subject line; also include your email address in the body of the email. Accepts photocopies, computer printouts, and simultaneous submissions if identified. SASE. Responds in 3–4 months.
Articles: 500–1,000 words. Informational, factual, and how-to articles; opinion and personal experience pieces. Topics include health and fitness, recreation, religion, social issues, education, and multicultural and ethnic issues.
Depts/columns: Staff written.

Sample Issue

32 pages (20% advertising): 12 articles; 4 depts/columns. Sample copy, free with 9x12 SASE (4 first-class stamps). Guidelines available.

- "The Heart of a Mother." Essay reflects on the author's love of his mother who cares for him as he struggles with muscular dystrophy.
- "Who Needs a Step-Dad?" Personal experience piece tells how the author's misdirected anger at her step-father changed after he gave her a thoughtful Christmas present.

Rights and Payment

One-time and reprint rights. Articles, $30–$60. Pays on publication. Provides 2 contributor's copies.

Editor's Comments

We are currently seeing too many articles related to grief, illness, and nostalgia. Material should be inspirational, practical, and optimistic. Please do not send preachy articles. We like articles that can provide great reading material for the entire family.

Fantastic Growth
Living Safety
Jack Smith, General Manager

Living Safety is published by the Canada Safety Council. The 32-page quarterly is entering its twenty-third year. "The growth has been nothing short of fantastic and last year, we printed over 600,000 copies for an adjusted quarterly circulation of around 150,000," says General Manager Jack Smith.

The magazine is read by Canadian families, and covers off-the-job safety issues including consumer goods, safety laws and regulations, and dangerous practices in the home, school, and the community. According to Smith, females between the ages of 32 and 38 comprise the magazine's largest demographic.

When asked if he sees any issues looming on the vast Canadian horizon, Smith says, "Our industry is fast-moving, particularly with new technologies. It is not always an easy task to predict what will be hot issues a year in advance."

But with the issues aligned with the seasons, writers should submit suitable articles at least six months in advance. Holidays, notable for their spikes in accidents, are good take-off points for safety information.

Smith says, "I look for a writer with some experience although we have published articles from new writers who showed a lot of maturity in their style. It is always important that the writer submit either an online or hard copy query. We absolutely reject full story proposals and those that are not concise. Simply put, we do not have time to read all of the manuscripts that are presented. So, if you are to be successful in freelancing for *Living Safety*, please write a brief, pointed synopsis and submit only a query, not a whole manuscript. It is unfortunate that we do not have the time to read all submissions, because I feel we have probably missed some excellent work. However, if we are going to apply a policy on writer queries then it will be applied across the board."

Living Safety

Canada Safety Council
1020 Thomas Spratt Place
Ottawa, Ontario K1G 5L5
Canada

General Manager: Jack Smith

Description and Readership

Published by the Canada Safety Council, this publication offers articles and tips on home, traffic, and recreational safety. Targeting Canadian corporate employees and their families, it covers timely public safety topics for company, off-the-job safety programs.
- **Audience:** All ages
- **Frequency:** Quarterly
- **Distribution:** Subscription
- **Circulation:** 100,000
- **Website:** www.safety-council.org

Freelance Potential

75% written by nonstaff writers. Publishes 25 freelance submissions yearly; 65% by unpublished writers, 10% by authors who are new to the magazine. Receives 2–3 queries monthly.

Submissions

Query with résumé and clips or writing samples. Accepts photocopies and computer printouts. SASE. Responds in 2 weeks.
Articles: 1,500–2,500 words. Informational articles. Topics include recreation, humor, traffic, school safety, and health issues.
Depts/columns: Word length varies. Safety news, research findings, opinions, and product recalls.
Other: Children's activities.

Sample Issue

32 pages (no advertising): 6 articles; 3 depts/columns; 1 kids' page. Sample copy, free with 9x12 SAE/IRC. Writers' guidelines available.
- "Keeping Your Home Office Safe." Article discusses safety precautions people should take when working from home.
- "Should I Stay or Should I Go?" Article takes a look at what to do before deciding to evacuate a burning high-rise.
- Sample dept/column: "Safety First" offers safety tips on tire maintenance, alarms, pools, and outdoor renovations.

Rights and Payment

All rights. Articles, to $500. Depts/columns, payment rate varies. Pays on acceptance. Provides 1–5 copies.

Editor's Comments

We are all about safety and primarily deal with prevention. We strive to inform and educate our readers on prevention, and believe that accidents are avoidable and preventable. Please do not send us any horrifying tales as the focus of an article. Instead, you may introduce an article with a story as a means of enhancing it.

Living with Teenagers

One Life Way Plaza
Nashville, TN 37234-0174

Editor: Ivey Beckman

Description and Readership

This publication from LifeWay Church Resources targets parents who are trying to raise their teens in a Christian home with biblical principles. Articles help parents connect with their teens by dealing with the everyday challenges as well as with the critical issues they face in today's society.
- **Audience:** Parents
- **Frequency:** Monthly
- **Distribution:** Subscription; religious instruction
- **Circulation:** 42,000
- **Website:** www.lifeway.com

Freelance Potential

90% written by nonstaff writers. Publishes 12 freelance submissions yearly. Receives 5 queries and unsolicited mss each month.

Submissions

Query with outline and statement of article's purpose; or send complete ms with résumé. Accepts photocopies and email submissions to ibeckman@lifeway.com. SASE. Response time varies.
Articles: 600–2,000 words. Informational, self-help, and how-to articles; profiles; interviews; and reviews. Topics include parenting; colleges; current events; health; fitness; recreation; religion; and social, spiritual, multicultural, and ethnic issues.
Depts/columns: Staff written.

Sample Issue

34 pages (no advertising): 7 articles; 8 depts/columns. Sample copy, free. Guidelines available.
- "Setting Healthy Boundaries." Article addresses the importance of establishing family boundaries related to protecting and enhancing good health.
- "What Teens Really Want." Article looks at the difficult parental job of discerning and meeting a teen's deeper needs.
- "Test of an Effective Father." Article offers guidance to fathers by pointing out common pitfalls and discussing ways to avoid them.

Rights and Payment

All rights with non-exclusive license to the writer. Pays on acceptance. Articles, $100–$300. Provides 3 author's copies.

Editor's Comments

Articles most likely to be accepted are written in a clear, readable style; address the concerns and needs of parents of teens; and support the Christian way of life.

Look-Look Magazine

6685 Hollywood Boulevard
Los Angeles, CA 90028

Associate Editor: Lauren Edson

Description and Readership
The target audience is 14- to 20-year-olds who need an editorial vehicle for publishing their fiction and nonfiction stories, essays, photographs, poems, art, and ruminations. Its stated purpose is to celebrate the culture of youth and to convey the ideas and talents of young people to influential readers.
- **Audience:** 14–Adult
- **Frequency:** 2 times each year
- **Distribution:** 95% newsstand; 5% subscription
- **Circulation:** 55,000
- **Website:** www.look-lookmagazine.com

Freelance Potential
99% written by nonstaff writers. Publishes 500 freelance submissions yearly; 100% by unpublished writers, 100% by authors who are new to the magazine.

Submissions
Query with submission. Accepts submissions through website.
Articles: To 2,000 words. How-to articles; profiles; interviews; photo essays; and personal experience pieces. Topics include the arts and popular culture.
Fiction: To 2,000 words. Genres include contemporary, humorous, and multicultural fiction.
Artwork: B/W and color prints and transparencies. Line art.
Other: Poetry. Submit seasonal material 4 months in advance.

Sample Issue
104 pages (5% advertising): 1 article; 5 stories; 4 photo essays; 1 interview. Sample copy, $5.95 with 9x12 SASE. Guidelines and editorial calendar available at website.
- "How to Be a Freedom Fighter." Article uses tongue-in-cheek humor to explain what it takes to be a successful freedom fighter.
- "The White Ranger." Story tracks a cinema employee's work week utilizing a personal diary format to record events, thoughts, activities, and progress through the days.
- "The Kid Stays in the Pixar." Interview explains the creative mind and world of Jason Deamer, a character designer with Pixar Animation Studio.

Rights and Payment
All rights. No payment. Provides 2 contributor's copies.

Editor's Comments
Our entire magazine is comprised of work by young amateur writers and artists. While we accept all types of formats and subject matter, we would like to see more submissions on political and environmental issues and more poetry about the breakup of relationships.

Los Angeles Family Magazine

Suite 312
17525 Ventura Boulevard
Encino, CA 91316

Editor: Megan Macmanus

Description and Readership
This regional publication is read regularly by more than 450,000 individuals living in and around Los Angeles. Each issue features a cover story, a family calendar, and topics related to child development, health, education, and pediatric medicine.
- **Audience:** Parents
- **Frequency:** Monthly
- **Distribution:** Controlled
- **Circulation:** 150,000
- **Website:** www.lafamily.com

Freelance Potential
85% written by nonstaff writers. Publishes 5 freelance submissions yearly; 15% by unpublished writers, 5% by authors who are new to the magazine. Receives 5 queries monthly.

Submissions
Query. Accepts email submissions to editor@lafamily.com. SASE. Responds in 2–6 weeks.
Articles: 500–800 words. Informational and how-to articles and personal experience pieces. Topics include nature, family issues, social issues, education, fitness, humor, recreation, travel, sports, current events, the arts, and regional news.
Depts/columns: 500 words. News and reviews.
Artwork: Color prints or transparencies.

Sample Issue
134 pages (65% advertising): 12 articles; 8 depts/columns. Sample copy, free with #10 SASE ($.37 postage). Guidelines and editorial calendar available at website.
- "Beijo: Kissed With Success." Article profiles a single mom who launched her own line of affordable handbags.
- "Pardon Me, Do You Have the Time?" Essay suggests parents try to step out of the fast lane once in a while and try putting religion back in their lives.
- Sample dept/column: "Mothermind" offers tips on how to feed a newborn baby the right way and make the experience a success for both mother and child.

Rights and Payment
One-time print and electronic rights. No payment. Provides up to 4 contributor's copies.

Editor's Comments
We are interested in regional coverage of family issues and current events as they relate to Southern Californians. Useful how-to's and hard-hitting investigative pieces are always on our wish list as well. We prefer an active voice, intelligent language, and please, correct grammar. We are not currently accepting any new column ideas.

Lowcountry Parent

1277 Stiles Bee Avenue
Charleston, SC 29412

Submissions Editor: Christina Bean

Description and Readership

Parenting issues, education, and regional events are featured in this magazine for families living in the Charleston, South Carolina, area. Its articles on child development cover the years from birth through young adulthood.
• **Audience:** Parents
• **Frequency:** 10 times each year
• **Distribution:** 80% schools; 20% controlled.
• **Circulation:** 38,000
• **Website:** www.lowcountryparent.com

Freelance Potential

90% written by nonstaff writers. Publishes many freelance submissions yearly; 40% by authors who are new to the magazine. Receives 100 unsolicited mss monthly.

Submissions

Query with sample pages; or send complete ms with biography. Accepts email submissions to editor@lowcountryparent.com. Responds in 3 days.
Articles: Word length varies. Informational and factual articles and personal experience pieces. Topics include parenting, child development, family issues, education, vacations, holidays, and pets.
Depts/columns: Word length varies. Infant, preteen, and teen development, health issues, and media reviews.
Artwork: B/W or color prints.
Other: Word length varies. Jokes, puzzles, and filler.

Sample Issue

30 pages (50% advertising): 5 articles; 7 depts/columns; 1 calendar of events. Sample copy, free. Guidelines available.
• "The Average Dad." Tongue-in-cheek description of the "average" father.
• "I Want Blue Food." Article suggests that the additives and dyes in today's intensely colored foods may be a cause of attention, sleep, and behavioral disorders.
• Sample dept/column: "Family Health" discusses the nutritional benefits of sports drinks versus water.

Rights and Payment

One-time rights. Pays on publication. Written material, $15-$100. Provides 3 contributor's copies.

Editor's Comments

We are always looking for writers that know what is happening in our area. Topics of interest to our readers continue to be parenting problems and solutions, peer pressure, self-esteem, and substance abuse. New writers are invited to try submitting a piece on local events and activities for families.

The Magazine of Fantasy & Science Fiction

P.O. Box 3447
Hoboken, NJ 07030

Editor: Gordon Van Gelder

Description and Readership

This publication has been around for more than 50 years, continuously appealing to the sci-fi and fantasy lover. Its digest-size makes it easy to put in a pocket or book bag. A lot is packed between its covers—novellas, short stories, and staff-written essays and reviews.
• **Audience:** YA–Adult
• **Frequency:** Monthly
• **Distribution:** Subscription; newsstand
• **Circulation:** 45,000
• **Website:** www.sfsite.com/fsf

Freelance Potential

90% written by nonstaff writers. Publishes 60–90 freelance submissions yearly; 10% by unpublished writers, 20% by authors who are new to the magazine. Receives 400–600 unsolicited mss monthly.

Submissions

Send complete ms. Accepts photocopies and computer printouts. No simultaneous or electronic submissions. SASE. Responds in 1 month.
Fiction: 1,000–25,000 words. Novellas, novelettes, and short stories. Genres include fantasy, science fiction, and humor.
Depts/columns: Staff written.

Sample Issue

162 pages (1% advertising): 3 novelettes; 5 short stories; 6 depts/columns. Sample copy, $5. Guidelines available.
• "How It Feels." Novella probes individual characters one by one to explain what it's really like to be possessed by aliens—or was it all a dream after all.
• "Kissing Frogs." Short story describes the fantasy relationship between a woman and her iridescent green frog, ending with surprises for both characters.
• "The Masked City." Short story searches the canals of Venice, slowly revealing the darker side to this fabled city of treasures and architectural splendors.

Rights and Payment

First world rights with option on anthology rights. Written material, $.05–$.07 per word. Pays on acceptance. Provides 2 contributor's copies.

Editor's Comments

Our need is for character-driven science fiction stories that are well-written for adults of all ages. Stories with even a slight element of science fiction are acceptable. We also need stories with a humorous slant—we never get enough humor.

Mahoning Valley Parent

Suite 210
100 DeBartolo Place
Youngstown, OH 44512

Editor & Publisher: Amy Leigh Wilson

Description and Readership
Distributed to parents, grandparents, educators, and other caregivers of children in northeastern Ohio, this publication offers timely information on family issues, school, health and nutrition.
- **Audience:** Parents
- **Frequency:** Monthly
- **Distribution:** Subscription; newsstand; schools
- **Circulation:** 50,000
- **Website:** www.forparentsonline.com

Freelance Potential
85% written by nonstaff writers. Publishes 35 freelance submissions yearly; 5% by unpublished writers, 20% by authors who are new to the magazine. Receives 21 unsolicited mss monthly.

Submissions
Send complete ms. Accepts photocopies, computer printouts, Macintosh or ASCII disk submissions, and email submissions to editor@mvparentmagazine.com. Retains all material on file for possible use; does not respond until publication. Include SASE if retaining ms is not acceptable.
Articles: 1,000–1,800 words. Informational and how-to articles; profiles; and reviews. Topics include regional news, current events, parenting, the environment, nature, crafts, travel, recreation, hobbies, and ethnic and multicultural subjects.
Depts/columns: Word length varies. Parenting issues, book reviews, events for kids.
Artwork: B/W and color prints.
Other: Seasonal material.

Sample Issue
50 pages (70% advertising): 6 articles; 5 depts/columns. Sample copy, free with 9x12 SASE. Writers' guidelines and editorial calendar available.
- "Home Is Where the Learning Starts." Article discusses how play activities at home can teach children life experiences.
- "Good Money Habits Start Early." Article offers advice on the importance of teaching kids how to manage money.
- Sample dept/column: "Special Mommy Chronicles" discusses how important it is to accept children the way they are.

Rights and Payment
One-time rights. Articles, $20–$50. Pays on publication. Provides tearsheets.

Editor's Comments
We are always on the lookout for well-written articles that target women who have young children at home. Please note that we have enough humor, slice-of-life, first-person stories.

The Majellan: Champion of the Family

P.O. Box 43
Brighton, Victoria 3186
Australia

Editor: Father Paul Bird, C. SS. R

Description and Readership
Written from a Catholic point of view, this publication offers residents of Australia and New Zealand articles that cover marriage, parenting, child development, and family life issues.
- **Audience:** Parents
- **Frequency:** Quarterly
- **Distribution:** 100% subscription
- **Circulation:** 28,000
- **Website:** www.majellan.org.au

Freelance Potential
60% written by nonstaff writers. Publishes 15 freelance submissions yearly; 10% by unpublished writers, 20% by authors who are new to the magazine. Receives 4 queries, 4 unsolicited mss monthly.

Submissions
Prefers complete ms; will accept query. Accepts photocopies, computer printouts, and email submissions to majellan@hotkey.net.ua (attachments in Microsoft Word or Rich Text format). SASE. Response time varies.
Articles: 750–1,500 words. Informational articles and personal experience pieces about marriage and family life.

Sample Issue
48 pages: 12 articles. Sample copy available.
- "The Myth of the Perfect Parent." Article discusses why some mothers feel guilty about admitting that mothering is a difficult task and offers insight into coping realistically.
- "Empty Nest." Personal experience piece explores ways to strengthen a marriage as kids grow older and get ready to leave the house.
- "Healing Family." Article discusses the importance of facing family challenges by forgiving and sharing with each other so the healing spirit of God can work.
- "It's Not about Food." Article discusses the underlying reasons behind eating disorders and offers suggestions to recognize the feelings involved.

Rights and Payment
Rights vary. Written material, $50–$80 (Australian). Pays on acceptance.

Editor's Comments
We look for articles that support strong Christian family values. Topics relating to strengthening communication and how to foster a happy, healthy family life are always welcome. Information for parents on how to face teen issues gets a second look here. Please note that we have enough articles on psychological problems such as depression.

Maryland Family

10750 Little Patuxent Parkway
Columbia, MD 21044

Editor: Betsy Stein

Description and Readership
Residents in the Baltimore area receive substantial information about family issues from pet ownership to college choices in this monthly publication. Area events, health, book reviews, and recipes complete the editorial mix.
- **Audience:** Maryland families
- **Frequency:** Monthly
- **Distribution:** Subscription; newsstand; other
- **Circulation:** 50,000
- **Website:** www.marylandfamilymagazine.com

Freelance Potential
40% written by nonstaff writers. Publishes 10 freelance submissions yearly; 10% by unpublished writers, 10% by authors who are new to the magazine. Receives 30–50 queries each month.

Submissions
Query with description of your expertise in proposed subject. Accepts photocopies and computer printouts. SASE. Responds in 1 month.
Articles: 800–1,000 words. Practical application pieces, how-to articles, and profiles. Topics include family issues, parenting, college, careers, music, summer camp, and national trends looked at from a local angle.
Depts/columns: 500–750 words. Health, education, books, cooking, crafts, money, recreation, safety, teens, and travel.
Artwork: Color prints and transparencies.
Other: News briefs on timely, local subjects and "Family Matters," 100–400 words. Submit seasonal material about holidays and events 2–3 months in advance.

Sample Issue
50 pages (50% advertising): 2 articles; 7 depts/columns; 1 calendar; 1 activity. Sample copy, free with 9x12 SASE.
- "Are You Ready for a Pet?" Article considers the balance between children's pleas for a pet and the practical realities of adding an animal to your lifestyle.
- "It's in the Bag." Article puts together a list of age-appropriate items to add to successful birthday party goodie bags.

Rights and Payment
First and electronic rights. Written material, payment rate varies. Pays on publication. Provides 1 contributor's copy.

Editor's Comments
We are a regional publication and therefore require inclusion of a Baltimore or Maryland connection in our pieces. We look for substantial coverage of current issues that are important to our readers.

Metro Parent Magazine

Suite 150
24567 Northwestern Highway
Southfield, MI 48075

Editor: Susan DeMaggio

Description and Readership
In print for over 18 years, this tabloid offers up-to-date material on parenting topics to families living in southeastern Michigan. It includes articles, activities, and other resourceful information on services and events in the region.
- **Audience:** Parents
- **Frequency:** Monthly
- **Distribution:** 75% newsstand; 25% subscription
- **Circulation:** 80,000
- **Website:** www.metroparent.com

Freelance Potential
66% written by nonstaff writers. Publishes 200 freelance submissions yearly; 25% by unpublished writers, 50% by authors who are new to the magazine. Receives 100 unsolicited mss each month.

Submissions
Send complete ms. Accepts email submissions to sdemaggio@ metroparent.com. SASE. Responds 1–2 days.
Articles: 1,500–2,500 words. Informational, regional, inspirational, and how-to articles; and interviews. Topics include parenting, family life, childbirth, education, social issues, child development, crafts, summer travel, family vacations, finances, fitness, health, and nature.
Fiction: Word length varies. Inspirational and contemporary fiction, humor, problem-solving stories, and stories about sports.
Depts/columns: 850–900 words. Crafts, computers, family fun, media reviews, product information, and women's health.

Sample Issue
96 pages (60% advertising): 5 articles; 14 depts/columns. Sample copy free.
- "Character Counts." Article discusses the importance of reinforcing good character traits in children and programs that focus on character education.
- "Hyper-Parenting." Article examines the downside of enrolling kids in too many activities, and offers ideas for better family planning towards living more balanced lives.

Rights and Payment
First rights. Articles and fiction, $150–$300. Depts/columns, $50–$100. Pays on publication. Provides 1 contributor's copy.

Editor's Comments
In addition to parents, our readers include teachers, social workers, and health-care providers. We are always looking for fresh articles on family-related issues as well as timely information on events in the region.

Midwifery Today

P.O. Box 2672
Eugene, OR 97402

Editor-in-Chief: Jan Tritten

Description and Readership

All types of birth practitioners read this magazine for information on all aspects of the birthing process, including natural childbirth and breastfeeding. Its audience comprises midwives, doctors, doulas, and birth educators. *Midwifery Today* also offers networking information, news, and media reviews.
- **Audience:** Childbirth practitioners
- **Frequency:** Quarterly
- **Distribution:** 80% subscription; 10% newsstand; 10% other
- **Circulation:** 10,000
- **Website:** www.midwiferytoday.com

Freelance Potential

90% written by nonstaff writers. Publishes 40+ freelance submissions yearly; 5% by unpublished writers, 5–10% by authors who are new to the magazine. Receives 12 queries monthly.

Submissions

Query with author background. Accepts email submissions to editorial@midwiferytoday.com (Microsoft Word or RTF files). No simultaneous submissions. SASE. Responds in 1 month.
Articles: 800–1,500 words. Informational and instructional articles; profiles; interviews; personal experience pieces; and media reviews. Topics include family and parenting issues, feminism, health and fitness, medical care and services, diet and nutrition, and multicultural and ethnic issues, all as they relate to childbirth.
Depts/columns: "Question of the Quarter," 100–800 words.
Artwork: B/W and color prints.

Sample Issue

72 pages (10% advertising): 25 articles; 8 depts/columns. Sample copy, $12.50. Guidelines and editorial calendar available.
- "Champagne and the Fetus Ejection Reflex." Article provides a medical perspective on protecting the perineum.
- "Easing the Baby Out." Article discusses the best techniques for pushing during delivery.
- Sample dept/column: "Media Reviews" looks at new books on waterbirth and holistic childbirth.

Rights and Payment

Joint rights. No payment. Provides 2 contributor's copies and a 1-year subscription.

Editor's Comments

We're interested in material on the use of herbal and homeopathic treatments in pregnancy, labor, delivery, and postpartum. We strive to provide a book's worth of information in every issue. Accurate information and sources are a must.

Momentum

National Catholic Educational Association
Suite 100
1077 30th Street NW
Washington, DC 20007-3852

Editor: Brian Gray

Description and Readership

Teachers and administrators read this magazine for its articles and viewpoints on catechetical education and trends, methodology, financial development, and management. It is the official journal of the National Catholic Educational Association.
- **Audience:** Teachers, school administrators, and parents
- **Frequency:** Quarterly
- **Distribution:** 100% controlled
- **Circulation:** 24,000
- **Website:** www.ncea.org

Freelance Potential

90% written by nonstaff writers. Publishes 55 freelance submissions yearly; 20% by unpublished writers, 80% by authors who are new to the magazine. Receives 7 unsolicited mss each month.

Submissions

Send complete ms with résumé and bibliography. Accepts computer printouts, disk submissions (Microsoft Word), and email submissions to momentum@ncea.org. SASE. Responds in 1–3 months.
Articles: 1,000–1,500 words. Informational and scholarly articles on private education. Topics include teacher and in-service education, educational trends, research, management, and public relations—all as they relate to Catholic education.
Depts/columns: Book reviews, 300 words. "Trends in Technology," 900 words. "From the Field," 700 words.

Sample Issue

84 pages (20% advertising): 16 articles; 7 depts/columns. Sample copy, free with 9x12 SASE ($1.05 postage). Writers' guidelines and editorial calendar available.
- "Connecting Curriculums and Culture." Article tells of a collaborative Spanish program that connects a college with an elementary school.
- "What Has Become of Sin?" Article discusses the need to recognize sin and confess to accept salvation.
- Sample dept/column: "DRE Directions" explains a catechetical movement, the Catechesis of the Good Shepard.

Rights and Payment

First rights. Articles, $75. Depts/columns, $50. Pays on publication. Provides 2 contributor's copies.

Editor's Comments

We need more articles on religious education programs in the parish for students attending public schools. Please make sure you stay within the word count requirements. We are receiving many articles that are too long.

MOMSense

2370 South Trenton Way
Denver, CO 80231-3822

Editor: Beth Jusino

Description and Readership
Written with a Christian perspective, this publication offers practical and inspiring articles on topics relating to motherhood. It is published by Mothers of Preschoolers International (MOPS).
- **Audience:** Mothers
- **Frequency:** 6 times each year
- **Distribution:** 95% subscription; 5% other
- **Circulation:** 100,000
- **Website:** www.mops.org

Freelance Potential
40% written by nonstaff writers. Publishes 20 freelance submissions yearly; 40% by unpublished writers, 40% by authors who are new to the magazine. Receives 8 queries, 33 unsolicited mss monthly.

Submissions
Query or send complete ms. Accepts computer printouts, and email submissions to MOMSense@mops.org (Microsoft Word attachments). Availability of artwork improves chance of acceptance. SASE. Response time varies.
Articles: 500–1,000 words. Informational articles; profiles; and personal experience pieces. Topics include parenting, religion, and humor.
Depts/columns: Word length varies. Parenting and family life articles.
Artwork: B/W and color prints and transparencies.
Other: Accepts seasonal material 6–12 months in advance.

Sample Issue
24 pages (no advertising): 8 articles; 6 depts/columns. Sample copy, free. Writers' guidelines available.
- "Meals on Wheels, Girlfriend Style." Essay tells how busy moms share their joy of cooking and friendship.
- "Buddy Barriers." Article talks about the changes friendships undergo when babies arrive, and offers strategies to overcome the challenges and stay connected to good friends.
- Sample dept/column: "Mentor Mom" discusses how much to teach a preschooler about making and keeping friends.

Rights and Payment
First rights. Payment policy and rates vary. Provides contributor's copies.

Editor's Comments
We are looking for articles for women that cover topics other than motherhood, as well as creative ideas for young children. We do not need devotional articles, or articles that do not have some sort of take-away or motivational value.

Monterey County Family

P.O. Box 2354
Salinas, CA 93902

Publisher: Cheryl Von Flue

Description and Readership
Parents of infants through teens are the target audience of this free resource publication for families living in California's Monterey County. It publishes informative articles on general parenting topics, event calendars, and a directory of businesses and services. Much of its content is published in Spanish, as well as English.
- **Audience:** Parents
- **Frequency:** Monthly
- **Distribution:** 30% schools; 70% other
- **Circulation:** 40,000
- **Website:** www.family-mc.com

Freelance Potential
40% written by nonstaff writers. Publishes 10 freelance submissions yearly; 10% by unpublished writers, 10% by authors who are new to the magazine. Receives 6 unsolicited mss monthly.

Submissions
Send complete ms. Accepts email submissions to MntryFam@aol.com (no attachments). SASE. Responds in 2 weeks.
Articles: 500–600 words. Informational and how-to articles. Topics include parenting and family issues, health, safety, gifted and special education, hobbies, crafts, nature, the environment, literacy, recreation, and community events.
Depts/columns: 500–600 words. Educational issues.
Artwork: B/W prints or transparencies. Line art.
Other: Activities, filler, and games. Submit seasonal material 2 months in advance.

Sample Issue
16 pages (33% advertising): 3 articles; 2 depts/columns; 1 school calendar; 1 community calendar. Sample copy, free with 9x12 SASE ($1.29 postage). Guidelines and theme list/editorial calendar available.
- "Building Blocks for Life." Article discusses strengthening bonds in early childhood through the school age years.
- "Children's Opportunities—Our Responsibilities." Article offers advice for selecting high-quality child care.

Rights and Payment
All rights. Payment rates and policy vary. Provides 1 copy.

Editor's Comments
Unsolicited materials and article ideas are welcome. We're primarily interested in articles on health, safety, education, literacy, and recreation for all age groups—infants through teens. Our goal is to help Monterey County families enjoy happy, healthy, successful lives.

Montessori Life

281 Park Avenue South
New York, NY 10010

Submissions: Mary Krever

Description and Readership
The official publication of the American Montessori Society, *Montessori Life* strives to provoke thought, promote professional growth, and provide a forum for discussion of major issues and ideas as they relate to the Montessori method of education.
- **Audience:** Educators; parents
- **Frequency:** Quarterly
- **Distribution:** 99% subscription; 1% other
- **Circulation:** 10,500
- **Website:** www.amshq.org

Freelance Potential
90% written by nonstaff writers. Publishes 40 freelance submissions yearly; 30% by unpublished writers, 30% by authors who are new to the magazine. Receives 10–20 unsolicited mss each month.

Submissions
Send complete ms. Accepts photocopies and computer print-outs. Prefers email submissions to mary@amshq.org. SASE. Responds in 3 months.
Articles: 1,000–4,000 words. Informational, academic, and how-to articles; profiles; interviews; and humor. Topics include educational trends, social issues, and family life—all with some connection to Montessori education.
Fiction: 1,000–1,500 words. Publishes allegorical fiction.
Depts/columns: 500–1,000 words. Montessori community news, events, media reviews, and parenting.

Sample Issue
50 pages (25% advertising): 11 articles; 3 depts/columns. Sample copy, $5 with 9x12 SASE. Guidelines available.
- "Random Patterns, Chance Designs." Article from a teacher's perspective traces her path toward the Montessori method, which is not simply a philosophy but a way of life to her.
- "Montessori and Constructivism." Article presents a comparison of these two educational approaches.
- Sample dept/column: "News from the UN" reports on a special ceremony that honored Dr. Maria Montessori with a peacemaker award.

Rights and Payment
All rights. Written material, $90 per published page. Pays on publication. Provides 1–5 contributor's copies.

Editor's Comments
Only articles on topics of interest to the Montessori community are appropriate for us. These would include academic articles by leading educators as well as personality profiles and parenting reflections. Our readers include parents as well as educators.

Mothering

P.O. Box 1690
Santa Fe, NM 87504

Senior Editor: Ashisha

Description and Readership
Subtitled "The Magazine of Natural Family Living," this publication's emphasis is on natural methods of childbirth and child raising. It blends practical advice with inspirational articles, most of which are submitted by its readers.
- **Audience:** Parents
- **Frequency:** 6 times each year
- **Distribution:** 70% subscription; 30% newsstand
- **Circulation:** 250,000
- **Website:** www.mothering.com

Freelance Potential
90% written by nonstaff writers. Publishes 100+ freelance submissions yearly; 20% by unpublished writers, 80% by authors who are new to the magazine. Receives 9 queries each month.

Submissions
Query with outline/synopsis. Accepts photocopies and computer printouts. SASE. Responds in 2–4 weeks.
Articles: 2,000 words. Informational and factual articles; profiles; and personal experience pieces. Topics include pregnancy, childbirth, midwifery, health, homeopathy, teen issues, and organic foods.
Depts/columns: Word length varies. Inspirational pieces; parenting news; health updates; book and product reviews.
Artwork: 5x7 B/W or color prints.
Other: Children's activities and arts and crafts. Poetry on motherhood and families. Submit seasonal material 6–8 months in advance.

Sample Issue
88 pages (35% advertising): 2 articles; 7 depts/columns. Sample copy, $5.95 with 9x12 SASE. Guidelines available.
- "The Flu Vaccine and You." Article offers a comprehensive look at the flu vaccine and the dangers of mercury poisoning.
- "The Undervalued Art of Vaginal Breech Birth." Discusses the rarity of vaginal breech births and why delivering a breech baby vaginally is a skill every birth attendant should learn.

Rights and Payment
First rights. Written material, $175+. Artwork, payment rate varies. Pays on publication. Provides 2 contributor's copies and a 1-year subscription.

Editor's Comments
Familiarize yourself with *Mothering*. We are more likely to publish your article if you are one of our readers. Think about the subjects you know well and the areas in which little information exists.

Mr. Marquis' Museletter

Box 29556
Maple-Ridge, British Columbia V2X 2V0
Canada

Editor: Kalen Marquis

Description and Readership

Formerly *Kwil Kids Quarterly*, this publication encourages young writers and artists to submit material and learn the connection between persistent trying and success. It encourages growth and creativity through practice and doing.
- **Audience:** 2–21 years
- **Frequency:** Quarterly
- **Distribution:** 100% subscription
- **Circulation:** 150

Freelance Potential

100% written by nonstaff writers. Publishes 40 freelance submissions yearly; 90% by unpublished writers, 90% by authors who are new to the magazine. Receives 40 queries and unsolicited mss monthly.

Submissions

Query with writing samples; or send complete ms. Accepts photocopies, computer printouts, simultaneous submissions if identified, and email submissions to kmarquis@sd42.ca. SASE. Responds in 4 months.
Articles: 300 words. Personal experience pieces and book reviews. Topics include nature, animals, pets, the arts, current events, history, multicultural and ethnic issues, music, and popular culture. Also features biographies of painters, writers, and inventors.
Fiction: 300 words. Genres include adventure; problem-solving stories; and contemporary, inspirational, and multicultural fiction.
Artwork: Line art.
Other: Poetry, 4–16 lines. Accepts seasonal material 6 months in advance.

Sample Issue

10 pages (no advertising): 3 poems; 5 stories; 2 depts/columns. Sample copy, $2 with #10 SASE. Guidelines available.
- "A Strange Night." Story recounts a dream-like experience that could have been real . . . or just a dream.
- "The Myth of Horcus the Snake." Story tells how it came to be that all snakes have to crawl on their bellies.
- "The Dog Who Wore Shoes." Poem dishes up a fanciful account of a dog who owns shoes for all occasions.

Rights and Payment

One-time rights. No payment. Provides 1 contributor's copy.

Editor's Comments

We would like to see more touching human interest stories and tributes to individuals. It is favorable if they are humorous and tug at the heartstrings.

Multicultural Review

6 Birch Hill Road
Ballston Lake, NY 12019

Editor-in-Chief: Lyn Miller-Lachmann

Description and Readership

Focusing on multicultual material and information, this trade journal and book review for librarians and educators provides bibliographic and ethnographic articles on different groups, as well as essays, news, and reviews.
- **Audience:** Teachers and librarians
- **Frequency:** Quarterly
- **Distribution:** 100% subscription
- **Circulation:** 5,000
- **Website:** www.mcreview.com

Freelance Potential

90% written by nonstaff writers. Publishes 200 freelance submissions yearly; 20% by unpublished writers, 20% by authors who are new to the magazine. Receives 66 queries monthly.

Submissions

Query with table of contents and writing samples. Accepts photocopies. SASE. Responds in 40 days.
Articles: 2,000–6,000 words. Informational articles and personal experience pieces. Topics include multiculturalism, ethnography, pedagogy, librarianship, education, and current issues in the U.S.
Depts/columns: News and announcements, word length varies. Book reviews, 200–500 words.
Other: Multicultural games.

Sample Issue

118 pages (8% advertising): 5 articles; 5 depts/columns; 148 reviews. Writers' guidelines and editorial calendar available.
- "Lessons Learned: A Glimpse into Japanese Schools and Life." Article tells of a teacher's trip to Japan and the inspiring lessons he learned and brought back to his students.
- "Teaching Cultural and Racial Understanding Through International Travel Courses." Article reports on experiences from students in a graduate study/international travel course.
- "Righteous Gentiles Among Nations." Article reviews books that focus on non-Jews that risked their lives to help Jews escape the Holocaust.

Rights and Payment

All rights. Articles and depts/columns, payment rate varies. Reviews, no payment. Pays on publication. Provides 1 contributor's copy; additional copies available upon request.

Editor's Comments

We are currently looking for more articles and bibliographies highlighting the works of independent publishers in the U.S. and Canada. Please do not send any theoretical articles on multicultural education.

MultiMedia & Internet Schools

Suite 100
10000 NE 7th Avenue
Vancouver, WA 98685

Editor: David Hoffman

Description and Readership

Library media specialists and others who use electronic resources with students exchange ideas through this publication. Articles stress how the technology helps students learn, and the requirements needed for it to happen.
- **Audience:** Librarians, teachers, and technology coordinators
- **Frequency:** Monthly
- **Distribution:** Unavailable
- **Circulation:** 12,000
- **Website:** www.infotoday.com/MMSchools

Freelance Potential

90% written by nonstaff writers. Publishes 20–24 freelance submissions yearly; 20% by unpublished writers, 20% by authors who are new to the magazine.

Submissions

Query or send complete ms. Accepts disk submissions and email submissions to hoffman@infotoday.com. Availability of artwork improves chance of acceptance. SASE. Responds in 6–8 weeks.
Articles: 1,500 words. Informational, factual, and how-to articles. Topics include K–12 education, the Internet, multimedia and electronic resources, technology-based tools, and curriculum integration.
Artwork: 300 dpi TIFF format.

Sample Issue

80 pages (15% advertising): 15 articles; 5 depts/columns. Sample copy and guidelines, $7.95 with 9x12 SASE.
- "Meet Me at the Fair." Article provides information on where to find a collection of materials related to past world's fairs, and describes several of the events that are available for research.
- "Classroom and Building Presentation Systems." Article features several new techniques and products that have revolutionized presentations.

Rights and Payment

First rights. Pays on publication. Written material, $.05 per word. Artwork, payment rate varies. Provides 2 contributor's copies.

Editor's Comments

We're looking for articles that emphasize Internet multimedia and other electronic resources and technology-based tools, and how they're integrated into library multimedia centers and school curricula. We particularly want to show how these tools have improved student learning.

Music Educators Journal

MENC
1806 Robert Fulton Drive
Reston, VA 20191

Editor: Frances S. Ponick

Description and Readership

Examples of successful music programs, methods, and teaching philosophies, many of them tried and used by music teachers, are offered in this journal published by MENC, the National Association for Music Education.
- **Audience:** Music teachers
- **Frequency:** 5 times each year
- **Distribution:** 100% membership
- **Circulation:** 80,000
- **Website:** www.menc.org

Freelance Potential

90% written by nonstaff writers. Publishes 40 freelance submissions yearly; 5% by unpublished writers. Receives 20 unsolicited mss monthly.

Submissions

Send 5 copies of complete ms. Accepts photocopies and computer printouts. SASE. Responds in 3 months.
Articles: 1,800–3,000 words. Instructional and informational articles; and historical studies of music education. Topics include teaching methods, professional philosophy, and current issues in music teaching and learning.
Depts/columns: Word length varies. Personal experience pieces, product reviews, commentary from music teachers, and MENC news.
Other: Submit seasonal material 8–12 months in advance.

Sample Issue

80 pages (40% advertising): 5 articles; 8 depts/columns. Sample copy, $6 with 9x12 SASE ($2.00 postage). Writers' guidelines available.
- "An Alternative Approach to Developing Music Literacy Skills in a Transient Society." Article suggests utilizing a mixed-system approach for a highly mobile student body.
- "Teaching Music as Democratic Practice." Article shows that democratic thinking and musical excellence are not mutually exclusive.
- Sample dept/column: "Idea Bank" provides personal thoughts and ideas that are helpful to teachers.

Rights and Payment

All rights. No payment. Provides 2 contributor's copies.

Editor's Comments

Music education must be the focus of any material submitted to us. Articles can be pertinent to music education in schools, colleges, universities, teacher education institutions, and/or local communities.

Growing in Faith & Friendship
My Friend
Sister Maria Grace Dateno, Editor

The editors at *My Friend* know that the middle-grade reader's world is expanding beyond home into the world of peers. They know that friendships are important and that kids can learn a lot about faith in seeing that Jesus is their friend, too. In fact, Editor Sister Maria Grace Dateno hopes readers "will consider the magazine itself as a friend."

While Dateno characterizes *My Friend* as "unabashedly Catholic" and likes to see stories with characters in a Catholic setting, obvious religious references are not necessary. Values must be evident but religious themes are often underlying rather than blatantly presented. Sister Dateno looks for stories that will grab kids' attention and present something different. A unique twist will please her as well as her readers.

Another element that appeals to Dateno is realistic dialogue. "If kids sound like real kids," she says, "that really grabs me." She also likes humor. Even if the story isn't funny, she believes humor can be used in the character's dialogue or thoughts. Especially if the issue's theme is heavy, a story with a light approach is appreciated. While adventure stories and the occasional mystery are used, most of the stories in *My Friend* are contemporary. Historical fiction is not accepted and neither are serials.

Dateno sees many stories geared toward the upper end of the middle-grade range but likes to include one story in each issue aimed at the seven- to nine-year-olds who also read the magazine. Plots for this group should be less complicated but interesting with clear character development.

My Friend

Pauline Book's & Media/Daughters of St. Paul
50 Saint Pauls Avenue
Boston, MA 02130-3491

Editor: Sister Maria Grace Dateno, FSP

Description and Readership
This religious publication for children uses humor, stories, and hands-on activities to provide a solid foundation in the Catholic faith. Each issue revolves around a theme which can include seasons, values, and challenging situations.
- **Audience:** 7–12 years
- **Frequency:** 10 times each year
- **Distribution:** 80% subscription; 20% newsstand
- **Circulation:** 9,000
- **Website:** www.myfriendmagazine.com

Freelance Potential
60% written by nonstaff writers. Publishes 30 freelance submissions yearly; 5% by unpublished writers, 65% by authors who are new to the magazine. Receives 100 unsolicited mss monthly.

Submissions
Send complete ms. Accepts photocopies and computer printouts. No email. SASE. Responds in 2 months.
Articles: 150–900 words. Informational, self-help, and how-to articles and biographies—all with some connection to the Catholic faith.
Fiction: 750–1,100 words. Genres include inspirational, contemporary, and multicultural fiction.
Depts/columns: Staff written.

Sample Issue
32 pages (no advertising): 1 article; 5 stories; 2 depts/columns; 4 activities; 2 comics. Sample copy, $2 with 9x12 SASE ($1.29 postage). Guidelines available.
- "Uniforms to the Rescue." Article tells how hearing about poor countries initiated a generous response from a student.
- "Lambros and His Easter Egg." Story demonstrates how several Easter traditions are celebrated in Greece.
- "St. Martin and the Monastery Mice." Story retells the legend of Brother Martin de Porres and his intelligent mice friends.

Rights and Payment
First worldwide publication rights. Written material, $80-$150. Pays on acceptance. Provides contributor's copies.

Editor's Comments
We continue to need stories that are fun and humorous, yet not necessarily directly related to a theme. Since September 11th, children are very sensitive to life's realities, and we appreciate an underlying awareness of current events and global tensions. We are also looking for multicultural stories, especially when they are connected with the various Hispanic cultures. Stories should have realistic dialogue using current lingo and good character development.

Nashville Christian Family

P.O. Box 1425
Nashville, TN 37065

Editor: Paula Morrison

Description and Readership
Published for Christian families in the Nashville area of Tennessee, this tabloid newspaper includes information on regional events and resources, profiles of successful Christians, articles on groups and individuals of interest to readers, and general interest pieces on family life, Christian living, parenting, and religion.
- **Audience:** Parents
- **Frequency:** Monthly
- **Distribution:** 95% newsstand; 5% subscription
- **Circulation:** 35,000

Freelance Potential
30% written by nonstaff writers. Publishes 60 freelance submissions yearly; 5% by unpublished writers, 2–3% by authors who are new to the magazine. Receives 8 queries monthly.

Submissions
Query with photos if applicable. Accepts photocopies and computer printouts. SASE. Responds in 1 month.
Articles: To 500 words. Informational and how-to articles; and personal experience pieces. Topics include regional news, travel, entertainment, recreation, animals, crafts, hobbies, health, fitness, and music.
Fiction: To 500 words. Genres include humorous and inspirational fiction.
Depts/columns: To 500 words. Marriage, careers, student issues, family finances, and profiles of church leaders.
Other: Activities. Submit seasonal material 2 months in advance.

Sample Issue
22 pages: 2 articles; 16 depts/columns; 1 calendar of events; 1 activity. Sample copy, free with 9x12 SASE ($3 postage). Editorial calendar available.
- "Chris Sanders." Profile of a professional football player who uses his job to advance his Christian beliefs.
- "Athlete Focus." Article highlights a young volleyball player who became a Christian at an FCA camp.
- Sample dept/column: "Great Family Dining" offers a review of a family-friendly restaurant in Nashville's historic Germantown district.

Rights and Payment
Rights vary. No payment. Provides 1 contributor's copy.

Editor's Comments
All submissions should have a Christian slant and relate to the Nashville area. We continue to need profiles of positive, inspiring Christians, practical information on raising a Christian family, and articles on local events.

Nashville Parent Magazine

2228 Metro Center Boulevard
Nashville, TN 37228

Editor: Susan B. Day

Description and Readership
This source of parenting information for families living in central Tennessee offers plainly spoken, easy-to-understand articles written to help parents better understand the needs of their children. It alerts parents to services and resources in the local area that can help them do a better job of parenting.
- **Audience:** Parents
- **Frequency:** Monthly
- **Distribution:** 50% newsstand; 10% subscription; 10% schools; 30% other
- **Circulation:** 73,000
- **Website:** www.parentworld.com

Freelance Potential
60% written by nonstaff writers. Publishes 40 freelance submissions yearly; 40% by authors who are new to the magazine. Receives 40 unsolicited mss monthly.

Submissions
Send complete ms. Accepts computer printouts, Macintosh disk submissions with hard copy, and email submissions to npinfo@nashvilleparent.com. Availability of artwork improves chance of acceptance. SASE. Responds in 2 weeks.
Articles: 800–1,000 words. Informational and how-to articles; profiles; interviews; photoessays; and personal experience pieces. Topics include parenting, family issues, current events, social issues, health, music, travel, recreation, religion, the arts, crafts, computers, and multicultural and ethnic issues.
Depts/columns: Staff written.
Artwork: B/W prints.
Other: Submit seasonal material related to Christmas, Easter, and Halloween 2 months in advance.

Sample Issue
102 pages (50% advertising): 9 articles; 11 depts/columns. Sample copy, free with 9x12 SASE. Guidelines available.
- "Cool Down! Beat the Heat with Backyard Water Fun." Article provides ideas for water activities and games.
- "Educational Activities for Young Explorers." Article lists fun ways to stimulate young minds.

Rights and Payment
One-time rights. Written material, $35. Pays on publication. Provides 3 contributor's copies.

Editor's Comments
As a local resource, we require all stories to be sourced within the community. We will supply some sources, but we expect writers to thoroughly research their stories.

NASSP Bulletin

National Association of Secondary School Principals
1904 Association Drive
Reston, VA 20191-1537

Editor

Description and Readership

This award-winning journal has served as a scholarly resource for middle school and high school principals for over 80 years. Timely, thought-provoking articles emphasize effective administration and leadership and cover a wide range of topics of enduring interest to educators.
- **Audience:** Secondary school educators and administrators
- **Frequency:** Quarterly
- **Distribution:** 100% subscription
- **Circulation:** 35,000
- **Website:** www.principals.org

Freelance Potential

98% written by nonstaff writers. Publishes 30 freelance submissions yearly; 2% by unpublished writers, 20% by authors who are new to the magazine. Receives 16 unsolicited mss monthly.

Submissions

Send complete ms with bibliography and abstract. Accepts computer printouts, IBM disk submissions, and email to bulletin@principals.org (Microsoft Word attachments). SASE. Responds in 4–6 weeks.
Articles: 4,000 words. Informational articles about education, school administration, and leadership.
Depts/columns: Word length varies. "Resource Review" features book and product reviews.

Sample Issue

100 pages: 9 articles; 3 depts/columns. Sample copy, free with 8x10 SASE. Guidelines available.
- "Teacher Portfolios Come of Age: A Preliminary Study." Article reports on a study that shows how teacher portfolios can be used not only in assessing teacher performance, but also in recruitment, selection, and professional development.
- "Peer Coaching: Veteran High School Teachers Take the Lead on Learning." Article describes a peer-coaching program at a suburban high school and its positive effects on the teachers, which included increased levels of trust, morale, and motivation.

Rights and Payment

All rights. No payment. Provides 2 contributor's copies.

Editor's Comments

Priority topics include alternative education; alternative scheduling effectiveness; discipline models; teacher effectiveness, recruitment, and retention; and visionary leadership. We publish articles on a wide variety of topics, however; prospective authors should not limit their submissions to these alone.

National Geographic Kids

National Geographic Society
1145 17th Street NW
Washington, DC 20036-4688

Executive Editor: Julie Agnone

Description and Readership

Each issue of this nonfiction magazine is packed with educational articles and colorful photos that cover nature, animals, geography, science, technology, and entertainment. It aims to make exploring the world fun, fresh, and exciting for kids.
- **Audience:** 6–14 years
- **Frequency:** 10 times each year
- **Distribution:** 100% subscription
- **Circulation:** 1.2 million
- **Website:** www.nationalgeographic.com/ngkids

Freelance Potential

85% written by nonstaff writers. Publishes 20 freelance submissions yearly; 1% by unpublished writers, 50% by authors who are new to the magazine. Receives 30 queries monthly.

Submissions

Query with relevant clips. No unsolicited mss. SASE. Response time varies.
Articles: Word length varies. Informational articles. Topics include geography, history, archaeology, paleontology, adventure, sports, natural history, science, technology, entertainment, and the environment.
Depts/columns: Word length varies. Fun facts, jokes, games, and amazing animals.
Other: Original game ideas.

Sample Issue

44 pages (20% advertising): 5 articles; 9 depts/columns. Sample copy, $3.95.
- "8 Animal Rascals." Article relates hilarious stories about mischievious animals.
- "Spy Kit." Article looks at historical spy stories, adding sidebars with movie spies, codes, and a quiz—it's the ultimate guide to secret sleuthing.
- Sample dept/column: "Amazing Animals" tells true stories about the achievements of animals.

Rights and Payment

All rights. Written material, payment rate varies. Artwork, $100–$600. Pays on acceptance. Provides 3–5 author's copies.

Editor's Comments

Although most of our story ideas come from staff writers, we welcome your queries for stories that have kid appeal. Make sure your proposal is based on a well-researched premise that has not been done by us before. We are looking for animals for our "Amazing Animals" section, which features unusual or remarkable pets and wild animals.

Nature Friend Magazine

2673 TR421
Sugarcreek, OH 44681

Editor: Marvin Wengerd

Description and Readership
Young children read this magazine for its stories and articles about the wonders of nature. It also helps them discover the relationship between God's creation and themselves. Each issue includes fiction, nonfiction, games, and poetry.
- **Audience:** 6–12 years
- **Frequency:** Monthly
- **Distribution:** 100% subscription
- **Circulation:** 12,000

Freelance Potential
80% written by nonstaff writers. Publishes 36 freelance submissions yearly; 5% by unpublished writers, 10% by authors who are new to the magazine. Receives 40–60 mss monthly.

Submissions
Send complete ms. Accepts photocopies and computer printouts. SASE. Response time varies.
Articles: 300–900 words. Informational and how-to articles. Topics include nature and wildlife.
Fiction: 300–900 words. Outdoor adventures and wholesome stories about wildlife, the environment, and enjoying God's creations.
Artwork: 4x6 or larger prints.
Other: Puzzles and projects related to nature and science.

Sample Issue
24 pages (no advertising): 4 articles; 3 depts/columns; 1 story. Sample copy, $2.50 with 9x12 SASE ($.87 postage). Guidelines available for $4 with 9x12 SASE.
- "Plates and Cups of Mud." Story about two children who use clay they find at the edge of a brook to make plates and cups.
- "Beware the Bull's Eye." Article explains how to recognize a deer tick and what to do if you find a rash on yourself that is shaped like a bull's eye.
- Sample dept/column: "Wondernose" answers the question: "What animal spends its mornings calling insults and making faces at its neighbors?"

Rights and Payment
One-time rights. Written material, $.05 per word. Pays on publication. Artwork, payment rate varies. Provides 1 tearsheet.

Editor's Comments
We look for writers who can deliver stories or articles that increase a child's awareness of God, teach spiritual lessons, or teach natural truths and facts. If your work fulfills one or more of these goals, we'd like to hear from you.

New Expression

Columbia College
Suite 207
600 South Michigan Avenue
Chicago, IL 60605

Editorial Advisor: Brent Watters

Description and Readership
With the intent of making sure that youth is heard and understood, this tabloid is written for and by teens. It promotes literacy and encourages free expression, while addressing real issues that confront young people every day.
- **Audience:** Teens–Adults
- **Frequency:** 9 times each year
- **Distribution:** 90% schools; 5% subscription; 5% other
- **Circulation:** 45,000
- **Website:** www.newexpression.org

Freelance Potential
20–25% written by nonstaff writers. Publishes 40–50 freelance submissions yearly; 50% by unpublished writers, 50% by authors who are new to the magazine. Receives 3–4 unsolicited mss monthly.

Submissions
Send complete ms. Accepts email submissions only to newexpress@aol.com. Availability of artwork improves chance of acceptance. Response time varies.
Articles: No word limit. Informational articles; reviews; and personal experience pieces. Topics include current events, music, popular culture, and social issues.
Depts/columns: News briefs.
Artwork: B/W JPEG files.
Other: Poetry.

Sample Issue
24 pages (10% advertising): 6 articles; 5 depts/columns; 1 calendar. Sample copy, $1. Writers' guidelines and editorial calendar available.
- "Teens Caught in Middle of War Over Sex Ed Policy." Article explores all the aspects of teens and sex, from sexually transmitted diseases and sex education in school, to television content and birth control methods.
- "Teens Overcoming Disabilities." Article profiles several teens who have overcome physical disabilities and learned how to cope successfully in life despite the challenges.
- Sample dept/column: "Entertainment" reviews summer movie releases.

Rights and Payment
All rights. No payment.

Editor's Comments
All material is written and edited by teens. Submissions must be articulate and accurate. We are interested in current news and social issues, college and career news, entertainment, business, and sports.

N.E.W. Kids

P.O. Box 45050
Madison, WI 53744-5050

Editor-in-Chief: Justine Kessler

Description and Readership
A local focus keeps this publication on target for families in the greater Green Bay, Wisconsin, region. It addresses general parenting issues, local events, and profiles of colorful residents. Travel, day trips, health, and family activities are also covered each month.
- **Audience:** Parents
- **Frequency:** Monthly
- **Distribution:** Schools; libraries; other
- **Circulation:** 28,000
- **Website:** www.ericksonpublishing.com

Freelance Potential
80% written by nonstaff writers. Publishes 40 freelance submissions yearly; 50% by authors who are new to the magazine. Receives 20 queries and unsolicited mss monthly.

Submissions
Query or send complete ms. Accepts photocopies, computer printouts, and disk submissions (RTF files). SASE. Response time varies.
Articles: To 1,000 words. Informational articles; profiles; and personal experience pieces. Topics include family issues, regional news, gifted and special education, health, sports, multicultural and social issues, the arts, colleges, careers, computers, crafts, hobbies, music, travel, and popular culture.
Depts/columns: To 750 words. Pediatric health.

Sample Issue
16 pages (60% advertising): 6 articles; 8 depts/columns. Sample copy, free with 9x12 SASE ($.77 postage). Guidelines and editorial calendar available.
- "The Path to Pearly Whites." Article details the steps parents can take to assure dental health in their children.
- "8 Questions Every Parent Should Ask When Choosing a Summer Camp." Article outlines important considerations for parents choosing a summer camp for their children.
- Sample dept/column: "Women's Health Today" looks at health issues that are currently in the news and important to today's women.

Rights and Payment
First rights negotiable. Written material, payment rate varies. Pays on publication.

Editor's Comments
While most of the ideas for articles are staff generated, we always welcome fresh ideas and new angles on subjects, written in a lively, imaginative manner. Family health, fitness, education, and area events are all important to our readers.

Aiming High
New Moon
Lacey Louwagie, Editor

As the name of this magazine implies, *New Moon* is for girls who want their dreams taken seriously. "We let girls tell the world who they are rather than adults telling them who they should be," says Editor Lacey Louwagie. This theme is evident in the fiction they publish. "Our fiction always features a strong girl as the main character, someone girls can relate to." Avoiding stereotypes is critical. A story where the central conflict is the girl finding the right shade of lipstick for the school dance won't work. "Girls' lives," says Louwagie, "are bigger than makeup and clothes."

What types of conflicts are acceptable? Conflicts that reflect the phases girls are going through in their middle-grade years. Relationships with parents and friends are key. A story in which a girl struggles while growing apart from a friend would catch Louwagie's attention. Boy/girl relationships, however, require caution. Simple friendships between boys and girls are always acceptable and stories where the main character shows an emerging awareness of the opposite sex are fine, too. While a hug or quick kiss might find its way onto *New Moon*'s pages, explicit sexual content will not.

All types of fiction are acceptable, including adventure, historical fiction, mystery, and humor. In fact, Louwagie says she doesn't see enough good humor. "A girl's sense of humor is different than an adult's sense of humor," says Louwagie. She adds that the best humor she sees is written by girls, and while *New Moon* publishes fiction written by adults, it encourages submissions from readers, too.

(See listing for *New Moon* on following page)

New Moon

The Magazine for Girls and Their Dreams

Suite 200
34 East Superior Street
Duluth, MN 55802

Editor: Lacey Louwagie

Description and Readership

With an editorial objective to help girls hold on to their dreams as they move into young adulthood, *New Moon* offers articles and stories that focus on girls, women, and female issues. Its editorial board is made up of girls ages 8 to 14 who have the final say on which submissions are accepted for publication.

- **Audience:** Girls, ages 8–14
- **Frequency:** 6 times each year
- **Distribution:** 90% subscription; 10% newsstand
- **Circulation:** 25,000
- **Website:** www.newmoon.org

Freelance Potential

20% written by nonstaff writers. Publishes 10–12 freelance submissions yearly; 50% by unpublished writers, 50% by authors who are new to the magazine. Receives 17 queries, 20–25 unsolicited mss monthly.

Submissions

Query or send complete ms. Accepts photocopies, computer printouts, and email submissions to girl@newmoon.org. SAS postcard. Does not return mss. Responds in 4–6 months.
Articles: 300–900 words. Informational and self-help articles; profiles; interviews; and personal experience pieces. Topics include college, careers, health, fitness, recreation, science, technology, and social issues.
Fiction: 900–1,200 words. Genres include contemporary, inspirational, multicultural, and ethnic fiction.
Depts/columns: Word length varies. Material about women and girls; opinion pieces.
Other: Poetry.

Sample Issue

50 pages (no advertising): 5 articles; 1 story; 22 depts/columns. Sample copy, $6.50. Guidelines available at website.
- "Lightning Bolts & Goddess Jolts." Article looks at a few of the cultures and religions that feature goddesses and heroines in their nature myths.
- Sample dept/column: "Herstory" introduces readers to Dian Fossey and her efforts to protect the gorillas of Africa.

Rights and Payment

First North American serial rights. Written material, payment rate varies. Pays on publication. Provides 3 author's copies.

Editor's Comments

We take girls very seriously, and our publication is structured to empower girls. Writers who understand our style, goals, and philosophy have the best chance of publication.

New York Family

Suite 302
141 Halstead Avenue
Mamaroneck, NY 10543

Regional Editor: Heather Hart

Description and Readership

Part of a national network of local parenting publications, *New York Family* provides service-oriented articles designed to meet the needs of families. In addition to covering local issues and publicizing local events and resources, it includes articles on a variety of parenting topics. This publication is distributed free of charge throughout the New York City area.

- **Audience:** Parents
- **Frequency:** 11 times each year
- **Distribution:** 96% controlled; 4% subscription
- **Circulation:** 50,000
- **Website:** www.parenthood.com

Freelance Potential

80% written by nonstaff writers. Publishes 40 freelance submissions yearly; 40% by authors who are new to the magazine. Receives 50 queries monthly.

Submissions

Query with clips. Accepts photocopies and computer printouts. SASE. Response time varies.
Articles: 800–1,200 words. Informational articles; profiles; interviews; photoessays; and personal experience pieces. Topics include gifted education, music, recreation, regional news, social issues, special education, travel, and women's interests.
Depts/columns: 400–800 words. News and reviews.

Sample Issue

62 pages: 2 articles; 1 story; 10 depts/columns; 1 calendar of events. Sample copy, free with 9x12 SASE. Writers' guidelines available.
- "Daddy Do-Right." Article surveys local dads about how fatherhood has changed since they were kids.
- "Birth Order." Article looks at birth-order research and the theory that typical traits are associated with each child.
- Sample dept/column: "Playing Smart" offers activities for making dinnertime a fun, bonding, learning experience for the whole family.

Rights and Payment

First rights. Pays on publication. Written material, $25–$200. Provides 1 contributor's copy.

Editor's Comments

The articles we publish offer solutions to parents. They speak directly to them about their familial concerns in the context that matters most: the local community where they live, work, and play. We look for authoritative features with national scope and local relevance.

New York Times Upfront

Scholastic Inc.
557 Broadway
New York, NY 10012-3999

Editor

Description and Readership
Articles in this collaborative effort between *The New York Times* and Scholastic Inc. are selected for timeliness, interest to teens, and relevance to history and social studies courses.
- **Audience:** 14–18 years
- **Frequency:** 18 times each year
- **Distribution:** 95% schools; 5% subscription
- **Circulation:** 250,000
- **Website:** www.upfrontmagazine.com

Freelance Potential
10% written by nonstaff writers. Publishes 2 freelance submissions yearly; 10% by authors who are new to the magazine. Receives 12 queries monthly.

Submissions
Query with résumé and published clips. Accepts photocopies and computer printouts. Availability of artwork improves chance of acceptance. SASE. Responds in 2–4 weeks only if interested.
Articles: 500–1,200 words. Informational articles, profiles, and interviews. Topics include popular culture, current events, social issues, history, careers, college, the arts, the environment, technology, science, politics, government, business, and multicultural subjects.
Depts/columns: Word length varies. News and trends, first-person accounts from teens.
Artwork: High-resolution color prints or transparencies.

Sample Issue
14 pages (18% advertising): 6 articles; 2 depts/columns. Sample copy, $2.25. Guidelines available.
- "Does God Belong in the Pledge?" Article highlights the question of whether or not school children should have to recite the Pledge of Allegiance containing the word "God."
- "When the Games Began." Article intertwines the history of the Olympic Games with findings of ancient games at excavation sites and the underlying philosophy of athletes.
- "Is the Group Responsible for the Individual's Crime?" Article weighs the ethics of holding an entire group responsible for the actions of one member.

Rights and Payment
All rights. All material, payment rate varies. Pays on publication.

Editor's Comments
We assume that young people are smart, aware, and interested in the world around them. Study either our magazine or website format prior to submitting material.

The Next Step Magazine

86 West Main Street
Victor, NY 14564

Editor-in-Chief: Laura Jeanne Hammond

Description and Readership
This magazine is mailed by request to high school guidance counselors in 34 states and Ontario, Canada. Written for high school juniors and seniors, it covers college and career choices as well as life skills.
- **Audience:** 14–21 years
- **Frequency:** 5 times each year
- **Distribution:** 100% controlled
- **Circulation:** 700,000
- **Website:** www.nextstepmagazine.com

Freelance Potential
35% written by nonstaff writers. Publishes 20 freelance submissions yearly.

Submissions
Query. Accepts email queries to laura@ nextSTEPmagazine.com. Response time varies.
Articles: 700–1,000 words. Informational, self-help, and how-to articles; profiles; interviews; personal experience pieces; humor; and essays. Topics include college planning, financial aid, campus tours, choosing a career, useful life skills, résumé writing, public speaking, computers, multicultural and ethnic issues, social issues, sports, and special education.

Sample Issue
82 pages: 3 articles. Sample copy available on website. Guidelines available.
- "Test Taking Myths." Article explains why standardized tests are not as important as many people think when it comes to the college admissions process.
- "The Ball's in Your Court." Article offers advice for navigating the athletic recruiting process and managing a college athletic career.
- "Test Drive Your School." Tells why summer programs are a great way to prepare for college and campus life.

Rights and Payment
All rights. Articles, payment rate varies. Pays on publication.

Editor's Comments
Our purpose is to prepare students for life after high school. From freelancers, we need articles on all aspects of the college-planning process, as well as life skills pieces. Career articles should address several careers available to those who study a particular degree. For example, an article on journalism careers could highlight jobs such as reporter, anchor, photojournalist, and editor. The best queries are specific, concise, and entertaining. We especially like to see pieces that include interviews with expert sources and college faculty.

Nick Jr. Family Magazine

7th Floor
1633 Broadway
New York, NY 10019

Deputy Editor: Wendy Smolen

Description and Readership
A general resource magazine for parents of children three to eleven, *Nick Jr. Family Magazine* is published by Nickelodeon and offers information on health, vacations, and parenting issues. Readers also find craft ideas, recipes, activities, and stories designed to promote interaction with children.
• **Audience:** Families
• **Frequency:** 9 times each year
• **Distribution:** 46% controlled; 53% subscription; 1% other
• **Circulation:** 1+ million
• **Website:** www.nickjr.com

Freelance Potential
40% written by nonstaff writers. Publishes 10 freelance submissions yearly; 50% are by authors who are new to the magazine. Receives 50 queries and unsolicited mss monthly.

Submissions
Query or send complete ms. Accepts photocopies and computer printouts. SASE. Responds in 3 months.
Articles: To 300 words. Informational and how-to articles. Topics include nature, the environment, music, social issues, popular culture, special education, animals, crafts, hobbies, pets, mathematics, current events, and multicultural subjects.
Fiction: Word length varies. Humor; adventure; and stories about nature, animals, and the environment.
Other: Activities and games.

Sample Issue
95 pages (35% advertising): 5 articles; 1 story; 6 depts/columns; 10 activities. Sample copy, $2.95 at newsstands.
• "Generation Overlap: The New Mother-Daughter Dynamic." Article explores how changing family roles create new perks for modern motherhood.
• "The Amazing, Blazing Sun." Read-together story describes the power of the sun and its benefits to the earth.
• Sample dept/column: "5 Things to Do With . . . . A Paper Bag" offers ideas for crafts made with paper bags.

Rights and Payment
All rights. Written material, payment rate varies. Pays on publication. Provides 10 contributor's copies.

Editor's Comments
Please become familiar with our content and format before submitting material. We are only interested in submissions relevant for children three to eleven years old, and their parents. Part of our editorial focus is to encourage activities such as crafts and stories that bring parents and children together. Currently, we are not interested in long fiction pieces.

No Crime

Suite 201
348 Fraser Street
North Bay, Ontario P1B 3W7
Canada

Managing Editor: Randall Meier

Description and Readership
This Canadian website is created by the group Young People's Press. Its mission is to bring parents and youth professionals helpful material on keeping young people away from crime as well as reports on alternatives to jail as a deterrent to youth crime.
• **Audience:** YA–Adult
• **Frequency:** 6 times each year
• **Distribution:** 100% Internet
• **Hits per Month:** 24,000
• **Website:** www.nocrime.net

Freelance Potential
75% written by nonstaff writers. Publishes 150–200 freelance submissions yearly; 70% by unpublished writers, 75% by authors who are new to the magazine.

Submissions
Send complete ms. Accepts email submissions to writeus@yyp.net. Responds immediately.
Articles: Word length varies. Informational articles and personal experience pieces. Topics include youth justice and crime, and community-based programs in crime prevention.

Sample Issue
10 articles. Guidelines available at website.
• "Breaking up Families, Building up Communities." Article examines the problems that lead young people to join gangs, and how youth professionals can combat these problems.
• "Young Offenders Learn Hard Lessons." Article features a personal look at the impact an experimental program has on helping keep at-risk youth away from crime.
• "Helping Youth Learn on Their Own." Article profiles a woman who works in schools developing resources that will steer young people away from crime.

Rights and Payment
Rights, payment rates, and policy vary.

Editor's Comments
Our audience includes men and women who work closely with schools and community groups to develop programs that offer an alternative to crime and suggest positive ways to influence youth who are at risk. Most of our writers have extensive experience in working with young people and can use successful examples from their own experiences. Remember that we are only focusing on issues related to Canada and Canadian young people. Our approach is very hands-on; we are practical rather than analytical.

Northern Michigan Family Magazine

☆

P.O. Box 1042
Indian River, MI 49749

Editor: Tina Sorensen

Description and Readership

This bimonthly parenting tabloid covers a wide range of issues important to parents with children up to the age of 16. Each issues features stories on local events, as well as news of regional services.
- **Audience:** Parents
- **Frequency:** 6 times each year
- **Distribution:** 100% controlled
- **Circulation:** 10,000

Freelance Potential

50% written by nonstaff writers. Publishes 20 freelance submissions yearly; 25% by unpublished writers, 50% by authors who are new to the magazine. Receives 100 queries and mss monthly.

Submissions

Query or send complete ms. Accepts photocopies, computer printouts, and simultaneous submissions if identified. Availability of artwork improves chance of acceptance. SASE. Response time varies.
Articles: 200–1,500 words. Informational, self-help, and how-to articles; profiles; interviews; and personal experience pieces. Topics include parenting, family life, gifted and special education, current events, music, nature, the environment, regional news, recreation, and social issues.
Depts/columns: Word length varies. Family news and resources, health information, area events, and perspectives from parents.

Sample Issue

22 pages: 4 articles; 10 depts/columns. Sample copy, free with 9x12 SASE. Guidelines available.
- "Is Your Home a Toxin-Free Zone?" Article discusses the hazards that can be found in simple, everyday products.
- Sample dept/column: "From Dad's Notepad" features an essay about the many chores at home that parents need to complete before even leaving for work.

Rights and Payment

All rights. Pays $10–$25 for unsolicited articles and reprints; pays $25–$100 for assigned articles. Payment policy varies.

Editor's Comments

For the coming year we need more submissions that relate to children's health issues such as food allergies. Also of interest are ideas for crafts and recipes for foods that kids can make on their own. Look for a topic that is in the news and find local experts to discuss it—all of our articles should have quotes from local experts. We are seeing too many personal essays on parenting experiences.

Northwest Baby & Child

15417 204th Avenue SE
Renton, WA 98059

Editor: Betty Freeman

Description and Readership

Issues involving parenting and pregnancy, family-related environmental concerns, family activities, and local events fill the pages of this Northwestern, U.S., tabloid. Its goal is to assist in the raising of young children, supporting the idea that there is no "one right way" to do so.
- **Audience:** Expectant and new parents
- **Frequency:** Monthly
- **Distribution:** 75% subscription; 10% schools; 5% subscription; 10% other
- **Circulation:** 28,000
- **Website:** www.nwbaby.com

Freelance Potential

50% written by nonstaff writers. Publishes 30 freelance submissions yearly; 10% by unpublished writers, 20% by authors who are new to the magazine. Receives 125 queries monthly.

Submissions

Query. Accepts email queries to editor@nwbaby.com (no attachments). Responds in 2–3 months if interested.
Articles: 750 words. Informational and how-to articles; personal experience pieces; profiles; and interviews. Topics include early education, party ideas, home-based businesses, pregnancy and childbirth, family life, travel holidays, and traditions.
Depts/columns: Word length varies. Health, parenting tips, activities, and regional resources.
Artwork: B/W and color prints and transparencies. Line art.

Sample Issue

12 pages (15% advertising): 6 articles; 4 depts/columns. Sample copy, free with 9x12 SASE ($.77 postage). Guidelines and editorial calendar available.
- "Gardens Galore." Article lists local-area gardens and nature collections to use for teaching nature to children.
- "A Secondborn's Quest for Power." Article relates the different needs in first- and second-born children when the next sibling arrives.
- Sample dept/column: "Parent to Parent" gives helpful hints to parents who want children to help with gardening tasks.

Rights and Payment

First rights. Written material, $10–$40. Pays on publication. Provides 1–2 contributor's copies.

Editor's Comments

At this time we would like to see more submissions about special needs children, the environment, and issues relating to new parents. If a piece is humorous, its overall substance must be educational.

Northwest Family News

Suite 204
16 West Harrison Street
Seattle, WA 98119

Publisher: Susan Petty

Description and Readership
Information on local events and resources, as well as advice on general parenting and family issues, fill the pages of this regional tabloid geared toward families residing in the state of Washington.
- **Audience:** Parents
- **Frequency:** Monthly
- **Distribution:** 20% subscription; 80% other
- **Circulation:** 56,200
- **Website:** www.nwfamily.com

Freelance Potential
80% written by nonstaff writers. Publishes 60 freelance submissions yearly; 10% by unpublished writers, 25% by authors who are new to the magazine. Receives 25 unsolicited mss each month.

Submissions
Send complete ms. Accepts email submissions to nwfamilysubmissions@earthlink.net and disk submissions (Microsoft Word). No hard copy. Responds only if interested.
Articles: To 900 words. Informational and how-to articles; profiles; interviews; humor; and personal experience pieces. Topics include family life, health, education, summer camp, travel, outdoor activities, grandparenting, teens and tweens, home improvement, interior decorating, and holiday traditions.
Depts/columns: To 700 words. Media reviews, crafts, travel tips, parenting, pets, gardening, health, and food.
Other: Submit seasonal material 4 months in advance.

Sample Issue
16 pages (30% advertising): 10 articles; 9 depts/columns. Sample copy, $1 with 9x12 SASE ($1.15 postage). Guidelines and editorial calendar available.
- "To Homeschool or Not to Homeschool? That is the Question." Article lists several resources that provide information about homeschooling and curriculums.
- "Moms in the Marketplace." Article discusses the realities for women who are reentering today's work force.
- Sample dept/column: "The Healthy Family" investigates the impact peer pressure has on a child's life.

Rights and Payment
One-time rights. Pays within 30 days of publication. Articles, $20–$40. Depts/columns, $10–$25.

Editor's Comments
We would like to see more human interest articles dealing with challenges facing families; and articles about kids and pets, and families living in northwest Washington state.

OC Family
The News Magazine for Parents

Suite 201
1451 Quail Street
Newport Beach, CA 92660

Editor: Craig Reem

Description and Readership
This Orange County resource for families, provides information on community events, health, family issues, and parenting. All of the content has some local relevance or reference, citing either an area expert or facility.
- **Audience:** Families
- **Frequency:** Monthly
- **Distribution:** Newsstand; subscription; controlled
- **Circulation:** 80,000
- **Website:** www.ocfamily.com

Freelance Potential
82% written by nonstaff writers. Publishes 50 freelance submissions yearly; 1% by unpublished writers, 1% by authors who are new to the magazine. Receives 8 queries monthly.

Submissions
Query. Accepts photocopies and email queries to OCFmag@aol.com. SASE. Responds in 1 month.
Articles: 800–2,500 words. Informational articles and profiles. Topics include education, the Internet, family activities, health, stay-at-home moms, fatherhood, sports, fine arts, regional food and dining, consumer interests, and grandparenting.
Depts/columns: Word length varies. Family life, personal finances, book and software reviews, and women's health.
Artwork: B/W and color prints.

Sample Issue
178 pages (60% advertising): 4 articles; 21 depts/columns; 2 directories; 2 guides. Sample copy, free. Editorial calendar available.
- "Thank You: Raise Polite Children in an Age of Rudeness." Article discusses today's cultural trend toward rudeness and how it can be overcome with parental example.
- "Pediatricians: The Calling to Heal Young Bodies." Article profiles the pediatric profession, analyzing its history, its appeals, and benefits.
- Sample dept/column: "Single Parenthood" presents different ways single parents can build a community of resources to help them cope with problems and situations.

Rights and Payment
One-time rights. Articles, $100–$500. Artwork, $90. Kill fee, $50. Pays 45 days after publication. Provides 3 copies.

Editor's Comments
Most of our authors are local, making it easy to include references that are relevant to our readers. Submissions that are news-oriented are the best bet for consideration. Topics cover all aspects of family matters.

Odyssey

Carus Publishing
Suite C
30 Grove Street
Peterborough, NH 03458

Senior Editor: Elizabeth E. Lindstrom

Description and Readership

Making science fascinating for middle-grade students is the goal of this publication. Each issue is theme-based and presents one subject from a variety of different angles. Thought-provoking activities that help drive the information home provide some fun in each issue.
- **Audience:** 10–16 years
- **Frequency:** 9 times each year
- **Distribution:** 100% subscription
- **Circulation:** 21,000
- **Website:** www.odysseymagazine.com

Freelance Potential

90% written by nonstaff writers. Publishes 40 freelance submissions yearly; 5% by unpublished writers, 25% by authors who are new to the magazine. Receives 12 queries monthly.

Submissions

Query with outline, biography, and clips or writing samples. Availability of artwork improves chance of acceptance. SASE. Responds in 5 months.
Articles: 750–1,000 words. Informational articles; interviews; and biographies.
Depts/columns: Word length varies. Science news.
Other: Activities, to 500 words. Seasonal material about notable astronomy or space events placed in current context, experiments, and science projects.

Sample Issue

50 pages (no advertising): 8 articles; 1 story; 7 depts/columns; 5 activities. Sample copy, $4.50 with 9x12 SASE (4 first-class stamps). Guidelines and theme list available.
- "Rebuilding the Food Pyramid." Article tries to make practical sense out of the conflicting nutritional information bombarding us today.
- "Math . . . . By Mouth." Article describes the chemical reasons people gain weight and shows the common sense relationship between eating incorrectly and obesity.
- Sample dept/column: "Fantastic Journeys" tells the story of one young woman's battle with an eating disorder.

Rights and Payment

All rights. Written material, $.20–$.25 per word. Other material, payment rate varies. Pays on publication. Provides 2 copies.

Editor's Comments

We are interested in articles rich in scientific accuracy and liveliness concerning the subject at hand. The inclusion of primary research, (such as interviews with scientists focusing on current research), is of primary interest to our magazine.

The Old Schoolhouse Magazine

Homeschool Families
P.O. Box 185
Cool, CA 95614

Publisher: Gena Suarez

Description and Readership

The purpose of this publication is to promote homeschooling and provide resources to help families accomplish positive and effective homeschooling experiences. The information is offered from a Christian perspective. Conference information, reports, trends, and political affairs are included.
- **Audience:** Homeschooling parents and families
- **Frequency:** Quarterly
- **Distribution:** Unavailable
- **Circulation:** 22,000
- **Website:** www.thehomeschoolmagazine.com

Freelance Potential

40% written by nonstaff writers. Publishes 100+ freelance submissions yearly; 75% by unpublished writers, 75% by authors who are new to the magazine. Receives 16 queries and unsolicited mss monthly.

Submissions

Query with outline, sample paragraphs, and biography. Accepts email queries to publishers@TOSmag.com. No simultaneous submissions. SASE. Response time varies.
Articles: 1,000–2,000 words. Informational and how-to articles; and personal experience pieces. Topics include homeschooling, education, family life, art, music, spirituality, literature, child development, teen issues, science, history, and mathematics.

Sample Issue

160 pages (40% advertising): 4 articles; 25 depts/columns. Sample copy available. Guidelines available at website.
- "Creation Answers: What Really Happened to Dinosaurs?" Article investigates the era of dinosaurs and what happened to them in the context of biblical references.
- "Make Time for a Tea Party." Article traces the legend of how tea became known and describes a homeschool field trip to learn all about tea and its customs.
- Sample dept/column: "Units with Kim" offers ideas on organizing home study units utilizing libraries, homeschooling catalogues, award-winning book lists, and favorite books.

Rights and Payment

First rights. Written material, $.05 per word. Artwork, payment rate varies. Pays on publication. Provides 2 contributor's copies.

Editor's Comments

We need more journalistic pieces and newsy items that include statistics and data. We welcome articles on all facets of homeschooling, including creative homemaking, child-raising, instruction, international news, and "getting it all done."

Once Upon a Time . . .

553 Winston Court
St. Paul, MN 55118

Editor/Publisher: Audrey B. Baird

Description and Readership
Considered a "backyard fence" for the industry, this highly specialized and focused publication offers encouragement and tips for children's writers and illustrators. Its pages are filled with articles that share successes, frustrations, information, and ideas from established writers and artists. Readers enjoy the nurturing tone and the nuts-and-bolts help.
- **Audience:** Children's writers and illustrators
- **Frequency:** Quarterly
- **Distribution:** 100% subscription
- **Circulation:** 1,000
- **Website:** http://members.aol.com/ouatmag

Freelance Potential
50% written by nonstaff writers. Publishes 160 freelance submissions yearly; 30% by unpublished writers, 20% by authors who are new to the magazine. Receives 25 unsolicited mss each month.

Submissions
Send complete ms. No queries. Accepts photocopies and computer printouts. SASE. Response time varies.
Articles: To 900 words. Informational, self-help, how-to, and personal experience articles. Topics include writing and illustrating for children.
Depts/columns: Staff written.
Artwork: B/W line art.
Other: Poetry, to 24 lines.

Sample Issue
32 pages (2% advertising): 17 articles; 14 poems; 14 depts/columns. Sample copy, $5. Guidelines available.
- "How to Find Your Inner Child." Article explains that being aware of our five senses can help bring us back to childhood experiences in order to use them as story springboards.
- "The Three P's to Getting Published." Article discusses how practice, persistence, and patience are keys to getting into print.
- "Your Writing Core." Article offers ideas for writers to use to tap into and reawaken experiences and memories.

Rights and Payment
One-time rights. No payment. Provides 2 contributor's copies; 5 copies for cover art.

Editor's Comments
We are interested in how-to articles concerning the process of writing and illustrating children's literature—except how to cope with rejection. Short articles of 100–400 words find their way into print faster than longer articles.

On Course

General Council of the Assemblies of God
1445 North Boonville Avenue
Springfield, MO 65802-1894

Assistant Editor: Heather Van Allen

Description and Readership
Teen readers find articles on contemporary issues that emphasize biblical approaches to life in *On Course*. It is distributed free of charge to teens across the nation who request it, as well as through Assemblies of God churches.
- **Audience:** 12–18 years
- **Frequency:** Quarterly
- **Distribution:** 100% controlled
- **Circulation:** 190,000
- **Website:** www.oncourse.ag.com

Freelance Potential
85% written by nonstaff writers. Publishes 20 freelance submissions yearly; 30% by unpublished writers, 40% by authors who are new to the magazine.

Submissions
Send résumé with clips or writing samples. All work is done on assignment only.
Articles: To 1,000 words. How-to articles, profiles, interviews, humor, and personal experience pieces. Topics include social issues, music, health, religion, sports, careers, college, and multicultural subjects.
Fiction: To 1,000 words. Genres include multicultural, ethnic, inspirational, and real-life fiction; humor; and stories about sports.
Depts/columns: Word length varies.
Artwork: Photography and other artwork by teens.
Other: Poetry written by teens.

Sample Issue
32 pages (33% advertising): 5 articles; 6 depts/columns. Sample copy, free. Guidelines and theme list available.
- "Flying Solo." Article discusses the positive points of the gift of singleness in contrast to the gift of marriage.
- "RJ Helton: Life after *American Idol*." Article brings readers up to date on this Gospel singer who gained fame as a contestant on *American Idol*.
- Sample dept/column: "NYM Focus" recounts personal experiences of students who took part in the Fine Arts Festival in Washington, DC.

Rights and Payment
First and electronic rights. Pays on publication. Articles, $.10 per word. Poetry and artwork, $50. Provides 5 copies.

Editor's Comments
We would welcome articles on financial planning and preparing for the future instead of the usual "don't give in to peer pressure" articles. Sexual purity is another overdone theme.

On the Line

Mennonite Publishing House
616 Walnut Avenue
Scottsdale, PA 15683-1999

Editor: Mary Clemens Meyer

Description and Readership
Targeting upper elementary and junior high school children, this magazine strives to emphasize the use of Christian values in solving everyday problems, and the importance of accepting others with differences.
- **Audience:** 9–14 years
- **Frequency:** Monthly
- **Distribution:** 90% subscription; 10% other
- **Circulation:** 5,000
- **Website:** www.mph.org/otl

Freelance Potential
90% written by nonstaff writers. Publishes 85 freelance submissions yearly; 10% by unpublished writers, 30% by authors who are new to the magazine. Receives 100 mss monthly.

Submissions
Send complete ms. Prefers email submissions to otl@mph.org. Accepts photocopies, computer printouts, and simultaneous submissions if identified. SASE. Responds in 1 month.
Articles: 350–500 words. Informational, how-to, and self-help articles; profiles; biographies; and photo essays. Topics include animals, history, sports, hobbies, crafts, and social and ethnic issues, environmental concerns, and peacemaking.
Fiction: 1,000–1,800 words. Genres include adventure; humor; mystery; and contemporary, ethnic, and multicultural fiction.
Artwork: Full-color.
Other: Interesting facts, recipes, quizzes, puzzles, jokes, and cartoons. Poetry, 3–24 lines. Submit seasonal material 4–6 months in advance.

Sample Issue
24 pages (no advertising): 1 article; 3 stories; 6 activities. Sample copy, $2 with 8x10 SASE (2 first-class stamps). Writers' guidelines available.
- "Blue Crew Mystery." Story tells how a boy solves the mystery of missing money from a clubhouse cashbox.
- "Theft-protected." Story of a boy who learns a lesson about fundraising after the money he collects is stolen.

Rights and Payment
One-time rights. Articles and fiction, $.04–$.05 per word. Puzzles and quizzes, $10–$15. Poetry, $10–$25. Cartoons, $10. Pays on acceptance. Provides 2 contributor's copies.

Editor's Comments
We could use more stories about homeschooled children. Also, we are always on the lookout for more puzzles. Please do not send any material on moving, and trying to earn money—we have enough on these topics.

Organic Family Magazine

P.O. Box 1614
Wallingford, CT 06492-1214

Editor: C. J. Wong

Description and Readership
Readers interested in living an organic life find articles on organic agriculture and the natural world in each issue of this magazine, which also offers poetry and short stories on living with environmental responsibility.
- **Audience:** Families
- **Frequency:** Quarterly
- **Distribution:** Unavailable
- **Circulation:** Unavailable
- **Website:** www.organicfamilymagazine.com

Freelance Potential
90% written by nonstaff writers. Publishes 80 freelance submissions yearly.

Submissions
Query or send complete ms. Prefers email submissions to sciencelibrarian@hotmail.com. Accepts photocopies and computer printouts. SASE. Response time varies.
Articles: Word length varies. Informational articles; interviews; and personal experience pieces. Topics include nature, organic agriculture, conservation, parenting, natural pet care, herbs, gardening, nutrition, progressive politics, health, wellness, and environmental issues.
Fiction: Word length varies. Stories about nature and the environment.
Depts/columns: Word length varies. New product reviews, recipes, profiles of conservation organizations, book reviews.
Other: Poetry.

Sample Issue
36 pages: 18 articles; 7 depts/columns; 1 poem; 1 contest.
- "Controlling Pests Naturally." Article suggests ways to avoid the use of insecticides, including hand-picking bugs off plants, spraying plants with a hose to wash insect pests away, and encouraging the presence of beneficial bugs.
- "Children First!" Personal essays reveals that a couple's decision to put the needs of their child first, and their own relationship second, nearly destroyed their marriage.
- Sample dept/column: "Organic Labeling: What Does It All Mean?" advises consumers to be wary of food labels.

Rights and Payment
One-time rights. No payment. Provides 1 contributor's copy.

Editor's Comments
Have you recently made a switch from a mainstream product to a more environmentally sound alternative? Do you have a passion for organic gardening? If so, you can be an inspiration to others. If you have an idea for an article, pitch it to us.

Our Children

National PTA
Suite 2100
330 North Wabash
Chicago, IL 60611-3690

Editor: Marilyn Anderson

Description and Readership
This official publication of the National PTA is read for straightforward information to help children lead happy, healthy, and productive lives. Current educational issues and concerns are part of its editorial mix.
- **Audience:** Parents, educators, school administrators
- **Frequency:** 6 times each year
- **Distribution:** 90% membership; 10% subscription
- **Circulation:** 31,000
- **Website:** www.pta.org

Freelance Potential
50% written by nonstaff writers. Publishes 18–20 freelance submissions yearly; 75% by authors who are new to the magazine. Receives 15–20 queries and unsolicited mss monthly.

Submissions
Query or send complete ms. Accepts email submissions to m_anderson@pta.org. No simultaneous submissions. Final submissions must be sent on disk. SASE. Responds in 2 months.
Articles: 600–1,100 words. Informational and how-to articles. Topics include education, child welfare, and family life.
Depts/columns: Word length varies. Short updates on parenting and education issues.
Artwork: 3x5 or larger color prints and slides.
Other: Submit seasonal material 3 months in advance.

Sample Issue
22 pages (no advertising): 4 articles; 1 interview; 9 depts/columns. Sample copy, $2.50 with 9x12 SASE ($1 postage). Guidelines and theme list available.
- "Is Science Valued at Your Child's Elementary School?" Article demonstrates how to evaluate if science is an important subject in a curriculum, and if not, how to improve it.
- "Helping Your Child Dream Big." Article outlines several steps to take with children to help them grow and nurture their dreams and aspirations.
- Sample dept/column: "Child Advocacy" alerts parents and PTA leaders to the problem of asbestos, how it can be discovered, and what can be done to solve the situation.

Rights and Payment
First rights. No payment. Provides 3 contributor's copies.

Editor's Comments
We would like to receive more submissions about after-school programs, ADHD, divorce, nutrition, educational funding, understanding the No Child Left Behind Act, and effective interaction with teachers.

Pack-O-Fun

Suite 375
2400 Devon
Des Plaines, IL 60018-4618

Managing Editor: Irene Mueller

Description and Readership
Designed to encourage creativity and make learning fun, this publication features craft projects and activities for elementary school age children. Most of its subscribers are teachers, parents, and group leaders who work with children.
- **Audience:** 6–12 years; parents; teachers
- **Frequency:** 6 times each year
- **Distribution:** 67% subscription; 33% newsstand
- **Circulation:** 130,000
- **Website:** www.craftideas.com

Freelance Potential
100% written by nonstaff writers. Publishes 8 freelance submissions yearly; 20% by unpublished writers, 40% by authors who are new to the magazine. Receives 42 queries and unsolicited mss monthly.

Submissions
Query or send complete ms with instructions and sketches if appropriate. Accepts photocopies. SASE. Responds in 4–6 weeks.
Articles: To 200 words. How-to and craft projects and party ideas.
Depts/columns: Word length varies. Art ideas; projects for children and adults to do together; ideas for vacation Bible school programs; and pictures of projects from readers.
Artwork: B/W line art.
Other: Activities, puzzles, games, skits, and poetry.

Sample Issue
66 pages (10% advertising): 14 crafts and activities; 4 depts/columns. Sample copy, $4.99 with 9x12 SASE (2 first-class stamps). Guidelines available.
- "It's a Watermelon Celebration." Features ideas for decoratively carving watermelons, as well as instructions for making a watermelon welcome sign for your front door.
- "Camp Crafts." Activities include making a ladybug and a bee with craft sticks.
- Sample dept/column: "Craft-a-Story" offers project ideas that relate to children's favorite stories, songs, or poems.

Rights and Payment
All rights. Written material, $10–$15. Artwork, payment rate varies. Pays 30 days after signed contract. Provides 3 contributor's copies.

Editor's Comments
We target grown-ups who enjoy making clever, low-cost craft projects for or with kids. We like projects that are innovative and use materials in a fresh and interesting way. The required materials should be affordable and readily available.

Parent and Preschooler Newsletter

North Shore Child & Family Guidance Center
480 Old Westbury Road
Roslyn Heights, NY 11577-2215

Editor: Neala S. Schwartzberg, Ph.D.

Description and Readership
The goal of this newsletter is to provide helpful information to persons caring for children from birth through age six. Featured articles are written by child psychologists, social workers, educators, and recognized experts in specialized fields.
- **Audience:** Parents, caregivers, and early childhood professionals
- **Frequency:** 10 times each year
- **Distribution:** 100% subscription
- **Circulation:** Unavailable
- **Website:** www.northshorechildguidance.org

Freelance Potential
90% written by nonstaff writers. Publishes 10 freelance submissions yearly; 70% by authors who are new to the magazine. Receives 5–6 queries monthly.

Submissions
Query with outline. Accepts disk submissions and email to nealas@panix.com. SASE. Responds in 1 week.
Articles: 2,000 words. Practical information and how-to articles. Topics include education, self-esteem, discipline, children's health, parenting skills, fostering cooperation through play, and coping with death.
Depts/columns: Staff written.

Sample Issue
8 pages (no advertising): 3 articles; 3 depts/columns. Sample copy, $3 with #10 SASE (1 first-class stamp). Writers' guidelines available.
- "Talk, Talk, Talk . . ." Article outlines communication differences between men and women and offers suggestions on how to improve one's understanding of each other.
- "Girls, Boys, and Books." Article explains how children's books not only demonstrate a culture's values, but how they work to socialize children into the values of society.

Rights and Payment
First world rights. Articles, $200. Pays on publication. Provides 10 contributor's copies.

Editor's Comments
Subscribers to our newsletter cover a wide range of child caregivers from new parents and librarians to professionals in early childhood development. It is an international resource with English and Spanish editions that address universal themes. The content in each issue combines theory and practical information intended to improve skills needed for parenting and child education. Articles should provide a positive approach to parenting issues.

ParenTeacher Magazine

P.O. Box 1246
Mount Dora, FL 32756

Editor: Carmen McGuiness

Description and Readership
This publication by Read America strives to provide quality instructional techniques for parents, teachers, clinicians, and other educational professionals interfacing with students.
- **Audience:** Parents, educators, and reading specialists
- **Frequency:** 6 times each year
- **Distribution:** 90% controlled; 10% subscription
- **Circulation:** 35,000
- **Website:** www.parenteacher.net

Freelance Potential
20% written by nonstaff writers. Publishes 100 freelance submissions yearly; 90% by unpublished writers, 100% by authors who are new to the magazine. Receives 166 unsolicited mss monthly.

Submissions
Send complete ms. Accepts computer printouts and email submissions to parenteacher@aol.com (no attachments). No simultaneous submissions. SASE. Responds in 1 month.
Articles: 500–1,500 words. Practical application articles; reviews; and read-aloud pieces. Topics include literature, reading, education, family, parenting, child development, homeschooling, health, nutrition, cooking, gardening, and travel.
Fiction: Word length varies. Short stories.
Artwork: Candid color photos or digital images.
Other: Poetry, to 500 words. Submit seasonal material 3 months in advance.

Sample Issue
26 pages (20% advertising): 10 articles; 1 calendar of events. Sample copy, $7.50 with 9x12 SASE. Guidelines available.
- "The Yoga Advantage." Article considers the growing popularity of yoga among school children and describes the benefits derived from this discipline.
- "Philately for Preschoolers: Stamp Collecting for Toddlers." Article describes one grandmother's surprise at the interest her 4-year-old grandson took in her stamp collection.

Rights and Payment
One-time rights. All material, payment rate varies. Pays on publication. Provides 1 contributor's copy.

Editor's Comments
We want to impact the educational system and change it to be more in line with the way children really learn. Our main focus is on literacy but we also welcome material about health, nutrition, general education, family life, children, and different cultures of the world.

Parentguide News

13th Floor
419 Park Avenue South
New York, NY 10016

Editor: Anne Marie Evola

Description and Readership

Parentguide is a tabloid newspaper that caters to the needs of parents with children under the age of twelve living in the New York City, Long Island, and New Jersey areas. Its articles and columns address national and local issues affecting health, education, and family life.

- **Audience:** Parents
- **Frequency:** Monthly
- **Distribution:** Subscription; controlled
- **Circulation:** 210,000
- **Website:** www.parentguidenews.com

Freelance Potential

85% written by nonstaff writers. Publishes 45 freelance submissions yearly; 20% by unpublished writers, 80% by authors who are new to the magazine. Receives 8 queries and unsolicited mss monthly.

Submissions

Query or send complete ms with résumé. Accepts photocopies and computer printouts. SASE. Responds in 3–4 weeks.
Articles: 750–1,500 words. Informational and self-help articles; personal experience pieces; profiles; and humor. Topics include parenting, family issues, social issues, current events, regional issues, popular culture, health, careers, computers, and science.
Depts/columns: 500 words. News on local schools and businesses, travel, reviews, and women's health.

Sample Issue

74 pages (39% advertising): 13 articles; 8 depts/columns; 2 directories; 1 calendar of events. Sample copy, free with 10x13 SASE. Guidelines available.

- "An Atmosphere of Tolerance." Article offers six tips for teaching children about interfaith and intercultural families.
- "Fatherhood: It's a Whole New Ballgame." Article compares being a father with various sporting metaphors.
- Sample dept/column: "In Season" suggests ways to make Father's Day special.

Rights and Payment

Rights negotiable. No payment. Provides 1+ contributor's copies.

Editor's Comments

Our editors are looking for personal experiences, advice, humorous anecdotes, and professional or newsworthy observations on parenting and family issues. New writers are invited to submit material on local family recreational activities and parenting topics.

Parenting

4th Floor
530 Fifth Avenue
New York, NY 10036

Submissions Editor

Description and Readership

Families with children under the age of twelve find useful child-rearing information and updates on pediatric health and behavior in this magazine. *Parenting* includes age-appropriate information on child development and tips for making the most of family time.

- **Audience:** Parents
- **Frequency:** 10 times each year
- **Distribution:** 90% subscription; 10% newsstand
- **Circulation:** 1.6 million
- **Website:** www.parenting.com

Freelance Potential

80% written by nonstaff writers. Publishes few freelance submissions yearly; 5% by unpublished writers, 10% by new authors. Receives 10 queries, 125 unsolicited mss monthly.

Submissions

Query or send complete ms. Accepts photocopies and computer printouts. SASE. Responds in 1–2 months.
Articles: 1,000–2,500 words. Informational, how-to, and self-help articles; profiles; and personal experience pieces. Topics include child development, behavior, health, pregnancy, childbirth, and family activities.
Depts/columns: 100–1,000 words. Parenting tips and advice; child development by age range; work and family; and health and beauty advice for moms.

Sample Issue

170 pages (50% advertising): 10 articles; 15 depts/columns. Sample copy, $5.95 (mark envelope Attn: Back Issues). Guidelines available.

- "How to Stop Fighting about Money." Article explains how to keep different spending or saving styles from hurting a marriage.
- "Time to Move?" Article offers advice for making a move to a new house as painless as possible.
- Sample depts/column: "Healthy Bites" tells why parents shouldn't worry too much about picky eaters and provides information on healthy crackers for kids.

Rights and Payment

First world rights with 2 months' exclusivity. Written material, payment rate varies. Pays on publication. Provides 1 contributor's copy.

Editor's Comments

We're interested in useful tools, in-depth information, reality-tested advice, and quick tips for parents. Departments offer the best opportunity for new writers.

Parenting New Hampshire

P.O. Box 1291
Nashua, NH 03061-1291

Editor: Beth Quarm Todgham

Description and Readership

Supporting New Hampshire families in their family efforts by sharing ideas, information, and news is the goal of this tabloid. It is well-rounded resource guide for common and not-so-common parenting issues, and local events.
- **Audience:** Parents
- **Frequency:** Monthly
- **Distribution:** 100% controlled
- **Circulation:** 27,500
- **Website:** www.parentingnh.com

Freelance Potential

70% written by nonstaff writers. Publishes 20–25 freelance submissions yearly; 20% by unpublished writers, 90% by authors who are new to the magazine. Receives 40 queries and unsolicited mss monthly.

Submissions

Query or send complete ms. Accepts photocopies, computer printouts, disk submissions, and email submissions to news@parentingnh.com. Availability of artwork improves chance of acceptance. SASE. Response time varies.
Articles: Word length varies. Informational and how-to articles; and profiles. Topics include family life, parenting, current events, sports, travel, education, popular culture, social issues, science, the environment, and college preparation.
Depts/columns: Word length varies. Child development, medical news, and parenting news.
Other: Submit seasonal material 2 months in advance.

Sample Issue

56 pages (42% advertising): 5 articles; 12 depts/columns. Sample copy, free. Editorial calendar available.
- "Plan Now for Your Child's Best Summer Ever!" Article simplifies the process of deciding what type of summer camp will provide the best experience for a child.
- "Scholarships and Financial Aid Help Make Summer Camp Affordable." Article reveals that a majority of summer camps offer some type of financial aid.

Rights and Payment

All rights. Articles, $25. Other material, payment rate varies. Pays on acceptance. Provides 3 contributor's copies.

Editor's Comments

We would like to see more articles exploring ways that families can have fun together, and submissions on early childhood development and education. Articles should be based on primary research with thoroughly covered topics.

Everyday Challenges
ParentLife, HomeLife
William Summey, Editor-in-Chief

ParentLife is just one of the thousands of Christian living resources that LifeWay sells and makes available online. Think of it as "one-stop shopping" for information about the world from a Christian viewpoint.

Ten years ago, *ParentLife* replaced two older magazines, *Living with Preschoolers* and *Living with Children*. Editor-in-Chief William Summey, says, "It was the success of *HomeLife Magazine*, also published by LifeWay, that led to the obvious need of a monthly parenting resource."

Summey, who recently received his doctorate with a dissertation on evangelical approaches to childrearing, says, "Our preference for nonfiction formats are a blend of personal life experiences with teachable advice that apply to other parents and sidebars that provide further information for readers. We want readers to have the best sources from professionals whether from medical doctors, professors, counselors, and the best faith-based materials."

HomeLife, enjoying a half century of publishing, currently reaches 375,000 readers. Its columns and articles offer practical advice and inspiration. Latino writers can contribute articles to LifeWay's Spanish quarterly, *La Familia Christiana de Hoy.*

Living with Teenagers, another magazine published by LifeWay, helps parents to use biblical principles in their relationships with their teens. Editor Sherrie Thomas says, "I seek to deal with the everyday challenges as well as the critical issues parents and teens face in their fast-paced world of music, movies, school, and sports."

(See listing for *ParentLife* on following page)

ParentLife

1 LifeWay Plaza
Nashville, TN 37234-0172

Editor-in-Chief: William Summey

Description and Readership
The Bible is the basis for finding solutions for the challenges of everyday living in this magazine published by LifeWay Christian Resources. Its information is pertinent to children through pre-teen years, and readers discover a wide range of material relevant to all types of families, including those with single parents, adopted or special needs children, and grandparents.
- **Audience:** Parents
- **Frequency:** Monthly
- **Distribution:** 90% churches; 10% subscription
- **Circulation:** 100,000
- **Website:** www.lifeway.com

Freelance Potential
90% written by nonstaff writers. Publishes 12 freelance submissions yearly; 5% by unpublished writers, 5% by authors who are new to the magazine. Receives 8 queries and unsolicited mss monthly.

Submissions
Query or send complete ms. Accepts computer printouts and email submissions to parentlife@lifeway.com. SASE.
Articles: 500–1,500 words. Informational and how-to articles; and personal experience pieces. Topics include family issues, religion, education, health, fitness, crafts, and hobbies.
Depts/columns: 500 words. Medical advice, family stories, crafts, and food.
Artwork: Color prints or transparencies.
Other: Accepts seasonal material for Christmas and Thanksgiving.

Sample Issue
50 pages (no advertising): 8 articles; 12 depts/columns.
Sample copy, $2.95 with 9x12 SASE. Guidelines available.
- "Wild at Heart." Article advances the theory that God has given every child a sense of adventure and the best thing a parent can do is to teach children how to face challenges, rather than avoid life's obsticles.
- Sample dept/column: "A Father's Thoughts" explains how important a father's blessing is to a child.

Rights and Payment
Non-exclusive rights. All material, payment rate varies. Pays on publication. Provides 1 contributor's copy.

Editor's Comments
We would like to receive more submissions on special needs children, concerns of single parenting and step parenting, adoption, and stay-at-home dads. Our vision is to transform families through biblical solutions.

Parents and Children Together Online

Suite 140
2805 East 10th Street
Bloomington, IN 47403

Editor: Mei-Yu Lu

Description and Readership
A Family Literacy Center project, this website's goal is to advance their cause by bringing parents and children together to enjoy the magic of reading. It features original stories and articles suitable for reading aloud with children from 5 to 14 years of age. A special parental section features resources for children's development and literacy learning.
- **Audience:** Parents and children
- **Frequency:** Irregular
- **Distribution:** Internet
- **Hits per month:** 10,000
- **Website:** www.reading.indiana.edu/www/famres/ pctogeth/index.shtml

Freelance Potential
75% written by nonstaff writers. Publishes 50–80 freelance submissions yearly; 40% by unpublished writers, 60% by authors who are new to the magazine. Receives 12–13 unsolicited mss monthly.

Submissions
Send complete ms. Accepts email submissions to reading@indiana.edu. Availability of artwork improves chance of acceptance. Response time varies.
Articles: 500–1,800 words. Informational articles that expand children's understanding of different lifestyles, cultures, and places. Also publishes articles for parents and children's writers and illustrators.
Fiction: Word length varies. Features gender inclusive stories that may be enjoyed by parents and children.
Depts/columns: Word length varies. Book reviews.
Artwork: 8x10 B/W and color prints. Line art.
Other: Literary activities for families; poetry.

Sample Issue
Guidelines available at website:
reading.indiana.edu/www/famres/pctogeth/wg.shtml.
- "Missolua Magic." Article presents the Missoula Children's Theatre, from Missoula, Montana, the largest touring children's theatre in the United States.
- "From Fluff to Fabric." Article demonstrates the process that turns wool into felt—a method used for thousands of years.

Rights and Payment
Electronic rights. No payment.

Editor's Comments
We would like more submissions dealing with multicultural and controversial issues in children's lives, including death, divorce, abuse, illness, and emotional problems.

Parents & Kids

Suite 294
2727 Old Canton Road
Jackson, MS 39216

Editor: Gretchen Cook

Description and Readership
Practical service articles for parents of children up to the age of 14 are featured in *Parents & Kids*, a regional publication reaching families in metropolitan Jackson and central Mississippi.
- **Audience:** Parents
- **Frequency:** 7 times each year
- **Distribution:** 66% schools; 34% controlled
- **Circulation:** 35,000
- **Website:** www.PandKmagazine.com

Freelance Potential
80% written by nonstaff writers. Publishes 80 freelance submissions yearly; 50% by unpublished writers. Receives 33 unsolicited mss monthly.

Submissions
Send complete ms. Accepts email submissions to pkmag@mindspring.com (in text of message and as Microsoft Word attachment). SASE. Responds in 6 weeks.
Articles: 700 words. Informational, self-help, and how-to articles. Topics include the arts, computers, crafts and hobbies, health, fitness, multicultural and ethnic issues, recreation, regional news, social issues, special education, sports, and travel.
Depts/columns: 500 words. Travel, cooking, computers.
Artwork: B/W prints or transparencies. Line art. Prefers electronic files; contact publisher for specifics.
Other: Submit seasonal material 3–6 months in advance.

Sample Issue
56 pages (54% advertising): 6 articles; 8 depts/columns; 1 activity planner. Sample copy, free with 9x12 SASE ($1.06 postage). Guidelines available at website.
- "Love Your Teen." Article lists subtle ways parents can show love for their teenagers.
- "Domestic Violence." Article looks at emotional, psychological, and physical abuse among families.
- Sample dept/column: "What's for Supper?" consists of recipes for an Italian-style Valentine's Day dinner.

Rights and Payment
One-time rights. Pays on publication. Articles and depts/columns, $25. Provides tearsheet.

Editor's Comments
Use a conversational tone in your article, and write it in the active voice at a sixth- to eighth-grade reading level. Localized parenting articles are much more likely to be accepted. Need local contacts? We may be able to help.

Parents Express
Pennsylvania Edition

290 Commerce Drive
Fort Washington, PA 19034

Submissions Editor: Daniel Sean Kaye

Description and Readership
Available free at various locations in Delaware Valley, Pennsylvania, this regional newspaper features information on local events, resources, and issues, including entertainment, education, and politics.
- **Audience:** Parents
- **Frequency:** Monthly
- **Distribution:** 50% schools; 50% other
- **Circulation:** 80,000
- **Website:** www.parents-express.net

Freelance Potential
50% written by nonstaff writers. Publishes 25–35 freelance submissions yearly; 25% by unpublished writers, 75% by authors who are new to the magazine. Receives many queries each month.

Submissions
Query with clips or writing samples. Accepts photocopies, computer printouts, and email queries to wdelucca@montgomerynews.com. Availability of artwork improves chance of acceptance. SASE. Responds in 1 month.
Articles: 300–1,000 words. Informational articles; profiles; interviews; and personal experience pieces. Topics include parenting and family life, health, politics, business, entertainment, music, education, and computers.
Depts/columns: 600–800 words Regional events and activities, book and product reviews, and local school news.
Artwork: B/W or color prints or transparencies.
Other: Submit seasonal material 2 months in advance.

Sample Issue
56 pages (62% advertising): 17 depts/columns; 3 events calendars. Sample copy, free with 10x13 SASE ($2.14 postage). Theme list available.
- Sample dept/column: "School News" explains how to find the right tutor, improve students' math skills, and keep kids safe and healthy.
- Sample dept/column: "Profiles in Parenting" Offers various child development and education concerns.

Rights and Payment
One-time rights. Articles, $35–$200. Depts/columns, payment rate varies. Pays on publication. Provides contributor's copies upon request.

Editor's Comments
We would like to see more in-depth, hard-core articles that deal with contemporary family issues. Writers living in the Delaware Valley are encouraged to submit material.

Parents Express

Southern New Jersey Edition

290 Commerce Drive
Fort Washington, PA 19034

Editor: Daniel Sean Kaye

Description and Readership

While there are a lot of serious articles about parenting in this publication, it also readily includes humorous items if there is an underlying nugget of wisdom useful to parents.
- **Audience:** Parents
- **Frequency:** Monthly
- **Distribution:** 30% schools; 10% subscription; 60% other
- **Circulation:** 80,000
- **Website:** www.parents-express.net

Freelance Potential

40% written by nonstaff writers. Publishes 50–60 freelance submissions yearly; 25% by unpublished writers, 75% by authors who are new to the magazine. Receives many queries each month.

Submissions

Query with clips or writing samples. Accepts photocopies, computer printouts, and email queries to dkaye@ montgomerynews.com. SASE. Responds in 1 month.
Articles: 300–1,000 words. Informational articles; profiles; interviews; and personal experience pieces. Topics include parenting, family life, child care, politics, business, education, and entertainment.
Depts/columns: 600–800 words. Regional events, book and product reviews, local school news, family field trips, crafts, and activities.
Artwork: B/W or color prints or transparencies.
Other: Submit seasonal material 2 months in advance.

Sample Issue

38 pages (62% advertising): 22 depts/columns; 1 calendar. Sample copy, free with 9x12 SASE. Editorial calendar available.
- Sample dept/column: "Homefront Journal" shares one mother's humorous experience in trying to understand and use the "codes" found in parenting publications for disciplining a child.
- Sample dept/column: "Dadography" looks at parenting through the eyes of a new father and tries to dispel preconceived fatherly notions.

Rights and Payment

One-time rights. Articles, $35–$200. Depts/columns, payment rate varies. Pays on publication. Provides contributor's copies.

Editor's Comments

Although many of our contributors live in the South Jersey area, it's not a prerequisite for submitting general parenting material. Our readership enjoys useful tips and entertaining material.

Parents Magazine

Gruner + Jahr
375 Lexington Avenue
New York, NY 10017

Editor

Description and Readership

This widely circulated parenting magazine strives to bring its readers practical, useful parenting information that appeals to a broad spectrum of families. It includes personal parenting experiences as well as advice from experts on such topics as health, behavior, and child development.
- **Audience:** Parents
- **Frequency:** Monthly
- **Distribution:** Subscription; newsstand
- **Circulation:** Unavailable
- **Website:** www.parents.com

Freelance Potential

20% written by nonstaff writers. Publishes 50 freelance submissions yearly. Receives 100 queries monthly.

Submissions

Query with clips. Accepts photocopies and computer printouts. SASE. Responds in 6 weeks.
Articles: Word length varies. Informational, self-help, and how-to articles; profiles; and personal experience pieces. Topics include gifted and special education, child development and behavior, health, fitness, social issues, travel, and multicultural and ethnic issues.
Depts/columns: Word length varies. Family issues, marriage and relationships, family cooking, and health and beauty for mothers.

Sample Issue

282 pages: 23 articles; 22 depts/columns. Sample copy, $3.50 with 9x12 SASE. Guidelines available at website.
- "Simple Secrets of Happy Families" Article discusses the importance of finding a community that fits your family, talking to your kids, caring for pets, and sharing chores.
- "Picky Eating: How to Respond." Article offers tips for helping your child develop a more tolerant attitude toward food.
- "10 Healthy Eating Habits for Babies and Toddlers." Article presents easy ways to teach young children good nutrition habits for life.

Rights and Payment

Rights policy varies. Written material, payment rate varies. Pays on publication.

Editor's Comments

Send us a one-page letter detailing the topic you'd like to address and your strategy for writing the story. Demonstrate that you are adept at doing research by mentioning the kind of sources you intend to use. All of our articles use expert advice and real parent examples.

Parents' Monthly

104 Appel Court
Folsom, CA 95630

Editor: Kandi Chong

Description and Readership
Family life in central and northern California is the focus of this magazine for parents, teachers, child-care providers, and other advocates for children ages newborn through teens. It prefers a local slant for area events and personalities, and well researched information on parenting issues.
- **Audience:** Families
- **Frequency:** Monthly
- **Distribution:** 90% newsstand;10% subscription
- **Circulation:** 55,000
- **Website:** www.parentsmonthlymagazine.com

Freelance Potential
50% written by nonstaff writers. Publishes 25 freelance submissions yearly; 50% by unpublished writers, 50% by new authors. Receives 80–85 queries monthly.

Submissions
Query. Accepts simultaneous submissions if identified. Availability of artwork improves chance of acceptance. SASE. Responds to queries in 1 month, to mss in 4–6 months.
Articles: 1,000 words. Informational and how-to articles; humor; profiles; and interviews. Topics include education, child development, parenting, community issues, and travel.
Depts/columns: Opinion pieces, 600 words. Local personality profiles, 600 words. Local parenting items, 150–300 words.
Artwork: Color prints, digital JPEG or TIFF.
Other: Submit seasonal material 6 months in advance.

Sample Issue
38 pages (57% advertising): 4 articles; 3 depts/columns. Sample copy, free with 9x12 SASE (3 first-class stamps). Guidelines and editorial calendar available.
- "Coed or Same Sex?" Article weighs the advantages and disadvantages of both types of children's summer camps.
- "Champions in Synch." Article spotlights the Sacramento synchronized swim team and what makes it special.
- Sample dept/column: "Theater Preview" describes the local Dale Scholl Dance/Art company in Sacramento.

Rights and Payment
One-time rights. Written material, $50–$300. Photos, $25–$50. Pays on publication. Provides 1 contributor's copy.

Editor's Comments
We would like to see submissions dealing with baby and toddler issues, arts with children, and homeschooling topics. We are not looking for personal experience pieces or those relating to discipline situations. Articles that have special appeal to families in the Sacramento and Stockton, California areas are preferred.

Parents' Press

1454 Sixth Street
Berkeley, CA 94710

Editor: Dixie Jordon

Description and Readership
This San Francisco Bay area parenting tabloid publishes articles on general parenting topics along with information on education, child development, health, and local events. *Parents' Press* primarily targets families with infants and toddlers, but it also offers material related to school-age and adolescent children.
- **Audience:** Parents
- **Frequency:** Monthly
- **Distribution:** 100% controlled
- **Circulation:** 75,000
- **Website:** www.parentspress.com

Freelance Potential
60% written by nonstaff writers. Publishes 10 freelance submissions yearly; 25% by authors who are new to the magazine. Receives 60 unsolicited mss monthly.

Submissions
Send complete ms. SASE. Responds in 2 months.
Articles: To 1,500 words. How-to and informational articles. Topics include child development, education, health, safety, party planning, and regional family events and activities.
Depts/columns: Staff written.
Artwork: B/W prints and transparencies. Line art.
Other: Submit seasonal material 2 months in advance.

Sample Issue
36 pages (63% advertising): 9 articles; 4 depts/columns; 1 event calendar; 1 school directory. Sample copy, $3 with 9x12 SASE ($1.93 postage). Guidelines and theme list/editorial calendar available.
- "Knock 'Em Dead." Article presents strategies for stay-at-home moms who are returning to the workplace.
- "The Good, the Bad, and the Unpretentious." Article provides reviews of Bay area waterslides.

Rights and Payment
All or second rights. Articles, $50–$500. Pays 45 days after publication.

Editor's Comments
We want informational, research-based articles on a broad spectrum of topics—from playground safety and early childhood behavior to adolescent health. You don't have to be an expert in the field you choose to write in, but you have to do your homework. Almost all of the material we publish has some sort of local angle or connection and we encourage interviews with local experts. At this time, we are not interested in reviewing personal essays from parents.

Partners

Christian Light Publications
P.O. Box 1212
Harrisburg, VA 22803-1212

Editor: Norma Plank

Description and Readership
Targeting Mennonite children, this publication features inspirational and character-building stories that focus on Christian values, living, and the joy of serving Christ. It also includes poetry and activities.
- **Audience:** 9–14 years
- **Frequency:** Monthly
- **Distribution:** Sunday schools; subscription
- **Circulation:** 6,562

Freelance Potential
98% written by nonstaff writers. Publishes 200–500 freelance submissions yearly; 5% by unpublished writers, 5% by authors who are new to the magazine. Receives 60–80 unsolicited mss monthly.

Submissions
Send complete ms. Prefers email submissions to partners@clp.org. Accepts photocopies, computer printouts, disk submissions, and simultaneous submissions if identified. SASE. Responds in 6 weeks.
Articles: 200–800 words. Informational articles. Topics include nature, customs, and biblical history.
Fiction: 400–1,600 words. Stories that emphasize Mennonite beliefs and biblical interpretations.
Other: Puzzles and activities with biblical themes; poetry. Submit seasonal material 6 months in advance.

Sample Issue
4 pages (no advertising): 2 stories; 2 poems; 1 activity. Sample copy, free with 9x12 SASE ($.78 postage). Writers' guidelines and theme list available.
- "Trust in the Lord." Story tells how a boy who struggles with arithmetic learns that he must trust in himself and the help of God to get through the challenges he faces.
- "No Bread in the Village." Story of a boy who is given a Bible to learn about Jesus after his village runs out of bread.

Rights and Payment
All, first, or one-time rights. Written material, $.02–$.07 per word. Poetry, $.25–$.75 per line. Pays on acceptance. Provides 1 contributor's copy.

Editor's Comments
Please note that we are a thematic publication. We seek stories that incorporate a biblical, spiritual lesson into a related theme. Remember, it is more effective to "show" the lesson than to "tell" it through conversation and explanation. Fiction writing must be faithful to the biblical accounts they reference.

Pediatrics for Parents

P.O. Box 63716
Philadelphia, PA 19147

Editor: Richard J. Sagall, M.D.

Description and Readership
Emphasizing childhood health care, this magazine stresses preventative care, accident prevention, and a common sense approach to children's health issues. Much of its content is written by medical and dental professionals.
- **Audience:** Parents
- **Frequency:** Monthly
- **Distribution:** 100% subscription
- **Circulation:** 2,000
- **Website:** www.pedsforparents.com

Freelance Potential
50% written by nonstaff writers. Publishes 12 freelance submissions yearly; 90% by unpublished writers, 10% by authors who are new to the magazine. Receives 3 queries and unsolicited mss monthly.

Submissions
Query or send complete ms. Prefers email submissions to articles@pedsforparents.com. Accepts photocopies and computer printouts. SASE. Response time varies.
Articles: 250–1,000 words. Informational articles. Topics include pregnancy and issues such as medical problems and advances, new treatments, wellness, prevention, and fitness as they relate to infants and children.
Depts/columns: Word length varies. New product information and article reprints.
Other: Filler, 150–200 words.

Sample Issue
12 pages (no advertising): 18 articles. Sample copy, $3. Guidelines available.
- "Early Explorers: When Toddlers Discover Their Sexual Selves." Article explains that a parent's natural response to young children's curiosity creates healthy sexual attitudes.
- "Protect Children from Acetaminophen Overdoses." Article emphasizes the difference between concentrated and regular types of acetaminophens.

Rights and Payment
First rights. Written material, $5–$50. Pays on publication. Provides 2 contributor's copies.

Editor's Comments
We are not a general parenting publication. We are interested in original, well-researched, and informative articles on medical subjects important to parents: disease processes and treatment approaches; wellness; prevention; and modes of interaction between children, parents, and medical professionals.

Piedmont Parent

P.O. Box 11740
Winston-Salem, NC 27116

Editor: Leanne MacDonald

Description and Readership

Parents, teachers, and other child-care providers find practical information with a regional twist in this tabloid that concentrates on children's issues from newborns to teens.
- **Audience:** Parents
- **Frequency:** Monthly
- **Distribution:** 100% newsstand
- **Circulation:** 33,000
- **Website:** www.piedmontparent.com

Freelance Potential

75% written by nonstaff writers. Publishes 60 freelance submissions yearly; 25% by unpublished writers, 50% by authors who are new to the magazine. Receives 25 unsolicited mss monthly.

Submissions

Send complete ms. Accepts email submissions to editor@piedmontparent.com and simultaneous submissions if identified. SASE. Responds in 2 months.
Articles: 600–900 words. Informational and how-to articles and interviews. Topics include child development, day care, summer camps, gifted and special education, local and regional news, science, social issues, sports, popular culture, health, and travel.
Depts/columns: 600–900 words. Health and news items.
Other: Family games and activities.

Sample Issue

36 pages (47% advertising): 6 articles; 4 depts/columns; 1 directory. Sample copy, free with 9x12 SASE ($1.50 postage). Guidelines and theme list available.
- "Should Your Teen Work?" Article focuses on high school students who work several hours a week in addition to carrying a full course schedule and extracurricular activities, and how parents can lay the groundwork for a more realistic approach to life.
- Sample dept/column: "Is My Kid OK?" discusses a parent's normal emotions and behavior when children leave home to begin their college experience.

Rights and Payment

One-time rights. Written material, $30. Pays on publication. Provides 1 tearsheet.

Editor's Comments

Our feature articles require thorough research, a minimum of three reliable sources, and knowledge of our target audience. We prefer email submissions.

Pikes Peak Parent

30 South Prospect Street
Colorado Springs, CO 80903

Managing Editor: Lisa Carpenter

Description and Readership

This free publication for families in the Colorado Springs, Colorado area offers articles on parenting, family issues, and child development. It also provides timely information on local events and resources that are available in the region.
- **Audience:** Parents
- **Frequency:** Monthly
- **Distribution:** Unavailable
- **Circulation:** 35,000
- **Website:** www.pikespeakparent.net

Freelance Potential

23% written by nonstaff writers. Publishes 10 freelance submissions yearly; 5% by authors who are new to the magazine.

Submissions

Query with writing samples. No unsolicited mss. Accepts photocopies, computer printouts, and email queries to parent@gazette.com. SASE. Response time varies.
Articles: 800–1,500 words. Informational and how-to articles. Topics include regional news, local resources, parenting, family life, travel, sports, social issues, and recreation.
Depts/columns: Word length varies. News, health, family issues, and calendar of events.

Sample Issue

30 pages (50% advertising): 4 articles; 8 depts/columns. Sample copy, free with 9x12 SASE.
- "Karate Kids." Article discusses the benefits of children learning karate and explains how it teaches them discipline, control, and self-defense while they are having fun.
- "Keeping Your Child Safe This Winter." Article reports on precautions parents can take to battle respiratory viruses during the winter season.
- "Where to Sled and Ski on a Whim." Article reports on local venues that are available for outdoor wintertime fun.
- Sample dept/column: "Family Daze" offers humorous insight into what to do with leftover holiday decorations.

Rights and Payment

Reprint rights. Written material, payment rate varies. Pays on publication. Provides 1 contributor's copy.

Editor's Comments

We would like to see more material written from a father's perspective. All material must have a strong local slant. We are always on the lookout for creative outdoor activities for children and families, as well as parenting tips. We suggest that all subject matters are well-researched prior to submitting your query.

Pittsburgh Parent

P.O. Box 374
Bakerstown, PA 15007

Editor: Patricia Poshard

Description and Readership
The general parenting tips in this regional publication cover topics pertinent to a range of family members: from education, and organizational skills, to health. Each issue also includes special events and a calendar of activities in and around the Pittsburgh, Pennsylvania area.
• **Audience:** Parents
• **Frequency:** Monthly
• **Distribution:** Subscription; newsstand; schools
• **Circulation:** 65,000

Freelance Potential
85% written by nonstaff writers. Publishes 50 freelance submissions yearly; 5% by authors who are new to the magazine. Receives 125 queries and unsolicited mss monthly.

Submissions
Query or send complete ms. Accepts photocopies and simultaneous submissions. SASE. Response time varies.
Articles: Cover story, 2,500–2,750 words. Other material, 400–900 words. Informational articles; profiles; and interviews. Topics include family issues, parenting, education, science, fitness, health, nature, the environment, college, computers, and multicultural subjects.
Depts/columns: Word length varies. Book reviews, teen topics, and news for families.
Other: Submit seasonal material 3 months in advance.

Sample Issue
38 pages (65% advertising): 6 articles; 7 depts/columns; 1 special section. Sample copy, free. Guidelines available.
• "The Do's & Don'ts of Divorce." Article presents the realities and pitfalls of divorce with the reminder that parents need to love their children more than they want to separate.
• "Underage Drinking." Article presents new research on the effects of drinking on a growing brain and provides resources for parents encountering this problem.
• Sample dept/column: "Teen Talk" explores ways to say "I love you" without embarrassing the teen.

Rights and Payment
First rights. All material, payment rate varies. Pays 30 days after publication. Provides 1 contributor's copy.

Editor's Comments
Any article submitted to *Pittsburgh Parent* should be related to the locale, either with information on the region or highlighting experts and resources from the area. Information on camp programs, physical fitness, and fresh perspectives on parenting are welcome. Please do not send personal experience pieces.

Plays
The Drama Magazine for Young People

P.O. Box 600160
Newton, MA 02460

Editor: Elizabeth Preston

Description and Readership
This digest-sized publication specializes in one-act dramas, with minimal scenery, appropriate for schoolchildren to perform. Content is wholesome and can be thoughtful or fun.
• **Audience:** 6–17 years
• **Frequency:** 7 times each school year
• **Distribution:** 100% subscription
• **Circulation:** 5,300
• **Website:** www.playsmag.com

Freelance Potential
100% written by nonstaff writers. Publishes 40–45 freelance submissions yearly; 25% by unpublished writers, 50% by authors who are new to the magazine. Receives 20–22 queries and unsolicited mss monthly.

Submissions
Query for adaptations of classics and folktales. Send complete ms for other material. Accepts photocopies and computer printouts. SASE. Responds to queries in 1 week, to mss in 2 weeks.
Fiction: One-act plays for high school, to 5,000 words; for middle school, to 3,750 words; for elementary school, to 2,500 words. Also publishes skits, monologues, and dramatized classics. Genres include historical and biographical drama, mystery, holiday plays, melodrama, comedy, and farce.
Depts/columns: Staff written.
Other: Submit material on secular holidays celebrated in school 4 months in advance.

Sample Issue
64 pages (5% advertising): 7 plays; 1 skit; 1 dramatized classic. Sample copy, free. Guidelines available.
• "A Little Bit O' Heaven." Play for upper grades centers around a mischievous leprechaun who drops in on a Manhattan party and creates some lively confusion.
• "The Monsters on Sycamore Street." Play for middle grades explores the strange habits of new neighbors that set rumors flying about the possibility of resident aliens.
• "War." Skit for upper grades questions the actors' different feelings about military service to generate a classroom discussion on the topic of war.

Rights and Payment
All rights. All material, payment rate varies. Pays on acceptance. Provides 1 contributor's copy.

Editor's Comments
We would like to see more plays written about friendship, dating, school, sports, and other topics relevant to today's students. Animal themes have become too prevalent.

Pockets

The Upper Room
1908 Grand Avenue
P.O. Box 340004
Nashville, TN 37203-0004

Editor: Lynn W. Gilliam

Description and Readership
Positive themes about relationships with God and how they weave through everyday situations permeate the messages in this non-denominational, children's magazine.
• **Audience:** 6–11 years
• **Frequency:** 11 times each year
• **Distribution:** 100% subscription
• **Circulation:** 98,000
• **Website:** www.pockets.org

Freelance Potential
80% written by nonstaff writers. Publishes 175–185 freelance submissions yearly; 40% by unpublished writers, 20% by authors who are new to the magazine. Receives 200 unsolicited mss monthly.

Submissions
Send complete ms. Accepts photocopies and computer printouts. SASE. Responds in 6 weeks.
Articles: 400–1,000 words. Informational articles; profiles; and personal experience pieces. Topics include holidays and multicultural subjects.
Fiction: 600–1,400 words. Stories that demonstrate Christian values that children can incorporate in solving life's everyday problems.
Depts/columns: Word length varies. Recipes and Scripture readings.
Other: Puzzles, activities, and games. Poetry.

Sample Issue
49 pages (no advertising): 2 articles; 6 stories; 7 depts/columns; 9 activities; 2 poems; 1 recipe. Sample copy, free with 9x12 SASE (4 first-class stamps). Writers' guidelines and theme list available at website.
• "Peacemakers at Work." Article praises a young girl's efforts to befriend a new student who is physically handicapped and from a different country.
• "Next of Kin." Story explores the excitement and enjoyment of finding "lost" members of a family tree.

Rights and Payment
First and second rights. Written material, $.14 per word. Poetry, $2 per line. Games, $25–$50. Pays on acceptance. Provides up to 5 contributor's copies.

Editor's Comments
We need more profiles of children involved in environmental, community, and peace and justice issues. We are also looking for more biographical sketches of persons whose lives reflect Christian commitment and values.

Pointe

23rd Floor
110 William Street
New York, NY 10038

Editor: Virginia Johnson

Description and Readership
Professional ballet dancers and serious ballet students turn to this magazine for in-depth stories of ballet companies around the world, news of summer tours and ballet festivals, and profiles of dancers and choreographers. Nutritional information for dancers and physical conditioning guidelines are other facets of its editorial content.
• **Audience:** YA–Adult
• **Frequency:** 6 times each year
• **Distribution:** 100% subscription
• **Circulation:** Unavailable
• **Website:** www.pointemagazine.com

Freelance Potential
50% written by nonstaff writers. Publishes 25 freelance submissions yearly; 15% by authors who are new to the magazine. Receives 10 queries monthly.

Submissions
Query. Accepts photocopies and computer printouts. Availability of artwork improves chance of acceptance. SASE. Responds in 2 months.
Articles: 1,000–2,000 words. Informational articles; profiles; interviews; personal experience pieces; and photo essays. Topics include health, nutrition, fitness, youth ballet, and international ballet companies.
Depts/columns: 700–1,200 words. Q&As, ballet-related news items, new product information, and ballet and music reviews.
Artwork: Accepts B/W prints or transparencies; prefers color.

Sample Issue
80 pages: 5 articles; 14 depts/columns; 1 festival guide. Sample copy, $4.99. Guidelines and editorial calendar available.
• "London's Other Ballet." Article profiles the English National Ballet, a company that is earning acclaim for its wide-ranging repertoire.
• "Real Life Dance: Work It Out." Article describes the workout routines that two dancers from San Francisco Ballet use to supplement their daily ballet regimen.

Rights and Payment
All rights. Articles, $200–$300. Depts/columns, $100–$150. Pays on acceptance. Provides 2 contributor's copies.

Editor's Comments
Topics related to the world of ballet, especially those that are international in scope, are what we seek. Recent issues have included articles on the future of ballet, making the most of ballet music, and dual careers of dancers/choreographers.

Positive Teens

SATCH Publishing
P.O. Box 1136
Boston, MA 02130-0010

Publisher/Editor-in-Chief: Susan Manning

Description and Readership
This magazine accentuates the positive aspects of today's youth. Many of the articles show how a young person met a challenge and used it to become a better person.
• **Audience:** 12–21 years
• **Frequency:** 6 times each year
• **Distribution:** Subscription; newsstand; other
• **Circulation:** 93,000
• **Website:** www.positiveteensmag.com

Freelance Potential
85% written by nonstaff writers. Publishes 150–200 freelance submissions yearly; 70% by unpublished writers, 80% by authors who are new to the magazine. Receives 50–60 unsolicited mss monthly.

Submissions
Query or send complete ms. Submissions published by teens under 18 must include parental consent. Accepts photocopies, computer printouts, disk submissions, email to info@positiveteensmag.com, and fax submissions to 617-522-2961. SASE. Responds in 2–3 months.
Articles: To 1,000 words. Informational articles; personal experience pieces; and opinion. Topics include education, friendship, social issues, health, spirituality, and relationships.
Fiction: 800–1,000 words.
Depts/columns: Word length varies. Sports, commentary, arts and entertainment, and book reviews.
Artwork: 8½ x11 B/W or color prints. Line art.
Other: Poetry.

Sample Issue
30 pages (no advertising): 4 articles; 8 depts/columns; 4 poems; 1 puzzle. Sample copy, $3.95 with 9x12 SASE. Writers' guidelines available.
• "Third Culture Kid." Article illustrates what it is like to spend several years in a different country.
• "Mind Over Matter." Article details the rigors of attending the Navy Seal Cadet Corps.
• Sample dept/column: "Having Our Say" looks at the importance of having love in a teen's life.

Rights and Payment
Permission for exclusive use for 18 months only. Written material, $5–$30. Artwork, payment rate varies (pays for work by teens and adults). Payment policy varies.

Editor's Comments
We would like to see more articles on sports, diversity, and global-related issues.

Potluck Children's Literary Magazine

P.O. Box 546
Deerfield, IL 60015-0546

Editor-in-Chief: Susan Napoli Picchietti

Description and Readership
Showcasing the works of young writers and artists from around the world, this journal features articles, short stories, poetry, book reviews, and artwork. It also includes information on writing skills, and the business of writing.
• **Audience:** 8–16 years
• **Frequency:** Quarterly
• **Distribution:** Unavailable
• **Circulation:** Unavailable
• **Website:** www.potluckmagazine.org

Freelance Potential
99% written by nonstaff writers. Publishes 130–133 freelance submissions yearly; 1% by unpublished writers, 99% by authors who are new to the magazine. Receives 200 unsolicited mss monthly.

Submissions
Send complete ms. Accepts photocopies, computer printouts, and email submissions to submissions@potluckmagazine.org. No simultaneous submissions. SASE. Response time varies.
Articles: Word length varies. Topics include writing, grammar, and character and story development.
Fiction: To 1,500 words. Genres include contemporary fiction, mystery, folktales, fantasy, and science fiction.
Artwork: 8½x11 color photocopies.
Other: Book reviews, to 250 words. Poetry, to 30 lines.

Sample Issue
48 pages (no advertising): 8 stories; 20 poems. Sample copy, $5.80. Writers' guidelines available with SASE, at website, and in each issue.
• "Shark Bait." Story tells how a new surfer overcomes his fear of riding a big wave after a friend tricks him into thinking there is a shark in the water.
• "Snowmen." Story features a mother telling her son about the kindness of strangers during a snowstorm, and how important it is to help others.
• "Winter Blues." Story describes a girl's gloomy feelings during the winter, and her longing for spring.

Rights and Payment
First rights. Provides 1 contributor's copy in lieu of payment.

Editor's Comments
We offer young voices a way to express their creativity, and, in addition, we provide educational and informational articles to help writing flourish. We do not encourage "I Am," "Color," or "Name" poems. Remember, all work must be original, unpublished, and not submitted elsewhere.

PrayKids!

P.O. Box 35004
Colorado Springs, CO 80935

Editorial Advisor: Sandie Higley

Description and Readership
Inspirational articles, Bible stories, and hands-on activities fill the pages of this middle-grade religious magazine. Its mission is to help children develop a life-long relationship with Jesus as they learn about prayer.
- **Audience:** 8–12 years
- **Frequency:** 6 times each year
- **Distribution:** Subscription; newsstand; schools
- **Circulation:** 40,000
- **Website:** www.praykids.com

Freelance Potential
50% written by nonstaff writers. Publishes 8–10 freelance submissions yearly; 5% by unpublished writers, 5% by authors who are new to the magazine. Receives 2–3 mss monthly.

Submissions
Send complete ms. Accepts computer printouts and email submissions to sandie.higley@navpress.com. SASE. Responds to queries in 6–8 weeks.
Articles: Bible stories on prayer, 500 words. Prayers to 100 words; articles by children whose experience in prayer had a far-reaching impact, 125–300 words.
Depts/columns: Word length varies. Information for parents and prayers.
Other: Puzzles, activities, and games on prayer.

Sample Issue
8 pages (no advertising): 1 article; 1 Bible story; 2 depts/columns. Sample copy, guidelines, and theme list available.
- "Praying in Style." Article discusses the many ways people have of praying and how they are all valid ways of reaching out to Jesus.
- "Scary Story Stopper." Personal essay by a young reader about how she overcame her fear of scary stories.
- Sample dept/column: "Walk the Talk" features an activity that teaches children about different styles of prayer.

Rights and Payment
First or reprint rights. Pays on acceptance. Written material, $.10 per word. Provides 2 contributor's copies.

Editor's Comments
We are interested in hearing about children's experiences where prayer has made a difference in their lives—particularly how it has helped them reach beyond their own world and needs. Stories from countries around the world are welcome. We invite prospective contributors to review back issues of our publication, as our focus is very specific. We see far too many submissions of Bible stories that do not relate to prayer.

Prehistoric Times

145 Bayline Circle
Folson, CA 95630-8077

Editor: Mike Fredericks

Description and Readership
Just about everything anyone wants to know about dinosaurs and other prehistoric mammals can be found in *Prehistoric Times*. Paleontological discoveries, collectible news, models of prehistoric animals, and reviews of children's and adult books are all found within its covers.
- **Audience:** YA–Adult
- **Frequency:** 6 times each year
- **Distribution:** Subscription; other
- **Circulation:** Unavailable
- **Website:** www.prehistorictimes.com

Freelance Potential
40% written by nonstaff writers. Publishes 25 freelance submissions yearly; 60% by unpublished writers, 40% by authors who are new to the magazine. Receives 4 unsolicited mss monthly.

Submissions
Send complete ms. Accepts email submissions to pretimes@aol.com (attach file). Response time varies.
Articles: 1,500–2,000 words. Informational articles. Topics include dinosaurs, paleontology, prehistoric life, drawing dinosaurs, and dinosaur-related collectibles.
Depts/columns: Word length varies. Interviews, field news, dinosaur models, media reviews, and in-depth descriptions of dinosaurs and other prehistoric species.

Sample Issue
56 pages (30% advertising): 9 articles; 1 story; 2 depts/columns; 1 interview; 2 book reviews. Guidelines available via email to pretimes@aol.com.
- "La Brea Tar Pits." Article highlights the Ranch La Brea Tar Pits in Los Angeles, California, where fossils of approximately 60 species have been found.
- "Revenge of the Movie Mammoths!" Article reports on all the different types of prehistoric mammals that have been featured on the big screen.
- Sample dept/column: "What's New in Review" details the newest dinosaur models.

Rights and Payment
All rights. All material, payment rate varies. Payment policy varies. Provides contributor's copies.

Editor's Comments
Our material is written for an adult audience with serious scientific interest in dinosaurs, other prehistoric animals such as sabertoothed cats and mammoths, and prehistoric life. We accept interviews with scientists and artists and information on collectibles and merchandise related to prehistoric times.

Primary Street

Urban Ministries
1551 Regency Court
Calumet City, IL 60409

Senior Editor: Judith Hull

Description and Readership

Primary Street targets African American children who receive religious education in urban areas. Each quarterly issue contains 13 four-page folders, with each folder stressing a specific Christian theme or value. The Bible stories are written to accommodate all levels of readers, beginning to advanced, and help the readers find solutions for everyday problems. The two activities in each issue reinforce its theme.

- **Audience:** 6–8 years
- **Frequency:** Quarterly
- **Distribution:** Unavailable
- **Circulation:** Unavailable
- **Website:** www.urbanministries.com

Freelance Potential

10% written by nonstaff writers. Publishes 48 freelance submissions yearly; 5% by unpublished writers, 4% by authors who are new to the magazine.

Submissions

All material is written by assignment. Query with résumé or writing samples. SASE. Response time varies.

Articles: Word length varies. How-to articles; photo essays; and personal experience pieces. Topics include nature, environment, animals, pets, crafts, hobbies, African history, multicultural, ethnic subjects, regional news, and social issues.

Depts/columns: Word length varies.

Artwork: B/W and color prints or transparencies.

Other: Puzzles, activities, fillers, games, and jokes.

Sample Issue

4 pages (no advertising): 1 story; 1 Bible story; 2 activities. Sample copy, $2.99 ordered from website. Writers' guidelines available.

- "David." Story revolves around an individual and demonstrates an everyday event that ties into the lesson featured in that issue.
- "Jesus Began His Work." Bible story states the central idea up front and follows up with a short story about Jesus illustrating the value being stressed.

Rights and Payment

All rights. Written material, payment rate varies. Pays on publication. Provides 1 contributor's copy.

Editor's Comments

Please obtain our guidelines and become familiar with our format before sending in a query. The lessons are based on International Sunday school lessons and all of our material is written on assignment.

Primary Treasure

Pacific Press Publishing
P.O. Box 5353
Nampa, ID 83653-5353

Editor: Aileen Andres Sox

Description and Readership

Published continuously since 1957, *Primary Treasure* features true stories that teach children Christian beliefs, values, and practices. It is a take-home paper for elementary school students who attend Sabbath School at Seventh-day Adventist Churches.

- **Audience:** 6–9 years
- **Frequency:** Weekly
- **Distribution:** 100% religious instruction
- **Circulation:** 30,000
- **Website:** www.pacificpress.com

Freelance Potential

85% written by nonstaff writers. Publishes 40–50 freelance submissions yearly; 10% by unpublished writers, 30% by authors who are new to the magazine. Receives 60 unsolicited mss monthly.

Submissions

Query for serials. Send complete ms for other submissions. Accepts photocopies, computer printouts, email submissions to ailsox@pacificpress.com, and simultaneous submissions if identified. SASE. Responds in 4 months.

Articles: 600–1,000 words. Features true stories about children in Christian settings and true, problem-solving pieces that help children learn about themselves in relation to God and others. All material must be consistent with Seventh-day Adventist beliefs and practices.

Other: Submit seasonal material 7 months in advance.

Sample Issue

16 pages (no advertising): 3 stories; 1 rebus story; 1 Bible lesson; 1 page of daily prayers; 2 activities. Sample copy, free with 9x12 SASE (2 first-class stamps). Guidelines available.

- "No Comprendo." Story features a bilingual boy who helps his hospital roommate by translating the doctor's questions into Spanish.
- "Light in the Darkness." Story about an elderly man who teaches a blind friend to carve animals out of wood.
- "Now I See!" Rebus retells the Bible story of how Ananias cured a blind man.

Rights and Payment

One-time rights. Written material, $25–$50. Pays on acceptance. Provides 3 contributor's copies.

Editor's Comments

We're interested in stories that speak to the experience, lifestyle, needs, and vocabulary of today's Christian child. Avoid stories that depict men and women in stereotypical roles. We are currently seeking more stories that feature dads.

Principal

1615 Duke Street
Alexandria, VA 22314

Associate Editor: Candice Johnson

Description and Readership

Established in 1921, this magazine for elementary and middle-level principals offers articles relating to school administration. Topics include meeting the needs of students, successful teaching and strategies, and other issues relating to effective leadership, education policy, and legislation.
• **Audience:** K–8 school administrators
• **Frequency:** 5 times each year
• **Distribution:** 100% controlled
• **Circulation:** 36,000
• **Website:** www.naesp.org

Freelance Potential

90% written by nonstaff writers. Publishes 20 freelance submissions yearly; 80% by authors who are new to the magazine. Receives 7 queries and unsolicited mss monthly.

Submissions

Query or send complete ms. Accepts computer printouts and email submissions to comdiv@naesp.org. SASE. Responds in 1 month.
Articles: 1,000–1,800 words. Informational and instructional articles; profiles; and opinion and personal experience pieces. Topics include elementary education, gifted and special education, parenting, mentoring, science, and computers.
Depts/columns: 750–1,500 words. Classroom management issues, legal issues, and technology.

Sample Issue

72 pages (30% advertising): 9 articles; 13 depts/columns. Sample copy, $8. Writers' guidelines and theme list available.
• "Living Well Is the Best Revenge." Article offers strategies that principals can use to help reduce stress and promote good physical and mental health.
• "Effective Teaching." Article reports on three major projects that analyze research-based knowledge about effective teaching and also describes other techniques and characteristics of good teaching.
• Sample dept/column: "The Reflective Principal" takes a look at the challenges a principal of a K-2 school overcomes during her first year in the position.

Rights and Payment

All rights. No payment. Provides 3 contributor's copies.

Editor's Comments

We are interested in seeing more articles on fundraising, technology applications, and the arts. Remember to avoid excessive documentation. Instead, provide a brief listing of your major references and or resources, including any useful websites.

Puget Sound Parent

Suite 215
123 NW 36th Street
Seattle, WA 98119

Editor: Wenda Reed

Description and Readership

This award-winning publication offers timely information on matters that concern parents of children and teens. Reports on developments in education, health issues, and child care that have national significance are typically presented with a local slant and include opinions of local experts. Announcements of Puget Sound-area events and attractions for parents or children are featured in each issue.
• **Audience:** Parents
• **Frequency:** Monthly
• **Distribution:** 100% newsstand
• **Circulation:** Unavailable
• **Website:** www.parenthood.com

Freelance Potential

80% written by nonstaff writers. Publishes 50+ freelance submissions yearly; 5% by unpublished writers, 10% by authors who are new to the magazine. Receives 20 queries monthly.

Submissions

Query with outline. Send queries for local stories to address above. Send queries on national interest stories to Editor, United Parenting Publications, 15400 Knoll Trail, Suite 400, Dallas, TX 75248. Accepts photocopies, computer printouts, and simultaneous submissions if identified. SASE. Responds in 2 weeks.
Articles: Word length varies. Informational, how-to, and personal experience articles. Topics include family and parenting issues, health, fitness, gifted and special education, regional news, travel, and social issues.
Depts/columns: Word length varies. Profiles, essays, and media reviews.

Sample Issue

34 pages: 2 articles; 5 depts/columns; 1 calendar of events. Sample copy, $3. Guidelines and theme list available.
• "'Good Divorce' Brings Hope, Protects Children." Article discusses how local couples and attorneys are finding ways to make divorce less traumatic for everyone involved.
• "Entertaining Solutions to Children's Birthday Parties." Article lists party places and entertainers in the Puget Sound area.
• Sample dept/column: "Education" reports on an outreach program for needy students in Tacoma.

Rights and Payment

Rights vary. Written material, payment rate varies. Pays on publication. Provides 2 contributor's copies.

Editor's Comments

One way of breaking in might be to publicize a local event of interest to our readers. Query us with your idea.

Queens Parent

256-33 Union Turnpike
Glen Oaks, NY 11004

Editor: Helen Freedman

Description and Readership

Queens Parent is published by the same company that produces *Big Apple Parent* and it often features the same articles that appear in *Big Apple Parent*. Each edition reports on local services, events in the metropolitan area, and issues relating to raising children.
- **Audience:** Parents
- **Frequency:** Monthly
- **Distribution:** 100% controlled
- **Circulation:** 68,000
- **Website:** www.parentsknow.com

Freelance Potential

95% written by nonstaff writers. Publishes 450 freelance submissions yearly; 25% by authors who are new to the magazine. Receives 75 queries, 75 unsolicited mss monthly.

Submissions

Query or send complete ms. Accepts photocopies, computer printouts, and email to hellonwheels@parentsknow.com. SASE. Responds to queries in 1 week.
Articles: 800–1,000 words. Informational and how-to articles; profiles; interviews; humor; and personal experience pieces. Topics include family issues, health, fitness, humor, nature, current events, gifted and special education, nutrition, crafts, and regional news.
Depts/columns: 750 words. News and reviews.
Other: Submit seasonal material 4 months in advance.

Sample Issue

80 pages: 5 articles; 4 depts/columns. Sample copy, free with 10x13 SASE. Guidelines available.
- "Oral Health Hygiene: A Priority During Pregnancy." Article addresses the oral health issues often faced by mothers-to-be, such as gum disease.
- Sample dept/column: "NewKidontheBlock" profiles a new yoga spa in Queens.

Rights and Payment

First New York Area rights. Articles, $50. Pays 2 months after publication. Provides 1 contributor's copy.

Editor's Comments

We continue to look for submissions that address controversial issues related to raising children. Investigative stories that include quotes from area experts are also a top priority. If you are interested in covering a standard parenting topic that is fine if you can offer a new twist or a different point of view. Regional coverage of new businesses that cater to parents are also welcome. We see too many personal experience essays.

Ranger Rick

National Wildlife Federation
11100 Wildlife Center Drive
Reston, VA 20190-5362

Editor: Gerald Bishop

Description and Readership

This award-winning magazine offers children a fun way to explore nature. Published by the National Wildlife Federation, it includes a mix of photo essays, articles, stories, puzzles, games, and activities.
- **Audience:** 7–12 years
- **Frequency:** Monthly
- **Distribution:** 100% subscription
- **Circulation:** 560,000
- **Website:** www.nwf.org/gowild

Freelance Potential

10% written by nonstaff writers. Publishes 1–2 freelance submissions yearly; 1% by authors who are new to the magazine. Receives 100 queries each month.

Submissions

Query with outline and sample paragraph. Response time varies.
Articles: To 900 words. Informational articles. Topics include nature, animals, the environment, outdoor adventure, dinosaurs, oceanography, and insects.
Fiction: To 900 words. Genres include mystery, adventure, fantasy, fables, and stories about nature.
Depts/columns: Staff written.
Artwork: 35mm color prints and illustrations.
Other: Puzzles on topics related to nature. Submit seasonal material 1 year in advance.

Sample Issue

40 pages (no advertising): 4 articles; 4 depts/columns; 1 cartoon. Writers' guidelines available.
- "Catch a Ride." Article explains how and why some animals carry their young and other animals around.
- "Cockroaches." Article offers facts about cockroaches and the different types of cockroach species in the world.
- "Reptile Safari." Essay describes a father/son adventure in central Oregon hunting for reptiles, then releasing what they catch.

Rights and Payment

Rights policy varies. All material, payment rate varies. Pays on acceptance. Provides 2 contributor's copies.

Editor's Comments

Send us a query for fresh ideas for unusual wildlife pieces and stories about unique animal behaviors. If you have a special qualification to write on a specific subject, make sure you let us know. Do not send us anything on wildlife rehabilitation, unless it's about threatened or endangered species. Also, we do not accept articles that focus on keeping wildlife as pets.

Read

Weekly Reader
200 First Stamford Place
Stamford, CT 06912

Managing Editor: Debra Dolan Nevins

Description and Readership

Read is distributed to middle-grade and high school students throughout the U.S. Each issue includes a play, a short story or narrative, and other material that provides a basis for classroom reading and discussion.

- **Audience:** 11–15 years
- **Frequency:** 18 times each year
- **Distribution:** 100% schools
- **Circulation:** 250,000
- **Website:** www.weeklyreader.com

Freelance Potential

60% written by nonstaff writers. Publishes 8–10 freelance submissions yearly; 10% by authors who are new to the magazine. Receives 75 unsolicited mss monthly.

Submissions

Send complete ms with résumé. Accepts photocopies, email submissions to sbarchers@weeklyreader.com, and simultaneous submissions if identified. SASE. Responds in 1–2 months.

Articles: 1,000–2,000 words. Informational and factual articles. Topics include popular culture, history, nature, the environment, science, and social issues. Also features biographies and humor.

Fiction: Word length varies. Genres include science fiction, historical and contemporary fiction, adventure, fantasy, folklore, mystery, romance, and animal stories.

Other: Language games. Submit seasonal material 9 months in advance.

Sample Issue

32 pages (no advertising): 1 article; 2 stories; 1 puzzle; 1 play. Sample copy, free with 5x7 SASE (3 first-class stamps). Guidelines available.

- "The Most Important Night of Melanie's Life." Story about a young girl who meets a boy and learns he may not be all that he seems to be.
- "The House That Ghosts Built." Article looks at the Winchester Mystery House, a home in California with stairs and doors that lead nowhere.

Rights and Payment

First North American and electronic one-time user rights. Written material, payment rate varies. Pays on acceptance. Provides 5 contributor's copies.

Editor's Comments

We want high-interest, thought-provoking, curriculum-relevant plays and fiction suitable for students age twelve to fourteen, as well as stories that portray current teen problems and world issues.

The Reading Teacher

International Reading Association
800 Barksdale Road
P.O. Box 8139
Newark, DE 19714-8139

Senior Editorial Assistant: Christina Lambert

Description and Readership

This peer-reviewed, professional journal features articles that discuss current practices, research, and trends in literacy education and related fields.

- **Audience:** Educators
- **Frequency:** 8 times each year
- **Distribution:** 100% subscription
- **Circulation:** 61,000
- **Website:** www.reading.org

Freelance Potential

99% written by nonstaff writers. Publishes 50 freelance submissions yearly; 20% by unpublished writers, 30% by authors who are new to the magazine. Receives 29 unsolicited mss monthly.

Submissions

Send 2 copies of complete ms in email attachment to rt@reading.org or on disk, and 2 hard copies; 1 copy of each must have author information removed. SASE. Responds in 2–3 months.

Articles: 1,000–1,500 words. Informational and how-to articles; and personal experience pieces. Topics include literacy, reading education, instruction techniques, classroom strategies, and educational technology.

Depts/columns: Word length varies. Teaching tips, book reviews, and short pieces on cultural diversity.

Sample Issue

73 pages (17% advertising): 4 articles; 5 depts/columns. Sample copy, $10. Guidelines available.

- "Teacher Rating of Oral Language and Literacy (TROLL)." Article examines the rating system that measures standards of speaking and listening skills.
- "Becoming Literary in the Technological Age." Article identifies the new literacies of the technological age, and explores a variety of tools available to teachers.
- Sample dept/column: "Instructional Materials" looks at a variety of reading materials available to help students with different levels of ability.

Rights and Payment

All rights. No payment. Provides 5 contributor's copies for articles, 2 for depts/columns.

Editor's Comments

We welcome submissions of articles, teaching tips, and filler. We are looking for material that helps educators gain insights and understanding about reading research and its application to classroom reading instruction. Send us your experiences in teaching reading and literacy.

Reading Today

International Reading Association
800 Barksdale Road
P.O. Box 8139
Newark, DE 19714-8139

Editor-in-Chief: John Mickles, Jr.

Description and Readership
Reading Today is mailed to members of the International Reading Association and strives to address the needs and interests of an audience involved in education at all levels. From pre-K through adult education, it is read by an international audience.
- **Audience:** IRA members
- **Frequency:** 6 times each year
- **Distribution:** 100% subscription
- **Circulation:** 80,000
- **Website:** www.reading.org

Freelance Potential
30% written by nonstaff writers. Publishes 25 freelance submissions yearly; 10% by unpublished writers, 25% by authors who are new to the magazine. Receives 15 mss monthly.

Submissions
Prefers query. Accepts complete ms. Accepts photocopies, computer printouts, and simultaneous submissions if identified. SASE. Responds in 1 month.
Articles: 500–1,000 words. Informational and factual articles and interviews. Topics include reading and education, grades K–12 and up.
Depts/columns: To 750 words. Classroom ideas, ideas for administrators and parents, and opinion pieces.
Artwork: B/W and color prints. Line art and cartoons.
Other: Puzzles, activities, and poetry.

Sample Issue
40 pages (30% advertising): 4 articles; 9 depts/columns. Sample copy, $6. Guidelines available.
- "Report Focuses on Girls' Education." A recent report from UNICEF stresses the need on an international level to improve the education of women and girls.
- "Called to Teaching." Article profiles an IRA member who was named the U.S. Teacher of the Year.
- Sample dept/column: "Parents & Reading" suggest ways parents can join in the promotion of reading during the Read Across America celebration.

Rights and Payment
One-time rights. Written material, $.20–$.30 per word. Pays on publication. Provides 3 contributor's copies.

Editor's Comments
Articles relating to use of children's literature in the classroom, exemplary or unusual school-wide reading programs, and school library programs top our current wish list. We see too many submissions that do not relate to our unique audience.

Real Sports

P.O. Box 8204
San Jose, CA 95155

Submissions Editor: Brian Styers

Description and Readership
All aspects of women's sports are covered by this online site with a particular focus on team sports at the professional, collegiate, and national levels. Its purpose is to raise the public awareness of women's athletics, the players, and the quality of the play, and to increase media coverage of games.
- **Audience:** 9–18 years
- **Frequency:** 6 times each year
- **Distribution:** 100% Internet
- **Hits per month:** Unavailable
- **Website:** www.real-sports.com

Freelance Potential
75% written by nonstaff writers. Publishes 40 freelance submissions yearly; 5% by unpublished writers, 50% by authors who are new to the magazine. Receives 2 queries monthly.

Submissions
Query with brief summary. No unsolicited mss. Accepts email queries to content@real-sports.com. SASE. Responds in 2–3 weeks.
Articles: 1,500–2,000 words. Informational and how-to articles; profiles; and interviews. Topics include training, tennis, track and field, basketball, baseball, skating, golf, skiing, soccer, and sports personalities.
Depts/columns: 750–1,000 words. Opinion pieces, book reviews, news, and profiles.

Sample Issue
Guidelines and theme list available online.
- "Faster, Higher, Stronger." Article updates the events, goals, and happenings in the second season of the United States Women's Soccer League.
- "Soccer 101." Article gives a prime time lesson on the basics of soccer—the field, the rules, the positions, and the ball play.
- "Opportunity Knocks." Article urges high school women to consider all the angles for playing sports in college, and gives suggestions for different levels of participation.

Rights and Payment
First rights. Written material, payment rate varies. Pays on publication. Provides 2–5 contributor's copies.

Editor's Comments
Sports activities involve a lot of passion, excitement, and personality, and we look for submissions that convey those same qualities to the reader. If you are interested in writing for our publication, a good place to start is to submit either a profile or interview featuring a woman in sports.

Recreational Ice Skating

Ice Skating Institute
Suite 140, 17120 North Dallas Parkway
Dallas, TX 75248-1187

Editor: Lori Fairchild

Description and Readership

Skaters of all ages and skill levels, as well as their parents and coaches, read this magazine for information on the various aspects of ice skating, including related health and fitness topics. It is published for members of the Ice Skating Institute, a non-profit organization that provides leadership, education, and services to the ice skating industry.
- **Audience:** 6 years–Adult
- **Frequency:** Quarterly
- **Distribution:** 99% membership; 1% schools
- **Circulation:** 50,000
- **Website:** www.skateisi.org

Freelance Potential

20% written by nonstaff writers. Publishes 10 freelance submissions yearly; 80% by unpublished writers, 90% by authors who are new to the magazine. Receives 1 query and unsolicited ms monthly.

Submissions

Query or send complete ms. Accepts photocopies, computer printouts, simultaneous submissions, and email submissions to dpowell@skateisi.org. SASE. Responds in 2–4 weeks.
Articles: 500–1,000 words. Informational and how-to articles; profiles; interviews; and personal experience pieces. Topics include ice skating techniques, team reviews, equipment, apparel, international skaters, and skating personalities.
Depts/columns: To 400 words. Health, fitness, skating news, and notes.
Other: Puzzles, games, cartoons. Poetry.

Sample Issue

38 pages (36% advertising): 5 articles; 6 depts/columns; 1 calendar of events. Sample copy, $4. Guidelines available.
- "Skaters Donate to Locks of Love." Article describes how two skaters donated their hair to a non-profit organization that donates hairpieces to children with medical problems.
- Sample dept/column: "Health & Fitness" focuses on the importance of preparation routines for both practice and competitions.

Rights and Payment

One-time rights. No payment. Provides contributor's copies.

Editor's Comments

Profiles of skaters and interviews with professional or competitive skaters are needed. We also like to see stories about unusual aspects of skating and unique skating programs. Material should appeal to skaters between the ages of six and fifteen, since they make up the majority of our audience.

Religion Teacher's Journal

P.O. Box 180
185 Willow Street
Mystic, CT 06355

Editor: Alison Berger

Description and Readership

This magazine enriches and empowers catechists and religion teachers in their important ministry of faith formation by providing practical up-to-date religious information, practice, and hands-on methods in catechism.
- **Audience:** Religion teachers
- **Frequency:** Monthly
- **Distribution:** 100% subscription
- **Circulation:** 32,000
- **Website:** www.religionteachersjournal.com

Freelance Potential

70% written by nonstaff writers. Publishes 35 freelance submissions yearly; 20% by unpublished writers, 20% by authors who are new to the magazine. Receives 2 queries, 3 unsolicited mss monthly.

Submissions

Query or send complete ms. Accepts computer printouts, disk submissions, and email submissions to aberger@ twentythirdpublications.com (Microsoft Word for Mac attachment). SASE. Responds to queries in 2–3 weeks, to mss in 3–4 weeks.
Articles: 1,300 words. Informational and how-to articles; personal experience pieces, plays, and theology. Topics include computers, crafts, hobbies, and teaching methods.
Depts/columns: 600 words. Prayers, youth ministry, computers, Scripture, Sunday Gospel, Catholic rites and rituals.
Other: 200–300 words. Activities, fillers, and games.

Sample Issue

38 pages (12% advertising): 7 articles; 13 depts/columns. Sample copy, $3.50 with 9x12 (3 first-class stamps) SASE. Guidelines and theme list available.
- "Twelve Ways to Advance a Child's Spiritual Life." Article offers practical suggestions that provide guidance in assisting children in their spiritual development.
- "The Life of a Leader." Article takes a look at the key moments in the life and papacy of Pope John Paul II.
- Sample dept/column: "Computer Bytes" offers websites for Easter craft ideas and recipes.

Rights and Payment

First North American serial rights. Articles, $50–$125. Depts/columns, $125. Fillers, $20. Pays on acceptance. Provides 3 contributor's copies.

Editor's Comments

We would like to see more concrete lesson ideas for church seasons, and sacrament preparation involving families.

Research in Middle Level Education

College of Education
Southwest Missouri State University
Springfield, MO 65804

Editor: David Hough

Description and Readership

Educators and librarians read this scholarly, peer-reviewed online journal for ideas and information on leadership roles relating to youth librarianship in schools and public libraries. The journal publishes research syntheses, integrative reviews, interpretations of research literature, case studies, and data-based studies.

- **Audience:** Educators
- **Frequency:** 2 times each year
- **Distribution:** 90% membership; 10% subscription
- **Hits per month:** 30,000
- **Website:** www.nmsa.org

Freelance Potential

95% written by nonstaff writers. Publishes 10 freelance submissions yearly; 90% by unpublished writers, 50% by authors who are new to the magazine. Receives 6 unsolicited mss each month.

Submissions

Send 5 full-blinded copies of complete ms including title and 150–200 word abstract. Accepts computer printouts. SASE. Responds in 1 week.
Articles: 1,500–2,500 words. Informational and factual articles; research results; case studies; and qualitative and quantitative studies. Topics include librarianship, education, professional development, and assessment and evaluation.

Sample Issue

Sample copy, $20; also available at website. Writers' guidelines available.

- "Attrition of Beginning Teachers and the Factors of Collaboration and School Setting." Article examines research that indicates beginning teachers leave the profession at a greater rate than veteran teachers, without the support of a collaborative group.
- "Advice and Student Agency in the Transition to Middle School." Study reveals themes of advice from eighth-grade students for students beginning sixth grade.

Rights and Payment

All rights. No payment. Provides 1 contributor's copy.

Editor's Comments

Although most of our readers are educators, submissions should be written as though for a general interest audience, rather than for an academic journal. We are looking for hands-on strategies and solutions for librarians to meet the challenges of education. We encourage writers to include anecdotes and specific examples of their programs, without academic or technical jargon.

Resource

6401 The Paseo
Kansas City, MO 64131

Assistant Editor: Shirley Smith

Description and Readership

Produced by the WordAction Publishing Company, *Resource* is written for Sunday school teachers and others involved in local church ministries. Teaching ideas, lesson plans, and activities appear along with articles written to inspire religious educators. Its editorial content follows the teachings of the Wesleyan-Holiness religious tradition.

- **Audience:** Sunday school teachers
- **Frequency:** Quarterly
- **Distribution:** 100% subscription
- **Circulation:** 30,000
- **Website:** www.nazarene.org

Freelance Potential

90% written by nonstaff writers. Publishes 100 freelance submissions yearly; 25% by authors who are new to the magazine. Receives 17 unsolicited mss monthly.

Submissions

Send complete ms. Accepts computer printouts and email submissions to ssmith@nazarene.org. SASE. Responds in 5 days.
Articles: 800 words. How-to and self-help articles and personal experience pieces. Topics include religion, education, and Sunday school lessons.

Sample Issue

24 pages (no advertising): 19 articles. Sample copy, free with 9x12 SASE. Guidelines available.

- "The Grafting of a Wild Shoot." Personal experience piece relates the story of 10-year-old boy who created trouble at summer camp but was changed by lessons he learned about Jesus and the Bible.
- "The Right Tools for the Job." Article explain how using the appropriate tools with preschool and kindergarten students can pave the way for successful learning experiences.
- "Good Relationships Require Cultivation." Offers ideas for making Sunday school more than just another activity for busy kids.

Rights and Payment

All rights. Written material, $.05 per word. Pays on publication. Provides 1 contributor's copy.

Editor's Comments

Our purpose is to provide information, training, and inspiration to those who are involved with Sunday school ministries. We would like to see ideas for ways to involve the local community in the church and likewise to get the church involved in the community. Articles about innovative, religious education for gifted and special needs children are also welcome.

Reunions Magazine

P.O. Box 11727
Milwaukee, WI 53211-0727

Editor: Edith Wagner

Description and Readership

Everything one needs to know about planning a reunion is offered in this publication. It has ideas for locations, games, entertainment, and planning. In addition, it contains many accounts of reunions submitted by its readers.
- **Audience:** Adults
- **Frequency:** 6 times each year
- **Distribution:** Subscription
- **Circulation:** 12,000
- **Website:** www.reunionsmag.com

Freelance Potential

75% written by nonstaff writers. Publishes 100 freelance submissions yearly; 50% by unpublished writers, 80% by authors who are new to the magazine. Receives 20–30 unsolicited queries and mss monthly.

Submissions

Query with outline; or send complete ms. Accepts photocopies, computer printouts, and email submissions to reunions@execpc.com. SASE. Responds in 12–18 months.
Articles: Word length varies. Factual, how-to, and personal experience articles; and profiles. Topics include organizing reunions, choosing reunion locations, activities, and genealogy.
Depts/columns: 250–1,000 words. Book reviews, resources, and opinions.
Artwork: Color prints, or JPEG or TIF files.
Other: Recipes, cartoons, and filler.

Sample Issue

68 pages (45% advertising): 16 articles; 5 depts/columns; 1 workbook. Sample copy, $2 with 9x12 SASE. Guidelines and editorial calendar available.
- "If You Plan It, Will They Come?" Article looks at different ways to increase the success of a reunion.
- "Merge Amid the Annals of History." Article itemizes the reasons for holding a reunion in the Shenandoah National Park in Virginia's Blue Ridge Mountains.
- Sample dept/column: "Scrapbook" offers ideas for several reunion venues.

Rights and Payment

One-time rights. Payment rate varies. Provides contributor's copies.

Editor's Comments

We are in constant need of descriptions of reunion activities, creative ideas, and the step-by-step process used from planning to event. We also encourage submission of well-focused photos from reunions and locales.

Richmond Parents Magazine

5511 Staples Mill RD #103
Richmond, VA 23228

Editor: Wayne Smith

Description and Readership

Now in print for more than 15 years, this Richmond-area tabloid provides information of interest to parents who are new to the area as well to long time residents. Coverage of local events and family resources is also found in each issue.
- **Audience:** Parents
- **Frequency:** Monthly
- **Distribution:** 100% controlled
- **Circulation:** 30,000
- **Website:** www.richmondparents.com

Freelance Potential

100% written by nonstaff writers. Publishes 8–10 freelance submissions yearly; 5% by authors who are new to the magazine. Receives 50 queries monthly.

Submissions

Query. Accepts disk submissions and email to wsmith@ richmondpublishing.com. Availability of artwork improves chance of acceptance. Responds in 1–3 weeks.
Articles: 600–1,000 words. Informational and self-help articles. Topics include health, recreation, parenting, family issues, and entertainment.
Depts/columns: Word length varies. Restaurant reviews, family-related news items, and media reviews.
Artwork: Color prints and transparencies.

Sample Issue

36 pages (15% advertising): 3 articles; 8 depts/columns. Sample copy, free. Editorial calendar available.
- "Magic in Mentoring." Article describes the benefits that come along with being a big brother or a big sister.
- "Say Spaaaaaa." Kid-friendly spa resorts are reviewed in this article.
- Sample dept/column: "Books to Loan" reviews the latest Newbery winner along with other current titles for children.

Rights and Payment

One-time rights. Written material, $.12 per word. Pays on publication.

Editor's Comments

Education, discipline, health topics, parents' needs, and regional events are all subjects that we cover regularly in our publication. Stories may have a national impact as long as they have some angle or slant that ties them to our region. Our readers want to be better parents and make their children's lives the best they can be. If you try your hand at a well-worn topic, such as potty training, make sure to give it a unique twist.

The Rock

Cook Communications
4050 Lee Vance View
Colorado Springs, CO 80918

Editor: Gail Rohlfing

Description and Readership

An in-class/take-home paper used in Sunday schools, *The Rock* includes daily devotions and Bible-based stories, activities, and features designed to help middle school children develop a relationship with God.
- **Audience:** 10–14 years
- **Frequency:** Weekly during the school year
- **Distribution:** 100% religious instruction
- **Circulation:** 65,000
- **Website:** www.cookministries.org

Freelance Potential

10% written by nonstaff writers. Publishes 2–3 freelance submissions yearly; 20% by unpublished writers, 100% by authors who are new to the magazine.

Submissions

Query with résumé and writing samples. SASE. Response time varies.
Articles: Word length varies. Informational articles; personal experience pieces; profiles; and interviews. Also publishes Bible lessons, allegories, and meditations.
Fiction: Word length varies. Genres include inspirational, contemporary, and historical fiction; adventure; real-life; and problem-solving stories.
Other: Puzzles, quizzes, activities, and poetry.

Sample Issue

8 pages (no advertising): 7 articles; 1 story; 8 depts/columns. Sample copy, $4 with 9x12 SASE ($.77 postage). Writers' guidelines available.
- "When It's Hard to Love My Friends." Article features comments from seven middle school students who discuss how God helps them deal with friendship problems.
- "A Gutsy Bird." Article points out that a South American bird, whose existence baffles scientists, is an example of the wonders of God's handiwork.
- "Job's Story: Suffering, Endurance, Faith in God." Bible study includes activities designed to help kids meditate on the various facets of the story of Job.

Rights and Payment

Rights negotiable. All material, payment rate varies. Pays on acceptance. Provides 1 contributor's copy.

Editor's Comments

The content of our Sunday school paper is based entirely on Scripture, because our goal is to help kids understand the messages of the Bible and to get to know God. If you feel drawn to do this kind of work, send us your query.

Ruminator Review

1648 Grand Avenue
St. Paul, MN 55105

Assistant Editor: Eleise Jones

Description and Readership

This theme-based literary tabloid offers reviews, essays, poems, and occasional fiction, focusing on non-mainstream authors and artists. The in-depth reviews are lengthy and often compare the perspectives found in two or more books.
- **Audience:** 14 years–Adult
- **Frequency:** Quarterly
- **Distribution:** Subscription; newsstands; schools
- **Circulation:** 30,000
- **Website:** www.ruminator.com

Freelance Potential

80% written by nonstaff writers. Of the freelance submissions yearly, 20% are by unpublished writers and 40% by authors who are new to the magazine. Receives 3 queries monthly.

Submissions

Does not accept unsolicited fiction or poetry. Query with writing sample. SASE. Responds in 2 weeks.
Articles: Word length varies. Personal experience pieces, profiles, interviews; and reviews. Topics include pets, the arts, crafts, hobbies, current events, history, multicultural and ethnic subjects, music, nature, the environment, popular culture, religion, science, social issues, sports, and travel.

Sample Issue

52 pages (15% advertising): 37 reviews; 3 essays; 3 interviews; 2 poems. Sample copy, $5. Guidelines available.
- "Religion Meets Ecology." Essay explores the historical relationship between religion and environmental issues, and the changes that are slowly occurring in churches' ecological awareness.
- "A Spell So Exquisite: An Interview with Terry Tempest Williams." Interview concentrates on the author's life influences and how they've shaped her writings.
- "Celestial Rhythms: Site Dance as Ritual." Essay discusses the unique ritualistic qualities of dance that is choreographed for a specific location rather than a traditional stage.

Rights and Payment

Rights vary. Written material, payment rate varies. Pays on publication. Provides 3 contributor's copies.

Editor's Comments

The material in each issue revolves around a central subject. Several aspects of the theme are explored through literary reviews, essays, poems, and interviews. We are interested in increasing our coverage of young adult fiction and educational books. Currently we are not accepting unpublished fiction, short stories, or poetry.

Sacramento/Sierra Parent

Suite 5
457 Grass Valley Highway
Auburn, CA 95603

Editor: Shelly Bokman Elia

Description and Readership

Editorial content encouraging healthy familial relationships is found in this regional publication. Information is geared toward families with children and grandchildren of all ages.
- **Audience:** Parents and grandparents
- **Frequency:** Monthly
- **Distribution:** 70% newsstand; 27% schools; 3% subscription
- **Circulation:** 55,000
- **Website:** www.ssparent.com

Freelance Potential

75% written by nonstaff writers. Publishes 75 freelance submissions yearly; 5–10% by unpublished writers, 70% by authors who are new to the magazine. Receives 65 queries each month.

Submissions

Query with list of topics and writing sample. Accepts email queries to ssparent@pacbell.net. Response time varies.
Articles: 700–1,000 words. Informational, how-to, and personal experience articles; and humor. Topics include fitness, family finance, family travel, learning disabilities, grandparenting, sports, adoption, and regional news.
Depts/columns: 400–500 words. Child development, opinions, and hometown highlights.
Other: Activities and filler. Submit seasonal material 2–3 months in advance.

Sample Issue

50 pages (50% advertising): 5 articles; 9 depts/columns. Sample copy, free with 10x12 SASE ($1.29 postage). Guidelines and editorial calendar/theme list available.
- "Growing a Healthy Middle School Boy." Article describes what is normal for a boy between 10 and 14 years of age, and some of the physical changes that are encountered during that period of life.
- "Decoding the Preschool Jargon." Article acts as a helpful glossary for understanding terms to describe preschool philosophies about child development and teaching.
- Sample dept/column: "Dad's World" provides a glimpse into issues faced by fathers.

Rights and Payment

Reprint rights. Articles, $50+. Depts/columns, $25–$40. Pays on publication. Provides contributor's copies.

Editor's Comments

We would like to see more submissions relating to personal experiences, overcoming challenges, infancy, and teens.

St. Louis Parent

P.O. Box 190287
St. Louis, MO 63119

Editor: Barb MacRobie

Description and Readership

This publication serving the St. Louis metropolitan area is available free of charge at grocery stores, libraries, schools, and various other locations. Its typical readers are mothers seeking child-rearing advice and information on local schools, camps, and other services for children and families.
- **Audience:** Parents
- **Frequency:** 10 times each year
- **Distribution:** Newsstands; hospitals; schools
- **Circulation:** 35,000

Freelance Potential

90% written by nonstaff writers. Publishes 30–50 freelance submissions yearly; 5% by unpublished writers. Receives 5 queries monthly.

Submissions

Query with résumé, outline, synopsis, and clips or writing samples. Accepts photocopies, computer printouts, and simultaneous submissions if identified. SASE. Response time varies.
Articles: 700 words. Informational and how-to articles. Topics include education; family health; safety; nutrition; child care; personal finances; and regional resources, services, and events.
Other: Submit seasonal material 6 months in advance.

Sample Issue

18 pages (40% advertising): 6 articles; 1 summer camp directory. Sample copy, free with 9x12 SASE ($1 postage). Guidelines and editorial calendar available.
- "Teaching Through Technology." Article discusses the current debate about whether schools should provide every student with access to a laptop computer.
- "Reasons for Test Anxiety." Article points out that prior negative experiences and poor study habits are among the reasons for test-taking anxiety; includes fear-quelling tips.
- "Taking a Year off after High School." Article explains why some young adults may greatly benefit from taking a year or two off before entering college.

Rights and Payment

All rights. Articles, $50. Other material, payment rate varies. Pays on acceptance. Provides 2 contributor's copies.

Editor's Comments

If you're a local writer, query us with your idea for an article on any topic of interest to parents with growing children. Education articles continue to be a strong need, particularly those that cite local schools or that quote local experts.

San Diego Family Magazine

P.O. Box 23960
San Diego, CA 92193

Publisher & Editor: Sharon Bay

Description and Readership
The focus of this publication is to enhance the quality of family life for members of the San Diego community. It emphasizes the importance and pleasures of parenting through educational articles and listings of regional resources.
• **Audience:** Parents
• **Frequency:** Monthly
• **Distribution:** 99% controlled; 1% other
• **Circulation:** 120,000
• **Website:** www.sandiegofamily.com

Freelance Potential
90% written by nonstaff writers. Publishes 50 freelance submissions yearly; 50% by unpublished writers. Receives 30–50 queries and unsolicited mss monthly.

Submissions
Query or send complete ms with a sample clip if available. Accepts photocopies, computer printouts, Macintosh disk submissions (Microsoft Word), and email submissions to bayview@thegroup.net. SASE. Responds to queries in 6–8 weeks, to mss in 2–3 months.
Articles: 750–1,000 words. Informational, how-to, and self-help articles. Topics include parenting, gifted and special education, family issues, travel, health, fitness, sports, and multicultural issues. Also publishes humorous articles.
Depts/columns: Word length varies. Book reviews, restaurant reviews, advice, health, and the home.
Artwork: 3x5 or 5x7 B/W glossy prints.

Sample Issue
146 pages (60% advertising): 25 articles; 14 depts/columns. Sample copy, $3.50 with 9x12 SASE ($1 postage). Writers' guidelines available.
• "Family Fun Night Is Back!" Article profiles two area families and the activities that bring their families together for one night a week.
• Sample dept/column: "Discover Science" explains how simple machines used every day really work.

Rights and Payment
First or second rights and all regional rights. Written material, $1.25 per published column inch. Pays on publication. Provides 1 contributor's copy.

Editor's Comments
Our editorial content has a definite San Diego county focus and our writing style strives to be positive and uplifting while addressing common parenting issues.

SchoolArts

Davis Publications
50 Portland Street
Worcester, MA 01608

Editor: Eldon Katter

Description and Readership
Since 1901, *SchoolArts* has been keeping art teachers at the cutting edge of art education by presenting information on innovative lessons, successful teaching units, and hands-on classroom activities. Most of the articles that appear in this magazine are written by art teachers.
• **Audience:** Teachers, grades K–12
• **Frequency:** 9 times each year
• **Distribution:** 100% subscription
• **Circulation:** 20,000
• **Website:** www.davis-art.com

Freelance Potential
90% written by nonstaff writers. Publishes 120 freelance submissions yearly; 60% by unpublished writers, 60% by authors who are new to the magazine. Receives 33 unsolicited mss monthly.

Submissions
Send complete ms with artwork. Accepts photocopies and computer printouts. SASE. Responds in 6 weeks.
Articles: Word length varies. Informational, how-to, and self-help articles. Topics include teaching art, techniques, art history, projects and activities, curriculum development, and art programs for the gifted, handicapped, or learning disabled.
Depts/columns: Word length varies. Media reviews, news, and technology updates.
Artwork: B/W prints or 35mm color slides. B/W line art.

Sample Issue
76 pages (40% advertising): 12 articles; 7 depts/columns; 7 ready-to-use resources. Sample copy, $3. Guidelines and editorial calendar available.
• "Art on the Go!" Article reports on a mobile art museum.
• "Kindergarten Explores the World of Art." Article describes an integrated curriculum that introduces kindergarten students to 10 artists and their works.
• Sample dept/column: "The Heart of Art City" profiles Utah's Springville Museum of Art.

Rights and Payment
First serial rights. Written material, $25–$150. Other material, payment rate varies. Pays on acceptance. Provides 3 copies.

Editor's Comments
Strive for a friendly, casual tone in your writing. Break complex processes into simple steps, point out problems teachers might encounter when attempting your activity, and suggest ways to adapt your idea to different grade levels.

The School Librarian's Workshop

1 Deerfield Court
Basking Ridge, NJ 07920

Editor: Ruth Toor

Description and Readership
In the fall of 2004, due to the explosion of information and technologies, *The School Librarian's Workshop* expanded its pages to 24, up from the previous 16 pages. Its goal is to be the most practical and useful of school library publications, and especially helpful in day-to-day operations.
- **Audience:** School Librarians
- **Frequency:** 6 times each year
- **Distribution:** 99% subscription; 1% other
- **Circulation:** 7,500+
- **Website:** www.school-librarians-workshop.com

Freelance Potential
20% written by nonstaff writers. Publishes 14 freelance submissions yearly; 30% by unpublished writers, 30% by authors who are new to the magazine. Receives 1–2 unsolicited mss monthly.

Submissions
Send 2 copies of complete ms. Prefers disk submissions (Microsoft Word). Accepts photocopies and computer printouts. No simultaneous submissions. SASE. Responds in 3 weeks.
Articles: To 1,000 words. Informational, how-to and practical application articles; profiles; and interviews. Topics include librarianship, special education, ethnic studies, computers, social and multicultural issues, and the environment.
Artwork: Line art.
Other: Submit seasonal material 8 months in advance.

Sample Issue
24 pages (no advertising): 12 articles; 1 dept/column; 1 puzzle page. Sample copy, free with 9x12 SASE. Guidelines and theme list available.
- "The Older Generation." Article describes several books about the lives of grandparents, and categorizes them according to students' ages.
- "When Authors Pay a Visit." Article provides a step-by-step process for librarians to use to make the most of inviting an author to visit a school.
- Sample dept/column: "On the Bulletin Board" coordinates ideas for a library's bulletin board with the month's theme.

Rights and Payment
First rights. No payment. Provides 3 contributor's copies.

Editor's Comments
We look for articles that deal with the practical aspects of library media programs for all grades. Several new departments were added in 2004, such as Reference Center, Marketing and Advocacy, and Professional Reading.

School Library Journal

360 Park Avenue South
New York, NY 10010

News & Features Editor: Rick Margolis

Description and Readership
Media specialists in schools, public libraries, and other types of libraries use this as a resource for improving library services. Book and media reviews add to its editorial mix.
- **Audience:** Librarians
- **Frequency:** Monthly
- **Distribution:** 100% subscription
- **Circulation:** 42,000
- **Website:** www.slj.com

Freelance Potential
80% written by nonstaff writers. Publishes 25 freelance submissions yearly; 60% by unpublished writers, 60% by authors who are new to the magazine. Receives 4–6 unsolicited mss monthly.

Submissions
Query or send complete ms. Accepts disk submissions (ASCII or Microsoft Word) and email submissions to rmargolis@reedbusiness.com. SASE. Responds to queries in 1 month, to mss in 3 months.
Articles: 1,500–2,500 words. Informational articles and interviews. Topics include children's and young adult literature, school library management, and library careers.
Depts/columns: 1,500–2,500 words. Book and media reviews; descriptions of successful library programs; and opinion pieces.
Artwork: Color prints, tables, charts, and cartoons.

Sample Issue
140 pages (25% advertising): 6 articles; 18 depts/columns; 1 calendar. Sample copy, $6.75. Guidelines available.
- "Here Comes Trouble." Article provides several suggestions for librarians to use when they are confronted by unruly teens who tend to disregard written library rules.
- "You Go, Girl." Article delivers reasons why librarians should get rid of the dumpy, bookish appearance and go for a trim, energetic look.
- Sample dept/column: "What Works" relates how one librarian introduced an online library unit.

Rights and Payment
First rights. Articles, $400. Depts/columns, $100–$200. Pays on publication. Provides 4 contributor's copies.

Editor's Comments
If you have had success with a program or other idea that improves overall library services, we would like to hear from you. We are also interested in articles describing librarians who have contributed to their students' success.

School Library Media Activities Monthly

17 East Henrietta Street
Baltimore, MD 21230-3910

Publisher: Paula Montgomery

Description and Readership
Established in 1984, this publication provides hands-on assistance to media specialists in their teaching roles. In addition to articles, it also offers software reviews, media production tips, and information on websites.
- **Audience:** School library and media specialists, grades K–8
- **Frequency:** 10 times each year
- **Distribution:** 100% subscription
- **Circulation:** 12,000
- **Website:** www.schoollibrarymedia.com

Freelance Potential
80% written by nonstaff writers. Publishes 30 freelance submissions yearly; 15% by unpublished writers, 25% by authors who are new to the magazine. Receives 4 queries and unsolicited mss monthly.

Submissions
Query or send complete ms. Accepts photocopies, disk submissions and email submissions to paulam@crinkles.com. SASE. Responds in 2 months.
Articles: 1,000–1,500 words. Informational and factual articles. Topics include media education, information technology, integrating curriculum materials, and library management.
Depts/columns: "Activities Almanac" features short descriptions of media activities. "Into the Curriculum" uses lesson plans. Also publishes media reviews and short articles on media production, and reading and listening skills.
Artwork: B/W transparencies and prints. Line art.

Sample Issue
52 pages (no advertising): 3 articles; 13 depts/columns. Guidelines available.
- "CultureGrams and StateGrams." Article discusses websites to help answer and find information about American states and foreign cultures.
- Sample dept/column: "Keeping Current" looks at ways librarians can develop an objective, nonevangelistic source of study for the world's religions to promote intercultural understanding.

Rights and Payment
All rights. All material, payment rate varies. Pays on publication. Provides 3+ contributor's copies.

Editor's Comments
We need practical articles that help them teach both students and teachers. Possible topics include using reference and trade books, audiovisual materials and equipment, computers and programs, and reference and research skills.

The School Magazine

P.O. Box 1928
Macquarie Centre, NSW 2113
Australia

Editor: Jonathan Shaw

Description and Readership
The School Magazine is a literary magazine for primary school children published by the New South Wales Department of Education and Training. Each issue contains four separate magazines, each one targeting a different educational level: 8–9-year-olds; 9–10-year-olds; 10–11-year-olds; and advanced readers in primary school.
- **Audience:** 6–12 years
- **Frequency:** 10 times each year
- **Distribution:** 100% subscription
- **Circulation:** 220,000

Freelance Potential
80% written by nonstaff writers. Publishes 100 freelance submissions yearly; 20% by unpublished writers, 30% by authors who are new to the magazine. Receives 83 mss monthly.

Submissions
Send complete ms. Accepts computer printouts. SAE/IRC. Responds in 6–8 weeks.
Articles: 800–2,000 words. Informational and factual articles. Topics include nature, pets, the environment, history, biography, science, technology, and multicultural issues.
Fiction: 800–2,000 words. Adventure; humor; fantasy; horror; mystery; folktales; stories about science and animals; problem-solving and real-life stories; and contemporary, multicultural, and historical fiction.
Depts/columns: Staff written.

Sample Issue
36 pages (no advertising): 1 article; 1 story; 3 poems; 5 depts/columns; 1 serial play; 2 activities; 2 comics. Sample copy, free with 9x12 SAE/IRC ($2 Australian postage). Writers' guidelines available.
- "Pemulwuy." Article recounts the life and legend of Pemulway of the Bidjigal people, the most famous warrior in all of Australian history.
- "Giving Mum a Hand." Story revolves around a reluctant choice made under parental pressure that turns out to be a life-saving decision.

Rights and Payment
One-time serial rights. Written material, $209 (Australian) per 1,000 words. Poetry, payment rate varies. Pays on acceptance. Provides 2 contributor's copies.

Editor's Comments
Fiction and nonfiction submissions are welcome. We operate within the non-sexist, multicultural, and Aboriginal policies of the Department of Education and Training.

Science Activities

Heldref Publications
1319 18th Street NW
Washington, DC 20036-1802

Managing Editor: Cheri Williams

Description and Readership
Science teachers for kindergarten through grade 12 find classroom-tested projects, experiments, and curriculum ideas in this magazine. All articles include an activity for students to do and most are accompanied by illustrative materials, such as photographs, tables, charts, and/or artist-rendered drawings.
- **Audience:** Science teachers
- **Frequency:** Quarterly
- **Distribution:** Subscription; schools; libraries
- **Circulation:** 1,200
- **Website:** www.heldref.org

Freelance Potential
80% written by nonstaff writers. Publishes 24 freelance submissions yearly; 50% by unpublished writers; 100% by authors who are new to the magazine. Receives 3–4 queries and unsolicited mss monthly.

Submissions
Query or send 2 copies of complete ms. Accepts photocopies and computer printouts. SASE. Responds in 3 months.
Articles: Word length varies. Informational and how-to articles. Topics include science, nature, technology, and computers.
Depts/columns: Word length varies. Book reviews, computer news, and classroom aids.
Artwork: B/W photos, prints, and slides. Line drawings and diagrams.

Sample Issue
48 pages (1% advertising): 4 articles; 3 depts/columns. Sample copy, $6 with 9x12 SASE. Guidelines available.
- "Flying Through the Standards with Bats." Article describes an integrated unit on bats and specifically addresses the National Science Education Standards.
- "The Art of Sorting: Using Venn Diagrams to Learn Science Process Skills." Article provides activities to teach students how to use sorting hoops and attribute blocks.
- Sample dept/column: "Computer News" details computer programs, CD-ROMs, and Internet sites for science classes.

Rights and Payment
All rights. No payment. Provides 2 contributor's copies.

Editor's Comments
We are looking for articles that incorporate the Internet and technology with science learning activities. Material should provide an introduction, materials procedure, and background information for doing a classroom activity. We are interested in articles on the Internet and science, ecology, insect studies, ocean life, human body systems, and motion and forces.

Science and Children

National Science Teachers Association
1840 Wilson Boulevard
Arlington, VA 22201-3000

Managing Editor: Monica Zerry

Description and Readership
Written for and by science teachers, *Science and Children* presents peer-reviewed feature articles that describe practical activities and instructional approaches to teaching science.
- **Audience:** Science educators, pre-K–grade 8
- **Frequency:** 8 times each year
- **Distribution:** 100% subscription
- **Circulation:** 23,000
- **Website:** www.nsta.org/pubs/sc

Freelance Potential
99% written by nonstaff writers. Publishes 80 freelance submissions yearly; 95% by unpublished writers, 95% by authors who are new to the magazine. Receives 30 unsolicited mss monthly.

Submissions
Accepts submissions from practicing educators only. Send 5 copies of complete ms. Accepts photocopies and IBM or Macintosh disk submissions. SASE. Responds in 6 months.
Articles: To 1,500 words. Informational and how-to articles; personal experience pieces; profiles; interviews; and reviews. Topics include science education, teacher training and techniques, astronomy, biology, physics, and Earth science.
Depts/columns: To 1,500 words. "Helpful Hints" and "In the Schools," to 500 words.
Other: Submit seasonal material 1 year in advance.

Sample Issue
68 pages (22% advertising): 5 articles; 14 depts/columns. Sample copy, free. Guidelines available.
- "On Observing the Weather." Informative article suggests real-life applications for weather observation activities, including reading the temperature, scanning the sky, and gauging wind speed.
- "Spiderific Learning Tools." Article explores the world of spiders with hands-on activities for students in grades four through six.
- Sample dept/column: "Finds & Sites" covers free or inexpensive materials, publications, and events of interest.

Rights and Payment
All rights. No payment. Provides 3 contributor's copies.

Editor's Comments
If you are an educator who is enthusiastic about elementary and middle-level science, you are invited to submit material that describes your experiences and insights into teaching. We would like to see successful classroom activities, interdisciplinary learning successes, and discussions of current issues and concerns in elementary science education.

The Science Teacher

National Science Teachers Association
1840 Wilson Boulevard
Arlington, VA 22201-3000

Managing Editor: Jennifer Henderson

Description and Readership
Articles on teaching techniques and theory appear along with practical ideas for hands-on classroom activities in this magazine from the National Science Teachers Association. It is primarily read by high school science teachers.
- **Audience:** Science educators, grades 7–12
- **Frequency:** 9 times each year
- **Distribution:** 100% controlled
- **Circulation:** 29,000
- **Website:** www.nsta.org/highschool

Freelance Potential
100% written by nonstaff writers. Publishes 50 freelance submissions yearly; 70% by unpublished writers, 30% by authors who are new to the magazine. Receives 30 unsolicited mss monthly.

Submissions
Send 3 copies of complete ms with copy on disk to Nadine Bowser, Manuscript Review Coordinator, at the address above; and 1 copy to Janet Gerking, Field Editor, 443 Valley Stream Drive, Geneva, FL 32732. SASE. Responds in 1 month.
Articles: 2,000 words. Informational articles; classroom projects; and experiments. Topics include science education, biology, earth science, space, computers, social issues, technology, and sports medicine.
Depts/columns: 500 words. Science updates, association news, and science careers.
Artwork: 5x7 or larger B/W glossy prints. Tables, diagrams, and line drawings.

Sample Issue
92 pages (40% advertising): 11 articles; 8 depts/columns. Sample copy, $4.25. Guidelines available.
- "An Interview with Animal Nutritionist Mark Edwards." Article profiles an animal nutritionist who works with the Zoological Society of San Diego.
- "Life Is Change." Describes a project that captures life processes and fosters K–12 curriculum collaboration.
- Sample dept/column: "Ask the Experts" provides a detailed explanation of how ice skates work.

Rights and Payment
First rights. No payment. Provides contributor's copies.

Editor's Comments
In your submission, we encourage you to share your complete teaching experience. Include descriptions of what you have done including what worked, and what didn't. Tell us what students were wondering about that led you to conduct the activity and explain how you know the students learned the material.

Science Weekly, Inc.

Suite 202
2141 Industrial Parkway
Silver Springs, MD 20904

Publisher: Dr. Claude Mayberry

Description and Readership
Each issue of *Science Weekly* is written for seven different reading levels and includes separate teaching notes with topic background information and related teaching projects for each educational level. A wide variety of challenging hands-on and self-discovery activities are designed to motivate and spark student interest and curiosity. A list of recommended reading and Internet resources are included in each issue.
- **Audience:** Students, grades K-6
- **Frequency:** 14 times each year
- **Distribution:** Subscription; schools
- **Circulation:** 200,000
- **Website:** www.scienceweekly.com

Freelance Potential
100% written by nonstaff writers; 80% by unpublished writers, 20% by authors who are new to the magazine.

Submissions
Query with résumé only. No unsolicited mss. All work is assigned to writers in the District of Columbia, Maryland, and Virginia. SASE. Response time varies.
Articles: Word length varies. Topics include space exploration, ecology, the environment, nature, biology, the human body, meteorology, ocean science, navigation, nutrition, photography, physical science, roller coasters, and secret codes.
Other: Theme-related puzzles, word games, and hands-on activities.

Sample Issue
4 pages (no advertising): 1 article; 6 activities. Sample copy, free with 9x12 SASE. Theme list available.
- "The Heart." Article explains how the human heart works, how it relates to the rest of the body, and what can be done to keep it healthy.
- Sample activity: "Weekly Problem" investigates a healthy heart rate and factors, such as resting or jumping, that contribute to a faster or slower pulse.

Rights and Payment
All rights. All material, payment rate varies. Pays on publication.

Editor's Comments
We like to work with new writers, but because one of our requirements is to have our contributors become involved with the editorial process for Science Weekly, they must live in the Washington, D.C., metropolitan area. A solid background in science and/or education is recommended, as well as an ability to write in a clear, creative, and compelling style. It is our policy not to accept unsolicited manuscripts.

Scouting

Boy Scouts of America
1325 West Walnut Hill Lane
P.O. Box 152079
Irving, TX 75015-2079

Editor: Jon C. Halter

Description and Readership
Boy Scout leaders turn to this magazine for its resourceful information on successful activity programs, leadership training, and events. It also includes profiles of outstanding leaders, essays on parenting, nature, and the environment.
- **Audience:** Scouting leaders
- **Frequency:** 6 times each year
- **Distribution:** 100% subscription
- **Circulation:** 1 million
- **Website:** www.scoutingmagazine.org

Freelance Potential
80% written by nonstaff writers. Publishes 5–10 freelance submissions yearly; 5% by unpublished writers, 15% by authors who are new to the magazine. Receives 50 queries monthly.

Submissions
Query with clips. Responds in 4–6 weeks.
Articles: 500–1,200 words. Informational and how-to articles; personal experience pieces; humor; profiles; and interviews. Topics include leadership, family issues, parenting, fitness, health, education, nature, and the environment.
Depts/columns: 500–700 words. Scouting events, anecdotes, and history; and family events.
Other: Puzzles.

Sample Issue
50 pages (33% advertising): 5 articles; 7 depts/columns. Sample copy, $2.50 with 9x12 SASE. Guidelines available.
- "Strictly for Scoutmasters" Article describes a course that examines the role of the Scoutmaster and offers methods for developing and improving the quality of troops.
- "Following the Footsteps of Lewis and Clark." Article takes a look at spots for hiking, paddling, and horseback riding along the historical Lewis and Clark trail.
- Sample dept/column: "Outdoor Smarts" looks at ten essential items for outdoor adventurers.

Rights and Payment
First North American serial rights. Articles, $500–$800. Other material, payment rate varies. Pays on acceptance. Provides 2 contributor's copies.

Editor's Comments
We seek information that will provide a positive influence on scouts. Articles covering scouting expeditions, teamwork, volunteerism, leadership, and other topics that relate to creating a rewarding scouting experience are of interest to us. We also include features on parenting issues since most volunteer scout leaders are parents of children of scout age.

Seattle's Child

Suite 215
123 NW 36th Street
Seattle, WA 98107

Editor: Wenda Reed

Description and Readership
For 25 years, *Seattle's Child* has been a source of community and parenting information for families with children up to the age of 12. Its articles, monthly events calendar, and coverage of local resources provide a wealth of useful, relevant information for families in the greater Seattle area.
- **Audience:** Parents
- **Frequency:** Monthly
- **Distribution:** 100% newsstand
- **Circulation:** Unavailable
- **Website:** www.seattleschild.com

Freelance Potential
80% written by nonstaff writers. Publishes 50+ freelance submissions yearly; 5% by unpublished writers, 10% by authors who are new to the magazine. Receives 20 queries monthly.

Submissions
Query with outline. Send queries for local stories to above address; send queries for national-interest stories to Editor, United Parenting Publications, 15400 Knoll Trail, Suite 400, Dallas, TX 75248. Accepts photocopies, computer printouts, and simultaneous submissions if identified. SASE. Responds in 2 weeks.
Articles: Word length varies. Informational and how-to articles; and personal experience pieces. Topics include family and parenting issues, fitness, regional news, travel, and social issues.
Depts/columns: Word length varies. Profiles, cooking, and media reviews.

Sample Issue
58 pages: 2 articles; 6 depts/columns; 1 calendar of events; 1 camp directory. Sample copy, $3. Guidelines and theme list available.
- "So Many Ways to Celebrate." Article offers tips for hosting a successful birthday party at home and includes a rundown of party supply stores in the greater Seattle area.
- Sample dept/column: "Education" looks at the fallout from the education reform law, No Child Left Behind.
- Sample dept/column: "Parenting People" profiles an area father of four who is leading one of the nation's largest grassroots marriage movements.

Rights and Payment
Rights vary. Written material, payment rate varies. Pays on publication. Provides 2 contributor's copies.

Editor's Comments
Articles on recently covered or overdone topics, and those that are too broad in scope or poorly written, are sure to be rejected.

Seek

Standard Publishing Company
8121 Hamilton Avenue
Cincinnati, OH 45231

Editor: Dawn A. Medill

Description and Readership

This publication is used in Sunday school classes and in church group discussions. Targeting older teens and adults, it features inspirational fiction and nonfiction, Christian testimonials, and discussions of timely religious issues.
- **Audience:** YA–Adult
- **Frequency:** Weekly
- **Distribution:** 100% religious education
- **Circulation:** 27,000
- **Website:** www.standardpub.com

Freelance Potential

70% written by nonstaff writers. Publishes 150–200 freelance submissions yearly; 80% by authors who are new to the magazine. Receives 250 unsolicited mss monthly.

Submissions

Send complete ms that relates to an upcoming theme (available at website). Prefers email submissions to seek@ standardpub.com. Accepts photocopies. No simultaneous submissions. SASE. Responds in 3–6 months.
Articles: 400–1,200 words. Inspirational, devotional, and personal experience pieces. Topics include religious and contemporary issues, Christian living, moral and ethical dilemmas, and controversial subjects.
Fiction: 400–1,200 words. Stories about coping with contemporary problems and religious beliefs; suspense; stories about sports; and humor.
Artwork: 8x10 B/W glossy prints.
Other: Filler, 250 words. Submit seasonal material 1 year in advance.

Sample Issue

8 pages (no advertising): 1 article; 2 stories; 1 Bible lesson. Sample copy, free with 6x9 SASE. Writers' guidelines available at website.
- "Tradition of Irises." Story about a woman who is comforted by the sight of irises in the springtime when she is homesick for her old house.
- "The Reunion." Story in which an elderly woman is helped with the upkeep of her farm by neighbors and family.

Rights and Payment

First and reprint rights. Written material, $.05 per word. Artwork, $50. Pays on acceptance. Provides 5 copies.

Editor's Comments

The purpose of our weekly paper is to provide spiritual enrichment. We look for writing that is wholesome, alive, vibrant, current, and relevant for today's reader.

Seventeen

13th Floor
1440 Broadway
New York, NY 10018

Features Editor: Leslie Heilbrunn

Description and Readership

For decades, young women have turned to *Seventeen* for the latest news from the world of fashion and for features related to beauty and fitness. Articles on social and international issues are another major component of the magazine. *Seventeen* is also known for publishing high-quality fiction on themes teens can relate to.
- **Audience:** 13–21 years
- **Frequency:** Monthly
- **Distribution:** 70% subscription; 30% newsstand
- **Circulation:** 2.35 million
- **Website:** www.seventeen.com

Freelance Potential

20% written by nonstaff writers. Publishes 20 freelance submissions yearly; 5% by unpublished writers, 40% by authors who are new to the magazine. Receives 46 queries, 200 unsolicited mss monthly.

Submissions

Query with outline and clips or writing samples. Send complete ms for fiction. No phone calls. Accepts photocopies, computer printouts, and simultaneous submissions if identified. SASE. Response time varies.
Articles: 650–3,000 words. Informational and self-help articles. Topics include relationships, dating, family issues, current events, social issues, friendship, and popular culture.
Fiction: 1,000–3,000 words. Stories that focus on teenage female experiences. Sponsors an annual short story contest.
Depts/columns: 500–1,000 words. Fashion, beauty, health, and fitness.
Other: Submit seasonal material 6 months in advance.

Sample Issue

214 pages (50% advertising): 3 articles; 1 story; 37 depts/ columns. Sample copy, $3.99 at newsstands. Writers' guidelines available.
- "A Fire Destroyed My Life." Article relates the experience of a young woman whose family was devastated by a wildfire.
- Sample dept/column: "Lifestyle" offers decorating tips, a flower-arranging strategy, and barbecue recipes.

Rights and Payment

First rights. Written material, $1–$1.50 per word. Pays on acceptance.

Editor's Comments

At this time, we could use more articles on fashion, beauty, health, and fitness, as well as reports on real-life issues of interest to young adult women.

SG Magazine

Suite C
950 Calle Amanecer
San Clemente, CA 92673

Editor: Robin Lass

Description and Readership
All aspects of board sports, including surfing, snowboarding, and skateboarding, are covered in this magazine for teenage girls. It also features material on beauty, fashion, fitness, and sport-related travel.
- **Audience:** 13–21 years
- **Frequency:** 6 times each year
- **Distribution:** Subscription; newsstand
- **Circulation:** 100,000
- **Website:** www.sgmag.com

Freelance Potential
30% written by nonstaff writers. Publishes 100 freelance submissions yearly.

Submissions
Query. Accepts computer printouts, and email submissions to sgmag@primedia.com. SASE. Responds in 2 months.
Articles: 1,500–2,000 words. How-to and informational articles; profiles; interviews; and personal experience pieces. Topics include surfing, skateboarding, snowboarding, skiing, the beach lifestyle, health, fitness, sports, travel, leisure, nutrition, recreation, and relationships.
Fiction: 300–800 words. Stories with snowboarding, skateboarding, and surfboarding themes.
Depts/columns: 300–800 words. Short profiles, skateboarding tips, fashion, beauty, travel, the environment, industry news, and reader-written poetry.

Sample Issue
114 pages (50% advertising): 4 articles; 16 depts/columns. Sample copy $2.99. Writers' guidelines available.
- "Life's Soundtrack." Article looks at the music of seven new bands who offer great summer listening.
- "Welcome to the Dollhouse." Article chronicles a trip to Guerrero, Mexico by three girl surfboarders sponsored by Billabong.
- Sample dept/column: "Babewatch" featurrofile of 18-year-old surf phenomenon, Jason Miller.

Rights and Payment
First rights. Pays on publication. All material, payment rate varies.

Editor's Comments
We need contributors who can write knowledgeably about all types of board sports in a way that appeals to teenage girls. You must be able to provide our readers with the sports and beach-lifestyle information they are looking for while using the language they are familiar with.

Sharing Space

521 North Broadway
P.O. Box 271
Nyack, NY 10960

Submissions Editor

Description and Readership
Creative Response to Conflict publishes this newsletter to illustrate the importance of using conflict resolution tactics in educational venues.
- **Audience:** Adults
- **Frequency:** 3 times each year
- **Distribution:** 25% schools; 25% subscription; 50% other
- **Circulation:** 3,000
- **Website:** www.ccrcglobal.org

Freelance Potential
40% written by nonstaff writers. Publishes 25 freelance submissions yearly; 20% by unpublished writers, 80% by authors who are new to the magazine. Receives 2–3 queries and unsolicited mss monthly.

Submissions
Query or send complete ms. Accepts photocopies, computer printouts, and disk submissions (Microsoft Word 5.1). SASE. Responds in 2 weeks.
Articles: Word length varies. Practical application, how-to, and personal experience pieces; profiles; read-aloud stories; and bilingual articles. Topics include special education, social issues, recreation, multicultural and ethnic issues, parenting, popular culture, technology, and current events.
Depts/columns: Word length varies. Short news items.
Other: Puzzles, activities, and games related to conflict resolution and problem-solving. Submit seasonal material 3 months in advance.

Sample Issue
8 pages (no advertising): 3 articles; 7 news briefs; 1 book review; 1 events calendar. Sample copy, $5 with 9x12 SASE.
- "Creative Responses to Bullying: Jockey Hollow Middle School." Article presents the case history of a Monroe, CT school's success in developing and implementing a conflict resolution program.
- "Adults First in Marlborough, CT: Working with the School Board." Article profiles a success that CRC had in working with a school board and school staff members in moving toward problem solving and conflict resolution.

Rights and Payment
Rights vary. No payment. Provides contributor's copies.

Editor's Comments
We look for articles that focus on programs that have successfully introduced or heightened cooperative communication, problem solving, awareness of bias or prejudice, affirmative behavior, and conflict resolution.

Sharing the Victory

Fellowship of Christian Athletes
8701 Leeds Road
Kansas City, MO 64129

Editor: Jill Ewert

Description and Readership
Published by the Fellowship of Christian Athletes, this magazine includes articles about athletes and coaches who speak out about their relationship with Jesus and aim to make a difference in their communities.
- **Audience:** Athletes and coaches, grades 7 and up
- **Frequency:** 9 times each year
- **Distribution:** 100% subscription
- **Circulation:** 80,000
- **Website:** www.fca.org

Freelance Potential
75% written by nonstaff writers. Publishes 30 freelance submissions yearly; 25% by unpublished writers, 10% by new authors. Receives 4 queries and unsolicited mss monthly.

Submissions
Query with outline/synopsis and clips or writing samples; or send complete ms. Accepts photocopies, computer printouts, and IBM disk submissions. Availability of artwork improves chance of acceptance. Response time varies.
Articles: To 1,200 words. Informational and factual articles; profiles; personal experience pieces; and interviews. Topics include sports, competition, training, and Christian education.
Depts/columns: Staff written.
Artwork: Color prints.
Other: Submit seasonal material 3–4 months in advance.

Sample Issue
38 pages (35% advertising): 7 articles; 7 depts/columns. Sample copy, $1 with 9x12 SASE (3 first-class stamps). Writers' guidelines available.
- "On a Mission." Article tells how members of a Minnesota basketball team gained faith in God that changed their lives while on a mission in Gutemala.
- "Off to a Quick Start." Article reports on the success of the first Christian Sports Camp organized by the Fellowship of Christian Athletes.
- "Lacrosse Training." Article discusses the growing number of Bible studies on college lacrosse teams in the Northeast and how they are impacting schools.

Rights and Payment
First serial rights. Articles, $150–$400. Pays on publication.

Editor's Comments
We are currently seeking more stories about female athletes. All articles should be connected somehow to the Fellowship of Christian Athletes. Articles should be accompanied by at least three sharp color photos.

SheKnows.com

719 Octavia Street
New Orleans, LA 70115

Editor: Jennifer Newton Reents

Description and Readership
SheKnows.com is an online publication that provides information on parenting children of all ages, pregnancy, childbirth, health, and a variety of other topics of interest to women. It was created by Coincide Media, which sponsors other websites such as *Pregnancy & Baby*, *GeoParent*, *Chef Mom*, and *LowCarb Energy*.
- **Audience:** Mothers
- **Frequency:** Monthly
- **Distribution:** 100% online
- **Circulation:** Unavailable
- **Website:** www.sheknows.com

Freelance Potential
90% written by nonstaff writers. Publishes 150 freelance submissions yearly.

Submissions
Query or send complete ms. Accepts submissions through the website only. Responds in 2 months.
Articles: 500–1,200 words. Informational, how-to, and factual articles; profiles; interviews; and personal experience pieces. Topics include parenting, fertility, pregnancy, maternity fashion trends, birth stories, pain management, depression, babies, toddlers, family issues, relationships, romance, entertainment, celebrities, work, health, hobbies, home decor, and money management.

Sample Issue
Sample copy and guidelines available at website.
- "When You Can't Be There: Twenty Ways to Stay Connected to Your Kids." Article offers ideas for ways to keep your relationship with your kids strong when you are travelling or working long hours.
- "Boy or Girl? The Mysteries of Gender Selection." Article reports on scientific research that relates to choosing the gender of a baby.

Rights and Payment
First electronic rights. Features, $25–$50. First-person pieces, $10. Pays on publication.

Editor's Comments
All of our sites are primarily freelance written. We like articles that are based on research and interviews. Writers should take a friendly, accessible approach. Originality and creativity—especially a unique twist on a more typical topic—are encouraged. We primarily use information from experts and features written by journalists with appropriate writing skills, although we will consider work by unpublished writers. Please don't send personal essays or opinion pieces at this time.

Shine Brightly

P.O. Box 7259
Grand Rapids, MI 49510

Managing Editor: Sara Lynne Hilton

Description and Readership
Articles and stories that are entertaining and teach a valuable lesson are included in this magazine for young girls. Material is written with a Christian slant. It is published by GEMS Girls' Clubs.
- **Audience:** 9–14 years
- **Frequency:** 9 times each year
- **Distribution:** 100% subscription
- **Circulation:** 14,000
- **Website:** www.gemsgc.org

Freelance Potential
70% written by nonstaff writers. Publishes 36 freelance submissions yearly; 20% by unpublished writers, 20% by authors who are new to the magazine. Receives 50 unsolicited mss monthly.

Submissions
Send complete ms. Accepts photocopies, computer printouts, and simultaneous submissions if identified. No email submissions. SASE. Responds in 1 month.
Articles: 50–500 words. How-to and informational articles; personal experience pieces; profiles; and humorous pieces. Topics include Christian life, community service, peer pressure, family life, social issues, and entertainment.
Fiction: 400–900 words. Genres include science fiction, contemporary fiction, mystery, romance, and adventure. Also publishes stories about nature, sports, and animals.
Depts/columns: Staff written.
Artwork: 5x7 or larger B/W and color prints.
Other: Puzzles, activities, and cartoons.

Sample Issue
24 pages (no advertising): 5 articles; 3 stories; 1 dept/column; 4 activity pages. Sample copy, $1 with 9x12 SASE ($.75 postage). Writers' guidelines available.
- "Meeting Marnie at the Top." Story tells of a girl who risks her friendship to stop a friend from getting hurt skiing.
- "The Science of Names." Article looks at the history of scientific names to describe plants and animals.

Rights and Payment
First, second, and simultaneous rights. Articles and fiction $.02–$.05 per word. Other material, payment rate varies. Pays on publication. Provides 2 contributor's copies.

Editor's Comments
We look for material that is fresh, and takes a realistic approach in dealing with contemporary social issues. Stories that focus on the idea of truth, with the Bible as the main source of absolute truth, continue to interest us.

Single Mother
A Support Group in Your Hands

National Organization of Single Mothers
P.O. Box 68
Midland, NC 28107-0068

Editor: Andrea Engber

Description and Readership
Published by the National Organization of Single Mothers and dedicated to helping single moms meet the challenges of daily life, this nonprofit newsletter offers information, emotional support, and advice.
- **Audience:** Single mothers
- **Frequency:** 6 times each year
- **Distribution:** Subscription; membership
- **Circulation:** Unavailable
- **Website:** www.singlemothers.org

Freelance Potential
10% written by nonstaff writers. Publishes 8 freelance submissions yearly. Receives 1–2 queries and unsolicited mss monthly.

Submissions
Query or send complete ms. Accepts photocopies and computer printouts. SASE. Response time varies.
Articles: Word length varies. Informational articles. Topics include parenting, money and time management, absent dads, dating, death, handling ex-families, pregnancy and childbirth, adoption, donor insemination, child support, paternity, custody, and visitation rights.
Depts/columns: Word length varies.

Sample Issue
8 pages (no advertising): 6 articles; 2 depts/columns. Sample copy, $2.95 with 9x12 SASE.
- "The Failing of Picture Perfect Parents." Article discusses ways to balance self, parenthood, and real life, and increase self-confidence as a parent.
- "Ending the Deadbeat Dilemma." Article suggests a way to locate deadbeat parents through motor vehicle renewals and new employment applications.
- Sample dept/column: "As I See It. . . ." is an opinion column that offers forum for discussing issues on raising children and teens.

Rights and Payment
Rights vary. Payment policy rates and policy vary.

Editor's Comments
We continue to need material that replaces previously held myths about single mothers with positive advice. We want research-backed information that supports the theory that children of single-parent households are well rounded, intelligent, and emotionally secure. Profiles and interviews with successful mothers outside of marriage will be considered, as will articles on moms from diverse social, economic, religious, and cultural backgrounds.

Skating

United States Figure Skating Association
20 First Street
Colorado Springs, CO 80906

Director of Publications: Amy Partain

Description and Readership
This magazine promotes the programs, personalities, and events of the U.S. Figure Skating Association. It reports on trends affecting the sport and covers skating competitions for its readers, most of whom are pre-teen and teenage girls active in the sport of figure skating.
• **Audience:** 5 years–Adult
• **Frequency:** 10 times each year
• **Distribution:** Subscription; other
• **Circulation:** 45,000
• **Website:** www.usfsa.org

Freelance Potential
70% written by nonstaff writers. Publishes 15 freelance submissions yearly; 10% by unpublished writers, 20% by authors who are new to the magazine. Receives 6 queries and unsolicited mss monthly.

Submissions
Query with résumé, clips or writing samples, and photo ideas; or send complete ms with photos or art ideas. Accepts photocopies, Macintosh Zip disk submissions, and email to skatingmagazine@usfsa.org. SASE. Responds in 1 month.
Articles: 750–2,000 words. Informational articles; profiles; and interviews. Topics include association news, competitions, techniques, personalities, and training.
Depts/columns: 600–800 words. Competition results, profiles of skaters and coaches, sports medicine, fitness, and technique tips.
Artwork: B/W or color prints, slides, or transparencies. Electronic images scanned at 300 dpi.

Sample Issue
60 pages: 4 articles; 11 depts/columns. Sample copy, $3 with 9x12 SASE. Guidelines available.
• "World Synchronized Skating Championships." Article covers the 2004 event held in Zagreb, Croatia.
• Sample dept/column: "Basic Skills" reports on Lace-Up for Leukemia, a fundraising event that benefits the Massachusetts chapter of The Leukemia and Lymphoma Society.

Rights and Payment
First serial rights. Articles, $75–$150. Depts/columns, $75. Artwork, payment rate varies. Pays on publication. Provides 5–10 contributor's copies.

Editor's Comments
Most of our articles are written by freelancers. We seek timely material that is representative of the USFSA, educational, and relevant to our figure skating audience.

Skipping Stones
A Multicultural Magazine

P.O. Box 3939
Eugene, OR 97403-0939

Editor: Arun N. Toké

Description and Readership
In print for over 15 years, this magazine celebrates and explores ecological and cultural richness and diversity. It offers articles and stories by both young and adult writers.
• **Audience:** 8–17 years; teachers; parents
• **Frequency:** 5 times each year
• **Distribution:** Subscription; newsstand; schools; libraries
• **Circulation:** 2,500
• **Website:** www.skippingstones.org

Freelance Potential
75% written by nonstaff writers. Publishes 200–250 freelance submissions yearly; 20% by unpublished adult writers, 80% by young authors. Receives 80+ unsolicited mss monthly.

Submissions
Send complete ms with cover letter. Accepts photocopies, computer printouts, Macintosh disk submissions, and simultaneous submissions if identified. Availability of artwork improves chance of acceptance. SASE. Responds in 3–4 months.
Articles: To 750 words. Essays and contemporary nonfiction. Topics include community service, family relationships, technology, problem-solving, sustainable living, disabilities, role models, and living abroad.
Fiction: To 750 words. Genres include multicultural, ethnic, inspirational, and historical fiction; humor; and folktales.
Depts/columns: 100–200 words. News, book reviews, opinion pieces, community action, and proverbs.
Artwork: B/W and color prints. Line art.
Other: Puzzles, activities, games, and jokes. Submit seasonal material 3 months in advance.

Sample Issue
36 pages (no advertising): 19 articles; 2 stories; 12 poems; 8 depts/columns. Sample copy, $5 with 9x12 SASE ($1 postage). Writers' guidelines and calendar available.
• "Women's Image in the Media." Article discusses how society's values pressure women to be thin.
• "Escaping Elephants." Story tells how elephants grow tired of the zoo and plan an escape out of the city.

Rights and Payment
First and reprint rights. No payment. Provides up to 4 contributor's copies and 25% discount on additional copies.

Editor's Comments
We aim to create an active experience for our readers that is relevant to local and global issues. Send us something that represents cultural and linguistic diversity that is presented in a fun and creative way. No adult poetry, please.

Slap

High Speed Productions
1303 Underwood Avenue
San Francisco, CA 94124

Editor: Mark Whiteley

Description and Readership
This magazine targets teens who are into skateboarding, street-style clothing, and the latest sounds from hip-hop, rap, and rock performers. Each issue includes photographs of the world's best skateboarders, interviews, product updates, and music reviews.
- **Audience:** YA
- **Frequency:** Monthly
- **Distribution:** 50% newsstand; 10% subscription; 40% other
- **Circulation:** 130,000
- **Website:** www.slapmagazine.com

Freelance Potential
20% written by nonstaff writers. Publishes 25+ freelance submissions yearly.

Submissions
Send complete ms. Accepts photocopies, computer printouts, IBM or Macintosh disk submissions, and simultaneous submissions if identified. Availability of artwork improves chance of acceptance. SASE. Responds in 2 months.
Articles: Word length varies. Informational and how-to articles; interviews; and personal experience pieces. Topics include skateboarding, contest reports and statistics, skateboard equipment, music, and recreation.
Depts/columns: Word length varies. Short news items, skateboarding tricks, and music reviews.
Artwork: 35mm B/W negatives; color prints and transparencies. B/W and color line art.
Other: Cartoons and comics about skateboarding and popular music.

Sample Issue
152 pages (40% advertising): 7 articles; 9 depts/columns. Sample copy, free with 9x12 SASE ($1.95 postage). Guidelines and editorial calendar available.
- "Skate Bros." Article profiles two skateboarding buddies; includes detailed photographs that show their skateboarding maneuvers.
- Sample dept/column: "Shorts" explains how a crew came together to build a skatepark in San Diego.

Rights and Payment
First rights. All material, payment rate varies. Pays on publication. Provides 1 contributor's copy.

Editor's Comments
Don't attempt a piece for us unless you're thoroughly familiar with the language of the streets and of skateboarders.

Social Studies and the Young Learner

C & I University of Texas
1 University Station, #D5700
Austin, TX 78712

Editor: Dr. Sherry Field

Description and Readership
Educators who work in the field of social studies turn to this professional journal for its articles on new trends in education, news, practical lesson ideas, read-aloud stories, activities, and games.
- **Audience:** Teachers
- **Frequency:** Quarterly
- **Distribution:** Subscription; newsstand
- **Circulation:** 15,000
- **Website:** www.socialstudies.org

Freelance Potential
95% written by nonstaff writers. Publishes 32 freelance submissions yearly; 30% by unpublished writers, 50% by authors who are new to the magazine. Receives 5 mss monthly.

Submissions
Send complete ms. Accepts photocopies and computer printouts. SASE. Responds to queries in 1 year.
Articles: To 2,000 words. Informational articles; profiles; and personal experience pieces. Topics include current events, gifted education, multicultural and ethnic subjects, social issues, history, and special education.
Fiction: Word length varies. Folktales; folklore; multicultural, ethnic, and historical fiction.
Depts/columns: To 500 words. Crafts and cooking.
Artwork: B/W and color prints and transparencies. Line art.
Other: Filler, puzzles, and activities.

Sample Issue
32 pages: 3 articles; 3 depts/columns. Sample copy, $7.50. Guidelines, theme list, and editorial calendar available.
- "Identifying with Ancestors: Tracking the History of America." Article outlines a project for use in fourth and fifth grade classrooms that will help children see how they connect with a rich cultural heritage.
- "Neighbors in Autumn: Service Learning with Elders." A teacher recounts how she developed a program for sixth graders to regularly visit a retirement home and spend time with the residents.

Rights and Payment
All rights. No payment.

Editor's Comments
Most of our writers are professional educators who can share their successful programs, opinions, and practical project ideas with other teachers. We are interested in hearing ideas that are appropriate for kindergarten through sixth grade education.

South Florida Parenting

5555 Nob Hill Road
Sunrise Hill, FL 33351

Managing Editor: Vicki McCash Brennan

Description and Readership

A mix of articles, tips, informational resources, and activities fills the pages of this regional magazine. Distributed free to parents, it covers a variety of parenting topics including child development, health, education, nutrition, finances, marriage issues, as well as travel destinations for the family.
• **Audience:** Parents
• **Frequency:** Monthly
• **Distribution:** Controlled; schools; other
• **Circulation:** 110,000
• **Website:** www.sfparenting.com

Freelance Potential

90% written by nonstaff writers. Publishes 150–180 freelance submissions yearly; 20% by authors who are new to the magazine. Receives 200+ unsolicited mss monthly.

Submissions

Send complete ms. Accepts photocopies, computer printouts, disk submissions, and email submissions to vmccash@ sfparenting.com. SASE. Responds in 2–3 months.
Articles: 800–2,000 words. Informational and how-to articles; profiles; interviews; and personal experience pieces. Topics include family life, travel, parenting, education, leisure, music, health, and regional events.
Depts/columns: To 750 words. Book, music, video, and product reviews; family finance; health; nutrition; and advice on infants and preteens.

Sample Issue

148 pages (60% advertising): 3 articles; 17depts/columns; 1 calendar. Guidelines available.
• "Telling Tales." Article discusses the benefits of storytelling, and offers ways to involve children in telling stories.
• "Natural Naples." Article highlights several natural environments that are available to explore in Florida.
• Sample dept/column: "Family Web" takes looks at several kid-friendly websites that teach children how to create and grow gardens.

Rights and Payment

One-time regional rights. Written material, $75–$300. Pays on publication. Provides copies upon request.

Editor's Comments

Topical features that are well-researched, well-written, and well-sourced are of interest to us. We are seeing too many personal essays with no real sourcing. Keep in mind that we provide up-to-date, regional information to parents that is reliable and useful.

Spider

The Magazine for Children

Cricket Magazine Group
P.O. Box 300, 315 Fifth Street
Peru, IL 61354

Associate Editor: Heather Delabre

Description and Readership

Launched in 1994, this popular magazine provides simple, lively stories and articles that young children love to read. It also includes poems and activities.
• **Audience:** 6–9 years
• **Frequency:** Monthly
• **Distribution:** Subscription; newsstand
• **Circulation:** 78,000
• **Website:** www.cricketmag.com

Freelance Potential

97% written by nonstaff writers. Publishes 50 freelance submissions yearly; 30% by unpublished writers, 50% by authors who are new to the magazine. Receives 200 unsolicited mss each month.

Submissions

Send complete ms; include biography for nonfiction. Accepts photocopies, computer printouts, and simultaneous submissions. SASE. Responds in 2–3 months.
Articles: 300–800 words. Informational and how-to articles; profiles; and interviews. Topics include animals, nature, science, technology, history, multicultural issues, foreign cultures, and the environment.
Fiction: 300–1,000 words. Easy-to-read stories. Genres include humor, fantasy, fairy tales, folktales, realistic and historical fiction, and science fiction.
Other: Puzzles, activities, games, and hidden pictures. Poetry, to 20 lines.

Sample Issue

34 pages (no advertising): 1 article; 4 stories; 2 poems; 4 activities. Sample copy, $4.95 with 9x12 SASE. Guidelines available.
• "Swamp Scramblers." Article describes how unique mudskipper fish are able to survive both on land and in the water.
• "The Case of the Vanishing TVs." Story features an iguana and a salamander who are detectives hired to solve a robbery at a warehouse.

Rights and Payment

All rights. Articles and fiction, $.25 per word. Poetry, to $3 per line. Other material, payment rate varies. Pays on publication. Provides 2 contributor's copies.

Editor's Comments

Humor submissions are always of interest to us. Other genres that we like to see include fantasy, folklore, and realistic fiction. We strive to make our magazine a fun-filled publication for independent readers. Make sure your writing style matches our young audience, and that activities are age-appropriate.

Spirit

Sisters of St. Joseph of Carondelet
1884 Randolph Avenue
St. Paul, MN 55105-1700

Editor: Joan Mitchell

Description and Readership
This Catholic publication for teens does not shy away from tackling difficult situations that can occur in anyone's life. Each issue revolves around the theme found in that Sunday's gospel. True accounts of teens facing real-life experiences and using faith to guide them toward solutions give readers examples of how to cope with their own challenges.
- **Audience:** YA
- **Frequency:** 28 times each year
- **Distribution:** 100% subscription
- **Circulation:** 30,000
- **Website:** www.goodgroundpress.com

Freelance Potential
50% written by nonstaff writers. Publishes 6–10 freelance submissions yearly; 50% by unpublished writers. Receives 16 queries and unsolicited mss monthly.

Submissions
Query or send complete ms. Accepts photocopies, computer printouts, and simultaneous submissions if identified. SASE. Responds to queries in 1 month, to mss in 6 months.
Articles: To 1,200 words. Informational and factual articles. Topics include peer pressure, moral dilemmas, social problems, risk taking, dating, eating disorders, drug and alcohol abuse, physical handicaps, family issues, community service, missionary work, and youth ministry. Also publishes profiles of adults who exemplify Christian values.
Fiction: To 1,200 words. Genres include contemporary fiction. Also publishes short stories about issues that affect teens.

Sample Issue
4 pages (no advertising): 2 articles; 1 story; 3 activities. Sample copy, free. Guidelines available.
- "A Day I Didn't Want to Begin." Article relates the story of a teen's attitude that changes when she discovers her mother is terminally ill.
- "Jesus' Resurrection: What Hope Does It Give Us?" Article discusses the meaning of the word "resurrection" and what this event in Jesus' life means for Catholics.

Rights and Payment
All rights. Written material, $200. Pays on publication. Provides 5–10 contributor's copies.

Editor's Comments
We like to receive submissions that address America's cultural diversity, current events, and problems in society, as well as youth service projects in parishes, schools, neighborhoods, or cities.

SportingKid

Suite 300
3650 Brookside Parkway
Alpharetta, GA 30022

Editor: Michael J. Pallerino

Description and Readership
Parents seeking an active, healthy lifestyle for their families find information that addresses this need in *SportingKid*. The magazine also reports in depth on a variety of youth sports. Profiles of professional athletes are featured along with interviews with youth players who are making their mark in the world of sports.
- **Audience:** Parents
- **Frequency:** 6 times each year
- **Distribution:** Subscription; newsstand
- **Circulation:** 400,000
- **Website:** www.sportingkid.com

Freelance Potential
20–30% written by nonstaff writers. Publishes 10 freelance submissions yearly; 10% by authors who are new to the magazine. Receives 50 queries monthly.

Submissions
Query or send complete ms. Accepts email submissions to editor@sportingkid.com. Queries must be pasted into the email message; manuscripts must be attached in a Microsoft Word document. SASE. Responds in 1 month.
Articles: Word length varies. Informational and how-to articles and personal experience pieces. Topics include sports played by children, coaching, and training.
Depts/columns: Word length varies. The culture of youth sports, new product information, profiles of prominent sports figures, and essays from a parent's perspective.

Sample Issue
44 pages: 5 articles; 5 depts/columns. Sample copy and guidelines available at website.
- "From the Word 'Go.'" Article reports on what the Nike company is doing to fight obesity and physical inactivity among kids.
- "The 'Gonzo' Factor." Article profiles Luis Gonzalez of the Arizona Diamondbacks.
- Sample dept/column: "Health & Wellness" recommends ways to avoid getting "Little League elbow."

Rights and Payment
First and electronic rights. All material, payment rate varies. Pays on publication.

Editor's Comments
We welcome articles on topics related to any youth sport, including those sports that may receive little or no coverage elsewhere. We cover all sports—from football and soccer to cycling, the martial arts, fencing, and table tennis.

Sports Illustrated for Kids

135 West 50th Street
New York, NY 10020-1393

Managing Editor: Neil Cohen

Description and Readership
Middle-grade readers enjoy this popular magazine for its articles, news, and exciting photos covering different sports topics, teams, and athletes.
- **Audience:** 8–14 years
- **Frequency:** Monthly
- **Distribution:** 71% subscription; 27% controlled; 2% newsstand
- **Circulation:** 1.1 million
- **Website:** www.sikids.com

Freelance Potential
30% written by nonstaff writers. Publishes 30 freelance submissions yearly. Receives 17 queries monthly.

Submissions
Query or send complete ms. Send for writers' guidelines to determine which department your material should be sent to. Responds in 2 months.
Articles: Lead articles and profiles, 500–700 words. Short features, 500–600 words. Topics include professional and aspiring athletes, fitness, health, safety, sports tips, hobbies, science, technology, and multicultural issues.
Depts/columns: Word length varies. Events coverage, humor, trivia, puzzles, and games.

Sample Issue
56 pages (24% advertising): 9 articles; 8 depts/columns; 1 calendar of events; 1 poster. Sample copy, $3.50 with 9x12 SASE to *Sports Illustrated for Kids*, P.O. Box 830609, Birmingham, AL 35283. Writers' guidelines available.
- "Heavy Hitter." Article profiles hard-hitting safety Roy Williams of the Dallas Cowboys.
- "Raising Baby Bulls." Article highlights the careers of Eddy Curry and Tyson Chandler, two young Chicago Bulls players who are helping the team return to greatness.
- Sample dept/column: "End Zone" offers a match quiz on universities and players.

Rights and Payment
All rights. Articles, $100–$1,500. Depts/columns, payment rate varies. Pays on acceptance. Provides author's copies.

Editor's Comments
While most of our articles are written by staff, we are always on the lookout for unusual stories or special interest stories. Presently, we are interested in articles on inspiring kid athletes. Articles must be written on a fifth-grade reading level. Please note that we do not accept fiction or poetry.

Stone Soup
The Magazine by Young Writers and Artists

P.O. Box 83
Santa Cruz, CA 95063

Editor: Gerry Mandel

Description and Readership
Established in 1973, Stone Soup has become one of the best known magazines to showcase the work of young writers. Children under the age of 14 are encouraged to submit their best stories, poems, essays, and reviews.
- **Audience:** 8–14 years
- **Frequency:** 6 times each year
- **Distribution:** 50% subscription; 25% newsstand; 25% schools
- **Circulation:** 20,000
- **Website:** www.stonesoup.com

Freelance Potential
100% written by nonstaff writers. Publishes 65 freelance submissions yearly; 90% by unpublished writers, 90% by authors who are new to the magazine. Receives 15,000 unsolicited mss monthly.

Submissions
Contributors must be under 14 years of age. No simultaneous submissions. Send complete ms. Responds in 6 weeks only if work is under consideration.
Fiction: To 2,500 words. Genres include science fiction; adventure; mystery; and multicultural, ethnic, and historical fiction.
Depts/columns: Word length varies. Book reviews.
Artwork: Color art.
Other: Poetry.

Sample Issue
48 pages (no advertising): 7 stories; 2 poems; 2 book reviews. Sample copy, $4. Guidelines available.
- "The Kingdom of Stones." Story tells of a budding friendship between two young girls who are new neighbors.
- "Piccadilly Dreams." Story follows a young girl whose dream comes true when her mother buys the girl a horse.
- Sample dept/column: "Book Reviews" critiques a new fantasy about a girl who dreams of becoming a warrior.

Rights and Payment
All rights. Stories and poems, $40. Book reviews, $40. Illustrations, $25. Pays on publication. Provides 2 copies.

Editor's Comments
We want to see stories and poems about the things you feel most strongly about. Whether your work is about imaginary situations or real ones, use your own experiences and observations to give your work depth and a sense of reality. If you would like to review a book for us, send a letter to Ms. Mandel telling her a little bit about yourself and why you want to be a book reviewer.

Story Friends

Mennonite Publishing Network
616 Walnut Avenue
Scottdale, PA 15683-1999

Editor: Susan Reith Swan

Description and Readership
Story Friends is a magazine for children that reinforces Christian values. It features articles and stories about God's creations, family values, and faith.
- **Audience:** 4–9 years
- **Frequency:** Monthly
- **Distribution:** 100% subscription
- **Circulation:** 6,000
- **Website:** www.mph.org

Freelance Potential
90% written by nonstaff writers. Publishes 80 freelance submissions yearly; 10% by unpublished writers, 50% by authors who are new to the magazine. Receives 83 unsolicited mss each month.

Submissions
Send complete ms. Accepts photocopies, computer printouts, and simultaneous submissions if identified. SASE. Responds in 2–3 months.
Articles: 125–300 words. Informational articles. Topics include nature, history, and religion.
Fiction: 300–800 words. Genres include contemporary and multicultural fiction that portray Christian family values, and stories about religious holidays.
Depts/columns: Book reviews, activities, puzzles, and recipes.
Artwork: Color slides and illustrations.
Other: Poetry, 6–12 lines.

Sample Issue
16 pages (no advertising): 3 stories; 5 depts/columns; 2 poems; 2 activities. Sample copy, free with 9x12 SASE (2 first-class stamps). Guidelines available.
- "The Two-Story Tree House." Story connects friendship, brotherhood, and compromise.
- Sample dept/column: "Solomon's Nature Wisdom" looks at how many of God's marvelous creatures use camouflage to blend in with their surroundings.

Rights and Payment
One-time rights. Fiction, $.03–$.05 per word. Other material, payment rate varies. Pays on acceptance. Provides 2 copies.

Editor's Comments
We always need stories, poems, and activities that speak to the needs of children. All material should provide positive ways to express love and caring, introduce readers to different cultures, reinforce the values taught by Christian families, and portray Jesus as a friend who cares.

Story Mates

Christian Light Publications
P.O. Box 1212
Harrisonburg, VA 22803-1212

Editor: Crystal Shanks

Description and Readership
Produced by Christian Light Publications, this weekly take-home story paper for young children of the Mennonite faith offers inspirational stories, Bible-based activities and puzzles, poems, and crafts that focus on God and living life in congruence with Christianity.
- **Audience:** 4–8 years
- **Frequency:** Monthly
- **Distribution:** Subscription; religious instruction
- **Circulation:** 6,200

Freelance Potential
90% written by nonstaff writers. Publishes 200 freelance submissions yearly. Receives 50 unsolicited mss monthly.

Submissions
Send complete ms. Accepts photocopies and computer printouts. SASE. Responds in 6 weeks.
Fiction: Stories related to Sunday school lessons and true-to-life stories, 800 words. Picture stories, 120–150 words.
Other: Biblical puzzles, activities, and crafts. Poetry, word length varies. Submit seasonal material 6 months in advance.

Sample Issue
4 pages (no advertising): 2 stories; 1 activity. Sample copy, free with 9x12 SASE ($.80 postage). Writers' guidelines and theme list available.
- "Ella's Sad Day." Story of a young girl who becomes unhappy after her puppy dies, and learns through Scripture that Jesus loves us even when we are sad.
- Sample dept/column: "The Passover" offers a crossword puzzle with words from the Bible that describe Passover.

Rights and Payment
First, reprint, or multiple-use rights. Fiction, $.03–$.05 per word. Poetry, $.35–$.75 per line. Other material, payment rate varies. Pays on acceptance. Provides 1 contributor's copy.

Editor's Comments
We are currently seeking full-page activities and picture stories. Remember, we target young children ages 4–8. Material must be suitable for that age range, and provide a lesson that shows them how to live in ways that please God. Stories must reflect a spiritual or biblical lesson and be in line with the faith of the Mennonites. Our articles and stories present God's word as truth. They are to build conviction and Christian character and to promote godly living. Writers must have a staunch appreciation for biblical truths as historically taught and practiced by conservative Mennonites. Writers must complete a questionnaire, which is provided when guidelines are requested.

Storytelling Magazine

National Storytelling Network
Suite 5
132 Boone Street
Jonesborough, TN 37659

Chair: Karen Dietz

Description and Readership

Anyone who uses storytelling—teachers, librarians, and professional storytellers—will find information of interest in this magazine. It contains news and applications of the oral storytelling tradition, as well as occasional stories suitable for oral telling.
- **Audience:** Adults
- **Frequency:** 6 times each year
- **Distribution:** 90% controlled; 10% newsstand
- **Circulation:** 6,000
- **Website:** www.storynet.org

Freelance Potential

80% written by nonstaff writers. Publishes 100 freelance submissions yearly; 50% by unpublished writers, 50% by authors who are new to the magazine. Receives 12–13 unsolicited mss monthly.

Submissions

Send complete ms. Accepts photocopies, disk submissions (Microsoft Word), and simultaneous submissions if identified. SASE. Responds in 4 months.
Articles: 1,000–2,000 words. Informational and how-to articles; and personal experience pieces. Topics include storytelling research and analysis, story origins, and ethnic and multicultural issues.
Depts/columns: 500 words. Noteworthy storytelling projects, resources, and reports on activities and events.

Sample Issue

46 pages (25% advertising): 12 articles; 2 stories; 7 depts/columns. Sample copy, $6 (includes postage).
- "Fun, Fun, Fun All the Way." Article attempts to dissect what humor is and looks at some of its different manifestations throughout the history of literature.
- "Laughing with Trickster." Story demonstrates American Indian humor by retelling an Abenaki tale.
- Sample dept/column: "Book Notes" reports on books of interest to National Storytelling Network (NSN) members.

Rights and Payment

First North American serial rights. No payment. Provides 2 contributor's copies.

Editor's Comments

We like to provide new ideas for storytelling sessions to our readers, so we would like to receive specific innovative applications of oral storytelling that can be duplicated. We would also like to receive reports of specific projects and events from the persons who organized them. We are not accepting freelance fiction.

Student Assistance Journal

Suite F
1270 Rankin Drive
Troy, MI 48083

Editor: Susan Hipsley

Description and Readership

This is a publication dedicated to provide helpful and timely information to professionals who work with youths. It addresses problems facing children today—including drug and alcohol abuse. Readers are student assistance personnel, educators, and treatment professionals.
- **Audience:** Student assistance personnel, K–12
- **Frequency:** 4 times each year
- **Distribution:** Unavailable
- **Circulation:** 10,000
- **Website:** www.prponline.net

Freelance Potential

90% written by nonstaff writers. Publishes 12 freelance submissions yearly; 50% by unpublished writers. Receives 3 queries monthly.

Submissions

Query if outside the field. Professionals should send complete ms. Accepts photocopies, computer printouts, IBM DOS-compatible disk submissions (WordPerfect), and simultaneous submissions. SASE. Responds only if interested.
Articles: 1,500 words. Informational and how-to articles; and personal experience pieces. Topics include high-risk students, special education programs, substance abuse prevention, legal issues, federal funding, and staff development.
Depts/columns: 750–800 words. Book reviews, events, commentaries, short news items, legal issues, media resources, and related research.

Sample Issue

34 pages (20% advertising): 3 articles; 9 depts/columns. Sample copy, free. Guidelines available.
- "When Do We Intervene?" Article examines the delicate balance between student assistance leaders who know when a student needs help and parents' denial of the facts.
- "Talking with Kids about Alcohol and Other Drugs." Article provides a format to use when talking to kids about drugs.
- Sample dept/column: "News You Can Use" provides practical information for student assistant professionals.

Rights and Payment

First rights. All material, payment rate varies. Pays on publication. Provides 5 contributor's copies.

Editor's Comments

We are looking for success stories that will help student assistance professionals, as well as articles on elementary prevention, innovative solutions to problems, and inspirational personal experiences.

Student Leader

Oxendine Publishing
P.O. Box 14081
Gainesville, FL 32604-2097

Associate Editor: John Lamothe

Description and Readership
Promoting effective student leadership among high school and college students is the goal of this publication. It wants to help students understand how being a fair, conscientious, and moral student leader ties into their future careers.
- **Audience:** College students
- **Frequency:** 3 times each year
- **Distribution:** Schools; subscription
- **Circulation:** 130,000
- **Website:** www.studentleader.com

Freelance Potential
10% written by nonstaff writers. Publishes 10 freelance submissions yearly; 50% by unpublished writers, 80% by authors who are new to the magazine. Receives 5 queries monthly.

Submissions
Query only. Accepts photocopies, computer printouts, and simultaneous submissions. Availability of artwork improves chance of acceptance. SASE. Responds in 6 weeks.
Articles: 1,000 words. Informational articles. Topics include organizational management, service projects, fund-raising, student motivation, interpersonal skills, promoting special events, editorial standards, communication, and volunteerism.
Depts/columns: 250 words. College and university group activities and short news items.
Artwork: Color prints and 35mm slides.

Sample Issue
32 pages (50% advertising): 8 articles; 1 dept/column. Sample copy, $3.50 with 9x12 SASE ($1.07 postage). Guidelines and editorial calendar available.
- "Shape up or Ship out: How to Handle a Lame Advisor." Article advises how to establish good relations with a student advisor.
- "SG vs. Administration: How to Heal an Ailing Relationship." Article discusses steps to take to solidify a positive working relationship with a college or university president.
- Sample dept/column: "FYI" brings readers up-to-date on a variety of college issues.

Rights and Payment
All rights. All material, payment rate varies. Pays on publication. Provides 1 contributor's copy.

Editor's Comments
Our focus is student leadership and the various aspects associated with it: organizational skills, fund-raising, ethical issues of student government, working with campus media, and building relationships with advisors and members of the administration.

Student Leadership

6400 Schroeder Road
P.O. Box 7895
Madison, WI 53707-7895

Editorial Assistant: Shelley Soceka

Description and Readership
This student leadership journal is published by the intervarsity Christian fellowship for Christian college students who participate in and lead student fellowship groups. Its mission is to bring readers news and information that will help them be better leaders.
- **Audience:** 18+ years
- **Frequency:** 3 times each year
- **Distribution:** 95% controlled; 5% subscription
- **Circulation:** 10,000
- **Website:** www.ivcf.org/slj

Freelance Potential
75% written by nonstaff writers. Publishes 1 freelance submission yearly. Receives 8 unsolicited mss monthly.

Submissions
Send complete ms. Accepts photocopies, computer printouts, and simultaneous submissions if identified. SASE. Responds in 6 months.
Articles: Word length varies. Informational, self-help, and how-to articles; and personal experience pieces. Topics include campus life, ministry, religion, leadership, student outreach programs, dating, relationships, popular culture, college, careers, and social issues.
Depts/columns: Word length varies. Trends and cultural observations, ideas and notes from chapters, and fellowship strategies.
Other: Poetry, no line limits.

Sample Issue
32 pages (no advertising): 5 articles; 4 depts/columns. Sample copy, $4 with 9x12 SASE ($1.25 postage). Guidelines and theme list available.
- "No Longer Color Blind." Article stresses the importance of discovering and acknowledging different cultures.
- "Yes, Lord." A staff worker for international students in the Boston area is interviewed.
- Sample dept/column: "Chapter Strategy" offers ideas for reaching out to students.

Rights and Payment
First rights. Written material, $50–$100. Pays on acceptance. Provides 2 contributor's copies.

Editor's Comments
Our readers are interested in suggestions for how to reach out to fellow students and encourage them to be part of the fellowship. They also like to hear from members who can share a success story or an idea for improving the work of the fellowship.

Suburban Parent

Middlesex Publications
850 Route 1
North Brunswick, NJ 08902

Editor: Melodie Dhondt

Description and Readership
Raising children involves educating, entertaining, and keeping them healthy and safe. This tabloid covers it all with information and local resources pertinent to families living in central New Jersey.
- **Audience:** Parents
- **Frequency:** Monthly
- **Distribution:** 96% controlled; 4% other
- **Circulation:** 78,000
- **Website:** www.NJParentWeb.com

Freelance Potential
80% written by nonstaff writers. Publishes 12 freelance submissions yearly; 20% by unpublished writers, 40% by authors who are new to the magazine. Receives 60 unsolicited mss monthly.

Submissions
Query with writing samples. Accepts photocopies, computer printouts, and simultaneous submissions if identified. Availability of artwork improves chance of acceptance. SASE. Responds in 2–8 weeks.
Articles: 700–1,000 words. Informational and how-to articles. Topics include family issues; parenting; pregnancy; childbirth; sports; careers; financial issues; cultural events; and restaurant, book, and media reviews.
Artwork: B/W or color prints.
Other: Submit seasonal material 4 months in advance.

Sample Issue
30 pages (60% advertising): 8 articles; 1 dept/column; 2 directories; 1 calendar. Sample copy, free with 9x12 SASE. Guidelines and editorial calendar available.
- "Ten Easy & Inexpensive Summer Activities." Article guides parents in the direction of family activities that are exciting but don't cost a lot of money.
- "Queasy Days of Summer." Article lists suggestions to reduce or eliminate motion sickness in children while riding in a car.
- "How to Become a Sidewalk Naturalist." Article describes activities to do with children on a walk.

Rights and Payment
Rights policy varies. Articles, $30. Artwork, payment rate varies. Pays on acceptance. Provides 1+ contributor's copies.

Editor's Comments
Check our editorial calendar for upcoming themes and if you have an idea that fits, query us. Please note that our material is geared toward parents.

Sugar

64 North Row
London W1K 7LL
England

Editor: Claire Irvin

Description and Readership
Girls age thirteen to eighteen read this fashion/celebrity magazine for its articles on teen life and coverage on such issues as beauty, health, fashion, and friendship. Much of it is devoted to teen idols and other celebrities.
- **Audience:** 13–18 years
- **Frequency:** Monthly
- **Distribution:** Subscription; newsstand
- **Circulation:** 363,000
- **Website:** www.sugarmagazine.co.uk

Freelance Potential
20% written by nonstaff writers. Publishes 60 freelance submissions yearly; 80% by unpublished writers, 100% by authors who are new to the magazine. Receives 4 queries monthly.

Submissions
Send résumé only. Accepts computer printouts. SAE/IRC. Responds in 1 month.
Articles: 1,200–1,800 words. Informational and self-help articles; profiles; and interviews. Topics include popular culture, music, health, fitness, fashion, beauty, and social issues.
Depts/columns: Word length varies. Advice and new product information.
Other: Quizzes. Submit seasonal material on Christmas and Valentine's Day 3 months in advance.

Sample Issue
138 pages (24% advertising): 7 articles; 25 depts/columns; 2 quizzes. Sample copy, £4.10. Guidelines available.
- "Are You Dying for a Fag?" Article investigates why teens continue to smoke despite health and social risks.
- "Gun Crime Put Me in Jail." Article profiles a young, black rap singer who served time for gun possession and now campaigns against gun violence.
- Sample dept/column: "How Embarrassing!" features stories from readers caught in unfortunate situations that caused them embarrassment.

Rights and Payment
All rights. Articles, $250. Depts/columns, payment rate varies. Pays on acceptance. Provides author's copies.

Editor's Comments
Our goal is to bring our readers the latest stories of interest to teens, as well as brief items and photos on hot looks, fashion, hair, and makeup. Much of our editorial is devoted to celebrity items and writers with inside contacts or information on famous U.S. or U.K. personalities are always welcome.

SuperScience

Scholastic Inc
555 Broadway
New York, NY 10012-3999

Editor: Nancy Honovich

Description and Readership
Real science presented in an interest-capturing format keeps middle-grade students fascinated while learning. Each issue contains a fictional science mystery based on real science facts. A teacher's guide is included each month.
- **Audience:** Teachers and students, grades 3–6
- **Frequency:** 8 times each year
- **Distribution:** 100% schools
- **Circulation:** 250,000
- **Website:** www.scholastic.com/superscience

Freelance Potential
75% written by nonstaff writers. Publishes 2 freelance submissions yearly; 50% by authors who are new to the magazine. Receives 1 query monthly.

Submissions
Query with résumé and clips. No unsolicited mss. Accepts photocopies. SASE. Response time varies.
Articles: 300–1,000 words. Informational and how-to articles; profiles; interviews; and personal experience pieces. Topics include earth, physical, and life science; health; technology; chemistry; and other areas of the science field.
Depts/columns: Word length varies. Science news.
Artwork: 8x10 B/W and color prints. Line art.
Other: Puzzles and activities.

Sample Issue
16 pages (no advertising): 2 articles; 1 story; 1 dept/column; 4 activities. Sample copy, free with 9x12 SASE. Guidelines and editorial calendar available.
- "Dinner Time!" Article looks at how some wild critters, such as spiders, fish, snakes, and giraffes, eat and process the foods they find.
- "The Case of the Switched Score." Story uses the physical properties of clay, used in lead pencils, to form the basis of a mystery plot.
- Sample activity: "Hands On" relates to the article on animal eating habits by showing how stomach enzymes help break down food.

Rights and Payment
First rights. Articles, $75–$600. Other material, payment rate varies. Pays on publication. Provides 2 contributor's copies.

Editor's Comments
We don't accept unsolicited manuscripts, but we suggest you check our editorial calendar and query with your area of expertise noted so we can match writers and assignments.

Surfing

Suite C
950 Calle Amanecer
San Clemente, CA 92673

Editor: Evan Slater

Description and Readership
Although some female surfers pick up this magazine, the average reader is a young adult male who has been surfing for approximately seven years. Readers consider this magazine an authority on the sport and consult it for high-intensity articles designed to help them improve their surfing skills and develop new ones.
- **Audience:** YA–Adult
- **Frequency:** Monthly
- **Distribution:** Newsstand; subscription
- **Circulation:** 105,000
- **Website:** www.surfingthemag.com

Freelance Potential
35% written by nonstaff writers. Publishes 15 freelance submissions yearly; 50% by unpublished writers. Receives 6 unsolicited mss monthly.

Submissions
Query or send complete ms. Accepts computer printouts, Macintosh disk submissions (Quark Xpress or Microsoft Word), and simultaneous submissions if identified. SASE. Responds in 1 month.
Articles: 2,000–3,000 words. Informational and how-to articles; profiles; and interviews. Topics include surfing techniques and equipment, destinations, surfing personalities, fashion, nature, the environment, and music.
Depts/columns: 35–500 words. Opinion pieces, photos, and new product information.
Artwork: Color prints.

Sample Issue
160 pages: 3 articles; 10 depts/columns. Sample copy, $3.99 at newsstands. Guidelines available.
- "Andy Rings the Bell." Article reports on the results of the Rip Curl Pro and profiles the surfers who placed in the final four.
- Sample dept/column: "Decode" explains the key points of a surfing move.
- Sample dept/column: "Rant" discusses a surfer's lament—crowds at the beach.

Rights and Payment
One-time rights. Written material, $.10–$.25 per word. Pays on publication. Provides 2 contributor's copies.

Editor's Comments
Writers should bring unique experiences to our readers. We'd like to see reports of news and developments in the world of surfing, as well as destination pieces.

Susquehanna Valley Parent

252 West 4th Street
Williamsport, PA 17701

Editor: Jessica Lamey

Description and Readership
Regional news and general information on families and parenting provide good resources for readers in the Susquehanna Valley area of Pennsylvania.
- **Audience:** Parents
- **Frequency:** Monthly
- **Distribution:** Subscription; newsstands; schools
- **Circulation:** 37,000
- **Website:** www.svparent.com

Freelance Potential
95% written by nonstaff writers. Publishes 50–100 freelance submissions yearly; 50% by unpublished writers, 50% by authors who are new to the magazine. Receives 10 unsolicited mss monthly.

Submissions
Send complete ms. Accepts photocopies, computer printouts, and Macintosh and ASCII disk submission. Retains all material for possible use; does not respond until publication. Include SASE if holding ms is not acceptable.
Articles: To 1,000 words. Informational and how-to articles; profiles; interviews; reviews; and personal experience pieces. Topics include parenting, regional news, current events, travel, recreation, hobbies, nature, and ethnic subjects.
Depts/columns: Word length varies. Health issues and parenting advice.
Artwork: B/W and color prints.
Other: Seasonal material.

Sample Issue
24 pages (50% advertising): 6 articles; 10 depts/columns; 3 activities; 1 calendar. Sample copy, free with 9x12 SASE. Guidelines and editorial calendar available.
- "Chiropractic Health: What Not to Do on Your Next Vacation." Article provides suggestions that will help make vacations pleasant, not overwhelming.
- "Animal Safety: Protecting Children and Responsible Ownership." Article suggests ways parents can help children avoid unpleasant encounters with animals.
- Sample dept/column: "Family Finance" offers tips for sound family money management.

Rights and Payment
One-time and electronic rights. Articles, $25. Artwork, payment rate varies. Pays on publication. Provides tearsheets.

Editor's Comments
All information, including general subject matter, should have a local slant to accommodate our readership.

SW Florida Parent & Child

5664 Jerez Court
Fort Myers, FL 33919

Editor: Connie Ramos-Williams

Description and Readership
This regional parenting paper now appears monthly and brings readers articles on a diverse range of subjects, from health and fitness, to family travel. All of its material covers topics of interest for families with young children who are living in southwest Florida.
- **Audience:** Parents
- **Frequency:** Monthly
- **Distribution:** 100% controlled
- **Circulation:** 20,000
- **Website:** www.swparentchild.com

Freelance Potential
50% written by nonstaff writers. Publishes 40–50 freelance submissions yearly; 5% by unpublished writers, 10% by authors who are new to the magazine. Receives 25 queries and unsolicited mss monthly.

Submissions
Query or send complete ms. Accepts photocopies and computer printouts. SASE. Response time varies.
Articles: Word length varies. Informational articles; profiles; and personal experience pieces. Topics include family issues, education, travel, sports, health, fitness, computers, and social and regional issues.
Depts/columns: Word length varies. Dining, travel, parenting, education, and nutrition.

Sample Issue
56 pages: 2 articles; 14 depts/columns. Guidelines available.
- "Tune-In to Fun When the TV's Off." Article offers ideas for activities that keep children busy without television.
- "Wee Workouts." Article profiles exercise programs in the area designed for very young children.
- Sample dept/column: "Grandparenting" suggests that grandparents take the time to tell grandchildren stories about their family history and family traditions.

Rights and Payment
All rights. Written material, $25–$40. Pays on publication.

Editor's Comments
As you will see when you read an issue, we cover a wide range of material in each issue; some in the form of regular columns, others as full-length articles. Any idea that you think will interest our readers will get consideration from our editors. Keep in mind that while we do run national stories on issues impacting family life, we always include material that will give the story a regional background. Most of our writers live in the area and have children or grandchildren of their own.

Swimming World and Junior Swimmer

Suite 200
90 Bell Rock Plaza
Sedona, AZ 86351

Editor-in-Chief: Dr. Phillip Whitten

Description and Readership

This official magazine of three swimming associations is acknowledged as "the Bible" of competitive swimming, and is the world's foremost authority on all aspects of competitive swimming. Readers find instruction, information, and inspiration for the sport.
- **Audience:** All ages
- **Frequency:** Monthly
- **Distribution:** 90% subscription; 10% newsstand
- **Circulation:** 59,000
- **Website:** www.swiminfo.com

Freelance Potential

75% written by nonstaff writers. Publishes 5–10 freelance submissions yearly; 5% by unpublished writers, 25% by authors who are new to the magazine. Receives 16+ queries monthly.

Submissions

Query. Accepts photocopies, computer printouts, disk submissions (WordPerfect 3.1), and email queries to swimworld@aol.com. Availability of artwork improves chance of acceptance. SASE. Responds in 2 months.
Articles: 500–3,500 words. Informational and how-to articles; interviews; profiles; and personal experience pieces. Topics include swimming, training, competition, medical advice, swim drills, nutrition, exercise physiology, and fitness.
Depts/columns: 500–750 words. Swimming news, new product reviews, and nutrition advice.
Artwork: Color prints and transparencies. Line art.
Other: Activities, games, and jokes. Submit seasonal material 1–2 months in advance.

Sample Issue

62 pages (30% advertising): 3 articles; 10 depts/columns. Sample copy, $4.50 with 9x12 SASE ($1.80 postage). Writers' guidelines available.
- "Stanford's Shining Light." Article profiles the senior captain of Stanford University's swim team and her quest for a place on the Olympic team.
- Sample dept/column: "Coaching" details a swimming stroke through description and photos.

Rights and Payment

All rights. Written material, $.12 per word. Artwork, payment rate varies. Pays on publication. Provides 2–5 author's copies.

Editor's Comments

Readers of our publication include swimmers, coaches, officials from around the world, and technical directors.

Synapse

25 Beacon Street
Boston, MA 02108

Editor

Description and Readership

Teens involved with the Young Religious Unitarian Universalists read and write for this publication which offers ideas for social change.
- **Audience:** 14–21 years
- **Frequency:** Twice each year
- **Distribution:** 100% subscription
- **Circulation:** 15,000
- **Website:** www.uua.org/YRUU

Freelance Potential

85% written by nonstaff writers. Of the freelance submissions published yearly, 90% are by unpublished writers.

Submissions

Send complete ms with résumé. Accepts disk submissions (Quark) and email submissions to YRUU@uua.org. SASE. Responds in 1 month.
Articles: Word length varies. Informational articles and personal experience and opinion pieces. Topics include current events, social issues, popular culture, regional events, youth programs, history, and ethnic and multicultural issues.
Depts/columns: Word length varies. Readings by Unitarian Universalist youth, sermons, homilies, religious and spiritual reflections, and social action news.
Artwork: B/W or color prints or transparencies. 3x5 line art.
Other: Puzzles, activities, games, and jokes related to Unitarian Universalism.

Sample Issue

40 pages (7% advertising): 7 articles; 10 depts/columns; 1 events calendar. Sample copy, free. Guidelines available.
- "Relearning History." Article looks at modern educational standards and values from a student's point of view after he realizes that his education was more of a straight jacket than a creative experience.
- "My Rant to an English Teacher." Article elucidates a student's feelings about being in high school and being coerced to think, do, and act the same as everyone else even though the writer saw the world differently.
- "Dark." Article philosophizes about the difference between light of day and dark of night and the reaction to each.

Rights and Payment

All rights. No payment.

Editor's Comments

We choose articles submitted by Unitarian Universalist youth, adults working with youth, and other interested parties. Some preference is given to new authors.

Syracuse Parent

5910 Firestone Drive
Syracuse, NY 13206

Editor: Mary Wasmund

Description and Readership

How-to, human interest, and general interest articles on parenting issues, as well as profiles of Syracuse-area individuals who positively impact family lives, appear regularly in the pages of this regional tabloid.
- **Audience:** Parents
- **Frequency:** 7 times each year
- **Distribution:** 70% controlled; 20% schools; 10% subscription
- **Circulation:** 22,500
- **Website:** www.syracuseparent.com

Freelance Potential

40% written by nonstaff writers. Publishes 15 freelance submissions yearly; 25% by unpublished writers, 10% by authors who are new to the magazine. Receives 8 queries monthly.

Submissions

Query. Accepts photocopies and computer printouts. SASE. Responds in 4–6 weeks.
Articles: 800–1,000 words. How-to, practical application, and personal experience pieces; interviews; humor; and profiles. Topics include family issues, parenting, animals, pets, education, current events, regional news, social issues, nature, computers, music, travel, and sports.
Depts/columns: Staff written.
Other: Submit seasonal and holiday material 3–4 months in advance.

Sample Issue

22 pages (50% advertising): 9 articles; 8 depts/columns. Sample copy, guidelines, and editorial calendar, $1 with 9x12 SASE.
- "Daytripping in CNY." Article reports on places of interest to families with young children.
- "Ice-Scream!" Article offers recipe for making homemade vanilla ice cream.
- Sample dept/column: "Single Parenting" offers practical suggestions on how to keep a civil relationship with the other parent for the child's benefit.

Rights and Payment

First rights. Articles, $25–$30. Pays on publication.

Editor's Comments

Our goal is to be the most in-depth and up-to-the minute source of information and ideas for families living in the Syracuse region. We prefer to use articles that include a strong regional angle, either in the way of a sidebar featuring local resources or opinions, or with strong original-source material used in interviews with experts in the region.

Take Five Plus

The General Council of the Assemblies of God
1445 North Boonville Avenue
Springfield, MO 65802-1894

Assistant Editor: Kimberly Stephens

Description and Readership

Three months of devotionals for teen members of the Assemblies of God congregations are found in each issue, encouraging readers to improve the presence of God in their lives. Each day's reading combines a short scene, a scriptural passage, and a question to stimulate thoughtful reflection.
- **Audience:** 12–19 years
- **Frequency:** Quarterly
- **Distribution:** 90% religious instruction; 10% subscription
- **Circulation:** 25,000
- **Website:** www.radiantlife.org

Freelance Potential

80% written by nonstaff writers. Of the freelance submissions published yearly, 5% are by unpublished writers and 10% are by authors new to the magazine.

Submissions

All material is assigned. Send letter of introduction with résumé, church background, and clips or writing samples. Accepts photocopies and computer printouts. SASE. Responds in 3 months.
Articles: 200–235 words. Daily devotionals based on scripture readings.
Artwork: Accepts material from teenagers only. 8x10 B/W prints and 35mm color slides. 8x10 or smaller color line art.
Other: Poetry by teens, to 20 lines.

Sample Issue

128 pages (no advertising): 90 devotionals; 3 poems. Guidelines and sample devotional available upon request for sample assignment.
- "The Potter's Hands." Devotional bases its lesson on Isaiah to teach how patience allows us to change from the inside, while learning what God wants us to do.
- "Because of Who He Is." Devotional uses a Psalm to show that God deserves our worship because he is God, and as such has the right to work changes in us.
- "Open Eyes." Devotional bases its message of spiritual insight on a passage from Luke.

Rights and Payment

First rights. Written material, $.05 per word. Artwork, payment rate varies. Pays on publication. Provides 2 contributor's copies.

Editor's Comments

All of our outside writing is done by contract. Freelancers who are interested in working for us must contact us for guidelines and sample assignments.

Tar Heel Junior Historian

North Carolina Museum of History
4650 Mail Service Center
Raleigh, NC 27699-4650

Editor: Doris McLean Bates

Description and Readership

Through a balanced selection of scholarly articles, photographs, and illustrations, *Tar Heel Junior Historian* presents the history of North Carolina to the students of the state. Its goal is to help local students better understand and appreciate their place in American history.
- **Audience:** 9–18 years
- **Frequency:** Twice each year
- **Distribution:** 100% North Carolina schools
- **Circulation:** 9,000
- **Website:** http://ncmuseumofhistory.org

Freelance Potential

50% written by nonstaff writers. Publishes 15 freelance submissions yearly; 40% by unpublished writers, 20% by authors who are new to the magazine.

Submissions

Query. No unsolicited mss. SASE. Response time varies.
Articles: 700–1,000 words. Informational articles; profiles; interviews; and personal experience pieces. Topics include regional history, and social, multicultural, and ethnic issues.
Fiction: Word length varies. Genres include historical, ethnic, and multicultural fiction; folktales; and folklore.
Artwork: B/W and color prints or transparencies. Line art.
Other: Puzzles, activities, and word games.

Sample Issue

38 pages (no advertising): 11 articles; 5 activities. Sample copy, $4 with 9x12 SASE ($2 postage). Guidelines and theme list available.
- "North Carolina Society in 1953 and in 2003." Article contrasts aspects of life in the year the Tar Heel Junior Historian Association was founded with life in the state today.
- "The Junior Historian Movement." Article traces the development of statewide junior historical societies from a successful beginning in 1938 through the present day.
- "Then and Now." Article spotlights THJHA members of past decades who reflect on how their junior historian experiences affected their lives.

Rights and Payment

All rights. No payment. Provides 10 contributor's copies.

Editor's Comments

The articles that appear in our magazine are written by expert scholars of North Carolina history. Each one is selected by the editor in consultation with conceptual editors and other experts. If you have the credentials to write for us, we will review your query.

Teacher Librarian

Box 34069
Department 343
Seattle, WA 98124-1069

Publisher: Dr. Ken Haycock

Description and Readership

School library professionals turn to this special publication for the latest news and trends related to making school libraries as efficient and broad in scope as possible.
- **Audience:** Professional librarians and educators
- **Frequency:** 5 times each year
- **Distribution:** 100% subscription
- **Circulation:** 10,000
- **Website:** www.teacherlibrarian.com

Freelance Potential

60% written by nonstaff writers. Publishes 10 freelance submissions yearly; 25% by unpublished writers, 50% by authors who are new to the magazine. Receives 6 queries and unsolicited mss monthly.

Submissions

Query or send complete ms with resumé, abstract, and bibliography. Accepts photocopies, computer printouts, disk submissions, and email submissions to admin@teacherlibrarian.com. SASE. Responds in 2 months.
Articles: 2,000+ words. Informational and analytical articles and profiles. Topics include library programming issues, audio/visual materials, cooperative teaching, and young adult services.
Depts/columns: Staff written.

Sample Issue

62 pages (20% advertising): 6 articles; 10 depts/columns. Guidelines and editorial calendar available.
- "Using International Literature to Enhance the Curriculum." Article offers suggestions on how to incorporate titles written by international writers into American curriculum for students in K–12.
- "Connecting with Aboriginal Students." Article stresses the need for finding ways to reach out to North American aboriginal students.
- Sample dept/column: "Author Portrait" profiles two sisters who work together as writers.

Rights and Payment

All rights. Written material, $100. Pays on publication. Provides 2 contributor's copies.

Editor's Comments

Submissions from professionals in library services are always welcome. If you feel you have a story that would benefit our readers and help them enhance their skills, program development, or program delivery, we would like to hear from you. Remember that all of our submissions are reviewed by members of our advisory board.

Teacher Magazine

Editorial Projects in Education
Suite 100
6935 Arlington Road
Bethesda, MD 20814

Features/Comment Editor

Description and Readership

Launched in 1989, *Teacher Magazine* is read by educators working in kindergarten through 12th grade classrooms. Its goal is to bring teachers the information they need to help shape the future of American education.
- **Audience:** Teachers
- **Frequency:** 6 times each year
- **Distribution:** Subscription; controlled
- **Circulation:** 120,000
- **Website:** www.teachermagazine.org

Freelance Potential

40% written by nonstaff writers. Publishes 35–40 freelance submissions yearly; 80% by unpublished writers, 20% by authors who are new to the magazine. Receives 40 unsolicited mss monthly.

Submissions

Send complete ms. Accepts computer printouts. SASE. Responds in 3 months.
Articles: To 3,000 words. Educational articles; commentaries; and personal experience and opinion pieces. Topics include K–12 education, professional development, classroom teaching, literacy, technology, and bilingual education.
Depts/columns: 1,000–1,250 words. "Viewpoints" features opinion pieces on precollegiate education. "First Person" offers school-related personal experiences.
Artwork: 8x10 B/W and color prints. Line art.
Other: Puzzles, activities, and poetry.

Sample Issue

72 pages: 6 articles; 12 depts/columns. Sample copy, $4. Guidelines available.
- "Great Expectations." A Chicago teacher draws on her own experiences pushing her students to succeed.
- "Free for All." Article takes a look at Summerhill, the boarding school that inspired education reformers in the 1960's.
- Sample dept/column: "Hidden Genius" examines the difficulties gifted students face in cookie-cutter classrooms.

Rights and Payment

First rights. Written material, payment rate varies. Pays on publication. Provides 3 contributor's copies.

Editor's Comments

You will most likely have a chance at getting published here with a piece for one of our columns. Opinion pieces in particular are frequently written by freelancers. In conjunction with our mission to help make American education the best it can be, we welcome innovative ideas from educators.

Teachers & Writers

7th Floor
5 Union Square West
New York, NY 10003-3306

Publications Director: Christopher Edgar

Description and Readership

Hoping to spark creative ideas for teaching the art of writing, this magazine offers innovative techniques and practical and theoretical methods for teachers of kindergarten to grade 12.
- **Audience:** Teachers
- **Frequency:** 6 times each year
- **Distribution:** 100% subscription
- **Circulation:** 3,000
- **Website:** www.twc.org

Freelance Potential

70% written by nonstaff writers. Publishes 25 freelance submissions yearly; 5% by unpublished writers, 50% by authors who are new to the magazine. Receives 10 unsolicited mss each month.

Submissions

Send complete ms. Accepts photocopies, computer printouts, and simultaneous submissions if identified. No email submissions. SASE. Response time varies.
Articles: 750–5,000 words. Practical and theoretical articles featuring innovative teaching ideas; and fresh approaches to familiar teaching methods. Topics include teaching writing in conjunction with the visual arts; teaching oral history; and teaching writing to senior citizens. Also publishes translations.
Depts/columns: Word length varies. Information on events and book reviews.
Other: Submit seasonal material 6 months in advance.

Sample Issue

28 pages (no advertising): 1 article; 5 depts/columns; 1 poem. Sample copy, $4. Guidelines available.
- "Letters to a Young Writer." Article tries to answer the question, "Why Do You Write?" asked of a writer who also teaches English literature courses.
- Sample dept/column: "Passwords" shows how the works of two poets help elementary children discover the wonderful world of creativity that's locked in their own minds.
- Sample dept/column: "The Literary Anatomy" analyzes the cinquain, a poetic form with a strict, regulated form.

Rights and Payment

First serial rights. Written material, $20 per printed column. Pays on publication. Provides 10 contributor's copies.

Editor's Comments

In addition to writing, we will consider submissions on related subjects, such as oral history, teaching writing in combination with visual art, and translation.

Teachers Interaction

Concordia Publishing House
3558 South Jefferson Avenue
St. Louis, MO 63118-3698

Editor: Thomas A. Nummela

Description and Readership
Sunday school teachers, pastors, educational directors, and superintendents read this Christian publication for information on how to share God's word with children in preschool through grade six classrooms.
- **Audience:** Sunday school teachers
- **Frequency:** Quarterly
- **Distribution:** 70% subscription; 30% churches
- **Circulation:** 12,000
- **Website:** www.cph.org

Freelance Potential
95% written by nonstaff writers. Publishes 20 freelance submissions yearly; 10% by unpublished writers, 20% by authors who are new to the magazine. Receives 4 mss monthly.

Submissions
Prefers email submissions to tom.nummela@cph.org. Accepts query or complete ms; include Social Security number. Accepts photocopies and computer printouts. SASE. Responds in 3 months.
Articles: To 1,100 words. How-to articles; and personal experience pieces. Topics include education, theology, teaching methods, and child development.
Depts/columns: 400 words. Mission stories, grade-specific teaching tips, and classroom ideas.
Other: Practical ideas for teachers, 100–200 words. Submit seasonal material 10 months in advance.

Sample Issue
28 pages (no advertising): 6 articles; 10 depts/columns. Sample copy, $4.99. Guidelines available.
- "30 Ways to Enhance Sunday School Visibility." Article provides practical ideas for increasing awareness of Sunday school and youth ministry activities.
- "The Pastor's Role in Sunday School." Article examines how pastors can actively affect the success of Sunday school.
- Sample dept/column: "The Adaptive Teacher" suggests how Sunday school teachers can best work with autistic students.

Rights and Payment
All rights. Articles, $55–$110. "The Teacher's Toolbox," $20–$40. Pays on publication. Provides 1 contributor's copy.

Editor's Comments
We give preference to articles that reflect the beliefs and practices of The Lutheran Church Mission , but do not require writers to be members of the church. We have a constant need for practical, original, creative teaching ideas that our readers can use.

Teachers of Vision

Christian Educators Association International
P.O. Box 41300
Pasadena, CA 91114

Contributing Editor: Judy Turpen

Description and Readership
As the official publication of the Christian Educators Association International, this inspirational magazine offers articles dealing with educational issues as well as organizational news.
It is read by Christian teachers who work in public schools.
- **Audience:** Christian teachers
- **Frequency:** 6 times each year
- **Distribution:** 75% controlled; 25% newsstand
- **Circulation:** 8,500
- **Website:** www.ceai.org

Freelance Potential
80% written by nonstaff writers. Publishes 20–25 freelance submissions yearly; 10% by unpublished writers, 40% by authors who are new to the magazine. Receives 4 unsolicited mss monthly.

Submissions
Send complete ms with brief biography. Accepts letter-quality computer printouts and disk submissions (RTF files or Microsoft Word) with hard copy. Prefers email submissions to judy@ceai.org (RTF files). SASE. Responds in 2–3 months.
Articles: 400–1,000 words. How-to articles, personal experience pieces, and documented reports, 800–1,000 words. Topics include issues related to Christian education, educational philosophy, and methodology. Interviews with noted Christian educators, 500–800 words. Teaching techniques, news, and special events, 400–500 words.
Depts/columns: 100–200 words. Reviews of books, videos, curricula, and other curricula resources for K–12 teachers.
Other: Submit seasonal material 4 months in advance.

Sample Issue
16 pages (1% advertising): 7 articles; 6 depts/columns. Sample copy, free with 9x12 SASE (4 first-class stamps). Writers' guidelines available.
- "A Teacher's Dilemma" Essay tells of a teacher who loses test papers from her new class and decides to tell her students the truth.
- Sample dept/column: "In God We Trust" explores using the Know-Want to Know-Learned chart as a classroom tool.

Rights and Payment
First and electronic rights. Articles, $20–$40. Reviews, $5. Pays on publication. Provides 3 contributor's copies.

Editor's Comments
We are currently seeking more articles in math/science areas. All material must have a Christian slant. Make sure you are up-to-date on trends in contemporary education.

Teaching PreK-8

40 Richards Avenue
Norwalk, CT 06854

Editorial Director: Patricia Broderick

Description and Readership
Kindergarten through eighth grade teachers will find ideas for tried and proven classroom projects, teaching strategies, and activities for all grade levels, as well as professional development help and information on pertinent technology for classroom use. Issues that affect classroom teaching are also included.
- **Audience:** Teachers, pre-K–grade 8
- **Frequency:** 8 times each year
- **Distribution:** 100% subscription
- **Circulation:** 107,000
- **Website:** www.teachingk-8.com

Freelance Potential
43% written by nonstaff writers. Publishes 40 freelance submissions yearly; 90% by authors who are new to the magazine. Receives 166 unsolicited mss monthly.

Submissions
Send complete ms. No simultaneous submissions. SASE. Responds in 1 month.
Articles: To 1,000 words. Informational and how-to articles and personal experience pieces. Topics include gifted and special education, curriculum development, educational trends, and teaching methods.
Depts/columns: Staff written.
Artwork: Color prints. No digital art.

Sample Issue
96 pages (50% advertising): 8 articles; 21 depts/columns; 1 calendar; 1 reproducible. Sample copy, $4.50 with 9x12 SASE (10 first-class stamps). Guidelines and theme list available.
- "Susan Striker: Outside the Lines." Article profiles the author of the Anti-Coloring Books that help foster creativity in kids by encouraging them to think in different ways.
- "Shake, Rattle, and Learn." Article shows how using songs from the fifties helps students build their skills while having fun at the same time.
- Sample dept/column: "Integrating Science in Your Classroom" demonstrates how science can be used to enhance most classroom subjects.

Rights and Payment
All rights. Written material, $20–$50. Artwork, payment rate varies. Pays on publication. Provides 2 contributor's copies.

Editor's Comments
Creative teaching is the crux of our publication, and we would like to see more submissions of classroom-tested ideas, programs, and projects, that utilize creativity in the classroom. Please do not send articles about testing standards.

Teaching Theatre

2343 Auburn Avenue
Cincinnati, OH 45219

Editor: James Palmarini

Description and Readership
Teachers seeking to enrich their theater arts classes find practical advice and inspiration in the articles that appear in this magazine. Material on professional development relevant to theater teachers appears along with reports on successful strategies other teachers have used in their middle school and high school classrooms.
- **Audience:** Theater teachers
- **Frequency:** Quarterly
- **Distribution:** 80% controlled; 20% other
- **Circulation:** 4,000
- **Website:** www.etda.org

Freelance Potential
60% written by nonstaff writers. Publishes 15–20 freelance submissions yearly; 20% by unpublished writers, 50% by authors who are new to the magazine. Receives 5 queries each month.

Submissions
Query with outline. Accepts photocopies and computer printouts. SASE. Responds in 1 month.
Articles: 1,000–3,000 words. Informational articles and personal experience pieces. Topics include theater education, the arts, and curriculum materials.
Depts/columns: Word length varies. "Promptbook" features classroom exercises, ideas, technical advice, and textbook or play suggestions.

Sample Issue
32 pages (no advertising): 3 articles; 2 depts/columns. Sample copy, $2 with 9x12 SASE ($2 postage). Guidelines available.
- "Analyzing the Work." Article argues that writing a critical response to a dramatic work is a necessary part of artistic exploration and craft development.
- "The Rasaboxes Exercise." Article describes an activity that involves a set of playing squares, each one representing an emotional state that the players "become" as they move through the squares.
- Sample dept/column: "Promptbook" explains how to create a timed improv show.

Rights and Payment
One-time rights. Written material, payment rate varies. Pays on publication. Provides 5 contributor's copies.

Editor's Comments
The teachers who read our magazine are experienced and skilled. They need material that goes beyond the basics—material far more substantial than general acting exercises.

Tech Directions

Prakken Publications
832 Phoenix Drive
P.O. Box 8623
Ann Arbor, MI 48107

Managing Editor: Susanne Peckham

Description and Readership

Professionals in technology, industrial, and vocational education turn to this magazine for information on teaching techniques, unusual projects, laboratory and classroom procedures, and issues facing the field.
- **Audience:** Teachers and administrators
- **Frequency:** 10 times each year
- **Distribution:** 98% controlled; 2% subscription
- **Circulation:** 43,000
- **Website:** www.techdirections.com

Freelance Potential

65% written by nonstaff writers. Publishes 60–70 freelance submissions yearly; 25% by unpublished writers, 40% by authors who are new to the magazine. Receives 10 unsolicited mss monthly.

Submissions

Query or send complete ms. Accepts photocopies, computer printouts, Macintosh disk submissions, and Macintosh-compatible email submissions to susanne@techdirections.com. SASE. Responds to queries in 1 week, to mss in 1 month.
Articles: To 3,000 words. Informational and how-to articles; and new product information. Topics include vocational and technical career education, technology, electronics, graphics, industrial arts, manufacturing, and computers.
Depts/columns: Word length varies. Legislative news, tool reviews, and new product reviews.

Sample Issue

32 pages (40% advertising): 7 articles; 10 depts/columns. Sample copy, $5 with 9x12 SASE (2 first-class stamps). Guidelines and editorial calendar available.
- "Vacuum Cannon!" How-to article explains the power of atmospheric pressure through a project to build a cannon out of an ordinary shop vac.
- "Career Directions." Article discusses the skills necessary for a successful job interview.
- Sample dept/column: "Mastering Computers" takes a look a some annoying web advertising methods.

Rights and Payment

All rights. Articles, $50 for first page, $25 for each additional page. Depts/columns, to $25. Pays on publication. Provides 3 contributor's copies.

Editor's Comments

We would like to see submissions on classroom projects that integrate science and technology, however, we have an abundance of computer articles.

Techniques

Connecting Education and Careers

1410 King Street
Alexandria, VA 22314

Editor: Susan Reese

Description and Readership

This magazine is published by the Association for Career and Technical Education to keep its members apprised of developments in the technical education field. It reports on legislation affecting career and technical education, offers in-depth features on issues and programs, profiles educators and other newsmakers, and covers ACTE events.
- **Audience:** Educators
- **Frequency:** 8 times each year
- **Distribution:** 80% membership; 15% schools; 5% subscription
- **Circulation:** 40,000
- **Website:** www.acteonline.org

Freelance Potential

50% written by nonstaff writers. Publishes 10–20 freelance submissions yearly; 15% by unpublished writers, 30% by authors who are new to the magazine. Receives 8 unsolicited mss monthly.

Submissions

Query or send complete ms on disk with hard copy. Accepts photocopies, computer printouts, and disk submissions (Microsoft Word). SASE. Responds in 4 months.
Articles: To 2,000 words. Informational and how-to articles; profiles; and reviews. Topics include technology, careers, education, computers, college, current events, science, math, and social issues.
Depts/columns: 500–850 words. Organizational news, opinion pieces, and legislative updates.
Artwork: Color prints and transparencies. Line art.
Other: Submit material about the end of the school year in March.

Sample Issue

62 pages (30% advertising): 8 articles; 5 depts/columns. Guidelines and theme list available at website.
- "Teacher Portfolios: Displaying the Art of Teaching." Article explains how to create a portfolio of accomplishments.
- "Tips for Writing Winning Résumés." Article offers guidelines teachers can use to help their students with this task.

Rights and Payment

All and Internet rights. Articles, payment rate varies. Depts/columns, $500. Pays on publication.

Editor's Comments

Your chances of publication dramatically increase if you submit an opinion piece to our "Forum" section, or a brief description of a successful program for "It Works."

Technology & Learning

CMP Media, Inc.
600 Harrison Street
San Francisco, CA 94107

Managing Editor: Michelle Thatcher

Description and Readership

Professionals involved with technology in kindergarten to grade 12 educational settings find cutting edge ideas and evaluations in this magazine. Readers are encouraged to consider new ways of using technology for teaching and inspiring students.
- **Audience:** Educators and technology coordinators
- **Frequency:** 11 times each year
- **Distribution:** 70% subscription; 30% newsstand
- **Circulation:** 85,000
- **Website:** www.techlearning.com

Freelance Potential

50–60% written by nonstaff writers. Publishes 44 freelance submissions yearly; 5% by authors who are new to the magazine. Receives 5–8 queries monthly.

Submissions

Query with outline and clips or writing samples. Accepts photocopies and computer printouts. SASE. Responds in 3 months.
Articles: 1,200–2,500 words. Informational and how-to articles. Topics include technology, education, research, teaching, and controversial issues in education and technology. Also publishes reviews of software used in education.
Depts/columns: To 600 words. News; classroom-tested teaching ideas; and technology primers.
Other: Comics.

Sample Issue

68 pages (40% advertising): 12 articles; 2 depts/columns; 1 pull-out calendar. Sample copy, $3 with 9x12 SASE ($3 postage). Guidelines and editorial calendar available.
- "Smart Tools: Making Technology Work." Article uses a Q&A format to describe how new technology can be used in a classroom setting.
- "7 Time-Saving Tools." Article summarizes how several innovative tools are being used by educators.
- "Show Him the Money." Article outlines how one school district created a more efficient and cost-effective plan for using technology in schools.

Rights and Payment

First rights. Articles, $400–$600. Software reviews, $150. Depts/columns, payment rate varies. Pays on publication. Provides 1 contributor's copy.

Editor's Comments

We are always looking for success stories for our "What Works" section that details the use of technology in innovative ways to help students and teachers.

Teen

3000 Ocean Park Boulevard
Santa Monica, CA 90405

Editor: Jane Fort

Description and Readership

Pre-teen and teenage girls enjoy this colorful glossy for its articles that cover the latest in fashion, entertainment, health, beauty, nutrition, and social issues.
- **Audience:** 12–16 years
- **Frequency:** Quarterly
- **Distribution:** 100% newsstand
- **Circulation:** 600,000
- **Website:** www.teenmag.com

Freelance Potential

60% written by nonstaff writers. Of the freelance submissions published yearly, 5% are by authors who are new to the magazine. Receives 10 queries monthly.

Submissions

Query for nonfiction. Send complete ms for fiction. Accepts photocopies, computer printouts, and simultaneous submissions. SASE. Responds in 2 months.
Articles: 800 words. Informational and how-to articles and personal experience pieces. Topics include relationships, beauty, fashion, music, popular culture, recreation, the arts, crafts, current events, and social issues.
Fiction: 1,000 words. Genres include romance and inspirational fiction.
Depts/columns: Word length varies. Advice.

Sample Issue

112 pages (10% advertising): 14 articles; 3 stories; 6 depts/columns. Sample copy, $3.99 at newsstands.
- "Dream Decoder." Article offers insight into figuring out the meaning behind dreams.
- "The Ultimate Friendship Rules." Article takes a look at ways to help keep a friendship strong.
- Sample dept/column: "Family Matters" offers solutions to family situations.

Rights and Payment

All rights. Written material, payment rate varies. Pays on publication. Provides 2 contributor's copies.

Editor's Comments

We cover topics that are of interest to teenage girls and look for queries with a unique hook. Make sure your writing style matches the voice of our readers, and that you are up-do-date with the young teen scene. Girls of this age look for material that they can relate to, and are eager to be informed on the latest, upcoming fashions and styles. They are beginning to explore relationships, and have a desire to learn about important issues and challenges that teens face in their lives.

Teenage Christian Magazine

P.O. Box 92
Hohenwald, TN 38462

Editor: Ben Forrest

Description and Readership
Centering around the issues that teens face today in their attempt to reconcile religion with the world around them, this online publication stresses positive ways to bring Christian values into the forefront of their lives. It is read by teens and the professionals in the ministry who work with them.
- **Audience:** YA–Adult
- **Frequency:** Unavailable
- **Distribution:** 100% Internet
- **Hits per month:** Unavailable
- **Website:** www.teenagechristian.net

Freelance Potential
50% written by nonstaff writers. Publishes 15–25 freelance submissions yearly. Receives 5 queries, 5 unsolicited mss monthly.

Submissions
Query or send complete ms. Accepts email submissions to teenagechristian@bellsouth.net. Response time varies.
Articles: 450–700 words. Informational articles; profiles; interviews; photoessays; and personal experience pieces. Topics include health, fitness, multicultural and ethnic topics, music, popular culture, religion, and social issues.
Depts/columns: Word length varies. Advice, sports, and music.

Sample Issue
Guidelines available at website.
- "Catching a Lesson with '*Big Fish*'." Article compares the lessons put forth in the movie *Big Fish* to the same type of situations many of us face on a daily basis.
- "How to Be a Terrific Friend." Article suggests several ways to improve relationships with friends, and relates them to specific Bible verses.
- "Celebrate Easter." Article illustrates how normal it is to develop an apathetic attitude toward traditional holy days, and provides ideas that will bring back the old excitement while celebrating them.

Rights and Payment
All rights. Payment policy and rate vary.

Editor's Comments
We are returning to print in July, 2004. We are specifically looking for articles on relationships, spiritual growth, entertainment, and sports. Two of our columns are good places to start: the *Music* column features interviews with Christian artists who are successfully combining professions with spiritual living; and the *Sports* column that gives insights into the minds and behavior of athletes who want to serve God.

Teen Countdown

Juvenile Diabetes Research Foundation
120 Wall Street, 19th Floor
New York, NY 10005

Editor: Sandy Dylak

Description and Readership
Launched in 2004, this magazine addresses the issues and concerns faced by teens with Type 1 diabetes. Published by the Juvenile Diabetes Research Foundation and sponsored by the Freestyle™ Blood Glucose Monitoring system, it offers articles on coping with diabetes, health, and making good choices. Each issue also includes an insert for younger children with Type 1 diabetes, *Countdown for Kids*.
- **Audience:** 12+ years
- **Frequency:** 2 times each year
- **Distribution:** Subscription; other
- **Circulation:** Unavailable
- **Website:** www.jdrf.org

Freelance Potential
25% written by nonstaff writers. Publishes 25 freelance submissions yearly.

Submissions
Query or send complete ms. Accepts photocopies and computer printouts. SASE. Response time varies.
Articles: Word length varies. Informational, factual and self-help articles; profiles; interviews; and personal experience pieces. Topics include coping with Type 1 diabetes, health, careers, college, popular culture, social issues, and diabetes research.
Depts/columns: Word length varies. Diabetes news, career profiles, and advice.

Sample Issue
22 pages: 2 articles; 3 depts/columns. Sample copy available.
- "How Can You Watch out for Yourself When Everyone Else Is Having Fun?" Article offers advice on how to deal with peer pressure and make the right decisions about alcohol, drugs, and dating.
- "Roundtable." Presents the thoughts of teenagers and experts about life with an insulin pump.
- Sample dept/column: "Life's Work" profiles a young emergency room nurse with diabetes who was inspired by the nurses who helped her as a child.

Rights and Payment
First North American serial rights. All material, payment rate varies. Pays on publication. Provides 1 contributor's copy.

Editor's Comments
Our magazine is for teenagers who are living every day with the challenges of diabetes. We're interested in articles that help our readers get through difficult situations, make good choices, and make a difference. We also publish information on the latest diabetes research.

Teen Graffiti

P.O. Box 452721
Garland, TX 75045-2721

Publisher: Sharon Jones-Scaife

Description and Readership
The mission of this new magazine is to become the voice of teenagers across the U.S. by providing a platform for the expression of their styles, concerns, ideas, talents, achievements, and community involvement endeavors. Contributions from teachers offering educational advice appear along with submissions from teens.
• **Audience:** 12–19 years
• **Frequency:** 6 times each year
• **Distribution:** 100% subscription
• **Circulation:** Unavailable
• **Website:** www.teengraffiti.com

Freelance Potential
60% written by nonstaff writers. Publishes 60 freelance submissions yearly.

Submissions
Query or send complete ms. Prefers email submissions to publish@teengraffiti.com. Accepts photocopies and computer printouts. SASE. Response time varies.
Articles: 250 words. Informational articles; personal experience and opinion pieces; and essays. Topics include college, careers, current events, popular culture, and social issues.
Depts/columns: 100–200 words. Educational tips, advice, and resourceful information from teachers of English, reading, science, math, writing, and computers. Teen-to-teen advice and book, music, and movie reviews.
Artwork: B/W or color prints accepted from teens only.
Other: Poetry written by teens.

Sample Issue
22 pages: 1 article; 12 depts/columns; 4 poems. Sample copy available. Guidelines included in each issue.
• "He Makes You Wanna Hollar!" Article profiles a 16-year-old high school junior, who is an up-and-coming star of comedy and entertainment in Dallas, Texas.
• Sample dept/column: "Teens Speak" features a 16-year-old girl's compilation of her top ten worst pick-up lines.
• Sample dept/column: "The Bookshelf" presents a review of *The Princess Diaries*.

Rights and Payment
One-time rights. No payment.

Editor's Comments
Only teachers who are council members of Teen Graffiti may contribute to our magazine. Council members serve on a volunteer basis; there are no time commitments or meetings to attend.

Teen Light

6118 Bend of River Road
Dunn, NC 28334

Publisher: Annette Dammer

Description and Readership
This Christian magazine provides a forum for teens to connect with each other through the written word. Appearing both online and in print format, it features devotionals, essays, poetry, testimonials, and useful resources.
• **Audience:** 10–21 years
• **Frequency:** Internet, weekly; print, quarterly
• **Distribution:** Internet; religious instruction; schools; subscription; churches
• **Circulation:** 2,000
• **Website:** www.teenlight.org

Freelance Potential
50% written by nonstaff writers. Publishes 24 freelance submissions yearly; 75% by unpublished writers, 50% by authors who are new to the magazine. Receives 20 queries monthly.

Submissions
Query with brief introduction. Accepts email submissions to publisher@teenlight.org (no attachments). SASE. Responds in 2 weeks.
Articles: To 500 words. Informational and self-help articles; profiles; devotionals; testimonials; journal entries; photo-essays; and personal experience pieces. Topics include the arts, biography, computers, college, health, gifted education, popular culture, and social issues.
Fiction: To 500 words.
Artwork: B/W and color JPEG files.
Other: Poetry. Submit seasonal material 6 months in advance.

Sample Issue
40 pages (15% advertising): 14 articles. Sample copy, $1.75 with SASE. Writers' guidelines available.
• "Savior in Space." Article discusses the faith of the astronauts of the Columbia tragedy, and how they knew God was with them in space.
• "Go for Your Dreams." Article explains how we should do what we can to make our dreams come true and not sit around and wait for them to happen.
• "Praying in Faith." A teen discusses her mission trip to Mexico and the importance of faith in having prayers answered.

Rights and Payment
Non-exclusive rights. No payment. Provides 3 author's copies.

Editor's Comments
We encourage teens to submit their views on world events, life experiences, and anything else they want to share with other teens. All material must be written with a Christian slant. Artwork and photos are also of interest to us.

Teen Tribute

71 Barber Greene Road
Don Mills, Ontario M3C 2AZ
Canada

Submissions: Robin Stevenson

Description and Readership

Movies, film industry news, celebrity profiles, and popular culture and entertainment are the focus of this publication. Its departments cover teen fashion and beauty, and its editorial content is written specifically for teens.
- **Audience:** 14–18 years
- **Frequency:** Quarterly
- **Distribution:** 90% newsstand; 10% subscription
- **Circulation:** 310,000
- **Website:** www.tribute.ca

Freelance Potential

10% written by nonstaff writers. Publishes 5–10 freelance submissions yearly; 1% by authors who are new to the magazine. Receives 2 queries monthly.

Submissions

Query with clips or writing samples. No unsolicited mss. Availability of artwork improves chance of acceptance. SAE/IRC. Responds in 1–2 months.
Articles: 400–500 words. Informational articles; profiles; interviews; and personal experience pieces Also publishes photoessays. Topics include movies, the film industry, entertainment, the arts, music, popular culture, and social issues.
Depts/columns: Word length varies. Beauty and fashion advice; media reviews.
Artwork: Color prints or transparencies.

Sample Issue

38 pages (50% advertising): 3 articles; 2 depts/columns. Sample copy, $1.95 Canadian with 9x12 SASE ($.86 Canadian postage).
- "Picture Perfect." Article offers an overview of Nicole Kidman's acting career and provides a look at her role in *The Stepford Wives*.
- "Sex Degrees." Article helps readers navigate through the sometimes confusing Hollywood dating scene.
- Sample dept/column: "Star Scoop" features gossip and updates on the personal lives of celebrities.

Rights and Payment

First North American serial rights. Written material, $75–$100 Canadian. Artwork, payment rate varies. Pays on acceptance. Provides 1 contributor's copy.

Editor's Comments

Most of the articles that appear in our magazine are written by our staff, but if you have first-hand, inside information about the contemporary entertainment scene, we would like to hear from you.

Teen Voices

P.O. Box 120-027
Boston, MA 02112-0027

Submissions Editor

Description and Readership

Written for and by teenage girls, this magazine is packed with writing, poetry, and artwork. It offers a forum for girls to express themselves, share their talents and ideas, and show how positive actions make a difference.
- **Audience:** Young adult women
- **Frequency:** Quarterly
- **Distribution:** Newsstand; other
- **Circulation:** 75,000
- **Website:** www.teenvoices.com

Freelance Potential

100% written by nonstaff writers. Publishes 150 freelance submissions yearly; 90% by unpublished writers, 90% by authors who are new to the magazine. Receives 330 unsolicited mss each month.

Submissions

Accepts articles written by teenage girls only. Send complete ms. Response time varies.
Articles: Word length varies. Informational and self-help articles. Topics include family relationships, teenage motherhood, the arts, popular culture, the media, surviving sexual assault, coping with disabilities and chronic illnesses, and experiences from teens around the world.
Fiction: Word length varies. Short stories.
Depts/columns: 500 words. News important to teens.
Artwork: B/W and color prints. Line art. Various art for features, as assigned.
Other: Poetry.

Sample Issue

56 pages (8% advertising): 7 articles; 4 poems; 9 depts/columns. Sample copy, $5. Writers' guidelines and editorial calendar available.
- "Bisexual, Proud & Fighting for Respect." Article takes a look at the lives of bisexual teens and shares their stories.
- "Sex Education: What Are They Teaching You?" Article discusses abstinence-only education vs. comprehensive sexual education in schools.
- Sample dept/column: "Shout! Notes" highlights the work of a teen program director.

Rights and Payment

First or one-time rights. No payment. Provides 5 copies.

Editor's Comments

We are currently seeking more quality short stories. Articles on self-esteem, popular culture, health, politics, racism, and other issues that are important to you are welcome.

Teenwire.com

434 West 33rd Street
New York, NY 10001

Editor: Susan Yudt

Description and Readership
Produced by the Planned Parenthood Federation of America, this website is committed to providing teens with facts about sexual health with the hope that it will aid them in making responsible choices.
- **Audience:** 13–21 years
- **Frequency:** Unavailable
- **Distribution:** Internet
- **Hits per month:** 400,000
- **Website:** www.teenwire.com

Freelance Potential
90% written by nonstaff writers. Publishes 100–156 freelance submissions yearly; 10% by unpublished writers, 25% by authors who are new to the magazine.

Submissions
Query with brief biography and clips or writing samples. Accepts email queries to twstaff@ppfa.org (type "Write for Teenwire" in the subject line). Responds in 1 week.
Articles: 500 words. Informational and factual articles; profiles; interviews; and Spanish pieces. Topics include teen relationships, sexual health, birth control, pregnancy, sexually transmitted diseases, teen activism, international youth issues, the arts, colleges, careers, current events, music, popular culture, recreation, social issues, and multicultural issues.
Other: Puzzles, games, and quizzes.

Sample Issue
Guidelines available at website.
- "Y Stay Friends with Your X." Article discusses how and when to stay friends with an ex when a relationship ends, and offers tips on changing a relationship into a friendship.
- "The Truth about Gay Guys." Article takes a look at myths and misconceptions about gay men.
- "Free 4 Life." Article profiles the life of television co-host Marie "Free" Wright and the Free4Life Foundation, which aims to encourage and strengthen the moral development of teens in Boston, MA.

Rights and Payment
All rights. Articles, $.50 per word to $250. Pays on acceptance.

Editor's Comments
We need more articles on teen culture/issues such as drugs, alcohol, and activism. We welcome inquires from freelance writers who are interested in writing for a teen audience. Freelancers can contribute to five feature sections: "In Focus," "Taking Action," "World Views," "Warehouse," and "TechKnow."

Texas Child Care

P.O. Box 162881
Austin, TX 78716-2881

Editor: Louise Parks

Description and Readership
This journal has been published for more than a quarter century. Its mission is to provide the latest information on all aspects of child development and child care. Published by the Texas Workforce Commission, its audience incudes parents, caregivers, foster parents, educators, state officials, and individuals involved in the management of family homes.
- **Audience:** Parents and caregivers
- **Frequency:** Quarterly
- **Distribution:** 80% controlled; 20% subscription
- **Circulation:** 32,000
- **Website:** www.childcarequarterly.com

Freelance Potential
50% written by nonstaff writers. Publishes 12–15 freelance submissions yearly; 10% by unpublished writers, 50% by authors who are new to the magazine. Receives 2–3 unsolicited mss monthly.

Submissions
Send complete ms. Accepts email submissions to editor@childcarequarterly.com. Responds in 3 weeks.
Articles: 2,500 words. Informational articles about child care, education, program administration, infant care, professional development, and issues and activities relating to school-age children.
Depts/columns: Word length varies. News and updates about child care, parenting, and licensing information.
Other: Submit seasonal material 6 months in advance.

Sample Issue
44 pages (no advertising): 6 articles; 5 depts/columns. Sample copy, $6.50. Guidelines available at website.
- "Fetal Alcohol Syndrome." Article explains this disease and its effects on a child's growth, nervous system, and physical features, and how it impacts behavior in the classroom.
- "Planning an Open House." Article suggests how caregivers can best present their facilities, staff, and programs, and offers ideas for parent-friendly activities.
- Sample dept/column: "Stuff & New Stuff" reviews new teacher resources and books for children.

Rights and Payment
All rights. No payment. Provides 2 contributor's copies.

Editor's Comments
We get a lot of submissions about literacy development—far more than we can use—and not nearly enough on the topics of math, assessment, science, and discovery. Ideally we want to see fresh, successful, classroom-tested materials.

Theory Into Practice

341 Ramseyer Hall
29 West Woodruff Avenue
Ohio State University
Columbus, OH 43210

Managing Editor: Ava M. Stinnett

Description and Readership
In print for over 40 years, this professional thematic journal provides perspectives and scholarly discussions on educational issues. Articles are based on concepts and ideas, and provide teachers with practical knowledge and applications.
- **Audience:** Educators
- **Frequency:** Quarterly
- **Distribution:** 65% schools/libraries; 35% other
- **Circulation:** 2,000
- **Website:** www.coe.ohio-state.edu/tip

Freelance Potential
100% written by nonstaff writers. Publishes 38 freelance submissions yearly; 10% by unpublished writers, 90% by authors who are new to the magazine. Receives 5 queries and unsolicited mss monthly.

Submissions
Query or send 2 copies of complete ms. Accepts photocopies. SASE. Responds in 1–2 months.
Articles: 3,000–4,000 words. Factual and informational articles. Topics include educational technology, cultural diversity, literary theory, teacher quality, cooperative learning, children's literature, mentoring, classroom communication, foreign languages, community service, and curriculum theory.

Sample Issue
142 pages (3% advertising): 11 articles. Sample copy, $12. Guidelines and theme list available.
- "Developing Self-Regulated Writers." Article discusses implementing effective writing instruction that uses self-regulation strategies to enhance students' development as life-long strategic learners.
- "How Classroom Teachers Can Help Students Learn and Teach Them How to Learn." Article takes a look at why students are ineffective learners and offers strategies to improve teaching so students achieve and learn more.

Rights and Payment
All rights. No payment. Provides 2 contributor's copies.

Editor's Comments
Issues of our publication are planned on a thematic basis and most articles are solicited; however we are always interested in outstanding articles on any educational topic. We welcome articles that are logically developed scholarly presentations of both theoretical and practical information. Technical writing should be avoided. We seek articles and reviews relevant to the achievement gap and gifted children.

Thrasher

1303 Underwood Avenue
San Francisco, CA 94124

Editor: Jake Phelps

Description and Readership
Teens who have a passion for skateboarding and snowboarding read *Thrasher*. It covers boarding locales, personalities, and techniques, often using graphic language and/or adult themes. Music industry reports are also included.
- **Audience:** 12–20 years
- **Frequency:** Monthly
- **Distribution:** 30% subscription; 30% newsstand; 40% other
- **Circulation:** 200,000
- **Website:** www.thrashermagazine.com

Freelance Potential
20% written by nonstaff writers. Publishes 20 freelance submissions yearly; 100% by unpublished writers. Receives 6–10 unsolicited mss monthly.

Submissions
Send complete ms. Accepts photocopies, computer printouts, IBM or Macintosh disk submissions, and simultaneous submissions if identified. Availability of artwork improves chance of acceptance. SASE. Responds in 1 month.
Articles: To 1,500 words. Informational articles; profiles; and interviews. Topics include skateboarding, snowboarding, sports, and music.
Fiction: To 2,500 words. Stories with skateboarding and snowboarding themes.
Depts/columns: 750–1,000 words. Skateboarding and snowboarding news, tips, and techniques.
Artwork: Color prints and transparencies. 35mm B/W negatives. B/W and color line art.

Sample Issue
248 pages (45% advertising): 14 articles; 11 depts/columns. Sample copy, $3.99. Guidelines available.
- "Ten Years of Thomas." Article chronicles the 10-year career of Jamie Thomas and describes the influence he has had on the sport of skateboarding.
- "High Noon at the Wallenberg Big Four." Article reports on a skateboarding event in Santa Monica, California.

Rights and Payment
First North American serial rights. Written material, $.10 per word. Artwork, payment rate varies. Pays on publication. Provides 2 contributor's copies.

Editor's Comments
If you want to write for our magazine, you have to be tuned-in to the board sports and music scene. Write in a style that reflects the language and tone of our readers.

Three Leaping Frogs

P.O. Box 2205
Carson City, NV 89702

Publisher: Ellen Hopkins

Description and Readership

Established in 2002, *Three Leaping Frogs* is a regional newspaper published for elementary school children who live in northern Nevada. Each issue includes articles on history, nature, animals, math, and biography—all with a Nevada focus when applicable. Stories and quizzes and games are also a regular feature in the newspaper.
- **Audience:** 7–12 years
- **Frequency:** 6 times each year
- **Distribution:** 100% schools
- **Circulation:** 25,000
- **Website:** www.junipercreekpubs.com

Freelance Potential

70% written by nonstaff writers. Publishes 50 freelance submissions yearly; 50% by unpublished writers, 60% by authors who are new to the magazine. Receives 16–40 mss monthly.

Submissions

Send complete ms. Accepts computer printouts and email submissions to 3leapingfrogs@junipercreekpubs.com. SASE. Responds in 3 months.
Articles: 500 words. Informational articles; profiles; and interviews. Topics include animals, nature, math, fitness, hobbies, biographies, history, and regional news.
Fiction: 1,000 words. Genres include mystery; adventure; humor; and historical, multicultural and science fiction.
Depts/columns: 300 words. Science experiments and advice.
Other: Puzzles, activities, games, and jokes. Poetry. Submit seasonal material 6 months in advance.

Sample Issue

8 pages (no advertising): 10 articles; 2 depts/columns; 2 puzzles. Sample copy, $1 with 9x12 SASE ($.57 postage). Guidelines and theme list available.
- "The Chinese Compass—An Invention That Changed History." Article explains the history behind the first compass, and its impact on history.
- "Amazing Inventions—The Ferris Wheel." The inventor of this amusement park special, George Ferris Jr., is profiled.
- Sample dept/column: "Go Figure" explains what a bank does with customers' money.

Rights and Payment

First rights. No payment. Provides 5 contributor's copies.

Editor's Comments

Keep in mind that we are a very small paper and rarely accept material that is more than 500 words long. We are interested in articles with Western themes at this time.

Tidewater Parent

Suite 102
1300 Diamond Springs Road
Virginia Beach, VA 23455

Editor: Jennifer O'Donnell

Description and Readership

This regional parenting publication caters to families living in the Hampton Roads metro area in Virginia. Distributed free through schools, child-care centers, hospitals, clinics, doctors' offices, and libraries, it publishes articles on health, education, and child development as well as product news, event updates, and resource reports.
- **Audience:** Parents
- **Frequency:** Monthly
- **Distribution:** 50% schools; 50% other
- **Circulation:** 48,000
- **Website:** www.tidewaterparent.com

Freelance Potential

90% written by nonstaff writers. Publishes 40 freelance submissions yearly; 10% by unpublished writers, 50% by authors who are new to the magazine. Receives 6 unsolicited mss monthly.

Submissions

Send complete ms. Will accept previously published mss that can be reprinted. Accepts photocopies and computer printouts. SASE. Response time varies.
Articles: 800–1,200 words. Informational and how-to articles. Topics include parenting, education, child health and development, family travel, and safety.
Depts/columns: Staff written.
Other: Send seasonal material 2–3 months in advance.

Sample Issue

36 pages (50% advertising): 2 articles; 8 depts/columns; 1 events calendar. Sample copy, $2. Writers' guidelines and theme list available.
- "Becoming a Family through Adoption." Article explores the legal issues adoptive parents face, as well as the practical health issues of adopted children.
- "House Calls." Article describes World Changers, a youth organization that helps cities throughout the U.S. take care of blighted houses.
- "Legal Uncertainty." Article reports on a new law that creates some confusion for same-sex couples.

Rights and Payment

Rights vary. Written material, $25. Kill fee, 50%. Pays on publication. Provides 1 contributor's copy.

Editor's Comments

Our magazine is the primary source of local parenting information for Tidewater Peninsula area families. We prefer articles that use a more informal, familiar tone that use real-life situations and people to gain the readers' attention.

Tiger Beat

Suite 700
6430 Sunset Boulevard
Hollywood, CA 90028

Editor: Leesa Coble

Description and Readership
This popular glossy offers teens the latest information on the young stars of the pop music, television, and film industries. Each issue is packed with articles, interviews, profiles, photos, quizzes, and the latest trends in beauty and fashion.
- **Audience:** 10–16 years
- **Frequency:** Monthly
- **Distribution:** 90% newsstand; 10% subscription
- **Circulation:** 200,000
- **Website:** www.tigerbeatmag.com

Freelance Potential
10% written by nonstaff writers. Publishes 10 freelance submissions yearly; 5% by unpublished writers, 10% by authors who are new to the magazine. Receives 8 queries monthly.

Submissions
Query with clips or writing samples. Accepts photocopies, computer printouts, and simultaneous submissions if identified. SASE. Responds in 2 months.
Articles: To 700 words. Interviews; and profiles. Topics include celebrities in the film, television, and recording industries.
Depts/columns: Word length varies. Gossip, advice, quizzes, fashion trends, and new product information.
Artwork: B/W and color prints or slides.
Other: Short updates on young celebrities. Submit seasonal material 3 months in advance.

Sample Issue
82 pages (12% advertising): 16 articles; 18 depts/columns; 20 posters. Sample copy, $3.99 at newsstands.
- "A Weekend with Chad." Article describes what actor Chad Murray likes to do on his weekends off.
- "The Name Game." Article takes a look at the meaning of some of the first names of famous stars.
- Sample dept/column: "Hollywood Hot Spot" offers the latest scoops on celebrities from the music, film, and television scenes.

Rights and Payment
All rights. Written material, $50–$200. Pays on publication. Provides 2 contributor's copies.

Editor's Comments
We provide our readers with the latest news, gossip, and information on what is going on with their favorite celebrities, as well as the ins and outs of fashion and beauty. Keep in mind that most of our readers are female. If you have an insider's angle for an exclusive interview with a top-tier celebrity, we welcome your query.

Time For Kids

Time-Life Building
22nd Floor
1271 Avenue of the Americas
New York, NY 10020

Editor: Martha Pickerill

Description and Readership
The children's version of this famous newsmagazine reports on news and current events in a format designed to engage younger readers. It comes in three versions; *Big Picture* is for kindergarten and first-grade students; *News Scoop* targets second and third graders; and *World Report* is aimed at children in fourth through sixth grade. Each issue covers a theme and includes theme-related writing activities and projects.
- **Audience:** 5–12 years
- **Frequency:** Weekly
- **Distribution:** 100% schools
- **Circulation:** 3.5 million
- **Website:** www.timeforkids.com

Freelance Potential
Less than 5% written by nonstaff writers. Publishes 1–3 freelance submissions yearly. Receives many queries monthly.

Submissions
Query with résumé. No unsolicited mss. SASE. Response time varies.
Articles: Word length varies. Informational and biographical articles. Topics include world news, current events, animals, education, health, fitness, science and technology, math, social studies, multicultural issues, music, popular culture, recreation, regional news, sports, travel, and social issues.
Depts/columns: Word length varies. Short news items and profiles.
Artwork: Color prints or transparencies.
Other: Theme-related activities.

Sample Issue
8 pages (no advertising): 3 articles; 3 depts/columns. Subscription, $3.95.
- "Marking a Civil Rights Milestone." Article reports on the 40th anniversary of the signing of the Civil Rights Act of 1964 and this Act's significance in U.S. history.
- Sample dept/column: "Who's News" interviews *Harry Potter* star Daniel Radcliffe and discusses how he is similar to, and different from, the character he plays.

Rights and Payment
All rights. Written material, payment rate varies. Pays on publication.

Editor's Comments
We are willing to consider submissions from authors who can write about current events and the news in a way that appeals to elementary school and middle-grade students. Contact us with your credentials before submitting an article.

Tiny Giant Magazine

23 Isabella Street
Toronto, Ontario M4Y 1M7
Canada

Submissions Editor: Jeff Denham

Description and Readership
Since its inception in 1940, this magazine has been present-ing the writing, photography, and illustrations of the youth of Canada. Staffed by teens, it is available as an e-zine and as a print publication. News articles on current events appear along with opinion pieces, poetry, fiction, and personal stories.
- **Audience:** 12–20 years
- **Frequency:** Quarterly
- **Distribution:** Unavailable
- **Circulation:** 165,000
- **Website:** www.tgmag.ca

Freelance Potential
50% written by nonstaff writers. Publishes 30 freelance submissions yearly; 50% by unpublished writers, 50% by authors who are new to the magazine. Receives 5 queries and unsolicited mss monthly.

Submissions
Accepts submissions from writers ages 12–20. Query with outline/synopsis; or send complete ms with author photo-graph and phone number. Accepts photocopies, computer printouts, Macintosh disk submissions, and email submis-sions to tgmag@tgmag.ca. SAE/IRC. Responds in 1 month.
Articles: Feature articles, to 1,000 words. Service articles and personal experience pieces, 500 words. Topics include con-temporary, multicultural, and social issues; popular culture; teen success; youth news; careers; families; and sexuality.
Fiction: 800 words. Genres include adventure and science fiction.
Depts/columns: 500 words. Opinion pieces, activities, and interviews.
Other: Poetry. Submit seasonal and sports material 3 months in advance.

Sample Issue
46 pages (8% advertising): 6 articles; 7 depts/columns; 1 poem. Sample copy, guidelines, and editorial calendar avail-able at website.
- "Reality TV: The New Fad?" Opinion piece questions the "reality" of these television programs.
- "Drugs: A Wasteful Facet." Personal experience piece reveals why one teen decided to stop using drugs.

Rights and Payment
First Canadian rights. No payment.

Editor's Comments
We love writers with a sense of humor but also seek work that is serious, smart, thoughtful, and non-conformist.

Tiny Tummies

P.O. Box 5756
Napa, CA 94581

Editor: Sanna Delmonico

Description and Readership
Straightforward information on food and nutrition keeps readers of this publication up to date on what's balanced and healthy to eat. It attempts to stay current with scientific stud-ies and any changes in basic nutrition news. Guidelines for raising healthy children, children's food issues, recipes, and good diet tips are important parts of its contents.
- **Audience:** Parents
- **Frequency:** 6 times each year
- **Distribution:** 100% subscription
- **Circulation:** 10,000
- **Website:** www.tinytummies.com

Freelance Potential
30% written by nonstaff writers. Publishes 10 freelance sub-missions yearly; 15% by authors who are new to the maga-zine. Receives 3 queries and unsolicited mss monthly.

Submissions
Query or send complete ms. SASE. Response time varies.
Articles: 750–1,000 words. Informational and how-to arti-cles; and personal experience pieces. Topics include nutri-tional information, menu ideas, health, family activities, and fitness.
Depts/columns: 200–300 words. Recipes, crafts, cookbook reviews, and new product information.

Sample Issue
12 pages (no advertising): 5 articles; 2 depts/columns. Sample copy, $1; also available at website.
- "Time to Rebuild the Food Pyramid." Article revisits the U.S. Department of Agriculture's Food Guide Pyramid to revise it according to new facts about nutrition and health.
- "Into the Mouths of Babies." Article reminds readers that Vitamin D is an essential ingredient in a child's daily nutri-tion to prevent rickets and promote bone strength.
- Sample dept/column: "In Season" highlights fresh foods that are available in the markets, and includes hints on choosing the best samples, food storage, and recipes.

Rights and Payment
Rights and payment policy vary.

Editor's Comments
We try to provide sound information concerning many of the current nutritional issues, such as organic foods, supplements, food bacteria, and mercury levels in certain fish. We also think that eating is a social activity, especially for families, and like to promote recipes and meal ideas that bring family members together before, during, and after eating.

Today's Catholic Teacher

Suite 300
2621 Dryden Road
Dayton, OH 45439

Editor-in-Chief: Mary Noschang

Description and Readership
Focusing on issues of interest to Catholic teachers from early childhood through junior high, this magazine offers timely information on curriculum, community needs, educational technology, trends, and administration.
- **Audience:** Educators, grades K–8
- **Frequency:** 6 times each year
- **Distribution:** 90% schools; 10% religious instruction
- **Circulation:** 50,000
- **Website:** www.peterli.com

Freelance Potential
95% written by nonstaff writers. Publishes 20 freelance submissions yearly; 50% by authors who are new to the magazine. Receives 16+ queries and unsolicited mss monthly.

Submissions
Query or send complete ms. Accepts photocopies, computer printouts, disk submissions with hard copy, email submissions to mnoschang@peterli.com, and simultaneous submissions if identified. SASE. Responds to queries in 1 month, to mss in 3 months.
Articles: 600–1,500 words. Informational, how-to, and self-help articles. Topics include curriculum development, testing, classroom management, administration, and national issues and trends.
Depts/columns: Word length varies. News items, software, teaching tools, and opinions.
Artwork: 8x10 B/W or color slides, prints, or transparencies.
Other: Classroom-ready reproducible activity pages.

Sample Issue
62 pages (45% advertising): 6 articles; 12 depts/columns. Sample copy, $3. Guidelines and editorial calendar available.
- "Everyday Assessment of Reading." Article outlines how to use daily assessments to improve reading achievement.
- "One Word at a Time." Article discusses programs that are helping to engage students and increase their vocabulary.
- Sample dept/column: "Today's Software" reviews an interactive CD-ROM on teasing, and one on science.

Rights and Payment
All rights. Written material, $100–$250. Pays on publication. Provides contributor's copies upon request.

Editor's Comments
We provide our readers with information on products and resources to help them become more effective educators. In addition to teachers, our readers also include principals, supervisors, superintendents, pastors, and parents.

Today's Christian Woman

465 Gundersen Drive
Carol Stream, IL 60188

Assistant Editor: Holly Robaina

Description and Readership
Christian women turn to this magazine for its inspirational articles on topics relating to health, spiritual growth, faith, personal relationships, and contemporary issues. It offers a biblical prospective on ways to cope with everyday challenges.
- **Audience:** Women
- **Frequency:** 6 times each year
- **Distribution:** Subscription; newsstand
- **Circulation:** 250,000
- **Website:** www.todayschristianwoman.com

Freelance Potential
90% written by nonstaff writers. Publishes 6 freelance submissions yearly. Receives 100 queries monthly.

Submissions
Query with summary and résumé. Accepts photocopies, and computer printouts. No simultaneous submissions. SASE. Responds in 2 months.
Articles: Informational and humorous articles, 1,000–1,800 words. Topics include families, parenting, friendship, marriage, health, self-help, single life, finances, and work. Issue-oriented articles, 1,800–2,000 words. Topics include infertility, homosexuality, ADHD, and negative effects of pornography. Personal experience pieces, 1,500 words. Topics include working through a difficult situation, event, or traumatic turning point. Also publishes practical spiritual-living articles.
Depts/columns: 100–300 words. Reviews, faith at work, and kids' humorous comments.

Sample Issue
80 pages (25% advertising): 10 articles; 12 depts/columns. Sample copy, $5 with 9x12 SASE ($3.19 postage). Writers' guidelines available.
- "What Every Women Needs to Know about Endometriosis." Article discusses a disease in women that often goes undetected and offers alternative treatments.
- "Family Ties." Article offers suggestions to help keep a family circle tight and remain connected to each other.
- Sample Dept/column: "Woman to Woman" offers ideas to help women relax.

Rights and Payment
First rights. Written material, $.20 per word. Pays on acceptance. Provides 2 contributor's copies.

Editor's Comments
We seek humorous and practical spiritual-life pieces, as well as articles on health topics. Please do not send us any more first-person, turning-point articles.

Today's Parent

8th Floor
1 Mount Pleasant Road
Toronto, Ontario M4Y 2YS
Canada

Managing Editor: Sarah Moore

Description and Readership
Mothers and fathers of children, infancy through age 14, turn to *Today's Parent* for practical and philosophical parenting articles. This widely circulated Canadian magazine offers feature articles on health, education, and child behavior.
- **Audience:** Parents
- **Frequency:** 11 times each year
- **Distribution:** Subscription; newsstand; other
- **Circulation:** 175,000
- **Website:** www.todaysparent.com

Freelance Potential
Of the freelance submissions published yearly, many are by unpublished writers and authors who are new to the magazine. Receives several queries monthly.

Submissions
Query with clips or writing samples; include information on article length. No unsolicited mss. Accepts photocopies and computer printouts. SAE/IRC. Response time varies.
Articles: 1,800–2,500 words. Informational, how-to, and self-help articles. Topics include parenting, family life, child development, health, nutrition, pregnancy, and childbirth.
Depts/columns: Word length varies. First-person parenting accounts and essays, cooking with kids, child behavior, teen issues, updates of interest to families.

Sample Issue
154 pages (15% advertising): 5 articles; 15 depts/columns; 1 special section on children's fiction. Sample copy, $4.50 Canadian at newsstands.
- "Does Early Mean Late?" Article examines the long-term health and developmental issues faced by very low birth-weight, premature babies.
- "Brain Trust." Article addresses issues associated with children's mental health.
- Sample dept/column: "Health" looks at truly healthy snacks for children, and ones that aren't as healthy as they sound.

Rights and Payment
All rights. Articles, $700–$1,500. Depts/columns, payment rate varies. Pays on publication. Provides 2 contributor's copies.

Editor's Comments
We do not try to dictate child-rearing approaches, but rather offer information and invite parents to adopt suggestions that may work for their families. We look for articles that respect parents' desire and ability to understand their children and make good parenting decisions.

Toledo Area Parent News

4120 Adams Street
Toledo, OH 46624

Editor

Description and Readership
Information on parenting issues and local events and resources fill the pages of this regional tabloid geared to the Toledo area. All of the material has a local slant, especially the available amusements, events, arts, and resources.
- **Audience:** Parents
- **Frequency:** Monthly
- **Distribution:** 100% controlled
- **Circulation:** 81,000
- **Website:** www.toledoparent.com

Freelance Potential
75% written by nonstaff writers. Publishes 10–15 freelance submissions yearly; 5% by unpublished writers, 25% by authors who are new to the magazine. Receives 8+ queries each month.

Submissions
Query with clips or send complete ms. Accepts photocopies and computer printouts. SASE. Responds in 1 month.
Articles: 700–2,000 words. Informational articles; profiles; and interviews. Topics include family issues, parenting, teen issues, education, social issues, health, and fitness.
Depts/columns: Word length varies. Brief news items related to family, and opinion essays.

Sample Issue
40 pages (60% advertising): 2 articles; 8 depts/columns; 1 calendar. Sample copy, free with 9x12 SASE. Guidelines available.
- "Toledo's MicroSociety." Article describes a unique program at an elementary school that demonstrates the usefulness of knowledge attained in school classes.
- Sample dept/column: "Parent Profile" features First Lady Hope Taft and her trip to Toledo to honor women and their considerable achievements.
- Sample dept/column: "Just Women" focuses on the trait in women to change moods quickly and without notice, catching loved ones offguard.

Rights and Payment
All rights. Written material, $30–$100. Pays on publication.

Editor's Comments
We would like to see more articles on health and discipline issues. General parenting information should be related to the local scene, either by profiling local people, or by quoting local experts. Residents in the Toledo area look for insights and information, and we are always interested in submissions that tackle current issues, with a local touch. Our goal is to help parents raise happy, healthy children.

Transitions Abroad

P.O. Box 745
Bennington, VT 05201

Submissions: Sherry Schwarz

Description and Readership
The focus of this publication is to be an informative resource for persons contemplating living or traveling abroad. Practical information, interesting personal experiences, events, economic and social issues, vacation opportunities, and travel issues all add to the editorial mix.
- **Audience:** YA–Adult
- **Frequency:** 6 times each year
- **Distribution:** 75% subscription; 25% newsstand
- **Circulation:** 20,000
- **Website:** www.transitionsabroad.com

Freelance Potential
95% written by nonstaff writers. Publishes 150–180 freelance submissions yearly; 30% by unpublished writers, 30% by authors who are new to the magazine. Receives 100 queries, 50 unsolicited mss monthly.

Submissions
Prefers query with outline; accepts complete ms with bibliography. Accepts photocopies, IBM disk submissions, and email submissions to editor@transitionsabroad.com. SASE. Responds in 1–2 months.
Articles: To 1,500 words. Informational and how-to articles. Topics include overseas travel for teens, families, and seniors, as well as overseas study and employment programs.
Depts/columns: Word length varies. Responsible travel, budget travel, and volunteer travel.

Sample Issue
64 pages (50% advertising): 37 articles; 3 depts/columns. Sample copy, $4.95. Guidelines and editorial calendar available at website.
- "Italy 101." Article gives practical information for traveling in Italy on a budget, and for better enjoyment of the local scenes by avoiding tourist traps.
- "Expatriate Life: Living Abroad Is a Lifetime of Learning." Article describes an American woman's experiences while living in Europe for thirty years.
- Sample dept/column: "Transitions Abroad" features one person's philosophy on traveling to other countries and his thoughtful experience in Myanmar.

Rights and Payment
First rights. Written material, $.05 per word. Artwork, payment rate varies. Pays on publication. Provides 2 copies.

Editor's Comments
Our readers are interested in active involvement, not in passive tourism. Sidebars should include additional information.

Treasure Valley Family ☆ Magazine

13191 West Scotfield Street
Boise, ID 83713-0899

Publisher: Liz Buckingham

Description and Readership
Families living in the Treasure Valley area of Idaho turn to this magazine for current information on local and regional events and news, resources, and suppliers. Its articles cover family issues, women's health, and child development.
- **Audience:** Parents
- **Frequency:** 10 times each year
- **Distribution:** 100% controlled
- **Circulation:** 18,500
- **Website:** www.boisefamily.com

Freelance Potential
100% written by nonstaff writers. Publishes 10 freelance submissions yearly; 5% by authors who are new to the magazine. Receives 17 unsolicited mss monthly.

Submissions
Send complete ms. Accepts email submissions to boisefamily@velocitus.net. Responds in 3–4 months.
Articles: To 1,500 words. How-to articles and personal experience pieces. Topics include regional news, gifted and special education, travel, health, hobbies, the arts, and recreation.
Fiction: Word length varies. Historical and inspirational fiction.
Depts/columns: 700–800 words. Regional news, family advocacy, book reviews, and crafts.
Artwork: Color prints and transparencies. Line art.
Other: Filler on health and safety, activities, and games. Submit seasonal material 6 months in advance.

Sample Issue
58 pages (45% advertising): 9 articles; 8 depts/columns. Sample copy, $1.50 with 9x12 SASE. Guidelines available.
- "Get Shakespearified!" Article highlights some of the events at the Idaho Shakespeare Festival.
- "To Market, to Market." Article praises local farmer's markets that provide fresh, wholesome fruit and vegetables.
- Sample dept/column: "Parenting with Passion" suggests cooking as a way to connect with children.

Rights and Payment
First rights. All material, payment rate varies. Pays on publication. Provides 2 contributor's copies.

Editor's Comments
Information on education in all forms, from special and gifted programs to local schools, remains at the top of our list of needs. The number of submissions we receive make acceptance very competitive, so make sure your article has a regional slant that will engage our readers.

Tulsa Kids Magazine

Suite 100
1820 South Boulder Avenue
Tulsa, OK 74119-4409

Editor: Betty Casey

Description and Readership
Families living in and around Tulsa, Oklahoma turn to this publication for its articles on parenting issues as well as its coverage of local events and reports on area resources.
• **Audience:** Families
• **Frequency:** Monthly
• **Distribution:** 80% newsstand; 16% schools
  3% religious instruction; 2% subscription
• **Circulation:** 20,000
• **Website:** www.tulsakids.com

Freelance Potential
99% written by nonstaff writers. Publishes 100+ freelance submissions yearly; 5% by unpublished writers, 1% by authors who are new to the magazine. Receives 100 mss monthly.

Submissions
Send complete ms. Accepts photocopies, computer printouts, disk submissions, and simultaneous submissions if identified. SASE. Responds in 2–3 months.
Articles: 500–800 words. Informational articles; profiles; interviews; humor; and personal experience pieces. Topics include family life, education, parenting, recreation, entertainment, college, health, fitness, careers, crafts, and social issues.
Depts/columns: 100–300 words. News, book reviews, safety, and family cooking.

Sample Issue
36 pages (50% advertising): 1 article; 8 depts/columns; 1 calendar. Sample copy, free with 10x13 SASE ($.75 postage). Guidelines available.
• "Moms on the Mother Road." Article offers ideas for a family vacation on the famous Route 66.
• "Route 66 Diner Delicacies." Article describes the great foods that can be sampled on a trip down Route 66.
• Sample dept/column: "Raising Responsible Children" addresses the summertime blues and how structure and chores can help children enjoy their summer vacation.

Rights and Payment
One-time rights. Written material, $25–$100. Payment policy varies. Provides 1 contributor's copy.

Editor's Comments
All of our material comes from freelance writers and we are always interested in hearing from writers who are new to us. Take a look at our publication to see the style and topics that work best for us, then tailor your article accordingly. We are interested in just about any subject that concerns parents parenting and family life in the Tulsa, Oklahoma area.

Turtle
Magazine for Preschool Kids

Children's Better Health Institute
1100 Waterway Boulevard
P.O. Box 567
Indianapolis, IN 46206-0567

Editor: Terry Harshman

Description and Readership
Written for preschool children, this magazine offers articles, illustrated stories, recipes, poems, and activities that combine fun and learning. Each issues teaches children about the fundamentals of health, nutrition, safety, and exercise. It is the sister publication to *Children's Playmate*.
• **Audience:** 2–5 years
• **Frequency:** 6 times each year
• **Distribution:** 100% subscription
• **Circulation:** 382,000
• **Website:** www.turtlemag.org

Freelance Potential
35% written by nonstaff writers. Publishes 20 freelance submissions yearly.

Submissions
Send complete ms. Accepts photocopies and computer printouts. SASE. Responds in 2–3 months.
Articles: To 500 words. Informational articles. Topics include science, health, fitness, and medicine.
Fiction: To 100 words for rebus stories. Genres include mystery; adventure; fantasy; humor; problem-solving stories; and contemporary, ethnic, and multicultural fiction.
Other: Puzzles, activities, and games. Poetry.

Sample Issue
36 pages (6% advertising): 3 stories; 10 activities; 1 rebus; 1 book review; 1 poem. Sample copy, $1.75 with 9x12 SASE. Guidelines available.
• "Backyard Zoo." Story follows a little boy as he visits with different animals and insects in his backyard after his father is unable to take him to the zoo.
• "Baby Animal Facts." Article takes a look at facts about how some baby animals act.
• "Fun Food: Frozen Banana Pops." Recipe gives directions on how to make yummy frozen treats.

Rights and Payment
All rights. Articles and fiction, $.22 per word. Other material, payment rate varies. Pays on publication. Provides up to 10 contributor's copies.

Editor's Comments
We are always on the lookout for articles that educate preschool children on health and fitness, activities that promote hand-eye coordination, simple crafts, games and puzzles that are fun and stimulate young minds, as well as recipes with easy directions for making healthy snacks. Make sure material is age-appropriate.

Tuscaloosa Christian Family

448 65th Street
Tuscaloosa, AL 35405

Editor: Craig Threlkeld

Description and Readership
Published for the local region, *Tuscaloosa Christian Family* promotes positive living. It provides its readers with inspirational literature, covers area entertainment, and reports on the latest news in healthy living. Profiles of family-minded individuals and organizations in the community are included as well, along with features that address parenting issues.
• **Audience:** Parents
• **Frequency:** Monthly
• **Distribution:** 95% newsstand; 5% other
• **Circulation:** 10,000

Freelance Potential
30% written by nonstaff writers. Publishes 60 freelance submissions yearly; 5% by unpublished writers, 2–3% by authors who are new to the magazine. Receives 8 queries each month.

Submissions
Query with photos if applicable. Accepts photocopies and computer printouts. SASE. Responds in 1 month.
Articles: 500 words. Informational and how-to articles; profiles; interviews; humor; and personal experience pieces. Topics include current events, health, fitness, recreation, regional news, religion, social issues, and travel.
Fiction: 500 words. Genres include inspirational and humorous fiction.
Depts/columns: 500 words. Book and music reviews, family finances, mission news, and working with youth.
Artwork: Color prints or transparencies.
Other: Activities. Submit seasonal material 2 months in advance.

Sample Issue
30 pages: 3 articles; 14 depts/columns; 1 calendar; 2 activities. Sample copy, free with 9x12 SASE ($3 postage). Editorial calendar available.
• "Last Call for 24-Hour Bars?" Article written in Q&A format focuses on a proposal by the interim president of the University of Alabama to limit the number of hours campus bars can remain open for business.
• Sample dept/column: "Money Matters" discusses tax issues.

Rights and Payment
Rights vary. No payment. Provides 1 contributor's copy.

Editor's Comments
If you're a local writer with an idea for an article with local connections, or if you would like to bring the community's attention to an outstanding Christian individual, query us.

Twins

Suite 101
11211 East Arapahoe Road
Centennial, CO 80112

Managing Editor: Sharon Withers

Description and Readership
Twins and other types of multiple births, which can be stressful and confusing situations for parents, are the focus for this publication that supplies support, practical information, and parenting tips and techniques.
• **Audience:** Parents
• **Frequency:** 6 times each year
• **Distribution:** 60% subscription; 37% controlled; 3% newsstand
• **Circulation:** 56,000
• **Website:** www.twinsmagazine.com

Freelance Potential
80% written by nonstaff writers. Publishes 80 freelance submissions yearly; 25% by authors who are new to the magazine. Receives 21 queries and unsolicited mss monthly.

Submissions
Query or send complete ms. Accepts photocopies, computer printouts, and simultaneous submissions if identified. SASE. Responds in 3 months.
Articles: 800–1,300 words. Informational and how-to articles; profiles; and personal experience pieces. Topics include parenting, family life, health, fitness, education, music, house and home, nutrition, sports, social issues, crafts, and hobbies.
Depts/columns: To 800 words. News, new product information, opinion pieces, and short items on child development.

Sample Issue
54 pages (30% advertising): 8 articles; 13 depts/columns. Sample copy, $5.50. Guidelines available.
• "Cognitive Catch-up in Premature Infants." Article examines the developmental challenges pre-term infants face in cognitive areas.
• "Conjoined Twins: Intimacy and Independence." Article explores the incidence of conjoined twins, the factors involved in their births, lifestyles, separation possibilities, and the increasing media focus on this phenomenon.
• Sample dept/column: "Zygosity Puzzle" presents information to suggest that twins are never identical.

Rights and Payment
All rights. All material, payment rate varies. Artwork, payment rate varies. Provides 1 contributor's copy.

Editor's Comments
We want all submissions to have a happy outcome, in addition to providing information, guidance, or resource material. Please write in a friendly and conversational style, and include sidebars if possible.

Twist

270 Sylvan Avenue
Englewood Cliffs, NJ 07632

Entertainment Editor: Jamie Harkin

Description and Readership

Upbeat articles on celebrities and news from the entertainment and fashion worlds appear in *Twist*. Its "Real Life" section tackles topics of a more serious nature. Focusing on teens who have overcome obstacles, it has covered such subjects as drunk driving, anorexia, and panic disorders.
- **Audience:** 14–19 years
- **Frequency:** 10 times each year
- **Distribution:** Subscription; newsstand
- **Circulation:** 1 million
- **Website:** www.twistmagazine.com

Freelance Potential

5% written by nonstaff writers. Publishes 120 freelance submissions yearly; 5% by unpublished writers, 5% by authors who are new to the magazine. Receives 25–30 queries monthly.

Submissions

Query. Accepts computer printouts. SASE. Responds in 2–3 weeks.
Articles: Word length varies. Informational articles; personal experience pieces; and humor. Topics include popular culture, music, current celebrities, fashion favorites, beauty tips, health, fitness, nutrition, sex, and relationships.
Depts/columns: Word length varies. Embarrassing moments, new fashion and beauty products, advice, and horoscopes.

Sample Issue

98 pages (25% advertising): 15 articles; 16 depts/columns. Sample copy, $2.99 with 9x12 SASE. Guidelines available.
- "The Real Difference between Mary-Kate and Ashley." Article written by a face-reader explains the relationship between facial features and character traits.
- "Stars Get Stressed out Too." Article shares celebrity tips for coping with stress.
- Sample dept/column: "Twist Investigation" outlines the risk factors and warning signs of an eating disorder.

Rights and Payment

First North American serial rights. Written material, payment rate varies. Pays on acceptance. Provides 2 author's copies.

Editor's Comments

We rarely accept freelance submissions. Our "Real Life" section continues to be the exception, however. A regular feature, "Real Life" stories profile teens who have overcome hardships in their lives. You might also consider submitting a quiz, another area more open to nonstaff writers.

U Magazine

United States Automobile Association
9800 Fredericksburg Road
San Antonio, TX 78288-0264

Editor: Shari Biediger

Description and Readership

This lively magazine is provided to children of United States Automobile Association members. Its goal is to educate preteens about relevant topics and help them prepare to become responsible adults. By including reader submissions, it reinforces the importance of their voices and ideas.
- **Audience:** 9–12 years
- **Frequency:** Quarterly
- **Distribution:** 99% controlled; 1% other
- **Circulation:** 440,000
- **Website:** www.usaa.com

Freelance Potential

20% written by nonstaff writers. Publishes 5 freelance submissions yearly. Receives 5 queries monthly.

Submissions

Query with résumé and clips or writing samples. Accepts photocopies. SASE. Responds in 6 weeks.
Articles: Word length varies. Informational, how-to, self-help, and personal experience pieces; profiles, and interviews. Topics include hobbies, history, mathematics, music, nature, the environment, popular culture, current events, science, technology, social issues, the arts, travel, money management, health, and safety issues.
Other: Puzzles, activities, games, and jokes.

Sample Issue

16 pages (no advertising): 3 articles; 1 dept/column; 6 activities. Sample copy, free with 9x12 SASE ($2 postage). Guidelines and theme list available.
- "Prepare Before U Pedal." Article describes ways to bike safely and includes testimonies from children whose bike helmets protected them from serious injury when they crashed.
- "Put Your Best Foot Forward." Article promotes walking as a means to a destination, gives several reasons why it is pleasurable, and tells how it can be done safely.
- Sample dept/column: "First Start" illustrates how youngsters can create a safe and secure online banking account.

Rights and Payment

All rights. Written material, payment rate varies. Pays on acceptance. Provides 25 contributor's copies.

Editor's Comments

We are looking for interactive/visual game ideas that are appropriate for our reading audience, and tie into one of our themes. We rarely publish fiction, poetry, or prose, but would consider such pieces if they are of high quality and applicable to a theme.

The Universe in the Classroom

Astronomical Society of the Pacific
390 Ashton Avenue
San Francisco, CA 94112

Editor: Suzanne Chippindale

Description and Readership
Published online, this newsletter is intended for use by teachers and others who want to share with children the wonders of the universe. Each issue focuses on a topic of current astronomical interest and includes a hands-on activity. In addition, it offers links for those who seek deeper exploration of a subject.
- **Audience:** Teachers
- **Frequency:** Quarterly
- **Distribution:** 100% Internet
- **Hits per month:** 10,000
- **Website:** www.astrosociety.org

Freelance Potential
90% written by nonstaff writers. Publishes 4 freelance submissions yearly; 50% by unpublished writers, 75% by authors who are new to the magazine. Receives 1 query each month.

Submissions
Query with outline. Accepts photocopies and computer printouts. Availability of artwork improves chance of acceptance. SASE. Responds in 1 month.
Articles: 3,000 words. Informational articles. Topics include astronomy, teaching methods, and astrobiology.
Artwork: Color prints and transparencies.
Other: Classroom activities.

Sample Issue
Sample copy available at website.
- "The Story of the Transit of Venus." Article reviews the history of the quest to measure the size of the solar system and how observation of the passage of Venus across the face of the sun helped scientists accomplish this.
- "It's Saturn Time!" Article provides guidelines for viewing Saturn during the winter and spring of 2004, when the planet appeared as a prominent feature in the night sky.
- "Making Your Own Astronomical Camera." Article shows how a one-time use camera can be modified and reloaded for astrophotography.

Rights and Payment
One-time rights. No payment.

Editor's Comments
Writing for us requires the ability to transform scientific information into accessible articles for an audience of teachers who may not have training in astronomy. A classroom activity to accompany your article is an important component, as are web links that make further study as close as a click away.

U*S*Kids

Children's Better Health Institute
P.O. Box 567
1100 Waterway Boulevard
Indianapolis, IN 46206-0567

Editor: Daniel Lee

Description and Readership
Articles, stories, and activities related to health and fitness, science and nature, and other interesting topics are included in this magazine.
- **Audience:** 6–8 years
- **Frequency:** 8 times each year
- **Distribution:** 100% subscription
- **Circulation:** 230,000
- **Website:** www.uskidsmag.com

Freelance Potential
50% written by nonstaff writers. Publishes 12 freelance submissions yearly; 70% by unpublished writers, 70% by authors who are new to the magazine. Receives 58 unsolicited mss each month.

Submissions
Send complete ms. Accepts photocopies and computer printouts. SASE. Responds in 6 weeks.
Articles: 400 words. Factual articles. Topics include health, fitness, science, the arts, computers, nature, the environment, and multicultural and ethnic issues.
Fiction: 300–400 words. Historical and contemporary fiction, mystery, fantasy, adventure, and folktales.
Depts/columns: Staff written.
Other: Puzzles and activities. Poetry, to 24 lines. Submit seasonal material 6 months in advance.

Sample Issue
36 pages (3% advertising): 5 articles; 1 story; 8 depts/columns. Sample copy, $2.95 with 9x12 SASE (2 first-class stamps). Writers' guidelines available.
- "The Mystery of the Message." Story tells of a boy's desire to learn the meaning of his mother's list of Italian words.
- "Smoking out the Truth." Article discusses the dangers of cigarettes and offers a science experiment.
- "The Fit Formula." Article explains a way to calculate if you are getting enough daily exercise.

Rights and Payment
All rights. Articles and fiction, to $.20 per word. Poetry, $25. Activities, payment rate varies. Pays on publication. Provides 5 contributor's copies.

Editor's Comments
We like to see material that sparks a child's imagination and creativity while they learn something new. Articles that cover healthy eating and exercise, as well as interesting facts about the world, are also of interest to us. Send us something lively and on a topic that kids will want to read.

U-Turn Magazine

9800 Fredericksburg Road
San Antonio, TX 78288

Editor: Shari Biediger

Description and Readership
U-Turn Magazine is written by the United Services Automobile Association, a company that offers banking, investing, and insurance services to military personnel. Its purpose is to help dependants of members at home and abroad become responsible adults.
- **Audience:** 13–17 years
- **Frequency:** Quarterly
- **Distribution:** 99% controlled; 1% other
- **Circulation:** 440,000
- **Website:** www.usaa.com

Freelance Potential
20% written by nonstaff writers. Publishes 5–10 freelance submissions yearly. Receives 5 queries monthly.

Submissions
Query with résumé and clips. Accepts photocopies and computer printouts. SASE. Responds in 6–8 weeks.
Articles: 800 words. Informational and how-to articles; profiles; interviews; and personal experience pieces. Topics include college, careers, saving and investing money, driving issues, relationships, and lifestyle issues.
Depts/columns: Word length varies. Expert advice; money management; quarterly events and information.

Sample Issue
32 pages: 3 articles; 7 depts/columns. Sample copy, free with 9x12 SASE ($1.80 postage). Guidelines available.
- "The D Word." Article discusses what to do when your parent is deployed and includes a personal experience piece from a teenage girl whose father is serving in Afghanistan.
- "On the Road to Find Out." Chronicles a trip taken by a high school junior to visit colleges and describes how he made his final choice.
- Sample dept/column: "First Start" explains the basics of a checking account.

Rights and Payment
All rights. Written material, payment rate varies. Pays on acceptance.

Editor's Comments
We have a large and active teen panel that helps us make our editorial decisions, and we often include material that is written by our readers. We will consider material by freelance writers who have good clips and send appropriate queries. After we assign articles, the editor and writer work closely to develop the direction of the article as it is researched. Many articles are design-driven.

U.25 Magazine

9800 Fredericksburg Road
San Antonio, TX 78288

Editor: Carol Barnes

Description and Readership
The dependents, ages 18–24, of members of the United Services Automobile Association (USAA), receive this magazine free of charge. Its purpose is to foster responsibility in young adults by covering topics such as careers, college, and money management. The USAA also publishes *U Magazine* for ages 9 to 12 and *U-Turn Magazine* for ages 13 to 17.
- **Audience:** 18–24 years
- **Frequency:** Quarterly
- **Distribution:** 100% controlled
- **Circulation:** 440,000
- **Website:** www.usaa.com

Freelance Potential
20% written by nonstaff writers. Publishes 5–10 freelance submissions yearly. Receives 5 queries monthly.

Submissions
Query with résumé and clips for feature articles. Send complete ms for shorter pieces. Accepts photocopies and computer printouts. SASE. Responds in 6–8 weeks.
Articles: 1,000 words. Shorter pieces, 300 words. Informational and how-to articles; profiles; interviews; and personal experience pieces. Topics include college, careers, saving and investing money, driving, and lifestyle issues.
Depts/columns: Word length varies. Short news items, USAA programs, and driving information.
Other: Activities, games.

Sample Issue
32 pages: 4 articles; 3 depts/columns. Sample copy, free with 9x12 SASE ($1.80 postage). Guidelines available.
- "Does It Take a Gimmick to Get a Job?" Article explains why old-fashioned professionalism is usually the best path to employment.
- "Weighty Issue." Article addresses the challenge of finding healthy, nutritious food when you're eating on a college campus food plan.
- Sample dept/column: "Road Scholar" offers driving and car maintenance tips.

Rights and Payment
All rights. Feature articles, $500. Other material, payment rate varies. Pays on acceptance.

Editor's Comments
Because we want to offer a fun and relevant magazine that features different styles of writing, we do accept a lot of freelance material. We like to include our readers as sources and subjects, but it is not mandatory to feature only readers.

Varsity Publications

Suite 300
12510 33rd Avenue NE
Seattle, WA 98125

Editor: Charles Beene

Description and Readership

Regional publications for youth and adult soccer and slo-pitch softball players and coaches are the specialty of this publisher. Its pages include national and local news, and profiles of teams, players, and coaches.
- **Audience:** YA–Adult
- **Frequency:** Monthly
- **Distribution:** 100% controlled
- **Circulation:** 200,000 (combined)
- **Website:** www.varsitycommunications.com

Freelance Potential

35% written by nonstaff writers. Publishes 100 freelance submissions yearly; 10% by unpublished writers. Receives 10 queries monthly.

Submissions

Query with résumé, outline, synopsis, and clips or writing samples. Accepts photocopies, computer printouts, and simultaneous submissions if identified. Availability of artwork improves chances of acceptance. SASE. Responds in 2–3 weeks.
Articles: 300–700 words. Informational and how-to articles; personal experience pieces; profiles; interviews; and humor. Topics include soccer, slo-pitch softball, equipment, uniforms, and health issues.
Fiction: Word length varies. Stories with softball and soccer themes.
Artwork: 3x5 B/W prints and 35mm color slides.
Other: Activities, puzzles, games, and filler. Submit material about tournaments 1–2 months in advance.

Sample Issue

24 pages (50% advertising): 6 articles; 5 depts/columns. Sample copy, free with 10x13 SASE. Writers' guidelines and theme list available.
- "Big Dreams and Hard Work Pay Off." First-person article about the success of a national soccer team member.
- "We Need Better Referees." Article suggests that young referees are a better match for young players.
- Sample dept/column: "Maher's Message" offers an opinion that no rules are necessary just to have fun.

Rights and Payment

Rights negotiable. Written material, $15–$40. Other material, payment rate varies. Pays on publication. Provides 1+ contributor's copies.

Editor's Comments

We seek writers with an understanding of coaching techniques. Profiles of young, up-and-coming players are needed.

Vegetarian Baby & Child

P.O. Box 388
Trenton, TX 75490

Editor: Melanie Wilson

Description and Readership

Parents who desire to raise vegetarian children look to this site for practical information, recipes, successful personal experiences, and product reviews, all geared toward making the effort as easy and as healthy as possible.
- **Audience:** Parents
- **Frequency:** Monthly
- **Distribution:** 100% Internet
- **Hits per month:** Unavailable
- **Website:** www.vegetarianbaby.com

Freelance Potential

95% written by nonstaff writers. Publishes 100–150 freelance submissions yearly. Receives 2 queries, 1–2 mss monthly.

Submissions

Query or send complete ms. Accepts photocopies, computer printouts, and email submissions to melanie@ vegetarianbaby.com (Microsoft Word attachments). SASE. Response time varies.
Articles: 350–1,500 words. Informational and how-to articles; personal experience pieces; profiles; and interviews. Topics include general nutrition, vegetarian pregnancy, dealing with friends and family, living with non-vegetarians, health, child care, activism, and support networks.
Depts/columns: Word length varies. Q&As, recipes, and book and new product reviews.
Other: Activities, games, and crafts for children.

Sample Issue

Writers' guidelines available at website.
- "Walt Disney World: A Place Where Veg Magic Happens." Article exalts the surprising vegetarian-friendly foods and attitudes found at Walt Disney World and area restaurants.
- "Pass the Hors D'Oeuvres, Please!" Article describes the success one mother had in allowing her six-year-old finicky child to make his own hors d'oeuvres to assure a balanced diet.
- "A Vegetarian in China." Article highlights the improved opportunities for vegetarians in China.

Rights and Payment

First rights. Articles, $10.

Editor's Comments

We look for articles dealing with all aspects of raising vegetarian/vegan children including health problems that have been overcome, how to deal with social and eating out issues, relationships with physicians and other healthcare professionals, challenges, original recipes, and tips for pursuing this lifestyle.

Vegetarianteen.com

P.O. Box 388
Trenton, TX 75490

Editor: Lucy Watkins

Description and Readership
Many of the articles in this online publication are written by teens for its teen audience. Visitors to the site find practical information relating to teens who follow vegetarian, vegan, semi-vegetarian, and raw food diets, and other topics important to teens following this lifestyle.
- **Audience:** Vegetarian teens and their parents
- **Frequency:** Monthly
- **Distribution:** 100% Internet
- **Hits per month:** Unavailable
- **Website:** www.vegetarianteen.com

Freelance Potential
95% written by nonstaff writers. Publishes 100–150 freelance submissions yearly; 50% by authors who are new to the magazine. Receives 20–25 queries, 10–15 unsolicited mss a year.

Submissions
Query or send complete ms. Accepts photocopies, computer printouts, and email submissions to melanie@ vegetarianbaby.com (Microsoft Word attachments). SASE. Response time varies.
Articles: 350–1,200 words. Informational and how-to articles; profiles; interviews; and personal experience pieces. Topics include fitness, family issues, animal activism, and nutrition.
Depts/columns: Word length varies. Recipes and book and product reviews.

Sample Issue
Sample issue available at website. Guidelines available.
- "Peaceful Activism: Do What You Can." Article portrays one young woman's plight as she tries to balance her desire to save unfortunate animals with a very limited income.
- "Starving Budgets, Obese Students." Article takes a hard, in-depth look at the typical American diet, its reliance on unhealthy fats and other ingredients, and the effect it is having on young people.
- "Vegetarian Vacation." Article offers ideas for maintaining a healthy diet even while vacationing in different countries.

Rights and Payment
Rights vary. All written material, $15.

Editor's Comments
We are giving teens a chance to be heard while gaining experience within the vegetarian movement. We also accept the writings of "tweens" between the ages of 10–12, and twenty-somethings who became vegetarians as teens, who were raised as vegetarians, or who have valuable words of wisdom to offer the visitors to our site.

VegFamily

8304 Green Clover Avenue
Las Vegas, NV 89149

Editor: Erin Pavlina

Description and Readership
VegFamily is an e-zine primarily for vegans, although other vegetarians will also find good information at the site. It is read primarily by mothers who are interested in raising vegan children, and offers links to playgroups, recipes, and other vegans.
- **Audience:** YA-Adult
- **Frequency:** Monthly
- **Distribution:** 100% Internet
- **Hits per month:** 30,000
- **Website:** www.vegfamily.com

Freelance Potential
50% written by nonstaff writers. Publishes 40 freelance submissions yearly; 90% by unpublished writers, 50% by writers who are new to the magazine. Receives 5 queries monthly.

Submissions
Query. Accepts email submissions to contact@ vegfamily.com. Responds in 1 week.
Articles: 500–1,500 words. Informational, self-help, and how-to articles; profiles, interviews, and personal experience pieces. Topics include health, fitness, nature, the environment, social issues, and vegan parenting. Publishes inspirational fiction; and stories about animals, nature, and the environment.
Depts/columns: Word length varies. Recipes, and book and product reviews.
Artwork: JPEG or GIF files.
Other: Activities. Submit seasonal material 2 months in advance.

Sample Issue
Guidelines available at website.
- "College Vegetarianism 101." Article offers suggestions for sticking to a vegetarian regime at college along with ideas to help make it easier.
- "Eat Your Way to Better Health." Article stresses how making the correct dietary choices can play a major role in keeping the entire family healthy.
- Sample dept/column: "Vegan Recipes" showcases recipes that adhere to a vegan format.

Rights and Payment
All electronic rights. Articles, $20. Pays on publication.

Editor's Comments
We need more submissions on natural parenting issues such as using cloth diapers, breastfeeding, homebirths, and co-sleeping. We would also like to see humorous accounts of a vegan lifestyle. Our tone is friendly and non-controversial.

Ventura County Parent Magazine

Suite O
3477-D Old Conejo Road
Newbury Park, CA 91320

Editor & Publisher: Hillary Lynn

Description and Readership

This award-winning publication provides parents in and around Ventura County, California with up-do-date information on educational development, health, social issues, new products, and local and regional events.
- **Audience:** Parents
- **Frequency:** Monthly
- **Distribution:** 89% controlled; 11% subscription
- **Circulation:** 37,000
- **Website:** www.vcparent.com

Freelance Potential

60% written by nonstaff writers. Publishes 40 freelance submissions yearly; 10% by unpublished writers, 10% by authors who are new to the magazine. Receives 250 queries, 8 unsolicited mss monthly.

Submissions

Query with sample paragraph or send complete ms. Accepts disk submissions (Macintosh compatible) and email submissions to info@vcparent.com. SASE. Responds to queries in 2 months, to mss in 6 weeks.
Articles: 1,000–1,500 words. Informational articles and personal experience pieces. Topics include animals, crafts, hobbies, pets, the arts, computers, current events, education, health, fitness, social issues, popular culture, and news.
Fiction: 1,000–1,500 words. Publishes real-life and problem-solving fiction.
Depts/columns: 600 words. Health and safety news, media reviews, and Internet tips.
Artwork: B/W or color prints. Line art.
Other: Activities and filler on local topics.

Sample Issue

30 pages (44% advertising): 2 articles; 7 depts/columns; 1 camp guide. Sample copy, free with 12x14 SASE. Writers' guidelines and theme list available.
- "Baby Showers." Article provides ideas and suggestions for planning and hosting the perfect baby shower.
- Sample dept/column: "Kreative Kids" offers directions for making Father's Day cards.

Rights and Payment

Exclusive regional rights. Written material, $35–$100. Artwork, payment rate varies. Pays on publication. Provides 1 copy.

Editor's Comments

We strive to provide listings to enhance community involvement. Material must be up-to-date and useful to families. Tips on safety issues and parenting topics interest us.

The Village Family

501 40th Street S
Fargo, ND 58103

Editor: Laurie Neill

Description and Readership

The Village Family is the only parenting publication serving the Fargo, North Dakota, and Moorhead, Minnesota, areas. In addition to articles on child care, this magazine also offers short humorous items, advice on money management, and information related to physical and mental well-being.
- **Audience:** Parents, 25–50 years
- **Frequency:** 6 times each year
- **Distribution:** Subscription; other
- **Circulation:** 25,000
- **Website:** www.thevillagefamily.org

Freelance Potential

70% written by nonstaff writers. Publishes 30 freelance submissions yearly.

Submissions

Query or send complete ms with brief author bio. Accepts photocopies, computer printouts, and email submissions to magazine@thevillagefamily.com. SASE. Response time varies.
Articles: To 1,500 words. Informational, self-help, and how-to articles; profiles; interviews; and personal experience pieces. Topics include current events, health, fitness, recreation, regional news, social issues, sports, and travel.
Depts/columns: Word length varies. Medical updates, media reviews, humorous essays, crafts, recipes, money matters, and family issues.

Sample Issue

46 pages: 4 articles; 1 story; 8 depts/columns. Writers' guidelines available.
- "Mom! I Can't Find My . . ." Article explores the topic of forgetfulness in children and offers strategies parents can use to teach their kids how to keep track of their belongings.
- "A New Year, a New You." Article shows how to start the new year off with resolutions that are about self-fulfillment rather than self-denial.
- Sample dept/column: "Time 4 Some Fun" offers instructions for making three heart-shaped craft items and a recipe for popcorn balls.

Rights and Payment

First and electronic rights. Written material, $.07–$.10 per word. Reprints, $30–$50. Pays on publication.

Editor's Comments

If you love to write about families, we'd love to see your work. You don't have to live in the local area to write for us. We often add quotes from local resources to articles written outside our distribution area.

Informational Needs of Teens
Voice of Youth Advocates (VOYA)
Cathi Dunn MacRae, Editor

"VOYA is the only publication exclusively serving the informational needs of teens," says Editor Cathi Dunn MacRae. It calls itself "The Library Magazine Serving Those Who Serve Young Adults." Voice of Youth Advocates has an amazing 99 percent subscription renewal rate. It reaches coordinators of teen programming, teen counselors, middle and high school teachers, and media specialists, including public and school librarians.

VOYA was founded in 1978 by two public librarians, Dorothy M. Broderick and Mary K. Chelton. It runs reviews of young adult books and articles about teen issues. And it works with teens through their reading and writing.

"We are an intellectual freedom journal," says MacRae. "We are anti-filtering. Subscribers want the teens they work with to have total access to information. Our readers guide and mentor teens, but do not direct them." They do so by "following the philosophies of youth participation and youth involvement."

When asked about her editorial needs, MacRae says, "I love articles about imaginative ways to encourage teens to take care of themselves, to become activists themselves." She is interested in publishing more articles that demonstrate community partnerships among various agencies and organizations serving teens. MacRae also hopes to attract psychologists, therapists, and social workers to write about the special challenges of working with teens and to include suggestions for supporting and collaborating with librarians and teachers.

VOYA writers must have experience working directly with teens in schools, libraries, youth centers, or other programs for teens. Anyone considering submission of an article to VOYA should first visit its website at www.voya.com.

Voice of Youth Advocates

Suite 200
4501 Forbes Boulevard
Lanham, MD 20706

Editor-in-Chief: Cathi Dunn MacRae

Description and Readership
Launched in 1978, this professional journal strives to meet the reading and information needs of teenagers. It provides teachers, librarians, and other youth workers with educational articles and reviews on library services, networking among agencies, teaching, and literature reviews.
- **Audience:** Professionals who work with youth
- **Frequency:** 6 times each year
- **Distribution:** 99% subscription; 1% other
- **Circulation:** 6,000
- **Website:** www.voya.com

Freelance Potential
85% written by nonstaff writers. Publishes 50 freelance submissions yearly; 70% by unpublished writers, 60% by authors who are new to the magazine. Receives 5 queries monthly.

Submissions
Query with résumé, synopsis, and market analysis. Accepts photocopies, computer printouts, and email queries to cmacrae@voya.com. SASE. Responds 2–4 months.
Articles: 800–3,000 words. Informational and how-to articles; interviews; book reviews; and book lists. We print one book list annually. Topics include young adult literature, contemporary authors, and library programs.
Other: Submit seasonal material 1 year in advance.

Sample Issue
80 pages (20% advertising): 4 articles; 160 book reviews. Sample copy, free with 9x12 SASE. Writers' guidelines available with SASE and at website.
- "Going All the Way." Article takes a look at the change over the years in first time sexual experiences of teens found in works of fiction.
- "Author Talk: Listening In." Article offers a discussion between young adult novelist Carolyn Maccullough and her editor, Deborah Brodie.

Rights and Payment
All rights. Articles, $50–$100. Pays on publication. Provides 3 contributor's copies.

Editor's Comments
We are seeking items for those beyond our major readership (librarians and teachers) who are interested in community partnerships and non-traditional interactions among youth advocates such as social workers, counselors, etc. We are receiving a lot of submissions of young adult literary criticism, as well as too many misdirected submissions from writers who have never examined our magazine.

Voices from the Middle

National Council of Teachers of English
1111 West Kenyon Road
Urbana, IL 61801-1096

Production Editor: Carol Schanche

Description and Readership

This professional journal addresses language arts educators, administrators, and curriculum directors who work with students in grades five through nine. Each issue is devoted to one topic or concept related to literacy and learning at the middle school level.
- **Audience:** Teachers
- **Frequency:** Quarterly
- **Distribution:** 90% subscription; 10% other
- **Circulation:** 11,000
- **Website:** www.ncte.org/pubs/journals/vm

Freelance Potential

100% written by nonstaff writers. Publishes 30 freelance submissions yearly; 60% by unpublished writers, 85% by authors who are new to the magazine. Receives 20 unsolicited mss monthly.

Submissions

Send 3 copies of complete ms. Accepts photocopies, computer printouts, and email submissions to cschanche@ncte.org (indicate issue for which you are submitting in the subject line). SASE. Responds in 3–5 months.
Articles: 2,500–4,000 words. Educational and personal experience articles related to the issue's theme. Topics include middle school language arts and English instruction.
Depts/columns: Staff written.
Artwork: B/W prints or transparencies. Line art.

Sample Issue

80 pages (9% advertising): 8 articles; 12 depts/columns. Sample copy, $6. Guidelines and theme list available.
- "Teaching ELL Students in Regular Classrooms at the Secondary Level." Article recommends strategies teachers can use to help English Language Learners adjust and succeed.
- "Preserving the Cultural Identity of the English Language Learner." Article discusses the importance of celebrating the multiple cultures and languages found in a diverse classroom.
- "Working Under Lucky Stars." Article presents language lessons for multilingual classrooms.

Rights and Payment

First and second rights. No payment. Provides 2 contributor's copies.

Editor's Comments

When possible, submissions should include material to help the reader visualize the classroom practice you are explaining, such as photos of students working, charts, or diagrams.

Washington Families Magazine

Suite 550
485 Spring Park Place
Herndon, VA 20170

Managing Editor: Marae Leggs

Description and Readership

This publication, targeting families in the Washington, D.C. area, is a well-rounded resource for information and ideas on parenting, indoor and outdoor events, health, and other general life-style issues.
- **Audience:** Parents
- **Frequency:** Monthly
- **Distribution:** 100% controlled
- **Circulation:** 100,000
- **Website:** www.familiesmagazines.com

Freelance Potential

50% written by nonstaff writers. Publishes 120 freelance submissions yearly; 50% by unpublished writers, 50% by authors who are new to the magazine. Receives 100 queries and unsolicited mss monthly.

Submissions

Query or send complete ms. Accepts Macintosh disk submissions and email to editor@familiesmagazines.com. SASE. Response time varies.
Articles: 500–700 words. How-to and self-help articles, and personal experience pieces. Topics include parenting, family life, relationships, health, fitness, crafts, hobbies, the arts, gifted and special education, music, travel, multicultural and ethnic issues, social issues, music, recreation, and travel.
Depts/columns: Word length varies. News for families.
Artwork: B/W prints or transparencies. Line art.
Other: Submit seasonal material 6 months in advance.

Sample Issue

114 pages (50% advertising): 14 articles; 2 depts/columns; 4 resource guides; 2 events calendars. Sample copy, $4 with 9x12 SASE. Guidelines and editorial calendar available.
- "New Vaccine to Help Infants." Article describes the combination vaccine, Pediarix, how it is to be given, and the conditions for which it is given.
- "Financial Planning for Baby." Article outlines many of the plans available that will ensure a good future for a child.
- Sample dept/column: "Going Places" details family events available in the Washington region.

Rights and Payment

Regional rights. Articles, $25. Depts/columns, payment rate varies. Pays on publication. Provides 1 contributor's copy.

Editor's Comments

We are always in need of submissions that deal with relationships, infertility issues, and fatherhood. While humor has its place, we do not use fluffy, "cute" pieces.

Washington Parent

Suite N720
4701 Sangamore Road
Bethesda, MD 20816

Editor: Margaret Hut

Description and Readership

Washington Parent serves as a local resource on topics of interest to parents of infants and children through age 18 who live in the Washington, D.C., metropolitan area. Family issues, child rearing, local events, and area resources are all included in its editorial mix.
- **Audience:** Families
- **Frequency:** Monthly
- **Distribution:** 93% controlled; 7% subscription
- **Circulation:** 75,000
- **Website:** www.washingtonparent.com

Freelance Potential

88% written by nonstaff writers. Publishes 120 freelance submissions yearly. Receives 38 queries monthly.

Submissions

Query. Accepts disk submissions (Microsoft Word or WordPerfect) and email submissions to washpar@washingtonparent.com (Microsoft Word or WordPerfect attachments). SASE. Response time varies.
Articles: 1,200–2,000 words. Informational and how-to articles. Topics include regional news and events, parenting, family issues, local entertainment, gifted and special education, child development, health, fitness, the environment, and multicultural and ethnic issues.
Depts/columns: Word length varies. Family travel, book and media reviews, education, topics relating to children with special needs, and short news items.

Sample Issue

118 pages (63% advertising): 8 articles; 10 depts/columns; 1 camp guide. Sample copy, guidelines, and theme list available.
- "Hands-On Dads." Article looks at how the role of fathering is changing, partly due to new expectations and partly due to changing parental realities.
- "No Child Left Behind." Article discusses the new law's impact on children with special needs.
- Sample dept/column: "In Our Own Backyard" finds lots of interesting bugs at the O. Orkin Insect Zoo.

Rights and Payment

First rights. Written material, payment rate varies. Pays on publication. Provides 3 contributor's copies.

Editor's Comments

Submissions to our publication—even general parenting or general interest pieces—should have a local twist. Our goal is to help educate and supply parents who live in the capital environs with helpful information.

Wee Ones E-Magazine

Editor: Jennifer Reed

Description and Readership

First appearing in 2001, this online kids magazine offers articles, stories, poems, and activities. It strives to bring families together reading and learning online.
- **Audience:** 5–10 years
- **Frequency:** 6 times each year
- **Distribution:** Internet
- **Circulation:** 40,000+
- **Website:** www.weeonesmag.com

Freelance Potential

100% written by nonstaff writers. Publishes 200 freelance submissions yearly; 50% by unpublished writers, 50% by authors who are new to the magazine. Receives 83 mss monthly.

Submissions

Send complete ms. Accepts email submissions to submissions@weeonesmag.com (no attachments unless you are an illustrator or submitting photos to accompany an article). Responds in 1–4 weeks.
Articles: 500 words. Informational and how-to articles. Topics include animals, pets, the arts, crafts, hobbies, current events, health, fitness, history, music, multicultural issues, nature, the environment, sports, travel, and recreation. Also publishes biographical articles.
Fiction: 500 words. Genres include contemporary, historical, and multicultural fiction; adventure; mystery; and suspense. Also publishes humor, sports stories, and read-aloud stories.
Artwork: Line art.
Other: Submit seasonal material 6 months in advance.

Sample Issue

Writers' guidelines available at website.
- "A Parent's Guide to Readiness Skills: Closure." Article discusses the benefits of building closure skills in children.
- "A Jarful of Sky." Article explains how light affects how we see color and offers a demonstrative experiment.
- "Terrible Tuesday." Story describes a young girl's fear of going to the doctor to get shots.

Rights and Payment

First electronic rights. Written material, $.05 per word. Pays on publication.

Editor's Comments

We are always looking for artwork, short poems, or articles by kids for "Kids Korner!" For adults, we are seeking character driven stories that children will be able to relate to, and nonfiction manuscripts on most topics. Currently, we would like to see more mysteries that are sports related.

Welcome Home

9493-C Silver King Court
Fairfax, VA 22031-4713

Manuscript Coordinator: Rebecca Lamey

Description and Readership
In print for over 21 years, this resourceful magazine features articles and tips on topics related to child development, parenting, education, and other family issues. It targets parents who are committed to stay at home with their children.
- **Audience:** Parents
- **Frequency:** Monthly
- **Distribution:** 98% subscription; 2% other
- **Circulation:** 14,000
- **Website:** www.FamilyAndHome.org

Freelance Potential
80% written by nonstaff writers. Publishes 50 freelance submissions yearly; 50% by unpublished writers, 50% by new authors. Receives 50 unsolicited mss monthly.

Submissions
Send complete ms with biography. Accepts photocopies and computer printouts. SASE. Responds in 3 months.
Articles: 500–1,500 words. Informational and self-help articles; personal experience pieces; and humor. Topics include parenting, marriage, education, household management and finances, travel, and recreation.
Depts/columns: 700–1,800 words. Book reviews, common problems and solutions, health and safety, media coverage of stay-at-home parents, and interviews.
Artwork: B/W prints. Line art.
Other: Poetry and filler. Submit seasonal material 9–12 months in advance.

Sample Issue
30 pages (3% advertising): 5 articles; 3 depts/columns; 3 poems. Writers' guidelines available.
- "Becoming Sleep Nourished." Article discusses how sleep deprivation can negatively impact family life, and offers ways to change routines at home to get enough rest.
- Sample dept/column: "Problems and Solutions" suggests ways to get young children to sit down and eat.

Rights and Payment
First or one-time rights. Limited payment. Provides 5 contributor's copies.

Editor's Comments
We are currently looking for anecdotes about parenting, stories about adoptive families, and informational pieces. We offer our readers supportive material that stresses the importance and value of parenting children.

Westchester Family

Suite 302
141 Halstead Avenue
Mamaroneck, NY 10543

Editor: Jean Sheff

Description and Readership
Westchester Family is a resource for parents who want to keep up with events in this New York City suburb, and who want the latest information and practical help on raising families. Local personalities, experts, issues, and resources are featured as well as general parenting tips.
- **Audience:** Parents
- **Frequency:** 11 times each year
- **Distribution:** 96% controlled; 4% subscription
- **Circulation:** 50,000
- **Website:** www.westchesterfamily.com

Freelance Potential
80% written by nonstaff writers. Publishes 40 freelance submissions yearly; 40% by authors who are new to the magazine. Receives 50 queries monthly.

Submissions
Query with clips. Accepts photocopies and computer printouts. SASE. Response time varies.
Articles: 800–1,200 words. Informational articles; humor; profiles; interviews, photo essays; and personal experience pieces. Topics include gifted education, music, recreation, regional news, social issues, and women's interests.
Depts/columns: 400–800 words. News and reviews.

Sample Issue
82 pages (52% advertising): 2 articles; 6 depts/columns; 1 calendar. Sample copy, free with 9x12 SASE. Writers' guidelines available.
- "Sesame Street Turns 35!" Article looks at the history of this popular children's television show, and considers what's in the works to keep it on top.
- "Mom-Preneurs." Article highlights several women in the community who have created lifestyles that enable them to be both parents and career women.
- Sample dept/column: "Health Notes" considers whether overweight children are the result of sedentary lives or being exposed to too many junk food advertisements.

Rights and Payment
First rights. Written material, $25–$200. Pays on publication. Provides 1 contributor's copy.

Editor's Comments
Knowledge of the Westchester area is a must for writers submitting material to our publication. Articles need to be well researched and accurate, and written in a style that is easy to read and informative. We don't shy away from hard-hitting, serious issues but we do not like subjects that are overdone.

Westchester Parent

Suite 21
901 North Broadway
North White Plains, NY 10603

Submissions Editor: Helen Freedman

Description and Readership

Parents residing in Westchester and Rockland, New York, and Stamford and Greenwich, Connecticut read this magazine for its articles on parenting issues, health, and child development.
- **Audience:** Parents
- **Frequency:** Monthly
- **Distribution:** 100% controlled
- **Circulation:** 66,000
- **Website:** www.parentsknow.com

Freelance Potential

90% written by nonstaff writers. Publishes 15 freelance submissions yearly; 5% by unpublished writers, 20% by authors who are new to the magazine. Receives 95 queries, 8 unsolicited mss monthly.

Submissions

Query or send complete ms. Accepts photocopies, computer printouts, and email submissions to reneé@parentsknow.com. SASE. Response time varies.
Articles: 800–1,000 words. Informational, self-help, and how-to articles; profiles; interviews; and personal experience pieces. Topics include parenting, family life, child development, animals, pets, the arts, computers, crafts, hobbies, current events, gifted and special education, health, fitness, recreation, regional news, and travel.
Depts/columns: 750 words. Short news items and local family outings.
Other: Submit seasonal material 4 months in advance.

Sample Issue

98 pages: 6 articles; 11 depts/columns. Sample copy, free with 10x13 SASE. Writers' guidelines available via email.
- "Joining a Sports League." Article discusses questions parents should ask before choosing a sports program for their kids.
- "New Phys. Ed. Guidelines." Article reports on the new physical activity guidelines for kids created in an effort to help combat childhood obesity.
- Sample dept/column: "Thoughts" tells of a mom's cleaning effort that stirs up childhood memories of thrown-out toys.

Rights and Payment

First New York area rights. Articles, $75. Depts/columns, payment rate varies. Pays 2 months after publication. Provides 1 contributor's copy.

Editor's Comments

We are always looking for well-written pieces on timely issues as well as family-related book, music, software, movie, television, toy, and online game reviews.

West Coast Families

224-280 Nelson Street
Vancouver, British Columbia V6B 2E2
Canada

Editor: Ingrid King

Description and Readership

Parents in the Vancouver area with an interest in the local products and services available for their families, pick up this free publication at schools, libraries, stores, and other selected locations.
- **Audience:** Families
- **Frequency:** Monthly
- **Distribution:** 93% controlled; 5% schools; 2% subscription
- **Circulation:** 50,000
- **Website:** www.westcoastfamilies.com

Freelance Potential

65% written by nonstaff writers. Publishes 10 freelance submissions yearly; 25% by authors who are new to the magazine. Receives 25 queries monthly.

Submissions

Query. Accepts photocopies, computer printouts, Macintosh disk submissions, and email submissions to info@ westcoastfamilies.com. SAE/IRC. Response time varies.
Articles: 600–800 words. Informational, self-help, and how-to articles; and personal experience pieces. Topics include family life, parenting, recreation, travel, religion, current events, health, fitness, education, sports, hobbies, science, technology, nature, animals, and pets.
Depts/columns: Staff written.
Other: Puzzles, activities, jokes, and games. Submit seasonal material 3 months in advance.

Sample Issue

28 pages (8% advertising): 7 articles; 4 depts/columns; 1 calendar; 1 camp guide; 2 contests. Sample copy, free with 9x12 SASE ($1.45 Canadian postage). Guidelines and editorial calendar available.
- "Behaviour Tips That Work!" Article reviews a book of parents tips for dealing with problems such as bossiness, bullying, and defiance.
- "Celebrate Bike Month with BEST." Article calls attention to the health and environmental benefits of bike riding.

Rights and Payment

Rights policy varies. Articles, $40–$60. Other material, payment rate varies. Pays on acceptance or publication. Provides contributor's copies upon request.

Editor's Comments

If you'd like to write for us, remember that our readers are educated, middle- to upper-income earners with an intense interest in family-related issues.

Western New York Family Magazine

Suite B
3147 Delaware Avenue
Buffalo, NY 14217

Editor & Publisher: Michele Miller

Description and Readership

Launched in 1984 as *Mother's Lifeline* newsletter, this publication serves as a resource for parents of children up to the age of 14 who live in Erie and Niagara counties. Its articles cover current parenting issues with a western New York tie-in.

- **Audience:** Parents
- **Frequency:** Monthly
- **Distribution:** Controlled; subscription
- **Circulation:** 26,500
- **Website:** www.wnyfamilymagazine.com

Freelance Potential

90% written by nonstaff writers. Publishes 60 freelance submissions yearly; 50% by unpublished writers, 50% by authors who are new to the magazine. Receives 65 unsolicited mss monthly.

Submissions

Send complete ms with short biography. Accepts photocopies, computer printouts, Macintosh disk submissions (Microsoft Word), email submissions to michele@wnyfamilymagazine.com (no attachments), and simultaneous submissions if identified. SASE. Responds if interested.
Articles: 600–2,500 words. How-to articles, personal experience pieces, humor, and first-person essays written by fathers. Topics include parenting, family issues, advice for working mothers, and information on regional events and activities.
Depts/columns: Staff written.
Other: Children's crafts and activities. Submit seasonal material 3 months in advance.

Sample Issue

62 pages (60% advertising): 8 articles; 9 depts/columns; 1 calendar of events; 3 directories. Sample copy, $2.50 with 9x12 SASE ($1.01 postage). Guidelines available.
- "Plan to Plant a 'Portable Garden' This Spring." Article gives instructions for creating a "pillow-pak" garden plot.
- "Celebrate & Learn." Article features a recipe and an activity for celebrating the festival of Purim and discusses the significance of this Jewish holiday.

Rights and Payment

First North American serial rights. Articles, $25–$150. Pays on publication. Provides 1 contributor's copy.

Editor's Comments

Because this is a regional publication, local writers are given preference. Please tell us about your parenting, grandparenting, and/or professional experience in your author bio.

What

108-93 Lombard Avenue
Winnipeg, Manitoba R3B 3B1
Canada

Editor: Barbara Chabai

Description and Readership

Material in *What* is an eclectic mix ranging from hard social commentary about the world and serious looks at popular culture to lighthearted comments and commentaries by teens and profiles of famous personalities.

- **Audience:** 14–18 years
- **Frequency:** 6 times each year
- **Distribution:** 100% schools
- **Circulation:** 250,000
- **Website:** www.whatmagnet.com

Freelance Potential

30% written by nonstaff writers. Publishes 25 freelance submissions yearly; 5% by unpublished writers, 20% by authors who are new to the magazine. Receives 20 queries monthly.

Submissions

Query with clips. No unsolicited mss. SAE/IRC. Response time varies.
Articles: 300–1,700 words. Informational and factual articles; humor; and profiles. Topics include current events, music, popular culture, entertainment, health, social issues, and relationships.
Depts/columns: 300–1,700 words. Ordinary teens in extraordinary situations, trends, and sports.
Artwork: Color prints or transparencies.

Sample Issue

30 pages (60% advertising): 7 articles; 4 depts/columns. Sample copy, $1.42 (Canadian) with 9x12 SAE/IRC. Guidelines and editorial calendar available.
- "Climate for Change." Article recounts life in Vietnam, one of the most disaster-prone countries in the world with monsoons, flooding, and loss of crops.
- "Technical Difficulties." Article demonstrates poor technological manners such as keeping a cell phone on while in a movie theater, and text messaging on a phone while talking to someone else in person.
- Sample dept/column: "Whatnot" provides information on new products.

Rights and Payment

First rights. Written material, to $500. Pays 30 days after publication. Provides 2 contributor's copies.

Editor's Comments

Teens are well aware of what's going on in the world. Submissions should be geared to the sophisticated element of this intelligent population with down-to-earth writing that isn't stuffy or overblown.

What If?

19 Lynwood Place
Guelph, Ontario N1G 2V9
Canada

Managing Editor: Mike Leslie

Description and Readership
Striving to inspire, enlighten, and entertain all readers, this magazine offers an outlet for teens to showcase their creativity through top-quality fiction, editorials, and poetry in any style. Most of its material is written by and for young Canadians.
- **Audience:** 12–21 years
- **Frequency:** 6 times each year
- **Distribution:** 60% schools; 20% subscription; 20% newsstand
- **Circulation:** 25,000
- **Website:** www.whatifmagazine.com

Freelance Potential
90% written by nonstaff writers. Publishes 125 freelance submissions yearly; 90% by unpublished writers, 90% by authors who are new to the magazine. Receives 125 unsolicited mss each month.

Submissions
Send complete ms with résumé. Accepts photocopies, computer printouts, email to whatif@rogers.com (Microsoft Word), and simultaneous submissions if identified. Availability of artwork improves chance of acceptance. SASE. Responds in 2 months.
Articles: To 500 words. Opinion pieces and editorials.
Fiction: To 3,000 words. Genres include mystery; suspense; fantasy; humor; and contemporary, inspirational, real-life, and science fiction.
Artwork: B/W drawings.
Other: Poetry, to 20 lines.

Sample Issue
48 pages (3% advertising): 4 articles; 7 stories; 8 poems. Sample copy, $6.50 with 9x12 SAE/IRC ($1.60 postage). Writers' guidelines available.
- "I Wrote This with a Pen and Oink." Story tells what happens in a town when pigs sprout wings and start flying.
- "An Urban Buzz." Story features a young man who is convinced he is communicating with aliens and ends up jumping to his death while thinking he is leaping into an alien world.

Rights and Payment
First rights. No payment. Provides 3 contributor's copies.

Editor's Comments
Most of our young adult contributions are contemporary fiction and we feature the works of both new and established writers. We are currently seeking humor, mystery, and suspense stories and would love to see more editorials and opinion pieces from young adults. Make sure your characters are teenagers and/or of interest to that age group.

What's Up Kids?

496 Melter Road
Ridgeville, Ontario LOS 1MO
Canada

Managing Editor: Susan Pennell-Sebekos

Description and Readership
This magazine is a resource for positive and practical information targeting parents of newborns through early teens. It stresses learning through enjoyable activities and contains contests, games, and other hands-on projects in every issue. It covers health, nutrition, exercise, and parenting tips.
- **Audience:** Parents and children
- **Frequency:** 6 times each year
- **Distribution:** Subscription; newsstand
- **Circulation:** 200,000
- **Website:** www.whatsupkids.com

Freelance Potential
80% written by nonstaff writers. Publishes 40 freelance submissions yearly; 5% by unpublished writers, 60% by authors who are new to the magazine. Receives 29 unsolicited mss each month.

Submissions
Query. SASE. Response time varies.
Articles: Word length varies. Informational articles. Topics include education, family issues, travel, fitness, nutrition, and health.
Depts/columns: Word length varies. Brief informational items on fathers, health, finance, and news.

Sample Issue
62 pages (15% advertising): 12 articles; 10 depts/columns; 1 kids' section.
- "Helping Children with Learning Disabilities." Article tackles the subject of learning disabilities by profiling the Arrowsmith School's techniques that are offered in several Canadian locations.
- "Yoga for Kids." Article explains the ways that yoga can benefit children—from proper breathing and meditative skills to relaxation and effective exercising.
- Sample dept/column: "What's up with Dad?" focuses attention on fathers and the issues that affect them as people and as parents.

Rights and Payment
All rights. Payment policy varies. Provides contributor's copies.

Editor's Comments
We need more submissions pertaining to topics of interest to 'tweens. We cover almost every subject that relates to raising children such as, environmental issues, safety, family fun, education, teaching sound financial principles to children, the influence of television on children, and reports on children's gear and equipment.

Winner

55 West Oak Ridge Drive
Hagerstown, MD 21740

Editor: Anita Jacobs

Description and Readership

Winner stresses how important drug prevention is to pre-teens. This magazine helps readers avoid getting started with drugs by providing helpful information about peer pressure and other solutions to everyday social challenges.
- **Audience:** 8–12 years
- **Frequency:** 9 times each year
- **Distribution:** 80% schools; 20% other
- **Circulation:** 15,000
- **Website:** www.winnermagazine.com

Freelance Potential

60% written by nonstaff writers. Publishes 50 freelance submissions yearly; 5% by unpublished writers, 20% by authors who are new to the magazine. Receives 8 queries monthly.

Submissions

Query with clips or writing samples. Email queries to editor@listenmagazine.org. SASE. Responds in 1 month.
Articles: 500–600 words. Informational, how-to, and self-help articles; and profiles. Topics include family issues; sports; peer pressure; tobacco, drug and alcohol abuse; life skills; social issues; and personal relationships.
Fiction: 600 words. True-life stories about positive lifestyles and problem solving.
Artwork: Color prints and transparencies. Line art.
Other: Puzzles, games, and filler.

Sample Issue

16 pages (no advertising): 2 articles; 2 stories; 5 activities; 1 comic. Sample copy, $2 with 9x12 SASE (2 first-class stamps). Guidelines available.
- "A Voyage through Inner Space." Article creates a story-like format as it explains what happens to the inside of a body when a person smokes a cigarette.
- "Detective Walton's Message." Article profiles a Canadian policeman/drug expert as he explains how children can avoid an accidental introduction to drugs.
- "Only Dummies Don't Wear Helmets." Story points out several reasons bike helmets should be worn.

Rights and Payment

First rights. Articles, $80. Pays on acceptance. Provides 3 contributor's copies.

Editor's Comments

We have found great advantage to publishing articles about a role model who is drug free and successful. We welcome short interviews with such personalities as well as factual articles about drugs, real-world advice, and cartoons.

Wire Tap Magazine

c/o Independent Media Institute
77 Federal Street
San Francisco, CA 94107

Submissions Editor

Description and Readership

Wire Tap Magazine is an e-zine that covers social, political, and cultural issues for teens. All of its material is written from a socially progressive point of view, and many of its articles are written by its readers.
- **Audience:** YA
- **Frequency:** Monthly
- **Distribution:** Electronic
- **Hits per month:** Unavailable
- **Website:** www.alternet.org/wiretap

Freelance Potential

95% written by nonstaff writers. Publishes 50 freelance submissions yearly. Receives 10 queries, 10 unsolicited mss each month.

Submissions

Query. Accepts photocopies, computer printouts, and email submissions to editor@wiretapmag.org (no attachments). SASE. Response time varies.
Articles: Word length varies. Informational and how-to articles; profiles; and interviews. Topics include politics, social issues, the environment, and consumer issues.

Sample Issue

Sample copy and guidelines available online.
- "Redeeming the Youth Vote." Article reports on how conservative and Christian groups in America are working hard to get conservative youth to vote.
- "A Youth Activist on the Road Out." Profiles Bremley Lyngdon, a former youth activist who now is working with the World Bank and getting a Ph.D. in sustainable development.
- "The Bitter Story of Your Favorite Sweets." Investigates how the West African chocolate industry and the Salvadoran sugar industry exploit child workers.

Rights and Payment

Electronic rights. Articles, $50–$100 for assigned pieces, no payment for unsolicited submissions.

Editor's Comments

We accept a small number of submissions from accomplished writers, but before you decide to send an article, please visit our website and get to know the style and tone of our editorial content. We're always interested in new ideas and investigations—tell us a story we haven't seen in mainstream press. Bear in mind that we have a national readership and we're looking for material that will appeal to readers from Seattle to Miami and anywhere in between.

With

The Magazine for Radical Christian Youth

P.O. Box 347
722 Main Street
Newton, KS 67114

Editor: Carol Duerksen

Description and Readership

In print for over 36 years, this inspirational magazine offers first-person stories, humor pieces, how-to articles, and realistic and speculative fiction. A magazine for Mennonite teens, it seeks to empower youth to be radically committed to a personal relationship with Jesus Christ.
- **Audience:** 15–18 years
- **Frequency:** 6 times each year
- **Distribution:** 100% subscription
- **Circulation:** 4,000

Freelance Potential

100% written by nonstaff writers. Publishes 60 freelance submissions yearly; 5% by unpublished writers, 5% by authors who are new to the magazine. Receives 83 queries and unsolicited mss monthly.

Submissions

Query with clips or writing samples for how-to and first-person stories. Send complete ms for other material. Accepts photocopies, computer printouts, and simultaneous submissions. SASE. Responds to queries in 1 month, to mss in 2 months.
Articles: How-to pieces, 800–1,500 words. First-person articles, 800–1,800 words. Sidebars for first-person articles, 100–600 words. Topics include religion, missions, contemporary social issues, and family life.
Fiction: 500–2,000 words. Contemporary, inspirational, and ethnic fiction.
Depts/columns: Word length varies. Media reviews.
Artwork: Photographs and illustrations.
Other: Meditations, 100–1,200 words. Poetry, to 50 lines. Cartoons. Submit seasonal material 6–8 months in advance.

Sample Issue

32 pages (9% advertising): 6 articles; 6 depts/columns; 2 poems. Sample copy, free with 9x12 SASE (4 first-class stamps). Guidelines and theme list available.
- "Christianity Was Just Another Thing to Sneer At." Essay reflects on author's past as a troubled young rebel and how Christianity saved his life.
- Sample dept/column: "Video Review" takes a look at the documentary, *Bowling for Columbine*.

Rights and Payment

Simultaneous and reprint rights. All material, payment rate varies. Pays on acceptance. Provides 2 contributor's copies.

Editor's Comments

Each issue of our magazine focuses on a theme related to the challenges and issues teens face in their every day lives.

Woman's Day

1633 Broadway
New York, NY 10019

Senior Features Editor: Ellen Breslau

Description and Readership

Millions of women in the United States pick up this magazine to discover practical information on health, cooking, decorating, entertaining, fitness, finance management, careers, interpersonal relationships, child rearing, and spirituality.
- **Audience:** Women
- **Frequency:** 17 times each year
- **Distribution:** Subscription; newsstand
- **Circulation:** 5.1 million
- **Website:** www.womansday.com

Freelance Potential

70% written by nonstaff writers. Publishes 20 freelance submissions yearly; 20% by authors who are new to the magazine. Receives 833 queries monthly.

Submissions

Query with clips or writing samples. No unsolicited mss. SASE. Responds in 1 month.
Articles: Parenting articles, to 400 words. Other material, 500–2,000 words. Informational and how-to articles; personal experience pieces; and true stories. Topics include health, humor, family life, marriage, relationships, lifestyles, child development, home safety, crafts, gardening, and religion.
Depts/columns: 50–850 words. Food, household tips, and decorating.

Sample Issue

156 pages (76% advertising): 19 articles; 18 depts/columns. Sample copy, $1.99 at newsstands. Writers' guidelines available with SASE.
- "Smile!" Article describes teeth whitening procedures and products from the drugstore to the dentist's chair.
- "Natural Remedies." Article looks at several common household items and foods that have a reputation for healing, and describes how to use them.
- Sample dept/column: "Wdcheckup" considers premenstrual dysphoric disorder (PMDD), a more severe form of PMS, and examines treatments that are available.

Rights and Payment

First North American Serial rights. Written material, payment rate varies. Pays on publication. Provides 1 contributor's copy.

Editor's Comments

We are interested in material that will help women improve their lives, including dramatic accounts of women who have survived a disaster or achieved something significant.

Women Today Magazine

P.O. Box 300, Stn A
Vancouver, British Columbia V6C 2x3
Canada

Editorial Administrator: Leah Jenvy

Description and Readership

This Canadian Internet magazine offers women information about contemporary issues from a Christian perspective. Articles cover beauty, fashion, health, relationships, parenting, finance, and well being. Last year it also launched a Chinese version and may expand into other languages.
- **Audience:** Women
- **Frequency:** Monthly
- **Distribution:** 100% Internet
- **Hits per Month:** 2.1 million
- **Website:** www.womentodaymagazine.com

Freelance Potential

60% written by nonstaff writers. Publishes 36–50 freelance submissions yearly; 15% by unpublished writers, 30% by authors who are new to the magazine. Receives 45–60 queries each month.

Submissions

Query or send complete ms. Accepts photocopies, computer printouts, and simultaneous submissions if identified. Availability of artwork improves chance of acceptance. SASE. Responds to queries in 1–2 weeks, to mss in 2–3 months.
Articles: To 1,000 words. Informational, self-help, and how-to articles; confession and personal experience pieces; humor; and true stories. Topics include careers, finances, family, self-esteem and relationships.
Depts/columns: 300–500 words. Cooking, health, fitness, beauty, and advice.

Sample Issue

44 pages (1–2% advertising): 11 articles; 11 depts/columns. Guidelines available at website.
- "Restore Your Self-Esteem." Article discusses and defines self-esteem and offers ideas for making life better by learning to like yourself.
- "Finding a Doctor." The best ways to find the right family physician for your family are outlined in this article.

Rights and Payment

One-time reprint rights. No payment.

Editor's Comments

Before querying us, please review our editorial calendar. We are always looking for new ideas and ways to develop what you see on the calendar. Our goal is to offer women information about the issues that affect them every day such as spirituality, marriage, finances, and more. We want to see writing that is uplifting, informative, and reflective of our connection to God.

Wonder Years

321 North Pine
Lansing, MI 48933

Publications Editor: Linda Wacyk

Description and Readership

This four-page publication is distributed throughout the state of Michigan. It regularly covers parenting and education topics of interest to families with children up to the age of 16. Subjects covered on a regular basis include health, fitness, special education, child development, and personal experiences.
- **Audience:** Parents
- **Frequency:** 6 times each year
- **Distribution:** 50% social service agencies; 30% schools; 20% subscription
- **Circulation:** 150,000
- **Website:** www.partnershipforlearning.org

Freelance Potential

80% written by nonstaff writers. Publishes 55 freelance submissions yearly; 5% by unpublished writers, 50% by authors who are new to the magazine. Receives 8 mss monthly.

Submissions

Send complete ms. Accepts email queries to wacykl@cablespeed.com. Responds 6–8 weeks.
Articles: 400–800 words. Informational and how-to articles; reviews; and personal experience pieces. Topics include heath, fitness, humor, music, nature, the environment, self-help, and parenting.
Artwork: Color prints or transparencies. Line art.
Other: Sidebars, briefs, 150–500 words. Submit seasonal material 6 months in advance.

Sample Issue

8 pages (no advertising): 8 articles. Sample copy, free with 9x12 SASE ($1 postage). Guidelines available.
- "Simply Grand." Article looks at the important role a grandparent can play in a young child's life.
- "Play Pretend." A craft that will help children "act out" different roles and emotions is described here.
- "Read." Article offers suggestions on how to slow a toddle down by reading to them.

Rights and Payment

First or reprint rights. All material, payment rate varies. Pays on acceptance. Provides 5 contributor's copies.

Editor's Comments

We would like to see more stories about how children learn an develop, and the practical ways parents can use to improve thi process. On the other hand, we get far too many submissions general discipline topics and general parenting advice. If you supply terrific photos along with your article, you will have a better chance of seeing your work in print.

Word Dance Magazine

P.O. Box 10804
Wilmington, DE 19850

Director: Stuart Ungar

Description and Readership
Self-described as "the magazine dedicated to the voice of today's youth," *Word Dance* provides a forum for self-expression for students from kindergarten through eighth grade. It encourages young writers to freely express themselves through mediums of poetry and articles relating travel and sports experiences.
- **Audience:** 6–14 years
- **Frequency:** Quarterly
- **Distribution:** 50% newsstand; 30% subscription; 20% schools
- **Circulation:** Unavailable
- **Website:** www.worddance.com

Freelance Potential
100% written by nonstaff writers. Publishes 250 freelance submissions yearly; 95% by unpublished writers. Receives 80+ unsolicited mss monthly.

Submissions
Send complete ms with permission form. No more than 10 submissions per class or 3 submissions per student. Accepts photocopies and computer printouts. SASE. Responds in 6–9 months.
Articles: To three pages. Topics include animals, pets, social issues, and travel.
Fiction: To three pages. Genres include fantasy, adventure, folktales, folklore, humor, and inspirational, multicultural, and ethnic fiction. Also publishes stories about animals, nature, the environment, and sports.
Artwork: Line art.
Other: Poetry, to 3 pages.

Sample Issue
2 pages (no advertising): 2 articles; 1 story; 11 poems. Sample copy, $4.95. Guidelines and editorial calendar available.
- "My Own Little World." First-person narrative explores the fine line between sports reality and fantasy.
- "Field Trip." Story recounts a dream set in the Kalahari desert in Africa with the narrator weaving between real experiences and imagined scenes.

Rights and Payment
rights. Pays $5 on publication. Provides contributor's a discounted rate.

Comments
submissions should be to the specific categories in We encourage young writers to express their the world, their travel experiences, and self-is also a special Haiku section.

Working Mother

27th Floor
60 East 42nd Street
New York, NY 10165

Parenting Editor: Caroline Howard

Description and Readership
This guide for busy mothers helps them meet the demands of family responsibilities while persuing employment outside the home.
- **Audience:** Mothers
- **Frequency:** Monthly
- **Distribution:** 90% subscription; 10% newsstand
- **Circulation:** 900,000
- **Website:** www.workingmother.com

Freelance Potential
50% written by nonstaff writers. Publishes 75 freelance submissions yearly; 30% by authors who are new to the magazine. Receives 75 queries, 150 unsolicited mss monthly.

Submissions
Prefers query. Accepts complete ms. Accepts photocopies and computer printouts. SASE. Responds to queries in 6–8 weeks, to mss in 2 months.
Articles: 1,500–2,000 words. Informational articles; profiles; interviews; humor; and personal experience pieces. Topics include child rearing, home and money management, health, family relationships, and job-related issues.
Depts/columns: Word length varies. Health, safety, finance, and career issues.
Other: Submit seasonal material 6 months in advance.

Sample Issue
84 pages (34% advertising): 2 articles; 1 photoessay; 17 depts/columns. Sample copy, $3.50 at newsstands. Guidelines available.
- "How to Advocate for Your Child." Article shares stories of moms who used work skills such as communication, empathy, flexibility, and negotiation to challenge the system and meet their kids' needs.
- Sample dept/column: "Go Home" offers short pieces on traveling with your toddler, playdate discipline, and sending kids to day camp.
- Sample dept/column: "Work in Progress" looks at ways to deal with financial setbacks.

Rights and Payment
All rights. Written material, payment rate varies. Pays on acceptance. Provides 2 contributor's copies.

Editor's Comments
The most successful queries are those that are timely, appropriately researched, engagingly written, and tailored to a situation or problem unique to our readers. Don't submit travel, beauty, food, or fashion pieces—these are staff written.

World Kid Magazine

3435 SW First Avenue
Miami, FL 33145

Editor: Luis F. Rodriguez

Description and Readership

Just as its name promises, this colorful magazine brings the world in all of its excitement to children. Upbeat writing is partnered with exciting photographs meant to entice and spark the interest of young readers.
- **Audience:** All ages
- **Frequency:** 6 times each year
- **Distribution:** Subscription; newsstand
- **Circulation:** 10,000
- **Website:** www.worldkidmag.com

Freelance Potential

40% written by nonstaff writers. Publishes 15–20 freelance submissions yearly.

Submissions

Query with clips or writing samples. Accepts email submissions to editor@worldkidmag.com. Responds in 2 weeks.
Articles: Word length varies. Informational articles. Topics include art, science, literature, fashion, sports, games, pop music, personalities, travel, photography, art and illustrations, museums, languages, cultures, performing arts, parenting, health, nature, personal care, and animals.
Fiction: Word length varies. Genres include adventure and multicultural fiction.
Other: Games.

Sample Issue

50 pages (no advertising): 8 articles; 1 dept/column; 1 funny page. Sample copy, guidelines, and editorial calendar, $4.50 with 9x12 SASE.
- "Petra." Article brings to life the Nigerian city of Petra, a long-lost city of the Nabateans, a tribe of Bedouins, now resplendent in its restoration since its rediscovery in 1813.
- "Antique Bisque Dolls." Article examines how bisque dolls manufactured in France and Germany in the late 1800s accurately reflect the fashions and hairstyles of those eras.
- "San Francisco." Photoessay documents several of the city's cultural and historical areas, punctuated with breathtaking photos.

Rights and Payment

All rights. Written material, payment rate varies. Pays on publication. Provides 10 contributor's copies.

Editor's Comments

We want to introduce children to the cultural wonders of the world, using top quality photos and vibrant language to portray the exciting possibilities that abound on earth. Almost any subject is accepted, except religion and politics.

Writers' Journal

P.O. Box 394
Perham, MN 56573

Editor: Leon Ogroske

Description and Readership

Novice and experienced writers turn to this magazine for its informational articles and tips on the skill of writing, independent publishing, and the business side of writing. Reviews on poetry, books and software, as well as contest information are also included.
- **Audience:** YA–Adult
- **Frequency:** 6 times each year
- **Distribution:** 90% newsstand; 10% subscription
- **Circulation:** 23,000
- **Website:** www.writersjournal.com

Freelance Potential

90% written by nonstaff writers. Publishes 60 freelance submissions yearly; 50% by unpublished writers, 70% by authors who are new to the magazine. Receives 23 queries and unsolicited mss monthly.

Submissions

Query or send complete ms. Accepts photocopies, and computer printouts. SASE. Responds 2–6 months.
Articles: 1,200–2,000 words. Informational and how-to articles; profiles; and interviews. Topics include fiction writing, travel writing, technical writing, business writing, writing skills, interviewing, researching, record keeping, and finances.
Depts/columns: Photography tips and marketing ideas, 1,200–2,000 words. Software reviews, 500–750.
Other: Poetry. Fiction contest, various genres.

Sample Issue

64 pages (10% advertising): 11 articles; 1 story; 9 depts/columns. Sample copy, $5 with 9x12 SASE. Writers' guidelines available.
- "Details! Details!" Article discusses the importance of choosing and using the correct details when writing a story.
- "What's Your Punctuation Personality?" Article offers a theory based on matching the excessive use of certain punctuation marks with different personalities.
- "Sample dept/column: "Photography Techniques" offers tips and techniques on photographing nature.

Rights and Payment

One-time rights vary. Written material, $20 plus 1-year subscription. Pays on publication. Provides contributor's copies.

Editor's Comments

We are looking for new and unusual freelance market ideas, as well as articles on developing stories. Remember, we are an instructional magazine. Our readers look to us to provide them with the information they need to get their work published.

YES Mag

Canada's Science Magazine for Kids

3968 Long Gun Place
Victoria, British Columbia V8N 3A9
Canada

Managing Editor: Jude Isabella

Description and Readership

This Canadian magazine is full of articles and fascinating photos that explore the wonderful world of science. It aims to captivate and inspire middle school children to pursue an interest in the field of science. It also includes information on the latest technology, books, and software.
- **Audience:** 8–14 years
- **Frequency:** 6 times each year
- **Distribution:** 85% subscription; 15% newsstand
- **Circulation:** 18,000
- **Website:** www.yesmag.ca

Freelance Potential

70% written by nonstaff writers. Publishes 30 freelance submissions yearly; 15% by unpublished writers, 50% by authors who are new to the magazine. Receives 15 queries monthly.

Submissions

Query. Accepts email submissions to editor@yesmag.ca. Response time varies.
Articles: Informational articles, 250 words. Features, 800–1,200 words. Short articles relating to the theme topic, 400–800 words. Topics include mathematics, science, and technology.
Depts/columns: 250 words. Short topics on recent science, technology, and environmental news.

Sample Issue

32 pages (9% advertising): 4 articles; 5 depts/columns. Sample copy, $4 with SAE/IRC. Guidelines and theme list available.
- "Giant River Otters." Article describes the activities of these endangered species who live in family groups in South America's wetlands.
- "Video Game Invasion." Article takes a look at the use of a new wave of computer technology—augemented reality—and how it will change the future of video games.
- Sample dept/column: "Sci and Tech Watch" reports on a camera able to watch bears and research species in the sea.

Rights and Payment

First rights. Written material, $.20 (Canadian) per word. Other material, payment rate varies. Pays on publication. Provides 1 contributor's copy.

Editor's Comments

We provide interesting information on science topics that kids love to read about. We want to make science fun, so kids will want to learn more. The only department open to freelancers is our "Science and Technology Watch." Reviews of software and books are done by our readers—kids.

Yin Magazine

9th Floor
730 Fifth Avenue
New York, NY 10019

Editor-in-Chief: Cindy Chen

Description and Readership

Glossy and chic, *Yin* is for the young, intelligent Asian woman who has a strong sense of self and personal style. It showcases issues and topics of interest to them—fashion, beauty, travel, world culture, current affairs, entertainment, celebrity personalities, and Asian profiles—all in a manner that is fresh, smart, and relevant.
- **Audience:** Asian women, 18–35 years
- **Frequency:** 6 times each year
- **Distribution:** Subscription; newsstand
- **Circulation:** Unavailable
- **Website:** www.yinmag.com

Freelance Potential

50% written by nonstaff writers. Publishes 15–20 freelance submissions yearly.

Submissions

Query or send complete ms. Accepts photocopies, computer printouts, and email submissions to editor@yinmag.com. SASE. Response time varies.
Articles: Word length varies. Informational articles; profiles; interviews; and personal experience pieces. Topics include fashion, beauty, travel, celebrity issues, health, culture, lifestyles, entertainment, and reviews.
Depts/columns: Word length varies. Reviews and fashion.

Sample Issue

66 pages (10% advertising): 9 articles; 4 depts/columns. Sample copy, $4.95 at newsstands. Guidelines available.
- "Go Go Girl: Chiaki Kuriyama." Article profiles a diminutive actress, one of the stars in the movie, "*Kill Bill,*" whose cute, young ways belie the killer she portrayed.
- "Top 10 Airport Goodbye Scenes." Article compiles the author's 10 all-time favorite airport departure scenes according to the "tears" factor.
- Sample dept/column: "Yin Reviews" offers critiques on films that are either directed by Asian professionals or feature stories that take place in Asian countries.

Rights and Payment

All rights. Written material, payment rate varies. Pays 1 month after publication.

Editor's Comments

We strive to be the magazine that Asian women turn to for information and support for their interests and lifestyles. Our goal is to reflect theAsian influences and trends in the world, and to serve as a voice for the knowledgeable, multi-ethnic Asian woman who wants to speak out and be heard.

YM

Gruner + Jahr Publishing
15 East 26th Street
New York, NY 10010

Managing Editor: Monica James

Description and Readership

This magazine for teenage girls covers all aspects of young adulthood. Popular culture, jobs, relationships, celebrities, fashion, beauty, healthful eating, and social issues are among the topics explored.
- **Audience:** 14–24 years
- **Frequency:** Monthly
- **Distribution:** Subscription; newsstand
- **Circulation:** 1.5 million
- **Website:** www.ym.com

Freelance Potential

20% written by nonstaff writers. Publishes 20–25 freelance submissions yearly; 10% by unpublished writers, 40% by authors who are new to the magazine. Receives 375 queries and unsolicited mss monthly.

Submissions

Query with résumé and clips or writing samples for articles. Send complete ms for essays. Accepts photocopies, computer printouts, and simultaneous submissions if identified. SASE. Responds in 2 months.
Articles: To 2,500 words. Informational and how-to articles; first-person narratives; profiles; and interviews. Topics include fashion, beauty, entertainment, celebrities, popular culture, dating, health, fitness, relationships, friendship, sexuality, and social issues.
Depts/columns: Staff written.
Other: Submit seasonal material 6 months in advance.

Sample Issue

172 pages (30% advertising): 6 articles; 24 depts/columns. Sample copy, $3.50 at newsstands. Guidelines available.
- "Lights, Camera, Not So Much Action." Personal experience piece relates what it was like to be an extra on a movie set.
- "Shia LaBeouf." Article profiles a successful young actor who, at the age of 12, pulled his own strings to get a shot at stardom.
- "Closet Preppy." Article follows the step-by-step process of a 16-year-old girl's bedroom makeover.

Rights and Payment

First North American serial rights. Written material, $100+. Pays on acceptance. Provides 1 contributor's copy.

Editor's Comments

Articles must be informative, but opinions of experts such as psychologists, authors, or teachers should be included only as supplements to the feelings and experiences of young women.

Young Adult Today

P.O. Box 436987
Chicago, IL 60643-6987

Submissions Editor: Katara A. Washington

Description and Readership

This publication is a study guide for African American young adults who live in urban areas and participate in Urban Ministries' Christian education program. Each issue features weekly lessons that include Scripture passages, study questions, and lesson applications.
- **Audience:** 18–24 years
- **Frequency:** Quarterly
- **Distribution:** 100% subscription
- **Circulation:** 19,000
- **Website:** www.urbanministries.com

Freelance Potential

95% written by nonstaff writers. Publishes 52 freelance submissions yearly; 50% by unpublished writers, 50% by authors who are new to the magazine. Receives 20 queries each month.

Submissions

Query with résumé. No unsolicited mss. All articles and Bible lessons are assigned. SASE. Responds in 2 months.
Articles: To 400 words. Lessons consist of discussion pieces, questions, devotional readings, and Bible study guides that explain how to apply the lessons learned from Scripture to modern life.

Sample Issue

80 pages (4% advertising): 1 article; 13 life application stories; 13 Bible study guides. Sample copy, $2.25 with 9x12 SASE ($.87 postage). Guidelines provided on assignment.
- "Not Impossible." Lesson drives home the point that trusting and obeying God, especially in the most trying of circumstances, will help believers enjoy all the benefits of their salvation.
- "Be Faithful to Teaching." Lesson teaches that growth in Christian maturity is an ongoing process and directs students to commit to applying God's word to their daily lives.

Rights and Payment

Rights negotiable. Written material, $150 per lesson. Pays on publication.

Editor's Comments

Our student lessons are designed to be stimulating and challenging for young adults seeking to grow in their Christian faith. Because this is a ministry to young African Americans, our lessons reflect their culture and our "Timely Insights" stories depict black youth. If you feel you are called to join us in our ministry, send us your résumé for consideration.

Young Adult Today Leader

P.O. Box 436987
Chicago, IL 60643

Submissions Editor: Katara A. Washington

Description and Readership
Urban Ministries, Inc., publishes this teacher's guide to its young adult Christian education program. The material produced by Urban Ministries includes Sunday school curriculum, vacation Bible school resources, books, videos, and music—all of which depict or speak to African Americans in the context of their culture.
- **Audience:** Teachers
- **Frequency:** Quarterly
- **Distribution:** Unavailable
- **Circulation:** 12,000
- **Website:** www.urbanministries.com

Freelance Potential
95% written by nonstaff writers. Publishes 52 freelance submissions yearly; 50% by unpublished writers, 50% by authors who are new to the magazine. Receives 20 queries each month.

Submissions
Query with résumé. All work is done on assignment only. No unsolicited mss. SASE. Responds in 2 months.
Articles: Devotionals, 400 words. Topics include current events and social issues as they relate to Christianity and the Bible.

Sample Issue
80 pages (no advertising): 1 article; 26 teaching plans with daily lessons. Sample copy, $2.25 with 9x12 SASE ($.87 postage). Guidelines available.
- "Learning to Live." Article cites the experiences of Sojourner Truth, Booker T. Washington, and the apostle Paul to show that developing our special God-given talent will help us find the meaning of life and the secret of contentment.
- "Choosing to Believe." Teaching plan with lesson enforces the point that God's message of salvation is just as urgent and compelling in this age of technology as it was when Jesus was alive on earth, and stresses that God gave us the freedom to choose what to believe.

Rights and Payment
Rights negotiable. Written material, $150. Pays on publication.

Editor's Comments
Ours is a special ministry to young adults of the Christian African American community. If you have been a leader in youth programs and feel you'd like to take part in ours, we invite you to submit a résumé. Study a sample issue to become familiar with the specific structure of our lessons.

YoungBucksOutdoors.com

P.O. Box 244022
Montgomery, AL 36124

Managing Editor: Dockery Austin

Description and Readership
This publication brings the great outdoors online for children interested in nature, hunting, fishing, and other outside activities. It stresses respect for all living creatures.
- **Audience:** 7 years–Adult
- **Frequency:** Weekly
- **Distribution:** 100% Internet
- **Hits per month:** 200,000
- **Website:** www.youngbucksoutdoors.com

Freelance Potential
60% written by nonstaff writers.

Submissions
Query with details about photo support. Accepts email submissions to daustin@buckmasters.com. Availability of artwork improves chance of acceptance. SASE. Responds to queries in 3 days.
Articles: 400 words. Informational and how-to articles; interviews; photoessays; and humor. Topics include animals, nature, health, fitness, the outdoors, recreation, science, technology, crafts, and sports.
Fiction: To 500 words. Genres include adventure and stories about nature, the environment, and animals.
Depts/columns: To 500 words. Gun safety, the human body, and insects.
Artwork: Color prints and transparencies.
Other: Puzzles. Submit seasonal material 4 months in advance.

Sample Issue
3 articles. Sample copy available at website. Writers' guidelines available.
- "Deer Rifles for Kids." Article explains the importance of fitting a child with the correct size rifle and what to consider when doing it.
- "Release That Lunker." Article relates a young boy's fishing experience and his decision to return a trophy trout back to the stream.
- Sample dept/column: "Wildlife" portrays the bloodhound and its characteristics.

Rights and Payment
First rights. All material, payment rate varies. Pays on publication.

Editor's Comments
We are always interested in interviews with a famous sports personality or celebrity who emphasizes interest in the outdoors. Don't be afraid of humor when it's appropriate.

Young Dancer

11th Floor
333 7th Avenue
New York, NY 10001

Editor: Susan Keough

Description and Readership

Premiering in 2004, this magazine is written for middle-grade kids with a passion and enthusiasm for all types of dance. Each issue includes profiles of young dancers, advice for competitive dancers, crafts related to dance, and general advice.
- **Audience:** 8–13 years
- **Frequency:** Monthly
- **Distribution:** Subscription; newsstand
- **Circulation:** Unavailable
- **Website:** www.youngdancer.com

Freelance Potential

70% written by nonstaff writers. Publishes 20 freelance submissions yearly.

Submissions

Query. SASE. Response time varies.
Articles: Word length varies. Informational articles; profiles; and personal experience pieces. Topics include dance, crafts, exercise, competition, nutrition.
Depts/columns: Word length varies. Crafts and fashion.

Sample Issue

40 pages: 6 articles; 3 depts/columns.
- "A Chance to Fly." A young dancer who has just captured a major role in a new production is profiled.
- "Competitive Edge." In this article, top dance professionals offer advice for young dancers.
- "A Little Pro." Young dancer Tara Sorine, a dancer with the New York City Ballet, is profiled.
- Sample dept/column: "Faux Pas" makes fun of embarrassing goofs.

Rights and Payment

All rights. Payment policy and rates vary. Provides copies.

Editor's Comments

As a new publication, we are interested in nurturing relationships with freelancers who we can use regularly. You need to have a background in dance or choreography and understand how to write for young readers in a way that is informative but now condescending. We are looking for features on young dancers and interviews with professional dancers. If you are crafty, send us an idea for a craft that relates to dance in some way—for example we featured a piece on how to make a dance bag. All sections of the magazine are open to new writers. While we do pay for material, we have no set fees. Send us a story that will grab our young readers' attention with its enthusiastic tone.

Young Money

Suite 310
2101 Park Center Drive
Orlando, FL 32835

Managing Editor: Daniel Jimenez

Description and Readership

Articles that help college students understand the concept of smart money management in the 21st century appear in *Young Money* magazine. Information about this complicated subject is presented in an easy-to-understand, entertaining format to appeal to its readers, many of whom are not business or finance majors.
- **Audience:** 18–24 years
- **Frequency:** Quarterly
- **Distribution:** 99% schools; 1% subscription
- **Circulation:** 200,000
- **Website:** www.youngmoney.com

Freelance Potential

90% written by nonstaff writers. Publishes 20 freelance submissions yearly; 50% by authors who are new to the magazine. Receives 10 queries monthly.

Submissions

Query with abstract. SASE. Responds in 10 days.
Articles: 350–800 words. Informational articles. Topics include money management, finances, saving, investing, credit cards, travel, car buying, and career searches. Also uses profiles of 18- to 24-year-old entrepreneurs.
Artwork: Color prints and transparencies.

Sample Issue

32 pages (25% advertising): 20 articles; 1 survey. Sample copy, free. Guidelines and editorial calendar available.
- "Conquering the Quarterlife Crisis." Article looks at the conflicts faced by young adults as they leave the security of a college campus and venture into the real world.
- "Missing in Action: Where Are the Women?" Article maintains that it is still a difficult climb for women seeking top management positions, despite the increased support and resources that have become available to them in recent years.
- "How to Avoid the Potholes of Vehicle Repair." Article lists basic maintenance rules that, if followed, could save thousands of dollars in car repair bills.

Rights and Payment

First rights. Articles, $100–$200. Pays on publication. Provides 2 contributor's copies.

Editor's Comments

Your own personal interest in the topic you're covering must come through in your writing. If you're excited about an issue related to money management or careers, your reader will be too. While everything we publish must contain accurate and authoritative information, it should be fun to read as well.

Young Rider

P.O. Box 8237
Lexington, KY 40533

Editor: Lesley Ward

Description and Readership
Young horse and pony lovers enjoy this magazine for its educational and entertaining articles and colorful photos on caring for horses and riding. It also includes fictional stories with horse themes.
- **Audience:** 6–14 years
- **Frequency:** 6 times each year
- **Distribution:** 70% subscription; 30% newsstand
- **Circulation:** 89,000
- **Website:** www.youngrider.com

Freelance Potential
20% written by nonstaff writers. Publishes 20 freelance submissions yearly; 30% by unpublished writers, 80% by authors who are new to the magazine. Receives 10 queries monthly.

Submissions
Query. Accepts computer printouts. SASE. Responds in 2 weeks.
Articles: Word length varies. Factual, informational, and how-to articles; and profiles. Topics include riding, horses, careers, training, technique, and horse care.
Fiction: 1,200 words. Stories that feature horses and youth themes.
Artwork: Color prints, transparencies, and high-resolution digital images.

Sample Issue
64 pages (28% advertising): 9 articles; 1 story; 3 depts/columns. Sample copy, $2.95 with 9x12 SASE ($1 postage). Guidelines and editorial calendar available.
- "Deworming." Article offers step-by-step instructions on how to deworm a horse or pony.
- "Feeding the Older Horse." Article discusses special dietary needs for older horses or ponies and offers tips on proper feeding care.
- "Trail Trials." Story tells of two boys who learn a lesson about each other while riding a judged trail ride.

Rights and Payment
First rights. Written material, $.10 per word. Artwork, payment rate varies. Pays on publication. Provides 2 contributor's copies.

Editor's Comments
We would like to see more on horsey celebrities and interesting horsey events and activities. Also, funny stories, with a bit of conflict, which will appeal to the 13-year-old age group is of interest to us. Make sure you write in the third person, and focus on kids. Please, no first-person stories about boring childhood riding experiences, or moralistic stories.

Young Salvationist

The Salvation Army
P.O. Box 269
Alexandria, VA 22313-0269

Editor-in-Chief: Marlene Chase

Description and Readership
Inspirational articles and stories that teach the Gospel of Jesus Christ are featured in this magazine. Published by the Salvation Army, it offers youths a way to deal with the challenges of adolescence by connecting with their Christian faith.
- **Audience:** 13–18 years
- **Frequency:** 10 times each year
- **Distribution:** 80% controlled; 20% subscription
- **Circulation:** 48,000
- **Website:** www.thewarcry.com

Freelance Potential
65% written by nonstaff writers. Publishes 66 freelance submissions yearly; 5% by unpublished writers, 10% by authors who are new to the magazine. Receives 66 unsolicited mss each month.

Submissions
Send complete ms. Accepts photocopies, computer printouts, simultaneous submissions, and email submissions to ys@usn.salavationarmy.org. SASE. Responds in 2 months.
Articles: 1,000–1,500 words. How-to, inspirational, and personal experience pieces; profiles; interviews; and humor. Topics include religion and issues of relevance to teens.
Fiction: 500–1,200 words. Genres include adventure, fantasy, romance, humor, and religious and science fiction—all written from a Christian perspective.
Other: Submit seasonal material 6 months in advance.

Sample Issue
22 pages (no advertising): 8 articles. Sample copy, free with 9x12 SASE (3 first-class stamps). Writers' guidelines and theme list available with #10 SASE or at website.
- "Need Some Polishing." Essay tells how a collector of old brass instruments is reminded that it is people, not things, who are truly valuable in life.
- "I'm So Mad, I Could Scream." Article takes a look at some of the reasons why we get angry, and offers positive ways to deal with our emotions.

Rights and Payment
First and reprint rights. Written material, $.15 per word for first rights, $.10 per word for reprint rights. Pays on acceptance. Provides 4 contributor's copies.

Editor's Comments
We would like to see features showing how youth are making a difference in society. We are also looking for more celebrity profiles. Please make sure articles are not preachy, and help readers face situations positively.

Your Stepfamily

10314 Tanager Trail
Brecksville, OH 44141

Editor: Karen Adolphson

Description and Readership
This online publication addresses the needs of the more than 90 million Americans who are members of a stepfamily. Readers find upbeat, positive information and help for various issues faced by blended families.
- **Audience:** Stepfamilies, therapists, clergy members, and educators
- **Frequency:** 6 times each year
- **Distribution:** 80% subscription; 20% other
- **Circulation:** Unavailable
- **Website:** www.yourstepfamily.com

Freelance Potential
75% written by nonstaff writers. Publishes 15+ freelance submissions yearly; 30% by unpublished writers, 50% by authors who are new to the magazine. Receives 10 mss monthly.

Submissions
Query or send complete ms. Accepts photocopies, computer printouts, and simultaneous submissions if identified. SASE. Responds in 2 weeks.
Articles: 500–2,500 words. Informational, self-help, and how-to articles; personal experience pieces; profiles; interviews; and reviews. Topics include family life, parenting, education, and social and multicultural issues.
Fiction: 500–2,500 words. Stories about stepfamilies.
Depts/columns: 500–2,500 words. Child development, family meals, dealing with ex-spouses, and book reviews.
Other: Poetry and original cartoons. Submit seasonal material 6 months in advance.

Sample Issue
5 articles; 8 short reads; 6 depts/columns.
- "Middler in the Haunted House." Article refers to the difficulties of being in a stepfamily faced by children ages 10 to 15 and provides ideas on how to help them cope with these challenging situations.
- "Food Fight!" Article tackles the inevitable problems of ingrained eating habits when stepchildren are put into new family situations and introduced to new traditions.

Rights and Payment
Prefers all rights; will negotiate. No payment. Provides 3 contributor's copies.

Editor's Comments
We would like to see more submissions dealing with adult stepchildren, teen stepchildren, legal issues, financial issues, and how extended family members relate to the presence of new spouses and stepchildren.

Youth & Christian Education Leadership

1080 Montgomery Avenue
Cleveland, TN 37311

Editor: Wanda Griffith

Description and Readership
Christian educators, pastors, outreach workers, youth pastors, and other ministry professionals find inspiration, information, and creative ideas for teaching religious studies in this publication.
- **Audience:** Adults
- **Frequency:** Quarterly
- **Distribution:** 100% subscription
- **Circulation:** 13,000
- **Website:** www.pathwaypress.org

Freelance Potential
80% written by nonstaff writers. Publishes 60 freelance submissions yearly; 5% by unpublished writers, 10% by authors who are new to the magazine. Receives 20 queries, 30 unsolicited mss monthly.

Submissions
Prefers complete ms with author biography. Accepts queries. Accepts disk submissions (Microsoft Word or WordPerfect) and email to Wanda_Griffith@pathwaypress.org. SASE. Responds in 3 weeks.
Articles: 500–1,000 words. Informational and how-to articles; profiles; interviews; and personal experience pieces. Topics include current events, humor, music, religion, social issues, psychology, family parenting, and multicultural and ethnic subjects.
Depts/columns: Staff written.

Sample Issue
32 pages (2% advertising): 9 articles; 7 depts/columns. Sample copy, $1 with 9x12 SASE (2 first-class stamps). Guidelines available.
- "Reaching Students Outside the Classroom." Article explains why one college educator believes interacting with her students outside the classroom setting has positive benefits for everyone.
- "Making Christian Education Fun!" Article narrates one pastor's many years of experience teaching Sunday school and the ways he has found to make it interesting.

Rights and Payment
First rights. Written material, $25–$50. Kill fee, 50%. Pays on publication. Provides 1–10 contributor's copies.

Editor's Comments
We are always interested in material that features successful Christian education ministries or focuses on individuals or groups who are advancing Christian education. Practical guidelines for effective ministry are also welcome.

Youth Today

4th Floor
1200 17th Street NW
Washington, DC 20036

Editor: Patrick Boyle

Description and Readership

This tabloid is a hands-on informational resource for persons involved in youth services nationwide. Content includes grants, programs, success stories, news of the industry, research analysis, and legislative issues concerning youth.
- **Audience:** Youth workers
- **Frequency:** 10 times each year
- **Distribution:** 75% subscription; 25% controlled
- **Circulation:** 26,000
- **Website:** www.youthtoday.org

Freelance Potential

50% written by nonstaff writers. Publishes 25 freelance submissions yearly; 10% by authors who are new to the magazine. Receives 3 queries monthly.

Submissions

Query with résumé and clips. SASE. Responds in 3 months.
Articles: 1,000–2,500 words. Informational articles; news and research reports; profiles of youth workers and youth programs; and business features. Topics include foster care, child abuse, youth program management, juvenile justice, job training and school-to-work programs, after-school programs and mentoring, and other social issues related to youth development.
Depts/columns: Book and video reviews; news briefs; opinion pieces; and people in the news.

Sample Issue

44 pages (50% advertising): 9 articles; 13 depts/columns. Sample copy, $5. Guidelines available.
- "Attracting Teens." Article compares successful and unsuccessful teen programs, highlighting an effective Boys & Girls Club regimen.
- "Research Watch." Article points out that urban and suburban children have basically the same types of behavior, sexual experiences, and drug abuse.
- Sample dept/column: "Youth Work Snapshots" provides an indepth look at Alternatives, Inc. in Chicago which offers youth and parent family services.

Rights and Payment

All rights. Written material, $.50–$.75 per word. Pays on acceptance. Provides 3 contributor's copies.

Editor's Comments

Our publication covers every aspect of youth services. We are looking for first-hand accounts of successful interactions with youth, and what really works to help them develop in a positive and well-balanced manner.

Youthworker

3rd Floor
104 Woodmont Boulevard
Nashville, TN 37205

Editor: Will Penner

Description and Readership

This Christian magazine is written for individuals involved in youth ministry. Each themed issue offers thoughtful articles written by experienced youth workers. Most, though not all, of the magazine's readers are associated with churches.
- **Audience:** Christian youth workers
- **Frequency:** 6 times each year
- **Distribution:** 100% subscription
- **Circulation:** 20,000
- **Website:** www.youthworker.com

Freelance Potential

50% written by nonstaff writers. Publishes 20 freelance submissions yearly; 10% by unpublished writers. Receives 60 queries monthly.

Submissions

Query. Accepts photocopies, computer printouts, disk submissions (Microsoft Word), fax submissions to 615-385-4112, and email submissions to will@youthspecialties.com (write "query" in the subject field). SASE. Responds in 6–8 weeks.
Articles: Word length varies. Informational and practical application articles and reviews. Topics include religious issues, adolescent research, education, family issues, popular culture, careers, college, music, and media.
Depts/columns: Word length varies. Reports on national and regional trends; and quotations that relate to youth workers.

Sample Issue

68 pages (30% advertising): 7 articles; 7 depts/columns. Sample copy, $8. Guidelines available at website.
- "With Great Power Comes Great Responsibility." Article looks at ways the inherent power of a youth worker has the potential to lead sheep astray and undermine ministry.
- "Bean Counting 101: Playing the Numbers Game." Article discusses the use of numbers in everyday life but points out that the value of time, objects, or an individual should not be based solely on numbers.

Rights and Payment

All rights. Written material, $15–$200. Pays on publication. Provides 1 contributor's copy.

Editor's Comments

Avoid how-to articles. It's fine to share what's worked for you, but don't assume it will work for others. Inspire your readers not by setting out to write an "inspirational" article, but by being transparent and honest in your writing—transparency and honesty are what inspire.

Additional Listings

Additional Listings

We have selected the following magazines to offer you additional publishing opportunities. These magazines range from general interest publications to women's magazines to craft and hobby magazines. While children, young adults, parents, or teachers may not be their primary target audience, these publications do publish a limited amount of material that relates to children and families.

These listings also serve to keep you informed of the magazines that would not be considered good markets at this time. Such listings would include magazines that were closed to queries and freelance submissions at the time we went to press, as well as magazines that are in the process of reviewing their focus.

As you review the listings that follow, use the Description and Readership section as your guide to the particular needs of each magazine. This section offers general information about the magazine and its readers' interests, as well as the type of material it usually publishes. The Freelance Potential section will provide information about the publication's receptivity to freelance manuscripts.

After you survey the listings to determine if your work meets the magazine's specifications, be sure to read a recent sample copy and the current writers' guidelines before submitting your material.

Adventures

6401 The Paseo
Kansas City, Mo 64131

Assistant Editor: Andrea Callison

Description and Readership
Published by the Church of the Nazarene, *Adventure* is used in Sunday school classes. Its goal is to help children make connections between lessons from the Bible and their everyday lives. Each issue includes a seven to eight page Bible story, which are written on assignment. Adventure will not be accepting submissions until 2006. Circ: Unavailable.
Website: www.wordaction.com

Freelance Potential
50% written by nonstaff writers. Publishes 15 freelance submissions yearly; 10% by unpublished writers, 10% by authors who are new to the magazine. Receives 25 queries monthly.
Submissions and Payment: Writers' guidelines and theme list available. Query. SASE. Responds in 4–6 weeks. Articles, word lengths and payment rates vary. Pays on acceptance. All rights. Provides 2 contributor's copies.

The ALAN Review

College of Liberal Arts & Sciences
Department of English
Arizona State University, P.O. Box 870302
Tempe, AZ 85287

Editor: James Blasingame

Description and Readership
Articles, commentaries, and research that explores teaching literature in middle, junior, and senior high school can be found in this journal. Read by members of the National Council of Teachers, it appears three times each year. Circ: 2,500.
Website: www.alan-ya.org

Freelance Potential
90% written by nonstaff writers. Publishes 25 freelance submissions yearly; 50% by unpublished writers. Receives 4 unsolicited mss monthly.
Submissions and Payment: Guidelines available in magazine. Sample copy, free. Send 3 copies of complete ms with disk (ASCII or Microsoft Word 5.1 or higher). Accepts simultaneous submissions if identified. Availability of artwork improves chance of acceptance. SASE. Responds in 2 months. Articles, to 3,000 words. Depts/columns, word length varies. No payment. All rights. Provides 2 contributor's copies.

AKC Family Dog

American Kennel Club
260 Madison Avenue
New York, NY 10016

Managing Editor: Erika Mansourian

Description and Readership
Lively, inspiring, and entertaining articles, essays, and current events about purebred dogs can be found in this quarterly publication. Topics include grooming, training, health care, behavior, nutrition, traveling, and fun activities. Circ: 40,000.
Website: www.akc.org

Freelance Potential
90% written by nonstaff writers. Publishes 50 freelance submissions yearly; 2% by unpublished writers, 10% by authors who are new to the magazine. Receives 5–10 queries monthly.
Submissions and Payment: Guidelines available. Sample copy, $3.95 with 9x12 SASE. Query with outline. Accepts computer printouts and email submissions to familydog@akc.org (Microsoft Word attachments). SASE. Responds in 1–2 months. Articles, 1,000–2,000 words. Depts/columns, staff written. Written material, $125–$500. Pays on publication. First North American serial rights.

Amazing Kids!

PMB 486
1158 26th Street
Santa Monica, CA 90403

Editor: Alyse Rome

Description and Readership
Dedicated to helping kids realize their amazing potential, this website of the non-profit educational organization Amazing Kids! sponsors this e-zine. It offers articles and artwork by children for their peers that seeks to inspire them to reach their full potential. The e-zine is written entirely by children and teen volunteers. Hits per month: 640,000.
Website: www.amazing-kids.org

Freelance Potential
40% written by nonstaff writers. Publishes 70 freelance submissions yearly; 90% by unpublished writers, 70% by authors who are new to the magazine. Receives 250 queries and unsolicited mss monthly.
Submissions and Payment: Sample copy available at website. Query or send complete ms. Accepts email submissions to info@amazing-kids.org. SASE. Response time varies. Articles, word length varies. No payment. All rights.

American History

Primedia
Suite D2, 741 Miller Drive SE
Leesburg, VA 20175

Editorial Director: Roger Vance

Description and Readership
This magazine appeals to a general readership with its popular, rather than scholarly, style and tone. While articles are firmly grounded in thorough research, they feature lively writing and strong human interest angles. Policy studies and hard-core pieces on military strategy are not accepted. *American History* is published six times each year. Circ: 100,000.
Website: www.thehistorynet.com

Freelance Potential
80% written by nonstaff writers. Publishes 30 freelance submissions yearly; 50% by authors who are new to the magazine. Receives 100 queries monthly.
Submissions and Payment: Sample copy and guidelines, $6 with return label. Query with 1–2 page proposal. Accepts photocopies and computer printouts. SASE. Responds in 10 weeks. Articles, 3,000 words; $.20 per word. Pays on acceptance. All rights. Provides 5 contributor's copies.

ASK
Arts & Sciences for Kids

Suite 1100
332 South Michigan Avenue
Chicago, IL 60604

Submissions Editor

Description and Readership
ASK is published nine times each year and is full of investigation and discovery for seven- to ten-year-old readers. Its articles cover topics such as dinosaurs, architecture, astronomy, biology, science, ancient history, art, and music and helps children understand the way the world works. Its pages also include cartoons, activities, and contests. The editors of *ASK* are assign material on a work-for-hire basis only. Circ: Unavailable.
Website: www.cricketmag.com

Freelance Potential
100% written by nonstaff writers.
Submissions and Payment: Sample copy available for purchase through website. Work for hire only. Send résumé and clips. No unsolicited mss. Response time varies. Articles, 400–600 words. Depts/columns, 200 words. Rights and payment policy varies.

The Apprentice Writer

Box GG
Susquehanna University
Selinsgrove, PA 17870-1001

Writers Institute Director: Gary Fincke

Description and Readership
The Apprentice Writer features creative works from high school students and includes fiction, poetry, plays, essays, photographs, and art. It appears once a year and includes material by young writers from across the United States.
Circ: 10,500.
Website: www.susque.edu/writers(click writers' institute)

Freelance Potential
100% written by nonstaff writers. Publishes 80 freelance submissions yearly; 95% by unpublished writers, 95% by authors who are new to the magazine. Receives 5,000 mss monthly.
Submissions and Payment: Sample copy, $3 with 9x12 SASE ($1.17 postage). Send complete ms. Accepts photocopies, computer printouts, and simultaneous submissions if identified. SASE. Responds during the month of May. Articles and fiction, 7,000 words. Poetry, no line limits. No payment. First rights. Provides 2 contributor's copies.

Baseball Parent

Suite 2204
4437 Kingston Pike
Knoxville, TN 37919-5226

Editor: Wayne Christensen

Description and Readership
This e-zine is updated six times each year for parents and coaches of youth baseball players. It features dates, locations, and contacts for weekend tournaments and youth World Series, articles on techniques and strategies, information on baseball camps, and profiles of successful coaches and teams. It is interested in material on off-season training, conditioning, and boosting self-esteem as well as finding college baseball programs. Hits per month: 25,000.
Website: www.baseball-parent.com

Freelance Potential
2% written by nonstaff writers. Publishes 1–3 freelance submissions yearly. Receives 1 unsolicited ms monthly.
Submissions and Payment: Sample copy available at website. Send complete ms. Accepts photocopies and computer printouts. SASE. Responds in 1 day. Articles, 2,000 words. Depts/columns, 1,000 words. No payment. All rights.

Beta Journal

National Beta Club
151 Beta Club Way
Spartenburg, SC 29306-3012

Editor: Lori Guthrie

Description and Readership
This monthly magazine is the official publication of the National Beta Club, a leadership service club for students in elementary school through high school. It features articles on the accomplishments of its members, community service, and character, as well as personal experience pieces. Circ: 300,000.
Website: www.betaclub.org

Freelance Potential
50% written by nonstaff writers. Publishes 2–4 freelance submissions yearly; 80% by unpublished writers. Receives 1 unsolicited mss monthly.
Submissions and Payment: Send complete ms. Accepts computer printouts. Availability of artwork improves chance of acceptance. SASE. Responds in 2 months. Articles and fiction, 700–1,000 words; $25–$50. B/W prints, transparencies, and line art; payment rate varies. Pays publication. Rights policy varies. Provides 10 contributor's copies.

Boutique Magazine

P.O. Box 1162
Newtown, PA 18940

Editor: Lynda Caravello

Description and Readership
Launched in 2004, *Boutique Magazine* targets affluent families with features that spotlight the latest clothes, shoes, toys, gifts, books, home decor, and accessories for children up to the age of 10. Its editors are looking for articles that provide readers with the information they need to find unique products for their children or grandchildren. Prospective writers must have experience in the industry. *Boutique* is published six times each year. Circ: Unavailable.
Website: www.boutiquemagazineonline.com

Freelance Potential
20% written by nonstaff writers. Publishes 12 freelance submissions yearly.
Submissions and Payment: Query or send complete ms. Accepts photocopies and computer printouts. SASE. Response time varies. Articles, word lengths and payment rates vary. Pays on publication. One-time rights.

Caledonia Times

Box 278
Prince Rupert, British Columbia V8J 3P6
Canada

Editor: Debby Shaw

Description and Readership
Targeting Christian young adults and adults, this Canadian magazine features fiction, nonfiction, and poetry with a Christian slant. It is published 10 times each year. The editors of *Caledonia Times* are interested in material from new and established writers that focuses on contemporary topics and issues related to religion and Christian life. Opinion pieces will be given preference, and submissions by young adults are especially welcome. Circ: 1,259.

Freelance Potential
90% written by nonstaff writers. Publishes many freelance submissions yearly. Receives many unsolicited mss monthly.
Submissions and Payment: Sample copy and guidelines, free with 8x10 SAE/IRC. Send complete ms. Accepts computer printouts. SAE/IRC. Responds in 2–4 weeks. Articles and fiction, 500–750 words. Depts/columns, word length varies. No payment. All rights. Provides 5 contributor's copies.

Canoe & Kayak Magazine

Suite 3
10526 NE 68th Street
Kirkland, WA 98033

Editor: Mike Kord

Description and Readership
Informative articles for canoeists and kayakers appear in this magazine that covers both flatwater and whitewater boating. It is published six times each year. Circ: 67,000.
Website: www.canoekayak.com

Freelance Potential
90% written by nonstaff writers. Publishes 25 freelance submissions yearly; 5% by unpublished writers, 25% by authors who are new to the magazine. Receives 20 queries and unsolicited mss monthly.
Submissions and Payment: Sample copy and guidelines, free with 9x12 SASE (7 first-class stamps). Query or send complete ms. Accepts computer printouts, IBM or Macintosh disk submissions, and email submissions to editor@canoekayak.com. SASE. Responds in 6–8 weeks. Articles, 700–2,500 words. Depts/columns, 500–1,200 words. Written material, $.13–$.50 per word. Pays on publication. All rights. Provides 1 copy.

Carolina Parent

Suite 201
5716 Fayetteville Road
Durham, NC 27713

Editor: Cathy Ashby

Description and Readership

Parents, educators, day-care and health-care providers, and other advocates for children up to the age of 18 find thoroughly researched articles on topics related to the family in this monthly publication. Each issue offers several feature articles that focus on the theme of the month. Circ: 55,000.
Website: www.carolinaparent.com

Freelance Potential

50% written by nonstaff writers. Publishes 40 freelance submissions yearly.
Submissions and Payment: Guidelines and editorial calendar available. Accepts queries from established writers. New writers, send complete ms. Accepts photocopies, computer printouts, and email submissions to editorial@ carolinaparent.com (Microsoft Word attachments). SASE. Response time varies. Articles, word length varies; $50–$75. Pays on publication. First and electronic rights.

Cat Fancy

Fancy Publications
3 Burroughs
Irvine, CA 92618

Editor: Susan Logan

Description and Readership

This monthly publication offers readers information on feline health, nutrition, grooming, behavior, and training as well as lifestyle articles and features on cat-related events. Circ: 270,000.
Website: www.catfancy.com

Freelance Potential

80% written by nonstaff writers. Publishes 75 freelance submissions yearly; 40% by unpublished writers, 5% by authors who are new to the magazine. Receives 25 unsolicited mss each month.
Submissions and Payment: Guidelines available. Query with clips. No unsolicited mss. Availability of artwork improves chance of acceptance. Accepts email queries to mwibe@ fancypubs.com. Responds in 1–3 months. Articles, 500–2,000 words. Depts/columns, 750 words. Artwork, 35mm slides. All material, payment rate varies. First rights. Pays on publication. Provides 2 contributor's copies.

Catalyst

Independent Reporting on Urban Schools

Suite 500
332 South Michigan Avenue
Chicago, IL 60604

Editor & Publisher: Linda Lenz

Description and Readership

This regional professional publication targets educators working in Chicago and its surrounding suburbs. *Catalyst* is published nine times each year and covers a wide range of educational subjects. Articles, essays, personal opinion pieces, and interviews are all found between its covers. It strives to bring its readers the latest educational news as well as successful classroom programs. Circ: 7,000.
Website: www.catalyst-chicago.org

Freelance Potential

20% written by nonstaff writers. Publishes 45 freelance submissions yearly; 20% by new authors. Receives 4 unsolicited submissions monthly.
Submissions and Payment: Sample copy and guidelines, $2. Query or send letter of introduction, résumé, and clips. SASE. Response time varies. Articles, to 2,300 words; $1,700. All rights. Pays on acceptance. Provides 1 contributor's copy.

Chickadee

Bayard Press Canada
2nd Floor, 49 Front Street East
Toronto, Ontario M5E 1B3
Canada

Submissions Editor

Description and Readership

Published ten times each year, information and new concepts about animals, science, sports, and social studies are featured in this magazine for beginning readers. Each theme-based issue includes articles, stories, word and math puzzles, science experiments, activities, and crafts. Circ: 85,000.
Website: www.owlkids.com

Freelance Potential

5% written by nonstaff writers. Publishes 1 freelance submission yearly; 5% by unpublished writers, 20% by authors who are new to the magazine. Receives 83 unsolicited mss each month.
Submissions and Payment: Sample copy, $4. Writers' guidelines and theme list available. Not currently accepting submissions. Check our website or send an SASE for updates to our submissions policy.

Child Life

Children's Better Health Institute
P.O. Box 567
Indianapolis, IN 46206-0567

Editor: Jack Gramling

Description and Readership

Published nine times each year, *Child Life* is designed to educate and entertain children ages nine to eleven, and to promote good health and physical fitness. Its articles cover academics, history, personal fitness, medicine, and science; and its pages also include poetry, puzzles, word games, and book reviews. Although most of its material now consists of reprints, its editors are interested in poetry and limericks written by children. Circ: 35,000.
Website: www.childlifemag.org

Freelance Potential

Publishes several freelance submissions each year.
Submissions and Payment: Guidelines available. Sample copy, $1.75 with 9x12 SASE (4 first-class stamps). Not currently accepting submissions for articles and stories; will consider poetry written by children. Accepts photocopies and computer printouts. SASE. Response time varies. No payment. All rights.

Chirp

Bayard Press Canada
2nd Floor, 49 Front Street East
Toronto, Ontario M5E 1B3
Canada

Submissions Editor

Description and Readership

This magazine introduces children ages two to six to the relationship between words and pictures. Published nine times a year, *Chirp* features puzzles, games, rhymes, stories, and songs to teach readers about letters, numbers, nature, and animals. It is not currently accepting submissions. Circ: 60,000.
Website: www.owlkids.com

Freelance Potential

10% written by nonstaff writers. Publishes 1–3 freelance submissions yearly; 1% by unpublished writers, 10% by authors who are new to the magazine. Receives many unsolicited mss each month.
Submissions and Payment: Sample copy, $3.50. Guidelines available. Not currently accepting submissions. Check our website or send an SASE for updates to our submissions policy.

The Christian Science Monitor

1 Norway Street
Boston, MA 02115

Kid Space Editor: Owen Thomas

Description and Readership

Published by the First Church of Christ, Scientist, this daily newspaper covers issues and events of broad public significance. It offers a mix of analytical pieces about timely events and stories that speak to the mind and heart. Circ: 80,000.
Website: www.csmonitor.com

Freelance Potential

30% written by nonstaff writers. Publishes 750 freelance submissions yearly; 60% by unpublished writers. Receives 500 queries monthly.
Submissions and Payment: Sample copy and guidelines, $.75. Query with résumé and clips for articles. Send complete ms for depts/columns. Accepts computer printouts and email submissions to homeforum@csmonitor.com. SASE. Responds in 1 month. Articles, to 1,000 words. Depts/columns, 400–800 words. All material, payment rate varies. Pays on publication. Exclusive rights. Provides 1 contributor's copy.

Cincinnati Family

Suite 900
895 Central Avenue
Cincinnati, OH 45202

Editor-in-Chief: Susan Brooke Day

Description and Readership

Parents seeking family activities or services in the Cincinnati area find a wealth of information in this monthly magazine. In addition, *Cincinnati Family* offers a varied selection of factual articles, personal experience pieces, profiles, and interviews that touch on topics such as college, careers, crafts, hobbies, current events, music, popular culture, recreation, social issues, sports, and travel. Self-help and how-to articles, humorous pieces, and regional news items are other features. Circ: 75,000.
Website: www.cincinnatifamilymagazine.com

Freelance Potential

75% written by nonstaff writers. Publishes 36 freelance submissions yearly.
Submissions and Payment: Query or send complete ms. Accepts photocopies and computer printouts. SASE. Response time varies. Articles and depts/columns, word lengths and payment rates vary. Pays on publication. First rights.

Class Act

P.O. Box 802-HP
Henderson, KY 42419

Editor

Description and Readership
Targeting English teachers of grades six through twelve, this publication appears monthly September through May and offers material that is practical and educational. It includes classroom games, tips and ideas, and activities. Circ: 300.
Website: http://classactpress.com

Freelance Potential
40% written by nonstaff writers. Publishes 20 freelance submissions yearly; 70% by unpublished writers, 80% by authors who are new to the magazine. Receives 8 unsolicited mss each month.
Submissions and Payment: Sample copy and guidelines, $3 with 9x12 SASE (1 first-class stamp). Send complete ms. Accepts photocopies and email submissions to classact@lightpower.net (no attachments). SASE. Responds in 1 month. Articles, 500–1,000 words; $10–$40. Pays on acceptance. All rights. Provides 1 contributor's copy.

Classic Toy Trains

21027 Crossroads Circle
Waukesha, WI 83187

Editor: Neil Besougloff

Description and Readership
Collectors of toy trains look forward to nine yearly issues of this magazine that delves into historical and current toy trains and accessories, including their care and repair. Circ: 68,000.
Website: www.classictoytrains.com

Freelance Potential
60% written by nonstaff writers. Publishes 40–50 freelance submissions yearly; 20% by unpublished writers, 20% by authors who are new to the magazine. Receives 8 queries, 5 unsolicited mss monthly.
Submissions and Payment: Sample copy, $4.95 ($3 postage). Prefers query. Accepts complete ms. Accepts photocopies, computer printouts, disk submissions (Microsoft Word), and email submissions to editor@classictoytrains.com. SASE. Responds in 3 months. Articles, 500–5,000 words; $75 per page. Depts/columns, word length and payment rate vary. Pays on acceptance. All rights. Provides 1 contributor's copy.

Clubhouse

P.O. Box 15
Berrien Springs, MI 49103

President/Editor: Elaine Trumbo

Description and Readership
This religious magazine is published monthly for nine- to twelve-year-old children. Short stories are a regular feature; genres include inspirational, real-life, problem-solving, and contemporary fiction. Nonfiction may be on topics such as nature, religion, pets, animals, and history. This year marks its return to reviewing freelance submissions. Circ: 500.
Website: www.yourstoryhour.org/clubhouse

Freelance Potential
85% written by nonstaff writers. Publishes several freelance submissions yearly; 75% by unpublished writers, 95% by authors who are new to the magazine.
Submissions and Payment: Sample copy, free with 6x9 SASE (2 first-class stamps). Send complete ms. Accepts photocopies and computer printouts. SASE. Response time varies. Articles and fiction, 1,500 words. B/W line art. All material, payment rate varies. Pays after publication. All rights.

Coins

700 East State Street
Iola, WI 54990

Editor: Robert Van Ryzin

Description and Readership
Focusing on coins and coin collecting, this monthly magazine features how-to and informational articles on commemoratives, world coins, collections, and values as well as the latest in coin news and events. Readers includes serious collectors, enthusiasts, and professionals. Articles on buying opportunities are welcome. Circ: 60,000.
Website: www.collect.com

Freelance Potential
40% written by nonstaff writers. Publishes 70 freelance submissions yearly; 1% by authors who are new to the magazine. Receives 3–5 queries monthly.
Submissions and Payment: Sample copy and guidelines, free. Query. Accepts photocopies and computer printouts. SASE. Responds in 1–2 months. Articles, 1,500–2,500 words; $.04 per word. Work for hire. Pays on publication. All rights. Provides contributor's copies upon request.

College and Junior Tennis

Port Washington Tennis Academy
100 Harbor Road
Port Washington, NY 10050

Webmaster: Marcia Frost

Description and Readership

This e-zine provides up-to-date results, rankings, and stories of young tennis players. Its readers include players, parents, and coaches, and its editors seek in-depth coverage and information on up-and-coming teen tennis players. Prospective writers must be familiar with the junior and college circuit. Hits per month: 500,000.
Website: www.collegeandjuniortennis.com

Freelance Potential

10% written by nonstaff writers. Publishes 4 freelance submissions yearly; 1% by authors who are new to the magazine. Receives 2 unsolicited mss monthly.
Submissions and Payment: Send complete ms. Accepts email submissions to marcia@collegeandjuniortennis.com. Responds in 2–14 days. Articles, to 700 words. Games and 1-page puzzles. Token payment for expenses, $25–$50. One-time rights.

Complete Woman

Suite 3434
875 North Michigan Avenue
Chicago, IL 60611-1901

Associate Editor: Diana Mirel

Description and Readership

Published six times each year, this magazine focuses heavily on love, sexuality, and relationships. Its editors welcome nonfiction submissions from freelancers on any topic of interest to contemporary women, especially in the areas of health and self-improvement. Circ: 350,000.
Website: www.associatedpub.com

Freelance Potential

90% written by nonstaff writers. Publishes 75 freelance submissions yearly; 20% by unpublished writers, 30% by authors who are new to the magazine. Receives 60 queries monthly.
Submissions and Payment: Sample copy, $3.99 at newsstands. Query or send complete ms with clips and résumé. Accepts photocopies, computer printouts, and simultaneous submissions if identified. SASE. Responds in 3 months. Articles, 800–1,200 words; payment rate varies. Pays on publication. Rights policy varies. Provides 3 contributor's copies.

Community Education Journal

Suite 91-A
3929 Old Lee Highway
Fairfax, VA 22030

Editor: Valerie A. Romney

Description and Readership

This quarterly journal serves as a forum for exchanging ideas and practices about community education. It welcomes theoretical inquires as well as descriptions of successful programs and research projects that are of use to community educators. Circ: 2,500.
Website: www.ncea.com

Freelance Potential

98% written by nonstaff writers. Publishes 24 freelance submissions yearly; 30% by unpublished writers, 60% by authors who are new to the magazine. Receives 1–2 unsolicited mss each month.
Submissions and Payment: Sample copy, guidelines, and theme list, $5. Send complete ms. Accepts email submissions to varomney@hotmail.com. Responds in 1–2 months. Written material, word length varies. No payment. All rights. Provides 5 contributor's copies.

Cyberteens Zeen

Able Minds, Inc.
1750-1 30th Street #170
Boulder, CO 80301

Editor

Description and Readership

Original, creative work by teens for teens is the focus of this electronic magazine. *Cyberteens Zeen* will consider short stories, personal experience pieces, articles, poems, editorials, media reviews, and website reviews. All topics are of interest, but humorous and positive material is preferred. Hits per month: Unavailable.
Website: www.cyberteens.com

Freelance Potential

100% written by nonstaff writers. Publishes 300 freelance submissions yearly. Receives many unsolicited mss monthly.
Submissions and Payment: Sample copy available at website. Query or send complete ms. Accepts photocopies, computer printouts, ad email submissions to editor@cyberteens.com (no attachments). SASE. Response time varies. All material, to 10 pages. Artwork, TIFF or JPEG format. No payment. All rights.

Dallas Teen

Lauren Publications
Suite 146
4275 Kellway Circle
Austin, TX 75001

Submissions Editor: Shelley Pate

Description and Readership

Issues related to parenting teenagers and activities that encourage family communication are included in this magazine. It targets families with teenage children in the Dallas, Texas area. Freelancers are welcome to submit articles on parenting topics, health related issues, media reviews, and family strengthening activities. Circ: Unavailable.
Website: www.dallaschild.com

Freelance Potential

60% written by nonstaff writers. Publishes 12–15 freelance submissions yearly; 20% by authors who are new to the magazine. Receives 20 queries monthly.
Submissions and Payment: Writers' guidelines available. Query with résumé. Accepts photocopies and computer printouts. SASE. Responds in 2–3 months. Articles, 1,000–2,500 words. Depts/columns, 800 words. Payment rate varies. Pays on publication. First rights.

Davey and Goliath

Devotions for Families on the Go

Augsburg Fortress Publishers
P.O. Box 1209
Minneapolis, MN 55440-1209

Development Editor: Arlene Flancher

Description and Readership

Designed to help families with children between the ages of five and eleven live out their Christian faith, this publication consists of daily devotionals based on the Bible. Formerly published as *Christ in Our Home*, it appears quarterly. Circ: 50,000.
Website: www.augsburgfortress.org

Freelance Potential

100% written by nonstaff writers. Publishes 30 freelance submissions yearly; 25% by unpublished writers, 75% by authors who are new to the magazine. Receives less than 1 query monthly.
Submissions and Payment: Sample copy and guidelines provided free to prospective writers. All work assigned on a contract basis. Query with 6x9 SASE (2 first-class stamps). Responds in 1 month. Articles and fiction, 100–125 words; payment rates vary. Pays on acceptance. All rights. Provides 2 contributor's copies.

Discoveries

WordAction Publishing Company
6401 The Paseo
Kansas City, MO 64131

Editorial Assistant: Julie Smith

Description and Readership

Discoveries is a weekly story paper for third and fourth grade Sunday school classrooms that directly correlates with the WordAction Sunday school curriculum. When it resumes review of freelance submissions in 2007, it will consider contemporary, true-to-life stories about 8- to 10-year-old children that demonstrate character-building traits and have a scriptural application. *Discoveries* is also interested in clever puzzles that relate to themed Sunday school lessons. Circ: 35,000.

Freelance Potential

70% written by nonstaff writers.
Submissions and Payment: Not currently accepting submissions. Will resume submission reviews in January 2007. Query or send complete ms. Accepts photocopies and computer printouts. SASE. Responds in 4–6 weeks. Articles, 150 words; $15. Pays on publication. Multiple-use rights. Provides 2 contributor's copies.

Discovery

John Milton Society for the Blind
475 Riverside Drive, Room 455
New York, NY 10115

Assistant Editor: Jennifer Glober

Description and Readership

Appearing four times each year, this magazine is published in braille and targets visually impaired young people between the ages of eight and eighteen. Each issue relates to a specific theme. Editorial material is selected from Christian and secular publications and reprinted here, and few freelance submissions are ever accepted. Fiction, nonfiction, games, puzzles, poetry, and prayers all appear on a regular basis in *Discovery*. Circ: 2,000.
Website: www.jmsblind.org

Freelance Potential

50% written by nonstaff writers. Publishes 10 freelance submissions yearly. Receives 5 unsolicited mss monthly.
Submissions and Payment: Guidelines available. Send complete ms. SASE. Responds in 3–6 months. Articles and fiction, 500–1,500 words. Filler, 10–150 words. Prayers and poetry, 5–30 lines. No payment. Reprint rights. Provides copies.

Discovery Trails

Gospel Publishing House
1445 North Boonville Avenue
Springfield, MO 65802-1894

Editor

Description and Readership
This quarterly Sunday school publication for fifth- and sixth-grade students recently changed to a comic book format. Each issue includes articles, stories, and activities that reinforce a spiritual lesson and emphasize Christian living. Circ: 20,000.
Website: www.radiantlife.org

Freelance Potential
95% written by nonstaff writers. Publishes 168 freelance submissions yearly; 30–40% by authors who are new to the magazine. Receives 83 unsolicited mss monthly.
Submissions and Payment: Guidelines available. Sample copy, free with 6x9 SASE. Send complete ms. Accepts photocopies, computer printouts, and email submissions to rl-discoverytrails@gph.org. SASE. Responds in 2–4 weeks. Articles, 200–400 words. Fiction, 700–800 words. Written material, $.07–$.10 per word. Pays on acceptance. All rights. Provides 3 contributor's copies.

Dog Fancy

Fancy Publications
P.O. Box 6050
Mission Viego, CA 92690-6050

Managing Editor: Michelle Iten

Description and Readership
Published monthly for dog owners, breeders, and fanciers, this magazine features informative articles on all breeds of dogs and their health, training, behavior, and care. It welcomes queries by freelance writers for well-written, practical material. Circ: 270,000.
Website: www.dogfancy.com

Freelance Potential
80% written by nonstaff writers. Publishes 20–25 freelance submissions yearly; 25% by authors who are new to the magazine. Receives 100 queries monthly.
Submissions and Payment: Guidelines available. Query with résumé outline, and writing samples. No unsolicited mss. Responds in 6–8 weeks. Articles, 1,200–1,800 words. Depts/columns, 650 words. All material, payment rate varies. Pays on publication. First North American rights. Provides 2 contributor's copies.

Dollhouse Miniatures

21027 Crossroads Circle
Waukesha, WI 53187

Editor: Melanie Buellesbach

Description and Readership
Dollhouse readers incude experienced miniaturists, as well as newcomers to the hobby. It welcomes queries from writers who know the market and can describe their projects in a way that will hook readers. Many of its stories are developed in-house and then assigned. Circ: 25,000.
Website: www.dhminiatures.com

Freelance Potential
75% written by nonstaff writers. Publishes 120 freelance submissions yearly; 30% by unpublished writers, 30% by authors who are new to the magazine. Receives 20 queries monthly.
Submissions and Payment: Guidelines available at website. Sample copy, $4.95 with 9x12 SASE ($1.95 postage). Query with outline. Accepts computer printouts and email submissions to editor@dhminiatures.com. SASE. Responds in 1 month. Articles and depts/columns, word lengths and payment rates vary. Pays on acceptance. All rights. Provides 1 copy.

Early Years

Suite 103
3035 Valley Avenue
Winchester, VA 22601

Submissions: Jennifer Hutchinson

Description and Readership
Distributed by teachers for parents of preschool and kindergarten children, this monthly newsletter offers practical articles and tips that promote school readiness and parent involvement. It is published by the Resources for Educators. Query only. It is not accepting submissions. Circ: 60,000.
Website: www.rfeonline.com

Freelance Potential
100% written by nonstaff writers. Publishes 80 freelance submissions yearly; 28% by unpublished writers. Receives 3 queries monthly.
Submissions and Payment: Sample copy, free with 9x12 SASE ($.77 postage). Query with résumé and clips. Accepts photocopies and computer printouts. SASE. Responds in 1 month. Articles, 225–300 words. Depts/columns, 175–200 words. Written material, $.60 per word. Pays on acceptance. All rights. Provides 5 contributor's copies.

Earthwatch Institute Journal

3 Clock Tower Place
Maynard, MA 01754-0075

Editor: Philip Johausson

Description and Readership

Earthwatch Institute's quarterly journal is designed to engage readers, including all constituents, members, volunteers, donors, and those with a shared vision of involvement in the field of science. It describes its mission as "finding solutions for a sustainable future" and features current Earthwatch projects which are generally written by scientists or journalists with a scientific background. Circ: 25,000.
Website: www.earthwatch.org

Freelance Potential

30% written by nonstaff writers. Publishes 2–3 freelance submissions yearly. Receives 4–5 queries, 2–3 unsolicited mss each month.
Submissions and Payment: Sample copy and writers' guidelines available. Query or send complete ms. SASE. Response time varies. Articles, $500–$1,000. Pays on publication. First rights.

The Education Revolution

417 Roslyn Road
Roslyn, NY 11577

Executive Director: Jerry Mintz

Description and Readership

This magazine is published by the Alternative Education Resource Organization, a nonprofit group founded in 1989 to advance learner-centered approaches to education. The quarterly is read by parents, educators, and school administrators interested in keeping abreast of the latest innovations in education. Each issue offers articles, job opportunities, and educational conferences related to alternative education. Freelancers with a background in education are welcome. Circ: 700.
Website: www.edrev.org

Freelance Potential

20% written by nonstaff writers. Publishes 10 freelance submissions yearly; 50% by authors who are new to the publication. Receives 15 queries monthly.
Submissions and Payment: Query. SASE. Responds in 1 month. Written material, word length varies. No payment.

EFCA Today

418 Fourth Street NE
Charlottesville, VA 22902

Editor: Diane Mc Dougall

Description and Readership

As the official leadership publication of the Evangelical Free Church of America, this quarterly journal is read by church leaders: pastors, elders, deacons, and ministry volunteers. A portion of each issue focuses on the cover theme, a topic designed to stimulate spiritual growth. Circ: 30,000.
Website: www.efca.org/magazine

Freelance Potential

90% written by nonstaff writers. Publishes several freelance submissions yearly.
Submissions and Payment: Sample copy and guidelines, $1 with 9x12 SASE (5 first-class stamps). Query. Accepts photocopies, computer printouts, and email submissions to dianemc@journeygroup.com. SASE. Response time varies. Articles, 200–700 words. Cover theme articles, 300–1,000 words. Written material, $.23 per word. Pays on acceptance. First rights.

Faith & Family

432 Washington Avenue
North Haven, CT 06473

Editorial Assistant: Robyn Lee

Description and Readership

Published quarterly and distributed throughout Catholic churches, *Faith & Family* offers a Catholic perspective on family life and contemporary issues that affect families. Its pages include articles on education, marriage, spirituality, and parenting, as well as profiles of outstanding Catholics. Circ: 32,000.
Website: www.faithandfamilymag.com

Freelance Potential

90% written by nonstaff writers. Publishes 35 freelance submissions yearly; 15% by unpublished writers, 10% by authors who are new to the magazine. Receives 25 unsolicited mss each month.
Submissions and Payment: Guidelines available. Sample copy, $3. Query via email to editor@faithandfamilymag.com. Responds in 2–3 months. Articles, 600–2,000 words. Depts/columns, word length varies. Written material, $.33 per word. Pays on acceptance. First North American serial rights.

FamilyRapp.com

Submissions: Cathy Baillie & Jane Rouse

Description and Readership
Parents with children between the ages of three and thirteen log on to this e-zine for informational and how-to articles that focus on parenting issues. Updated weekly, the online publication also deals with the topics of gifted and special education, social issues, health, and family holidays. Book reviews are included, as well as profiles, interviews, and personal experience essays. It publishes approximately seven articles per week. Hits per month: Unavailable.
Website: www.familyrapp.com

Freelance Potential
80% written by nonstaff writers. Publishes 350 freelance submissions yearly. Receives 40 queries monthly.
Submissions and Payment: Sample copy available at website. Send complete ms. Accepts email submissions to info@familyrapp.com. Response time varies. Articles, 500–1,000 words. No payment. One-time and electronic rights.

Fantastic Stories of the Imagination ⊗

P.O. Box 329
Brightwaters, NY 11718

Editor-in-Chief: Edward J. McFadden

Description and Readership
Science fiction, fantasy, light horror, poetry, and book reviews appear in this quarterly publication. Due to an overload of material, it will not be accepting freelance submissions until 2008. Circ: 7,000.
Website: www.dnapublications.com

Freelance Potential
100% written by nonstaff writers. Publishes 50 freelance submissions yearly; 10% by unpublished writers. Receives 450 unsolicited mss monthly.
Submissions and Payment: Sample copy and guidelines, $5 with 9x12 SASE. Send complete ms. Accepts photocopies and computer printouts. SASE. Responds in 1–8 weeks. Fiction, 2,000–15,000 words. Depts/columns, word length varies. Poetry, no line limits. Written material, $.01–$.05 per word. Payment policy varies. First North American serial rights. Provides 1 contributor's copy.

Family Safety & Health

1121 Spring Lake Drive
Itsaca, IL 60143

Editor: Bob Vavra

Description and Readership
In an effort to make the public more aware of preventable hazards present in the home, at the workplace, in recreational areas, and in motor vehicles, this quarterly publication presents informative articles in an easy-to-understand style. While safety issues are its main concern, articles also cover the topics of nutrition, health, and fitness. The editors no longer review unsolicited material, but writers who submit résumés may be considered for writing assignments. Circ: 700,000.
Website: www.nsc.org/pubs/fsh.htm

Freelance Potential
5% written by nonstaff writers. Publishes 5 freelance submissions yearly; 20% by authors who are new to the magazine.
Submissions and Payment: Guidelines and editorial calendar available. Send résumé only. All writing is done on a work-for-hire basis. Written material, payment rate varies. Pays on acceptance. All rights.

Farm & Ranch Living

5925 County Lane
Greendale, WI 53129

Editor: Nick Pabst

Description and Readership
This bimonthly publication is interested in photo-illustrated stories about present day farmers and ranchers, traditional or unique, and 4-H members. Circ: 350,000.
Website: www.farmandranchliving.com

Freelance Potential
90% written by nonstaff writers. Publishes 36 freelance submissions yearly; 50% by unpublished writers, 50% by authors who are new to the magazine. Receives 10 queries and unsolicited mss monthly.
Submissions and Payment: Sample copy, $2. Query or send complete ms. Accepts photocopies, computer printouts, and email submissions to editors@farmandranchliving.com. Artwork improves chance of acceptance. SASE. Responds in 6 weeks. Articles, 1,200 words. Depts/columns, 350 words. Written material, $10–$150. Color prints, slides, or transparencies. Pays on publication. One-time rights. Provides 1 copy.

FineScale Modeler

21027 Crossroads Circle
P.O. Box 1612
Waukesha, WI 53187

Editor: Mark Thompson

Description and Readership
FineScale Modeler is published 10 times each year for modelers at all levels of skill. Feature articles focus on technique, and the majority are written by experienced modelers. Submissions on any how-to aspect of modeling are welcome. Circ: 80,000.
Website: www.finescale.com

Freelance Potential
85% written by nonstaff writers. Publishes 40 freelance submissions yearly; 20% by authors who are new to the magazine. Receives 30 queries, 10–20 unsolicited mss monthly.
Submissions and Payment: Sample copy, $3.95 with 9x12 SASE. Query or send complete ms. No simultaneous submissions. Accepts photocopies, computer printouts, and disk submissions with hard copy. SASE. Responds in 1–4 months. Articles, 750–3,000 words. Depts/columns, word length varies. Written material, $40–$60 per page. Pays on acceptance. All rights. Provides 1 contributor's copy.

Gball

2488 North Triphammer Road
Ithaca, NY 14850

Editor-in-Chief: Eleanor Frankel

Description and Readership
This electronic magazine targets girls who play basketball. The website includes profiles of professional, college, and high school players and teams; interviews with coaches; tips for improving technique; and information on basketball camps. Freelance writers with experience in the sport are encouraged to submit material of interest to passionate basketball enthusiasts. Hits per month: Unavailable.
Website: www.gballmag.com

Freelance Potential
10% written by nonstaff writers. Of the freelance submissions published yearly; 20% by new authors.
Submissions and Payment: Query with résumé and clips. Accepts email to eleanor_frankel@momentummedia.com. Responds in 2 months. Articles, 2,000 words; $1,000–$2,000. Depts/columns, word length varies; $600. Pays on publication. First rights.

Gay Parent Magazine

P.O. Box 750852
Forest Hills, NY 11375-0852

Editor: Angeline Acain

Description and Readership
Gay and lesbian parents read this magazine for its articles and resources on issues related to gay-headed families. Appearing every other month, it seeks material on gay family vacations and activities. All material must be written by gay parents or about gay parenting. Circ: 10,000.
Website: www.gayparentmag.com

Freelance Potential
1% written by nonstaff writers. Publishes 3 freelance submissions yearly; 100% by authors who are new to the magazine. Receives 2 unsolicited mss monthly.
Submissions and Payment: Sample copy and guidelines, $3.50. Send complete ms. Prefers email submissions to acain@gis.net. Availability of artwork improves chances of acceptance. Response time varies. Articles, 500–1,000 words. Color prints or transparencies. Written material, $50. Pays on publication. One-time rights. Copies available upon request.

Girlfriend Magazine

35-51 Mitchell Street
McMahons Point, New South Wales 2000
Australia

Editor: Sandra Barker

Description and Readership
Directed at teenage girls, this monthly magazine explores topics such as college, careers, social issues, and popular culture. Personal experience pieces, puzzles, games, activities, and problem-solving fiction round out each issue. Circ: 112,000.
Website: www.girlfriend.com.au

Freelance Potential
30% written by nonstaff writers. Publishes 36 freelance submissions yearly; 25% by unpublished writers, 15% by authors who are new to the magazine.
Submissions and Payment: Sample copy, $4.80. Send complete ms. Accepts photocopies, computer printouts, and email submissions to girlfriendonline@pacpubs.com.au. SAE/IRC. Responds in 3 weeks. Articles, 1,500–2,000 words. Fiction, 2,000 words. Depts/columns, 500 words. Color prints or transparencies. All material, payment rate varies. Pays on publication. Exclusive rights. Provides 3 contributor's copies.

Good Housekeeping

Hearst Corporation
250 West 55th Street
New York, NY 10019

Executive Editor: Judith Coyne

Description and Readership

Focusing on women's health, fashion, beauty, and style as well as home decorating and remodeling, gardening, food and entertainment, this monthly magazine publishes informative articles, how-to pieces, and inspirational personal experience stories. Circ: 6 million.
Website: www.goodhousekeeping.com

Freelance Potential

80% written by nonstaff writers. Publishes 50+ freelance submissions yearly. Receives 1,500–2,000 queries monthly.
Submissions and Payment: Guidelines available. Sample copy, $5.50 at newsstands. Query with résumé and clips for nonfiction; SASE. Send complete ms for fiction; mss not returned. Accepts computer printouts. Responds in 4–6 weeks. Articles, 750–2,500 words; to $2,000. Essays, to 1,000 words; to $750. Pays on acceptance. All rights for nonfiction; first North American serial rights for fiction. Provides 1 copy.

Grandparents Magazine

281 Rosedale Avenue
Wayne, PA 19087

Editor: Katrina Hayday Wester

Description and Readership

This e-zine was created to cater to the needs of grandparents. Updated monthly, it helps grandparents enhance their relationships with their grandchildren by providing activity ideas and product reviews. Informational articles, personal experience pieces, profiles, interviews, and life lessons are among the features found at this website, along with links to message forums. Typical topics that are regularly covered include health, fitness, recreation, religion, social issues, and traveling with grandchildren. Circ: Unavailable.
Website: www.grandparentsmagazine.net

Freelance Potential

Publishes several freelance submissions yearly.
Submissions and Payment: Sample copy and guidelines available at website. Query. SASE. Accepts email queries to content@grandparentsmagazine.net. Response time varies. Articles, word length varies. No payment. Electronic rights.

Grrr!

c/o PETA
501 Front Street
Norfolk, VA 23510

Editorial Coordinator: Robyn Wesley

Description and Readership

The organization People for the Ethical Treatment of Animals (PETA) publishes this quarterly for children between eight and fourteen. Its goal is to get children to respect animals and take an interest in animal rights and treatment. Each issue offers a mix of articles, interviews, personal experience pieces, and profiles of activists. All editorial material is produced on assignment and very little of it comes from freelancers. Queries are welcome, but unsolicited manuscripts will not be considered. Circ: 55,000.
Website: www.petakids.com

Freelance Potential

5% written by nonstaff writers. Publishes few freelance submissions yearly. Receives 1 query monthly.
Submissions and Payment: Sample copy, free. Query. No unsolicited mss. Responds in 1 month. Articles, word length, and payment rate vary. Payment policy varies. All rights.

Haunted Attraction

P.O. Box 220286
Charlotte, NC 28222

Editor-in-Chief: Leonard Pickel

Description and Readership

This special interest magazine appeals to the entertainment industry related to haunted houses, hay rides, and other seasonal attractions. It is especially interested in how-to articles related to events and informational articles on creating attractions. Circ: 3,000.
Website: www.hauntedattraction.com

Freelance Potential

90% written by nonstaff writers. Publishes 18 freelance submissions yearly; 5% by unpublished writers, 75% by authors who are new to the magazine. Receives 20 queries yearly.
Submissions and Payment: Guidelines available. Sample copy, $6.95. Query. Accepts disk submissions (Word) and email submissions (Word) to editor@hauntedattraction.com. SASE. Responds in 1 week. Articles, 3,000 words. Color prints and transparencies. No payment. Print and web rights. Provides 5 contributor's copies.

The High School Journal

CB#3500 University of North Carolina
Editorial Office, School of Education
Chapel Hill, NC 27599

Submissions Editor

Description and Readership
Published for professionals in the field of secondary education, this journal offers reports, research, and informed opinions on education and adolescent development. It is interested in articles on contemporary issues affecting high school students. Circ: 1,500.
Website: www.muse.jhu.edu/

Freelance Potential
100% written by nonstaff writers. Publishes 20–30 freelance submissions yearly; 25% by unpublished writers, 85% by authors who are new to the magazine. Receives 27 unsolicited mss monthly.
Submissions and Payment: Sample copy and guidelines, $7.50 with 9x12 SASE. Send 3 copies of ms. Accepts photocopies and computer printouts. SASE. Responds in 3 months. Articles, 1,500–2,500 words. Depts/columns, 300–400 words. No payment. All rights. Provides 2 contributor's copies.

Home & School Connection

Suite 103
3035 Valley Avenue
Winchester, VA 22601

Submissions: Jennifer Hutchinson

Description and Readership
Parenting and education issues are the focus of this monthly newsletter. It features informative articles and practical tips on family, school, and social issues; special needs; and communication skills. Circ: 3 million.
Website: www.rfeonline.com

Freelance Potential
100% written by nonstaff writers. Publishes 80 freelance submissions yearly; 28% by unpublished writers, 14% by authors who are new to the magazine. Receives 3 unsolicited mss monthly.
Submissions and Payment: Sample copy, free with 9x12 SASE ($.77 postage). Query with résumé and 3 clips. SASE. Responds in 4 weeks. Articles, 225–300 words. Depts/columns, 175–200 words. Written material, $.60 per word. Pays on acceptance. All rights. Provides 5 contributor's copies.

High School Years

Suite 103
3035 Valley Avenue
Winchester, VA 22601

Submissions: Jennifer Hutchinson

Description and Readership
Published monthly for parents of high school students, this newsletter offers information on helping young adults succeed in school. Each issues includes articles on career choices, college, reading, math, and parenting. Circ: 300,000.
Website: www.rfeonline.com

Freelance Potential
100% written by nonstaff writers. Publishes 80 freelance submissions yearly; 28% by unpublished writers. Receives 3 unsolicited mss monthly.
Submissions and Payment: Sample copy, free with 9x12 SASE. Guidelines and editorial calendar available. Query with résumé and 3 clips. SASE. Responds in 4 weeks. Articles, 225–300 words. Depts /columns, 175–200 words. Written material, $.60 per word. Pays on acceptance. All rights. Provides 5 contributor's copies.

Hot Rod

6420 Wilshire Boulevard
Los Angeles, CA 90048

Editor: David Frieburger

Description and Readership
In print since 1948, this special interest magazine offers hot rod car enthusiasts how-to and technical articles, and personal experience pieces on racing, custom cars, collecting, and repairs. It also includes product reviews and profiles of drivers. Appearing monthly, it seeks writers that know all the facets of hot rod cars and racing. Circ: 680,000.
Website: www.hotrod.com

Freelance Potential
15% written by nonstaff writers. Publishes 24 freelance submissions yearly. Receives 24 queries monthly.
Submissions and Payment: Sample copy, $3.50 at newsstands. Guidelines available. Query. SASE. Response time varies. Articles, 3,000 characters per page; $250–$300 per page. Depts/columns, word length varies; $100 per page. B/W and color prints and 35mm color transparencies; payment rate varies. Pays on publication. All rights.

I.D.

Cook Communications Ministries
4050 Lee Vance View
Colorado Springs, CO 80918

Editor: Gail Rohlfing

Description and Readership

Stories related to Bible studies can be found in this weekly Sunday school take-home paper distributed to students ages 15 to 17. It includes profiles and interviews as well as how-to articles and personal experience pieces on topics related to careers, health, nature, recreation, social issues, religion, and sports. Circ: 100,000.
Website: www.cookministries.org

Freelance Potential

30% written by nonstaff writers. Publishes 25 freelance submissions yearly.
Submissions and Payment: Guidelines available. Query with résumé. All articles are assigned. Accepts photocopies and computer printouts. SASE. Responds in 6 months. Articles, 600–1,200 words; $50–$300 depending on experience. Color and B/W prints; payment rate varies. Pays on acceptance. Rights policy varies. Provides 1 contributor's copy.

Indian Life Newspaper

P.O. Box 3765
RPO Redwood Centre
Winnipeg, Manitoba R2L 1L6
Canada

Editor: Viola Fehr

Description and Readership

This bimonthly tabloid covers issues relative to the lives of Christian North American Natives. It would like to see more positive news stories about Native Americans and first-person stories that give hope. Circ: 20,000.
Website: www.indianlife.org

Freelance Potential

80% written by nonstaff writers. Publishes 10 freelance submissions yearly; 1% by unpublished writers, 2% by authors who are new to the magazine. Receives 35 queries and unsolicited mss each month.
Submissions and Payment: Sample copy, $2.50 with #9 SAE (4 first-class stamps). Prefers query. Accepts complete ms. Accepts photocopies, disk submissions, and email submissions to jim.editor@indianlife.org. SAE/IRC. Responds in 1 month. Articles, 300–1,500 words. Written material, $.05 per word. Pays on publication. First rights. Provides 15 copies.

I Love Cats

16 Meadow Hill Lane
Armonk, NY 10504

Editor: Lisa Allmendinger

Description and Readership

This bimonthly publication appears in a digest format and covers a wide range of topics related to cats and to the owners of cats. It regularly reports on health issues, breeds, behavior, and products. Both fiction and nonfiction submissions are welcome. Circ: 50,000.
Website: www.iluvcats.com

Freelance Potential

50% written by nonstaff writers. Publishes 100 freelance submissions yearly; 25% by unpublished writers, 85% by authors who are new to the magazine. Receives 150 queries, 400+ unsolicited mss monthly.
Submissions and Payment: Sample copy and guidelines, $6 with 6x9 SASE. Query or send ms. Accepts computer printouts and email to yankee@izzy.net. SASE. Responds in 1–2 months. Articles and fiction, 500–1,000 words; $25–$150. Pays on publication. All rights. Provides 1 contributor's copy.

Inside Kung-Fu

CFW Enterprises
4201 Vanowen Place
Burbank, CA 91505

Editor: Dave Cater

Description and Readership

Individuals who are training in Chinese martial arts or who have a strong interest in the martial arts find articles on technique, profiles of prominent practitioners, and information on health and fitness as they relate to martial arts training in each issue of this monthly magazine. Circ: 110,000.
Website: www.cfwenterprises.com

Freelance Potential

80% written by nonstaff writers. Publishes 100 freelance submissions yearly; 25% by unpublished writers, 75% by authors who are new to the magazine. Receives 42 queries monthly.
Submissions and Payment: Sample copy and guidelines, $2.95 with 9x12 SASE. Query. Accepts computer printouts, IBM or Macintosh disk submissions, and email queries to davecater@cfwenterprises.com. SASE. Responds in 4–6 weeks. Articles, 1,500. Depts/columns, 750 words. Written material, payment rate varies. Pays on publication. First rights.

Jam Rag

Suite 240
22757 Woodward
Ferndale, MI 48220

Co-Editor & Publisher: Tom Ness

Description and Readership
Jam Rag appears monthly and covers the music scene in Michigan. Its audience includes both young adults and adults interested in music reviews as well as in the careers of local musicians and bands. Circ: 12,000.
Website: www.jamrag.com

Freelance Potential
70% written by nonstaff writers. Publishes 250 freelance submissions yearly; 50% by unpublished writers, 50% by authors who are new to the magazine. Receives 20 mss monthly.
Submissions and Payment: Sample copy and guidelines, free with 9x12 SASE ($.75 postage). Query or send complete ms. Accepts photocopies, computer printouts, disk submissions, and simultaneous submissions. Availability of artwork improves chance of acceptance. SASE. Response time varies. Articles, word length varies, $10–$50. Pays on publication. One-time rights. Provides 1 contributor's copy.

Justine Magazine

Suite 430
6263 Poplar Avenue
Memphis, TN 38119

Editorial Director/Publisher: Jana Pettey

Description and Readership
This quarterly magazine, launched in 2004, targets high school girls between the ages of 13 and 18. What sets it apart from typical teen magazines is its editorial content, which is wholesome, tasteful, and entertaining. Recent issues have featured craft projects and fashion and beauty tips. Articles have focused on subjects such as redecorating a bedroom, dealing with family dilemmas, self-confidence, healthful eating, and making the most of Friday nights. Circ: Unavailable.
Website: www.justinemagazine.com

Freelance Potential
15–20% written by nonstaff writers. Publishes 20–30 freelance submissions yearly.
Submissions and Payment: Query with résumé and clips. Accepts photocopies and computer printouts. SASE. Response time varies. Articles and depts/columns, word lengths and payment rates vary. Pays 30 days after publication. Rights vary.

Kansas 4-H Journal

116 Umberger Hall
KSU
Manhattan, KS 66506-3417

Editor: Rhonda Atkinson

Description and Readership
This journal is published 10 times each year for Kansas 4-H members, parents, and leaders. Its purpose is to bring together 4-H members from all counties in Kansas and to report on statewide programs, topics, and concerns. All sections of the journal are open to submissions from 4-H families or from experts in youth development training. Circ: 14,000.

Freelance Potential
60% written by nonstaff writers. Publishes 100 freelance submissions yearly; 10% by unpublished writers, 20% by authors who are new to the magazine. Receives 58 queries and unsolicited mss monthly.
Submissions and Payment: Sample copy and editorial calendar, $5. Query or send complete ms. Accepts photocopies and computer printouts. SASE. Response time varies. Articles, 500 words; payment rate varies. Payment policy varies. Rights negotiable.

Keyboard

2800 Campus Drive
San Mateo, CA 94403

Editor: Ernie Rideout

Description and Readership
Targeting serious musicians, this monthly magazine offers how-to and technical articles as well as profiles of artists. Topics related to keyboard music, instruments, and players are included. How-to articles on equipment usage provides the best opportunities for freelance writers. Circ: 71,000.
Website: www.keyboardmag.com

Freelance Potential
10–20% written by nonstaff writers. Publishes 15 freelance submissions yearly; 1% by authors who are new to the magazine. Receives 60 unsolicited mss monthly.
Submissions and Payment: Sample copy and guidelines, free with 9x12 SASE. Send complete ms with résumé. Accepts photocopies and computer printouts. SASE. Responds in 3 months. Articles, 500–3,000 words. Depts/columns, 400–800 words. All material, payment rate varies. Pays on acceptance. All rights. Provides 5 contributor's copies.

Kickoff Magazine

23rd Floor
110 William Street
New York, NY 10038

Editor: Mitchell Lavnick

Description and Readership
Football players and fans of the sport who range in age from seven to fourteen enjoy this monthly magazine's informative, in-depth features. How-to articles on teamwork, technique, and coaching appear along with profiles of teams and interviews with players. Writers with coaching or playing experience are invited send a submission. Circ: 80,000.
Website: www.kickoffmag.com

Freelance Potential
20% written by nonstaff writers. Publishes 5 freelance submissions yearly.
Submissions and Payment: Query with clips; or send complete ms. Accepts photocopies, computer printouts, and Macintosh disk submissions. SASE. Responds in 3 months. Articles, to 1,000 words. Depts/columns, word length varies. Written material, payment rate varies. Pays 2 months after acceptance. All rights.

Kids

341 East Lancaster Avenue
Downington, PA 19335

Editor: Bob Ludwick

Description and Readership
Published for parents and students living in Chester County, Pennsylvania, this monthly tabloid features information on local elementary and middle school education. *Kids* will consider material on teachers, youth, and progams that have made a positive impact on the lives of students. Its editors prefer that prospective writers live in the Chester County area. Circ: 43,000.

Freelance Potential
90% written by nonstaff writers. Publishes 120 freelance submissions yearly; 20% by unpublished writers. Receives several queries monthly.
Submissions and Payment: Editorial calendar available. Sample copy, free with 9x12 SASE. Query with résumé. Accepts photocopies and computer printouts. SASE. Responds in 1 week. Articles and depts/columns, to 500 words. No payment. All rights. Provides 2 contributor's copies.

Kidsandkaboodle.com

1169 Mount Rushmore Way
Lexington, KY 40515

Editor: Jennifer Anderson

Description and Readership
Kidsandkaboodle is an online magazine for families living in central Kentucky. Many of its articles have helpful links and associated activities. It is interested in receiving research-type articles on health issues for children, family concerns, single parenting, seasonal safety, and child development. Hits per month: 50,000.
Website: www.kidsandkaboodle.com

Freelance Potential
10% written by nonstaff writers. Publishes 10 freelance submissions yearly; 50% by unpublished writers, 50% by authors who are new to the magazine. Receives 3–4 unsolicited mss each month.
Submissions and Payment: Sample copy available at website. Send complete ms. Accepts email submissions to editor@kidsandkaboodle.com. Response time varies. Written material, word length varies. Payment policy varies. All rights.

Kid's Directory

P.O. Box 21226
Little Rock, AR 72221-1226

Publisher: Jennifer Robins

Description and Readership
In publication for more that twelve years, this digest-sized, regional directory is distributed throughout central Arkansas to families with children ages thirteen and under. The directory highlights goods and resources applicable to parenting and family services. Its editors seek local freelance writers to review children's books, software, videos, and music, as well as articles on family events, entertainment, and travel options. Prospective authors must be familiar with family resources in the central Arkansas area, and be able to cover topics of interest with originality and flair. Circ: 19,000.

Freelance Potential
100% written by nonstaff writers. Publishes 6 freelance submissions yearly. Receives 2 queries, 2 unsolicited mss monthly.
Submissions and Payment: Sample copy, free with 6x9 SASE ($1.06 postage). Query or send complete ms. Response time varies. Articles, word lengths and payment rates vary. All rights.

Kids Discover

12th Floor
149 Fifth Avenue
New York, NY 10010-6801

Editor: Stella Sands

Description and Readership

Started in 1991, this high-end publication is written for children between the ages of six and twelve. Each monthly issue focuses on an individual theme and covers a wide range of related subjects. Articles are complimented by graphics and photographs. Some of the topics covered in recent issues relate to geology, lakes, ecology, the Mississippi river, World War I, Ancient Egypt, the Industrial Revolution, Ellis Island, and George Washington. Its sister publication, *Kids Discover 2*, is written for children from ages one to three. The magazine usually works with its regular writers and does not accept any freelance submissions. All articles are assigned. Circ: 500,000.

Freelance Potential

100% written by nonstaff writers. Receives 10 queries monthly.
Submissions and Payment: Not accepting queries or unsolicited mss at this time. Send résumé only. All work is assigned.

The Kids Hall of Fame® News

3 Ibsen Court
Dix Hills, NY 11746

Publisher: Victoria Nesnick

Description and Readership

Published quarterly, this magazine showcases the works of young adults under the age of 20 who have achieved extraordinary things. It aims to provide all children with positive peer role models, who inspire and motivate them to reach their full potential. Circ: 8,000.
Website: www.thekidshalloffame.com

Freelance Potential

40% written by nonstaff writers. Publishes 300 freelance submissions yearly; 10% by unpublished writers, 20% by authors who are new to the magazine. Receives 100 unsolicited mss monthly.
Submissions and Payment: Sample copy, free. Send complete ms. Accepts photocopies and computer printouts. Availability of artwork improves chances of acceptance. SASE. Responds in 1–2 months. Articles, 1,000–2,000 words. All material, payment rate varies. Pays on acceptance. Rights policy varies.

Kiwibox.com

Suite 1602
330 West 38th Street
New York, NY 10018

Submissions Editor: Jasmine Kurjakovie

Description and Readership

Targeting girls between the ages of 14 and 21, *Kiwibox* is a website developed for teens by teens. It features material written by high school and college students that covers music, movies, sports, TV, dating, travel, games, health, career choices, life issues, fashion, beauty, celebrities, technology, education, and popular culture. It would like to see submissions of original fiction and self-help articles, and will consider material that is hip, hot, and trendy, or thoughtful and serious. Hits per month: 1 million.
Website: www.kiwibox.com

Freelance Potential

90% written by nonstaff writers.
Submissions and Payment: Sample copy available at website. Send complete ms. Accepts email submissions to editor@ kiwibox.net. Responds in 2 weeks. Articles, 350 words. Fiction, word length varies. No payment. All rights.

The Lamp-Post

1106 West 16th Street
Santa Ana, CA 92706

Senior Editor: David G. Clark

Description and Readership

The C.S. Lewis Society of Southern California publishes this special interest publication which is devoted to articles, essays, and fiction related to author C.S. Lewis. *The Lamp-Post* appears four times each year. Most of its editorial is devoted to articles on Lewis, his circle of friends, and those who influenced him. It does publish fiction and poetry on occasion. Circ: 100.

Freelance Potential

80% written by nonstaff writers. Publishes 30–40 freelance submissions yearly; 20% by unpublished writers, 50% by authors who are new to the magazine. Receives 3–4 unsolicited submissions monthly.
Submissions and Payment: Sample copy, $4. Send ms. Accepts email to dgclark@adelphia.net (Microsoft Word or rich text format). Responds in 2 days. Articles and fiction, length varies. No payment. Rights policy varies. Provides 2 copies.

LAPregnancy.com

1007 Montana Avenue #831
Santa Monica, CA 90403

Editor

Description and Readership
Up-to-the-minute information to help expectant mothers during their pregnancy is provided through this website. Spotlighting businesses in the Los Angeles area, the site reports on baby stores, mother and baby classes, and other resources. It offers reviews of new products related to pregnancy and articles on health and fitness. Exercises for pregnant women are featured, along with exercises designed to help women through the post-pregnancy period. Hits per month: Unavailable.
Website: www.LAPregnancy.com

Freelance Potential
50% written by nonstaff writers. Publishes 50 freelance submissions yearly. Receives 30 queries monthly.
Submissions and Payment: Query. Accepts email queries to Belly@LAPregnancy.com. SASE. Response time varies. Articles, word length varies. No payment. Electronic rights.

Leaders in Action

CSB Ministries
P.O. Box 150
Wheaton, IL 60189

Managing Editor: B. J. Slinger

Description and Readership
Read by adult leaders of the Christian Service Brigade, this magazine includes articles on leadership training, religious service, and program development. Not currently accepting submissions. Will resume in 2005. Circ: 6,000.
Website: www.csbministries.org

Freelance Potential
25% written by nonstaff writers. Publishes 8–10 freelance submissions yearly; 25% by unpublished writers. Receives 3–4 queries monthly.
Submissions and Payment: Resuming reviews in 2005. Sample copy, $1.50 with 9x12 SASE ($1.01 postage). Query with clips or writing samples. Accepts photocopies, computer printouts, and simultaneous submissions. SASE. Responds in 1 week. Articles, to 1,000 words; $.05–$.10 per word. Pays on publication. First rights. Provides 2 contributor's copies.

The Lion

Lions Clubs International
300 22nd Street
Oak Brook, IL 60523-8842

Senior Editor: Robert Kleinfelder

Description and Readership
Informational articles that report on the activities of Lions Clubs, family-oriented essays, and profiles of notable members appear in this magazine that is published ten times each year. It currently seeks more humorous articles, as well as submissions on social issues and disabilities. Circ: 500,000.
Website: www.lionsclub.org

Freelance Potential
40% written by nonstaff writers. Publishes 40 freelance submissions yearly; 5% by unpublished writers, 20% by authors who are new to the magazine. Receives 20 queries, 5 unsolicited mss monthly.
Submissions and Payment: Sample copy and guidelines, free. Prefers query; accepts complete ms. Accepts photocopies and computer printouts. SASE. Responds to queries in 10 days, to mss in 2 months. Articles, 300–2,200 words; $100–$700. Pays on acceptance. All rights. Provides 4–10 copies.

Long Island Woman

P.O. Box 176
Malverne, NY 11565

Publisher: Arie Nadboy

Description and Readership
Women across Long Island pick up this free monthly publication for information on the issues that concern them, such as business, finance, health, fashion, and travel. Book reviews and interviews with inspiring women appear regularly. Circ: 40,000.
Website: www.liwomanonline.com

Freelance Potential
40% written by nonstaff writers. Publishes 15 freelance submissions yearly; 5% by unpublished writers, 15% by authors who are new to the magazine. Receives 50 mss monthly.
Submissions and Payment: Sample copy and guidelines, $5 with 9x12 SASE. Send complete ms. Accepts photocopies, computer printouts, and email submissions to editor@ liwomanonline.com. SASE. Responds in 2 months. Articles, 600–1,000 words. Depts/columns, 500–800 words. Written material, $35–$150. Pays on publication. One-time and electronic rights. Provides 1 tearsheet.

Metro Parent

P.O. Box 13660
Portland, OR 97213

Editor: Marie Sherlock

Description and Readership

Distributed throughout the Portland area, this monthly publication offers parents insightful information for raising their kids and spotlights local activities, outings, and family events. Circ: 32,000.
Website: www.metro-parent.com

Freelance Potential

75% written by nonstaff writers. Publishes 50 freelance submissions yearly; 5% by unpublished writers. Receives 20 queries monthly.
Submissions and Payment: Sample copy, guidelines, and theme list, $2. Query with outline. Accepts photocopies, computer printouts, simultaneous submissions if identified, and email submissions to editor@metro-parent.com. SASE. Responds in 1 month. Articles and depts/columns, word lengths and payment rates vary. Pays on publication. Rights policy varies.

Middle Years

Suite 103
3035 Valley Avenue
Winchester, VA 22601

Submissions Editor: Jennifer Hutchinson

Description and Readership

Targeting parents of children in middle school, this monthly newsletter offers practical, informational articles and tips on issues related to parent involvement in education and improving basic parenting skills. It is currently not accepting complete manuscript; query only. Circ: 1 million.
Website: www.rfeonline.com

Freelance Potential

100% written by nonstaff writers. Publishes 80 freelance submissions yearly. Receives 3 queries monthly.
Submissions and Payment: Sample copy and writers' guidelines, free with 9x12 SASE ($.77 postage). Query with résumé and 3 clips. Accepts photocopies and computer printouts. SASE. Responds in 1 month. Articles, 225–300 words. Fiction, 1,000 words. Depts/columns, 175–200 words. Written material, $.60 per word. Pays on acceptance. All rights. Provides 5 contributor's copies.

Model Airplane News

Air Age Publishing
100 East Ridge Road
Ridgefield, CT 06877-4606

Editor-in-Chief: Debra Cleghorn

Description and Readership

In print since 1929, this monthly magazine focuses on model airplanes. It includes articles on building and flying models, detailed reviews of kits, and the latest in technology. It is particularly interested in how-to articles. Circ: 95,000.
Website: www.modelairplanenews.com

Freelance Potential

90% written by nonstaff writers. Publishes 100 freelance submissions yearly; 33% by authors who are new to the magazine. Receives 12–24 queries monthly.
Submissions and Payment: Sample copy and guidelines, $3.50 with 9x12 SASE. Query with outline and biography describing model experience. Accepts photocopies and computer printouts. Availability of artwork improves chance of acceptance. SASE. Responds in 6 weeks. Articles, 1,700–2,000 words; $175–$600. Pays on publication. All rights. Provides up to 6 copies.

Mommy Too! Magazine

2525 Booker Creek Road #13B
Chapel Hill, NC 27514

Editor: Jennifer James

Description and Readership

African American and Latina mothers log on to this monthly online magazine to read timely, well-written articles, essays, fiction, and poetry. Prospective writers need not be mothers of color to submit their work, but all material must relate to the e-zine's overall themes of motherhood, parenting, and family life. Hits per month: Unavailable.
Website: www.mommytoo.com

Freelance Potential

35% written by nonstaff writers. Publishes 50–60 freelance submissions yearly.
Submissions and Payment: Sample copy and guidelines available at website. Query or send complete ms. Accepts submissions through the website and email submissions to mommytoo@email.com. Response time varies. Articles, 600 words minimum. Essays, fiction, and poetry, word length varies. No payment. Electronic rights.

Moms Help Moms

Editor

Description and Readership
Working, work-at-home, and stay-at-home moms turn to this electronic publication for its infomational and how-to articles, interviews, and essays on topics related to parenting, relationships, business, child safety, health, child development, child care, school, time savers, pregnancy, and women's health. If you have a fresh idea for a resourceful article that will be useful to busy moms, send us a query. It does not accept fiction. Circ: Unavailable.
Website: www.momshelpmoms.com

Freelance Potential
85% written by nonstaff writers. Publishes 36–40 freelance submissions yearly. Receives 160+ queries monthly.
Submissions and Payment: Query. No unsolicited mss. Accepts email to articles@momshelpmoms.com. Response time varies. Articles and depts/columns, word lengths vary. No payment. Electronic rights.

Muse

Suite 1000
332 South Michigan Avenue
Chicago, IL 60604

Editor

Description and Readership
Published ten times each year by *Smithsonian Magazine* and the Cricket Magazine Group, *Muse* is a nonfiction magazine for children ages eight to fourteen. Each issue includes articles with website recommendations, photos, cartoons, and contests. Articles explain ideas and concepts to young readers so that they will learn to understand how the world works. Topics include art, science, nature, math, history, and technology. All material is commissioned. This publication is not currently accepting unsolicited submissions. Circ: 60,000.
Website: www.cricketmag.com

Freelance Potential
90% written by nonstaff writers. All articles are commissioned from experienced authors.
Submissions and Payment: Send résumé and clips. Response time varies. Articles, to 1,500 words. Depts/columns, word length varies. Rights and payment policy varies.

National Pal Copsnkids Chronicles

National Association of Police Athletic Leagues
Suite 201, 618 U.S. Highway 1
North Palm Beach, FL 33408

Creative Services Editor

Description and Readership
With four issues a year, this magazine caters to individuals working in Police Athletic Leagues in the U.S. Topics covered on a regular basis incude violence prevention, social and ethnic topics, sports, and crime prevention. It strives to provide the latest concepts regarding youth programs designed to improve quality of life and show young people alternatives to crime and violence. Reports on successful programs as well as ideas for games and competitions are also found in each issue. Circ: 21,000.
Website: www.nationalpal.org

Freelance Potential
75% written by nonstaff writers.
Submissions and Payment: Sample copy, free. Query or send complete ms. Accepts computer printouts and email submissions to copnkid@nationalpal.org. SASE. Response time varies. Articles, word length varies. No payment. All rights.

Natural Jewish Parenting

P.O. Box 466
Sharon, MA 02067

Editor: Yael Resnick

Description and Readership
This magazine's focus is on Jewish spirituality and natural family living. It will resume publishing quarterly print editions and electronic material this year. Circ: 5,000.
Website: www.naturaljewishparenting.com

Freelance Potential
90% written by nonstaff writers. Publishes 40 freelance submissions yearly; 50% by unpublished writers, 80% by authors who are new to the magazine. Receives 8 unsolicited mss each month.
Submissions and Payment: Guidelines available. Sample copy, $5 with 9x12 SASE ($1.65 postage). Send complete ms. Accepts computer printouts and email submissions to njpmail@mindspring.com. SASE. Responds in 1–2 months. Articles, 1,000–3,500 words. Depts/columns, 500–1,500 words. Written material, $.04–$.05 per word. Pays on publication. First and second rights. Provides 1 contributor's copy.

Neapolitan Family Magazine

P.O. Box 110656
Naples, FL 34108

Editor

Description and Readership

Distributed to families residing in Naples, Florida, this monthly family and parenting magazine offers articles on topics realted to education, parenting, and travel. It also includes local resources and a calendar of events. Circ: 10,000.
Website: www.NeapolitanFamilyMagazine.com

Freelance Potential

95% written by nonstaff writers. Publishes 10–12 freelance submissions yearly. Receives 10–15 queries, 25–30 unsolicited mss monthly.
Submissions and Payment: Guidelines and editorial calendar available at website. Sample copy, free with 9x12 SASE. Query or send complete ms. Prefers email submissions to NeapolitanFamily@aol.com. Will accept photocopies and computer printouts. SASE. Responds in 1 month. Articles and depts/columns, word lengths and payment rates vary. Pays on publication. Rights policy varies.

The Numismatist

American Numismatic Association
818 North Cascade Avenue
Colorado Springs, CO 80903-3279

Editor & Publisher: Barbara J. Gregory

Description and Readership

As the official publication of the American Numismatic Association, this collectors' magazine offers informational articles on medals, paper money, and coins. It appears monthly and is read by collectors of all levels. Circ: 29,500.
Website: www.money.org

Freelance Potential

60% written by nonstaff writers. Publishes 36 freelance submissions yearly; 20% by unpublished writers, 10% by authors who are new to the magazine. Receives 4 mss monthly.
Submissions and Payment: Sample copy and guidelines, free with 9x12 SASE ($2.50 postage). Send complete ms with biography. Accepts email submissions to magazine@money.org, photocopies, computer printouts, and disk submissions. SASE. Responds in 8–10 weeks. Articles, to 3,500 words; $3.60 per published column inch. Pays on publication. Perpetual but non-exclusive rights. Provides 5 copies.

Our Little Friend

Pacific Press Publishing
P.O. Box 5353
Nampa, ID 83653-5353

Editor: Aileen Andres Sox

Description and Readership

Distributed to children ages one through six at Sabbath school at a Seventh-day Adventist Church, this weekly publication offers Bible lessons and stories that teach children Christian values, beliefs, and practices. Circ: 46,000.
Website: www.pacificpress.com

Freelance Potential

100% written by nonstaff writers. Publishes 50 freelance submissions yearly; 10% by unpublished writers, 10% by new authors. Receives 40+ unsolicited mss monthly.
Submissions and Payment: Guidelines available on website or by mail. Sample copy, free with 9x12 SASE (2 first-class stamps). Send ms. Accepts photocopies, computer printouts, simultaneous submissions, and email submissions to ailsox@ pacificpress.com. SASE. Responds in 4 months. Articles and fiction, 500–650 words. Written material, $25–$50. Pays on acceptance. One-time rights. Provides 3 author's copies.

Owl

2nd Floor
49 Front Street East
Toronto, Ontario M5E 1B3
Canada

Submissions Editor

Description and Readership

Owl is a magazine of discovery for children ages eight and up. It appears nine times each year and has articles on animals, natural phenomena, science, people, sports, conservation, and technology. It is not accepting submissions until further notice. Circ: 104,000.
Website: www.owlkids.com

Freelance Potential

60% written by nonstaff writers. Publishes 1–3 freelance submissions yearly; 5% by unpublished writers, 10% by new authors. Receives 50 queries and mss monthly.
Submissions and Payment: Sample copy, $4.28. Not currently accepting submissions. Check our website or send an SASE for updates to our submissions policy.

ParentingHumor.com

P.O. Box 2128
Weaverville, NC 28787

Editor

Description and Readership
Dedicated to the lighter side of parenting, this weekly online publication offers humorous articles on parenting issues as well as crafts. It includes topics on pregnancy, ages and stages of child development, relationships, fashion, health, beauty, and cooking. It is under new ownership, and has a new look. Parents are welcome to share their funny stories and advice. Hits per month: Unavailable.
Website: www.parentinghumor.com

Freelance Potential
98% written by nonstaff writers. Publishes 250 freelance submissions yearly. Receives 25 queries monthly.
Submissions and Payment: Writers' guidelines and submission form available at website. Accepts email to staff@parentinghumor.com. Response time varies. Articles, to 700 words. No payment. One-time electronic rights. Offers an author's biography and a link to the author's website.

Parents' Choice

Parents Choice Foundation
Suite 303
201 West Padonia Road
Timonium, MD 21093

Editor: Claire Green

Description and Readership
Parents' Choice features reviews and information on children's books, videos, toys, audio tapes, software, television programs, and magazines. Its readers are interested in identifying the best products for children of different ages, skills, and interests. This e-zine is published by Parent's Choice Foundation, a non-profit organization that helps parents participate in their children's learning experiences. Circ: 300,000.
Website: www.parents-choice.org

Freelance Potential
100% written by nonstaff writers. Publishes 4 freelance submissions yearly; 90% by unpublished writers, 15% by authors who are new to the magazine.
Submissions and Payment: Query or send complete ms. Accepts photocopies, computer printouts, and simultaneous submissions if identified. SASE. Response time varies. Articles, 800–1,000 words; $200–$400. Pays on acceptance. All rights.

Passport

WordAction Publishing
6401 The Paseo
Kansas City, MO 64131

Editorial Assistant: Julie J. Smith

Description and Readership
This weekly paper used for religious education programs is for pre-teens to take home. All of its content conforms to the teachings of the Church of the Nazarene and relates to the lesson of the day. Please note that it is not currently accepting submissions. Circ: 55,000.
Website: www.nazarene.org

Freelance Potential
90% written by nonstaff writers. Publishes 30 freelance submissions yearly; 20% by unpublished writers, 20% by new authors. Receives 20 queries and unsolicited mss monthly.
Submissions and Payment: Sample copy, free with 5x7 SASE. Query with author information. Accepts photocopies and computer printouts. SASE. Responds in 4–6 weeks. Articles, 400–500 words. Fiction, 600–800 words. Written material, $15–$30. Pays on publication. Multiple use rights. Provides 4 contributor's copies.

Pogo Stick

1300 Kicker Road
Tuscaloosa, AL 35404

Editor: Lillian Kopaska-Merkel

Description and Readership
Established in 2004 and published four times each year, *Pogo Stick* is a new magazine for children up to the age of 17. Its pages are filled with stories, poems, jokes, art, and puzzles written by children. Its editors encourage submissions of contemporary, multicultural, and ethnic fiction; and fantasy; as well as adventure stories; mystery; and poetry. Submissions from adults will not be considered. Circ: Unavailable.

Freelance Potential
Of the submissions published, 100% are by authors who are new to the magazine.
Submissions and Payment: Guidelines available. Sample copy, $3. Send complete ms. Three manuscripts per child per submission. Accepts photocopies and computer printouts. SASE. Responds in 1 month. Written material, to 2,000 words. No payment. All rights. Provides 1 contributor's copy.

Prairie Messenger

Box 190
100 College Drive
Muenster, Saskatchewan S0K 2Y0
Canada

Associate Editor: Maureen Weber

Description and Readership

Prairie Messenger is celebrating its 100th year in print. This weekly tabloid is read by individuals interested in the Catholic Church. Most of the material found in each issue relates daily life situations to the teachings of the church. Circ: 7,300.
Website: www.stpeters.sk.ca/prairie_messenger

Freelance Potential

40% written by nonstaff writers. Publishes 3 freelance submissions yearly. Receives 2 queries and unsolicited mss monthly.
Submissions and Payment: Sample copy and guidelines, $1 with 9x12 SAE/IRC. Query or send complete ms. Accepts email submissions to pm.canadian@stpeters.sk.ca. Responds in 1 month. Articles, 700 words; payment rate varies. Depts/columns, 700 words; $50 (Canadian). Color prints or transparencies and line art; rates vary. Pays at the end of each month. First rights.

Preschool Playhouse

Urban Ministries
P.O. Box 436987
Chicago, IL 60409

Editor: Katherine Steward

Description and Readership

Published quarterly, this publication provides children ages two to five living in urban areas with Biblical and contemporary stories to teach them about Christian solutions to situations they may face in their daily lives. Topics include animals, crafts, African American history, multicultural issues, nature and the environment, religion, and social issues.
Circ: Unavailable.
Website: www.urbanministries.com

Freelance Potential

80% written by nonstaff writers. Publishes 48 freelance submissions yearly.
Submissions and Payment: Sample copy and guidelines available. Send résumé with clips or writing samples. All material written on assignment. SASE. Response time varies. Articles and depts/columns, word lengths and payment rates vary. Pays on publication. All rights. Provides 1 contributor's copy.

Quilt It for Kids

Suite A
741 Corporate Circle
Golden, CO 80401-5622

Editor-in-Chief: Vivian Ritter

Description and Readership

Ten times each year, *Quilter's Newsletter Magazine* publishes *Quilt It for Kids,* a magazine filled with quick and easy projects that even inexperienced quilters can complete. Each issue offers step-by-step instructions for making full-size quilts, wall hangings, pillows, and other items designed to delight children of all ages. Columns on techniques cover applique, embroidery, binding, and other quilting embellishments. Circ: 50,000.
Website: www.quiltersnewsletter.com

Freelance Potential

80% written by nonstaff writers. Publishes 15 freelance submissions yearly; 10% by unpublished writers.
Submissions and Payment: Sample copy, $5.99. Send ms. Accepts photocopies and computer printouts. SASE. Responds in 2 months. Articles, to 800 words. Depts/columns, word length varies. 35mm color prints or transparencies. All material, rates vary. Pays on publication. First rights. Provides 3 copies.

Racquetball

1685 West Uintah
Colorado Springs, CO 80904

Executive Assistant: Heather Fender

Description and Readership

Racquetball players, coaches, and tournament directors read this colorful glossy for its national and local tournament coverage, profiles of players, features, and tips on strategy and techniques. Published by the United States Racquetball Association, it appears six times each year. It welcomes personality profiles of outstanding players. Circ: 40,000.
Website: www.racqmag.com

Freelance Potential

25% written by nonstaff writers. Publishes 10 freelance submissions yearly.
Submissions and Payment: Sample copy and guidelines, $4. Prefers query; accepts complete ms. Accepts photocopies and computer printouts. SASE. Responds in 9 weeks. Articles, 1,500–2,000 words. Depts/columns, 500–1,000 words. Written material, $.03–$.07 per word. Pays on publication. One-time rights.

Radio Control Boat Modeler

Air Age Publishing
100 East Ridge Road
Ridgefield, CT 06877-4606

Executive Editor: Gerry Yarrish

Description and Readership

Covering all facets of radio-controlled boats, this magazine offers readers articles on building and racing boats; construction projects; product reviews; and racing event coverage. It appears seven times each year. Circ: 53,000.
Website: www.rcboatmodeler.com

Freelance Potential

60% written by nonstaff writers. Publishes 20–25 freelance submissions yearly; 75% by unpublished writers. Receives 15 queries monthly.
Submissions and Payment: Sample copy and guidelines, free with 9x12 SASE. Query with outline and brief biography. Accepts email queries to rcboatmodeler@airage.com, photocopies and computer printouts. Availability of artwork improves chance of acceptance. B/W prints and 35mm slides. SASE. Responds in 1–3 months. Articles, 1,000–2,000 words; $50–$500. Pays on publication. All rights. Provides 2 copies.

Radio Control Car Action

Air Age Publishing
100 East Ridge Road
Ridgefield, CT 06877-4606

Technical Editor: Peter Vieira

Description and Readership

This colorful magazine offers articles that cover all aspects of radio-controlled electric and gas model cars. It includes how-to articles, painting and detailing articles, product reviews, conversion kits, scratch-built projects, and event coverage. It appears monthly. Circ: 140,000.
Website: www.rccaraction.com

Freelance Potential

50% written by nonstaff writers. Publishes 50 freelance submissions yearly. Receives 35 unsolicited mss monthly.
Submissions and Payment: Sample copy and guidelines, $4.50. Send complete ms with available artwork. Accepts photocopies, computer printouts, and disk submissions (ASCII). Accepts 35mm color slides for complete projects; B/W prints for step-by-step articles. SASE. Responds in 2 months. Articles, 700–1,500 words; $75–$500. Pays on publication. All rights. Provides 2 contributor's copies.

Read, America!

3900 Glenwood Avenue
Golden Valley, MN 55422

Editor & Publisher: Roger Hammer

Description and Readership

Read, America! is a quarterly newsletter sent to reading and literacy program leaders and professionals. It features news and feature stories aimed at adult program coordinators, and poems and short stories for children. Submissions should be interesting and motivating, spiritual but not religious, and thoughtful. Themes should focus on reading, literacy, and comprehension. Circ: 10,000.

Freelance Potential

50% written by nonstaff writers. Publishes 100 freelance submissions yearly; 80% by unpublished writers, 100% by authors who are new to the magazine. Receives 125 unsolicited mss monthly.
Submissions and Payment: Sample copy and guidelines, $7.50. Send complete ms. No simultaneous submissions. SASE. Responds in 2 months. Articles and fiction, to 1,000 words. Written material, to $50. Pays on acceptance. All rights.

Redbook

Hearst Corporation
224 West 57th Street
New York, NY 10019

Articles Department

Description and Readership

Married women between the ages of 25 and 44 find information tailored to their needs and interests in this monthly magazine. Articles cover contemporary social issues, marriage (with an emphasis on strengthening the relationship), and parenting topics such as children's health and behavioral issues. First-person essays are also featured. Circ: 2.3 million.
Website: www.redbookmag.com

Freelance Potential

5% written by nonstaff writers. Publishes 10 freelance submissions yearly; 2% by unpublished writers. Receives 830+ queries and unsolicited mss monthly.
Submissions and Payment: Sample copy, $2.99 at newsstands. Query with clips. Accepts photocopies and computer printouts. SASE. Responds in 3–4 months. Articles, 1,000–3,000 words; $.75–$1 per word. Depts/columns, 1,000–1,500 words; payment rate varies. Pays on acceptance. All rights.

Reptiles

P.O. Box 6050
Mission Viejo, CA 92690

Editor: Russ Case

Description and Readership

Reptiles is read by individuals who own reptiles as well as by veterinarians and others who treat and/or breed amphibians or reptiles. It is published monthly and brings readers the latest information on the care and health of these creatures. Circ: 50,000.
Website: www.reptilesmagazine.com

Freelance Potential

60% written by nonstaff writers. Publishes 55 freelance submissions yearly; 50% by unpublished writers, 40% by authors who are new to the magazine. Receives 10 queries monthly.
Submissions and Payment: Sample copy, $3.99 at newsstands. Query or send complete ms. Accepts photocopies and computer printouts. No simultaneous submissions. SASE. Responds in 2–3 months. Articles and depts/columns, word length and payment rates vary. Payment policy varies. First North American serial rights. Provides contributor's copies.

The Saturday Evening Post

1100 Waterway Boulevard
Indianapolis, IN 46202

Executive Editor: Ted Kreiter

Description and Readership

Published bimonthly, this magazine features health information relating to disease, medical problems, prevention, and modern medical solutions. It is interested in personal experience pieces and self-help articles. Circ: 450,000.
Website: www.satevepost.org

Freelance Potential

10% written by nonstaff writers. Publishes 10 freelance submissions yearly; 10% by unpublished writers. Receives 30–40 queries, 200 unsolicited mss monthly.
Submissions and Payment: Sample copy and guidelines, $4. Query with slips for articles; send complete ms for fiction. Accepts photocopies, computer printouts, and simultaneous submissions if identified. SASE. Responds in 3–8 weeks. Articles, to 3,000 words; $250–$400. Fiction, 2,500–3,000 words; payment rate varies. Short humor, 10–200 words; $15. Pays on publication. All rights. Provides 1 contributor's copy.

Rugby Magazine

Suite 1200
459 Columbus Avenue
New York, NY 10024

Editor: Ed Hagerty

Description and Readership

In publication since 1976, this monthly magazine for rugby enthusiasts features information on U.S. championship games, national team standings, profiles of outstanding coaches and players, as well as news of the international circuit. Circ: 10,500.
Website: www.rugbymag.com

Freelance Potential

50% written by nonstaff writers. Publishes 50 freelance submissions yearly; 40% by unpublished writers. Receives 50 unsolicited mss monthly.
Submissions and Payment: Sample copy and guidelines, $4 with 9x12 SASE ($1.70 postage). Query or send complete ms. Accepts photocopies, computer printouts, disk submissions, and email to rugbymag@aol.com. SASE. Responds in 2 weeks. Written material, word length and payment rates vary. Pays on publication. All rights. Provides 3 contributor's copies.

Scholastic Choices

Scholastic Inc.
557 Broadway
New York, NY 10012-3999

Editor: Bob Hugel

Description and Readership

Six times each year, students in middle school through high school receive this publication that is distributed as a classroom resource. Focusing on life skills, it delves into the areas of personal responsibility, decision making, health, and social issues. Circ: 200,000.
Website: www.scholastic.com

Freelance Potential

90% written by nonstaff writers. Publishes 30–40 freelance submissions yearly; 10% by unpublished writers. Receives 5 queries, 5 unsolicited mss monthly.
Submissions and Payment: Sample copy, guidelines, and editorial calendar, free with 9x12 SASE. Query or send complete ms. Accepts photocopies and computer printouts. SASE. Responds to queries in 3 months, to mss in 2 months. Articles and fiction, 500–1,000 words; payment rates vary. Pays on publication. All rights. Provides 10 contributor's copies.

Scholastic DynaMath

Scholastic Inc.
557 Broadway Room 4052
New York, NY 10012-3999

Editor: Matt Friedman

Description and Readership
Fun and educational math activities can be found in this magazine that is distributed to children in grades three through six. It appears eight times each year. Articles must focus on linking math to its usage in every day life. Circ: 200,000.
Website: www.scholastic.com

Freelance Potential
10% written by nonstaff writers. Publishes 5 freelance submissions yearly; 25% by unpublished writers, 25% by authors who are new to the magazine. Receives 4 queries and unsolicited mss monthly.
Submissions and Payment: Sample copy and guidelines, $4 with SASE. Query with outline and synopsis; or send complete ms. Accepts photocopies, computer printouts, and simultaneous submissions if identified. SASE. Responds in 1–2 months. Articles, to 600 words; $250–$400. Puzzles: $25–$50. Pays on acceptance. All rights. Provides 3 contributor's copies.

Scholastic Math Magazine

Scholastic Inc.
557 Broadway
New York, NY 10012-3999

Editor

Description and Readership
This educational magazine offers middle-grade students a way to connect math concepts with their daily lives and helps to develop their problem-solving skills. Published 14 times each year, it seeks material that relates math to video games, technology, music, television, the movies, and sports. Articles should be interesting and easy-to-follow. Circ: 200,000.
Website: www.scholastic.com

Freelance Potential
40% written by nonstaff writers. Publishes 3 freelance submissions yearly; 5% by unpublished writers. Receives 2 queries each month.
Submissions and Payment: Sample copy and guidelines, free with 9x12 SASE (3 first-class stamps). Query. Accepts photocopies and computer printouts. SASE. Responds in 2–3 months. Articles, 600 words; $300+. Depts/columns, 140 words; $35. Pays on publication. All rights.

Scholastic News

555 Broadway
New York, NY 10012

Submissions Editor, editions 1–3: Rebecca Bonder
Submissions Editor, editions 4–6: Suzanne Freemon

Description and Readership
This timely weekly newspaper keeps readers in tune with what is going on in the world. Targeting elementary students, it includes articles and essays on topics such as current events, politics, history, health, fitness, social issues, sports, science, and technology. Distributed to schools, it offers an edition for grades one through 3 and another for grades four through six. Circ: Unavailable.
Website: www.scholastic.com

Freelance Potential
5% written by nonstaff writers.
Submissions and Payment: Query or send complete ms with résumé. Accepts photocopies, computer printouts, and simultaneous submissions if identified. SASE. Availability of artwork improves chance of acceptance. Responds in 1–3 months. Articles, to 500 words; $75–$500. Pays on publication. All rights. Provides 3+ contributor's copies.

Scholastic Parent & Child

Scholastic Inc.
557 Broadway
New York, NY 10012-3999

Editor: Pam Abrams

Description and Readership
Published every other month this magazine from Scholastic Publishing keeps parents informed of the latest information in child learn and development. It is read by parents of children in pre-school or day care programs. Circ: 1.2 million.
Website: www.parentandchildonline.com

Freelance Potential
25% written by nonstaff writers. Publishes 10–15 freelance submissions yearly; 10% by unpublished writers. Receives 5 queries, 5 unsolicited mss monthly.
Submissions and Payment: Sample copy and guidelines, free with 9x12 SASE. Query or send complete ms. Accepts photocopies and computer printouts. SASE. Responds to queries in 3 months, to mss in 2 months. Articles and fiction, 500–1,000 words; payment rates vary. Pays on publication. All rights. Provides contributor's copies.

Scholastic Scope

Scholastic Inc.
557 Broadway
New York, NY 10012-3999

Senior Managing Editor: Mary Harvey

Description and Readership
From this well-known publisher of educational books and magazines for kids of all ages comes *Scholastic Scope*, a classroom publication read by students in junior and senior high school. It publishes 18 issues annually during the school year. Each issue includes both fiction and nonfiction, with all material geared toward topics of interest to teens. Circ: 550,000.
Website: www.scholastic.com

Freelance Potential
45% written by nonstaff writers. Publishes few freelance submissions yearly; 2% by unpublished writers, 10% by authors who are new to the magazine. Receives 17–25 mss monthly.
Submissions and Payment: Query with clips, outline/synopsis, and résumé for nonfiction. Accepts photocopies and computer printouts. SASE. Response time varies. Articles, 1,000 words; $100+. Pays on acceptance. Rights negotiable. Provides contributor's copies on request.

SchoolNet Magazine

Room 441
155 Queen Street
Ottawa, Ontario K1A 0H5
Canada

Submissions Editor

Description and Readership
Designed to help teachers integrate information and communication technology (ICT) into the classrooms, this magazine offers articles on practices and innovative uses of technology for learning, partnerships, the latest technological resources, and exploring the Internet. It also includes creative classroom projects, and interviews and profiles of experts. A Canadian publication, readers include teachers, parents, students, librarians, and school board members. It is interested in articles on using ICT as a tool for learning. Circ: Unavailable.
Website: www.schoolnet.ca

Freelance Potential
80% written by nonstaff writers. Publishes 10 freelance submissions yearly.
Submissions and Payment: Query. Accepts photocopies and computer printouts. SAE/IRC. Response time varies. Written material, word lengths and payment rates varies. Rights vary.

Science World

Scholastic Inc.
557 Broadway
New York, NY 10012-3999

Editor: Mark Bergman

Description and Readership
Students in junior high and high school are the target audience for this magazine. Published by Scholastic, it appears 13 times each year and offers a variety of exciting articles related to life science, earth science, and physical science as well as science news. Circ: 400,000.
Website: www.scholastic.com

Freelance Potential
50% written by nonstaff writers. Publishes 30 freelance submissions yearly; 10% by authors who are new to the magazine. Receives 5 queries monthly.
Submissions and Payment: Sample copy and guidelines, free with 9x12 SASE. All articles are assigned. Query with list of publishing credits and clips or writing samples. SASE. Responds in 2 months. Articles, to 750 words; $200–$650. Depts/columns, 200 words; $100–$125. Pays on acceptance. All rights. Provides 2 contributor's copies.

Scott Stamp Monthly

Scott Publishing Company
P.O. Box 828
Sidney, OH 45365

Editor: Michael Baadke

Description and Readership
This well-known monthly tabloid is read by amateur stamp collectors as well as dealers and other experts. Its editorial is devoted to covering the latest sales and auctions as well as reporting on unusual stamps. Circ: 22,000.
Website: www.scottonine.com

Freelance Potential
100% written by nonstaff writers. Publishes 120 freelance submissions yearly; 10% by unpublished writers, 15% by new authors. Receives 15 queries and unsolicited mss monthly.
Submissions and Payment: Sample copy and guidelines, $3.50 with 9x12 SASE ($1.95 postage). Prefers query. Accepts mss. Accepts computer printouts and disk submissions (Microsoft Word). SASE. Responds in 1 month. Articles, 1,200–2,000 words; $75–$150. Depts/columns, word lengths and payment rates vary. Pays on publication. First North American serial rights. Provides 2 contributor's copies.

Sesame Street Magazine ☆

One Lincoln Plaza
New York, NY 10023

Editor: Rebecca Herman

Description and Readership

This educational magazine is published 11 times each year for children ages two to five. Humorous fiction and animal stories and nonfiction on the topics of pets, animals, music, the arts, crafts, health, and fitness appear in each issue. Muppet characters are featured in each story, article, and activity. Because it does not accept freelance submissions, prospective writers who wish to approach this magazine should introduce themselves with a query letter that details their qualifications. *Sesame Street Magazine* has been in publication since 1970. Circ: 800,000.
Website: www.sesamestreet.com

Freelance Potential

100% written by staff writers. Receives 4 queries monthly.
Submissions and Payment: Query only. No unsolicited submissions. Articles and fiction, word length and payment rates vary. Payment and rights policy vary.

Shameless Magazine ☆

P.O. Box 68548
360A Bloor Street W
Toronto, Ontario M5S 1X1
Canada

Editor: Nicole Cohen

Description and Readership

Launched in 2004, *Shameless Magazine* targets teen girls seeking more than what typical teen magazines dish out. *Shameless Magazine's* readers—feminists, intellectuals, artists, and activists—find women's success stories and profiles of strong role models along with articles on music, arts and crafts, sports, travel, technology, and alternative style. It is is published three times each year. Circ: Unavailable.
Website: www.shamelessmag.com

Freelance Potential

30% written by nonstaff writers. Publishes 25 freelance submissions yearly.
Submissions and Payment: Guidelines available at website. Query with clips. Prefers email to submit@shamelessmag.com. Accepts photocopies and computer printouts. SAE/IRC. Response time varies. Articles, 650–2,000 words. Profiles, 300–500 words. No payment. First and electronic rights.

Simply You Magazine ☆

P.O. Box 284
Phillips, WI 54555-0284

Editor: Lynne

Description and Readership

This web publication is written for a teenage audience and provides an outlet for information, views, and interests of today's teens. It strives to provide articles and fiction that will enhance teens' bodies, minds, and spirits. Quizzes and message boards are also found on the site. Most of the individuals who visit the site are between 14 and 21 years old. Circ: 10,000.
Website: www.simplyyoumagazine.com

Freelance Potential

25% written by nonstaff writers. Publishes 20 freelance submissions yearly; 50% by unpublished writers, 70% by authors who are new to the magazine. Receives 2 queries monthly.
Submissions and Payment: Sample copy, $5 with business-sized SASE. Send complete ms. Accepts email to yourfriends@ simplyyoumagazine.com. Responds in 1–2 months. Articles, word length varies. No payment. All rights. Provides 1 copy.

Sister 2 Sister

P.O. Box 41148
Washington, DC 20018

Publisher: Jamie Foster Brown

Description and Readership

Profiles, interviews, media reviews, and articles targeting young adult and adult black women are the focus of this monthly magazine. Its editors are interested in informational and personal experience pieces on the music and entertainment industry, celebrities, and popular culture. Circ: 100,000.
Website: www.s2smagazine.com

Freelance Potential

40% written by nonstaff writers. Publishes 120 freelance submissions yearly. Receives 10 queries monthly.
Submissions and Payment: Sample copy and guidelines, $2.95 with 9x12 SASE ($1.52 postage). Prefers letter of introduction with résumé; accepts query. Accepts photocopies and computer printouts. SASE. Responds in 1–3 weeks if interested. Articles, 1,500 words. Depts/columns, 350 words. All material, payment rate varies. Pays on publication. First North American serial rights. Provides 2 contributor's copies.

Skiing

Suite 200
929 Pearl Street
Boulder, CO 80302

Executive Editor: Evelyn Spence

Description and Readership
This magazine with a strong editorial focus on skiing covers other winter adventure sports as well, such as ice skating, tobogganing, and dogsledding. New writers have a good shot at publication with a contribution to one of our departments. *Skiing* is published seven times each year. Circ: 403,000.
Website: www.skiingmag.com

Freelance Potential
60% written by nonstaff writers. Publishes 50 freelance submissions yearly; 2% by unpublished writers, 5% by authors who are new to the magazine. Receives 12 queries monthly.
Submissions and Payment: Sample copy and guidelines, $2.50 with 9x12 SASE ($1 postage). Query with clips or writing samples. No simultaneous submissions. SASE. Responds in 2–4 months. Articles and depts/columns, word length varies. Written material, $.75 per word. Pays on acceptance. First-time universal and all media rights. Provides author's copies.

SloppyNoodle.com

P.O. Box 468053
Atlanta, GA 31146

Editor: Stephen Isaac

Description and Readership
Christian teens explore this online publication for its articles and advice on issues related to evolution, God, faith, relationships, entertainment, substance abuse, sex, and violence prevention. It also includes devotionals, media reviews, poetry, and personal experience pieces. It welcomes articles by freelance writers. Hits per month: 3,000+.
Website: www.sloppynoodle.com

Freelance Potential
90% written by nonstaff writers. Publishes several freelance submissions yearly; 60% by unpublished writers, 10% by authors who are new to the magazine. Receives 50 queries, several unsolicited mss monthly.
Submissions and Payment: Sample issues and guidelines available at website. Query or send complete ms via email through website. Response time varies. Written material, word length varies. No payment. Rights vary.

Sonoma Parents Journal

P.O. Box 351
Philo, CA 95466

Managing Editor: Renée Mezzanatto

Description and Readership
Timely articles on parenting children from infancy to adolescence are the mainstay of this regional monthly. In addition, *Sonoma Parents Journal* keeps its readers up to date on community resources such as daycare programs, private schools, and extracurricular activities. Circ: 47,000.
Website: www.theparentsjournal.com

Freelance Potential
40% written by nonstaff writers. Publishes 20 freelance submissions yearly; 10% by unpublished writers. Receives 10+ unsolicited mss monthly.
Submissions and Payment: Writers' guidelines and editorial calendar available. Send complete ms. Accepts email submissions to renee@theparentsjournal.com (text only attachments). SASE. Response time varies. Articles and depts/columns, word lengths and payment rates vary. Pays on publication. One-time rights.

Sparkle

P.O. Box 7259
Grand Rapids, MI 49510

Managing Editor: Sara Lynne Hilton

Description and Readership
This magazine is designed for girls in grades one through three. Each of the quarterly issues features games, puzzles, stories, crafts, recipes, and science projects. It is published by the girls' club, GEMS (Girls Everywhere Meeting the Savior), and is filled with material that relates Christian faith to the real world. Circ: 2,700.
Website: www.gemsgc.org

Freelance Potential
85% written by nonstaff writers. Publishes 8 freelance submissions yearly; 50% by unpublished writers, 50% by authors who are new to the magazine. Receives 50 mss monthly.
Submissions and Payment: Guidelines available. Send complete ms. SASE. Responds in 4–6 weeks. Articles, 50–500 words. Fiction, 400–900 words. Depts/columns, 500 words. Written material, $.03–$.05 per word. Pays on publication. Rights policy varies. Provides 2 contributor's copies.

Storyworks

Scholastic Inc.
555 Broadway
New York, NY 10012-3999

Assistant Editor: Lauren Tarsh

Description and Readership

Children in grades three to five enjoy this publication from Scholastic for its fiction and nonfiction excerpts, poetry, interesting facts, and interviews with well-known authors. It also includes grammar, writing, and vocabulary activities. It is published six times each year. While most of its work is done in-house, it will consider queries from published writers for short pieces on topics related to books, reading, or writing for children. Circ: 270,000.
Website: www.scholastic.com/storyworks

Freelance Potential

60% written by nonstaff writers. Receives 20 queries monthly.
Submissions and Payment: Query. No unsolicited mss. SASE. Responds in 3 months. Articles, 500–1,500 words. Fiction, 1,000–1,500 words. Written material, payment rate varies. Pays on acceptance. Second rights. Provides contributor's copies upon request.

Surfer

33046 Calle Avidor
San Juan Capistrano, CA 92675

Editor: Chris Mauro

Description and Readership

Published monthly for serious surfers, this magazine includes photos of surfers and surfing, lifestyle articles, travel pieces, interviews, and the latest surfer news. New writers have the best chance with its "People Who Surf" column. Circ: 110,000.
Website: www.surfermag.com

Freelance Potential

75% written by nonstaff writers. Publishes 24 freelance submissions yearly; 1% by unpublished writers. Receives 60 queries monthly.
Submissions and Payment: Sample copy, $1 with 9x12 SASE. Query or send complete ms. Accepts photocopies, computer printouts, and Macintosh disk submissions. No simultaneous submissions. SASE. Responds in 6–8 weeks. Articles, 1,500–2,500 words. Depts/columns, to 1,000 words. Written material, $.20–$.35 per word. Pays on publication. First North American serial rights.

SuperTwins

P.O. Box 306
East Islip, NY 11730

Editor: Maureen A. Doolan Boyle

Description and Readership

Published by MOST (Mothers of Supertwins), Inc., this quarterly magazine is available to members of MOST as well as to non-members. Its articles are geared toward families with twins and multiples up to elementary-school age. Along with factual information, issues include recipes and crafts for kids and essays from fathers and grandparents. Circ: Unavailable.
Website: www.MOSTonline.org

Freelance Potential

15–20% written by nonstaff writers. Publishes 30–40 freelance submissions yearly.
Submissions and Payment: Sample copy, $5 with 9x12 SASE. Query or send complete ms. Accepts photocopies, computer printouts, and email submissions to info@mostonline.org. No simultaneous submissions. SASE. Response time varies. Articles and depts/columns, word length and payment rate vary. Pays on publication. Rights vary. Provides 2 copies.

Teaching Elementary Physical Education

Human Kinetics Publishers
P.O. Box 5076
Champaign, IL 61825-5076

Editor: Steve Stork

Description and Readership

Physical educators working with elementary and middle school children are the target audience of this bimonthly publication. It covers topics related to health and fitness as well as the latest information relating to physical education, fitness testing, and assessment. Circ: 4,000+.
Website: www.humankinetics.com

Freelance Potential

100% written by nonstaff writers. Publishes 78 freelance submissions yearly; 20% by unpublished writers, 30% by authors who are new to the magazine. Receives 8 mss monthly.
Submissions and Payment: Sample copy and guidelines, $4 with 9x12 SASE. Query with clips; or send complete ms. Accepts photocopies and computer printouts. SASE. Responds in 1–4 weeks. Articles, 2–12 double-spaced pages. Depts/columns, 200–500 words. No payment. First or one-time rights. Provides 1 contributor's copy.

Teen People

Time Life Building
35th Floor
Rockefeller Center
New York, NY 10020-1393

Editor

Description and Readership

The publishers of *People* magazine produce *Teen People*, which is tailored for an audience of teen and pre-teen readers with its focus on young celebrities. It features profiles, interviews, and updates on well-known and up-and-coming stars of the television, film, and music industries. Music reviews and fashion and beauty tips are other regular features. If you are a seasoned writer or journalist with an idea you think is right for *Teen People*, address a query to the appropriate editor on the masthead. Circ: 1.6 million.
Website: www.teenpeople.com

Freelance Potential

Publishes few freelance submissions.
Submissions and Payment: Sample copy, $3.99 at newsstands. Query. SASE. Response time varies. Articles and depts/columns, word lengths and payment rates vary. Pays on acceptance. All rights.

Teens on Target

Word Aflame Publications
8855 Dunn Road
Hazelwood, MO 63042-2299

Submissions: Lisa Henson

Description and Readership

The United Pentecostal Church International owns and operates the company that publishes *Teens on Target*, a Sunday school take-home paper. Published quarterly in weekly editions, it buys freelance material for three years, then recycles it for seven years. At this time, it is not considering freelance submissions. Visit its website for updates on this policy, and for information about what its needs will be when it once again seeks freelance material. Circ: 8,000.
Website: www.upci.org

Freelance Potential

85% written by nonstaff writers. Publishes 75 freelance submissions yearly; 50% by unpublished writers, 40% by authors who are new to the magazine.
Submissions and Payment: Sample copy and guidelines, free with #10 SASE. Not accepting freelance queries or submissions at this time.

Teens in Motion News

P.O. Box 1264
Santa Clara, CA 95052

Editor: Pamela Costa

Description and Readership

Short stories of all genres and articles on any topic of interest to teens appear in this quarterly publication, which is entirely written by teens. Self-help articles, personal experience pieces, and opinion essays are among the submissions that are most welcome, as the magazine's main objective is to allow teens to voice their concerns and share their experiences. Teens aiming for journalism careers may wish to submit column ideas, thus gaining valuable experience. Circ: Unavailable.

Freelance Potential

80% written by nonstaff writers. Publishes 50–100 freelance submissions yearly; 95% by unpublished writers. Receives 5 queries monthly.
Submissions and Payment: Query with clips or writing samples. Accepts photocopies and computer printouts. SASE. Responds in 1 month. Articles, 500 words; payment rate varies. Pays on publication. Rights vary. Provides 2 copies.

Teen Times

1910 Association Drive
Reston, VA 20191

Communications Manager: Beth Carpenter

Description and Readership

Members and advisors of Family, Career, and Community Leaders of America read this quarterly magazine that serves as a classroom resource in middle schools and high schools. In addition to keeping members informed of the activities and achievements of chapters across the country, it covers topics such as careers, health, fitness, and recreation. Circ: 220,000.
Website: www.fcclainc.org

Freelance Potential

50% written by nonstaff writers. Publishes 20 freelance submissions yearly; 100% by unpublished writers.
Submissions and Payment: Sample copy and editorial calendar available with 9x12 SASE. Query or send complete ms. Accepts photocopies and computer printouts. Availability of artwork improves chance of acceptance. SASE. Response time varies. Articles and depts/columns, word lengths vary. No payment. All rights. Provides contributor's copies upon request.

Today's Christian

465 Gundersen Drive
Carol Stream, IL 60188

Submissions Editor

Description and Readership
Short stories of faith, inspirational articles, and personal experience pieces on living a Christian life are the mainstay of this bimonthly digest publication. Circ: 185,000.
Website: www.todayschristian.net

Freelance Potential
30% written by nonstaff writers. Publishes 25–30 freelance submissions yearly; 10% by unpublished writers, 10% by authors who are new to the magazine.. Receives 150 unsolicited mss each month.
Submissions and Payment: Sample copy, free with 6x9 SASE (4 first-class stamps). Send complete ms. Accepts photocopies, computer printouts, and email submissions to tceditor@ christianreader.net (no attachments). SASE. Responds in 2 months. Articles, 700–2,800 words. Depts/columns, word length varies. Written material, $.15–$.25 per word. Pays on acceptance. First serial rights. Provides 2 contributor's copies.

Toy Farmer

7496 106th Avenue SE
LaMoure, ND 58458-9404

Editorial Assistant: Cheryl Hegvik

Description and Readership
This magazine offers articles, profiles, and events relating to collecting farm toys. Published monthly, it strives to bring collectors together worldwide to share the fun and information on the hobby. Circ: 27,000.
Website: www.toyfarmer.com

Freelance Potential
100% written by nonstaff writers. Publishes 50 freelance submissions yearly; 20% by unpublished writers, 20% by authors who are new to the magazine; 40% by experts. Receives several queries monthly.
Submissions and Payment: Guidelines and editorial calendar available. Sample copy, $5 with 9x12 SASE. Query with writing samples. Accepts computer printouts and disk submissions. SASE. Responds in 1 month. Articles, 1,500 words. Depts/columns, 800 words. Written material, $.10 per word. Pays on publication. First rights. Provides 2 author's copies.

Toy Tips Magazine

9663 Santa Monica Boulevard
Beverly Hills, CA 90210

Publisher: Marianne M. Szymanski

Description and Readership
Focusing on toys, this quarterly publication provides parents with academic research on industry trends, popularity, safety, and the benefits of play to children and adults. It offers information on toys that help develop and advance a child's skills. Circ: 3 million.
Website: www.toytips.com

Freelance Potential
15% written by nonstaff writers. Publishes 4 freelance submissions yearly; 5% by authors who are new to the magazine. Receives 2–4 queries, 2 unsolicited mss monthly.
Submissions and Payment: Sample copy and guidelines, $3 with 9x12 SASE. Query or send complete ms. Accepts email submissions to comments@toytips.com. Availability of artwork improves chance of acceptance. SASE. Responds in 1 month. Articles and depts/columns, 200 words. Color prints or transparencies. No payment. All rights. Provides 10 copies.

True Love

Sterling/McFadden Publishing
11th Floor
333 Seventh Avenue
New York, NY 10001

Editor-in-Chief: Alison Way

Description and Readership
First-person stories of light romance, inspiration, and current social concerns are featured in this monthly magazine for women. It seeks evocative stories involving real people and stories that shed new light on different perspectives. Stories with a twist will get a second look here. Circ: 200,000.
Website: www.truestorymail.com

Freelance Potential
100% written by nonstaff writers. Publishes 120 freelance submissions yearly; 40% by unpublished writers. Receives 35 unsolicited mss monthly.
Submissions and Payment: Sample copy, $2.99 at newsstands. Guidelines available. Send complete ms. No simultaneous submissions. Accepts photocopies and computer printouts. SASE. Responds in 6–9 months. Articles, 2,000–10,000 words; $.03 per word; no byline. Poetry, to 24 lines; $2 per line. Pays on publication. All rights. Provides 1 copy.

Vegetarian Journal

P.O. Box 1463
Baltimore, MD 21203

Managing Editor: Debra Wasserman

Description and Readership

This quarterly magazine is written for vegetarians, as well as those interested in healthy cooking without meat products. Each issue offers recipes, articles on health, fitness, natural foods, and nutrition. All writers with a knowledge about vegetarianism or an interest in related nutrition are welcome. Circ: 20,000.
Website: www.vrg.org

Freelance Potential

50% written by nonstaff writers. Publishes 12 freelance submissions yearly; 5% by unpublished writers, 15% by authors who are new to the magazine. Receives 8–10 queries and unsolicited mss monthly.
Submissions and Payment: Guidelines available. Query or send complete ms. Accepts photocopies and computer printouts. SASE. Response time varies. Written material, word length, and payment rate vary. Pays on acceptance. First rights.

Volta Voices

Alexander Graham Bell Association for the
Deaf and Hard of Hearing
3417 Volta Place NW
Washington, DC 20007-2778

Editor: Michelle Van Derhoff

Description and Readership

This magazine is published six times each year for individuals who are deaf or hard of hearing, parents of hearing-impaired children, and the professionals who work with them. It seeks articles on hearing loss, speech/language pathology, social services, and education. Circ: 5,500.
Website: www.agbell.org

Freelance Potential

90% written by nonstaff writers. Publishes 6 freelance submissions yearly; 50% by unpublished writers. Receives 2 unsolicited mss monthly.
Submissions and Payment: Sample copy, free with 9x12 SASE ($.58 postage). Send complete ms. Accepts computer printouts and Macintosh disk submissions (Microsoft Word or WordPerfect 5.1) with hard copy. SASE. Responds in 1–3 months. Articles, 500–2,000 words. No payment. All rights. Provides 2 contributor's copies.

Vibrant Life

55 West Oak Ridge Drive
Hagerstown, MD 21740

Editor: Charles Mills

Description and Readership

Published six times each year, *Vibrant Life* covers topics related to healthy lifestyles and fitness. Its audience is interested in articles that relate to these topics while incorporating a Christian lifestyle. Circ: 28,500.
Website: www.vibrantlife.com

Freelance Potential

90% written by nonstaff writers. Publishes 35–45 freelance submissions yearly; 10% by unpublished writers, 25% by new authors. Receives 30 queries, 25–35 unsolicited mss monthly.
Submissions and Payment: Sample copy and guidelines, $1 with 9x12 SASE (3 first-class stamps). Prefers complete ms; accepts queries. Accepts photocopies, computer printouts, and simultaneous submissions. SASE. Responds in 2 months. Articles, 1,000 words. Depts/columns, word length varies. Written material, $50–$400. Pays on acceptance. First world and reprint rights. Provides 3 contributor's copies.

WaterSki

Suite 200
460 North Orlando Avenue
Winter Park, FL 32789

Editor: Todd Ristorcelli

Description and Readership

Targeting small pleasure-craft owners and water-ski sportsmen, this magazine features information on boating and skiing technique, new products, training, and safety. Circ: 90,000.
Website: www.waterskimag.com

Freelance Potential

10% written by nonstaff writers. Publishes 6–10 freelance submissions yearly; 10% by unpublished writers. Receives 1 query, 1 unsolicited mss monthly.
Submissions and Payment: Sample copy and guidelines, $3 with 9x12 SASE. Query with résumé, outline, and clips; or send complete ms. Accepts photocopies, computer printouts, and IBM disk submissions. SASE. Responds in 2 months. Articles, 1,000–2,500 words; $300–$500. Depts/columns, 650–850 words; payment rate varies. Artwork, $75–$500. Pays on publication. Kill fee, 50%. First or one-time rights. Provides 10 contributor's copies.

The Water Skier

USA Water Ski
1251 Holy Cow Road
Polk City, FL 33686-8200

Editor: Scott Atkinson

Description and Readership
Published seven times each year by USA Water Ski, the governing body for organized water skiing in the U.S., this magazine offers information on the sport of water skiing for all levels of enthusiasts. It is interested in receiving information on competitions, profiles of professional and amateur water skiers, and sport-related fiction. Circ: 35,000.
Website: www.usawaterski.org

Freelance Potential
25% written by nonstaff writers. Publishes 3–5 freelance submissions yearly; 60% by authors who are new to the magazine. Receives 1 query monthly.
Submissions and Payment: Sample copy, $1.25 with 9x12 SASE. Query. SASE. Responds in 1 month. Articles, 1,000 words. Fiction, 500–1,000 words. Written material, payment rate varies. Pays on publication. All rights. Provides 1 contributor's copy.

Wild West

Primedia History Group
Suite D-2
741 Miller Drive SE
Leesburg, VA 20175

Editor: Greg Lalire

Description and Readership
Established in 1988, this magazine appears six times a year and offers articles showcasing the history of the great American West. Topics include expeditions, outlaws, Native Americans, and guns. It seeks well-written, accurate articles on topics related to the Wild West. Circ: 80,000.
Website: www.thehistorynet.com

Freelance Potential
90% written by nonstaff writers. Publishes 60 freelance submissions yearly; 10% by unpublished writers, 30% by authors who are new to the magazine. Receives 25 queries monthly.
Submissions and Payment: Sample copy and guidelines, $6. Query with résumé, outline, illustration ideas, source lists, and clips or writing samples. Accepts photocopies and computer printouts. SASE. Responds in 4–6 months. Articles, to 3,500 words; $300. Depts/columns, to 2,000 words; $150. Pays on publication. All rights.

World Around You

#6 Kendall School
Gallaudet University
800 Florida Avenue NE
Washington, DC 20002

Editor: Cathryn Carroll

Description and Readership
This magazine is published five times each year by Gallaudet University, the world's only university for undergraduate students who are deaf or hard of hearing. *World Around You* provides information on careers, reports on the achievements of hearing-impaired adults and young adults, and publishes personal experience pieces. Many of its contributors are hearing-impaired. Circ: 3,000.
Website: www.gallaudet.edu

Freelance Potential
10% written by nonstaff writers. Publishes 3–5 freelance submissions yearly. Receives 4 queries monthly.
Submissions and Payment: Sample copy, $2. Query. Accepts photocopies, computer printouts, and simultaneous submissions if identified. SASE. Responds in 1 month. Written material, word lengths and payment rates vary. Pays on publication. Rights negotiable. Provides 5 contributor's copies.

World Pulse Magazine

5935 NE Skidmore
Portland, OR 97218

Editor

Description and Readership
Based on the premise that women and children are transforming the world, this magazine covers human rights, the global economy, the environment, and other urgent international issues. News and feature stories, essays, fiction, and poetry are written by accomplished women journalists. Circ: Unavailable.
Website: www.worldpulsemagazine.com

Freelance Potential
15% written by nonstaff writers. Publishes 15–20 freelance submissions yearly.
Submissions and Payment: Guidelines available. Query with brief author bio and 2–4 clips. Accepts email submissions to editor@worldpulsemagazine.com. SASE. Responds in 3 months. Articles, 1,000–2,500 words. Fiction and poetry, word length varies. Depts/columns, 200–1,200 words. All material, payment rates and policy vary. Rights policy varies. Provides 1 contributor's copy and a 1-year subscription.

Young & Alive

P.O. Box 6097
Lincoln, NE 68506

Editor: Gaylena Gibson

Description and Readership

Published quarterly for sight-impaired young adults, this magazine features entertaining stories and articles with a Christian slant. *Young & Alive* is currently not accepting submissions. Circ: 25,000.
Website: www.christianrecord.org

Freelance Potential

90% written by nonstaff writers. Publishes 50 freelance submissions yearly; 5–10% by authors who are new to the magazine. Receives 40–50 queries and unsolicited mss monthly.
Submissions and Payment: Sample copy, free with 8x10 SASE (5 first-class stamps). Guidelines available. Accepts queries. Accepts photocopies, computer printouts, and simultaneous submissions. SASE. Responds in 11–12 months. Articles, 800–1,400 words. Depts/columns, word length varies. Written material, $.03–$.05 per word. Pays on acceptance. One-time rights. Provides 2 contributor's copies.

Young Voices

P.O. Box 2321
Olympia, WA 98507

Submissions Editor

Description and Readership

Short stories, essays, poetry, drawings, and photographs created by students in elementary through high school are published in this quarterly magazine. Work from students whose schools subscribe to *Young Voices* receives first priority. Circ: 3,000.
Website: www.youngvoicesmagazine.com

Freelance Potential

100% written by nonstaff writers. Publishes 150 freelance submissions yearly; 95% by unpublished writers. Receives 333 unsolicited mss monthly.
Submissions and Payment: Sample copy and guidelines, $4. Send complete ms. Accepts photocopies, computer printouts, simultaneous submissions if identified, and submissions sent through the website. SASE. Responds in 1 month. Articles and fiction, word lengths vary; $25–$300. B/W prints and line art, payment rate varies. Pays on acceptance. One-time rights. Provides 1–4 contributor's copies.

Your Child

155 Fifth Avenue
New York, NY 10010-6802

Editor: Kay E. Pomerantz

Description and Readership

The United Synagogue of Conservative Judaism publishes this newsletter three times each year for parents of young Jewish children. Believing that the key to the survival of Conservative Judaism is Jewish education, both formal and informal, *Your Child* focuses on informal education: the Jewish content of a child's life at home. Circ: 3,000.
Website: www.usjc.org

Freelance Potential

Of the freelance submissions published yearly, 50% are by unpublished writers.
Submissions and Payment: Sample copy, free with 9x12 SASE ($.55 postage). Send complete ms. Accepts photocopies. Availability of artwork improves chance of acceptance. SASE. Response time varies. Articles, word length varies. 8x10 B/W prints and transparencies; line art. No payment. All rights. Provides 1 contributor's copy.

ZooGoer

Friends of the National Zoo Communications Office
National Zoological Park
3001 Connecticut Avenue NW
Washington, DC 20008

Associate Editor: Brendan Horton

Description and Readership

Six times each year, this magazine enlightens readers who are interested in natural history, biological research, wildlife conservation, botany, and nature travel. Circ: 30,000.
Website: www.fonz.org

Freelance Potential

85% written by nonstaff writers. Publishes 16 freelance submissions yearly; 10% by unpublished writers, 2% by authors who are new to the magazine. Receives 2 queries, 1 unsolicited ms monthly.
Submissions and Payment: Guidelines available. Query with synopsis and clips or writing sample; or send complete ms. Accepts computer printouts, disk submissions (WordPerfect), and email submissions to zoogoer@fonz.org. SASE. Responds in 1–2 months. Articles, 2,500–3,000 words. Depts/columns, 800–1,500 words. Written material, $.50 per word. Pays on publication. First rights. Provides 5–8 contributor's copies.

Contests and Awards

Selected Contests and Awards

Entering a writing contest will provide you with a chance to have your work read by established writers and qualified editors. Winning or placing in a contest or an award program can open the door to publication and recognition of your writing. If you don't win, try to read the winning entry if it is published; doing so will give you some insight into how your work compares with its competition.

For both editors and writers, contests generate excitement. For editors, contests are a source to discover new writers. Entries are more focused because of the contest guidelines, and therefore more closely target an editor's current needs.

For writers, every contest entry is read, often by more than one editor, as opposed to unsolicited submissions that are often relegated to a slush pile.

And you don't have to be the grand-prize winner to benefit—non-winning manuscripts are often purchased by the publication for future issues.

To be considered for the contests and awards that follow, your entry must fulfill all of the requirements mentioned. Most are looking for unpublished article or story manuscripts, while a few require published works. Note special entry requirements, such as whether or not you can submit the material yourself, need to be a member of an organization, or are limited in the number of entries you can send. Also, be sure to submit your article or story in the standard manuscript submission format.

For each listing, we've included the address, the contact, a description, the entry requirements, the deadline, and the prize. In some cases, the 2005 deadlines were not available at press time. We recommend that you write to the addresses provided or visit the websites to request an entry form and the contest guidelines, which usually specify the current deadline.

Amazing Kids! Annual Essay Contest

Amazing Kids!
PMB 485
1158 26th Street
Santa Monica, CA 90403

Description
Held annually, this essay contest is sponsored by the Internet publication *Amazing Kids!* It is open to children and young adults ages 5 to 17 and consists of a different theme each year.
Website: www.amazing-kids.org
Length: No length requirements.
Requirements: No entry fees. Prefers email submissions to essays@amazing-kids.org. Will accept photocopies and computer printouts. All entries must include author's name, address, and a parent or guardian's permission to enter the contest. Visit the website or send an SASE for complete guidelines and current theme.
Prizes: Winners receive publication of their essays in the September issue of *Amazing Kids!*
Deadline: August 15.

Amy Writing Awards

The Amy Foundation
P.O. Box 16091
Lansing, MI 48901

Description
The Amy Writing Awards recognize creative writing that presents the biblical position on issues affecting the world today in a sensitive, thought-provoking manner. The competition is open to all writers and eligible entries will have been published in a secular, non-religious publication, but must contain Scripture.
Website: www.amyfound.org
Length: No length requirements.
Requirements: No entry fee. All entries must contain quotes from the Bible. Send an SASE or visit the website for complete guidelines.
Prizes: First-place winner receives a cash award of $10,000.
Deadline: December 31.

Isaac Asimov Award

University of South Florida
School of Mass Communications
4202 East Fowler
Tampa, FL 33620

Description
Open to undergraduate students, this annual award looks to promote and encourage the writing of high-quality science fiction and fantasy. It accepts previously unpublished entries only.
Website: www.asimovs.com
Length: 1,000–10,000 words.
Requirements: Open to full-time college students only. Entry fee, $10. Limit three entries per competition. Entries should include a cover sheet with author's name, address, and university. Author's name should not appear on the entry itself.
Prizes: Winner receives a cash prize of $500 and will be considered for publication in *Asimov's Science Fiction Magazine*.
Deadline: December 15.

AuthorMania.com Writing Contests

Cindy Thomas
AuthorMania.com
Rt. 4 Box 201-A
Buna, TX 77612

Description
AuthorMania.com sponsors a fiction contest and poetry contest each year. The contests are open to writers living in the U.S. and look for original, unpublished material. Entries must be written in English and may be on any subject, but must not include violence or hate.
Website: www.authormania.com
Length: Fiction, to 5,000 words. Poetry, no length limits.
Requirements: Entry fee, $20. Multiple entries will be accepted provided each is accompanied by a separate entry fee. Accepts photocopies and computer printouts. Manuscripts will not be returned. Send an SASE or visit the website for complete guidelines.
Prizes: Fiction contest winner receives a cash award of $1,000. Poetry contest winner receives a cash award of $400.
Deadline: May 31. Winner will be announced in June.

AWA Contests

Cumberland College
6000 College Station Drive
Williamsburg, KY 40769

Description
Open to members of the Appalachian Writers Association, these contests present several different awards in categories that include short story, essay, and playwriting. They accept previously unpublished material only.
Length: Lengths vary for each award category.
Requirements: No entry fee. Entrants may submit up to 3 entries per category. Accepts photocopies and computer printouts. Submit two copies of each entry. Manuscripts will not be returned. Visit the website or send an SASE for specific category guidelines and further information.
Prizes: First-place winners in each award category receive a cash award of $100. Second- and third-place winners receive cash awards of $50 and $25, respectively.
Deadline: June 1.

Baker's Plays High School Playwriting Contest

Baker's Plays
P.O. Box 699222
Quincy, MA 02269-9222

Description
Sponsored by Baker's Plays, this annual contest accepts submissions from high school students only. It looks to acknowledge playwrights at the high school level and to insure the future of American theater. It is recommended that each entry receive a public reading or production prior to submission.
Website: www.bakersplays.com
Length: No length requirements.
Requirements: No entry fee. Plays must be accompanied by the signature of a sponsoring high school English teacher. Accepts photocopies and computer printouts. Include an SASE for return of manuscript. Visit the website or send an SASE for complete guidelines and entry form.
Prizes: Cash prizes ranging between $100 and $500 are awarded. The first-place winner will also have their play produced.
Deadline: January 30.

Waldo M. and Grace C. Bonderman Youth Theatre Playwriting Competition

Indiana University–Purdue University at Indianapolis
CA305, 425 University Blvd., Suite 309
Indianapolis, IN 46202-5140

Description
This competition accepts plays that are intended for a young audience (third grade through high school). Scripts previously produced are not eligible for this competition.
Website: www.liberalarts.iupui.edu/bonderman
Length: 45-minute running time.
Requirements: No entry fee. Limit one entry per competition. Accepts photocopies and computer printouts. For dramatizations or adaptations, written proof is required that the original work is in the public domain or that permission has been granted by the copyright holder. Send an SASE or visit the website for more details.
Prizes: Awards will be presented to 10 finalists. Four cash awards of $1,000 are also awarded to the playwrights whose plays are selected for development.
Deadline: September 1.

ByLine Magazine Contests

Contests, *ByLine* Magazine
P.O. Box 130596
Edmond, OK 73013-0001

Description
Sponsored by *ByLine*, these contests are presented each month in various categories including children's story, personal essay, genre fiction, and character sketch.
Website: www.bylinemag.com/contests.html
Length: Lengths vary according to category.
Requirements: Fees vary according to category but range from $3 to $5. Multiple entries are accepted. Accepts photocopies and computer printouts. Send an SASE or visit the website for complete category information and further guidelines.
Prizes: Cash prizes ranging from $10 to $70 are presented to the winners. Runners-up also receive cash awards in each category. Winning entries for the Annual Literary Awards are published in *ByLine*, and receive a cash award of $250.
Deadline: Deadlines vary according to category.

Calliope Fiction Contest

Calliope
Sandy Raschke, Fiction Editor
P.O. Box 466
Moraga, CA 94556-0466

Description
Held annually, this contest accepts entries of short fiction that display creativity, good storytelling, and appropriate use of language for the target audience.
Length: To 2,500 words.
Requirements: Entry fee, $2 per story for non-subscribers; first entry is free for subscribers. Limit 5 entries per competition. Accepts photocopies and computer printouts. Manuscript will not be returned. Enclose an SASE for winners' list. Send an SASE for current contest theme and complete guidelines.
Prizes: First-place winner receives a cash award of $75. Second- and third-place winners receive $25 and $10, respectively. All winners are published in *Calliope* (requires one-time rights). Winners also receive certificates and a 1-year subscription to *Calliope*.
Deadline: Entries are accepted between April 15 and September 30.

CAPA Competition

Connecticut Authors and Publishers
223 Buckingham Street
Oakville, CT 06779

Description
Open to residents of Connecticut, this annual competition is open to previously unpublished entries only. It accepts entries in the categories of children's story, short story, personal essay, and poetry.
Website: http://aboutcapa.com
Length: Children's stories and short stories, to 2,000 words. Personal essays, to 1,500 words. Poetry, to 30 lines.
Requirements: Entry fee, $10 for 1 story or essay or up to 3 poems. Multiple entries are accepted. Submit four copies of manuscript. Manuscripts will not be returned. Visit the website or send an SASE for complete guidelines.
Prizes: First-place winner in each category receives a cash prize of $100. Second-place winners receive a cash award of $50.
Deadline: May 31.

Children's Writer Contests

Children's Writer
95 Long Ridge Road
West Redding, CT 06896-1124

Description
Each year, *Children's Writer* sponsors two contests with different themes for original, unpublished fiction and nonfiction. Entries are selected and judged on originality, writing quality, characterization, plot, and age-appropriateness.
Website: www.childrenswriter.com
Length: Requirements vary for each contest; usually 500–1,000 words.
Requirements: Entry fee, $10 for non-subscribers (entry fee includes an 8-month subscription); no entry fee for subscribers. Multiple entries are accepted. Manuscripts are not returned. Visit the website or send an SASE for current themes and further requirements.
Prizes: Cash prizes vary per contest. Winning entries are published in *Children's Writer*.
Deadline: February and October of each year.

CNW/FFWA Florida State Writing Competition

CNW/FFWA
P.O. Box A
North Stratford, NH 03590

Description
This annual competition is open to all writers and presents awards in several categories including children's literature short story, children's nonfiction, novel chapter, nonfiction book chapter, and poetry.
Website: www.writers-editors.com
Length: Vary according to category.
Requirements: Entry fees vary for each category. Multiple entries are accepted, as long as each entry is accompanied by an entry fee. Use paper clips only. Author's name must not appear on manuscript. Send an SASE or visit the website for complete contest guidelines, specific category information, and official entry form.
Prizes: First- through third-place winners will be awarded in each category. Winners receive cash awards ranging from $50 to $100.
Deadline: March 15.

Dragonfly Spirit Writing ☆ for Children Short Story Contest

331 Elmwood Drive, Suite 4-#261
Moncton, New Brunswick E1A 7Y1
Canada

Description

Sponsored by *Dragonfly Spirit*, this annual contest is open to writers who have not yet been published in the genres of children's or young adult fiction.

Website: www.dragonflyspirit.com

Length: To 2,000 words.

Requirements: Entry fee, $7. Accepts photocopies and computer printouts. Manuscripts will not be returned. Include target age range on entry. Send an SASE or visit the website for complete competition guidelines.

Prizes: First-place winner receives a cash prize of $225. Second- and third-place winners receive cash prizes of $50 and $25, respectively. Winning entries will be published on the *Dragonfly Spirit* website.

Deadline: September 30.

Shubert Fendrich Memorial Playwriting Contest

Pioneer Drama Service, Inc.
P.O. Box 4267
Englewood, CO 80155-4267

Description

Open to writers who have not been published by Pioneer Drama Service, this contest honors its winners with publication and a royalty advance. Plays may be on any subject that is appropriate for family viewing.

Website: www.pioneerdrama.com

Length: Running time, 20 to 90 minutes.

Requirements: No entry fee. Cover letter must accompany all submissions. Include title, synopsis, cast list breakdown, proof of production, number of sets and scenes, and, if applicable, musical score and tape. Any writers currently published by Pioneer Drama Service are not eligible. Send SASE for contest guidelines and information.

Prizes: Winner receives $1,000 royalty advance in addition to publication.

Deadline: March 1. Winners will be announced in June.

Focus on Writers Contest

3rd Floor
828 I Street
Sacramento, CA 95814

Description

Open to residents of California, this competition offers writers the opportunity to test their writing talents against other writers. It looks for high-quality, unpublished submissions of short stories, nonfiction articles, books/articles for children, and first chapter of a young adult novel.

Website: www.saclib.org

Length: Length limits vary for each category.

Requirements: Entry fee, $5. Multiple entries are accepted. Accepts photocopies and computer printouts. Author's name should not be included on manuscript. Include a 3x5 index card with author's name, address, and title of entry. Send an SASE or visit the website for guidelines.

Prizes: First-place winners in each category receive $200. Second- and third-place winners receive $100 and $50, respectively.

Deadline: August 31.

Friends of the Library Writing Contest

130 North Franklin
Decatur, IL 62523

Description

Held annually, this contest accepts material in the categories of fiction, juvenile fiction, essay, and poetry (both rhymed and unrhymed). It is co-sponsored by Hutton Publications and the Decatur Public Library.

Website: www.decatur.lib.il.us

Length: Fiction and juvenile fiction, to 3,000 words. Essay, to 2,000 words. Poetry, to 40 lines.

Requirements: Entry fee, $3 per piece. Limit 5 entries per competition. Accepts photocopies and computer printouts. Include an SASE for winners' list. Send an SASE or visit the website for complete guidelines and category information.

Prizes: Winners in each category receive cash prizes ranging from $20 to $50.

Deadline: September 25.

Submissions Received: Receives 180 submissions per competition.

Frontiers in Writing Contest

Panhandle Professional Writers
P.O. Box 8066
Amarillo, TX 79114

Description
Held annually, the Frontiers in Writing Contest presents awards in several categories including juvenile/young adult short story; juvenile/young adult novel; historical novel, and screenplay. The competition is open to all writers and accepts original, unpublished work only.
Length: Varies for each category.
Requirements: No entry fee. Accepts photocopies and computer printouts. Author's name must not be on manuscript. Include an entry form (available at website or with an SASE) with each submission.
Prizes: First-place winners in the short story categories receive $75; novel category winners receive $100. Second- and third-place winners receive cash awards ranging from $25 to $75.
Deadline: April 1.

John Gardner Memorial Prize for Fiction

Harpur Palate
English Department, Binghamton University
Box 6000
Binghamton, NY 13902-6000

Description
Honoring John Gardner for his dedication to the creative writing program at Binghamton University, this award is presented annually. It welcomes the previously unpublished short stories in any genre.
Website: http://harpurpalate.binghamton.edu
Length: To 8,000 words.
Requirements: Entry fee, $10 (checks should be made out to *Harpur Palate*). Multiple entries are accepted under separate cover only. Include a cover letter with name, address, phone number, email address, and title. Manuscripts will not be returned. Send an SASE or visit the website for further information.
Prizes: Winner receives a cash award of $500 and publication in *Harpur Palate*.
Deadline: March 1.

Lorian Hemingway Short Story Competition

P.O. Box 993
Key West, FL 33041

Description
The Lorian Hemingway Short Story Competition encourages writers who have not yet achieved major success in the world of publishing.
Website: www.shortstorycompetition.com
Length: To 3,000 words.
Requirements: Entry fee, $10 postmarked by May 1; $15 per submission postmarked between May 1 and May 15. Multiple entries are accepted. Accepts photocopies and computer printouts. Send an SASE for complete guidelines and further information.
Prizes: First-place winner receives a cash award of $1,000. Second- and third-place winners each receive a cash award of $500.
Deadline: May 15.

Highlights for Children Fiction Contest

Fiction Contest
803 Church Street
Honesdale, PA 18431

Description
With a commitment to raise the quality of writing for children, this competition is held annually and looks for well-written short stories for children ages two through twelve. Stories should not contain violence, crime, or derogatory humor.
Website: www.highlights.com
Length: To 500 words.
Requirements: No entry fee. Multiple entries accepted. Accepts photocopies and computer printouts. Include SASE for manuscript return. Send SASE for further guidelines.
Prizes: Winners receive a cash award of $1,000 and publication in *Highlights for Children* (requires all rights).
Deadline: Entries must be postmarked between January 1 and February 28.
Submissions Received: Receives 2,000 submissions each competition; 40% by unpublished writers.

Insight Writing Contest

Insight Magazine
55 West Oak Ridge Drive
Hagerstown, MD 21740-7390

Description

This annual contest values and recognizes the mechanics of good writing, particularly that with a spiritual message. It accepts entries of short nonfiction and poetry that is of interest to young people ages 14 to 22.
Website: www.insightmagazine.com
Length: From 1,500 to 2,000 words (no longer than seven pages).
Requirements: No entry fee. Accepts photocopies and computer printouts. Author's name must not be included on the manuscript. Include cover letter with title, category, name, address, phone number, and Social Security number. Multiple submissions accepted. Include SASE for return of entry.
Prizes: Winners receive cash awards ranging from $150 to $250 and publication in *Insight*. All other entries will be considered for purchase.
Deadline: June 1.

Milkweed Fiction Prize

Milkweed Editions
Suite 400
430 First Avenue North
Minneapolis, MN 55401-1473

Description

The Milkweed Fiction Prize is presented to the most exemplary work of literary fiction that is accepted by Milkweed Editions during each calendar year. Manuscripts can be a collection of short stories or individual stories previously published in magazines or anthologies.
Website: www.milkweed.org
Length: No length requirement.
Requirements: No entry fee. Manuscripts previously submitted to Milkweed Editions should not be resubmitted. Individual stories previously published in magazines or anthologies are eligible.
Prizes: Winner receives a $10,000 cash advance.
Deadline: Ongoing.

Magazine Merit Awards

The Society of Children's Book Writers & Illustrators
8271 Beverly Boulevard
Los Angeles, CA 90048

Description

Open to SCBWI members, these awards look to honor previously published fiction and nonfiction. The purpose of these awards is to recognize outstanding original magazine work for young people published during that calendar year.
Website: www.scbwi.org
Length: No length requirements.
Requirements: No entry fee. SCBWI members only. Submit 4 copies of the published work showing proof of publication date. Include 4 cover sheets with member's name as listed by SCBWI, mailing address, phone number, entry title, category, name of publication, and date of issue.
Prizes: Winners in each category receive a plaque. Honor certificates are also awarded.
Deadline: Entries are accepted between January 31 and December 15 of each year.

National Children's Theatre Festival

Actors' Playhouse at Miracle Theatre
3140 S. Peoria #295
Aurora, CO 80014

Description

This festival invites the submission of original musical scripts targeting children ages 5 to 12. Entries are judged on content, music, and originality.
Website: www.actorsplayhouse.org
Length: 45–60 minute running time.
Requirements: Entry fee, $10. Multiple submissions are accepted under separate cover. Accepts photocopies and computer printouts. Include an SASE for return of manuscript. Visit the website or send an SASE for guidelines.
Prizes: Winner receives a cash award of $500 and a full production of their play (requires performance rights for a limited time).
Deadline: August 1.

NEFSA Short Story Contest

P.O. Box 809
Framingham, MA 01701-0809

Description
Sponsored by the New England Science Fiction Association, this annual contest accepts original entries of science fiction or fantasy from writers who have not sold a story of any length to a professional publication.
Website: www.nefsa.org/storycon.html
Length: To 7,500 words.
Requirements: No entry fee. Multiple entries are accepted. Accepts photocopies, computer printouts, and email submissions (Microsoft Word) to storycontest@nesfa.org. Author's name should not appear on manuscript itself. Include a separate cover sheet with author's name, address, and title. Send an SASE or visit the website for complete competition guidelines.
Prizes: Winner receives a plaque and a $50 gift certificate for the NEFSA Press.
Deadline: October 15.

NWA Nonfiction Contest

National Writers Association
3140 S. Peoria #295
Aurora, CO 80014

Description
Sponsored by the National Writers Association, this competition looks to recognize high-quality work in the field of nonfiction. It accepts original, unpublished work only.
Website: www.nationalwriters.com
Length: To 5,000 words.
Requirements: Entry fee, $18. Multiple entries are accepted under separate cover. Accepts photocopies and computer printouts. All entries must be accompanied by an entry form (available with an SASE or at the website).
Prizes: First-place winner receives $200. Second- and third-place winners receive $100 and $50, respectively.
Deadline: December 31.
Submissions Received: Receives 100 submissions per competition; 35% by unpublished writers.

NWA Short Story Contest

National Writers Association
3140 S. Peoria #295
Aurora, CO 80014

Description
The purpose of this annual contest is to encourage the development of creative skills, recognize and reward outstanding ability in short story writing. It accepts previously unpublished entries only.
Website: www.nationalwriters.com
Length: To 5,000 words.
Requirements: Entry fee, $15. Multiple entries are accepted under separate cover. Accepts photocopies and computer printouts. All entries must be accompanied by an entry form (available with an SASE or at the website).
Prizes: First-place winner receives $250. Second- and third-place winners receive $100 and $50, respectively.
Deadline: July 1.
Submissions Received: Receives 200 submissions per competition; 65% by unpublished writers.

Pacific Northwest Writers Association Literary Contest

P.O. Box 2016
Edmonds, WA 98020-9516

Description
Held each year, these contests are sponsored by the Pacific Northwest Writers Association and accept entries in several categories including juvenile/young adult novel, juvenile short story, adult genre novel, and nonfiction/memoir.
Website: www.pnwa.org
Length: Length limits vary for each category.
Requirements: Entry fee, $35 for members; $45 for nonmembers. Limit one entry per category. Accepts photocopies and computer printouts. Send two copies of manuscript. Author's name should not appear on manuscript. Include a 3x5 index card with author's name, address, and title of entry. Send an SASE or visit the website for guidelines and specific category information.
Prizes: Winners in each category receive a cash prize of $1,000 and publication of their entry.
Deadline: February 28.

Pockets Annual Fiction Contest

Box 340004
1908 Grand Avenue
Nashville, TN 37203-0004

Description
The purpose of this annual contest is to discover new writers who can add a fresh perspective on children's literature. It accepts original, short story entries.
Website: www.pockets.org
Length: From 1,000 to 1,400 words.
Requirements: No entry fee. Multiple entries are accepted. Accepts computer printouts. Send an SASE for return of manuscript. Visit the website or send an SASE for complete competition guidelines.
Prizes: Winner receives a cash award of $1,000 and publication in *Pockets Magazine*.
Deadline: August 15.
Submissions Received: Receives 1,000 submissions each competition; 50% by unpublished writers.

Science Fiction/ Fantasy Short Story Contest

Science Fiction Writers of the Earth
P.O. Box 121293
Fort Worth, TX 76121

Description
This annual contest looks to promote the writing of science fiction and fantasy. The contest is open to writers who have not yet received payment for publication in these genres.
Website: www.flash.net/~swfoe
Length: From 2,000 to 7,500 words.
Requirements: Entry fee, $5 for first entry; $2 for each subsequent entry. Accepts photocopies and computer printouts. Send an SASE or visit the website for complete guidelines.
Prizes: First-place winner receives publication on the SFWOE website. First- through third-place winners receive cash awards ranging from $50 to $200. Special awards are also presented for outstanding work from younger authors.
Deadline: October 30.

Seven Hills Writing Contests

Tallahassee Writers Association
P.O. Box 32328
Tallahassee, FL 32315

Description
Sponsored by the Tallahassee Writers Association, these annual contests accept entries in the categories of short story, memoir, and children's literature. It accepts unpublished entries only.
Website: www.twaonline.com
Length: To 2,500 words.
Requirements: Entry fee, $15 for members; $20 for nonmembers. Multiple entries are accepted. Accepts photocopies and computer printouts. Send an SASE or visit the website for further guidelines.
Prizes: Winning entries will be published in *Seven Hills* and receive honor certificates.
Deadline: October 1.

Seventeen Magazine Fiction Contest

Seventeen Magazine
13th Floor
1440 Broadway
New York, NY 10018

Description
Seventeen Magazine sponsors this annual fiction contest that is open to writers ages 13 to 21. It accepts original, unpublished entries only.
Website: www.seventeen.com
Length: To 3,500 words.
Requirements: No entry fee. Multiple entries are accepted. Accepts photocopies and computer printouts. Send an SASE or visit the website for complete guidelines.
Prizes: Winners will receive cash awards and publication in *Seventeen Magazine*.
Deadline: April 30. Winners are announced in the summer.

Side Show Anthology Fiction Contest

Somersault Press
404 Vista Heights Road
El Cerrito, CA 94530

Description

Side Show, a fiction anthology, promotes this annual contest that accepts works of fiction in any genre. The competition looks for work of high literary merit to award with publication and cash prizes.
Length: No length requirements.
Requirements: Entry fee, $12.50. One entry fee covers several manuscripts provided that they are included in the same envelope. Accepts photocopies and computer printouts. Submissions that include an SASE will be critiqued if requested.
Prizes: First-place winners receive publication of their story in *Side Show* and a cash prize of $100. Second-place winner receives a cash prize of $75 and third-place winner receives a cash prize of $50
Deadline: Ongoing.

Southwest Writers Contests

Southwest Writers Workshop
Suite 106
8200 Mountain Road NE
Albuquerque, NM 87110

Description

Recognizing and encouraging distinctiveness in writing, the Southwest Writers Workshop sponsors these annual contests in several categories including middle-grade short story, children's picture book, screenplay, genre story, and young adult short story.
Website: www.southwestwriters.org
Length: Varies for each category.
Requirements: Entry fee, $25 for members; $45 for non-members. Accepts photocopies and computer printouts. Multiple entries are accepted under separate cover. Author's name should only appear on entry form (available at website or with an SASE). Send an SASE or visit the website for complete category information and further guidelines.
Prizes: Winners receive cash awards ranging from $75 to $150.
Deadline: May 1.

Skipping Stones Awards

Skipping Stones
P.O. Box 3939
Eugene, OR 97403

Description

These annual awards look to cultivate awareness of our multicultural world without perpetuating stereotypes or biases. Entries should promote cooperation, non-violence, and an appreciation of nature. Entries may be published magazine articles, books, or educational videos.
Website: www.efn.org/~skipping
Length: No length requirements.
Requirements: Entry fee, $50. Send 4 copies of each entry. Only entries produced in the preceding year are eligible. Send an SASE or visit the website for complete guidelines.
Prizes: Cash prizes are awarded to first- through fourth place winners. Winners are announced in April and reviewed in the summer issue of *Skipping Stones*.
Deadline: January 15.

Stepping Stones Writing Contest

P.O. Box 8863
Springfield, MO 65801-8863

Description

This annual contest promotes writing for children by giving writers an opportunity to submit their work for competition. Entries are judged on clarity, punctuation, grammar, and imagery that are suitable for children. All entries must be unpublished and may be either fiction or poetry.
Length: Fiction, to 1,500 words. Poetry, to 30 lines.
Requirements: Entry fee, $8 for first entry; $3 for each additional entry. Multiple entries are accepted under separate cover only. Accepts photocopies and computer printouts. For additional information and official entry forms, send an SASE.
Prizes: First-place winner receives a cash award of $140 and publication in *Hodge Podge*. Second- through fourth-place winners receive cash awards ranging from $15 to $50.
Deadline: July 31.

Sydney Taylor Manuscript Competition

Association of Jewish Libraries
c/o Rachel Glasser
315 Maitland Avenue
Teaneck, NJ 07666

Description
This annual award was established to encourage aspiring writers of Jewish children's books. It was first awarded in 1985 and looks for fiction manuscripts for ages 8 to 11. Entries must have a universal appeal and should reveal positive aspects of Jewish life.
Website: www.jewishlibraries.org
Length: From 64 to 200 pages.
Requirements: No entry fee. Limit one entry per competition. Accepts photocopies and computer printouts. Send an SASE or vsit the website for complete guidelines and submission information.
Prizes: Winner receives cash awards of $1,000 and possible publication.
Deadline: December 31.
Submissions Received: Receives 5–30 submissions each competition; 100% by unpublished writers.

Utah Original Writing Competition

617 E. South Temple
Salt Lake City, UT 84102

Description
Established in 1958, this annual competition looks to promote and reward excellence from Utah's finest writers. The competition presents awards in several categories including juvenile book, juvenile essay, short story, and general non-fiction. It accepts previously unpublished work from Utah writers only.
Website: http://arts.utah.gov/literature/comprules.html
Length: Varies for each category.
Requirements: No entry fee. Limit one entry per category. Accepts photocopies and computer printouts. Manuscripts will not be returned. Send an SASE or visit the website for complete category guidelines.
Prizes: Winners receive cash prizes ranging from $300 to $5,000.
Deadline: June 25. Winners are notified in September.

Vegetarian Essay Contest

The Vegetarian Resource Group
P.O. Box 1463
Baltimore, MD 21203

Description
This annual contest looks to educate young people on the vegetarian and vegan lifestyles. It offers prizes in three age categories: 14–18; 9–13; and 8 and under. Entrants should base their submissions on interviews, research, or personal opinion. Entrants need not be vegetarian to enter.
Website: www.vrg.org
Length: 2–3 pages.
Requirements: No entry fee. Limit one entry per competition. Accepts photocopies, computer printouts, and handwritten entries. Send an SASE or visit the website for complete guidelines.
Prizes: Winners in each category receive a $50 savings bond and publication in *The Vegetarian Journal* (requires all rights).
Deadline: May 1. Winners are announced at the end of the year.

Jackie White Memorial ☆ National Playwriting Competition

309 Parkade Avenue
Columbia, MO 65202

Description
This annual competition looks to encourage the writing of family-friendly plays. It accepts quality, unpublished scripts that are suitable for both children and adults and that challenge the talents of the participating actors.
Website: http://cec.missouri.org
Length: Full-length plays only; running time, 1 to 1½ hours.
Requirements: Entry fee, $10. Multiple entries are accepted. Accepts photocopies and computer printouts. Include a brief synopsis of the play. Send an SASE for return of manuscript. Visit the website or send an SASE for guidelines.
Prizes: Winner receives a cash award of $500 and the possible production of the winning entry.
Deadline: June 1.
Submissions Received: Receives 40 submissions each competition; 50% by unpublished authors.

Tennessee Williams One-Act Play Competition

Tennessee Williams New Orleans Literary Festival
UNO Lakefront
New Orleans, LA 70118

Description
Held annually, this competition looks to celebrate and honor previously unpublished playwrights. Entries should be one-act plays that demonstrate the strength of the work.
Website: www.tennesseewilliams.org
Length: One act.
Requirements: Entry fee, $15 per piece. Accepts photocopies, computer printouts, and multiple submissions. All entries must be typed and must include an entry form, available with an SASE or at the website. Send an SASE or visit the website for guidelines.
Prizes: Winner receives a cash prize of $1,000 and a reading and staging of their winning entry.
Deadline: December 5. Winners will be announced during the annual festival in March or April.

Paul A. Witty Short Story Award

International Reading Association
P.O. Box 8139
Newark, DE 19714-8139

Description
This award recognizes an author whose original short story is first published in a children's magazine or periodical. Entries should serve as a literary standard that encourages young people to read periodicals. The competition is held annually.
Website: www.reading.org
Length: No length requirements.
Requirements: No entry fees. Accepts photocopies accompanied by a copy of the periodical. No more than three entries per magazine. Publishers or authors may nominate a short story and send it to the designated Paul A. Witty Award Subcommittee Chair. For additional information and award guidelines, send an SASE, or email exec@reading.org.
Prizes: $1,000 given to winner at the annual IRA Convention.
Deadline: December 1.

Women in the Arts Annual Contests

Women in the Arts
P.O. Box 2907
Decatur, IL 62524

Description
Offering awards in several categories including essay, fiction, fiction for children, poetry and plays, these contests are held annually. The competition is open to all writers and accepts original, previously unpublished work only.
Length: Essay, fiction, and fiction for children, to 1,500 words. Plays, one act. Poetry, to 32 lines.
Requirements: Entry fee, $2 per submission. Accepts photocopies and computer printouts. Include a cover letter with author's name, address, home phone number, title of work, category of entry, and word count (for fiction). All entries will be subject to blind judging. Manuscripts are not returned.
Prizes: Winners receive cash prizes ranging from $15 to $30.
Deadline: November 1.
Submissions Received: Receives 200 submissions each competition.

John Wood Community ☆ College Creative Writing Contest

1301 S. 48th Street
Quincy, IL 62305

Description
Sponsored by John Wood Community College, this contest accepts entries in several categories including nonfiction, fiction, traditional rhyming poetry, and non-rhyming poetry. This competition focuses on promoting the work of beginning writers.
Website: www.jwcc.edu
Length: Nonfiction and fiction, to 2,000 words. Poetry, limit 2 pages.
Requirements: Entry fees range from $5 to $7 depending on category. Accepts photocopies and computer printouts. Author's name should not be included on manuscript itself. Include a 3x5 index card with author's name, address, and telephone number.
Prizes: Cash prizes are awarded to the first- through third-place winners. All winners may also receive publication of their winning entries.
Deadline: April 2.

Writers at Work Fellowship Competition

P.O. Box 540370
North Salt Lake, UT 84054-0370

Description
Open to writers who have not yet published a book-length volume of original work, this competition accepts entries in the categories of fiction, nonfiction, and poetry.
Website: www.writersatwork.org
Length: Fiction and nonfiction, to 5,000 words. Poetry, to 10 pages (up to 6 poems).
Requirements: Entry fee, $15. Accepts photocopies and computer printouts. Multiple entries are accepted under separate cover only. Indicate contest category on outside envelope. Manuscripts will not be returned. Visit the website or send an SASE for complete guidelines.
Prizes: Winners in each category receive a cash prize of $1,500 and publication in *Quarterly West*. Honorable mentions are also awarded.
Deadline: March 1.

Writer's Digest Annual Writing Competition

4700 East Galbraith Road
Cincinnati, OH 45236

Description
This competition accepts works in several categories including children's fiction, feature article, genre short story, memoir/personal essay, and stage play script. It accepts original, unpublished work only.
Website: www.writersdigest.com
Length: Children's fiction, to 2,000 words. Other categories, word lengths vary.
Requirements: Entry fee, $10. Multiple submissions are accepted under separate cover. Accepts photocopies and computer printouts. Author's name, address, phone numbers, and category should appear in the upper left corner of the first page. Manuscripts are not returned. Visit the website or send an SASE for complete category list and guidelines.
Prizes: Cash prizes vary for each category.
Deadline: May 31.

The Writing Conference, Inc. Writing Contests

P.O. Box 664
Ottawa, KS 66067-0664

Description
Open to children and young adults, these contests accept entries of short stories, short nonfiction, and poetry. The goal of these contests is to encourage a love of writing among young people.
Website: www.writingconference.com
Length: No length requirements.
Requirements: No entry fee. Limit one entry per competition. Accepts photocopies and computer printouts. Visit the website or send an SASE for further information.
Prizes: Winners in each category receive publication in *The Writer's Slate*.
Deadline: January. Winners are announced in February.
Submissions Received: Receives 250 submissions per competition; 100% by unpublished writers.

Writing for Children Competition

Writers' Union of Canada
3rd Floor, 40 Wellington Street East
Toronto, Ontario M5E 1C7
Canada

Description
Open to citizens of Canada who have not yet published a book, this competition looks to discover, encourage, and promote new and emerging writers. Entries must target children, and may be either fiction or nonfiction.
Website: www.writersunion.ca
Length: To 1,500 words.
Requirements: Entry fee, $15 per piece. Multiple entries are accepted. Accepts photocopies and computer printouts. Send an SASE or visit the website for complete competition guidelines.
Prizes: Winner receives a cash prize of $1,500 and the Writers' Union of Canada will submit the winning entry to several children's publishers.
Deadline: April. Winner is announced in June.

Indexes

2005 Market News

New Listings ☆

American Adrenaline
American Kids Parenting Magazine
American Libraries
Asimov's Science Fiction
AWA Contests
Baltimore's Child
Bay State Parent
Boutique Magazine
Brooklyn Parent
Busy Family Network
Cadet Quest
CAPA Competition
Carolina Parent
Catholic Library World
Children and Families
Church Worship
Cincinnati Family
Classic Toy Trains
Columbus Parent
Davey and Goliath
Dragonfly Spirit Writing for Children Short Story Contest
Dragon Magazine
Eclectic Homeschool Online
EFCA Today
Elementary School Writer
Family Doctor
FamilyRapp.com
Fit Pregnancy

Gay Parent Magazine
Grandparents Magazine
Guideposts Sweet 16
Gumbo Magazine
Haunted Attraction Magazine
High School Writer (Senior)
Imperial County Family
Justine Magazine
Kickoff Magazine
Know Your World Extra
The Lamp-Post
Library Sparks
The Lion
Long Island Woman
Look-Look Magazine
Los Angeles Family Magazine
Metro Parent (OR)
Mommy Too! Magazine
Mr. Marquis' Museletter
NEFSA Short Story Contest
New Moon
The Next Step Magazine
Northern Michigan Family Magazine
Organic Family Magazine
Parents & Kids Magazine
Pogo Stick
Pointe

Quilt It for Kids
Religion Teacher's Journal
Scholastic Parent and Child
Science Fiction/Fantasy Short Story Contest
Sesame Street Magazine
Shameless
SheKnows.com
Side Show Anthology Fiction Contest
Simply You Magazine
SuperTwins
Teen Countdown
Teen Graffiti
Today's Christian
Treasure Valley Family Magazine
U-Turn Magazine
U.25 Magazine
The Village Family
Jackie White Memorial National Playwriting Competition
John Wood Community College Creative Writing Contest
World Pulse Magazine
Yin Magazine
Young Dancer

2005 Market News (cont.)

Deletions and Name Changes

Baby Years Magazine: Ceased publication

Beckett Anime Collector: Unable to locate

Best of Dragon Ball Z: Ceased publication

Birmingham Family Times: Unable to locate

Black Parenting Today: Ceased publication

Boise Family Magazine: See **Treasure Valley Family Magazine**

Boy Crazy!: Ceased publication

Capital District Parent: Merged with **Hudson Valley Parent**

Child Care Business: Ceased publication

Christian Library Journal: Ceased publication

Christian Reader: See Today's Christian

Christ in Our Home for Families with Kids: See Davey & Goliath

Connecticut Family: Ceased publication

County Families Magazine: Ceased publication

The Crystal Ball: Ceased Publication.

Dallas Family: Ceased publication

Dream/Girl: Ceased publication

Early Childhood Educational Journal: Unable to locate

Equality Today: Ceased publication

Familes on the Go: Unable to locate

Family Times: See **Metro Parent (OR)**

Health and You: Ceased publication

Hullabaloo: Ceased publication

Island Parent Magazine: Unable to locate

Just Weird Enough: Ceased publication

kidsworld Magazine: No response

Latina Magazine: Removed at editor's request

Long Island Parenting News: No response

MaMaMedia: No response

Middle School Journal: No response

Multiple Moments: Unable to locate

MyParenTime.com: No response

Myria: Merged into **SheKnows.com**

Northern Nevada Family: Ceased publication

Northern Virginia Parent: Ceased publication

Our Kids Atlanta: Ceased publication

PetLife: Ceased publication

Rainy Day Corner: Ceased publication.

Relational Child and Youth Care Practice: No response

r*w*t: Ceased publication

Soccer Jr.: Ceased publication

Student Press Review: No response

Teaching Exceptional Children: No response

Team NYI Webzine: Ceased publication

Teenpreneur: Ceased publication

That's My Baby: Unable to locate

Virginia Writing: No response

Writes of Passage: Ceased publication

Xpress: Removed at editor's request

Youth Update: Ceased publication

Youth World Views: No response

Fifty+ Freelance

You can improve your chances of selling by submitting to magazines that fill their pages with freelance material. Of the 618 freelance markets listed in this directory, we have listed 182 markets that buy at least 50% of their contents from nonstaff writers, and that publish at least 35% of their freelance material from writers who are new to the magazine. Of course, there are no guarantees; but if you approach these magazines with well-written manuscripts targeted to their subject, age range, and word-limit requirements, you can increase your publication odds.

Abilities
Able Ezine
Adoptive Families
Alateen Talk
American Careers
American History
American Kids Parenting Magazine
American Libraries
American String Teacher
AppleSeeds
The Apprentice Writer
Art & Activities
Austin Family
Babybug
Bay Area Baby
Boys' Quest
Busy Family Network
Calliope
Camping Magazine
Canadian Children's Literature
Characters
Chicago Parent
Child
Child Care Information Exchange
Childhood Education
Children and Families
Children's Magic Window
Children's Ministry
Child Welfare Report
Circles of Peace, Circles of Justice
The Claremont Review
The Clearing House
Club Connection
Clubhouse
College Bound Teen Magazine
College Outlook
Columbus Parent
Community Education Journal
Connect
Creative Kids
Cricket
Dance Magazine
Dane County Kids
Davey and Goliath
Devo'Zine
Dig

Dimensions
Dimensions of Early Childhood
Dogs for Kids
Dovetail
Dramatics
Drink Smart
East of the Web
The Edge
Educational Horizons
Education Forum
Elementary School Writer
The EMMC Recorder
English Journal
Exceptional Parent
Faces
Face Up
The Family Digest
Farm & Ranch Living
Faze Teen
Footsteps
Fox Valley Kids
Games
Georgia Family
Gifted Education Press Quarterly
Go-Girl
Going Forth
Green Teacher
Grit
Group
Guideposts Sweet 16
Haunted Attraction
Highlights for Children
The High School Journal
High School Writer (Junior Edition)
High School Writer (Senior Edition)
Home Education Magazine
Home Times
Hopscotch
Hudson Valley & Capital District Parent
Inside Kung-Fu
Insight
InTeen
InTeen Teacher
Jack And Jill
Jam Rag
Journal of School Health

Kansas School Naturalist
Keynoter
Kids Life Magazine
Kids VT
Ladybug
Leadership for Student Activities
Leading Edge
Learning Guide
Live
Look-Look Magazine
Lowcountry Parent
Metro Parent Magazine
Momentum
Mothering
Mr. Marquis' Museletter
My Friend
Nashville Parent Magazine
National Geographic Kids
N.E.W. Kids
New York Family
No Crime
Northern Michigan Family Magazine
On Course
Our Children
Pack-O-Fun
Parent and Preschooler Newsletter
Parentguide News
Parenting New Hampshire
Parents and Children Together Online
Parents Express– Pennsylvania Edition
Parents Express– Southern New Jersey Edition
Parents' Monthly
Piedmont Parent
Plays
Positive Teens
Potluck Children's Literary Magazine
Principal
Read, America
Real Sports
Reptiles
Research in Middle Level Education
Reunions Magazine

Ruminator Review
Sacramento/Sierra Parent
SchoolArts
School Library Journal
Science Activites
Science and Activities
Seek
Social Studies and the Young Learner
Spider
Stone Soup
Story Friends
Storytelling Magazine
Suburban Parent
SuperScience
Susquehanna Valley Parent
Teacher Librarian
Teachers & Writers
Teachers of Vision
Teaching Theatre
Tech Directions
Teen Light
Teen Voices
Texas Child Care
Theory Into Practice
Three Leaping Frogs
Tidewater Parent
Tiny Giant Magazine
Today's Catholic Teacher
The Universe in the Classroom
U*S*Kids
Vegetarianteen.com
VegFamily
Voice of Youth Advocates
Voices from the Middle
Washington Families
Wees Ones E-Magazine
Welcome Home
Westchester Family
Western New York Family Magazine
What If?
What's Up Kids?
Wonder Years
Writers' Journal
YES Mag
Young Adult Today
Young Adult Today Leader
Young Money
Your Stepfamily

Category Index

To help you find the appropriate market for your manuscript or query letter, we have compiled a category and subject index listing magazines according to their primary editorial interests. Pay close attention to the markets that overlap. For example, when searching for a market for your rock-climbing adventure story for 8- to 12-year-old readers, you might look under the categories "Adventure Stories" and "Middle-grade (Fiction)." If you have an idea for an article about blue herons for early readers, look under the categories "Animals/Pets" and "Early Reader (Nonfiction)" to find possible markets. Always check the magazine's listing for explanations of specific needs.

For your convenience, we have listed below all of the categories that are included in this index. If you don't find a category that exactly fits your material, try to find a broader term that covers your topic.

Adventure Stories
Animals (Fiction)
Animals/Pets
  (Nonfiction)
Audio/Video
Bilingual (Nonfiction)
Biography
Boys' Magazines
Canadian Magazines
Career/College
Child Care
Computers
Contemporary Fiction
Crafts/Hobbies
Current Events
Drama
Early Reader (Fiction)
Early Reader (Nonfiction)
Education/Classroom
Factual/Informational
Fairy Tales
Family/Parenting
Fantasy
Folktales/Folklore
Games/Puzzles/Activities
Geography
Gifted Education

Girls' Magazines
Health/Fitness
Historical Fiction
History
Horror
How-to
Humor (Fiction)
Humor (Nonfiction)
Inspirational Fiction
Language Arts
Mathematics
Middle-grade (Fiction)
Middle-grade (Nonfiction)
Multicultural/Ethnic
  (Fiction)
Multicultural/Ethnic
  (Nonfiction)
Music
Mystery/Suspense
Nature/Environment
  (Fiction)
Nature/Environment
  (Nonfiction)
Personal Experience
Photo Essays
Popular Culture
Preschool (Fiction)

Preschool (Nonfiction)
Profile/Interview
Read-aloud Stories
Real-life/Problem-solving
Rebus
Recreation/Entertainment
Regional
Religious (Fiction)
Religious (Nonfiction)
Reviews
Romance
Science Fiction
Science/Technology
Self-help
Services/Clubs
Social Issues
Special Education
Sports (Fiction)
Sports (Nonfiction)
Travel
Western
Writing
Young Adult (Fiction)
Young Adult (Nonfiction)
Young Author (Fiction)
Young Author
  (Nonfiction)

Factual/Informational

Personal Experience

Special Education

Sports (Fiction)

Sports (Nonfiction)

Magazine and Contest Index

The following codes have been used to indicate each publication's readership: **YA**=Young adults, **A**=Adults, **E**=Educators (including librarians, teachers, administrators, student group leaders, and child-care professionals), **F**=Family (general interest), **P**=Parents. We have listed age ranges when specified by the editor.

If you do not find a particular magazine, turn to Market News on page 336.

★ indicates a newly listed magazine